*Political Facts of the United States Since 1789*

# POLITICAL FACTS
# OF THE UNITED STATES
# SINCE 1789

## Erik W. Austin

*With the assistance of* Jerome M. Clubb

*New York*
Columbia University Press
*1986*

**Library of Congress Cataloging-in-Publication Data**

Austin, Erik W.
  Political facts of the United States since 1789

  Bibliography: p.
  1. United States—Politics and government—
Miscellanea. 2. United States—Politics and
government—Statistics. I. Clubb, Jerome M.,
1928–   . II. Title.
E183.A97  1986      320.973        86-2605
ISBN 0-231-06094-7 (alk. paper)

Columbia University Press
New York  Guildford, Surrey
Copyright © 1986 by Erik W. Austin

Printed in the United States of America

# CONTENTS

PREFACE                                                        xi
INTRODUCTION                                                    1

**CHAPTER 1: NATIONAL LEADERSHIP**                             5
*The Executive Branch*                                         6
  Order of Succession to the Presidency              8
  Table 1.1. Presidents of the United States,
    1789–1985                               10
  Table 1.2. Vice Presidents of the United States,
    1789–1985                               13
  Table 1.3. Assassinations and Attempts on
    Major U.S. Political Figures, 1835–1981  15
  Table 1.4. Cabinet Officers, 1789–1985              16

*The Judicial Branch*                                          29
  Table 1.5. Justices of the Supreme Court of the
    United States, 1789–1985                 30

*The Legislative Branch*                                       34
  Table 1.6. Presidents Pro Tempore of the
    United States Senate, 1789–1985          35
  Table 1.7. Majority Leaders of the United
    States Senate, 1911–1985                 38
  Table 1.8. Majority Whips of the United States
    Senate, 1913–1985                        38
  Table 1.9. Minority Leaders of the United
    States Senate, 1911–1985                 39
  Table 1.10. Minority Whips of the United
    States Senate, 1915–1985                 39

Table 1.11. Chairmen of Major Committees in the United States Senate, 1875–1985    40

Table 1.12. Speakers of the United States House of Representatives, 1789–1985    42

Table 1.13. Majority Leaders of the United States House of Representatives, 1899–1985    43

Table 1.14. Majority Whips of the United States House of Representatives, 1899–1985    43

Table 1.15. Minority Leaders of the United States House of Representatives, 1899–1985    44

Table 1.16. Minority Whips of the United States House of Representatives, 1899–1985    44

Table 1.17. Chairmen of Major Committees in the United States House of Representatives, 1875–1985    45

Table 1.18. Congressional Bills Introduced and Passed, 1789–1984    47

Table 1.19. Congressional Bills Vetoed, 1789–1984    49

Table 1.20. Partisan Composition of the United States Senate, 1789–1985    50

Table 1.21. Partisan Composition of the United States House of Representatives, 1789–1985    53

Table 1.22. Salaries of Executive Branch Officers and Supreme Court Justices, 1789–1983    58

Table 1.23. Salaries of United States Senators and Representatives, 1789–1985    60

*Organizational Charts of the United States Government, 1984*    61

Chart A. Executive    62

Chart B. Judicial    63

Chart C. Legislative: House    64

Chart D. Legislative: Senate    65

**CHAPTER 2: STATE POLITICS**                              66

*State Government*                                          66

    Table 2.1. States of the United States              68

    Table 2.2. Population of States, 1790–1980          70

    Table 2.3. United States Territories and
      Possessions                                   75

**CHAPTER 3: PARTIES AND ELECTIONS**                       78

*Elections and Election Procedures*                        78

*Political Parties*                                        82

*The Vote for President of the United States*              92

    Table 3.1. National Electoral and Popular Vote
      Cast for President, 1789–1984                 94

    Table 3.2. Electoral Vote Cast for President, by
      State, 1789–1984                             101

    Table 3.3. Popular Vote Cast for President, by
      State, 1824–1984                             128

*The Vote for the United States Senate*                   181

    Table 3.4. National Popular Vote Cast for
      United States Senator, 1908–1984             182

    Table 3.5. Vote Cast for United States Senator,
      by State, 1908–1984                          184

*The Vote for the United States House of
  Representatives*                                  241

    Table 3.6. National Popular Vote Cast for
      United States Representative, 1824–1984       242

    Table 3.7. Vote Cast for United States
      Representatives, by State, 1824–1984          244

    Table 3.8. Apportionment to the United States
      Congress, 1787–1980                          358

    Table 3.9. Presidential Election Campaign Costs,
      1860–1984                                    363

    Table 3.10. American Presidential Conventions,
      1832–1984                                    364

Table 3.11. Qualifications for Suffrage,
1776–1981                                              370

Table 3.12. National Voter Turnout,
1824–1984                                              378

Table 3.13. Voter Turnout for Presidential
Elections, 1824–1984                                   381

Table 3.14. Party Identification of the
Electorate, 1937–1984                                  388

Table 3.15. Use of Voting Devices, 1982                390

**CHAPTER 4: FOREIGN AFFAIRS**                         392

Table 4.1. United States Recognition of Foreign
Nations                                                393

Table 4.2. United States Ambassadors to
Selected Nations                                       395

Table 4.3. Current United States Ambassadors           407

Table 4.4. United States Economic Assistance,
1946–1982                                              412

**CHAPTER 5: ARMED FORCES**                            415

Table 5.1. Military Personnel on Active Duty,
1789–1982                                              416

Table 5.2. Heads of Branches of the United
States Armed Services, 1775–1984                       418

Table 5.3. American Military Personnel and
Casualties During Selected Wars                        421

Table 5.4. Total Costs of United States Wars           422

**CHAPTER 6: WEALTH, REVENUE,
TAXATION, AND PUBLIC
EXPENDITURE**                                          424

Table 6.1. Per Capita Personal Income by State,
1929–1982                                              425

Table 6.2. Federal Government Receipts, by
Source, 1789–1982                                      430

Table 6.3. Federal, State, and Local
Government Expenditure, by Function,
1902–1981                                              436

Table 6.4A. Outlays of the Federal Government
     by Major Function, 1789–1899              446
Table 6.4B. Outlays of the Federal Government
     by Major Function, 1900–1939              450
Table 6.4C. Outlays of the Federal Government
     by Major Function, 1940–1967              451
Table 6.4D. Outlays of the Federal Government
     by Major Function, 1968–1982              457
**CHAPTER 7: DEMOGRAPHIC INFORMATION**  460
Table 7.1. Annual Estimated Population of the
     United States, 1790–1983                  461
Table 7.2. Population of the United States By
     Sex and Race, 1790–1980                   463
Table 7.3. Black Population, by State,
     1790–1980                                 466
Table 7.4. Total Number of Immigrants
     Arriving Annually in the United States,
     1820–1980                                 470
Table 7.5. Number of Immigrants from Selected
     Countries Arriving in the United States by
     Decade, 1820–1980                         472
Table 7.6. Estimated Civilian Labor Force in
     the United States and Percentage of Labor
     Force Unemployed, 1900–1982               475
Table 7.7. Estimated Civilian Labor Force and
     Percentage of Labor Force Unemployed, by
     State, 1930–1980                          476
**APPENDIX**                                   481
*Declaration of Independence*                  481
*Constitution of the United States*            485
**SOURCES**                                    509

# PREFACE

In preparing this work, a variety of published and unpublished sources were used. To the degree possible; the sources employed have been cited, both to express gratitude to others and to indicate where readers can go for additional and more comprehensive information. The citations, however, are not meant to be a comprehensive bibliography of sources of political facts for the United States. A complete bibliography would extend to several hundred pages and is beyond the scope of this volume.

The effort to collect and compile the information in this book spanned more than a decade and was a truly cooperative effort. I would like to first acknowledge the contributions of Jerome M. Clubb under whose intellectual aegis the book was begun. His immense knowledge of the political history of the U.S., as well as his acute sense of the relative importance of the factual components of our political system, were instrumental in forging the design of this volume. Certainly without Jerry the book would not have lifted off its launching pad. I will remain deeply in his debt for his intellectual contributions to this book as well as for his involvement in many other aspects of my own professional development.

Many others contributed as well to the successful execution of the volume. We all benefited greatly from the comments of three anonymous readers who examined a detailed outline for the volume. Unfortunately, we were not in every case able to implement their many valuable suggestions and criticisms. I also benefited from the comments and suggestions of numerous friends, colleagues, and former teachers. Usual practices will be violated here by not listing these individuals by name; the list would be embarrassingly lengthy and would risk attributing to others faults, errors, and omissions for which I alone am responsible. I do, however, wish to express gratitude to the colleagues who have assisted me in assembling the information and preparing the final manuscript: Susan Wyman, Phyllis Avery, Mary Vardigan, Sylvia Jenkins, Donna Gotts, Toby Bobbitt, and Dennis O'Connor.

*Political Facts of the United States Since 1789*

# Introduction

Our addition to already overcrowded bookshelves of still another compilation of facts requires at least a word of justification. That justification lies in the purpose of this modest volume. We have attempted to assemble basic facts to aid those interested to understand and interpret the political system as well as the historical and contemporary political events of the United States. We have designed this collection to meet the needs of all those who for vocational or avocational reasons seek to comprehend and make sense of the political life of the United States.

While numerous compilations of facts concerning United States politics are available, they are frequently in cumbersome multivolume formats which are difficult to use. Such compilations, moreover, are often highly specialized, and the immense stores of rich and detailed information they provide are frequently confined to relatively limited topics. Thus the quest for needed information often requires one to consult a number of these compilations. Because of their size and cost, these numerous compilations for the most part are to be found only in large, well-equipped libraries.

We have not, of course, attempted to provide a substitute for such massive compilations. The effort to do so would, of course, defeat its own purposes. We have undertaken here only the more modest, but in some ways more difficult, task of providing a useful intermediate reference tool.

The preceding comments, of course, expose the contradictory nature of our effort. Although the canons governing book titles dictate otherwise, the demands of accuracy would require the addition of the words "Some Selected" to the title of this volume. Since the volume cannot be comprehensive in the material that it includes, we have attempted to select for inclusion those materials that are most useful and important for interpreting and understanding the politics of the United States. In preparing the volume we have drawn heavily upon standard compilations. But we have also drawn upon many scholarly works and have brought together factual information that is otherwise to be found only by consulting a large number of individual studies. The United States historically and at present lacks a central agency with responsibility for collecting and compiling voting records of the countless elections that are held each year. Thus the election returns compiled in this volume have been gleaned from little known and limited-edition state and local publications and from unpublished sources. Some of the information provided here is currently available in no other published form. But however extensive our search for factual information, this volume is by no means comprehensive and its quality and utility are entirely dependent upon the adequacy of the criteria we have used in selecting information for inclusion.

This volume of political facts spans the years from the founding of the nation to 1985, a period of some 200 years. But in our efforts to select materials for inclusion in this volume we have been forced to conclude, as have others before us, that the political and governmental systems of the United States must, indeed, be the most complex of any modern or not-so-modern nation. Complexity results in part from the multilayered nature of government in the United States, with its national (federal), state, and local levels. It also results from the division of the national government into three co-equal branches— legislative, executive, and judicial—a division that is paralleled at the state level of government and, to a lesser degree, at the local level as well. Since exercise of certain governmental powers is restricted to the states, a diversity of practice and statute from state to state adds a further dimension of complexity to the political life of the United States.

One product of complexity, compounded by the sheer geographical size of the United States, is the very large number of elected and appointed officials who serve in the government at any given time and the much larger number who have served throughout our history. Well over 10,000 individuals have been elected to the two houses of Congress since the founding of the nation, and the number elected to the various state legislatures is many times larger. The number of elected state governors in the history of the nation runs into the thousands; and if we add the other elected officials of the states, the elected mayors, council members and other officials of cities, and the elected officials of the counties and other jurisdictions, the number of office holders and elections verges on the astronomical. If we consider also the widespread use of popular referenda at the state and local levels to decide policy issues and the increasing use of popular elections to nominate candidates for public office it might seem that the citizens of the United States and its many governmental jurisdictions do little else but vote and hold office.

Complexity, size, and diversity have required rigorous and exclusive criteria for selecting information for inclusion and have resulted in a volume that leaves out much more than it includes. This has another consequence as well: while we have attempted to emphasize facts rather than interpretation, the content of this volume is heavily colored by our own interpretations. Our interpretations obviously weigh most heavily in the selection of material for inclusion. In general we have placed primary emphasis upon politics and government at the national level; we have placed substantially less emphasis on the state level and virtually none on the politics and government of cities, municipalities, and other local jurisdictions. The numerous local, state, and national administrative and regulatory agencies and officials pass unnoticed even though they are often of major importance to the operation of politics and government.

At first glance, the justification for these relative emphases may appear self evident. Aside from simple and practical considerations of space, however, the decision to place primary emphasis upon national politics and government may be less defensible than it at first seems. In fact, the politics and government of the states and localities play a major role in shaping life in the nation and politics at these levels and also exert heavy influence on national politics and government. Moreover, a compilation prepared in the mid nineteenth century undoubtedly would have placed substantially greater emphasis upon the states and less on the national level. In those years the states were simply of greater importance in relation to national politics and government than is now the case. Thus while our emphases may be adequate for the contemporary period, they may also in some sense falsify history. Our decision to deemphasize urban politics might also be faulted. The simple fact is that politics and government in the major cities are often from many perspectives more significant than those of thinly populated states, and indeed, a similar compilation assembled in the 1990s might justifiably place primary emphasis upon the major urban agglomerations of the nation. In the long run, however, justification for our decision to place primary emphasis upon the national level must rest upon considerations of space, the diversity and extent of relevant information at the other levels, and the likely interests and needs of readers.

# CHAPTER ONE
## *National Leadership*

The United States is characterized by a highly complex form of government consisting of several levels, the highest of which is the national, or federal, government. At the next level down are the 50 state governments. The states were intended by the authors of the national Constitution to be semi-autonomous and semi-selfgoverning units, and certain governmental powers are reserved by the Constitution to the various states. Since the founding of the nation, however, the governmental power and authority of the states have diminished while those of the national government have increased. Even so, national and state governmental powers overlap in numerous ways and questions bearing upon the power, authority, and jurisdiction of the national government as opposed to those of the states remain a continuing source of political debate, controversy, and legal action.

Below the state level are a variety of local governments. The most prominent of these are municipalities, cities, towns, and counties. The structure and powers of the governments of these units vary widely from state to state, from region to region, and in some instances depend upon the size of the unit. In general, however, governments at this level can enact statutes and ordinances, impose administrative regulations, levy taxes, exercise certain police powers, and hold original jurisdiction in various criminal and civil cases. Within municipalities, cities, and counties there are often a variety of additional governmental units such as school districts, sewer and water districts, and in some instances police and fire districts. The governmental powers of these units are limited and highly specialized. In general, governmental power at this level is confined to taxation and imposition of administrative regulations for specific and usually narrowly defined purposes.

The form of the national government is defined by the Constitution of the United States which was drafted in 1787 and ratified in 1788. Through the years the Constitution has been substantially modified by explicit amendment, interpretation, precedent, and practice; but the formal structure of national government which it defines for the United States remains essentially as originally mandated. Under the Constitution the national government is divided into three separate branches: the legislative, the executive, and the judicial. Legislative powers are vested in the two houses of Congress (the House of Representatives and the Senate), executive powers in the President, and judicial powers in the Supreme Court and in the inferior federal courts that were subsequently created.

Although the Constitution created three separate branches of government, the governmental powers it assigned to each are overlapping. In this way, a system was developed which limits the independent power and authority of each branch. While the power to enact legislation is assigned to Congress, to become law congressional acts must be signed by, and are subject to veto by, the President. Congressional acts vetoed by the President become law only if passed again by Congress, this time by a two-thirds vote in both houses. The President is assigned power to make appointments to such governmental positions as cabinet offices, the federal judiciary, and various diplomatic posts. Such appointments must be approved (confirmed) by a two-thirds vote in the Senate. Similarly, while the President may enter into treaties with other nations, confirmation by a two-thirds vote of the Senate is required for them to go into effect. Although it is not explicitly provided by the Constitution, interpretation and precedent has accorded to the federal courts, ultimately to the Supreme Court, the power to declare unconstitutional and hence null and void laws passed by Congress and signed by the President. State laws are subject to the same process of "judicial review" by federal courts.

## The Executive Branch

The executive branch of the United States government consists of two elected officials (the President and Vice President) and numerous appointed officers. The President is charged by the Constitution to "take care that the laws be faithfully executed"; this responsibility includes the day-to-day administration and enforcement of laws that are passed by Congress. To assist the President in the performance of these tasks, a number of departments have been created. The heads of these departments are appointed by the President "by and with the advice and consent of the Senate." Included among the officials appointed by the President are cabinet officers, ambassadors, public ministers and consuls, justices of the Supreme Court as well as thousands of other judges, and military officers.

Presidents and Vice Presidents are elected to four-year terms. Before ratification (in 1951) of the Twenty-Second Amendment to the Constitution, no limit was imposed upon the number of terms a President could serve. That amendment, however, imposed a two-term limitation on Presidential tenure. Selection of the President and Vice President is through a complicated electoral process. Voters in the various states of the United States choose members of an "electoral college" (electors) equal to the number of Senators and Representatives allotted to each state. The electors then formally cast their ballots for the Presidential and Vice Presidential candidates to whom they were pledged in the popular election. Originally, the Constitution specified that each elector would cast two votes for President, with the candidate receiving the most votes becoming President, and the candidate receiving the next highest number becoming Vice President. The Twelfth Amendment to the Constitution (1804) changed that practice and directed the electors to cast one of their votes specifically for President and one for Vice President. To be elected, a candidate must receive a majority of the electoral votes cast in the election. If a candidate does not receive a majority of the electoral votes (as occurred twice, in 1800 and 1824), the House of Representatives is empowered to choose the President from among the candidates receiving the highest numbers of electoral votes. Because of the reliance upon electoral rather than popular votes in determining the winner, it is possible for a candidate to be elected President with less than a majority of the popular votes cast for the office; "minority" Presidents have been elected fifteen times, usually in elections in which minor-party candidates received a significant share of the popular votes cast.

The Constitution of the United States makes no mention of political parties as the mechanism by which candidates or electors are chosen. Political parties did, however, appear as early as 1800 and assumed the function of nominating candidates and Presidential electors. Thus the Presidential candidates and electors have usually represented political parties or factions. Yet there is no provision in the Constitution to prevent electors from repudiating their pre-election pledges to specific candidates (or political parties), and such repudiations have occurred several times in American political history.

Candidates for the Presidency and Vice Presidency must, according to the Constitution, be natural-born citizens of the United States, must have been residents of the United States for fourteen years, and must be at least 35 years of age.

The heads of the major executive departments collectively form the President's cabinet. Cabinet-level departments numbered only five at the time of the founding of the Republic (the Departments of State, Treasury, Justice, War, and Post Office). New cabinet departments were created as follows:

| | |
|---|---|
| Navy (1798) | Health, Education and Welfare (1953) |
| Interior (1849) | Housing and Urban Development (1965) |
| Agriculture (1889) | Transportation (1966) |
| Commerce and Labor (1903) | Energy (1977) |
| Commerce (1913) | Health and Human Services (1979) |
| Labor (1913) | Education (1979) |
| Defense (1947) | |

The tables that follow offer pertinent facts relating to the executive branch of government. The section entitled Order of Succession to the Presidency presents a verbatim account of the law that provides the rules for succession; it also shows the actual order of succession to the Presidency by office. Tables 1.1, 1.2, and 1.4 list, respectively, the Presidents, Vice Presidents, and cabinet officers of the United States from 1789 to 1985. Table 1.3 contains information on assassinations and assassination attempts on major United States political figures.

## Order of Succession to the Presidency

### Law on Succession to the Presidency

If by reason of death, resignation, removal from office, inability, or failure to qualify there is neither a president nor vice president to discharge the powers and duties of the office of president, then the Speaker of the House of Representatives shall upon his resignation as speaker and as representative, act as president. The same rule shall apply in the case of the death, resignation, removal from office, or inability of an individual acting as president.

If at the time when a speaker is to begin the discharge of the powers and duties of the office of president there is no speaker, or the speaker fails to qualify as acting president, then the president pro tempore of the Senate, upon his resignation as president pro tempore and as senator, shall act as president.

An individual acting as president shall continue to act until the expiration of the then current presidential term, except that (1) if his discharge of the powers and duties of the office is founded in whole or in part in the failure of both the president-elect and the vice president-elect to qualify, then he shall act only until a president or vice president qualifies, and (2) if his discharge of the powers and duties of the office is founded in whole or in part on the inability of the president or vice president, then he shall act only until the removal of the disability of one of such individuals.

If, by reason of death, resignation, removal from office, or failure to qualify, there is no president pro tempore to act as president, then the officer of the United States who is highest on the following list, and who is not under disability to discharge the powers and duties of president, shall act as president; the secretaries of state, treasury, defense, attorney general; secretaries of interior, agriculture, commerce, labor, health and human services, housing and urban development, transportation, energy, education.
(Legislation approved July 18, 1947; amended Sept. 9, 1965, Oct. 15, 1966, Aug. 4, 1977, and Sept. 27, 1979.)

## Order of Succession to the Presidency
### (as of September 27, 1979)

1 Vice President
2 Speaker of the House
  of Representatives
3 President Pro Tempore
  of the Senate
4 Secretary of State
5 Secretary of the Treasury
6 Secretary of Defense
7 Attorney General
8 Secretary of the Interior

9 Secretary of Agriculture
10 Secretary of Commerce
11 Secretary of Labor
12 Secretary of Health and
   Human Services
13 Secretary of Housing and
   Urban Development
14 Secretary of Transportation
15 Secretary of Energy
16 Secretary of Education

Table 1.1

Presidents of the United States, 1789-1985

| Name | Dates of Birth-Death | State of Birth | Home State | Party | Term of Service | Religious Affiliation |
|---|---|---|---|---|---|---|
| George Washington | 1732-1799 | Va. | Va. | Federalist | 4/30/1789-3/3/1797 | Episcopalian |
| John Adams | 1735-1826 | Mass. | Mass. | Federalist | 3/4/1797-3/3/1801 | Unitarian |
| Thomas Jefferson | 1743-1826 | Va. | Va. | Dem-Rep | 3/4/1801-3/3/1809 | Episcopalian |
| James Madison | 1751-1836 | Va. | Va. | Dem-Rep | 3/4/1809-3/3/1817 | Episcopalian |
| James Monroe | 1758-1831 | Va. | Va. | Dem-Rep | 3/4/1817-3/3/1825 | Episcopalian |
| John Q. Adams | 1767-1848 | Mass. | Mass. | Dem-Rep | 3/4/1825-3/3/1829 | Unitarian |
| Andrew Jackson | 1767-1845 | S.C. | Tenn. | Democrat | 3/4/1829-3/3/1837 | Methodist |
| Martin Van Buren | 1782-1862 | N.Y. | N.Y. | Democrat | 3/4/1837-3/3/1841 | Dutch Reformed |
| William H. Harrison[a] | 1773-1841 | Va. | Ohio | Whig | 3/4/1841-4/4/1841 | Episcopalian |
| John Tyler[b] | 1790-1862 | Va. | Va. | Whig | 4/6/1841-3/3/1845 | Episcopalian |
| James K. Polk | 1795-1849 | N.C. | Tenn. | Democrat | 3/4/1845-3/3/1849 | Methodist |
| Zachary Taylor[c] | 1784-1850 | Va. | Ky. | Whig | 3/4/1849-7/9/1850 | Episcopalian |
| Millard Fillmore[d] | 1800-1874 | N.Y. | N.Y. | Whig | 7/10/1850-3/3/1853 | Unitarian |
| Franklin Pierce | 1804-1869 | N.H. | N.H. | Democrat | 3/4/1853-3/3/1857 | Episcopalian |
| James Buchanan | 1791-1868 | Pa. | Pa. | Democrat | 3/4/1857-3/3/1861 | Presbyterian |
| Abraham Lincoln[e] | 1809-1865 | Ky. | Ill. | Republican | 3/4/1861-4/15/1865 | Presbyterian |
| Andrew Johnson[f] | 1808-1875 | N.C. | Tenn. | Democrat | 4/15/1865-3/3/1869 | Methodist |
| Ulysses S. Grant | 1822-1885 | Ohio | Ohio | Republican | 3/4/1869-3/3/1877 | Methodist |
| Rutherford B. Hayes | 1822-1893 | Ohio | Ohio | Republican | 3/4/1877-3/3/1881 | Methodist |

Table 1.1 (continued)

| Name | Dates of Birth-Death | State of Birth | Home State | Party | Term of Service | Religious Affiliation |
|---|---|---|---|---|---|---|
| James A. Garfield[e] | 1831-1881 | Ohio | Ohio | Republican | 3/4/1881-9/19/1881 | Christian Church |
| Chester A. Arthur[g] | 1830-1886 | Vt. | N.Y. | Republican | 9/20/1881-3/3/1885 | Episcopalian |
| Grover Cleveland | 1837-1908 | N.J. | N.Y. | Democrat | 3/4/1885-3/3/1889 3/4/1893-3/3/1897 | Presbyterian |
| Benjamin Harrison | 1833-1901 | Ohio | Ohio | Republican | 3/4/1889-3/3/1893 | Presbyterian |
| William McKinley[e] | 1843-1901 | Ohio | Ohio | Republican | 3/4/1897-9/14/1901 | Methodist |
| Theodore Roosevelt[h] | 1858-1919 | N.Y. | N.Y. | Republican | 9/14/1901-3/3/1909 | Dutch Reformed |
| William H. Taft | 1857-1930 | Ohio | Ohio | Republican | 3/4/1909-3/3/1913 | Unitarian |
| Woodrow Wilson | 1856-1924 | Va. | N.J. | Democrat | 3/4/1913-3/3/1921 | Presbyterian |
| Warren G. Harding[i] | 1865-1923 | Ohio | Ohio | Republican | 3/4/1921-8/2/1923 | Baptist |
| Calvin Coolidge[j] | 1872-1933 | Vt. | Mass. | Republican | 8/3/1923-3/3/1929 | Congregationalist |
| Herbert Hoover | 1874-1964 | Iowa | N.Y. | Republican | 3/4/1929-3/3/1933 | Friends |
| Franklin D. Roosevelt[k] | 1882-1945 | N.Y. | N.Y. | Democrat | 3/4/1933-4/12/1945 | Episcopalian |
| Harry S Truman[l] | 1884-1972 | Mo. | Mo. | Democrat | 4/12/1945-1/20/1953 | Baptist |
| Dwight D. Eisenhower | 1890-1969 | Texas | Kans. | Republican | 1/20/1953-1/20/1961 | Presbyterian |
| John F. Kennedy[e] | 1917-1963 | Mass. | Mass. | Democrat | 1/20/1961-11/22/1963 | Roman Catholic |
| Lyndon B. Johnson[m] | 1908-1973 | Texas | Texas | Democrat | 11/22/1963-1/20/1969 | Christian Church |
| Richard M. Nixon[n] | 1913- | Calif. | Calif. | Republican | 1/20/1969-8/9/1974 | Friends |
| Gerald R. Ford[o] | 1913- | Neb. | Mich. | Republican | 8/9/1974-1/20/1977 | Episcopalian |
| Jimmy Carter | 1924- | Ga. | Ga. | Democrat | 1/20/1977-1/20/1981 | Baptist |
| Ronald W. Reagan | 1911- | Ill. | Cal. | Republican | 1/20/1981-date | Presbyterian |

[a]William H. Harrison caught pneumonia during his inauguration and died April 4, 1841 after serving only 31 days.

[b]John Tyler was Harrison's Vice President and, on the latter's death, succeeded to the Presidency on April 6, 1841.

[c]Zachary Taylor died in office July 9, 1850 after serving only 16 months.

[d]Millard Fillmore was Taylor's Vice President and, on the latter's death, succeeded to the Presidency on July 10, 1850.

[e]President assassinated while in office (see Table 1.3 "Assassinations and Attempts on Major U.S. Political Figures, 1835-1981").

[f]Andrew Johnson was Lincoln's Vice President and, on the latter's assassination, succeeded to the Presidency on April 15, 1865.

[g]Chester A. Arthur was Garfield's Vice President and, on the latter's assassination, succeeded to the Presidency on September 20, 1881.

[h]Theodore Roosevelt was McKinley's Vice President and, on the latter's assassination, succeeded to the Presidency on September 14, 1901.

[i]Warren G. Harding, returning from a trip to Alaska, became ill and died on August 2, 1923.

[j]Calvin Coolidge was Harding's Vice President, and on the latter's death, succeeded to the Presidency on August 3, 1923.

[k]Franklin D. Roosevelt died during his fourth term in office, on April 12, 1945.

[l]Harry S Truman was Roosevelt's Vice President and, on the latter's death, succeeded to the Presidency on April 12, 1945.

[m]Lyndon B. Johnson was Kennedy's Vice President and, on the latter's assassination, succeeded to the Presidency on November 22, 1963.

[n]Richard M. Nixon was the only President to resign from office. He resigned on August 9, 1974 as a result of the Watergate scandal.

[o]Gerald R. Ford was the first President never elected to either the Presidency or Vice Presidency. Ford replaced Spiro Agnew as Nixon's Vice President on October 12, 1973 and, upon Nixon's resignation, succeeded to the Presidency on August 9, 1974.

Table 1.2

Vice Presidents of the United States, 1789-1985

| Name | Dates of Birth-Death | State of Birth | Home State | Party | Term of Service |
|---|---|---|---|---|---|
| John Adams[a] | 1735-1826 | Mass. | Mass. | Federalist | 4/30/1789-3/3/1797 |
| Thomas Jefferson[a] | 1743-1826 | Va. | Va. | Dem-Rep | 3/4/1797-3/3/1801 |
| Aaron Burr | 1756-1836 | N.J. | N.Y. | Anti-Fed. | 3/4/1801-3/3/1805 |
| George Clinton[b] | 1739-1812 | N.Y. | N.Y. | Dem-Rep | 3/4/1805-4/20/1812 |
| Elbridge Gerry[c] | 1744-1814 | Mass. | Mass. | Dem-Rep | 3/4/1813-11/23/1814 |
| Daniel D. Tompkins | 1774-1825 | N.Y. | N.Y. | Dem-Rep | 3/4/1817-3/3/1825 |
| John C. Calhoun[d] | 1782-1850 | S.C. | S.C. | Dem-Rep | 3/4/1825-12/28/1832 |
| Martin Van Buren[a] | 1782-1862 | N.Y. | N.Y. | Democrat | 3/4/1833-3/3/1837 |
| Richard M. Johnson | 1781-1850 | Ky. | Ky. | Democrat | 3/4/1837-3/3/1841 |
| John Tyler[e] | 1790-1862 | Va. | Va. | Whig | 3/4/1841-4/4/1841 |
| George M. Dallas | 1792-1864 | Pa. | Pa. | Democrat | 3/4/1845-3/3/1849 |
| Millard Fillmore[f] | 1800-1874 | N.Y. | N.Y. | Whig | 3/4/1849-7/9/1850 |
| William R. King[g] | 1786-1853 | N.C. | Ala. | Democrat | 3/4/1853-4/18/1853 |
| John C. Breckinridge | 1821-1875 | Ky. | Ky. | Democrat | 3/4/1857-3/3/1861 |
| Hannibal Hamlin | 1809-1891 | Me. | Me. | Republican | 3/4/1861-3/3/1865 |
| Andrew Johnson[h] | 1808-1875 | N.C. | Tenn. | Democrat | 3/4/1865-4/15/1865 |
| Schuyler Colfax | 1823-1885 | N.Y. | Ind. | Republican | 3/4/1869-3/3/1873 |
| Henry Wilson[i] | 1812-1875 | N.H. | Mass. | Republican | 3/4/1873-11/22/1875 |
| William A. Wheeler | 1819-1887 | N.Y. | N.Y. | Republican | 3/4/1877-3/3/1881 |
| Chester A. Arthur[j] | 1830-1886 | Vt. | N.Y. | Republican | 3/4/1881-9/19/1881 |
| Thomas A. Hendricks[k] | 1819-1885 | Ohio | Ind. | Democrat | 3/4/1885-11/25/1885 |
| Levi P. Morton | 1824-1920 | Vt. | N.Y. | Republican | 3/4/1889-3/3/1893 |
| Adlai E. Stevenson | 1835-1914 | Ky. | Ill. | Democrat | 3/4/1893-3/3/1897 |
| Garret A. Hobart[l] | 1844-1899 | N.J. | N.J. | Republican | 3/4/1897-11/21/1899 |
| Theodore Roosevelt[m,a] | 1858-1919 | N.Y. | N.Y. | Republican | 3/4/1901-9/14/1901 |
| Charles W. Fairbanks | 1852-1918 | Ohio | Ind. | Republican | 3/4/1905-3/3/1909 |
| James S. Sherman[n] | 1855-1912 | N.Y. | N.Y. | Republican | 3/4/1909-10/30/1912 |
| Thomas R. Marshall | 1854-1921 | Ind. | Ind. | Democrat | 3/4/1913-3/3/1921 |
| Calvin Coolidge[o,a] | 1872-1933 | Vt. | Mass. | Republican | 3/4/1921-8/3/1923 |
| Charles G. Dawes | 1865-1951 | Ohio | Ill. | Republican | 3/4/1925-3/3/1929 |
| Charles Curtis | 1860-1936 | Kans. | Kans. | Republican | 3/4/1929-3/3/1933 |
| John N. Garner | 1868-1967 | Texas | Texas | Democrat | 3/4/1933-1/20/1941 |
| Henry A. Wallace | 1888-1965 | Iowa | Iowa | Democrat | 1/20/1941-1/20/1945 |
| Harry S Truman[p,a] | 1884-1972 | Mo. | Mo. | Democrat | 1/20/1945-4/12/15 |
| Alben W. Barkley | 1877-1956 | Ky. | Ky. | Democrat | 1/20/1949-1/20/1953 |
| Richard M. Nixon[a] | 1913- | Calif. | Calif. | Republican | 1/20/1953-1/20/1961 |
| Lyndon B. Johnson[q,a] | 1908-1973 | Texas | Texas | Democrat | 1/20/1961-11/22/1963 |
| Hubert H. Humphrey | 1911-1978 | S. Dak. | Minn. | Democrat | 1/20/1965-1/20/1969 |

Table 1.2 (continued)

| Name | Dates of Birth-Death | State of Birth | Home State | Party | Term of Service |
|------|---------------------|----------------|------------|-------|-----------------|
| Spiro T. Agnew[r] | 1913- | Md. | Md. | Republican | 1/20/1969-10/10/1973 |
| Gerald R. Ford[s] | 1913- | Neb. | Mich. | Republican | 12/6/1973-8/9/1974 |
| Nelson A. Rockefeller[t] | 1908-1979 | Me. | N.Y. | Republican | 12/19/1974-1/20/1977 |
| Walter F. Mondale | 1928- | Minn. | Minn. | Democrat | 1/20/1977-1/20/1981 |
| George Bush | 1924- | Mass. | Texas | Republican | 1/20/1981-date |

[a]Subsequently elected President.

[b]George Clinton died on April 20, 1812, leaving the office unoccupied for over 10 months.

[c]Elbridge Gerry died on November 23, 1814, leaving the office unoccupied for over 2 years.

[d]John C. Calhoun resigned on December 28, 1832 in order to become a U.S. Senator, leaving the office unoccupied for over 2 months.

[e]As a result of Harrison's death, John Tyler assumed the Presidency on April 4, 1841, leaving the Vice Presidency unoccupied for nearly 4 years.

[f]As a result of Taylor's death, Millard Fillmore assumed the Presidency on July 9, 1850, leaving the Vice Presidency unoccupied for over 2.5 years.

[g]William R. King died on April 18, 1853, leaving the office unoccupied for nearly 4 years.

[h]As a result of Lincoln's assassination, Andrew Johnson assumed the Presidency on April 15, 1865, leaving the Vice Presidency unoccupied for almost 4 years.

[i]Henry Wilson died on November 22, 1875, leaving the office unoccupied for over a year.

[j]As a result of Garfield's assassination, Chester A. Arthur assumed the Presidency on September 19, 1881, leaving the Vice Presidency unoccupied for almost 3.5 years.

[k]Thomas A. Hendricks died on November 25, 1885, leaving the office unoccupied for over 3 years.

[l]Garret A. Hobart died on November 21, 1899, leaving the office unoccupied for over a year.

[m]As a result of McKinley's assassination, Theodore Roosevelt assumed the Presidency on September 14, 1901, leaving the Vice Presidency unoccupied for nearly 3.5 years.

[n]James S. Sherman died on October 30, 1912, leaving the office unoccupied for over 4 months.

[o]As a result of Harding's death, Calvin Coolidge assumed the Presidency on August 2, 1923, leaving the Vice Presidency unoccupied for over 1.5 years.

[p]As a result of Roosevelt's death, Harry S Truman assumed the Presidency on April 12, 1945, leaving the Vice Presidency unoccupied for nearly 4 years.

[q]As a result of Kennedy's assassination, Lyndon B. Johnson assumed the Presidency on November 22, 1963, leaving the Vice Presidency unoccupied for over a year.

[r]Spiro T. Agnew resigned on October 10, 1973.

[s]Gerald R. Ford replaced Agnew on December 6, 1973 according to the procedure specified in the 25th Amendment to the Constitution of the United States (1967). As a result of Nixon's resignation, Ford then assumed the Presidency on August 9, 1974.

[t]Nelson Rockefeller was appointed by Gerald R. Ford on December 19, 1974.

Table 1.3

Assassinations and Attempts on Major U.S. Political Figures,
1835-1981

| Political Figure | Attack Date | Location | Assailant | Birthplace |
|---|---|---|---|---|
| ANDREW JACKSON | 1/30/1835 | Washington | Richard Lawrence | England |
| ABRAHAM LINCOLN[*] | 4/14/1865 | Washington | John Wilkes Booth | Baltimore |
| JAMES A. GARFIELD[*] | 7/2/1881 | Washington | Charles Guiteau | Freeport, Ill. |
| WILLIAM MCKINLEY[*] | 9/6/1901 | Buffalo | Leon Czolgosz | Alpena, Mich.[a] |
| Theodore Roosevelt | 10/14/1912 | Milwaukee | John Schrank | Bavaria |
| Franklin D. Roosevelt | 2/15/1933 | Miami | Giuseppe Zangara | Sicily |
| Huey Long[*] | 9/8/1935 | Baton Rouge | Carl Weiss | Baton Rouge |
| HARRY S TRUMAN[b] | 11/1/1950 | Washington | Oscar Collazo | Puerto Rico |
|  |  |  | Griselio Torresola |  |
| JOHN F. KENNEDY[*] | 11/22/1963 | Dallas | Lee Harvey Oswald | New Orleans |
| Malcolm Little (Malcolm X)[*] | 2/21/1965 | New York | Unknown | Omaha |
| Martin Luther King[*] | 4/4/1968 | Memphis | James Earl Ray | Alton, Ill. |
| Robert F. Kennedy[*] | 6/5/1968 | Los Angeles | Sirhan Sirhan | Jerusalem |
| George Wallace[c] | 5/15/1972 | Laurel, Md. | Arthur Bremer | Milwaukee |
| RICHARD M. NIXON[d] | 2/22/1974 | Baltimore | Samuel Byck | Philadelphia |
| GERALD R. FORD | 9/5/1975 | Sacramento | Lynette Fromme | Los Angeles |
| GERALD R. FORD | 9/20/1975 | San Francisco | Sara Jane Moore | Charleston, W. Va. |
| RONALD REAGAN | 3/30/1981 | Washington | John Hinckley | Denver |

Note: Names of U.S. Presidents at the time of the assassination or attempt are shown in full capitals. The other seven were: Theodore Roosevelt, former President and Presidential candidate in 1912; Franklin D. Roosevelt, President-elect; Huey Long, Senator from Louisiana; Malcolm X, Black Nationalist leader; Martin Luther King, Civil Rights leader; Robert F. Kennedy, Senator from New York and Presidential candidate; and George Wallace, Governor of Alabama and Presidential candidate.

[*] Killed by assassin.

[a] Mother came to Alpena from Czechoslovakia one month before Czolgosz was born.

[b] Truman was never actually attacked; his assailants were stopped before they entered the White House.

[c] George Wallace was permanently paralyzed because of his injuries.

[d] Byck never actually attacked President Nixon; he intended to crash a commercial plane into the White House but was stopped after trying to commandeer the plane.

16

Table 1.4

Cabinet Officers, 1789-1984

| President | Secretary | Home State | Date Appointed |
|---|---|---|---|
| | | | |

### Secretaries of State

| President | Secretary | Home State | Date Appointed |
|---|---|---|---|
| Washington | John Jay | New York | 1789 |
| Washington | Thomas Jefferson | Virginia | 1789 |
| Washington | Edmund Randolph | Virginia | 1794 |
| Washington | Timothy Pickering | Pennsylvania | 1795 |
| J. Adams | Timothy Pickering | Pennsylvania | 1795 |
| J. Adams | John Marshall | Virginia | 1800 |
| Jefferson | James Madison | Virginia | 1801 |
| Madison | Robert Smith | Maryland | 1809 |
| Madison | James Monroe | Virginia | 1811 |
| Monroe | John Quincy Adams | Massachusetts | 1817 |
| J. Q. Adams | Henry Clay | Kentucky | 1825 |
| Jackson | Martin Van Buren | New York | 1829 |
| Jackson | Edward Livingston | Louisiana | 1831 |
| Jackson | Louis McLane | Delaware | 1833 |
| Jackson | John Forsyth | Georgia | 1834 |
| Van Buren | John Forsyth | Georgia | 1837 |
| W. H. Harrison | Daniel Webster | Massachusetts | 1841 |
| Tyler | Daniel Webster | Massachusetts | 1841 |
| Tyler | Abel P. Upshur | Virginia | 1843 |
| Tyler | John C. Calhoun | South Carolina | 1844 |
| Polk | John C. Calhoun | South Carolina | 1845 |
| Polk | James Buchanan | Pennsylvania | 1845 |
| Taylor | James Buchanan | Pennsylvania | 1849 |
| Taylor | John M. Clayton | Delaware | 1849 |
| Fillmore | John M. Clayton | Delaware | 1850 |
| Fillmore | Daniel Webster | Massachusetts | 1850 |
| Fillmore | Edward Everett | Massachusetts | 1852 |
| Pierce | William L. Marcy | New York | 1853 |
| Buchanan | William L. Marcy | New York | 1857 |
| Buchanan | Lewis Cass | Michigan | 1857 |
| Buchanan | Jeremiah S. Black | Pennsylvania | 1860 |
| Lincoln | Jeremiah S. Black | Pennsylvania | 1861 |
| Lincoln | William H. Seward | New York | 1861 |
| A. Johnson | William H. Seward | New York | 1865 |
| Grant | Elihu B. Washburne | Illinois | 1869 |
| Grant | Hamilton Fish | New York | 1869 |
| Hayes | Hamilton Fish | New York | 1877 |
| Hayes | William M. Evarts | New York | 1877 |
| Garfield | William M. Evarts | New York | 1881 |
| Garfield | James G. Blaine | Maine | 1881 |
| Arthur | James G. Blaine | Maine | 1881 |
| Arthur | F. T. Frelinghuysen | New Jersey | 1881 |
| Cleveland | F. T. Frelinghuysen | New Jersey | 1885 |
| Cleveland | Thomas F. Bayard | Delaware | 1885 |
| B. Harrison | Thomas F. Bayard | Delaware | 1889 |
| B. Harrison | James G. Blaine | Maine | 1889 |
| B. Harrison | John W. Foster | Indiana | 1892 |
| Cleveland | Walter Q. Gresham | Illinois | 1893 |
| Cleveland | Richard Olney | Massachusetts | 1895 |
| McKinley | Richard Olney | Massachusetts | 1897 |
| McKinley | John Sherman | Ohio | 1897 |
| McKinley | William R. Day | Ohio | 1898 |
| McKinley | John Hay | District of Columbia | 1898 |
| T. Roosevelt | John Hay | District of Columbia | 1901 |
| T. Roosevelt | Elihu Root | New York | 1905 |
| T. Roosevelt | Robert Bacon | New York | 1909 |
| Taft | Robert Bacon | New York | 1909 |

Table 1.4 (continued)

| President | Secretary | Home State | Date Appointed |
|-----------|-----------|------------|----------------|

## Secretaries of State

| President | Secretary | Home State | Date Appointed |
|-----------|-----------|------------|----------------|
| Taft | Philander C. Knox | Pennsylvania | 1909 |
| Wilson | Philander C. Knox | Pennsylvania | 1913 |
| Wilson | William J. Bryan | Nebraska | 1913 |
| Wilson | Robert Lansing | New York | 1915 |
| Wilson | Bainbridge Colby | New York | 1920 |
| Harding | Charles E. Hughes | New York | 1921 |
| Coolidge | Charles E. Hughes | New York | 1923 |
| Coolidge | Frank B. Kellogg | Minnesota | 1925 |
| Hoover | Frank B. Kellogg | Minnesota | 1929 |
| Hoover | Henry L. Stimson | New York | 1929 |
| F. D. Roosevelt | Cordell Hull | Tennessee | 1933 |
| F. D. Roosevelt | E. R. Stettinius, Jr. | Virginia | 1944 |
| Truman | E. R. Stettinius, Jr. | Virginia | 1945 |
| Truman | James F. Byrnes | South Carolina | 1945 |
| Truman | George C. Marshall | Pennsylvania | 1947 |
| Truman | Dean G. Acheson | Connecticut | 1949 |
| Eisenhower | John Foster Dulles | New York | 1953 |
| Eisenhower | Christian A. Herter | Massachusetts | 1959 |
| Kennedy | Dean Rusk | New York | 1961 |
| L. B. Johnson | Dean Rusk | New York | 1963 |
| Nixon | William P. Rogers | New York | 1969 |
| Nixon | Henry A. Kissinger | District of Columbia | 1973 |
| Ford | Henry A. Kissinger | District of Columbia | 1974 |
| Carter | Cyrus R. Vance | New York | 1977 |
| Carter | Edmund J. Muskie | Maine | 1980 |
| Reagan | Alexander M. Haig, Jr. | Connecticut | 1981 |
| Reagan | George P. Shultz | California | 1982 |

## Secretaries of Treasury

| President | Secretary | Home State | Date Appointed |
|-----------|-----------|------------|----------------|
| Washington | Alexander Hamilton | New York | 1789 |
| Washington | Oliver Wolcott | Connecticut | 1795 |
| J. Adams | Oliver Wolcott | Connecticut | 1797 |
| J. Adams | Samuel Dexter | Massachusetts | 1801 |
| Jefferson | Samuel Dexter | Massachusetts | 1801 |
| Jefferson | Albert Gallatin | Pennsylvania | 1801 |
| Madison | Albert Gallatin | Pennsylvania | 1809 |
| Madison | George W. Campbell | Tennessee | 1814 |
| Madison | Alexander J. Dallas | Pennsylvania | 1814 |
| Madison | William H. Crawford | Georgia | 1816 |
| Monroe | William H. Crawford | Georgia | 1817 |
| J. Q. Adams | Richard Rush | Pennsylvania | 1825 |
| Jackson | Samuel D. Ingham | Pennsylvania | 1829 |
| Jackson | Louis McLane | Delaware | 1831 |
| Jackson | William J. Duane | Pennsylvania | 1833 |
| Jackson | Roger B. Taney | Maryland | 1833 |
| Jackson | Levi Woodbury | New Hampshire | 1834 |
| Van Buren | Levi Woodbury | New Hampshire | 1837 |
| W. H. Harrison | Thomas Ewing | Ohio | 1841 |
| Tyler | Thomas Ewing | Ohio | 1841 |
| Tyler | Walter Forward | Pennsylvania | 1841 |
| Tyler | John C. Spencer | New York | 1843 |
| Tyler | George M. Bibb | Kentucky | 1844 |
| Polk | Robert J. Walker | Mississippi | 1845 |
| Taylor | William M. Meredith | Pennsylvania | 1849 |
| Fillmore | Thomas Corwin | Ohio | 1850 |
| Pierce | James Guthrie | Kentucky | 1853 |

Table 1.4 (continued)

| President | Secretary | Home State | Date Appointed |
|---|---|---|---|
| | | Secretaries of Treasury | |
| Buchanan | Howell Cobb | Georgia | 1857 |
| Buchanan | Phillip F. Thomas | Maryland | 1860 |
| Buchanan | John A. Dix | New York | 1861 |
| Lincoln | Salmon P. Chase | Ohio | 1861 |
| Lincoln | William P. Fessenden | Maine | 1864 |
| Lincoln | Hugh McCulloch | Indiana | 1865 |
| A. Johnson | Hugh McCulloch | Indiana | 1865 |
| Grant | George S. Boutwell | Massachusetts | 1869 |
| Grant | William A. Richardson | Massachusetts | 1873 |
| Grant | Benjamin H. Bristow | Kentucky | 1874 |
| Grant | Lot M. Morrill | Maine | 1876 |
| Hayes | John Sherman | Ohio | 1877 |
| Garfield | William Windom | Minnesota | 1881 |
| Arthur | Charles J. Folger | New York | 1881 |
| Arthur | Walter Q. Gresham | Indiana | 1884 |
| Arthur | Hugh McCulloch | Indiana | 1884 |
| Cleveland | Daniel Manning | New York | 1885 |
| Cleveland | Charles S. Fairchild | New York | 1887 |
| B. Harrison | William Windom | Minnesota | 1889 |
| B. Harrison | Charles Foster | Ohio | 1891 |
| Cleveland | John G. Carlisle | Kentucky | 1893 |
| McKinley | Lyman J. Gage | Illinois | 1897 |
| T. Roosevelt | Lyman J. Gage | Illinois | 1901 |
| T. Roosevelt | Leslie M. Shaw | Iowa | 1902 |
| T. Roosevelt | George B. Cortelyou | New York | 1907 |
| Taft | Franklin MacVeagh | Illinois | 1909 |
| Wilson | William G. McAdoo | New York | 1913 |
| Wilson | Carter Glass | Virginia | 1918 |
| Wilson | David F. Houston | Missouri | 1920 |
| Harding | Andrew W. Mellon | Pennsylvania | 1921 |
| Coolidge | Andrew W. Mellon | Pennsylvania | 1923 |
| Hoover | Andrew W. Mellon | Pennsylvania | 1929 |
| Hoover | Ogden L. Mills | New York | 1932 |
| F. D. Roosevelt | William H. Woodin | New York | 1933 |
| F. D. Roosevelt | Henry Morgenthau, Jr. | New York | 1934 |
| Truman | Fred M. Vinson | Kentucky | 1945 |
| Truman | John W. Snyder | Missouri | 1946 |
| Eisenhower | George M. Humphrey | Ohio | 1953 |
| Eisenhower | Robert B. Anderson | Connecticut | 1957 |
| Kennedy | C. Douglas Dillon | New Jersey | 1961 |
| L. B. Johnson | C. Douglas Dillon | New Jersey | 1963 |
| L. B. Johnson | Henry H. Fowler | Virginia | 1965 |
| L. B. Johnson | Joseph W. Barr | Indiana | 1968 |
| Nixon | David M. Kennedy | Illinois | 1969 |
| Nixon | John B. Connally | Texas | 1970 |
| Nixon | George P. Shultz | Illinois | 1972 |
| Nixon | William E. Simon | New Jersey | 1974 |
| Ford | William E. Simon | New Jersey | 1974 |
| Carter | W. Michael Blumenthal | Michigan | 1977 |
| Carter | G. William Miller | Rhode Island | 1979 |
| Reagan | Donald T. Regan | New York | 1981 |
| Reagan | James Baker | Texas | 1985 |

Table 1.4 (continued)

| President | Secretary | Home State | Date Appointed |
|-----------|-----------|------------|----------------|

Secretaries of War[a]

| President | Secretary | Home State | Date Appointed |
|-----------|-----------|------------|----------------|
| Washington | Henry Knox | Massachusetts | 1789 |
| Washington | Timothy Pickering | Pennsylvania | 1795 |
| Washington | James McHenry | Maryland | 1796 |
| J. Adams | James McHenry | Maryland | 1797 |
| J. Adams | Samuel Dexter | Massachusetts | 1800 |
| Jefferson | Henry Dearborn | Massachusetts | 1801 |
| Madison | William Eustis | Massachusetts | 1809 |
| Madison | John Armstrong | New York | 1813 |
| Madison | James Monroe | Virginia | 1814 |
| Madison | William H. Crawford | Georgia | 1815 |
| Monroe | John C. Calhoun | South Carolina | 1817 |
| J. Q. Adams | James Barbour | Virginia | 1825 |
| J. Q. Adams | Peter B. Porter | New York | 1828 |
| Jackson | John H. Eaton | Tennessee | 1829 |
| Jackson | Lewis Cass | Ohio | 1831 |
| Jackson | Benjamin F. Butler | New York | 1837 |
| Van Buren | Joel R. Poinsett | South Carolina | 1837 |
| W. H. Harrison | John Bell | Tennessee | 1841 |
| Tyler | John Bell | Tennessee | 1841 |
| Tyler | John C. Spencer | New York | 1841 |
| Tyler | James M. Porter | Pennsylvania | 1843 |
| Tyler | William Wilkins | Pennsylvania | 1844 |
| Polk | William L. Marcy | New York | 1845 |
| Taylor | George W. Crawford | Georgia | 1849 |
| Fillmore | Charles M. Conrad | Louisiana | 1850 |
| Pierce | Jefferson Davis | Mississippi | 1853 |
| Buchanan | John B. Floyd | Virginia | 1857 |
| Buchanan | Joseph Holt | Kentucky | 1861 |
| Lincoln | Simon Cameron | Pennsylvania | 1861 |
| Lincoln | Edwin M. Stanton | Pennsylvania | 1862 |
| A. Johnson | Edwin M. Stanton | Pennsylvania | 1865 |
| A. Johnson | John M. Schofield | Illinois | 1868 |
| Grant | John A. Rawlins | Illinois | 1869 |
| Grant | William T. Sherman | Ohio | 1869 |
| Grant | William W. Belknap | Iowa | 1869 |
| Grant | Alphonso Taft | Ohio | 1876 |
| Grant | James D. Cameron | Pennsylvania | 1876 |
| Hayes | George W. McCrary | Iowa | 1877 |
| Hayes | Alexander Ramsey | Minnesota | 1879 |
| Garfield | Robert T. Lincoln | Illinois | 1881 |
| Arthur | Robert T. Lincoln | Illinois | 1881 |
| Cleveland | William C. Endicott | Massachusetts | 1885 |
| B. Harrison | Redfield Proctor | Vermont | 1890 |
| B. Harrison | Stephen B. Elkins | West Virginia | 1891 |
| Cleveland | Daniel S. Lamont | New York | 1893 |
| McKinley | Russell A. Alger | Michigan | 1897 |
| McKinley | Elihu Root | New York | 1899 |
| T. Roosevelt | Elihu Root | New York | 1901 |
| T. Roosevelt | William H. Taft | Ohio | 1904 |
| T. Roosevelt | Luke E. Wright | Tennessee | 1908 |
| Taft | Jacob M. Dickinson | Tennessee | 1909 |
| Taft | Henry L. Stimson | New York | 1911 |
| Wilson | Lindley M. Garrison | New Jersey | 1913 |
| Wilson | Newton D. Baker | Ohio | 1916 |
| Harding | John W. Weeks | Massachusetts | 1921 |
| Coolidge | John W. Weeks | Massachusetts | 1923 |
| Coolidge | Dwight F. Davis | Missouri | 1925 |

Table 1.4 (continued)

| President | Secretary | Home State | Date Appointed |
|-----------|-----------|------------|----------------|

### Secretaries of War[a]

| President | Secretary | Home State | Date Appointed |
|-----------|-----------|------------|----------------|
| Hoover | James W. Good | Illinois | 1929 |
| Hoover | Patrick J. Hurley | Oklahoma | 1929 |
| F. D. Roosevelt | George H. Dern | Utah | 1933 |
| F. D. Roosevelt | Harry H. Woodring | Kansas | 1937 |
| F. D. Roosevelt | Henry L. Stimson | New York | 1940 |
| Truman | Robert P. Patterson | New York | 1945 |
| Truman | Kenneth C. Royall | North Carolina | 1947 |

[a]This office was discontinued in 1947. The War Department then became the Department of the Army and was made part of the Defense Department, whose head holds a cabinet position.

### Secretaries of the Navy[b]

| President | Secretary | Home State | Date Appointed |
|-----------|-----------|------------|----------------|
| J. Adams | Benjamin Stoddert | Maryland | 1798 |
| Jefferson | Benjamin Stoddert | Maryland | 1801 |
| Jefferson | Robert Smith | Maryland | 1801 |
| Madison | Paul Hamilton | South Carolina | 1809 |
| Madison | William Jones | Pennsylvania | 1813 |
| Madison | Benjamin Williams Crowninshield | Massachusetts | 1814 |
| Monroe | Benjamin Williams Crowninshield | Massachusetts | 1817 |
| Monroe | Smith Thompson | New York | 1818 |
| Monroe | Samuel L. Southard | New Jersey | 1823 |
| J. Q. Adams | Samuel L. Southard | New Jersey | 1825 |
| Jackson | John Branch | North Carolina | 1829 |
| Jackson | Levi Woodbury | New Hampshire | 1831 |
| Jackson | Mahlon Dickerson | New Jersey | 1834 |
| Van Buren | Mahlon Dickerson | New Jersey | 1837 |
| Van Buren | James K. Paulding | New York | 1838 |
| W. H. Harrison | George E. Badger | North Carolina | 1841 |
| Tyler | George E. Badger | North Carolina | 1841 |
| Tyler | Abel P. Upshur | Virginia | 1841 |
| Tyler | David Henshaw | Massachusetts | 1843 |
| Tyler | Thomas W. Gilmer | Virginia | 1844 |
| Tyler | John Y. Mason | Virginia | 1844 |
| Polk | George Bancroft | Massachusetts | 1845 |
| Polk | John Y. Mason | Virginia | 1846 |
| Taylor | William B. Preston | Virginia | 1849 |
| Fillmore | William A. Graham | North Carolina | 1850 |
| Fillmore | John P. Kennedy | Maryland | 1852 |
| Pierce | James C. Dobbin | North Carolina | 1853 |
| Buchanan | Isaac Toucey | Connecticut | 1857 |
| Lincoln | Gideon Welles | Connecticut | 1861 |
| A. Johnson | Gideon Welles | Connecticut | 1865 |
| Grant | Adolph E. Borie | Pennsylvania | 1869 |
| Grant | George M. Robeson | New Jersey | 1869 |
| Hayes | Richard W. Thompson | Indiana | 1877 |
| Hayes | Nathan Goff, Jr. | West Virginia | 1881 |
| Garfield | William H. Hunt | Louisiana | 1881 |
| Arthur | William H. Hunt | Louisiana | 1881 |
| Arthur | William E. Chandler | New Hampshire | 1882 |
| Cleveland | William C. Whitney | New York | 1885 |
| B. Harrison | Benjamin F. Tracy | New York | 1889 |
| Cleveland | Hilary A. Herbert | Alabama | 1893 |
| McKinley | John D. Long | Massachusetts | 1897 |

Table 1.4 (continued)

| President | Secretary | Home State | Date Appointed |
|-----------|-----------|------------|----------------|

### Secretaries of the Navy[b]

| President | Secretary | Home State | Date Appointed |
|-----------|-----------|------------|----------------|
| T. Roosevelt | John D. Long | Massachusetts | 1901 |
| T. Roosevelt | William H. Moody | Massachusetts | 1902 |
| T. Roosevelt | Paul Morton | Illinois | 1904 |
| T. Roosevelt | Charles J. Bonaparte | Maryland | 1905 |
| T. Roosevelt | Victor H. Metcalf | California | 1906 |
| T. Roosevelt | Truman H. Newberry | Michigan | 1908 |
| Taft | George von L. Meyer | Massachusetts | 1909 |
| Wilson | Josephus Daniels | North Carolina | 1913 |
| Harding | Edwin Denby | Michigan | 1921 |
| Coolidge | Edwin Denby | Michigan | 1923 |
| Hoover | Charles Francis Adams | Massachusetts | 1929 |
| F. D. Roosevelt | Claude A. Swanson | Virginia | 1933 |
| F. D. Roosevelt | Charles Edison | New Jersey | 1940 |
| F. D. Roosevelt | Frank Knox | Illinois | 1940 |
| F. D. Roosevelt | James V. Forrestal | New York | 1944 |
| Truman | James V. Forrestal | New York | 1945 |

[b]This office was discontinued in 1945. The Navy Department then became a branch of the Defense Department, whose head holds a cabinet position.

### Secretaries of Defense

| President | Secretary | Home State | Date Appointed |
|-----------|-----------|------------|----------------|
| Truman | James V. Forrestal | New York | 1947 |
| Truman | Louis A. Johnson | West Virginia | 1949 |
| Truman | George C. Marshall | Pennsylvania | 1950 |
| Truman | Robert A. Lovett | New York | 1951 |
| Eisenhower | Charles E. Wilson | Michigan | 1953 |
| Eisenhower | Neil H. McElroy | Ohio | 1957 |
| Eisenhower | Thomas S. Gates, Jr. | Pennsylvania | 1959 |
| Kennedy | Robert S. McNamara | Michigan | 1961 |
| L. B. Johnson | Robert S. McNamara | Michigan | 1963 |
| L. B. Johnson | Clark M. Clifford | Maryland | 1968 |
| Nixon | Melvin R. Laird | Wisconsin | 1969 |
| Nixon | Elliot L. Richardson | Massachusetts | 1973 |
| Nixon | James R. Schlesinger | Virginia | 1973 |
| Ford | James R. Schlesinger | Virginia | 1974 |
| Ford | Donald H. Rumsfeld | Illinois | 1975 |
| Carter | Harold Brown | California | 1977 |
| Reagan | Caspar W. Weinberger | California | 1981 |

### Attorneys General

| President | Secretary | Home State | Date Appointed |
|-----------|-----------|------------|----------------|
| Washington | Edmund Randolph | Virginia | 1789 |
| Washington | William Bradford | Pennsylvania | 1794 |
| Washington | Charles Lee | Virginia | 1795 |
| J. Adams | Charles Lee | Virginia | 1797 |
| Jefferson | Levi Lincoln | Massachusetts | 1801 |
| Jefferson | John Breckenridge | Kentucky | 1805 |
| Jefferson | Caesar A. Rodney | Delaware | 1807 |
| Madison | Caesar A. Rodney | Delaware | 1809 |
| Madison | William Pinkney | Maryland | 1811 |
| Madison | Richard Rush | Pennsylvania | 1814 |
| Monroe | Richard Rush | Pennsylvania | 1817 |
| Monroe | William Wirt | Virginia | 1817 |

Table 1.4 (continued)

| President | Secretary | Home State | Date Appointed |
|-----------|-----------|------------|----------------|
| | | | |

### Attorneys General

| President | Secretary | Home State | Date Appointed |
|-----------|-----------|------------|----------------|
| J. Q. Adams | William Wirt | Virginia | 1825 |
| Jackson | John McP. Berrien | Georgia | 1829 |
| Jackson | Roger B. Taney | Maryland | 1831 |
| Jackson | Benjamin F. Butler | New York | 1833 |
| Van Buren | Benjamin F. Butler | New York | 1837 |
| Van Buren | Felix Grundy | Tennessee | 1838 |
| Van Buren | Henry D. Gilpin | Pennsylvania | 1840 |
| W. H. Harrison | John J. Crittenden | Kentucky | 1841 |
| Tyler | John J. Crittenden | Kentucky | 1841 |
| Tyler | Hugh S. Legare | South Carolina | 1841 |
| Tyler | John Nelson | Maryland | 1843 |
| Polk | John Y. Mason | Virginia | 1845 |
| Polk | Nathan Clifford | Maine | 1846 |
| Polk | Isaac Toucey | Connecticut | 1848 |
| Taylor | Reverdy Johnson | Maryland | 1849 |
| Fillmore | John J. Crittenden | Kentucky | 1850 |
| Pierce | Caleb Cushing | Massachusetts | 1853 |
| Buchanan | Jeremiah S. Black | Pennsylvania | 1857 |
| Buchanan | Edwin M. Stanton | Pennsylvania | 1860 |
| Lincoln | Edward Bates | Missouri | 1861 |
| Lincoln | James Speed | Kentucky | 1864 |
| A. Johnson | James Speed | Kentucky | 1865 |
| A. Johnson | Henry Stanbery | Ohio | 1866 |
| A. Johnson | William M. Evarts | New York | 1868 |
| Grant | Ebenezer R. Hoar | Massachusetts | 1869 |
| Grant | Amos T. Akerman | Georgia | 1870 |
| Grant | George H. Williams | Oregon | 1871 |
| Grant | Edward Pierrepont | New York | 1875 |
| Grant | Alphonso Taft | Ohio | 1876 |
| Hayes | Charles Devens | Massachusetts | 1877 |
| Garfield | Wayne MacVeagh | Pennsylvania | 1881 |
| Arthur | Benjamin H. Brewster | Pennsylvania | 1881 |
| Cleveland | Augustus Garland | Arkansas | 1885 |
| B. Harrison | William H. H. Miller | Indiana | 1889 |
| Cleveland | Richard Olney | Massachusetts | 1893 |
| Cleveland | Judson Harmon | Ohio | 1895 |
| McKinley | Joseph McKenna | California | 1897 |
| McKinley | John W. Griggs | New Jersey | 1898 |
| McKinley | Philander C. Knox | Pennsylvania | 1901 |
| T. Roosevelt | Philander C. Knox | Pennsylvania | 1901 |
| T. Roosevelt | William H. Moody | Massachusetts | 1904 |
| T. Roosevelt | Charles J. Bonaparte | Maryland | 1906 |
| Taft | George W. Wickersham | New York | 1909 |
| Wilson | J. C. McReynolds | Tennessee | 1913 |
| Wilson | Thomas W. Gregory | Texas | 1914 |
| Wilson | A. Mitchell Palmer | Pennsylvania | 1919 |
| Harding | Harry M. Daugherty | Ohio | 1921 |
| Coolidge | Harry M. Daugherty | Ohio | 1923 |
| Coolidge | Harlan F. Stone | New York | 1924 |
| Coolidge | John G. Sargent | Vermont | 1925 |
| Hoover | William D. Mitchell | Minnesota | 1929 |
| F. D. Roosevelt | Homer S. Cummings | Connecticut | 1933 |
| F. D. Roosevelt | Frank Murphy | Michigan | 1939 |
| F. D. Roosevelt | Robert H. Jackson | New York | 1940 |
| F. D. Roosevelt | Francis Biddle | Pennsylvania | 1941 |
| Truman | Tom C. Clark | Texas | 1945 |
| Truman | J. Howard McGrath | Rhode Island | 1949 |
| Truman | J. P. McGranery | Pennsylvania | 1952 |

Table 1.4 (continued)

| President | Secretary | Home State | Date Appointed |
|---|---|---|---|
| | | | |

### Attorneys General

| President | Secretary | Home State | Date Appointed |
|---|---|---|---|
| Eisenhower | H. Brownell, Jr. | New York | 1953 |
| Eisenhower | William P. Rogers | Maryland | 1957 |
| Kennedy | Robert F. Kennedy | Massachusetts | 1961 |
| L. B. Johnson | Robert F. Kennedy | Massachusetts | 1963 |
| L. B. Johnson | Nicholas deB. Katzenbach | Illinois | 1965 |
| L. B. Johnson | Ramsey Clark | Texas | 1967 |
| Nixon | John N. Mitchell | New York | 1969 |
| Nixon | Richard G. Kleindienst | Arizona | 1972 |
| Nixon | Elliot L. Richardson | Massachusetts | 1973 |
| Nixon | William B. Saxbe | Ohio | 1974 |
| Ford | William B. Saxbe | Ohio | 1974 |
| Ford | Edward H. Levi | Illinois | 1975 |
| Carter | Griffin B. Bell | Georgia | 1977 |
| Carter | Benjamin R. Civiletti | Maryland | 1979 |
| Reagan | William French Smith | California | 1981 |
| Reagan | Edwin Meese III | California | 1985 |

### Secretaries of the Interior

| President | Secretary | Home State | Date Appointed |
|---|---|---|---|
| Taylor | Thomas Ewing | Ohio | 1849 |
| Fillmore | Thomas M. T. McKennan | Pennsylvania | 1850 |
| Fillmore | Alex H. H. Stuart | Virginia | 1850 |
| Pierce | Robert McClelland | Michigan | 1853 |
| Buchanan | Jacob Thompson | Mississippi | 1857 |
| Lincoln | Caleb B. Smith | Indiana | 1861 |
| Lincoln | John P. Usher | Indiana | 1863 |
| A. Johnson | John P. Usher | Indiana | 1865 |
| A. Johnson | James Harlan | Iowa | 1865 |
| A. Johnson | Orville H. Browning | Illinois | 1866 |
| Grant | Jacob D. Cox | Ohio | 1869 |
| Grant | Columbus Delano | Ohio | 1870 |
| Grant | Zachariah Chandler | Michigan | 1875 |
| Hayes | Carl Schurz | Missouri | 1877 |
| Garfield | Sam J. Kirkwood | Iowa | 1881 |
| Arthur | Sam J. Kirkwood | Iowa | 1881 |
| Arthur | Henry M. Teller | Colorado | 1882 |
| Cleveland | Lucius Q. C. Lamar | Mississippi | 1885 |
| Cleveland | William F. Vilas | Wisconsin | 1888 |
| B. Harrison | John W. Noble | Missouri | 1889 |
| Cleveland | Hoke Smith | Georgia | 1893 |
| Cleveland | David R. Francis | Missouri | 1896 |
| McKinley | Cornelius N. Bliss | New York | 1897 |
| McKinley | Ethan A. Hitchcock | Missouri | 1898 |
| T. Roosevelt | Ethan A. Hitchcock | Missouri | 1901 |
| T. Roosevelt | James R. Garfield | Ohio | 1907 |
| Taft | Richard A. Ballinger | Washington | 1909 |
| Taft | Walter L. Fisher | Illinois | 1911 |
| Wilson | Franklin K. Lane | California | 1913 |
| Wilson | John B. Payne | Illinois | 1920 |
| Harding | Albert B. Fall | New Mexico | 1921 |
| Harding | Hubert Work | Colorado | 1923 |
| Coolidge | Hubert Work | Colorado | 1923 |
| Coolidge | Roy O. West | Illinois | 1929 |
| Hoover | Ray Lyman Wilbur | California | 1929 |
| F. D. Roosevelt | Harold L. Ickes | Illinois | 1933 |
| Truman | Harold L. Ickes | Illinois | 1945 |

Table 1.4 (continued)

| President | Secretary | Home State | Date Appointed |
|-----------|-----------|------------|----------------|
| | | | |

### Secretaries of the Interior

| President | Secretary | Home State | Date Appointed |
|-----------|-----------|------------|----------------|
| Truman | Julius A. Krug | Wisconsin | 1946 |
| Truman | Oscar L. Chapman | Colorado | 1950 |
| Eisenhower | Douglas McKay | Oregon | 1953 |
| Eisenhower | Fred A. Seaton | Nebraska | 1956 |
| Kennedy | Stewart L. Udall | Arizona | 1961 |
| L. B. Johnson | Stewart L. Udall | Arizona | 1963 |
| Nixon | Walter J. Hickel | Alaska | 1969 |
| Nixon | Rogers C. B. Morton | Maryland | 1971 |
| Ford | Rogers C. B. Morton | Maryland | 1974 |
| Ford | Thomas S. Kleppe | North Dakota | 1975 |
| Carter | Cecil D. Andrus | Idaho | 1977 |
| Reagan | James G. Watt | Colorado | 1981 |
| Reagan | William P. Clark | California | 1983 |
| Reagan | Donald Hodel | Oregon | 1985 |

### Secretaries of Agriculture

| President | Secretary | Home State | Date Appointed |
|-----------|-----------|------------|----------------|
| Cleveland | Norman J. Colman | Missouri | 1889 |
| B. Harrison | Jeremiah M. Rusk | Wisconsin | 1889 |
| Cleveland | J. Sterling Morton | Nebraska | 1893 |
| McKinley | James Wilson | Iowa | 1897 |
| T. Roosevelt | James Wilson | Iowa | 1901 |
| Taft | James Wilson | Iowa | 1909 |
| Wilson | David F. Houston | Missouri | 1913 |
| Wilson | Edward T. Meredith | Iowa | 1920 |
| Harding | Henry C. Wallace | Iowa | 1921 |
| Coolidge | Henry C. Wallace | Iowa | 1923 |
| Coolidge | Howard M. Gore | West Virginia | 1924 |
| Coolidge | W. M. Jardine | Kansas | 1925 |
| Hoover | Arthur M. Hyle | Missouri | 1929 |
| F. D. Roosevelt | Henry A. Wallace | Iowa | 1933 |
| F. D. Roosevelt | Claude R. Wickard | Indiana | 1940 |
| Truman | Clinton P. Anderson | New Mexico | 1945 |
| Truman | Charles F. Brannan | Colorado | 1948 |
| Eisenhower | Ezra Taft Benson | Utah | 1953 |
| Kennedy | Orville L. Freeman | Minnesota | 1961 |
| L. B. Johnson | Orville L. Freeman | Minnesota | 1963 |
| Nixon | Clifford M. Hardin | Indiana | 1969 |
| Nixon | Earl L. Butz | Indiana | 1971 |
| Ford | Earl L. Butz | Indiana | 1974 |
| Carter | Bob Bergland | Minnesota | 1977 |
| Reagan | John R. Block | Illinois | 1981 |

Table 1.4 (continued)

| President | Secretary | Home State | Date Appointed |
|---|---|---|---|
| | | **Secretaries of Commerce and Labor** | |
| T. Roosevelt | George B. Cortelyou | New York | 1903 |
| T. Roosevelt | Victor H. Metcalf | California | 1904 |
| T. Roosevelt | Oscar S. Straus | New York | 1906 |
| Taft | Charles Nagel | Missouri | 1909 |
| | | **Secretaries of Labor** | |
| Wilson | William B. Wilson | Pennsylvania | 1913 |
| Harding | James J. Davis | Pennsylvania | 1921 |
| Coolidge | James J. Davis | Pennsylvania | 1923 |
| Hoover | James J. Davis | Pennsylvania | 1929 |
| Hoover | William N. Doak | Virginia | 1930 |
| F. D. Roosevelt | Frances Perkins | New York | 1933 |
| Truman | L. B. Schwellenback | Washington | 1945 |
| Truman | Maurice J. Tobin | Massachusetts | 1949 |
| Eisenhower | Martin P. Durkin | Illinois | 1953 |
| Eisenhower | James P. Mitchell | New Jersey | 1953 |
| Kennedy | Arthur J. Goldberg | Illinois | 1961 |
| Kennedy | W. Willard Wirtz | Illinois | 1962 |
| L. B. Johnson | W. Willard Wirtz | Illinois | 1963 |
| Nixon | George P. Shultz | Illionis | 1969 |
| Nixon | James D. Hodgson | California | 1970 |
| Nixon | Peter J. Brennan | New York | 1973 |
| Ford | Peter J. Brennan | New York | 1974 |
| Ford | John T. Dunlop | California | 1975 |
| Ford | W. J. Usery, Jr. | Georgia | 1976 |
| Carter | F. Ray Marshall | Texas | 1977 |
| Reagan | Raymond J. Donovan | New Jersey | 1981 |
| Reagan | William E. Brock III | Tennessee | 1985 |
| | | **Secretaries of Commerce** | |
| Wilson | William C. Redfield | New York | 1913 |
| Wilson | Josh. W. Alexander | Missouri | 1919 |
| Harding | Herbert C. Hoover | California | 1921 |
| Coolidge | Herbert C. Hoover | California | 1923 |
| Coolidge | William F. Whiting | Massachusetts | 1928 |
| Hoover | Robert P. Lamont | Illinois | 1929 |
| Hoover | Roy D. Chapin | Michigan | 1932 |
| F. D. Roosevelt | Daniel C. Roper | South Carolina | 1933 |
| F. D. Roosevelt | Harry L. Hopkins | New York | 1939 |
| F. D. Roosevelt | Jesse Jones | Texas | 1940 |
| F. D. Roosevelt | Henry A. Wallace | Iowa | 1945 |
| Truman | Henry A. Wallace | Iowa | 1945 |
| Truman | W. Averell Harriman | New York | 1947 |
| Truman | Charles Sawyer | Ohio | 1948 |
| Eisenhower | Sinclair Weeks | Massachusetts | 1953 |
| Eisenhower | Lewis L. Strauss | New York | 1958 |
| Eisenhower | Frederick H. Mueller | Michigan | 1959 |
| Kennedy | Luther H. Hodges | North Carolina | 1961 |
| L. B. Johnson | Luther H. Hodges | North Carolina | 1963 |
| L. B. Johnson | John T. Connor | New Jersey | 1965 |
| L. B. Johnson | Alex B. Trowbridge | New Jersey | 1967 |

Table 1.4 (continued)

| President | Secretary | Home State | Date Appointed |
|---|---|---|---|
| | | **Secretaries of Commerce** | |
| L. B. Johnson | C. R. Smith | New York | 1968 |
| Nixon | Maurice H. Stans | Minnesota | 1969 |
| Nixon | Peter G. Peterson | Illinois | 1972 |
| Nixon | Frederick B. Dent | South Carolina | 1973 |
| Ford | Frederick B. Dent | South Carolina | 1974 |
| Ford | Rogers C. B. Morton | Maryland | 1975 |
| Ford | Elliot L. Richardson | Massachusetts | 1976 |
| Carter | Juanita M. Kreps | North Carolina | 1977 |
| Carter | Philip M. Klutznick | Illinois | 1979 |
| Reagan | Malcolm Baldrige | Connecticut | 1981 |
| | | **Secretaries of Health, Education and Welfare**[c] | |
| Eisenhower | Oveta Culp Hobby | Texas | 1953 |
| Eisenhower | Marion B. Folsom | New York | 1955 |
| Eisenhower | Arthur S. Flemming | Ohio | 1958 |
| Kennedy | Abraham A. Ribicoff | Connecticut | 1961 |
| Kennedy | Anthony J. Celebrezze | Ohio | 1962 |
| L. B. Johnson | Anthony J. Celebrezze | Ohio | 1963 |
| L. B. Johnson | John W. Gardner | New York | 1965 |
| L. B. Johnson | Wilbur J. Cohen | Michigan | 1968 |
| Nixon | Robert H. Finch | California | 1969 |
| Nixon | Elliot L. Richardson | Massachusetts | 1970 |
| Nixon | Casper W. Weinberger | California | 1973 |
| Ford | Casper W. Weinberger | California | 1974 |
| Ford | Forrest D. Mathews | Alabama | 1975 |
| Carter | Joseph A. Califano, Jr. | District of Columbia | 1977 |
| Carter | Patricia Roberts Harris | District of Columbia | 1979 |

[c]The Department of Health, Education and Welfare was divided by Congress on September 27, 1979 into the Department of Health and Human Services and the Department of Education.

| President | Secretary | Home State | Date Appointed |
|---|---|---|---|
| | | **Secretaries of Health and Human Services** | |
| Carter | Patricia Roberts Harris | District of Columbia | 1979 |
| Reagan | Richard S. Schweiker | Pennsylvania | 1981 |
| Reagan | Margaret M. Heckler | Massachusetts | 1983 |
| | | **Secretaries of Education** | |
| Carter | Shirley Hufstedler | California | 1979 |
| Reagan | Terrel Bell | Utah | 1981 |
| Reagan | William J. Bennett | North Carolina | 1985 |

Table 1.4 (continued)

| President | Secretary | Home State | Date Appointed |
|-----------|-----------|------------|----------------|
| Secretaries of Housing and Urban Development | | | |
| L. B. Johnson | Robert C. Weaver | Washington | 1966 |
| L. B. Johnson | Robert C. Wood | Massachusetts | 1968 |
| Nixon | George W. Romney | Michigan | 1969 |
| Nixon | James T. Lynn | Ohio | 1973 |
| Ford | James T. Lynn | Ohio | 1974 |
| Ford | Carla Anderson Hills | California | 1975 |
| Carter | Particia Roberts Harris | District of Columbia | 1977 |
| Carter | Moon Landrieu | Louisiana | 1979 |
| Reagan | Samuel R. Pierce, Jr. | New York | 1981 |
| Secretaries of Transportation | | | |
| L. B. Johnson | Alan S. Boyd | Florida | 1966 |
| Nixon | John A. Volpe | Massachusetts | 1969 |
| Nixon | Claude S. Brinegar | California | 1973 |
| Ford | Claude S. Brinegar | California | 1974 |
| Carter | Brock Adams | Washington | 1977 |
| Carter | Neil E. Goldschmidt | Oregon | 1979 |
| Reagan | Andrew L. Lewis, Jr. | Pennsylvania | 1981 |
| Reagan | Elizabeth Hanford Dole | Kansas | 1983 |
| Secretaries of Energy | | | |
| Carter | James R. Schlesinger | Virginia | 1977 |
| Carter | Charles Duncan, Jr. | Wyoming | 1979 |
| Reagan | James B. Edwards | South Carolina | 1981 |
| Reagan | Donald P. Hodel | Oregon | 1982 |
| Reagan | John S. Herrington | California | 1985 |
| Postmasters General[d] | | | |
| Washington | Samuel Osgood | Massachusetts | 1789 |
| Washington | Timothy Pickering | Pennsylvania | 1791 |
| Washington | Joseph Habersham | Georgia | 1795 |
| J. Adams | Joseph Habersham | Georgia | 1797 |
| Jefferson | Joseph Habersham | Georgia | 1801 |
| Jefferson | Gideon Granger | Connecticut | 1801 |
| Madison | Gideon Granger | Connecticut | 1809 |
| Madison | Return J. Meigs, Jr. | Ohio | 1814 |
| Monroe | Return J. Meigs, Jr. | Ohio | 1817 |
| Monroe | John McLean | Ohio | 1823 |
| J. Q. Adams | John McLean | Ohio | 1825 |
| Jackson | William T. Barry | Kentucky | 1829 |
| Jackson | Amos Kendall | Kentucky | 1835 |
| Van Buren | Amos Kendall | Kentucky | 1837 |
| Van Buren | John M. Niles | Connecticut | 1840 |
| W. H. Harrison | Francis Granger | New York | 1841 |
| Tyler | Francis Granger | New York | 1841 |
| Tyler | Charles A. Wickliffe | Kentucky | 1841 |
| Polk | Cave Johnson | Tennessee | 1845 |
| Taylor | Jacob Collamer | Vermont | 1849 |
| Fillmore | Nathan K. Hall | New York | 1850 |

Table 1.4 (continued)

| President | Secretary | Home State | Date Appointed |
|---|---|---|---|
| Postmasters General[d] | | | |
| Fillmore | Samuel D. Hubbard | Connecticut | 1852 |
| Pierce | James Campbell | Pennsylvania | 1853 |
| Buchanan | Aaron V. Brown | Tennessee | 1857 |
| Buchanan | Joseph Bolt | Kentucky | 1859 |
| Buchanan | Horatio King | Maine | 1861 |
| Lincoln | Montgomery Blair | District of Columbia | 1861 |
| Lincoln | William Dennison | Ohio | 1864 |
| A. Johnson | William Dennison | Ohio | 1865 |
| A. Johnson | Alex W. Randall | Wisconsin | 1866 |
| Grant | John A. J. Creswell | Maryland | 1869 |
| Grant | James W. Marshall | Virginia | 1874 |
| Grant | Marshall Jewell | Connecticut | 1874 |
| Grant | James N. Tyner | Indiana | 1876 |
| Hayes | David McK. Key | Tennessee | 1877 |
| Hayes | Horace Maynard | Tennessee | 1880 |
| Garfield | Thomas L. James | New York | 1881 |
| Arthur | Timothy O. Howe | Wisconsin | 1881 |
| Arthur | Walter Q. Gresham | Indiana | 1883 |
| Arthur | Frank Hatton | Iowa | 1884 |
| Cleveland | William F. Vilas | Wisconsin | 1885 |
| Cleveland | Don M. Dickinson | Michigan | 1888 |
| B. Harrison | John Wanamaker | Pennsylvania | 1889 |
| Cleveland | Wilson S. Bissel | New York | 1893 |
| Cleveland | William L. Wilson | West Virginia | 1895 |
| McKinley | James A. Gary | Maryland | 1897 |
| McKinley | Charles E. Smith | Pennsylvania | 1898 |
| T. Roosevelt | Charles E. Smith | Pennsylvania | 1901 |
| T. Roosevelt | Henry C. Payne | Wisconsin | 1902 |
| T. Roosevelt | Robert J. Wynne | Pennsylvania | 1904 |
| T. Roosevelt | George B. Cortelyou | New York | 1905 |
| T. Roosevelt | George von L. Meyer | Massachusetts | 1907 |
| Taft | Frank H. Hitchcock | Massachusetts | 1909 |
| Wilson | Albert S. Burleson | Texas | 1913 |
| Harding | Will H. Hays | Indiana | 1921 |
| Harding | Hubert Work | Colorado | 1922 |
| Harding | Harry S. New | Indiana | 1923 |
| Coolidge | Harry S. New | Indiana | 1923 |
| Hoover | Walter F. Brown | Ohio | 1929 |
| F. D. Roosevelt | James A. Farley | New York | 1933 |
| F. D. Roosevelt | Frank C. Walker | Pennsylvania | 1940 |
| Truman | Robert E. Hannegan | Missouri | 1945 |
| Truman | Jesse M. Donaldson | Missouri | 1947 |
| Eisenhower | A. E. Summerfield | Michigan | 1953 |
| Kennedy | J. Edward Day | California | 1961 |
| Kennedy | John A. Gronouski | Wisconsin | 1963 |
| L. B. Johnson | John A. Gronouski | Wisconsin | 1963 |
| L. B. Johnson | Lawrence F. O'Brien | Massachusetts | 1965 |
| L. B. Johnson | W. Marvin Watson | Texas | 1968 |
| Nixon | Winton M. Blount | Alabama | 1969 |

[d]This department was replaced by an independent agency, whose head is not a cabinet member.

# The Judicial Branch

The structure of the United States judiciary reflects the federal nature of government established by the Constitution. The judicial structure includes several tiers (local, state, and federal), each with its own jurisdiction, powers, and responsibilities. The federal judiciary has jurisdiction concerning disputes which either involve the federal Constitution or pertain to issues where not all the parties to the dispute are within state or local jurisdictions; examples of the latter would include disputes between state governments, or citizens of different states. Other legal disputes are settled within the jurisdiction of the state and local court systems with right of appeal to the federal judiciary.

At the federal level the District Courts represent the court of original jurisdiction. There are at present over 90 Federal Court Districts, at which over 300 judges preside. Appellate responsibility is delegated to the Court of Appeals, established by Congress in 1891. There exist 11 "circuits" for this Court, on which over 70 judges sit. The highest level of the federal judiciary is the United States Supreme Court; it is the final appellate court in the nation and also has original jurisdiction in cases involving ambassadors and other foreign agents, as well as disputes in which a state government is a party. The Supreme Court originally consisted of six members; acts of Congress subsequently changed its size five times until 1869, when the number was fixed at nine members.

All federal judges are appointed by the President "by and with the advice and consent of the Senate." The President appoints (and replaces) a chief judge or justice of each jurisdiction who acts as the presiding officer in deliberations of more than one judge. Federal judges hold office for life once appointed, conditional upon their "good behavior." Impeachment and removal from office of federal judges are the responsibilities of Congress. Allowable grounds for such action are treason, bribery, or "other high crimes and misdemeanors." The House of Representatives has impeached (indicted) nine federal judges over the years and the Senate has convicted and thus removed four judges.

## *Justices of the Supreme Court of the United States*

The following table lists all Justices who have served on the Supreme Court of the United States from 1789 to the present. Only those persons who actually served on the Supreme Court are listed; numerous other judges were nominated by various Presidents to serve on the Court, but their nominations were not confirmed by the United States Senate. When the position of Chief Justice has become vacant, Presidents have usually nominated for that position men not currently serving on the Court, rather than elevating Associate Justices already serving on the Supreme Court. Exceptions to this practice are noted in table 1.5 below.

Table 1.5

Justices of the Supreme Court of the United States, 1789-1985

| Name | Date of Birth | Date of Death | Home State | Dates Served | Reason for Leaving Court |
|------|---------------|---------------|------------|--------------|--------------------------|
| John Jay* | 1745 | 1829 | New York | 9/26/1789-6/29/1795 | Resigned |
| John Rutledge | 1739 | 1800 | South Carolina | 9/26/1789-3/5/1791 | Resigned |
| William Cushing | 1732 | 1810 | Massachusetts | 9/26/1789-9/13/1810 | Death |
| James Wilson | 1742 | 1789 | Pennsylvania | 9/26/1789-8/28/1798 | Death |
| John Blair | 1732 | 1800 | Virginia | 9/26/1789-1/27/1796 | Resigned |
| James Iredell | 1751 | 1799 | North Carolina | 2/10/1890-10/2/1799 | Death |
| Thomas Johnson | 1732 | 1819 | Maryland | 11/7/1791-3/4/1793 | Resigned |
| William Paterson | 1745 | 1806 | New Jersey | 3/4/1793-9/9/1806 | Death |
| Samuel Chase | 1741 | 1811 | Maryland | 1/27/1796-6/19/1811 | Death |
| Oliver Ellsworth* | 1745 | 1807 | Connecticut | 3/4/1796-9/30/1800 | Resigned |
| Bushrod Washington | 1762 | 1829 | Virginia | 12/20/1798-11/26/1829 | Death |
| Alfred Moore | 1755 | 1810 | North Carolina | 12/10/1799-3/1804 | Resigned |
| John Marshall* | 1755 | 1835 | Virginia | 1/27/1801-7/6/1835 | Death |
| William Johnson | 1771 | 1834 | South Carolina | 3/24/1804-8/11/1834 | Death |
| Henry B. Livingston | 1757 | 1823 | New York | 12/17/1806-3/18/1823 | Death |
| Thomas Todd | 1765 | 1826 | Kentucky | 3/3/1807-2/7/1826 | Death |
| Joseph Story | 1779 | 1845 | Massachusetts | 11/18/1811-9/10/1845 | Death |
| Gabriel Duval | 1752 | 1844 | Maryland | 11/18/1811-1/15/1835 | Resigned |
| Smith Thompson | 1768 | 1843 | New York | 12/19/1823-12/18/1843 | Death |
| Robert Trimble | 1777 | 1826 | Kentucky | 5/9/1826-8/25/1828 | Death |
| John McLean | 1785 | 1861 | Ohio | 3/7/1829-4/4/1861 | Death |

Table 1.5 (continued)

| Name | Date of Birth | Date of Death | Home State | Dates Served | Reason for Leaving Court |
|------|------|------|------|------|------|
| Henry Baldwin | 1780 | 1844 | Pennsylvania | 1/6/1830-4/21/1844 | Death |
| James M. Wayne | 1790 | 1867 | Georgia | 1/9/1835-7/5/1867 | Death |
| Roger B. Taney[*] | 1777 | 1864 | Maryland | 3/15/1836-10/12/1864 | Death |
| Philip P. Barbour | 1783 | 1841 | Virginia | 3/15/1836-2/24/1841 | Death |
| John Catron | 1786 | 1865 | Tennessee | 3/8/1837-5/30/1865 | Death |
| John McKinley | 1780 | 1852 | Alabama | 9/25/1837-7/19/1852 | Death |
| Peter V. Daniel | 1784 | 1860 | Virginia | 3/2/1841-6/30/1860 | Death |
| Samuel Nelson | 1792 | 1873 | New York | 2/14/1845-11/28/1872 | Resigned |
| Levi Woodbury | 1789 | 1851 | New Hampshire | 11/20/1845-9/4/1851 | Death |
| Robert C. Grier | 1794 | 1870 | Pennsylvania | 8/4/1846-1/31/1870 | Resigned |
| Benjamin Curtis | 1809 | 1874 | Massachusetts | 12/29/1851-9/30/1857 | Resigned |
| John A. Campbell | 1806 | 1889 | Alabama | 3/25/1853-4/1861 | Resigned |
| Nathan Clifford | 1803 | 1881 | Maine | 1/12/1858-7/25/1881 | Death |
| Noah H. Swayne | 1804 | 1884 | Ohio | 1/24/1862-1/24/1881 | Resigned |
| Samuel F. Miller | 1816 | 1890 | Iowa | 7/16/1862-10/13/1890 | Death |
| David Davis | 1815 | 1886 | Illinois | 12/8/1862-3/7/1877 | Resigned |
| Stephen J. Field | 1816 | 1899 | California | 3/10/1863-12/1/1897 | Resigned |
| Salmon P. Chase[*] | 1808 | 1873 | Ohio | 12/6/1864-5/7/1873 | Death |
| William Strong | 1808 | 1895 | Pennsylvania | 2/18/1870-12/14/1880 | Resigned |
| Joseph P. Bradley | 1806 | 1892 | New Jersey | 3/21/1870-1/22/1892 | Death |
| Ward Hunt | 1810 | 1886 | New York | 12/11/1872-1/7/1882 | Resigned |
| Morrison R. Waite[*] | 1816 | 1888 | Ohio | 1/21/1874-3/23/1888 | Death |
| John M. Harlan | 1833 | 1911 | Kentucky | 11/29/1877-10/14/1911 | Death |
| William B. Woods | 1824 | 1887 | Georgia | 12/21/1880-5/14/1887 | Death |
| Stanley Matthews | 1824 | 1889 | Ohio | 5/12/1881-2/11/1889 | Death |
| Horace Gray | 1828 | 1902 | Massachusetts | 12/20/1881-7/9/1902 | Resigned |
| Samuel Blatchford | 1820 | 1893 | New York | 3/27/1882-7/7/1893 | Death |
| Lucius Q. C. Lamar | 1825 | 1893 | Mississippi | 1/16/1888-1/23/1893 | Death |
| Melville W. Fuller[*] | 1833 | 1910 | Illinois | 7/20/1888-7/4/1910 | Death |
| Henry B. Brown | 1836 | 1913 | Michigan | 12/29/1890-5/28/1906 | Resigned |
| George Shiras, Jr. | 1832 | 1924 | Pennsylvania | 7/26/1892-2/23/1903 | Resigned |
| David J. Brewer | 1837 | 1910 | Kansas | 7/26/1892-2/23/1903 | Resigned |
| Howell E. Jackson | 1832 | 1895 | Tennessee | 2/18/1893-8/8/1895 | Death |
| Edward D. White[a] | 1845 | 1921 | Louisiana | 2/19/1894-5/19/1921 | Death |
| Rufus W. Peckham | 1838 | 1909 | New York | 12/9/1895-10/24/1909 | Death |
| Joseph McKenna | 1843 | 1926 | California | 1/21/1898-1/5/1925 | Resigned |
| Oliver W. Holmes | 1841 | 1935 | Massachusetts | 12/4/1902-1/12/1932 | Resigned |
| William R. Day | 1849 | 1923 | Ohio | 2/23/1903-11/13/1922 | Resigned |
| William H. Moody | 1853 | 1917 | Massachusetts | 12/12/1906-11/20/1910 | Resigned |

Table 1.5 (continued)

| Name | Date of Birth | Date of Death | Home State | Dates Served | Reason for Leaving Court |
|------|---------------|---------------|------------|--------------|--------------------------|
| Horace H. Lurton | 1844 | 1914 | Tennessee | 12/20/1909–7/12/1914 | Death |
| Charles E. Hughes[b] | 1862 | 1948 | New York | 5/2/1910–6/10/1916 | Resigned |
| Willis Van Devanter | 1859 | 1951 | Wyoming | 12/15/1910–6/2/1937 | Resigned |
| Joseph R. Lamar | 1857 | 1916 | Georgia | 12/15/1910–1/2/1916 | Death |
| Mahlon Pitney | 1858 | 1924 | New Jersey | 2/19/1912–12/31/1922 | Resigned |
| James C. McReynolds | 1862 | 1946 | Tennessee | 8/29/1914–1/31/1941 | Resigned |
| Louis D. Brandeis | 1856 | 1941 | Massachusetts | 6/1/1916–2/13/1939 | Resigned |
| John H. Clark | 1857 | 1945 | Ohio | 7/24/1916–9/18/1922 | Resigned |
| William H. Taft[*] | 1857 | 1930 | Connecticut | 6/30/1921–2/3/1930 | Resigned |
| George Sutherland | 1862 | 1942 | Utah | 9/5/1922–1/17/1938 | Resigned |
| Pierce Butler | 1866 | 1939 | Minnesota | 12/21/1922–11/16/1939 | Death |
| Edward T. Sanford | 1865 | 1930 | Tennessee | 1/29/1923–3/8/1930 | Death |
| Harlan F. Stone[c] | 1872 | 1946 | New York | 2/5/1925–4/22/1946 | Death |
| Charles E. Hughes[*] | 1862 | 1948 | New York | 2/13/1930–7/1/1941 | Resigned |
| Owen J. Roberts | 1875 | 1955 | Pennsylvania | 5/20/1930–7/31/1945 | Resigned |
| Benjamin N. Cardozo | 1870 | 1938 | New York | 2/24/1932–7/9/1938 | Death |
| Hugo L. Black | 1886 | 1971 | Alabama | 8/17/1937–9/17/1971 | Resigned |
| Stanley F. Reed | 1884 | 1980 | Kentucky | 1/25/1938–2/25/1957 | Resigned |
| Felix Frankfurter | 1882 | 1965 | Massachusetts | 1/17/1938–8/28/1962 | Resigned |
| William O. Douglas | 1898 | 1980 | Connecticut | 4/4/1939–11/12/1975 | Resigned |
| Frank Murphy | 1890 | 1949 | Michigan | 1/15/1940–7/19/1949 | Resigned |
| James F. Byrnes | 1879 | 1972 | South Carolina | 6/12/1941–10/3/1942 | Resigned |
| Robert H. Jackson | 1892 | 1954 | New York | 7/7/1941–10/9/1954 | Death |
| Wiley B. Rutledge | 1894 | 1949 | Iowa | 2/8/1943–9/10/1949 | Death |
| Harold H. Burton | 1888 | 1964 | Ohio | 9/19/1945–10/13/1958 | Resigned |
| Fred M. Vinson[*] | 1890 | 1953 | Kentucky | 6/20/1946–9/8/1953 | Death |
| Tom C. Clark | 1899 | 1967 | Texas | 8/19/1949–6/12/1967 | Death |
| Sherman Minton | 1890 | 1965 | Indiana | 10/4/1949–10/15/1956 | Resigned |
| Earl Warren | 1891 | 1974 | California | 3/1/1954–6/23/1969 | Resigned |
| John M. Harlan | 1899 | 1977 | New York | 3/16/1955–9/23/1971 | Resigned |
| William J. Brennan | 1906 | --- | New Jersey | 3/19/1957–date | Still serving |
| Charles E. Whittaker | 1901 | 1973 | Missouri | 3/19/1957–4/1/1962 | Resigned |
| Potter Stewart | 1915 | --- | Ohio | 5/5/1959–7/3/1981 | Resigned |
| Byron R. White | 1917 | --- | Colorado | 4/11/1962–date | Still serving |
| Arthur J. Goldberg | 1908 | --- | Illinois | 9/25/1962–7/25/1965 | Resigned |
| Abe Fortas | 1910 | 1982 | Tennessee | 8/11/1965–5/14/1969 | Resigned |
| Thurgood Marshall | 1908 | --- | New York | 8/30/1967–date | Still serving |
| Warren E. Burger[*] | 1907 | --- | Minnesota | 6/9/1969–date | Still serving |

Table 1.5  (continued)

| Name | Date of Birth | Date of Death | Home State | Dates Served | Reason for Leaving Court |
|------|------|------|------|------|------|
| Harry A. Blackmun | 1908 | --- | Minnesota | 5/12/1970–date | Still serving |
| Lewis F. Powell | 1907 | --- | Virginia | 12/6/1971–date | Still serving |
| William H. Rehnquist | 1924 | --- | Arizona | 12/10/1971–date | Still serving |
| John Paul Stevens | 1920 | --- | Illinois | 12/17/1975–date | Still serving |
| Sandra Day O'Connor | 1930 | --- | Arizona | 9/21/1981–date | Still serving |

[*]Served as Chief Justice.

[a]Served as Associate Justice, 1894-1910; Chief Justice, 1910-1921.

[b]Served as Associate Justice, 1910-1916, when he resigned to run for President of the United States. Appointed as Chief Justice in 1930 and served until 1941.

[c]Served as Associate Justice, 1925-1941; Chief Justice, 1941-1946.

# The Legislative Branch

The function of setting national policy through enactment of laws and statutes is vested in the United States Congress. The Constitution established a bicameral form of legislature, consisting of the Senate and the House of Representatives. Two representatives from each state serve in the Senate, balanced by proportional representation based upon state population in the House of Representatives. Certain forms of legislative action originate in or are confined to one chamber or the other (for example, appropriations measures must be initiated in the House, while only the Senate acts to confirm Presidential appointments). In general, however, legislation must pass through both chambers, receive a majority of the votes cast in each house, and be signed by the President to become law. Legislation passed by Congress is also subject to a Presidential veto, which may be overridden by a two-thirds majority vote in each house.

Members of the House of Representatives have generally been popularly elected for two-year terms. United States Senators were usually chosen by their respective state legislatures until 1913, when the Seventeenth Amendment to the Constitution was adopted. This amendment required the direct popular election of Senators for six-year terms of office. While the entire membership of the House of Representatives is elected every two years, only a third of the Senate is elected at each two-year period. United States Representatives must be at least 25 years old and have seven or more years of citizenship; they must reside in the state from which they are chosen. United States Senators must be 30 and have nine or more years of citizenship; they must also reside in the state which they represent.

The chief officers of each house are chosen by its members, with one exception: the presiding officer of the Senate is the Vice President of the United States (who may vote only to break a tie in a recorded vote). The Senate elects one of its members as President Pro Tempore, who becomes the presiding officer in the absence of the Vice President. At the beginning of each Congress, the members of the House of Representatives elect the Speaker of the House, who serves as presiding officer. The Speaker is a member of the House—and, in practice, a member of the majority party—and has the right to vote on issues before the House. Although Speakers are elected at the beginning of each Congress, they are frequently reelected Speaker in subsequent Congresses if their party retains a majority. In both chambers the respective political parties elect their floor leaders (called Majority and Minority Leaders and Whips) who perform much of the work of mobilizing members and organizing roll call (record) voting. Seniority within the chamber and capacity to influence individual members have usually been attributes of the leaders of the two chambers.

Much of the business of each of the two chambers of Congress is carried out in committees, both standing and temporary. The committees and their staffs draft legislation, collect information, and hold hearings which frequently involve a form of investigating activity, and influence the scheduling of legislation for consideration by the full House or Senate. Committee activity usually secures or prevents passage of legislation by the House or Senate. Committees are chaired by members of the majority party of each of the chambers, usually those with the greatest seniority on the Committee.

Tables 1.6 through 1.11 focus upon the United States Senate and provide rosters of all Presidents Pro Tempore, Majority Leaders and Whips, Minority Leaders and Whips, and chairmen of major Senate committees from 1789 to 1985. Tables 1.12 through 1.17 offer similar information about the United States House of Representatives; these tables list Speakers of the House, Majority Leaders and Whips, Minority Leaders and Whips, and chairmen of major House committees. Table 1.18 displays the total number of measures introduced and the total number of measures enacted during each of the 98 Congresses, while table 1.19 tabulates the number of congressional bills vetoed during each President's term in office.

Table 1.6

Presidents Pro Tempore of the United States Senate, 1789-1985

| Name | State | Party | Congresses | Years Served |
|------|-------|-------|------------|--------------|
| John Langdon | New Hampshire | Dem-Rep | 1st | 1789-1791 |
| Richard Henry Lee | Virginia | Unknown | 2nd | 1792 |
| John Langdon | New Hampshire | Dem-Rep | 2nd | 1792-1793 |
| Ralph Izard | South Carolina | Unknown | 3rd | 1794-1795 |
| Henry Tazewell | Virginia | Unknown | 3rd-4th | 1795-1796 |
| Samuel Livermore | New Hampshire | Unknown | 4th | 1796-1797 |
| William Bingham | Pennsylvania | Unknown | 4th | 1797 |
| William Bradford | Rhode Island | Unknown | 5th | 1797 |
| Jacob Read | South Carolina | Federalist | 5th | 1797-1798 |
| Theodore Sedgwick | Massachusetts | Federalist | 5th | 1798 |
| John Laurance | New York | Unknown | 5th | 1798 |

Table 1.6 (continued)

| Name | State | Party | Congresses | Years Served |
|------|-------|-------|------------|--------------|
| James Ross | Pennsylvania | Federalist | 5th | 1799 |
| Samuel Livermore | New Hampshire | Unknown | 6th | 1799-1800 |
| Uriah Tracy | Connecticut | Federalist | 6th | 1800 |
| John E. Howard | Maryland | Federalist | 6th | 1800-1801 |
| James Hillhouse | Connecticut | Federalist | 6th | 1801 |
| Abraham Baldwin | Georgia | Federalist | 7th | 1801-1802 |
| Stephen R. Bradley | Vermont | Dem-Rep | 7th | 1802-1803 |
| John Brown | Kentucky | Unknown | 8th | 1803-1804 |
| Jesse Franklin | North Carolina | Dem-Rep | 8th | 1804-1805 |
| Joseph Anderson | Tennessee | Dem-Rep | 8th | 1805 |
| Samuel Smith | Maryland | Dem-Rep | 9th-10th | 1805-1808 |
| Stephen R. Bradley | Vermont | Dem-Rep | 10th | 1808-1809 |
| John Milledge | Georgia | Unknown | 10th | 1809 |
| Andrew Gregg | Pennsylvania | Unknown | 11th | 1809-1810 |
| John Gaillard | South Carolina | Dem-Rep | 11th | 1810-1811 |
| John Pope | Kentucky | Dem-Rep | 11th | 1811 |
| William H. Crawford | Georgia | Dem-Rep | 12th | 1812-1813 |
| Joseph B. Varnum | Massachusetts | Dem-Rep | 13th | 1813-1814 |
| John Gaillard | South Carolina | Dem-Rep | 13th-15th | 1814-1819 |
| James Barbour | Virginia | Anti-Dem | 15th-16th | 1819-1820 |
| John Gaillard | South Carolina | Dem-Rep | 16th-19th | 1820-1826 |
| Nathaniel Macon | North Carolina | Dem-Rep | 19th-20th | 1826-1827 |
| Samuel Smith | Maryland | Democrat | 20th-21st | 1828-1831 |
| Littleton W. Tazewell | Virginia | Democrat | 22nd | 1832 |
| Hugh L. White | Tennessee | Unknown | 22nd-23rd | 1832-1834 |
| George Poindexter | Mississippi | Unknown | 23rd | 1834-1835 |
| John Tyler | Virginia | Unknown | 23rd | 1835 |
| William R. King | Alabama | Democrat | 24th-27th | 1836-1841 |
| Samuel L. Southard | New Jersey | Whig | 27th | 1841-1842 |
| Willie P. Mangum | North Carolina | Whig | 27th-28th | 1842-1845 |
| Ambrose H. Sevier | Alabama | Democrat | 29th | 1845 |
| David R. Atchison | Missouri | Whig | 29th-31st | 1846-1850 |
| William R. King | Alabama | Democrat | 31st-32nd | 1850-1852 |
| David R. Atchison | Missouri | Whig | 32nd-33rd | 1852-1854 |
| Lewis Cass | Michigan | Democrat | 33rd | 1854 |
| Jesse D. Bright | Indiana | Democrat | 33rd-34th | 1854-1856 |
| Charles E. Stuart | Michigan | Democrat | 34th | 1856 |
| James M. Mason | Virginia | Democrat | 34th-35th | 1856-1857 |
| Thomas J. Rusk | Texas | Democrat | 35th | 1857 |
| Benjamin Fitzpatrick | Alabama | Democrat | 35th-36th | 1857-1860 |
| Jesse D. Bright | Indiana | Democrat | 36th | 1860-1861 |
| Solomon Foot | Vermont | Republican | 36th-38th | 1861-1864 |
| Daniel Clark | New Hampshire | Republican | 38th | 1864-1865 |
| Lafayette S. Foster | Connecticut | Republican | 39th | 1865-1867 |
| Benjamin F. Wade | Ohio | Republican | 39th-40th | 1867-1869 |
| Henry B. Anthony | Rhode Island | Republican | 41st-42nd | 1869-1873 |
| Matthew H. Carpenter | Wisconsin | Republican | 43rd | 1873-1875 |
| Henry B. Anthony | Rhode Island | Republican | 43rd | 1875 |
| Thomas W. Ferry | Michigan | Republican | 44th-45th | 1875-1879 |
| Allen G. Thurman | Ohio | Democrat | 46th | 1879-1881 |
| Thomas F. Bayard | Delaware | Democrat | 47th | 1881 |
| David Davis | Illinois | Republican | 47th | 1881-1883 |
| George F. Edmunds | Vermont | Republican | 47th-48th | 1883-1885 |
| John Sherman | Ohio | Republican | 49th | 1885-1887 |
| John J. Ingalls | Kansas | Republican | 49th-51st | 1887-1891 |
| Charles F. Manderson | Nebraska | Republican | 51st-52nd | 1889-1893 |
| Isham G. Harris | Tennessee | Democrat | 52nd-53rd | 1893-1895 |
| Matt W. Ransom | North Carolina | Democrat | 53rd | 1895 |

Table 1.6 (continued)

| Name | State | Party | Congresses | Years Served |
|------|-------|-------|-----------|-------------|
| William P. Frye | Maine | Republican | 54th-62nd | 1896-1911 |
| Charles Curtis | Kansas | Republican | 62nd | 1911* |
| Henry Cabot Lodge | Massachusetts | Republican | 62nd | 1912 |
| Frank G. Brandegee | Connecticut | Republican | 62nd | 1912 |
| Augustus O. Bacon | Georgia | Democrat | 62nd | 1912-1913 |
| Jacob H. Gallinger | New Hampshire | Republican | 62nd | 1912-1913 |
| James P. Clark | Arkansas | Democrat | 63rd-64th | 1913-1915 |
| Willard Saulsbury | Delaware | Democrat | 64th-65th | 1916-1919 |
| Albert B. Cummins | Iowa | Republican | 66th-68th | 1919-1925 |
| George H. Moses | New Hampshire | Republican | 69th-72nd | 1925-1933 |
| Key Pittman | Nevada | Democrat | 73rd-76th | 1933-1940 |
| William H. King | Utah | Democrat | 76th | 1940-1941 |
| Pat Harrison | Mississippi | Democrat | 77th | 1941 |
| Carter Glass | Virginia | Democrat | 77th-78th | 1941-1945 |
| Kenneth McKellar | Tennessee | Democrat | 79th | 1945-1947 |
| Arthur H. Vandenberg | Michigan | Republican | 80th | 1947-1949 |
| Kenneth McKellar | Tennessee | Democrat | 81st-82nd | 1949-1953 |
| Styles Bridges | New Hampshire | Republican | 83rd | 1953-1955 |
| Walter F. George | Georgia | Democrat | 84th | 1955-1957 |
| Carl Hayden | Arizona | Democrat | 85th-90th | 1957-1969 |
| Richard B. Russell | Georgia | Democrat | 91st | 1969-1971 |
| Allen J. Ellender | Louisiana | Democrat | 92nd | 1971-1973 |
| James O. Eastland | Mississippi | Democrat | 93rd-95th | 1973-1979 |
| Warren G. Magnuson | Washington | Democrat | 96th | 1979-1981 |
| Strom Thurmond | South Carolina | Republican | 97th-99th | 1981-date |

*After the resignation of William P. Frye as President Pro Tempore on April 27, 1911 and his subsequent death on August 8, 1911, the Senate failed to elect a President Pro Tempore for the remainder of the Congress. So temporary designations were made from time to time. August O. Bacon, a Democrat, and Jacob H. Gallinger, a Republican, alternated in the office for most of 1912 and 1913.

Table 1.7

Majority Leaders of the United States Senate, 1911-1985[*]

| Name | State | Party | Congresses | Years Served |
|------|-------|-------|-----------|--------------|
| Shelby M. Cullom | Illinois | Republican | 62nd | 1911-1913 |
| John W. Kern | Indiana | Democrat | 63rd-64th | 1913-1917 |
| Thomas S. Martin | Virginia | Democrat | 65th | 1917-1919 |
| Henry Cabot Lodge | Massachusetts | Republican | 66th-68th | 1919-1924 |
| Charles Curtis | Kansas | Republican | 68th-71st | 1924-1929 |
| James E. Watson | Indiana | Republican | 71st-72nd | 1929-1933 |
| Joseph T. Robinson | Arkansas | Democrat | 73rd-74th | 1933-1937 |
| Alben W. Barkley | Kentucky | Democrat | 75th-79th | 1937-1947 |
| Wallace H. White, Jr. | Maine | Republican | 80th | 1947-1949 |
| Scott W. Lucas | Illinois | Democrat | 81st | 1949-1951 |
| Ernest W. McFarland | Arizona | Democrat | 82nd | 1951-1953 |
| Robert A. Taft | Ohio | Republican | 83rd | 1953[a] |
| William F. Knowland | California | Republican | 83rd | 1953-1955 |
| Lyndon B. Johnson | Texas | Democrat | 84th-86th | 1955-1961 |
| Mike Mansfield | Montana | Democrat | 87th-94th | 1961-1977 |
| Robert C. Byrd | West Virginia | Democrat | 95th-96th | 1977-1981 |
| Howard H. Baker | Tennessee | Republican | 97th-98th | 1981-1985 |
| Robert Dole | Kansas | Republican | 99th | 1985-date |

[*]Prior to 1911, party leadership in the Senate was informally exercised through caucuses, with dominant factions assuming the function of selecting a floor leader. Cullum was the first officially designated Majority Leader.

[a]Robert Taft died in July of 1953 and was succeeded by William F. Knowland.

Table 1.8

Majority Whips of the United States Senate, 1913-1985

| Name | State | Party | Congresses | Years Served |
|------|-------|-------|-----------|--------------|
| J. Hamilton Lewis | Illinois | Democrat | 63rd-65th | 1913-1919 |
| Charles Curtis | Kansas | Republican | 66th-68th | 1919-1924 |
| Wesley L. Jones | Washington | Republican | 68th-70th | 1924-1929 |
| Simeon D. Fess | Ohio | Republican | 71st-72nd | 1929-1933 |
| J. Hamilton Lewis | Illinois | Democrat | 73rd-75th | 1933-1939 |
| Sherman Minton | Indiana | Democrat | 76th | 1939-1941 |
| Lister Hill | Alabama | Democrat | 77th-79th | 1941-1947 |
| Kenneth Wherry | Nebraska | Republican | 80th | 1947-1949 |
| Francis J. Myers | Pennsylvania | Democrat | 81st | 1949-1951 |
| Lyndon B. Johnson | Texas | Democrat | 82nd | 1951-1953 |
| Leverett Saltonstall | Massachusetts | Republican | 83rd | 1953-1955 |
| Earle C. Clements | Kentucky | Democrat | 84th | 1955-1957 |
| Mike Mansfield | Montana | Democrat | 85th-86th | 1957-1961 |
| Hubert H. Humphrey | Minnesota | Democrat | 87th-88th | 1961-1965 |
| Russell B. Long | Louisiana | Democrat | 89th-90th | 1965-1969 |
| Edward M. Kennedy | Massachusetts | Democrat | 91st | 1969-1971 |
| Robert C. Byrd | West Virginia | Democrat | 92nd-94th | 1971-1977 |
| Alan Cranston | California | Democrat | 95th-96th | 1977-1981 |
| Theodore Stevens | Alaska | Republican | 97th-98th | 1981-1985 |
| Alan K. Simpson | Wyoming | Republican | 99th | 1985-date |

Table 1.9

Minority Leaders of the United States Senate, 1911-1985[*]

| Name | State | Party | Congresses | Years Served |
|------|-------|-------|------------|--------------|
| Thomas S. Martin | Virginia | Democrat | 62nd | 1911-1913 |
| Jacob H. Gallinger | New Hampshire | Republican | 63rd-64th | 1913-1917 |
| Henry Cabot Lodge | Massachusetts | Republican | 65th | 1917-1919 |
| Thomas S. Martin | Virginia | Democrat | 66th | 1919 |
| Oscar W. Underwood | Alabama | Democrat | 66th-67th | 1919-1923 |
| Joseph T. Robinson | Arkansas | Democrat | 68th-72nd | 1923-1933 |
| Charles McNary | Oregon | Republican | 73rd-78th | 1933-1945 |
| Wallace H. White, Jr. | Maine | Republican | 79th | 1945-1947 |
| Alben W. Barkley | Kentucky | Democrat | 80th | 1947-1949 |
| Kenneth S. Wherry | Nebraska | Republican | 81st-82nd | 1949-1951 |
| Styles Bridges | New Hampshire | Republican | 82nd | 1951-1953 |
| Lyndon B. Johnson | Texas | Democrat | 83rd | 1953-1955 |
| William F. Knowland | California | Republican | 84th-85th | 1955-1959 |
| Everett McKinley Dirksen | Illinois | Republican | 86th-91st | 1959-1969 |
| Hugh Scott | Pennsylvania | Republican | 91st-94th | 1969-1977 |
| Howard Baker | Tennessee | Republican | 95th-96th | 1977-1981 |
| Robert C. Byrd | West Virginia | Democrat | 97th-99th | 1981-date |

[*]Prior to 1911, party leadership in the Senate was informally exercised through caucuses, with dominant factions assuming the function of selecting a floor leader. Martin was the first officially designated Minority Leader.

Table 1.10

Minority Whips of the United States Senate, 1915-1985

| Name | State | Party | Congresses | Years Served |
|------|-------|-------|------------|--------------|
| James W. Wadsworth, Jr. | New York | Republican | 64th | 1915 |
| Charles Curtis | Kansas | Republican | 64th-65th | 1915-1919 |
| Peter G. Gerry | Rhode Island | Democrat | 66th-70th | 1919-1929 |
| Morris Sheppard | Texas | Democrat | 71st-72nd | 1929-1933 |
| Felix Hebert | Rhode Island | Republican | 73rd | 1933-1943 |
| Kenneth Wherry | Nebraska | Republican | 78th-79th | 1943-1947 |
| Scott W. Lucas | Illinois | Democrat | 80th | 1947-1949 |
| Leverett Saltonstall | Massachusetts | Republican | 81st-82nd | 1949-1953 |
| Earle C. Clements | Kentucky | Democrat | 83rd | 1953-1955 |
| Leverett Saltonstall | Massachusetts | Republican | 84th | 1955-1957 |
| Everett McKinley Dirksen | Illinois | Republican | 85th | 1957-1959 |
| Thomas H. Kuchel | California | Republican | 86-90th | 1959-1969 |
| Hugh Scott | Pennsylvania | Republican | 91st | 1969 |
| Robert P. Griffin | Michigan | Republican | 91st-94th | 1969-1977 |
| Theodore Stevens | Alaska | Republican | 95th-96th | 1977-1981 |
| Alan Cranston | California | Democrat | 97th-99th | 1981-date |

Table 1.11

Chairmen of Major Committees in the
United States Senate, 1875-1985

| Congress | Years | Chairman | State | Party |
|---|---|---|---|---|

### Judiciary Committee

| Congress | Years | Chairman | State | Party |
|---|---|---|---|---|
| 44th–45th | 1875-1879 | George F. Edmunds | Vermont | Republican |
| 46th | 1879-1881 | Allen G. Thurman | Ohio | Democrat |
| 47th–51st | 1881-1891 | George F. Edmunds | Vermont | Republican |
| 52nd | 1891-1893 | George F. Hoar | Massachusetts | Republican |
| 53rd | 1893-1895 | James L. Pugh | Alabama | Democrat |
| 54th–58th | 1895-1905 | George F. Hoar | Massachusetts | Republican |
| 59th–62nd | 1905-1913 | Clarence D. Clark | Wyoming | Republican |
| 63rd–65th | 1913-1919 | Charles A. Culberson | Texas | Democrat |
| 66th–67th | 1919-1923 | Knute Nelson | Minnesota | Republican |
| 68th | 1923-1925 | Frank B. Brandegee | Connecticut | Republican |
| 69th | 1925-1927 | Albert B. Cummins | Iowa | Republican |
| 70th–72nd | 1927-1933 | George W. Norris | Nebraska | Republican |
| 73rd–76th | 1933-1941 | Henry F. Ashurst | Arizona | Democrat |
| 77th–78th | 1941-1945 | Fredrick Van Nuys | Indiana | Democrat |
| 79th | 1945-1947 | Pat McCarran | Nevada | Democrat |
| 80th | 1947-1949 | Alexander Wiley | Wisconsin | Republican |
| 81st–82nd | 1949-1953 | Pat McCarran | Nevada | Democrat |
| 83rd | 1953-1955 | William Langer | North Dakota | Republican |
| 84th | 1955-1957 | Harley M. Kilgore | West Virginia | Democrat |
| 85th–95th | 1957-1979 | James O. Eastland | Mississippi | Democrat |
| 96th | 1979-1981 | Edward M. Kennedy | Massachusetts | Democrat |
| 97th–99th | 1981-date | Strom Thurmond | South Carolina | Republican |

### Foreign Relations Committee

| Congress | Years | Chairman | State | Party |
|---|---|---|---|---|
| 44th | 1875-1877 | Simon Cameron | Pennsylvania | Republican |
| 45th | 1877-1879 | Hanibal Hamlin | Maine | Republican |
| 46th | 1879-1881 | William W. Eaton | Connecticut | Democrat |
| 47th | 1881-1883 | William Windom | Minnesota | Republican |
| 48th–49th | 1883-1887 | John F. Miller | California | Republican |
| 50th–52nd | 1887-1893 | John Sherman | Ohio | Republican |
| 53rd | 1893-1895 | John T. Morgan | Alabama | Democrat |
| 54th | 1895-1897 | John Sherman | Ohio | Republican |
| 55th–56th | 1897-1901 | Cushman K. Davis | Minnesota | Republican |
| 57th–62nd | 1901-1913 | Shelby M. Cullom | Illinois | Republican |
| 63rd | 1913-1915 | Augustus O. Bacon | Georgia | Democrat |
| 64th–65th | 1915-1919 | William J. Stone | Missouri | Democrat |
| 66th–68th | 1919-1925 | Henry Cabot Lodge | Massachusetts | Republican |
| 69th–72nd | 1925-1933 | William E. Borah | Idaho | Republican |
| 73rd–76th | 1933-1941 | Key Pittman | Nevada | Democrat |
| 77th | 1941-1943 | Walter F. George | Georgia | Democrat |
| 78th–79th | 1943-1947 | Tom Connally | Texas | Democrat |
| 80th | 1947-1949 | Arthur H. Vandenberg | Michigan | Republican |
| 81st–82nd | 1949-1953 | Tom Connally | Texas | Democrat |
| 83rd | 1953-1955 | Alexander Wiley | Wisconsin | Republican |
| 84th | 1955-1957 | Walter F. George | Georgia | Democrat |
| 85th | 1957-1959 | Theodore Francis Green | Rhode Island | Democrat |
| 86th–93rd | 1959-1975 | J. W. Fulbright | Arkansas | Democrat |
| 94th–95th | 1975-1979 | John Sparkman | Alabama | Democrat |
| 96th | 1979-1981 | Frank Church | Idaho | Democrat |
| 97th–98th | 1981-1985 | Charles Percy | Illinois | Republican |
| 99th | 1985-date | Richard G. Lugar | Indiana | Republican |

41

Table 1.11 (continued)

| Congress | Years | Chairman | State | Party |
|---|---|---|---|---|

### Appropriations Committee

| | | | | |
|---|---|---|---|---|
| 44th-45th | 1875-1879 | William Windom | Minnesota | Republican |
| 46th | 1879-1881 | Henry G. Davis | West Virginia | Democrat |
| 47th-52nd | 1881-1893 | William B. Allison | Iowa | Republican |
| 53rd | 1893-1895 | Francis M. Cockrell | Missouri | Democrat |
| 54th-60th | 1895-1909 | William B. Allison | Iowa | Republican |
| 61st | 1909-1911 | Eugene Hale | Maine | Republican |
| 62nd | 1911-1913 | Francis E. Warren | Wyoming | Republican |
| 63rd-65th | 1913-1919 | Thomas S. Martin | Virginia | Democrat |
| 66th-71st | 1919-1931 | Francis E. Warren | Wyoming | Republican |
| 72nd | 1931-1933 | Fredrick Hale | Maine | Republican |
| 73rd-79th | 1933-1947 | Carter Glass | Virginia | Democrat |
| 80th | 1947-1949 | Styles Bridges | New Hampshire | Republican |
| 81st-82nd | 1949-1953 | Kenneth McKellar | Tennessee | Democrat |
| 83rd | 1953-1955 | Styles Bridges | New Hampshire | Republican |
| 84th-90th | 1955-1969 | Carl Hayden | Arizona | Democrat |
| 91st | 1969-1971 | Richard B. Russell | Georgia | Democrat |
| 92nd | 1971-1973 | Allen J. Ellender | Louisiana | Democrat |
| 93rd-95th | 1973-1979 | John L. McClellan | Arkansas | Democrat |
| 96th | 1979-1981 | Warren G. Magnuson | Washington | Democrat |
| 97th-99th | 1981-date | Mark O. Hatfield | Oregon | Republican |

### Armed Services Committee
#### (Military Affairs)

| | | | | |
|---|---|---|---|---|
| 44th | 1875-1877 | John A. Logan | Illinois | Republican |
| 45th | 1877-1879 | George E. Spencer | Alabama | Republican |
| 46th | 1879-1881 | Theodore F. Randolph | New Jersey | Democrat |
| 47th-49th | 1881-1887 | John A. Logan | Illinois | Republican |
| 50th-52nd | 1887-1893 | Joseph R. Hawley | Connecticut | Republican |
| 53rd | 1893-1895 | Edward C. Walthall | Mississippi | Democrat |
| 54th-58th | 1895-1905 | Joseph R. Hawley | Connecticut | Republican |
| 59th-61st | 1905-1911 | Francis E. Warren | Wyoming | Republican |
| 62nd | 1911-1913 | Henry A. DuPont | Delaware | Republican |
| 63rd | 1913-1915 | Joseph F. Johnston | Alabama | Democrat |
| 64th-65th | 1915-1919 | George E. Chamberlain | Oregon | Democrat |
| 66th-69th | 1919-1927 | James W. Wadsworth | New York | Republican |
| 70th-72nd | 1927-1933 | David A. Reed | Pennsylvania | Republican |
| 73rd-76th | 1933-1941 | Morris Sheppard | Texas | Democrat |
| 77th-78th | 1941-1945 | Robert R. Reynolds | North Carolina | Democrat |
| 79th | 1945-1947 | Elbert D. Thomas | Utah | Democrat |
| 80th | 1947-1949 | Chan Gurney | South Dakota | Republican |
| 81st | 1949-1951 | Millard E. Tydings | Maryland | Democrat |
| 82nd | 1951-1953 | Richard B. Russell | Georgia | Democrat |
| 83rd | 1953-1955 | Leverett Saltonstall | Massachusetts | Republican |
| 84th-90th | 1955-1969 | Richard B. Russell | Georgia | Democrat |
| 91st-96th | 1969-1981 | John C. Stennis | Mississippi | Democrat |
| 97th-98th | 1981-1985 | John Tower | Texas | Republican |
| 99th | 1985-date | Barry Goldwater | Arizona | Republican |

Table 1.12

Speakers of the United States
House of Representatives, 1789-1985

| Name | State | Party | Congresses | Years Served |
|------|-------|-------|-----------|--------------|
| Frederick A. C. Muhlenberg | Pennsylvania | Federalist | 1st | 1789-1791 |
| Jonathan Trumbull | Connecticut | Federalist | 2nd | 1791-1793 |
| Frederick A. C. Muhlenberg | Pennsylvania | Federalist | 3rd | 1793-1795 |
| Jonathan Dayton | New Jersey | Federalist | 4th-5tn | 1795-1799 |
| Theodore Sedgwick | Massachusetts | Federalist | 6th | 1799-1801 |
| Nathaniel Macon | North Carolina | Dem-Rep | 7th-9th | 1801-1807 |
| Joseph B. Varnum | Massachusetts | Dem-Rep | 10th-11th | 1807-1811 |
| Henry Clay | Kentucky | Dem-Rep | 12th-13th | 1811-1814 |
| Landon Cheves | South Carolina | Dem-Rep | 13th | 1814-1815 |
| Henry Clay | Kentucky | Dem-Rep | 14th-16th | 1815-1820 |
| John W. Taylor | New York | Dem-Rep | 16th | 1820-1821 |
| Philip P. Barbour | Virginia | Dem-Rep | 17th | 1821-1823 |
| Henry Clay | Kentucky | Dem-Rep | 18th | 1823-1825 |
| John W. Taylor | New York | Dem-Rep | 19tn | 1825-1827 |
| Andrew Stevenson | Virginia | Democrat | 20th-23rd | 1827-1834 |
| John Bell | Tennessee | Whig | 23rd | 1834-1835 |
| James K. Polk | Tennessee | Democrat | 24th-25th | 1835-1839 |
| Robert M. T. Hunter | Virginia | Democrat | 26th | 1839-1841 |
| John White | Kentucky | Whig | 27th | 1841-1843 |
| John W. Jones | Virginia | Democrat | 28th | 1843-1845 |
| John W. Davis | Indiana | Democrat | 29th | 1845-1847 |
| Robert C. Winthrop | Massachusetts | Whig | 30th | 1847-1849 |
| Howell Cobb | Georgia | Democrat | 31st | 1849-1851 |
| Linn Boyd | Kentucky | Democrat | 32nd-33rd | 1851-1855 |
| Nathaniel P. Banks | Massachusetts | American | 34th | 1855-1857 |
| James L. Orr | South Carolina | Democrat | 35th | 1857-1859 |
| William Pennington | New Jersey | Whig | 36th | 1859-1861 |
| Galusha A. Grow | Pennsylvania | Republican | 37th | 1861-1863 |
| Schuyler Colfax | Indiana | Republican | 38th-40th | 1863-1869 |
| Theodore M. Pomeroy | New York | Republican | 40th | 1869 |
| James G. Blaine | Maine | Republican | 41st-43rd | 1869-1875 |
| Michael C. Kerr | Indiana | Democrat | 44th | 1875-1876 |
| Samuel J. Randall | Pennsylvania | Democrat | 44th-46th | 1876-1881 |
| J. Warren Keifer | Ohio | Republican | 47th | 1881-1883 |
| John G. Carlisle | Kentucky | Democrat | 48th-50th | 1883-1889 |
| Thomas B. Reed | Maine | Republican | 51st | 1889-1891 |
| Charles F. Crisp | Georgia | Democrat | 52nd-53rd | 1891-1895 |
| Thomas B. Reed | Maine | Republican | 54th-55th | 1895-1899 |
| David B. Henderson | Iowa | Republican | 56th-57th | 1899-1903 |
| Joseph G. Cannon | Illinois | Republican | 58th-61st | 1903-1911 |
| Champ Clark | Missouri | Democrat | 62nd-65th | 1911-1919 |
| Frederick H. Gillett | Massachusetts | Republican | 66th-68th | 1919-1925 |
| Nicholas Longworth | Ohio | Republican | 69th-71st | 1925-1931 |
| John N. Garner | Texas | Democrat | 72nd | 1931-1933 |
| Henry T. Rainey | Illinois | Democrat | 73rd | 1933-1935 |
| Joseph W. Byrns | Tennessee | Democrat | 74th | 1935-1936 |
| William B. Bankhead | Alabama | Democrat | 74th-76th | 1936-1940 |
| Sam Rayburn | Texas | Democrat | 76th-79th | 1940-1947 |
| Joseph W. Martin, Jr. | Massachusetts | Republican | 80th | 1947-1949 |
| Sam Rayburn | Texas | Democrat | 81st-82nd | 1949-1953 |
| Joseph W. Martin, Jr. | Massachusetts | Republican | 83rd | 1953-1955 |
| Sam Rayburn | Texas | Democrat | 84th-87th | 1955-1961 |
| John W. McCormack | Massachusetts | Democrat | 87th-91st | 1962-1971 |
| Carl Albert | Oklahoma | Democrat | 92nd-94th | 1971-1977 |
| Thomas P. O'Neill, Jr. | Massachusetts | Democrat | 95th-99th | 1977-date |

Table 1.13

Majority Leaders of the United States*
House of Representatives,   1899-1985

| Name | State | Party | Congresses | Years Served |
|------|-------|-------|------------|--------------|
| Sereno E. Payne | New York | Republican | 56th-61st | 1899-1911 |
| Oscar W. Underwood | Alabama | Democrat | 62nd-63rd | 1911-1915 |
| Claude Kitchin | North Carolina | Democrat | 64th-65th | 1915-1919 |
| Franklin W. Mondell | Wyoming | Republican | 66th-67th | 1919-1923 |
| Nicholas Longworth | Ohio | Republican | 68th | 1923-1925 |
| John Q. Tilson | Connecticut | Republican | 69th-71st | 1925-1931 |
| Henry T. Rainey | Illinois | Democrat | 72nd | 1931-1933 |
| Joseph W. Byrns | Tennessee | Democrat | 73rd | 1933-1935 |
| William B. Bankhead | Alabama | Democrat | 74th | 1935-1937 |
| Sam Rayburn | Texas | Democrat | 75th-76th | 1937-1941 |
| John W. McCormack | Massachusetts | Democrat | 76th-79th | 1941-1947 |
| Charles A. Halleck | Indiana | Republican | 80th | 1947-1949 |
| John W. McCormack | Massachesutts | Democrat | 81st-82nd | 1949-1953 |
| Charles A. Halleck | Indiana | Republican | 83rd | 1953-1955 |
| John W. McCormack | Massachusetts | Democrat | 84th-87th | 1955-1961 |
| Carl Albert | Oklahoma | Democrat | 87th-91st | 1962-1971 |
| Thomas P. O'Neill, Jr. | Massachusetts | Democrat | 92nd-94th | 1971-1977 |
| James Wright | Texas | Democrat | 95th-99th | 1977-date |

*
Sereno Payne was the first House member to be officially designated Majority Leader.
Previously, the chairman of the Ways and Means Committee was looked upon as floor leader.
Occasionally the Speaker of the House had designated someone other than the Ways and Means
Chairman to serve as leader.  The Speaker selected the Majority Leader until 1911.  After
a "revolt" against Speaker Cannon in 1909-1910, House members took on the authority of
selecting a leader through party caucuses or conferences.

Table 1.14

Majority Whips of the United States
House of Representatives, 1899-1985

| Name | State | Party | Congresses | Years Served |
|------|-------|-------|------------|--------------|
| James A. Tawney | Minnesota | Republican | 56th-58th | 1899-1905 |
| James E. Watson | Indiana | Republican | 59th-60th | 1905-1909 |
| John W. Dwight | New York | Republican | 61st | 1909-1911 |
| --- | --- | --- | 62nd | 1911-1913 |
| Thomas M. Bell | Georgia | Democrat | 63rd | 1913-1915 |
| --- | --- | --- | 64th-65th | 1915-1919 |
| Harold Knutson | Minnesota | Republican | 66th-67th | 1919-1923 |
| Albert H. Vestal | Indiana | Republican | 68th-71st | 1923-1931 |
| John McDuffie | Alabama | Democrat | 72nd | 1931-1933 |
| Arthur H. Greenwood | Indiana | Democrat | 73rd | 1933-1935 |
| Patrick J. Boland | Pennsylvania | Democrat | 74th-77th | 1935-1942 |
| Robert Ramspeck | Georgia | Democrat | 77th-78th | 1942-1945 |
| John J. Sparkman | Alabama | Democrat | 79th | 1945-1947 |
| Leslie C. Arends | Illinois | Republican | 80th | 1947-1949 |
| J. Percy Priest | Tennessee | Democrat | 81st-82nd | 1949-1953 |
| Leslie C. Arends | Illinois | Republican | 83rd | 1953-1955 |
| Carl Albert | Oklahoma | Democrat | 84th-87th | 1955-1962 |
| Hale Boggs | Louisiana | Democrat | 87th-91st | 1962-1971 |
| Thomas P. O'Neill, Jr. | Massachusetts | Democrat | 92nd-93rd | 1971-1973 |
| John J. McFall | California | Democrat | 93rd-94th | 1973-1977 |
| John Brademas | Indiana | Democrat | 95th-96th | 1977-1981 |
| Thomas S. Foley | Washington | Democrat | 97th-99th | 1981-date |

Table 1.15

Minority Leaders of the United States[*]
House of Representatives, 1899-1985

| Name | State | Party | Congresses | Year Served |
|------|-------|-------|-----------|-------------|
| James D. Richardson | Tennessee | Democrat | 56th-57th | 1899-1903 |
| John Sharp Williams | Mississippi | Democrat | 58th-60th | 1093-1909 |
| Champ Clark | Missouri | Democrat | 61st | 1909-1911 |
| James R. Mann | Illinois | Republican | 62nd-65th | 1911-1919 |
| Champ Clark | Missouri | Democrat | 66th | 1919-1921 |
| Claude Kitchin | North Carolina | Democrat | 67th | 1921-1923 |
| Finis J. Garrett | Tennessee | Democrat | 68th-70th | 1923-1929 |
| John N. Garner | Texas | Democrat | 71st | 1929-1931 |
| Bertrand H. Snell | New York | Republican | 72nd-75th | 1931-1939 |
| Joseph W. Martin, Jr. | Massachusetts | Republican | 76th-79th | 1939-1947 |
| Sam Rayburn | Texas | Democrat | 80th | 1947-1949 |
| Joseph W. Martin, Jr. | Massachusetts | Republican | 81st-82nd | 1949-1953 |
| Sam Rayburn | Texas | Democrat | 83rd | 1953-1955 |
| Joseph W. Martin, Jr. | Massachusetts | Republican | 84th-85th | 1955-1959 |
| Charles A. Halleck | Indiana | Republican | 86th-88th | 1959-1965 |
| Gerald R. Ford | Michigan | Republican | 89th-92nd | 1965-1973 |
| John J. Rhodes | Arizona | Republican | 93rd-96th | 1973-1981 |
| Robert H. Michel | Illinois | Republican | 97th-99th | 1981-1987 |

[*]Although first identifiable as early as 1883, the position of Minority Leader became officially recognized in 1899. After 1911, the selection was made by the party conferences or caucuses, with the choice usually being the candidate the minority party had nominated for the Speakership of the House.

Table 1.16

Minority Whips of the United States
House of Representatives, 1899-1985

| Name | State | Party | Congresses | Years Served |
|------|-------|-------|-----------|--------------|
| Oscar W. Underwood | Alabama | Democrat | 56th | 1899-1901 |
| James T. Lloyd | Missouri | Democrat | 57th-60th | 1901-1909 |
| --- | --- | --- | 61st | 1909-1911 |
| John W. Dwight | New York | Republican | 62nd | 1911-1913 |
| Charles H. Burke | South Dakota | Republican | 63rd | 1913-1915 |
| Charles M. Hamilton | New York | Republican | 64th-65th | 1915-1919 |
| --- | --- | --- | 66th | 1919-1921 |
| William A. Oldfield | Arkansas | Democrat | 67th-70th | 1921-1928 |
| John McDuffie | Alabama | Democrat | 70th-71st | 1928-1931 |
| Carl G. Bachmann | West Virginia | Republican | 72nd | 1931-1933 |
| Harry L. Englebright | California | Republican | 73rd-77th | 1933-1943 |
| Leslie C. Arends | Illinois | Republican | 78th-79th | 1943-1947 |
| John W. McCormack | Massachusetts | Democrat | 80th | 1947-1949 |
| Leslie C. Arends | Illinois | Republican | 81st-82nd | 1949-1953 |
| John W. McCormack | Massachusetts | Democrat | 83rd | 1953-1955 |
| Leslie C. Arends | Illinois | Republican | 84th-93rd | 1955-1975 |
| Robert H. Michel | Illinois | Republican | 94th-96th | 1975-1981 |
| Trent Lott | Mississippi | Republican | 97th-99th | 1981-date |

Table 1.17

Chairmen of Major Committees in the
United States House of Representatives, 1875-1985

| Congresses | Years | Chairman | State | Party |
|------------|-------|----------|-------|-------|

### Ways and Means Committee

| Congresses | Years | Chairman | State | Party |
|------------|-------|----------|-------|-------|
| 44th | 1875-1877 | William R. Morrison | Illinois | Democrat |
| 45th-46th | 1877-1881 | Fernando Wood | New York | Democrat |
| 47th | 1881-1883 | William D. Kelley | Pennsylvania | Republican |
| 48th-49th | 1883-1887 | William D. Morrison | Illinois | Democrat |
| 50th | 1887-1889 | Roger Q. Mills | Texas | Democrat |
| 51st | 1889-1891 | William McKinley | Ohio | Republican |
| 52nd | 1891-1893 | William M. Springer | Illinois | Democrat |
| 53rd | 1893-1895 | William L. Wilson | West Virginia | Democrat |
| 54th-55th | 1895-1899 | Nelson Dingley | Maine | Republican |
| 56th-61st | 1899-1911 | Sereno E. Payne | New York | Republican |
| 62nd-63rd | 1911-1915 | Oscar W. Underwood | Alabama | Democrat |
| 64th-65th | 1915-1919 | Claude Kitchin | North Carolina | Democrat |
| 66th-67th | 1919-1923 | Joseph W. Fordney | Michigan | Republican |
| 68th-69th | 1923-1927 | William R. Green | Iowa | Republican |
| 70th-71st | 1927-1931 | Willis C. Hawley | Oregon | Republican |
| 72nd | 1931-1933 | James W. Collier | Mississippi | Democrat |
| 73rd-79th | 1933-1947 | Robert L. Doughton | North Carolina | Democrat |
| 80th | 1947-1949 | Harold Knutson | Minnesota | Republican |
| 81st-82nd | 1949-1953 | Robert L. Doughton | North Carolina | Democrat |
| 83rd | 1953-1955 | Daniel A. Reed | New York | Republican |
| 84th-85th | 1955-1959 | Jere Cooper | Tennessee | Democrat |
| 86th-93rd | 1959-1975 | Wilbur D. Mills | Arkansas | Democrat |
| 94th-96th | 1975-1981 | Al Ulman | Oregon | Democrat |
| 97th-99th | 1981-date | Dan Rostenkowski | Illinois | Democrat |

### Rules Committee

| Congresses | Years | Chairman | State | Party |
|------------|-------|----------|-------|-------|
| 44th-46th | 1875-1881 | Samuel J. Randall | Pennsylvania | Democrat |
| 47th | 1881-1883 | J. Warren Keifer | Ohio | Republican |
| 48th-50th | 1883-1889 | John G. Carlisle | Kentucky | Democrat |
| 51st | 1889-1891 | Thomas B. Reed | Maine | Republican |
| 52nd-53rd | 1891-1895 | Charles F. Crisp | Georgia | Democrat |
| 54th-55th | 1895-1899 | Thomas B. Reed | Maine | Republican |
| 56th-57th | 1899-1903 | David B. Henderson | Iowa | Republican |
| 58th-61st | 1903-1911 | Joseph G. Cannon | Illinois | Republican |
| 62nd-64th | 1911-1917 | Robert L. Henry | Texas | Democrat |
| 65th | 1917-1919 | Edward W. Pou | South Carolina | Democrat |
| 66th-67th | 1919-1923 | Philip Campbell | Kansas | Republican |
| 68th-71st | 1923-1931 | Bertrand H. Snell | New York | Republican |
| 72nd-73rd | 1931-1935 | Edward W. Pou | South Carolina | Democrat |
| 74th-75th | 1935-1939 | John J. O'Connor | New York | Democrat |
| 76th-79th | 1939-1947 | Adolph J. Sabath | Illinois | Democrat |
| 80th | 1947-1949 | Leo E. Allen | Illinois | Republican |
| 81st-82nd | 1949-1953 | Adolph J. Sabath | Illinois | Democrat |
| 83rd | 1953-1955 | Leo E. Allen | Illinois | Republican |
| 84th-89th | 1955-1967 | Howard W. Smith | Virginia | Democrat |
| 90th-92nd | 1967-1973 | William M. Colmer | Mississippi | Democrat |
| 93rd-94th | 1973-1977 | Ray J. Madden | Indiana | Democrat |
| 95th | 1977-1979 | James J. Delaney | New York | Democrat |
| 96th-97th | 1979-1983 | Richard Bolling | Missouri | Democrat |
| 98th-99th | 1983-date | Claude Pepper | Florida | Democrat |

Table 1.17 (continued)

| Congresses | Years | Chairman | State | Party |
|------------|-------|----------|-------|-------|

### Appropriations Committee

| | | | | |
|------------|-------|----------|-------|-------|
| 44th | 1875-1877 | William S. Holman | Indiana | Democrat |
| 45th-46th | 1877-1881 | John D. C. Atkins | Tennessee | Democrat |
| 47th | 1881-1883 | Frank Hiscock | New York | Republican |
| 48th-50th | 1883-1889 | Samuel J. Randall | Pennsylvania | Democrat |
| 51st | 1889-1891 | Joseph G. Cannon | Illinois | Republican |
| 52nd | 1891-1893 | William S. Holman | Indiana | Democrat |
| 53rd | 1893-1895 | Joseph D. Sayers | Texas | Democrat |
| 54th-57th | 1895-1903 | Joseph G. Cannon | Illinois | Democrat |
| 58th | 1903-1905 | James A. Hemenway | Indiana | Republican |
| 59th-61st | 1905-1911 | James A. Tawney | Minnesota | Republican |
| 62nd-65th | 1911-1919 | John J. Fitzgerald | New York | Democrat |
| 66th-67th | 1919-1923 | James W. Good | Iowa | Republican |
| 68th-69th | 1923-1927 | Martin B. Madden | Illinois | Republican |
| 70th | 1927-1929 | Daniel R. Anthony | Kansas | Republican |
| 71st | 1929-1931 | William R. Wood | Indiana | Republican |
| 72nd | 1931-1933 | Joseph W. Byrns | Tennessee | Democrat |
| 73rd-75th | 1933-1939 | James P. Buchanan | Texas | Democrat |
| 76th-77th | 1939-1943 | Edward T. Taylor | Colorado | Democrat |
| 78th-79th | 1943-1947 | Clarence Cannon | Missouri | Democrat |
| 80th | 1947-1949 | John Taber | New York | Republican |
| 81st-82nd | 1949-1953 | Clarence Cannon | Missouri | Democrat |
| 83rd | 1953-1955 | John Taber | New York | Republican |
| 84th-88th | 1955-1965 | Clarence Cannon | Missouri | Democrat |
| 89th-95th | 1965-1979 | George H. Mahon | Texas | Democrat |
| 96th-99th | 1979-date | Jamie L. Whitten | Mississippi | Democrat |

### Armed Services Committee
### (Military Affairs)

| | | | | |
|------------|-------|----------|-------|-------|
| 44th-45th | 1875-1879 | Henry B. Banning | Ohio | Democrat |
| 46th | 1879-1881 | William A. J. Sparks | Illinois | Democrat |
| 47th | 1881-1883 | Thomas J. Henderson | Illinois | Republican |
| 48th | 1883-1885 | William S. Rosencrans | California | Democrat |
| 49th | 1885-1887 | Edward S. Bragg | Wisconsin | Democrat |
| 50th | 1887-1889 | Richard W. Townshend | Illinois | Democrat |
| 51st | 1889-1891 | Byron M. Cutcheon | Michigan | Republican |
| 52nd-53rd | 1891-1895 | Joseph H. Outhwaite | Ohio | Democrat |
| 54th-61st | 1895-1911 | John A. T. Hull | Iowa | Republican |
| 62nd-64th | 1911-1917 | James Hay | Virginia | Democrat |
| 65th | 1917-1919 | S. Herbert Dent | Alabama | Democrat |
| 66th-68th | 1919-1925 | Julius Kahn | California | Republican |
| 69th-70th | 1925-1929 | John M. Morin | Pennsylvania | Republican |
| 71st | 1929-1931 | W. Frank James | Michigan | Republican |
| 72nd-74th | 1931-1937 | John J. McSwain | South Carolina | Democrat |
| 75th | 1937-1939 | Lister Hill | Alabama | Democrat |
| 76th-79th | 1939-1947 | Andrew J. May | Kentucky | Democrat |
| 80th | 1947-1949 | Walter G. Andrews | New York | Republican |
| 81st-82nd | 1949-1953 | Carl Vinson | Georgia | Democrat |
| 83rd | 1953-1955 | Dewey Short | Missouri | Republican |
| 84th-88th | 1955-1965 | Carl Vinson | Georgia | Democrat |
| 89th-91st | 1965-1971 | L. Mendel Rivers | South Carolina | Democrat |
| 92nd-93rd | 1971-1975 | F. Edward Hebert | Louisiana | Democrat |
| 94th-98th | 1975-1985 | Melvin Price | Illinois | Democrat |
| 99th | 1985-date | Les Aspin | Wisconsin | Democrat |

Table 1.18

Congressional Bills Introduced and Passed,
1789-1984

| Congress | Years | Measures Introduced | | | Measures Enacted | | |
|---|---|---|---|---|---|---|---|
| | | Total | Bills | Joint Resolutions | Total | Public | Private |
| 1st | 1789-1791 | 144 | 144 | --- | 118 | 108 | 10 |
| 2nd | 1791-1793 | 105 | 105 | --- | 77 | 65 | 12 |
| 3rd | 1793-1795 | 122 | 122 | --- | 127 | 103 | 24 |
| 4th | 1795-1797 | 132 | 132 | --- | 85 | 75 | 10 |
| 5th | 1797-1799 | 234 | 234 | --- | 155 | 137 | 18 |
| 6th | 1799-1801 | 157 | 157 | --- | 112 | 100 | 12 |
| 7th | 1801-1803 | 161 | 161 | --- | 95 | 80 | 15 |
| 8th | 1803-1805 | 217 | 217 | --- | 111 | 93 | 18 |
| 9th | 1805-1807 | 219 | 219 | --- | 106 | 90 | 16 |
| 10th | 1807-1809 | 266 | 266 | --- | 105 | 88 | 17 |
| 11th | 1809-1811 | 348 | 348 | --- | 119 | 94 | 25 |
| 12th | 1811-1813 | 406 | 406 | --- | 209 | 170 | 39 |
| 13th | 1813-1815 | 400 | 400 | --- | 273 | 185 | 88 |
| 14th | 1815-1817 | 465 | 465 | --- | 298 | 173 | 125 |
| 15th | 1817-1819 | 507 | 507 | --- | 257 | 156 | 101 |
| 16th | 1819-1821 | 480 | 480 | --- | 208 | 117 | 91 |
| 17th | 1821-1823 | 492 | 492 | --- | 238 | 136 | 102 |
| 18th | 1823-1825 | 498 | 481 | 17 | 335 | 141 | 194 |
| 19th | 1825-1827 | 622 | 609 | 13 | 266 | 153 | 113 |
| 20th | 1827-1829 | 632 | 612 | 20 | 235 | 134 | 101 |
| 21st | 1829-1831 | 856 | 842 | 14 | 369 | 152 | 217 |
| 22nd | 1831-1833 | 1,000 | 976 | 24 | 462 | 191 | 271 |
| 23rd | 1833-1835 | 993 | 946 | 47 | 390 | 128 | 262 |
| 24th | 1835-1837 | 1,107 | 1,055 | 52 | 459 | 144 | 315 |
| 25th | 1837-1839 | 1,631 | 1,566 | 65 | 532 | 150 | 382 |
| 26th | 1839-1841 | 1,122 | 1,081 | 41 | 147 | 55 | 92 |
| 27th | 1841-1843 | 1,210 | 1,146 | 64 | 524 | 201 | 323 |
| 28th | 1843-1845 | 1,085 | 979 | 106 | 279 | 142 | 137 |
| 29th | 1845-1847 | 1,051 | 956 | 95 | 303 | 142 | 161 |
| 30th | 1847-1849 | 1,433 | 1,305 | 128 | 446 | 176 | 270 |
| 31st | 1849-1851 | 1,080 | 978 | 102 | 167 | 109 | 58 |
| 32nd | 1851-1853 | 1,167 | 1,011 | 156 | 306 | 137 | 169 |
| 33rd | 1853-1855 | 1,660 | 1,552 | 108 | 540 | 188 | 352 |
| 34th | 1855-1857 | 1,608 | 1,515 | 93 | 433 | 157 | 276 |
| 35th | 1857-1859 | 1,686 | 1,544 | 142 | 312 | 129 | 183 |
| 36th | 1859-1861 | 1,746 | 1,595 | 151 | 370 | 157 | 213 |
| 37th | 1861-1863 | 1,661 | 1,370 | 291 | 521 | 428 | 93 |
| 38th | 1863-1865 | 1,708 | 1,402 | 306 | 515 | 411 | 104 |
| 39th | 1865-1867 | 2,248 | 1,864 | 484 | 714 | 427 | 287 |
| 40th | 1867-1869 | 3,723 | 3,003 | 720 | 765 | 354 | 411 |
| 41st | 1869-1871 | 5,314 | 4,466 | 848 | 769 | 470 | 299 |
| 42nd | 1871-1873 | 5,943 | 5,725 | 218 | 1,012 | 531 | 481 |
| 43rd | 1873-1875 | 6,434 | 6,252 | 182 | 859 | 415 | 444 |
| 44th | 1875-1877 | 6,230 | 6,001 | 229 | 580 | 278 | 302 |
| 45th | 1877-1879 | 8,735 | 8,413 | 322 | 746 | 303 | 443 |
| 46th | 1879-1881 | 10,067 | 9,481 | 586 | 650 | 372 | 278 |
| 47th | 1881-1883 | 10,704 | 10,194 | 510 | 761 | 419 | 342 |
| 48th | 1883-1885 | 11,443 | 10,961 | 482 | 969 | 284 | 685 |
| 49th | 1885-1887 | 15,002 | 14,618 | 384 | 1,452 | 424 | 1,028 |
| 50th | 1887-1889 | 17,078 | 16,664 | 414 | 1,824 | 570 | 1,254 |
| 51st | 1889-1891 | 19,630 | 19,163 | 467 | 2,251 | 611 | 1,640 |
| 52nd | 1891-1893 | 14,893 | 14,518 | 375 | 722 | 398 | 324 |

Table 1.18 (continued)

| Congress | Years | Measures Introduced | | | Measures Enacted | | |
|---|---|---|---|---|---|---|---|
| | | Total | Bills | Joint Resolutions | Total | Public | Private |
| 53rd | 1893-1895 | 12,226 | 11,796 | 430 | 711 | 463 | 248 |
| 54th | 1895-1897 | 14,585 | 14,114 | 471 | 948 | 434 | 514 |
| 55th | 1897-1899 | 18,463 | 17,817 | 646 | 1,437 | 552 | 885 |
| 56th | 1899-1901 | 20,893 | 20,409 | 484 | 1,942 | 443 | 1,499 |
| 57th | 1901-1903 | 25,460 | 25,007 | 453 | 2,790 | 480 | 2,31 |
| 58th | 1903-1905 | 26,851 | 26,504 | 347 | 4,041 | 575 | 3,466 |
| 59th | 1905-1907 | 34,879 | 34,524 | 355 | 7,024 | 775 | 6,249 |
| 60th | 1907-1909 | 38,388 | 37,981 | 407 | 646 | 411 | 235 |
| 61st | 1909-1911 | 44,363 | 43,921 | 442 | 884 | 595 | 289 |
| 62nd | 1911-1913 | 38,032 | 37,459 | 573 | 716 | 530 | 186 |
| 63rd | 1913-1915 | 30,053 | 29,367 | 686 | 700 | 417 | 283 |
| 64th | 1915-1917 | 30,052 | 29,438 | 614 | 684 | 458 | 226 |
| 65th | 1917-1919 | 22,594 | 21,919 | 675 | 453 | 405 | 48 |
| 66th | 1919-1921 | 21,967 | 21,222 | 745 | 594 | 470 | 124 |
| 67th | 1921-1923 | 19,889 | 19,133 | 756 | 930 | 654 | 276 |
| 68th | 1923-1925 | 17,462 | 16,884 | 578 | 996 | 707 | 289 |
| 69th | 1925-1927 | 23,799 | 23,250 | 549 | 1,423 | 879 | 544 |
| 70th | 1927-1929 | 23,897 | 23,238 | 659 | 1,722 | 1,145 | 577 |
| 71st | 1929-1931 | 24,453 | 23,652 | 801 | 1,522 | 1,009 | 513 |
| 72nd | 1931-1933 | 21,382 | 20,501 | 881 | 843 | 516 | 327 |
| 73rd | 1933-1934 | 14,370 | 13,774 | 596 | 975 | 539 | 436 |
| 74th | 1935-1936 | 18,754 | 17,819 | 935 | 1,724 | 987 | 737 |
| 75th | 1937-1938 | 16,156 | 15,120 | 1,036 | 1,759 | 919 | 840 |
| 76th | 1939-1941 | 16,105 | 15,174 | 931 | 1,662 | 1,005 | 657 |
| 77th | 1941-1942 | 11,334 | 10,793 | 541 | 1,485 | 850 | 635 |
| 78th | 1943-1944 | 8,334 | 7,845 | 489 | 1,157 | 568 | 589 |
| 79th | 1945-1946 | 10,330 | 9,748 | 582 | 1,625 | 733 | 892 |
| 80th | 1947-1948 | 10,797 | 10,108 | 689 | 1,363 | 906 | 457 |
| 81st | 1949-1951 | 14,988 | 14,219 | 769 | 2,024 | 921 | 1,103 |
| 82nd | 1951-1952 | 12,730 | 12,062 | 668 | 1,617 | 594 | 1,023 |
| 83rd | 1953-1954 | 14,952 | 14,181 | 771 | 1,783 | 781 | 1,002 |
| 84th | 1955-1956 | 17,687 | 16,782 | 905 | 1,921 | 1,028 | 893 |
| 85th | 1957-1958 | 19,112 | 18,205 | 907 | 1,720 | 936 | 784 |
| 86th | 1959-1960 | 18,261 | 17,230 | 1,031 | 1,292 | 800 | 492 |
| 87th | 1961-1962 | 18,376 | 17,230 | 1,146 | 1,569 | 885 | 684 |
| 88th | 1963-1964 | 17,480 | 16,079 | 1,401 | 1,026 | 666 | 360 |
| 89th | 1965-1966 | 24,003 | 22,483 | 1,520 | 1,283 | 810 | 473 |
| 90th | 1967-1968 | 26,460 | 24,786 | 1,674 | 1,002 | 640 | 362 |
| 91st | 1969-1971 | 26,303 | 24,631 | 1,672 | 941 | 695 | 246 |
| 92nd | 1971-1972 | 22,969 | 21,363 | 1,606 | 768 | 607 | 161 |
| 93rd | 1973-1974 | 23,396 | 21,950 | 1,446 | 772 | 649 | 123 |
| 94th | 1975-1976 | 21,096 | 19,762 | 1,334 | 729 | 588 | 141 |
| 95th | 1977-1978 | 19,387 | 18,045 | 1,342 | 803 | 633 | 170 |
| 96th | 1979-1980 | 12,583 | 11,722 | 861 | 736 | 613 | 123 |
| 97th | 1981-1982 | 11,490 | 10,582 | 908 | 529 | 473 | 56 |
| 98th | 1983-1984 | 10,559 | 9,537 | 1,022 | 491 | 460 | 31 |

Table 1.19

Congressional Bills Vetoed,
1789-1984

| Period | President | Total Vetoed Bills |
|--------|-----------|--------------------|
| 1789-1797 | George Washington | 2 |
| 1797-1801 | John Adams | 0 |
| 1801-1809 | Thomas Jefferson | 0 |
| 1809-1817 | James Madison | 7 |
| 1817-1825 | James Monroe | 1 |
| 1825-1829 | John Q. Adams | 0 |
| 1829-1837 | Andrew Jackson | 12 |
| 1839-1841 | Martin Van Buren | 1 |
| 1841 | William H. Harrison | 0 |
| 1841-1845 | John Tyler | 10 |
| 1845-1849 | James Polk | 3 |
| 1849-1850 | Zachary Taylor | 0 |
| 1850-1853 | Millard Fillmore | 0 |
| 1853-1857 | Franklin Pierce | 9 |
| 1857-1861 | James Buchanan | 7 |
| 1861-1865 | Abraham Lincoln | 6 |
| 1865-1869 | Andrew Johnson | 29 |
| 1869-1877 | Ulysses Grant | 93 |
| 1877-1881 | Rutherford Hayes | 13 |
| 1881 | James Garfield | 0 |
| 1881-1885 | Chester Arthur | 12 |
| 1885-1889 | Grover Cleveland | 414 |
| 1889-1893 | Benjamin Harrison | 44 |
| 1893-1897 | Grover Cleveland | 170 |
| 1897-1901 | William McKinley | 42 |
| 1901-1909 | Theodore Roosevelt | 82 |
| 1909-1913 | William Taft | 39 |
| 1913-1921 | Woodrow Wilson | 44 |
| 1921-1923 | Warren Harding | 6 |
| 1923-1929 | Calvin Coolidge | 50 |
| 1929-1933 | Herbert Hoover | 37 |
| 1933-1945 | Franklin Roosevelt | 635 |
| 1945-1953 | Harry Truman | 250 |
| 1953-1961 | Dwight Eisenhower | 181 |
| 1961-1963 | John Kennedy | 21 |
| 1963-1969 | Lyndon Johnson | 30 |
| 1969-1974 | Richard Nixon | 42 |
| 1974-1977 | Gerald Ford | 72 |
| 1977-1981 | Jimmy Carter * | 31 |
| 1981-1984 | Ronald Reagan | 28 |

*Ronald Reagan's total does not include any pocket vetoes from the 98th Congress.

## *Partisan Composition of the United States Congress*

The partisan division of each chamber of Congress is documented in the following tables (1.20 and 1.21), which record the number of seats held by members of the various parties at the beginning of the first session of each Congress. Deaths, resignations, and replacement of Senators and Representatives during a term of a Congress have often changed the partisan composition of these legislative bodies; in some çases, control of a chamber has been altered by such changes in membership. Until the 1830s, when a system of formal parties became established in the nation, the identification of partisan allegiance of elected members of Congress was imperfect and is subject to scholarly dispute.

Table 1.20

Partisan Composition of the
United States Senate, 1789-1985

| Congress | Years | Federalist | Democratic Republican | Anti-Federalist | Other Parties | Unknown or No Party | Total Seats |
|----------|-------|------------|-----------------------|-----------------|---------------|---------------------|-------------|
| 1st | 1789-1791 | 14 | 7 | 1 | 1 | 3 | 26 |
| 2nd | 1791-1793 | 13 | 10 | 2 | 1 | 3 | 29 |
| 3rd | 1793-1795 | 8 | 9 | -- | 1 | 12 | 30 |
| 4th | 1795-1775 | 14 | 11 | -- | 1 | 6 | 32 |
| 5th | 1797-1799 | 16 | 7 | -- | 1 | 8 | 32 |
| 6th | 1799-1801 | 17 | 9 | -- | -- | 6 | 32 |
| 7th | 1801-1803 | 15 | 11 | -- | 1 | 5 | 32 |
| 8th | 1803-1805 | 9 | 21 | -- | -- | 4 | 34 |
| 9th | 1805-1807 | 10 | 24 | -- | -- | -- | 34 |
| 10th | 1807-1809 | 9 | 23 | -- | -- | 2 | 34 |
| 11th | 1809-1811 | 8 | 22 | -- | -- | 4 | 34 |
| 12th | 1811-1813 | 9 | 22 | -- | -- | 5 | 36 |
| 13th | 1813-1815 | 10 | 22 | -- | -- | 4 | 36 |
| 14th | 1815-1817 | 11 | 19 | -- | 1 | 7 | 38 |
| 15th | 1817-1819 | 12 | 22 | -- | 3 | 5 | 42 |
| 16th | 1819-1821 | 9 | 28 | -- | 4 | 5 | 46 |
| 17th | 1821-1823 | 4 | 32 | -- | 4 | 8 | 48 |
| 18th | 1823-1825 | 5 | 32 | -- | 4 | 7 | 48 |
| 19th | 1825-1827 | 4 | 34 | -- | 4 | 6 | 48 |
| 20th | 1827-1829 | 2 | 33 | -- | 7 | 5 | 47 |

Table 1.20 (continued)

| Congress | Years | Democratic | Whig | National Republican | Federalist | Other Parties | Unknown or No Party | Total Seats |
|----------|-------|-----------|------|---------------------|------------|---------------|---------------------|-------------|
| 21st | 1829-1831 | 33 | -- | 6 | 3 | 6 | -- | 48 |
| 22nd | 1831-1833 | 28 | -- | 3 | 1 | 14 | 2 | 48 |
| 23rd | 1833-1835 | 27 | 11 | 5 | -- | 2 | 3 | 48 |
| 24th | 1835-1837 | 33 | 14 | 2 | -- | 2 | 1 | 52 |
| 25th | 1837-1839 | 38 | 11 | 1 | -- | 1 | 1 | 52 |
| 26th | 1839-1841 | 34 | 15 | -- | 1 | 1 | -- | 51 |
| 27th | 1841-1843 | 22 | 28 | -- | -- | 2 | -- | 52 |
| 28th | 1843-1845 | 23 | 27 | -- | -- | 1 | -- | 51 |
| 29th | 1845-1847 | 30 | 23 | -- | -- | 2 | -- | 55 |
| 30th | 1847-1849 | 34 | 21 | -- | -- | 2 | 1 | 58 |
| 31st | 1849-1851 | 32 | 25 | -- | -- | 4 | -- | 61 |
| 32nd | 1851-1853 | 37 | 23 | -- | -- | 2 | -- | 62 |

Table 1.20 (continued)

| Congress | Years | Democratic | Whig | Republican | Populist | Other Parties | Total Seats |
|----------|-------|-----------|------|------------|----------|---------------|-------------|
| 33rd | 1853-1855 | 41 | 20 | -- | -- | 1 | 62 |
| 34th | 1855-1857 | 40 | 13 | 6 | -- | 3 | 62 |
| 35th | 1857-1859 | 40 | 6 | 16 | -- | 4 | 66 |
| 36th | 1859-1861 | 36 | 3 | 23 | -- | 4 | 66 |
| 37th | 1861-1863 | 25 | 2 | 26 | -- | 3 | 56 |
| 38th | 1863-1865 | 11 | 1 | 34 | -- | 6 | 52 |
| 39th | 1865-1867 | 13 | -- | 33 | -- | 6 | 52 |
| 40th | 1867-1869 | 11 | -- | 49 | -- | 6 | 66 |
| 41st | 1869-1871 | 11 | -- | 57 | -- | 6 | 74 |
| 42nd | 1871-1873 | 17 | -- | 53 | -- | 4 | 74 |
| 43rd | 1873-1875 | 19 | -- | 51 | -- | 3 | 73 |
| 44th | 1875-1877 | 26 | -- | 44 | -- | 5 | 75 |
| 45th | 1877-1879 | 32 | -- | 40 | -- | 4 | 76 |
| 46th | 1879-1881 | 40 | -- | 32 | -- | 4 | 76 |
| 47th | 1881-1883 | 36 | -- | 36 | -- | 3 | 75 |
| 48th | 1883-1885 | 36 | -- | 38 | -- | 2 | 76 |
| 49th | 1885-1887 | 34 | -- | 40 | -- | 2 | 76 |
| 50th | 1887-1889 | 37 | -- | 38 | -- | 1 | 76 |
| 51st | 1889-1891 | 37 | -- | 51 | -- | -- | 88 |
| 52nd | 1891-1893 | 38 | -- | 45 | 1 | 1 | 85 |
| 53rd | 1893-1895 | 44 | -- | 41 | 2 | 1 | 88 |
| 54th | 1895-1897 | 40 | -- | 45 | 3 | 2 | 90 |
| 55th | 1897-1899 | 35 | -- | 49 | 3 | 3 | 90 |
| 56th | 1899-1901 | 27 | -- | 57 | -- | 5 | 89 |
| 57th | 1901-1903 | 29 | -- | 55 | -- | 6 | 90 |
| 58th | 1903-1905 | 32 | -- | 57 | -- | 1 | 90 |
| 59th | 1905-1907 | 31 | -- | 58 | -- | 1 | 90 |
| 60th | 1907-1909 | 31 | -- | 61 | -- | -- | 92 |
| 61st | 1909-1911 | 32 | -- | 60 | -- | -- | 92 |
| 62nd | 1911-1913 | 44 | -- | 51 | -- | -- | 95 |
| 63rd | 1913-1915 | 51 | -- | 45 | -- | -- | 96 |

Table 1.20 (continued)

| Congress | Years | Democratic | Republican | Progessive | Farmer Labor | Other Parties | Total Seats |
|----------|-------|------------|------------|------------|--------------|---------------|-------------|
| 64th | 1915-1917 | 56 | 40 | -- | -- | -- | 96 |
| 65th | 1917-1919 | 54 | 42 | -- | -- | -- | 96 |
| 66th | 1919-1921 | 47 | 49 | -- | -- | -- | 96 |
| 67th | 1921-1923 | 37 | 58 | -- | -- | 1 | 96 |
| 68th | 1923-1925 | 42 | 51 | -- | -- | 3 | 96 |
| 69th | 1925-1927 | 40 | 53 | -- | 1 | 2 | 96 |
| 70th | 1927-1929 | 47 | 44 | -- | 1 | 2 | 94 |
| 71st | 1929-1931 | 40 | 53 | -- | 1 | 2 | 96 |
| 72nd | 1931-1933 | 47 | 46 | -- | 1 | 2 | 96 |
| 73rd | 1933-1935 | 60 | 35 | -- | 1 | -- | 96 |
| 74th | 1935-1937 | 69 | 25 | -- | 1 | 1 | 96 |
| 75th | 1937-1939 | 76 | 17 | 1 | 2 | -- | 96 |
| 76th | 1939-1941 | 70 | 24 | 1 | 2 | -- | 96 |
| 77th | 1941-1943 | 66 | 29 | -- | -- | -- | 96 |
| 78th | 1943-1945 | 57 | 38 | 1 | -- | -- | 96 |

Table 1.20 (continued)

| Congress | Years | Democratic | Republican | Other Parties | Total Seats |
|----------|-------|------------|------------|---------------|-------------|
| 79th | 1945-1947 | 57 | 39 | -- | 96 |
| 80th | 1947-1949 | 45 | 51 | -- | 96 |
| 81st | 1949-1951 | 54 | 42 | -- | 96 |
| 82nd | 1951-1953 | 49 | 47 | -- | 96 |
| 83rd | 1953-1955 | 47 | 49 | -- | 96 |
| 84th | 1955-1957 | 48 | 48 | -- | 96 |
| 85th | 1957-1959 | 49 | 47 | -- | 96 |
| 86th | 1959-1961 | 66 | 34 | -- | 100 |
| 87th | 1961-1963 | 65 | 35 | -- | 100 |
| 88th | 1963-1965 | 67 | 33 | -- | 100 |
| 89th | 1965-1967 | 68 | 32 | -- | 100 |
| 90th | 1967-1969 | 64 | 36 | -- | 100 |
| 91st | 1969-1971 | 57 | 43 | -- | 100 |
| 92nd | 1971-1973 | 54 | 44 | 2 | 100 |
| 93rd | 1973-1975 | 56 | 42 | 2 | 100 |
| 94th | 1975-1977 | 60 | 37 | 3 | 100 |
| 95th | 1977-1979 | 61 | 38 | 1 | 100 |
| 96th | 1979-1981 | 58 | 41 | 1 | 100 |
| 97th | 1981-1983 | 46 | 53 | 1 | 100 |
| 98th | 1983-1985 | 46 | 54 | -- | 100 |
| 99th | 1985-1987 | 47 | 53 | -- | 100 |

Table 1.21

Partisan Composition of the United States
House of Representatives, 1789-1985

| Congress | Years | Federalist | Democratic Republican | Democratic | Anti-Federalist | National Republican | Whig | Other Parties | Unknown or No Party | Total Seats |
|---|---|---|---|---|---|---|---|---|---|---|
| 1st | 1789-1791 | 27 | 12 | -- | 3 | -- | -- | 1 | 22 | 65. |
| 2nd | 1791-1793 | 32 | 15 | -- | 6 | -- | -- | -- | 15 | 68 |
| 3rd | 1793-1795 | 37 | 35 | -- | 4 | -- | -- | -- | 30 | 106 |
| 4th | 1795-1797 | 41 | 46 | -- | 4 | -- | -- | -- | 24 | 106 |
| 5th | 1797-1799 | 43 | 34 | -- | 6 | -- | -- | -- | 23 | 106 |
| 6th | 1799-1801 | 44 | 38 | -- | 10 | -- | -- | -- | 19 | 105 |
| 7th | 1801-1803 | 24 | 44 | -- | 2 | -- | -- | -- | 34 | 104 |
| 8th | 1803-1805 | 28 | 69 | -- | 4 | -- | -- | -- | 41 | 142 |
| 9th | 1805-1807 | 27 | 79 | -- | 6 | -- | -- | -- | 34 | 146 |
| 10th | 1807-1809 | 28 | 78 | -- | 5 | -- | -- | -- | 31 | 142 |
| 11th | 1809-1811 | 44 | 71 | -- | 5 | -- | -- | -- | 23 | 142 |
| 12th | 1811-1813 | 38 | 90 | -- | 3 | -- | -- | -- | 9 | 143 |
| 13th | 1813-1815 | 63 | 99 | -- | 1 | -- | -- | 2 | 12 | 177 |
| 14th | 1815-1817 | 60 | 89 | -- | 1 | -- | -- | 4 | 28 | 185 |
| 15th | 1817-1819 | 31 | 114 | -- | -- | -- | -- | 7 | 36 | 182 |
| 16th | 1819-1821 | 18 | 103 | -- | -- | -- | -- | 10 | 39 | 170 |
| 17th | 1821-1823 | 17 | 112 | -- | -- | -- | -- | 14 | 43 | 186 |
| 18th | 1823-1825 | 17 | 121 | -- | -- | -- | -- | 29 | 47 | 214 |
| 19th | 1825-1827 | 13 | 116 | -- | -- | 9 | -- | 35 | 40 | 213 |
| 20th | 1827-1829 | 13 | 117 | -- | -- | 21 | -- | 34 | 27 | 212 |
| 21st | 1829-1831 | 3 | -- | 133 | -- | 15 | -- | 38 | 24 | 213 |
| 22nd | 1831-1833 | 3 | -- | 136 | -- | 13 | -- | 51 | 10 | 213 |
| 23rd | 1833-1835 | -- | -- | 149 | -- | -- | 77 | 10 | 4 | 240 |
| 24th | 1835-1837 | -- | -- | 148 | -- | -- | 84 | 8 | -- | 240 |
| 25th | 1837-1839 | -- | -- | 136 | -- | -- | 101 | 6 | -- | 243 |
| 26th | 1839-1841 | -- | -- | 131 | -- | -- | 108 | 2 | -- | 241 |
| 27th | 1841-1843 | -- | -- | 103 | -- | -- | 133 | 3 | 1 | 240 |
| 28th | 1843-1845 | -- | -- | 143 | -- | -- | 73 | 2 | -- | 218 |

Table 1.21 (continued)

| Congress | Years | Democratic | Whig | Republican | American | Greenback | Populist | Other Parties | Unknown or No Party | Total Seats |
|---|---|---|---|---|---|---|---|---|---|---|
| 29th | 1845-1847 | 147 | 75 | -- | 4 | -- | -- | 2 | -- | 228 |
| 30th | 1847-1849 | 112 | 109 | -- | 1 | -- | -- | 6 | -- | 228 |
| 31st | 1849-1851 | 117 | 105 | -- | 1 | -- | -- | 9 | -- | 232 |
| 32nd | 1851-1853 | 136 | 87 | -- | -- | -- | -- | 9 | -- | 233 |
| 33rd | 1853-1855 | 157 | 68 | 4 | 1 | -- | -- | 8 | -- | 234 |
| 34th | 1855-1857 | 85 | 61 | 39 | 41 | -- | -- | 8 | -- | 234 |
| 35th | 1857-1859 | 132 | 22 | 68 | 13 | -- | -- | 2 | -- | 237 |
| 36th | 1859-1861 | 98 | 12 | 107 | 15 | -- | -- | 6 | -- | 238 |
| 37th | 1861-1863 | 48 | 8 | 110 | -- | -- | -- | 18 | -- | 184 |
| 38th | 1863-1865 | 76 | 5 | 88 | -- | -- | -- | 15 | -- | 184 |
| 39th | 1865-1867 | 40 | 7 | 131 | -- | -- | -- | 10 | -- | 188 |
| 40th | 1867-1869 | 48 | 2 | 166 | -- | -- | -- | 8 | -- | 224 |
| 41st | 1869-1871 | 69 | 1 | 169 | -- | -- | -- | 4 | -- | 243 |
| 42nd | 1871-1873 | 98 | -- | 140 | -- | -- | -- | 5 | -- | 243 |
| 43rd | 1873-1875 | 86 | -- | 201 | -- | -- | -- | 6 | -- | 293 |
| 44th | 1875-1877 | 174 | -- | 111 | -- | -- | -- | 8 | -- | 293 |
| 45th | 1877-1879 | 156 | -- | 137 | -- | -- | -- | -- | -- | 293 |
| 46th | 1879-1881 | 150 | -- | 137 | -- | 4 | -- | 2 | -- | 293 |
| 47th | 1881-1883 | 129 | -- | 151 | -- | 4 | -- | 10 | -- | 293 |
| 48th | 1883-1885 | 199 | -- | 118 | -- | -- | -- | 8 | -- | 325 |
| 49th | 1885-1887 | 183 | -- | 140 | -- | 1 | -- | 1 | -- | 325 |
| 50th | 1887-1889 | 168 | -- | 154 | -- | -- | -- | 3 | -- | 325 |
| 51st | 1889-1891 | 152 | -- | 176 | -- | -- | -- | 3 | -- | 331 |
| 52nd | 1891-1893 | 236 | -- | 87 | -- | -- | 4 | 5 | -- | 332 |
| 53rd | 1893-1895 | 217 | -- | 126 | -- | -- | 7 | 6 | -- | 356 |
| 54th | 1895-1897 | 96 | -- | 253 | -- | -- | 8 | -- | -- | 357 |
| 55th | 1897-1899 | 126 | -- | 207 | -- | -- | 12 | 12 | -- | 357 |
| 56th | 1899-1901 | 162 | -- | 189 | -- | -- | 3 | 3 | -- | 357 |
| 57th | 1901-1903 | 153 | -- | 198 | -- | -- | 3 | 3 | -- | 357 |
| 58th | 1903-1905 | 172 | -- | 210 | -- | -- | -- | 4 | -- | 386 |
| 59th | 1905-1907 | 135 | -- | 251 | -- | -- | -- | -- | -- | 386 |
| 60th | 1907-1909 | 167 | -- | 224 | -- | -- | -- | -- | -- | 391 |
| 61st | 1909-1911 | 172 | -- | 219 | -- | -- | -- | -- | -- | 391 |

Table 1.21 (continued)

| Congress | Years | Democratic | Republican | Socialist | Progressive | Farmer Labor | American Labor | Other Parties | Total Seats |
|---|---|---|---|---|---|---|---|---|---|
| 62nd | 1911-1913 | 230 | 162 | 1 | — | — | — | 1 | 394 |
| 63rd | 1913-1915 | 291 | 143 | — | — | — | — | 1 | 435 |
| 64th | 1915-1917 | 231 | 199 | 1 | 2 | — | — | 2 | 435 |
| 65th | 1917-1919 | 215 | 217 | 1 | 2 | — | — | — | 435 |
| 66th | 1919-1921 | 192 | 239 | 1 | — | — | — | 3 | 435 |
| 67th | 1921-1923 | 130 | 302 | 1 | — | — | — | 2 | 435 |
| 68th | 1923-1925 | 205 | 226 | 1 | — | 1 | — | 2 | 435 |
| 69th | 1925-1927 | 183 | 247 | 1 | — | 3 | — | 1 | 435 |
| 70th | 1927-1929 | 194 | 238 | 1 | — | 1 | — | — | 435 |
| 71st | 1929-1931 | 164 | 270 | — | — | 1 | — | — | 435 |
| 72nd | 1931-1933 | 217 | 217 | — | — | 1 | — | — | 435 |
| 73rd | 1933-1935 | 313 | 117 | — | — | 5 | — | — | 435 |
| 74th | 1935-1937 | 322 | 103 | — | 7 | 3 | — | — | 435 |
| 75th | 1937-1939 | 334 | 89 | — | 7 | 5 | — | — | 435 |
| 76th | 1939-1941 | 261 | 168 | — | 2 | 1 | 1 | 2 | 435 |
| 77th | 1941-1943 | 267 | 162 | — | 3 | 1 | 1 | 1 | 435 |
| 78th | 1943-1945 | 221 | 209 | — | 2 | 1 | 1 | 1 | 435 |
| 79th | 1945-1947 | 243 | 191 | — | 1 | — | 1 | — | 435 |
| 80th | 1947-1949 | 188 | 246 | — | — | — | 1 | — | 435 |
| 81st | 1949-1951 | 263 | 171 | — | — | — | 1 | — | 435 |
| 82nd | 1951-1953 | 235 | 199 | — | — | — | — | 1 | 435 |
| 83rd | 1953-1955 | 213 | 221 | — | — | — | — | 1 | 435 |
| 84th | 1955-1957 | 232 | 203 | — | — | — | — | — | 435 |
| 85th | 1957-1959 | 235 | 200 | — | — | — | — | — | 435 |
| 86th | 1959-1961 | 282 | 153 | — | — | — | — | — | 435 |
| 87th | 1961-1963 | 263 | 174 | — | — | — | — | — | 435 |
| 88th | 1963-1965 | 259 | 176 | — | — | — | — | — | 435 |
| 89th | 1965-1967 | 295 | 140 | — | — | — | — | — | 435 |
| 90th | 1967-1969 | 247 | 188 | — | — | — | — | — | 435 |

Table 1.21 (continued)

| Congress | Years | Democratic | Republican | Socialist | Progressive | Farmer Labor | American Labor | Other Parties | Total Seats |
|---|---|---|---|---|---|---|---|---|---|
| 91st | 1969-1971 | 242 | 193 | -- | -- | -- | -- | -- | 435 |
| 92nd | 1971-1973 | 254 | 181 | -- | -- | -- | -- | -- | 435 |
| 93rd | 1973-1975 | 242 | 193 | -- | -- | -- | -- | -- | 435 |
| 94th | 1975-1977 | 291 | 144 | -- | -- | -- | -- | -- | 435 |
| 95th | 1977-1979 | 292 | 143 | -- | -- | -- | -- | -- | 435 |
| 96th | 1979-1981 | 276 | 159 | -- | -- | -- | -- | -- | 435 |
| 97th | 1981-1983 | 242 | 192 | -- | -- | -- | -- | -- | 435 |
| 98th | 1983-1985 | 269 | 166 | -- | -- | -- | -- | 1 | 435 |
| 99th | 1985-1987 | 253 | 182 | -- | -- | -- | -- | -- | 435 |

# Salaries of Public Officials

In the following tables (1.22 and 1.23), the salaries of major officeholders in the government of the United States are recorded over time. The dates presented are those at which changes in the salaries of various officials were mandated by legislative action. In addition to the salaries listed in the tables below, most of the officials were entitled to additional funds to cover travel and other expenses incurred in the performance of their duties. Among the additions to statutory salaries are allowances for office expenses, stationery and communications, and (for members of Congress and the Vice President) the "franking" privilege. The latter allows authorized persons to send official mail without charge, using a facsimile signature rather than a postage stamp to authorize its delivery by the U.S. Postal Department. Additional salary was also awarded to the Speaker of the House of Representatives for official leadership duties, and to various other officials (Vice President, President Pro Tempore of the Senate) for their temporary service in the place of other officials (e.g., the President, Vice President, etc.).

Officials whose salaries are presented in the first table below are:

President
Vice President

Supreme Court:
    Chief Justice
    Associate Justices

Cabinet Officers:
    Secretary of State
    Secretary of the Treasury
    Secretary of War
    Attorney General
    Secretary of the Navy
    Postmaster General
    Secretary of the Interior

Table 1.22

Salaries of Executive Branch Officers
and Supreme Court Justices, 1789-1985

| Year | Pres. | Vice Pres. | Supreme Court | | Cabinet Officers | | | | | | |
|---|---|---|---|---|---|---|---|---|---|---|---|
| | | | Chief Justice | Assoc. Justice | Sec. State | Sec. Tres. | Sec. War | Att. Gen. | Sec. Navy | Post M. General | Sec. Int. |
| 1789 | $25,000 | $5,000 | $4,000 | $3,500 | $3,500 | $3,500 | $3,000 | $1,500 | --- | $1,500 | --- |
| 1791 | 25,000 | 5,000 | 4,000 | 3,500 | 3,500 | 3,500 | 3,000 | 1,900 | --- | 1,500 | --- |
| 1792 | 25,000 | 5,000 | 4,000 | 3,500 | 3,500 | 3,500 | 3,000 | 1,900 | --- | 2,000 | --- |
| 1794 | 25,000 | 5,000 | 4,000 | 3,500 | 3,500 | 3,500 | 3,000 | 1,900 | --- | 2,400 | --- |
| 1797 | 25,000 | 5,000 | 4,000 | 3,500 | 3,500 | 3,500 | 3,000 | 2,400 | --- | 2,400 | --- |
| 1798 | 25,000 | 5,000 | 4,000 | 3,500 | 3,500 | 3,500 | 3,000 | 2,400 | --- | 2,400 | --- |
| 1799 | 25,000 | 5,000 | 4,000 | 3,500 | 3,500 | 3,500 | 3,000 | 3,000 | 3,000 | 3,000 | --- |
| 1819 | 25,000 | 5,000 | 5,000 | 4,500 | 5,000 | 5,000 | 4,500 | 3,500 | 4,500 | 4,000 | --- |
| 1827 | 25,000 | 5,000 | 5,000 | 4,500 | 6,000 | 6,000 | 6,000 | 3,500 | 6,000 | 6,000 | --- |
| 1830 | 25,000 | 5,000 | 5,000 | 4,500 | 6,000 | 6,000 | 6,000 | 4,000 | 6,000 | 6,000 | --- |
| 1849 | 25,000 | 5,000 | 5,000 | 4,500 | 6,000 | 6,000 | 4,000 | 6,000 | 6,000 | 6,000 | 6,000 |
| 1853 | 25,000 | 8,000 | 5,000 | 4,500 | 8,000 | 8,000 | 8,000 | 8,000 | 8,000 | 8,000 | 8,000 |

Table 1.22 (continued)

| Year | Pres. | Vice Pres. | Chief Justice | Assoc. Justice | Cabinet Officers[a] |
|------|-------|-----------|---------------|----------------|---------------------|
| 1854 | $25,000 | $8,000 | $5,000 | $4,500 | $8,000 |
| 1856 | 25,000 | 8,000 | 6,500 | 6,000 | 8,000 |
| 1871 | 25,000 | 8,000 | 8,500 | 8,000 | 8,000 |
| 1873[b] | 50,000 | 10,000 | 10,500 | 10,000 | 10,000 |
| 1874 | 50,000 | 8,000 | 10,500 | 10,000 | 8,000 |
| 1903 | 50,000 | 8,000 | 13,000 | 12,500 | 8,000 |
| 1907 | 50,000 | 12,000 | 13,000 | 12,500 | 12,000 |
| 1909 | 75,000 | 12,000 | 13,000 | 12,500 | 12,000[c] |
| 1912 | 75,000 | 12,000 | 15,000 | 14,500 | 12,000 |
| 1926 | 75,000 | 15,000 | 20,500 | 20,000 | 15,000 |
| 1946 | 75,000 | 15,000 | 25,500 | 25,000 | 15,000 |
| 1949 | 100,000 | 30,000 | 25,500 | 25,000 | 22,500 |
| 1955 | 100,000 | 35,000 | 35,500 | 35,000 | 25,000 |
| 1964 | 100,000 | 43,000 | 40,000 | 39,500 | 35,000 |
| 1969 | 200,000 | 62,500 | 62,500 | 60,000 | 60,000 |
| 1975 | 200,000 | 65,600 | 62,500 | 60,000 | 63,000 |
| 1976 | 200,000 | 68,800 | 65,600 | 63,000 | 66,000 |
| 1977 | 200,000 | 75,000 | 75,000 | 72,000 | 66,000 |
| 1978 | 200,000 | 75,000 | 75,000 | 72,500 | 66,000 |
| 1979 | 200,000 | 79,100 | 75,000 | 72,500 | 69,600 |
| 1980 | 200,000 | 79,100 | 84,675 | 81,288 | 69,600 |
| 1982 | 200,000 | 79,100 | 96,800 | 93,000 | 69,600 |
| 1983 | 200,000 | 91,000 | 96,800 | 93,000 | 80,100 |

[a] In 1853, pay was equalized for all cabinet officers.

[b] This increase was the result of the famous "Salary Grab" act passed by Congress in 1873. Public outcry against it was strong and for the most part the raises were rescinded the next year.

[c] The salary of the Secretary of State was temporarily reduced to $8,000 so Philander C. Knox, Pennsylvania Senator from 1905-1909, could take office in accordance with the Constitutional requirement that no Senator or Representative be appointed to an office which had received a salary increase (see the U.S. Constitution, Article I, Section 6).

Table 1.23

Annual Salaries of the United States Senators
and Representatives,
1789-1985

| Year | Salary |
|------|--------|
| 1789[a] | $6 per diem |
| 1816[b] | $1,500 per year |
| 1817 | $8 per diem |
| 1856 | $3,000 per year |
| 1866 | $5,000 per year |
| 1873[c] | $7,500 per year |
| 1874 | $5,000 per year |
| 1907 | $7,500 per year |
| 1925 | $10,000 per year |
| 1932[d] | $9,000 per year |
| 1933 | $8,500 per year |
| 1935 | $10,000 per year |
| 1947 | $12,500 per year |
| 1955 | $22,500 per year |
| 1964 | $30,000 per year |
| 1969 | $42,500 per year |
| 1975 | $44,600 per year |
| 1976 | $46,800 per year |
| 1977 | $57,500 per year |
| 1979 | $60,700 per year |
| 1983 | $69,800 per year |

[a]Salaries of United States Senators were raised in 1795
to $7 per diem but in 1796 were returned to $6 per diem.

[b]In 1816 Congress raised its own salary to $1,500 per
year. Public outcry forced the repeal of this increase
on 1817.

[c]The "Salary Grab" act of 1873 raised Congressional
salaries to $7,500 but public criticism forced its
repeal in 1874.

[d]Salary decreases for members of Congress in 1932 and
1933 followed reduction of salaries of all federal
employees at the height of the Great Depression.

# Organizational Charts of the United States Government, 1984

The following charts depict the organizational structure of the three branches of the U.S. government: the executive branch (chart A); the judicial branch (chart B); and the legislative branch, which is broken down into two separate parts—one for the House of Representatives (chart C) and one for the Senate (chart D).

**EXECUTIVE**

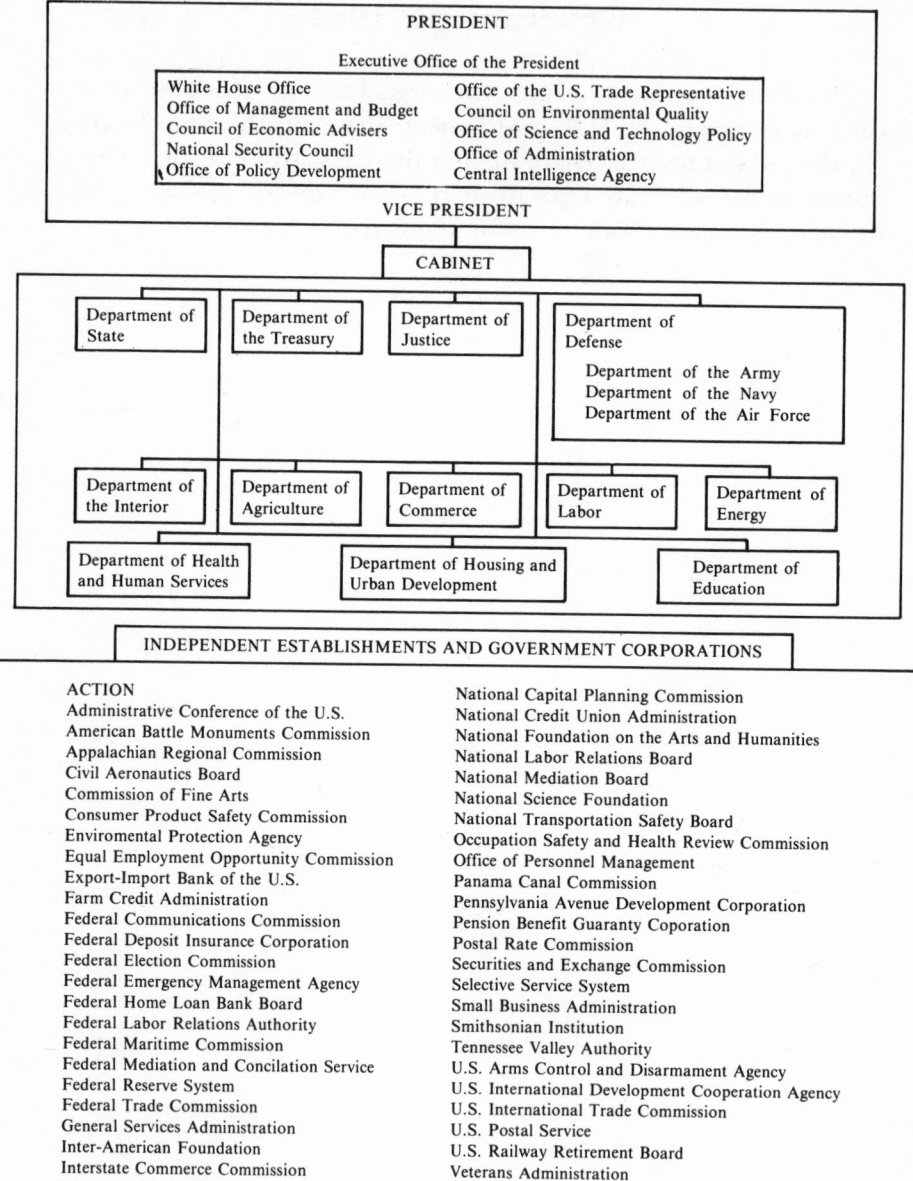

**PRESIDENT**

Executive Office of the President

| | |
|---|---|
| White House Office | Office of the U.S. Trade Representative |
| Office of Management and Budget | Council on Environmental Quality |
| Council of Economic Advisers | Office of Science and Technology Policy |
| National Security Council | Office of Administration |
| Office of Policy Development | Central Intelligence Agency |

**VICE PRESIDENT**

**CABINET**

Department of State

Department of the Treasury

Department of Justice

Department of Defense

Department of the Army
Department of the Navy
Department of the Air Force

Department of the Interior

Department of Agriculture

Department of Commerce

Department of Labor

Department of Energy

Department of Health and Human Services

Department of Housing and Urban Development

Department of Education

**INDEPENDENT ESTABLISHMENTS AND GOVERNMENT CORPORATIONS**

ACTION
Administrative Conference of the U.S.
American Battle Monuments Commission
Appalachian Regional Commission
Civil Aeronautics Board
Commission of Fine Arts
Consumer Product Safety Commission
Enviromental Protection Agency
Equal Employment Opportunity Commission
Export-Import Bank of the U.S.
Farm Credit Administration
Federal Communications Commission
Federal Deposit Insurance Corporation
Federal Election Commission
Federal Emergency Management Agency
Federal Home Loan Bank Board
Federal Labor Relations Authority
Federal Maritime Commission
Federal Mediation and Concilation Service
Federal Reserve System
Federal Trade Commission
General Services Administration
Inter-American Foundation
Interstate Commerce Commission
National Aeronautics and Space Administration

National Capital Planning Commission
National Credit Union Administration
National Foundation on the Arts and Humanities
National Labor Relations Board
National Mediation Board
National Science Foundation
National Transportation Safety Board
Occupation Safety and Health Review Commission
Office of Personnel Management
Panama Canal Commission
Pennsylvania Avenue Development Corporation
Pension Benefit Guaranty Coporation
Postal Rate Commission
Securities and Exchange Commission
Selective Service System
Small Business Administration
Smithsonian Institution
Tennessee Valley Authority
U.S. Arms Control and Disarmament Agency
U.S. International Development Cooperation Agency
U.S. International Trade Commission
U.S. Postal Service
U.S. Railway Retirement Board
Veterans Administration

**Chart A.** Organization of the Executive Branch

**JUDICIAL**

**Chart B.** Organization of the Judicial Branch

**LEGISLATIVE**

**UNITED STATES HOUSE OF REPRESENTATIVES**

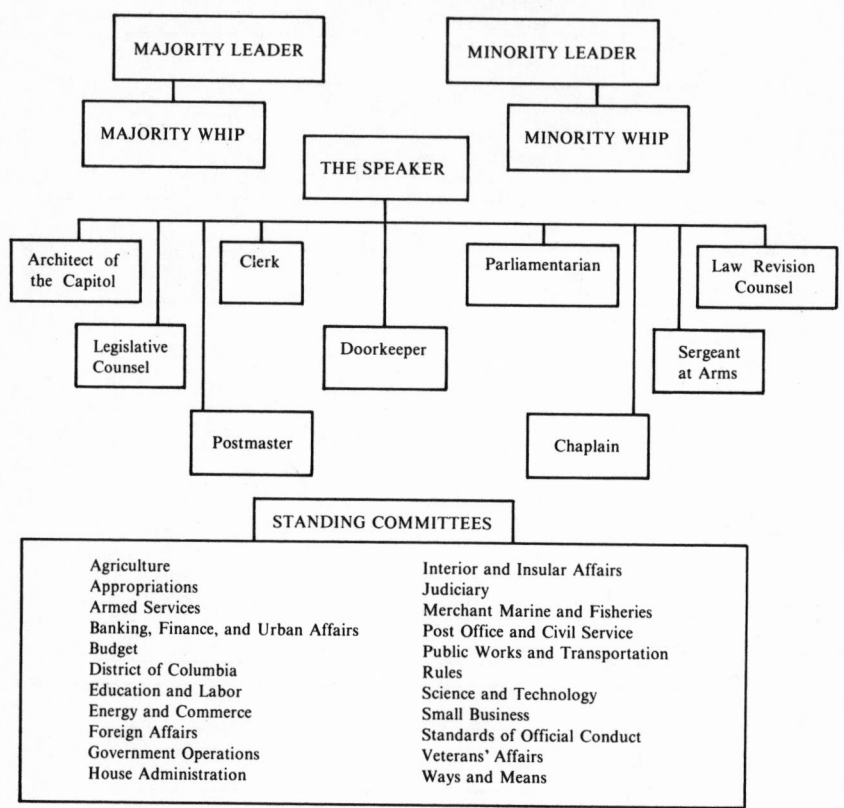

**Chart C.** Organization of the House of Representatives

**LEGISLATIVE**

**UNITED STATES SENATE**

```
                        ┌─────────────────────┐
                        │   VICE PRESIDENT    │
                        └─────────────────────┘

  ┌──────────┐    ┌──────────────────────┐    ┌──────────┐
  │ MAJORITY │    │ PRESIDENT PRO TEMPORE│    │ MINORITY │
  │  LEADER  │    │                      │    │  LEADER  │
  └──────────┘    └──────────────────────┘    └──────────┘

┌──────────┐ ┌──────────┐      ┌──────────┐  ┌──────────┐ ┌──────────┐
│Secretary │ │ Majority │      │ Chaplain │  │ Minority │ │ Sergeant │
│          │ │Secretary │      │          │  │Secretary │ │ at Arms  │
└──────────┘ └──────────┘      └──────────┘  └──────────┘ └──────────┘

  ┌──────────┐  ┌──────────┐  ┌──────────────┐ ┌──────────┐
  │ Assistant│  │  Legal   │  │ Legislative  │ │ Assistant│
  │ Majority │  │ Counsel  │  │  Counsel     │ │ Minority │
  │  Leader  │  │          │  │              │ │  Leader  │
  └──────────┘  └──────────┘  └──────────────┘ └──────────┘
```

**STANDING COMMITTEES**

| | |
|---|---|
| Agriculture, Nutrition, and Forestry | Finance |
| Appropriations | Foreign Relations |
| Armed Services | Governmental Affairs |
| Banking, Housing, and Urban Affairs | Judiciary |
| Budget | Labor and Human Resources |
| Commerce, Science, and Transportation | Rules and Administration |
| Energy and Natural Resources | Small Business |
| Environment and Public Works | Veterans' Affairs |

**Chart D.**  Organization of the Senate

# CHAPTER TWO
## *State Politics*

## State Government

The Constitution of the United States provides that all powers not specifically granted to the federal government are the province of the various states. For many years after the formation of the nation, the state governments were in many respects considerably more powerful than the federal government. While the federal government, especially in the twentieth century, has come to be the preeminent policymaking body of the American political system, state governments have retained a large number of powers and prerogatives which they perform in many instances alongside similar functions carried out by the federal government. The individual state governments have power to raise and spend money, to provide for the welfare of their citizens, and—within broad limits—to choose and pursue courses of policy action independently of those of other states and the federal government. There is rarely uniformity of purpose or action among the various state governments, which reflects the diversity of the states and the many local influences, interests, and points of view they represent. In political and governmental terms, much of the power of the American people is vested in state and local hands, and national political organizations often resemble agglomerations of many state and local political parties, organizations, and interests.

The form of government of the individual states, as in the case of the federal government, is defined by state constitutions. In general, these constitutions resemble the federal constitution and establish three separate branches of government. The chief executive officers of the states are the governors, who have been popularly elected in most states throughout most of the history of the nation. While elected federal government officials have uniform terms of office and responsibilities under the Constitution, the governors and other officers of the various states are elected according to a pastiche of state constitutional requirements and for terms and at times that vary widely from one state to the other. Governors exercise the executive powers of the state governments, although the extent of their power has varied immensely across time and in the different states.

Both legislative and judicial systems, which to a large degree resemble the federal pattern, also exist at the state level. The legislative functions in most states are performed by bicameral legislatures, although in the early years of the twentieth century several states adopted a single legislative body (unicameral) for their lawmaking functions. A hierarchical system of courts also exists within the various states ranging from municipal or local courts through Courts of Appeals to State Supreme Courts.

Political affairs in the various states have often been controlled for long periods of time by particular parties, factions, or interest groups within particular states. Candidates for public office at all levels, including those seeking positions in the federal government, have had to win the approval of state and local organizations or face difficult challenges in attaining elective or appointive office. The politics of most states usually have been highly partisan, with one political party generally being dominant in particular areas for extended periods of time. Since the mid-nineteenth century the Republican party has dominated the local political affairs of much of the New England region as well as vast segments of the Midwestern United States and those states located west of the Great Plains. The Democratic party has exercised hegemony over the Southern United States for much of the past 130 years; in addition, many urban areas in the Northern and Western states became Democratic in the years following the turn of the century, a condition which remains to the present day.

The following three tables provide a variety of facts about the states and territories of the United States. In table 2.1 are found selected historical and contemporary facts about each of the states. Table 2.2 records the population of each state as enumerated in the decennial censuses of 1790–1980, including estimates of the population of states when they were still in their territorial (pre-statehood) stage of development. Dashes (—) have been used in this table to indicate that no reliable population figures for a state are available. Table 2.3 contains descriptive and statistical information about territories and possessions of the United States.

Table 2.1

States of the United States

| State | Capital | Land Area in Square Miles in 1970 | Year Settled | Date of Territorial Formation | Date of Admission into the Union |
|---|---|---|---|---|---|
| Alabama | Montgomery | 50,708 | 1702 | Mar. 3, 1817 | 1819 |
| Alaska | Juneau | 566,432 | 1784 | Aug. 24, 1912 | 1959 |
| Arizona | Pheonix | 113,417 | 1848 | Feb. 24, 1863 | 1912 |
| Arkansas | Little Rock | 51,945 | 1785 | Mar. 2, 1819 | 1836 |
| California | Sacramento | 156,361 | 1769 | --- | 1850[c] |
| Colorado | Denver | 103,766 | 1858 | Feb. 28, 1861 | 1876 |
| Connecticut | Hartford | 4,862 | 1635 | --- | 1788[a] |
| Delaware | Dover | 1,982 | 1683 | --- | 1787[a] |
| Dist. of Columbia | Washington | 61 | | --- | ---[d] |
| Florida | Tallahassee | 54,090 | 1565 | Mar. 30, 1822 | 1845 |
| Georgia | Atlanta | 58,073 | 1733 | --- | 1788[a] |
| Hawaii | Honolulu | 6,425 | | Apr. 30, 1900 | 1959 |
| Idaho | Boise | 82,677 | 1842 | Mar. 3, 1863 | 1890 |
| Illinois | Springfield | 55,748 | 1720 | Feb. 3, 1809 | 1818 |
| Indiana | Indianapolis | 36,097 | 1733 | May 7, 1800 | 1816 |
| Iowa | Des Moines | 55,941 | 1788 | June 12, 1838 | 1846 |
| Kansas | Topeka | 81,787 | 1727 | May 30, 1854 | 1861 |
| Kentucky | Frankfort | 39,650 | 1774 | --- | 1792[e] |
| Louisiana | Baton Rouge | 44,930 | 1699 | Mar. 3, 1805 | 1812 |
| Maine | Augusta | 30,920 | 1624 | --- | 1820 |
| Maryland | Annapolis | 9,891 | 1634 | --- | 1788[a] |
| Massachusetts | Boston | 7,826 | 1620 | --- | 1788[a] |
| Michigan | Lansing | 56,817 | 1668 | Jan. 11, 1805 | 1837 |
| Minnesota | St. Paul | 79,289 | 1805 | Mar. 3, 1849 | 1858 |
| Mississippi | Jackson | 47,296 | 1699 | Apr. 7, 1798 | 1817 |
| Missouri | Jefferson City | 68,995 | 1735 | Mar. 3, 1805 | 1821 |
| Montana | Helena | 145,587 | 1809 | May 26, 1864 | 1889 |
| Nebraska | Lincoln | 76,483 | 1847 | May 30, 1854 | 1867 |
| Nevada | Carson City | 109,889 | 1850 | Mar. 2, 1861 | 1864 |
| New Hampshire | Concord | 9,027 | 1623 | --- | 1788[a] |
| New Jersey | Trenton | 7,521 | 1664 | --- | 1787[a] |
| New Mexico | Santa Fe | 121,412 | 1605 | Sept. 9, 1850 | 1912 |
| New York | Albany | 47,831 | 1614 | --- | 1788[a] |
| North Carolina | Raleigh | 48,798 | 1650 | --- | 1789[a] |
| North Dakota | Bismark | 69,273 | 1766 | Mar. 2, 1861 | 1889 |
| Ohio | Columbus | 40,975 | 1788 | May 7, 1800 | 1803 |
| Oklahoma | Oklahoma City | 68,782 | 1889 | May 2, 1890 | 1907 |
| Oregon | Salem | 96,184 | 1811 | Aug. 14, 1848 | 1859 |

69

Table 2.1 (continued)

| State | Capital | Land Area in Square Miles in 1970 | Year Settled | Date of Territorial Formation | Date of Admission into the Union |
|---|---|---|---|---|---|
| Pennsylvania | Harrisburg | 44,966 | 1682 | --- | 1787a |
| Rhode Island | Providence | 1,049 | 1636 | --- | 1790[a] |
| South Carolina | Columbia | 30,225 | 1670 | --- | 1788[a] |
| South Dakota | Pierre | 75,955 | 1856 | Mar. 2, 1861 | 1889 |
| Tennessee | Nashville | 41,328 | 1757 | May 26, 1790 | 1796 |
| Texas | Austin | 262,134 | 1691 | Dec. 29, 1845 | 1845 |
| Utah | Salt Lake City | 82,096 | 1847 | Sept. 9, 1850 | 1896 |
| Vermont | Montpelier | 9,267 | 1724 | --- | 1791 |
| Virginia | Richmond | 39,780 | 1607 | --- | 1788[a] |
| Washington | Olympia | 66,570 | 1811 | Mar. 2, 1853 | 1889 |
| West Virginia | Charleston | 24,070 | 1727 | --- | 1863[b] |
| Wisconsin | Madison | 54,464 | 1766 | Apr. 20, 1836 | 1848 |
| Wyoming | Cheyenne | 97,203 | 1834 | July 25, 1868 | 1890 |

[a]Original state.

[b]Not a territory, admitted as a state when it split from Virginia during the Civil War.

[c]Mexico ceded to U.S. by the Treaty of Guadalupe Hidalgo on February 2, 1848.

[d]Not a state, established by Congressional acts in 1790 and 1791.

[e]Not a territory, prior to admission as a state it was under the control of Virginia.

Table 2.2

Population of States, 1790-1980
(in Thousands)

| State | 1790 | 1800 | 1810 | 1820 | 1830 |
|---|---|---|---|---|---|
| Alabama | --- | 1[a] | 9[a] | 128 | 310 |
| Alaska | --- | --- | --- | --- | --- |
| Arizona | --- | --- | --- | --- | --- |
| Arkansas | --- | --- | 1 | 14 | 30 |
| California | --- | --- | --- | --- | --- |
| Colorado | --- | --- | --- | --- | --- |
| Connecticut | 238 | 251 | 262 | 275 | 298 |
| Dist. of Columbia | --- | 14 | 24 | 33 | 40 |
| Delaware | 59 | 64 | 73 | 73 | 77 |
| Florida | --- | --- | --- | --- | 35 |
| Georgia | 83 | 163 | 252 | 341 | 517 |
| Hawaii | --- | --- | --- | --- | --- |
| Idaho | --- | --- | --- | --- | --- |
| Illinois | --- | --- | 12 | 55 | 157 |
| Indiana | --- | 6 | 25 | 147 | 343 |
| Iowa | --- | --- | --- | --- | --- |
| Kansas | --- | --- | --- | --- | --- |
| Kentucky | 74 | 221 | 407 | 564 | 688 |
| Louisiana | --- | --- | 77 | 153 | 216 |
| Maine | 97 | 152 | 229 | 298 | 399 |
| Maryland | 320 | 342 | 381 | 407 | 447 |
| Massachusetts | 379 | 423 | 472 | 523 | 610 |
| Michigan | --- | --- | 5 | 9 | 32 |
| Minnesota | --- | --- | --- | --- | --- |
| Mississippi | --- | 8[a] | 31[a] | 75 | 137 |
| Missouri | --- | --- | 20 | 67 | 140 |
| Montana | --- | --- | --- | --- | --- |
| Nebraska | --- | --- | --- | --- | --- |
| Nevada | --- | --- | --- | --- | --- |
| New Hampshire | 142 | 184 | 214 | 244 | 269 |
| New Jersey | 181 | 211 | 246 | 278 | 321 |
| New Mexico | --- | --- | --- | --- | --- |
| New York | 340 | 589 | 959 | 1,373 | 1,919 |
| North Carolina | 394 | 478 | 556 | 639 | 738 |
| North Dakota | --- | --- | --- | --- | --- |
| Ohio | --- | 45 | 231 | 581 | 938 |
| Oklahoma | --- | --- | --- | --- | --- |
| Oregon | --- | --- | --- | --- | --- |
| Pennsylvania | 434 | 602 | 810 | 1,049 | 1,348 |
| Rhode Island | 69 | 69 | 77 | 83 | 97 |
| South Carolina | 249 | 346 | 415 | 503 | 581 |
| South Dakota | --- | --- | --- | --- | --- |
| Tennessee | 36 | 106 | 262 | 423 | 682 |
| Texas | --- | --- | --- | --- | --- |
| Utah | --- | --- | --- | --- | --- |
| Vermont | 85 | 154 | 218 | 236 | 281 |
| Virginia | 692 | 808 | 878 | 938 | 1,044 |
| Washington | --- | --- | --- | --- | --- |
| West Virginia | 56 | 79 | 105 | 137 | 177 |
| Wisconsin | --- | --- | --- | --- | --- |
| Wyoming | --- | --- | --- | --- | --- |

Table 2.2 (continued)

| State | 1840 | 1850 | 1860 | 1870 | 1880 |
|---|---|---|---|---|---|
| Alabama | 591 | 772 | 964 | 997 | 1,263 |
| Alaska | --- | --- | --- | --- | 33 |
| Arizona | --- | --- | --- | 10 | 40 |
| Arkansas | 98 | 210 | 435 | 484 | 803 |
| California | --- | 93 | 380 | 560 | 865 |
| Colorado | --- | --- | 34 | 40 | 194 |
| Connecticut | 310 | 371 | 460 | 537 | 623 |
| Dist. of Columbia | 44 | 52 | 75 | 132 | 178 |
| Delaware | 78 | 92 | 112 | 125 | 147 |
| Florida | 54 | 87 | 140 | 188 | 269 |
| Georgia | 691 | 906 | 1,057 | 1,184 | 1,542 |
| Hawaii | --- | --- | --- | --- | --- |
| Idaho | --- | --- | --- | 15 | 33 |
| Illinois | 476 | 851 | 1,712 | 2,540 | 3,078 |
| Indiana | 686 | 988 | 1,350 | 1,681 | 1,978 |
| Iowa | 43 | 192 | 675 | 1,194 | 1,625 |
| Kansas | --- | --- | 107 | 364 | 996 |
| Kentucky | 780 | 982 | 1,156 | 1,321 | 1,649 |
| Louisiana | 352 | 518 | 708 | 727 | 940 |
| Maine | 502 | 583 | 628 | 627 | 649 |
| Maryland | 470 | 583 | 687 | 781 | 935 |
| Massachusetts | 738 | 995 | 1,231 | 1,457 | 1,783 |
| Michigan | 212 | 398 | 749 | 1,184 | 1,637 |
| Minnesota | --- | 6 | 172 | 440 | 781 |
| Mississippi | 376 | 607 | 791 | 828 | 1,132 |
| Missouri | 384 | 682 | 1,182 | 1,721 | 2,168 |
| Montana | --- | --- | --- | 21 | 39 |
| Nebraska | --- | --- | 26 | 123 | 452 |
| Nevada | --- | --- | 7 | 42 | 62 |
| New Hampshire | 285 | 318 | 326 | 318 | 347 |
| New Jersey | 373 | 490 | 672 | 906 | 1,131 |
| New Mexico | --- | $62^d$ | $94^e$ | 92 | 120 |
| New York | 2,429 | 3,097 | 3,881 | 4,383 | 5,083 |
| North Carolina | 753 | 869 | 993 | 1,071 | 1,400 |
| North Dakota | --- | --- | $5^g$ | $2^g$ | $37^g$ |
| Ohio | 1,519 | 1,980 | 2,340 | 2,665 | 3,198 |
| Oklahoma | --- | --- | --- | --- | --- |
| Oregon | --- | $12^f$ | 52 | 91 | 175 |
| Pennslyvania | 1,724 | 2,312 | 2,906 | 3,522 | 4,283 |
| Rhode Island | 109 | 148 | 175 | 217 | 277 |
| South Carolina | 594 | 669 | 704 | 706 | 996 |
| South Dakota | --- | --- | --- | $12^g$ | $98^g$ |
| Tennessee | 829 | 1,003 | 1,110 | 1,259 | 1,542 |
| Texas | --- | 213 | 604 | 819 | 1,592 |
| Utah | --- | 11 | 40 | 87 | 144 |
| Vermont | 292 | 314 | 315 | 331 | 332 |
| Virginia | 1,025 | 1,119 | 1,220 | 1,225 | 1,513 |
| Washington | --- | $1^f$ | $12^h$ | 24 | 75 |
| West Virginia | 225 | 302 | 377 | 442 | 618 |
| Wisconsin | 31 | 305 | 776 | 1,055 | 1,315 |
| Wyoming | --- | --- | --- | 9 | 21 |

Table 2.2 (continued)

| State | 1890 | 1900 | 1910 | 1920 | 1930 |
|---|---|---|---|---|---|
| Alabama | 1,513 | 1,829 | 2,138 | 2,348 | 2,646 |
| Alaska | 32 | 64 | 64 | 55 | 59[b] |
| Arizona | 88 | 123 | 204 | 334 | 436 |
| Arkansas | 1,128 | 1,312 | 1,574 | 1,752 | 1,854 |
| California | 1,213 | 1,485 | 2,378 | 3,427 | 5,677 |
| Colorado | 413 | 540 | 799 | 940 | 1,036 |
| Connecticut | 746 | 908 | 1,115 | 1,381 | 1,607 |
| Delaware | 168 | 185 | 202 | 223 | 238 |
| Dist. of Columbia | 230 | 279 | 331 | 438 | 487 |
| Florida | 391 | 529 | 753 | 968 | 1,468 |
| Georgia | 1,837 | 2,216 | 2,609 | 2,896 | 2,909 |
| Hawaii | --- | 154 | 192 | 256 | 368 |
| Idaho | 89 | 162 | 326 | 432 | 445 |
| Illinois | 3,826 | 4,822 | 5,639 | 6,485 | 7,631 |
| Indiana | 2,192 | 2,516 | 2,701 | 2,930 | 3,239 |
| Iowa | 1,912 | 2,232 | 2,225 | 2,404 | 2,471 |
| Kansas | 1,428 | 1,470 | 1,691 | 1,769 | 1,881 |
| Kentucky | 1,859 | 2,147 | 2,290 | 2,417 | 2,615 |
| Louisiana | 1,119 | 1,382 | 1,656 | 1,799 | 2,102 |
| Maine | 661 | 694 | 742 | 768 | 797 |
| Maryland | 1,042 | 1,188 | 1,295 | 1,450 | 1,632 |
| Massachusetts | 2,239 | 2,805 | 3,366 | 3,852 | 4,250 |
| Michigan | 2,094 | 2,421 | 2,810 | 3,668 | 4,842 |
| Minnesota | 1,310 | 1,751 | 2,076 | 2,387 | 2,564 |
| Mississippi | 1,290 | 1,551 | 1,797 | 1,791 | 2,010 |
| Missouri | 2,679 | 3,107 | 3,293 | 3,404 | 3,629 |
| Montana | 143 | 243 | 376 | 549 | 538 |
| Nebraska | 1,063 | 1,066 | 1,192 | 1,296 | 1,378 |
| Nevada | 47 | 42 | 82 | 77 | 91 |
| New Hampshire | 377 | 412 | 431 | 443 | 465 |
| New Jersey | 1,445 | 1,884 | 2,537 | 3,156 | 4,041 |
| New Mexico | 160 | 195 | 327 | 360 | 423 |
| New York | 6,003 | 7,269 | 9,114 | 10,385 | 12,588 |
| North Carolina | 1,618 | 1,894 | 2,206 | 2,559 | 3,170 |
| North Dakota | 191 | 319 | 577 | 647 | 681 |
| Ohio | 3,672 | 4,158 | 4,767 | 5,759 | 6,647 |
| Oklahoma | 259 | 790 | 1,657 | 2,028 | 2,396 |
| Oregon | 318 | 414 | 673 | 783 | 954 |
| Pennsylvania | 5,258 | 6,302 | 7,665 | 8,720 | 9,631 |
| Rhode Island | 346 | 429 | 543 | 604 | 687 |
| South Carolina | 1,151 | 1,340 | 1,515 | 1,684 | 1,739 |
| South Dakota | 349 | 402 | 584 | 637 | 693 |
| Tennessee | 1,768 | 2,021 | 2,185 | 2,338 | 2,617 |
| Texas | 2,236 | 3,049 | 3,897 | 4,663 | 5,825 |
| Utah | 211 | 277 | 373 | 449 | 508 |
| Vermont | 332 | 344 | 356 | 352 | 360 |
| Virginia | 1,656 | 1,854 | 2,062 | 2,309 | 2,422 |
| Washington | 357 | 518 | 1,142 | 1,357 | 1,563 |
| West Virginia | 763 | 959 | 1,221 | 1,464 | 1,729 |
| Wisconsin | 1,693 | 2,069 | 2,334 | 2,632 | 2,939 |
| Wyoming | 63 | 93 | 146 | 194 | 226 |

Table 2.2 (continued)

| State | 1940 | 1950 | 1960 | 1970 | 1980 |
|---|---|---|---|---|---|
| Alabama | 2,833 | 3,062 | 3,267 | 3,444 | 3,394 |
| Alaska | 73[c] | 129 | 226 | 300 | 402 |
| Arizona | 499 | 750 | 1,302 | 1,771 | 2,718 |
| Arkansas | 1,949 | 1,910 | 1,786 | 1,923 | 2,286 |
| California | 6,907 | 10,586 | 15,717 | 19,953 | 23,668 |
| Colorado | 1,123 | 1,325 | 1,754 | 2,207 | 2,890 |
| Connecticut | 1,709 | 2,007 | 2,535 | 3,032 | 3,108 |
| Delaware | 267 | 318 | 446 | 548 | 594 |
| Dist. of Columbia | 663 | 802 | 764 | 757 | 638 |
| Florida | 1,897 | 2,771 | 4,952 | 6,789 | 9,746 |
| Georgia | 3,124 | 3,445 | 3,943 | 4,590 | 5,463 |
| Hawaii | 423 | 500 | 633 | 769 | 965 |
| Idaho | 525 | 589 | 667 | 713 | 944 |
| Illinois | 7,897 | 8,712 | 10,081 | 11,114 | 11,427 |
| Indiana | 3,428 | 3,934 | 4,662 | 5,194 | 5,490 |
| Iowa | 2,538 | 2,621 | 2,758 | 2,824 | 2,914 |
| Kansas | 1,801 | 1,905 | 2,179 | 2,247 | 2,364 |
| Kentucky | 2,846 | 2,945 | 3,038 | 3,219 | 3,661 |
| Louisiana | 2,364 | 2,684 | 3,257 | 3,641 | 4,206 |
| Maine | 847 | 914 | 969 | 992 | 1,125 |
| Maryland | 1,821 | 2,343 | 3,101 | 3,922 | 4,217 |
| Massachusetts | 4,317 | 4,691 | 5,149 | 5,689 | 5,737 |
| Michigan | 5,256 | 6,372 | 7,823 | 8,875 | 9,262 |
| Minnesota | 2,792 | 2,982 | 3,414 | 3,805 | 4,076 |
| Mississippi | 2,184 | 2,179 | 2,178 | 2,217 | 2,521 |
| Missouri | 3,785 | 3,955 | 4,320 | 4,677 | 4,917 |
| Montana | 559 | 591 | 675 | 694 | 787 |
| Nebraska | 1,316 | 1,326 | 1,411 | 1,483 | 1,570 |
| Nevada | 110 | 160 | 285 | 489 | 800 |
| New Hampshire | 492 | 533 | 607 | 738 | 921 |
| New Jersey | 4,160 | 4,835 | 6,067 | 7,168 | 7,365 |
| New Mexico | 532 | 681 | 951 | 1,1016 | 1,303 |
| New York | 13,479 | 14,830 | 16,782 | 18,237 | 17,558 |
| North Carolina | 3,572 | 4,062 | 4,556 | 5,082 | 5,882 |
| North Dakota | 642 | 620 | 632 | 618 | 653 |
| Ohio | 6,908 | 7,947 | 9,706 | 10,652 | 10,798 |
| Oklahoma | 2,336 | 2,233 | 2,328 | 2,559 | 3,025 |
| Oregon | 1,090 | 1,521 | 1,769 | 2,091 | 2,633 |
| Pennsylvania | 9,900 | 10,498 | 11,319 | 11,794 | 11,864 |
| Rhode Island | 713 | 792 | 859 | 947 | 947 |
| South Carolina | 1,900 | 2,117 | 2,383 | 2,591 | 3,122 |
| South Dakota | 643 | 653 | 681 | 666 | 691 |
| Tennessee | 2,916 | 3,292 | 3,567 | 3,924 | 4,591 |
| Texas | 6,415 | 7,711 | 9,580 | 11,197 | 14,229 |
| Utah | 550 | 689 | 891 | 1,059 | 1,461 |
| Vermont | 359 | 378 | 390 | 444 | 511 |
| Virginia | 2,678 | 3,319 | 3,967 | 4,648 | 5,347 |
| Washington | 1,736 | 2,379 | 2,853 | 3,409 | 4,132 |
| West Virginia | 1,902 | 2,006 | 1,860 | 1,744 | 1,950 |
| Wisconsin | 3,138 | 3,435 | 3,952 | 4,418 | 4,706 |
| Wyoming | 251 | 291 | 330 | 332 | 470 |

## 74

Table 2.2 (continued)

---

[a]Population of those parts of Mississippi Territory now in present State.

[b]Census taken October 1, 1929.

[c]Census taken October 1, 1939.

[d]Data for Territory of New Mexico, which included parts of present states of Arizona and New Mexico, and smaller parts of Colorado and Nevada.

[e]Includes population of area taken to form part of Arizona Territory in 1863.

[f]Population total of those parts of Oregon Territory taken to form part of Washington Territory in 1853 and 1859 excluded from Oregon; this population included under Washington.

[g]North and South Dakota comprised Dakota Territory.

[h]Includes population of Idaho and parts of Montana and Wyoming.

Table 2.3

United States Territories and Possessions

---

OUTLYING UNITED STATES AREAS
(all residents have U.S. citizenship)

| | | |
|---|---|---|
| Puerto Rico | Location: | Easternmost island of Caribbean Island Chain, Greater Antilles |
| | Area: | 3,435 sq. mi. |
| | Population: | 3,196,520 (1980) |
| | Status: | Commonwealth. A directly elected Resident Commissioner in House of Representatives may vote in committee only. |
| | History: | Ceded to U.S. as a result of the Treaty of Paris, December 10, 1898, ending Spanish-American War. Puerto Rico became a Commonwealth on July 25, 1952 by an Act of Congress. |
| Virgin Islands | Location: | East of Puerto Rico at the western end of the Lesser Antilles in the Caribbean |
| | Area: | 133 sq. mi. for 50 islands. St. Croix, St. Thomas, St. John are the largest. |
| | Population: | 95,000 (1980) |
| | Status: | Unincorporated territory administered by Department of the Interior. Residents have one delegate in the House of Representatives who may vote in committee only. |
| | History: | The Virgin Islands were purchased from Denmark for $25 million effective March 31, 1917. |
| American Samoa | Location: | South Pacific, 2,300 miles southwest of Hawaii, 2,150 miles east of Australia |
| | Area: | 76 sq. mi. for seven islands, Tutuila, Aunuu, Manua Islands (Tau, Olosega, Ofu), Rose, and Swain Island 210 miles northwest. |
| | Population: | 31,171 (1980) |
| | Status: | United States ownership administered by Department of Interior since 1951. Non-voting delegate to the U.S. Congress elected beginning in 1980. |
| | History: | Pago Pago became a U.S. Coaling Station in 1872 through a commercial treaty. The six islands of Samoa became a territory of the U.S. as a result of an 1899 treaty with Great Britain and Germany which was confirmed by local chiefs in 1900 and 1904. Swain Island was annexed in 1925 by a congressional resolution. |
| Guam | Location: | West Central Pacific, 1,500 miles east of the Philippines |
| | Area: | 209 sq. mi. |
| | Population: | 106,000 (1980) |
| | Status: | Guam is an unincorporated territory administered by the Department of Interior. A 1972 law gives Guam one delegate to the House of Representatives who may vote in committee only. |
| | History: | Guam was ceded to the United States by Spain as a result of the Treaty of Paris, December 10, 1898, which ended the Spanish-American War. |
| Guantanamo Bay, Cuba | Location: | Southeastern Cuba |
| | Area: | 30 sq. mi. |
| | Status: | U.S. lease in perpetuity terminated only by mutual agreement or U.S. abandonment of the area. It is a U.S. naval base under the jurisdiction of the U.S. Navy. |
| | History: | As a result of the Spanish-American War and the Treaty of Paris, December 10, 1898, ending the war, Cuba became an independent republic under the protection of the U.S. On May 10, 1902, U.S. troops formally withdrew, but a 1903 treaty gave the U.S. control of Guantanamo Bay. That status was reaffirmed in 1934 by a treaty, the Platt Amendment, which stipulated the present conditions of U.S ownership in return for the U.S. relinquishing the power to intervene in the domestic affairs of Cuba. |

Table 2.3 (continued)

---

| Wake, Wilkes and Peale Islands | | |
|---|---|---|
| | Location: | Central Pacific, 2,000 mi. west of Hawaii and 1,290 mi. east of Guam |
| | Area: | 3 sq. mi. |
| | Population: | 300 (1980) |
| | Status: | Possessions formerly administered by the Federal Aviation Administration. They have been administered by the U.S. Air Force since 1972. |
| | History: | General F. V. Greene, commanding the 2d Detachment of the Philippine Expedition took possession of Wake Island on July 4, 1898. Formal possession of the uninhabited island occurred in 1899. |

| Midway Islands (Sand, Eastern) | | |
|---|---|---|
| | Location: | North Pacific, 1,150 mi. northwest of Hawaii |
| | Area: | 2 sq. mi. |
| | Population: | 2,256 (1980) |
| | Status: | Possession administered by the Navy Department. |
| | History: | The Midway Islands were annexed in 1867, except Sand Island which was claimed in 1858 under the Guano Island Act of 1856, which stipulated that the U.S. could take possession of uninhabited Guano Islands. |

## MISCELLANEOUS ISLANDS AND HOLDINGS

| Johnston Atoll | | |
|---|---|---|
| | Location: | Southwest of Hawaii |
| | Area: | 1 sq. mi. |
| | Population: | 300 (1980) |
| | Status: | Operated by U.S. Nuclear Defense Agency. |
| | History: | The Atoll was claimed in 1858 under the Guano Island Act of 1865. |

| Kingman Reef | | |
|---|---|---|
| | Location: | South of Hawaii |
| | Population: | Uninhabited |
| | Status: | U. S. Navy Administration |
| | History: | The reef was annexed by an Act of Congress in 1922. |

| Howland, Jarvis, & Baker Islands | | |
|---|---|---|
| | Location: | South of Hawaii |
| | Population: | Uninhabited |
| | Status: | U.S. Department of the Interior Administration |
| | History: | This island was claimed in 1934 under terms of the Guano Island Act of 1856. |

| Navassa | | |
|---|---|---|
| | Location: | Between Jamaica and Haiti |
| | Area: | 2 sq. mi. |
| | Population: | Uninhabited |
| | Status: | U.S. Department of the Interior Administration |
| | History: | This island was claimed in 1865 under terms of the Guano Island Act of 1856. |

## UNITED NATIONS TRUSTEESHIP HELD BY UNITED STATES

| Territory of the Pacific Islands | | |
|---|---|---|
| | | This includes three major island groups in the Western Pacific, the Caroline Islands, the Marshall Islands, and the Mariana Islands (except Guam). |
| | Area: | 715.8 sq. mi. |
| | Population: | 116,662 (1980) |
| | Status: | In 1885 most of the islands were claimed by Germany, and were sold to Germany by Spain in 1898 at the time of the Spanish-American War. After the outbreak of World War I, Japan occupied the islands and a League of Nations mandate was awarded to Japan after the war. The islands were the scene of bitter fighting during World War II. Afterwards, the islands were designated a trust territory by the United Nations (1947) |

---

Table 2.3 (continued)

under the administration of the United States. Since 1951 they have been administered by the Department of the Interior, but the Marianas became a Commonwealth on June 17,1975. Plans for independence are underway for the Caroline and Marshall Islands. The islands are scattered over three million square miles of Micronesia.

DISPUTED ISLANDS

Line Islands, Phoenix Islands, & Ellice Islands
Location: South Pacific
Status: Possession of these three South Pacific islands is disputed by the United States and the United Kingdom. The islands are being administered by the United Kingdom. The Ellice Islands became independent of the United Kingdom on October 1, 1978.

Tokelau Islands & Northern Cook Islands
Location: South Pacific
Status: Possession of these South Pacific islands is disputed by the United States and New Zealand, but administered by New Zealand.

FORMER POSSESSIONS, TRUSTEESHIPS

Swan Islands
Location: 97 miles northeast of Honduras
Status: Claimed by the United States in 1863 under the Guano Island Act, but Honduras also claimed ownership. The United States reorganized Honduras' sovereignty on September 1, 1972.

Ryukyu Islands including Okinawa
Location: 400 miles south of Japan
Status: Came under U.S. jurisdiction as a result of the peace treaty with Japan in 1945. By agreement, all but Okinawa were returned to Japan on June 26, 1968. Okinawa was returned to Japan on May 15, 1972.

Corn Islands
Location: 30 miles off the southeast coast of Nicaragua
Status: Was leased for 99 years from Nicaragua in 1916 along with a perpetual right to build a ship for the canal payment of $3 million. The canal rights and lease of the islands were relinquished on April 25, 1971.

Philippine Islands
Location: Off southeast coast of Asia, south of Taiwan
Status: The Philippine Islands became a possession of the United States as a result of the Spanish-American War of 1898. The Treaty of Paris ending the war provided for payment of $20 million to Spain for the islands. After a delay caused by World War II, the Philippines became independent on July 4, 1946.

Quita Sueno Bank, Ronlajor Lay, Serrana Bank, Seranilla Bank
Location: In the Caribbean between Nicaragua and Jamaica
Status: These uninhabited islands were returned to Colombia in 1972 by a treaty which took effect on September 17, 1981.

Panama Canal Zone
Location: Central Panama, strip 5 mi. wide running from the Atlantic to the Pacific Ocean
Area: 553 sq. mi. total
Population: 44,198 (1970)
Status: United States Government Reservation
History: A November 18, 1903 treaty between the newly independent Republic of Panama granted the United States sovereignty over the Canal Zone. On April 18, 1978 the U.S. Senate voted to turn the Panama Canal Zone over to Panama on December 31, 1999.

# CHAPTER THREE
## *Parties and Elections*

Election practices and procedures have varied widely during the history of the United States. The Constitution provides only general requirements governing the selection of elected federal officials—the President, Vice President, members of Congress—and includes no provisions bearing upon the selection of state and other officials. The dates and modes of conducting elections and the qualifications for voting were in general left to the states, and practices, have been highly diverse in these and other respects. Historically, however, the trend has been toward increasing similarity of electoral practices. Virtually from the beginning of the nation, political parties and factions have played an informal and formal role in both the nomination and selection of elective officials. Here again, the role of political parties in the electoral process has varied widely from state to state and from one time to another.

## Elections and Election Procedures

The timing and methods of conducting elections, the qualifications required of voters, and the terms of elected state officials have undergone major changes during the course of American history. In general, change has brought greater standardization of practices and extended to a larger and larger portion of the national population the formal right to vote for officials at all levels of government. Particularly during the middle decades of the twentieth century, the federal government has acted to eliminate informal and formal state and local limitations on the exercise of voting rights. At the same time, administrative changes in the twentieth century, such as personal registration requirements, have made the act of voting more difficult and have contributed to a reduction of citizen participation in the electoral process.

## *Methods of Choosing Officials*

The President and Vice President of the United States are chosen indirectly through the mechanism of the Electoral College (see chapter 1). Presidential electors were popularly elected in only four of the original thirteen states in 1789; in the remainder of the states, electors were chosen by the respective state legislatures. By 1860, in all but one state (South Carolina) presidential electors were chosen directly in popular elections held every four years; after 1860 all states chose electors by popular election. Electors chosen in each of the states assembled in December following the election and chose the President and Vice President by majority vote. On two occasions (the elections of 1800 and 1824), no candidate received a majority of the electoral votes and the House of Representatives chose the President in keeping with provisions of the Constitution.

Each state has two Senators. Senators were chosen by the various state legislatures from 1789 to 1913. In that year, the 17th Amendment to the Constitution was ratified, changing the method of choosing Senators to popular election. Senate seats are divided into three "classes," with a different class elected to six-year terms every two years.

Members of the U.S. House of Representatives have been popularly elected in the various states since 1789. The number of Representatives of each state is determined by population. With a few exceptions, states have established representational constituencies (Congressional Districts) within their boundaries and one Representative is chosen from each district.

Governors of the states were chosen by state legislatures in eight of the thirteen original states in 1789; by 1870 all states held popular elections for governor. The terms of office of state governors display the greatest variance of the major elective offices in the United States: one-, two-, three-, and four-year terms of office have all been common in several states over time. Many states elected governors annually in the eighteenth and early nineteenth centuries. Later, however, two- and then four-year gubernatorial terms became the most widely accepted practice.

## *Times of Elections*

The major elected officers in the United States were chosen at widely varying times of the year throughout much of the nineteenth century. Elections for governor, U.S. Representative, Senator (elected by the legislatures), and even President were held in different months in various states. Congressmen were frequently elected in odd-numbered years in many states, and Congressional sessions often began before some states had held elections for that session. By the 1870s, however, most states had standardized dates of election and elected most officials on the first Tuesday after the first Monday in November of even numbered years. When popular election of Senators was adopted, most states held Senatorial elections on this same uniform date. In the twentieth century the trend has been toward elections of governors in non-Presidential election years. Thus, in the contemporary period, most states hold elections for President, U.S. Representative, and Senator (if required) on the same day in November of a year (e.g., 1984), and elections for governor, U.S. Representative and Senator (if required) two years later.

The terms of office and the timing of elections to state legislatures and other elective state offices have also varied over time and from state to state. In general, however, elections to these offices also occur on the first Tuesday after the first Monday in November of even numbered years. Elections to municipal and local offices are marked by considerable variation. Two- and four-year terms are common, but the date of election varies widely from state to state and from one local jurisdiction to the other.

## *Methods of Voting*

Voice voting was the accepted method of casting votes in the late eighteenth century. By the end of the first decade of the nineteenth century, however, most states had abolished this method in favor of the secret ballot. With the rise of formal political parties in the nineteenth century, voters, as they entered the polling places, were often handed paper ballots that listed only the candidates of one party. Gradually, the state-printed "Australian" ballot, which listed the candidates of all parties, was adopted in the late-nineteenth and early-twentieth centuries. By the mid-twentieth century, paper ballots were still used in many areas, but automatic vote tabulating machines, as well as punch card and other electronically countable forms of recording votes, are now most common.

## Suffrage and Other Voting Requirements

In 1789 voting in the United States was limited to adult white male citizens who could demonstrate some form of property-holding status (such as real estate), or personal wealth, or payment of taxes. Since then, the franchise has been greatly extended. The movement toward a more democratic electoral system had, by the 1830s, removed the property qualification from voting eligibility in virtually all states. A number of constitutional amendments further extended the franchise for the nation as a whole: the Fifteenth Amendment (1870) gave the right to vote to newly freed male Negro slaves; the Nineteenth (1920) granted suffrage to women; and the Twenty-Sixth Amendment (1971) lowered the voting age from 21 to 18 years of age.

Most of these alterations in the composition of the eligible electorate were enacted by the federal government and were of national scope. A number of these suffrage extensions, however, came into practice in particular states before they were adopted for the nation as a whole. Wyoming allowed women to vote in certain elections as early as 1869, and in various other states and territories women had at least limited eligibility to vote before the adoption of the Nineteenth Amendment. In Georgia, the voting age was lowered in 1944 to 18. On the other hand, formal and informal practices in various states also worked to reduce the impact of these extensions of the right to vote or, in some cases, to effectively prevent their implementation.

Near the end of the nineteenth century and continuing into the twentieth, a number of procedural requirements were implemented throughout the nation which had a dampening effect upon voter participation. In general these requirements were introduced as means to reduce vote fraud and prevent illegal voting. Among these reforms were more stringent, and more vigorously enforced, requirements for time in residence within a jurisdiction as a qualification for voting there. Prohibitions against voting by noncitizens were also stiffened and more vigorously enforced. Personal registration was introduced, which required the individual to formally register as a potential voter several weeks or months before the date of the election. Residency and registration requirements vary widely among states and localities and from one level of office to another but work in general to reduce participation in elections.

Particularly in the late nineteenth and early twentieth centuries, devices specifically intended to restrict the exercise of the franchise were adopted in southern and some other states. Among the most widespread of these devices were the prepayment of a poll tax and the requirement that literacy be demonstrated as a condition for voting. Such requirements significantly reduced voter participation. When supplemented in some areas by differential enforcement on racial grounds and by informal actions, they worked effectively to prevent participation by black citizens in elections. Since the 1950s, action has been taken by the federal government to eliminate these bars to participation in elections. The poll tax was banned by the Twenty-Fourth Amendment (1964) and Civil Rights legislation has looked toward extension and more vigorous enforcement of the right to vote. Residency and personal preregistration requirements remain in effect, although some effort, largely through the action of citizen groups, has been made to make registration less difficult and more automatic.

# Political Parties

Political parties and factions were viewed as undesirable by the framers of the United States Constitution. Indeed, one of the goals that underlay the structure of government provided by the Constitution was the avoidance of parties and factions. Nevertheless, they appeared shortly after the founding of the nation and have persisted. The political arena has generally been dominated by two "major" parties (with various other "minor," or "third," parties appearing or disappearing after brief political lives), although major parties have been replaced by others. However, with the formation of the modern Republican party in 1854, the present-day party system was formed and the Democratic and Republican parties became the major contestants for political power.

Although political parties appeared in the early days of the nation, they did not develop into the highly disciplined and well organized structures characteristic of some other nations. Nonetheless, parties play a major role in the conduct of government and politics both in official and unofficial ways. They play a major role in the organization and conduct of political campaigns and raise funds to support the efforts of their candidates to gain election to office. The parties provide a principal organizational structure for government at the national, state, and (to a somewhat lesser degree) the municipal and local levels, although party members in office have not been in most eras as highly disciplined as party members in other nations. Moreover, the parties have also constituted the primary mechanism for nomination to candidacy for elective office.

### The Nomination Process

During the earlier days of the nation, nominations of candidates for elective office were largely made by notable figures within the parties or factions. In the early decades of the nineteenth century, this "caucus" system was replaced by a system of conventions. In operation the convention system has varied widely from state to state and from one historical era to the next. In its best developed form, reached in some states in the latter nineteenth century, this system involved local, state, and national party conventions. At the local level party members or elected delegates met in convention to nominate candidates to local offices, drafted a "platform" stating party goals, positions, principles, and policies, and elected delegates to the state party convention. At the state convention the process was repeated: candidates to state office were nominated, a platform adopted, and delegates to the national convention selected. At the national convention, the party's candidates for President and Vice President were nominated and a national platform adopted.

Even in the latter nineteenth century the convention system did not reach this somewhat idealized form throughout the nation. Conventions were and remain, however, central elements in the nominating process. The national conventions not only constitute a means to select Presidential and Vice Presidential nominees but also serve as major symbolic events. The major elements are the opening addresses, including the "keynote speech," which is intended to set the tone for the convention and the following campaign; the nominating and seconding speeches, which introduce the contenders for nomination; the call, or calls, of the roll of the state delegations through which each delegation casts its ballots for one or the other of the contenders and which continues for as many separate ballots as are required to select a nominee; and the introduction, debate, and adoption of the platform. The conventions are intended as occasions for reconciliation of differences within the parties, as demonstrations of unanimity, as the opening events of the campaigns, and as the beginning of the process of rallying the electorate for the coming election.

While party conventions, and particularly national conventions, continue to be major and highly significant events in national politics, the nominating process was modified beginning in the early twentieth century through the institution of "direct primaries" in many states. Although primaries differ in form, degree of contest, and political relevance, they are popular nominating elections in which voters select from among potential candidates those individuals whom they wish to have represent the parties as candidates for particular elective offices. In some states, primaries are "open," and voters may choose to select candidates for either or both parties; in other states primaries are "closed" and voters may select candidates only for the party in which they are registered.

Not all states hold Presidential primaries, and the significance of the primaries varies in those states that do. Some states hold only "preference" primaries, in which voters choose from among the potential candidates, but do not obligate state delegates to the national convention to reflect their choice. In other states, the results of primaries bind all or part of the state delegation to support a particular individual for a fixed number of ballots or until the delegation is "released" by that individual and thereby freed to support another contender. Despite these variations and the fact that before 1976 no contender had ever received through the primaries alone sufficient support to secure the nomination, presidential primaries have been of major importance in selecting the candidates. Extensive reforms of the rules governing the conduct of primaries were implemented in the early 1970s (particularly in the Democratic party); these changes were intended to make the party primaries and "caucuses" more responsive to public sentiment and secure wider participation in the process of choosing candidates. The contests in New Hampshire,

Florida, Wisconsin, Massachusetts, New York, Texas, Oregon, California, and Ohio are considered to be some of the most important of the presidential primaries. With the increased media attention that accompanied the selection process in 1976 and subsequent elections, primaries which were held early in the campaign season (particularly the Iowa caucuses and the New Hampshire primary, both occurring in February) took on added importance as bellwethers of the aspirations of various contenders. Presidential primaries and caucuses are thus important quadrennial components of politics in the nation.

## Major Parties, 1789–1854

The two predominant political factions for the first twenty years after the founding of the nation were the Federalists and the Democratic-Republicans. The Federalists included the groups who favored the adoption of the Federal Constitution and who were considered the advocates of urban and commercial interests. The Democratic-Republicans developed as the organized opposition to the Federalists. Successors to the Anti-Federalists, the Democratic-Republicans coalesced around Thomas Jefferson; members of this party were widely identified at the time as Republicans or Jeffersonians, were seen as advocates of rural and agrarian interests, and favored expanding democracy by the extension of suffrage and popular control of the government.

By 1816 the Federalist Party had become so weak that it was unable to contest elections except at the local level. The Democratic-Republicans became the only major party, and nominated all of the major Presidential candidates during this "Era of Good Feeling" (1816 to 1824). There remained factions within that party, however, split roughly along the same rural-urban, agrarian-commercial lines that had separated the Federalists from the Democratic-Republicans. By 1824 these factions had taken on sectional trappings as well, with John Quincy Adams of Massachusetts acting as the leader of the northeastern segment and Andrew Jackson of Tennessee heading the rural, agrarian, and largely southern and western wing. The Jackson wing of the Democratic-Republican party retained the name Democratic-Republican which after 1828 was shortened to Democratic (although it was also called the Jacksonian or the Jacksonian Democratic

Party while Jackson served as President). The Adams wing took the name National Republican Party and as such that party maintained a separate existence only until 1832. In 1834, a loose federation of individuals and interests opposed to the Jacksonian philosophy of government formed the Whig Party. For the next twenty years (or until 1854) the Whig and the Democratic parties contested largely with each other for control of the government. Several largely ephemeral minor parties also appeared during this period. The Anti-Masonic Party was active primarily in the Northern states in the early 1830s and involved resentment of elitist prerogatives and trappings symbolized by the Masonic Order. Two additional minor parties, the Liberty and Free Soil parties, organized around opposition to Negro slavery in the United States. While attracting considerable attention in the press, these parties received only a small percentage of the vote cast in the elections they contested and elected only a small number of Representatives to Congress. They were strongest in the New England and Mid-Atlantic states, with strength in the Great Lakes states as well. The American Party (Know Nothing Party) was one of the most successful minor parties in this period. Appearing in the mid 1850s, this party capitalized upon nativist and anti-immigrant feelings occasioned by large-scale migration to the United States from other nations during that decade. The Know Nothing Party attracted individuals from both the Whig and Democratic parties, and during two years in the mid 1850s was able to elect seven governors, five United States Senators, and 43 members of the House of Representatives. The party eventually divided over the slavery issue, with its members returning to the major parties as well as to a new party, the Republican.

## Political Parties, 1854–1900

The Republican Party was formed in 1854 and rapidly rose to major party status, replacing the Whig Party, which went out of existence shortly thereafter. The Republicans collected adherents in the Northern states, largely from among former Whig Party members as well as from members of the Northern wing of the Democratic Party who were dissatisfied with adherence to the Southern position on slavery. The Republican Party ran candidates for election in 1854, nominated a Presidential candidate in 1856, and in 1860 elected its nominee, Abraham Lincoln, to the Presidency, as a result of the division of the Democratic Party into Northern and Southern wings. Lincoln's election was viewed by most Southern Democrats as a precipitant of the American Civil War, which followed shortly.

During the Civil War the Republican Party ruled political affairs in the North with nearly complete control of national public offices. After the War the Republican administration attempted to nurture Republican parties in the Southern states by building upon newly enfranchised black voters and succeeded in controlling Southern political affairs for a number of years. By the mid 1870s, however, most Southern states were again predominantly Democratic in political affiliation. The Democratic and Republican parties remained the chief protagonists in national and local politics thereafter, competing in some areas on a relatively even basis but with major areas of strength in the North (Republican) and the South (Democrat).

Minor parties were numerous during the second half of the nineteenth century. The Liberal Republicans Party was a short-lived party that ran a Presidential candidate in opposition to Republican Ulysses S. Grant in 1872. The Greenback Party came into existence with currency reform as a central issue. Greenbackers drew support from farmers and workers in industry, who had been hit especially hard by the Depression of 1873. As a solution to their economic woes they opposed a return to the gold standard in currency and advocated the retention of paper money (called greenbacks) that was thought to be inflationary and beneficial to these groups. The Party ran Presidential candidates in 1876, 1880, and 1884. Party strength was centered in the agrarian South and Midwest with some support in the industrial cities of the East. In the Congressional elections of 1878 the Greenback Party polled over a million votes and elected fourteen members to the United States House of Representatives. The party declined in popularity as a measure of prosperity returned and by the mid-1880s was no longer a significant factor in electoral politics.

Two minor parties which came into existence in the latter half of the nineteenth century remain in existence today, the Prohibition Party and the Socialist Labor Party. The Prohibition Party has been in existence longer than any minor party in American political history. Its basic tenet was, and is, the abolition of alcoholic beverages. The party ran candidates in a number of national elections in the late nineteenth and early twentieth centuries, but never received more than 2.5 percent of the popular vote. The influence of the Prohibition Party was most strongly felt when in 1919, partly because of its initiative, the sale of alcoholic beverages was prohibited by the Eighteenth Amendment and the Volsted Act. Prohibition remained the law of the land for fourteen years thereafter, although often more in spirit than in fact. The Socialist Labor Party was the earliest socialist political organization in the United States. It first ran candidates for the Presidency in 1892 and has done so in every election thereafter. The party's support for socialist principles and its militant advocacy of revolution has never gained significant electoral support.

The Peoples or Populist Party was among the most significant minor parties of the forty years following the American Civil War. The party was organized in 1891 and persisted for seventeen years. Considered by some electoral scholars as a descendant of the Greenback movement, the Populists were strongest numerically in the Southern and Midwestern farming states. The party proposed a number of radical (for their time) reforms of the government and economy, all directed to improvement of the condition of the farmers and, to a lesser degree, industrial labor. Included among these reforms were government ownership of railroads, free coinage of silver, and a number of social and political reforms including a graduated income tax, direct election of Senators, and the eight-hour working day. The Populist Party's best showing was in 1892, when it received over eight percent of the Presidential vote and the party candidate, James B. Weaver, carried five Western States. The party's strength grew in 1894, resulting in the election of six United States Senators and seven members of the House of Representatives. When the Democratic Party in 1896 adopted most of the Populist agrarian reforms in its national campaign platform, the Populists abandoned their own party label and endorsed the Democratic candidate, William Jennings Bryan. In the election of 1896 the Democrat and Populist fusion ticket carried states in the Western United States but Bryan was defeated. The Populist Party continued to run candidates for a number of years but was never again a significant force.

### Political Parties, 1900–1984

The Republican Party dominated national politics for more than thirty years following the election of 1896 and was able to elect

Presidential candidates and majorities in Congress during most of the period. The only interruptions in Republican control of the Presidency came in 1912 and 1916 when Democrat Woodrow Wilson was elected thanks to a split within the Republican Party. The Great Depression resulted in a political realignment in the nation and elevated the Democrats to dominance. The Presidencies of Franklin D. Roosevelt began a series of Democratic successes throughout the nation that was broken only intermittently by Republican victories. From the 1930s to the early 1980s, a majority of voters identified themselves with the Democratic party. During this period two Republican presidents were elected (Dwight D. Eisenhower and Richard M. Nixon), but their victories signified personal popularity of these men or division in the Democratic ranks rather than the return to power of a Republican majority. Democrats remained in control of both chambers of Congress for all but two of the fourteen years of the Eisenhower and Nixon Presidencies. In the period from the 1930s to the 1970s, the Republican Party remained strong in rural areas and in the less densely populated environs of the large cities, while the sources of Democratic electoral strength continued to be anchored in the South and in the large cities of the nation.

Changes in the Depression-born political alignment began to appear in the early 1960s with the deterioration of the South as a Democratic bastion. Republican candidates in the South increased their share of the vote in elections from the Presidency down to local races, with attendant loss of the former Democratic hegemony in this region. Sizable nationwide shifts of voters toward allegiance to the Republican Party have been observed in very recent years, accompanying the Presidential victories of Ronald W. Reagan in 1980 and 1984, and the Republican wresting of partisan control of the U.S. Senate from the Democrats in 1980. Considerable debate in both scholarly and journalistic circles has left unresolved the question of whether there was a Republican "realignment" among the U.S. electorate in the early 1980s.

A number of minor parties came into existence in the twentieth century but, with two exceptions, were singularly unsuccessful in gaining significant electoral strength. The Socialist Party was formed in 1901 and has continued until the present time. The party, which advocates traditional socialist goals, reached its zenith in 1920, when Eugene V. Debs, the Presidential candidate, received nearly a million votes (approximately six percent of the total votes cast). The Socialist

Party's advocacy of pacifism resulted in some successes before America entered World War I but probably contributed to its lack of popularity thereafter. While the Party has run candidates in most Presidential elections after 1920, it has been unable to gain more than 0.5 percent of the vote.

The Progressive (or "Bull Moose") Party of 1912 centered upon Theodore Roosevelt and voiced opposition to the conservative course followed by the Republican Party after Roosevelt's retirement from the Presidency. The Progressive Party nominated Roosevelt in 1912, and succeeded in winning more than four million votes (over 27 percent of the popular vote). Roosevelt's candidacy in 1912, however, split the Republican Party and enabled Democrat Woodrow Wilson to gain the Presidency. In 1916 the Progressive Party was unsuccessful in persuading Roosevelt to lead its ticket and the party passed out of existence.

In 1924 another party, also called the Progressive Party, led by Wisconsin Senator Robert M. LaFollette, appeared and advocated much the same reformist goals that had earlier been major planks in the Bull Moose platform. In the campaign of 1924 LaFollette received 16 percent of the popular vote in the nation, but Progressive Party strength was centered in the rural and agrarian sections of the country and LaFollette carried only one state. The party ceased to exist after 1925.

The Communist Party also came into existence in the United States in the interwar period, and fielded its first Presidential slate in 1924. As a consequence of widespread popular distrust and anti-Communist governmental actions, the party ceased overt political activity in the United States after 1940. The party again ran candidates for the Presidency beginning in 1968, but has never received a significant number of votes.

Splitting off from the Communist Party in 1938, the Socialist Workers Party was formed by followers of the views of Leon Trotsky. The Party has consistently advocated radical social and economic change and has remained active since its formation; the electoral successes of the party have been even less significant than those of the Communist Party (never more than 0.1 percent of the popular vote for President).

The 1948 Presidential election marked the appearance of two additional (and ephemeral) political parties. These were the Progressive Party, with Henry Wallace as its Presidential candidate, and the States Rights Democratic Party with Strom Thurmond as its Presidential candidate. Both parties were formed in reaction to the policies of the Democrats and their nomination of Harry S Truman. The States Rights Democratic Party, popularly known as the Dixiecrats, was composed of conservative Southern elements that opposed the civil rights policies of Truman and Northern Democrats. The party gained support only in the South, where it won the electoral votes of four states, but only two percent of the popular vote nationally. The party ceased to exist after the election of 1948 and most of its members returned to the Democratic Party.

Unlike the Dixiecrats, the Wallace Progressives of 1948 contended that the Truman administration was not sufficiently liberal or progressive, especially in the areas of foreign affairs and civil rights. Although the Progressive Party ran in nearly all states, Wallace received less than 2.5 percent of the popular vote, with most of that vote coming from the state of New York. The Progressive Party ran candidates in the following four years but received virtually no electoral support and vanished after 1952.

The American Independent Party was formed in 1968 by Alabama Governor George C. Wallace in opposition to the directions taken by the Democratic Party. With strong racial undertones, the party sought to capitalize upon the frustrations and anger of white, especially blue-collar, voters in reaction to the civil rights and antiwar movements of the 1960s. The party's strength was centered largely in the southern and western states. In the election of 1968, Wallace received nearly 10 million popular votes and won the electoral votes of five southern states. His candidacy contributed to the election of the Republican nominee in that year, Richard M. Nixon, who gained the Presidency with less than 50 percent of the popular vote. Wallace renewed his allegiance to the Democratic Party after the 1968 election and in so doing considerably weakened the appeal of the American Independent Party. Although the party nominated a Presidential slate in 1972, it received slightly over one percent of the popular vote and no electoral votes. The party was effectively out of existence by the late 1970s.

In 1980 John B. Anderson of Illinois mounted a relatively strong Independent campaign for the Presidency. Although a Republican who had served ten terms in the U.S. House of Representatives, Anderson pitched his Presidential campaign at independent voters as well as at Democrats and Republicans who were dissatisfied with their parties' respective choices for President (Jimmy Carter and Ronald W. Reagan). The Anderson campaign and "middle-of-the-road" positions did not win strong support anywhere in the nation; its appeal to young, relatively liberal and affluent voters garnered less than six million votes (under 7 percent of those cast). Anderson himself seemingly vanished from the national political scene after the 1980 election.

# The Vote For President of the United States

The three tables which follow record the popular and electoral votes cast for President of the U.S. from 1789 to 1984. In table 3.1, national-level votes (electoral and popular) are presented for each candidate for the Presidency at each election. Before 1824, the manner of choosing electors and of recording popular votes cast for Presidential electors varied considerably from state to state. The popular vote totals for elections in that period, because of comparability problems, have therefore not been included in the table. From 1789 to 1800, votes were cast for an undifferentiated list of candidates; the person receiving the largest number of electoral votes was chosen President and the second-highest vote-getter became Vice President. Thus, table 3.1 records candidates for both President and Vice President until 1804. Identification of the party affiliation of candidates in the early elections (1789–1800) is tenuous for that nascent stage of party formation in the country.

Table 3.2 contains the electoral votes cast for any candidate for the Presidency (and Vice Presidency from 1789–1800) in each of the states. The partisan identification of each candidate, where known, can be found in table 3.1. In table 3.3 are found the popular votes cast for the major candidates in each of the states. Votes for minor candidates or parties have been aggregated into the "other" category for each election displayed in the table. Dashes (—) have been inserted for a state for the time before that state was in the Union; for instances where the election returns could not be recovered; and for

South Carolina for the elections of 1824 to 1860, since presidential electors in that state were chosen by the state legislature until after the Civil War.

Table 3.1

National Electoral and Popular Vote Cast for President,
1789-1984

| Year | Number of States | Presidential Candidates | Party | Electoral Vote | Popular Vote |
|------|------|------|------|------|------|
| 1789 | 10 | George Washington | Federalist | 69 | |
| | | John Adams | Federalist | 34 | |
| | | John Jay | Federalist | 9 | |
| | | R. H. Harrison | Unknown | 6 | |
| | | John Rutledge | Unknown | 6 | |
| | | John Hancock | Unknown | 4 | |
| | | George Clinton | Democratic-Republican | 3 | |
| | | Samuel Huntington | Unknown | 2 | |
| | | John Milton | Unknown | 2 | |
| | | James Armstrong | Federalist | 1 | |
| | | Benjamin Lincoln | Unknown | 1 | |
| | | Edward Telfair | Unknown | 1 | |
| | | (not voted) | | 12 | |
| 1792 | 15 | George Washington | Federalist | 132 | |
| | | John Adams | Federalist | 77 | |
| | | George Clinton | Democratic-Republican | 50 | |
| | | Thomas Jefferson | Democratic-Republican | 4 | |
| | | Aaron Burr | Democratic-Republican | 1 | |
| 1796 | 16 | John Adams | Federalist | 71 | |
| | | Thomas Jefferson | Democratic-Republican | 68 | |
| | | Thomas Pinckney | Federalist | 59 | |
| | | Aaron Burr | Anti-Federalist | 30 | |
| | | Samuel Adams | Democratic-Republican | 15 | |
| | | Oliver Ellsworth | Federalist | 11 | |
| | | George Clinton | Democratic-Republican | 7 | |
| | | John Jay | Independent- Federalist | 5 | |
| | | James Iredell | Federalist | 3 | |
| | | George Washington | Federalist | 2 | |
| | | John Henry | Independent | 2 | |
| | | Samuel Johnston | Independent-Federalist | 2 | |
| | | Charles C. Pinckney | Independent-Federalist | 1 | |
| 1800 | 16 | Thomas Jefferson | Democratic-Republican | 73 | |
| | | Aaron Burr | Democratic-Republican | 73 | |
| | | John Adams | Federalist | 65 | |
| | | Charles C. Pinckney | Federalist | 64 | |
| | | John Jay | Federalist | 1 | |
| 1804 | 17 | Thomas Jefferson | Democratic-Republican | 162 | |
| | | Charles C. Pinckney | Federalist | 14 | |
| 1808 | 17 | James Madison | Democratic-Republican | 122 | |
| | | Charles C. Pinckney | Federalist | 47 | |
| | | George Clinton | Independent-Republican | 6 | |
| | | (not voted) | | 1 | |
| 1812 | 18 | James Madison | Democratic-Republican | 128 | |
| | | De Witt Clinton | Fusion | 89 | |
| | | (not voted) | | 1 | |
| 1816 | 19 | James Monroe | Republican | 183 | |
| | | Rufus King | Federalist | 34 | |
| | | (not voted) | | 4 | |

Table 3.1 (continued)

| Year | Number of States | Presidential Candidates | Party | Electoral Vote | Popular Vote |
|------|------|------|------|------|------|
| 1820 | 24 | James Monroe | Republican | 231 | |
| | | John Q. Adams | Independent-Republican | 1 | |
| | | (not voted) | | 3 | |
| 1824 | 24 | John Q. Adams | National-Republican | 84 | 108,740 |
| | | Andrew Jackson | Democrat | 99 | 153,544 |
| | | Henry Clay | Democrat | 37 | 47,136 |
| | | William H. Crawford | Democrat | 41 | 46,618 |
| 1828 | 24 | Andrew Jackson | Democrat | 178 | 647,286 |
| | | John Q. Adams | National-Republican | 83 | 508,064 |
| 1832 | 24 | Andrew Jackson | Democrat | 219 | 687,502 |
| | | Henry Clay | National-Republican | 49 | 530,189 |
| | | William Wirt | Anti-Masonic | 7 | |
| | | John Floyd | Nullifiers | 11 | |
| | | (not voted) | | 2 | |
| 1836 | 26 | Martin Van Buren | Democrat | 170 | 765,483 |
| | | William H. Harrison | Whig[a] | 73 | |
| | | Hugh L. White | Whig[a] | 26 | 739,795 |
| | | Daniel Webster | Whig[a] | 14 | |
| | | Willie P. Mangum | Anti-Jackson | 11 | |
| 1840 | 26 | William H. Harrison | Whig | 234 | 1,274,624 |
| | | Martin Van Buren | Democrat | 60 | 1,127,781 |
| 1844 | 26 | James K. Polk | Democrat | 170 | 1,338,464 |
| | | Henry Clay | Whig | 105 | 1,300,097 |
| | | James G. Birney | Liberty | -- | 62,300 |
| 1848 | 30 | Zachary Taylor | Whig | 163 | 1,360,967 |
| | | Lewis Cass | Democrat | 127 | 1,222,342 |
| | | Martin Van Buren | Free Soil | -- | 291,263 |
| 1852 | 31 | Franklin Pierce | Democrat | 254 | 1,601,117 |
| | | Winfield Scott | Whig | 42 | 1,385,453 |
| | | John P. Hale | Free Soil | -- | 155,825 |
| 1856 | 31 | James Buchanan | Democrat | 174 | 1,832,955 |
| | | John C. Fremont | Republican | 114 | 1,339,932 |
| | | Millard Fillmore | American | 8 | 871,731 |
| 1860 | 33 | Abraham Lincoln | Republican | 180 | 1,865,593 |
| | | John C. Breckinridge | Democrat (S) | 72 | 848,356 |
| | | Stephen A. Douglas | Democrat | 12 | 1,382,713 |
| | | John Bell | Constitutional Union | 39 | 592,906 |
| 1864 | 36 | Abraham Lincoln | Republican | 212 | 2,206,938 |
| | | George B. McClellan | Democrat | 21 | 1,803,787 |
| | | (not voted) | | 81 | |
| 1868 | 37 | Ulysses S. Grant | Republican | 214 | 3,013,421 |
| | | Horatio Seymour | Democrat | 80 | 2,706,829 |
| | | (not voted) | | 23 | |

Table 3.1 (continued)

| Year | Number of States | Presidential Candidates | Party | Electoral Vote | Popular Vote |
|------|---------|---------------------|-------|----------|--------|
| 1872 | 37 | Ulysses S. Grant | Republican | 286 | 3,596,745 |
|      |    | Horace Greeley | Democrat | b | 2,843,446 |
|      |    | Charles O'Connor | Straight Democrat | -- | 29,489 |
|      |    | Thomas A. Hendricks | Independent-Democrat | 42 | |
|      |    | B. Gratz Brown | Democrat | 18 | |
|      |    | Charles J. Jenkins | Democrat | 2 | |
|      |    | David Davis | Democrat | 1 | |
|      |    | (not voted) | | 17 | |
| 1876 | 38 | Rutherford B. Hayes | Republican | 185 | 4,036,572 |
|      |    | Samuel J. Tilden | Democrat | 184 | 4,284,020 |
|      |    | Peter Cooper | Greenback | -- | 81,737 |
| 1880 | 38 | James A. Garfield | Republican | 214 | 4,453,295 |
|      |    | Winfield S. Hancock | Democrat | 155 | 4,414,082 |
|      |    | James B. Weaver | Greenback-Labor | -- | 308,578 |
|      |    | Neal Dow | Prohibition | | 10,305 |
| 1884 | 38 | Grover Cleveland | Democrat | 219 | 4,879,507 |
|      |    | James G. Blaine | Republican | 182 | 4,850,293 |
|      |    | Benjamin F. Butler | Greenback-Labor | -- | 175,370 |
|      |    | John P. St. John | Prohibition | -- | 150,369 |
| 1888 | 38 | Benjamin Harrison | Republican | 233 | 5,447,129 |
|      |    | Grover Cleveland | Democrat | 168 | 5,537,857 |
|      |    | Clinton B. Fisk | Prohibition | -- | 249,506 |
|      |    | Anson J. Streeter | Union Labor | -- | 146,935 |
| 1892 | 44 | Grover Cleveland | Democrat | 277 | 5,555,426 |
|      |    | Benjamin Harrison | Republican | 145 | 5,182,690 |
|      |    | James B. Weaver | People's | 22 | 1,029,846 |
|      |    | John Bidwell | Prohibition | -- | 264,133 |
|      |    | Simon Wing | Socialist Labor | -- | 21,164 |
| 1896 | 45 | William McKinley | Republican | 271 | 7,102,246 |
|      |    | William J. Bryan | Democrat | 176 | 6,492,559 |
|      |    | John M. Palmer | National Democrat | -- | 133,148 |
|      |    | Joshua Levering | Prohibition | -- | 132,007 |
|      |    | Charles H. Matchett | Socialist Labor | -- | 36,274 |
|      |    | Charles E. Bentley | Nationalist | -- | 13,969 |
| 1900 | 45 | William McKinley | Republican | 292 | 7,218,491 |
|      |    | William J. Bryan | Democrat | 155 | 6,356,734 |
|      |    | John C. Wooley | Prohibition | -- | 208,914 |
|      |    | Eugene V. Debs | Socialist | -- | 87,814 |
|      |    | Wharton Barker | People's | -- | 50,373 |
|      |    | Joseph F. Malloney | Socialist Labor | -- | 39,739 |
| 1904 | 45 | Theodore Roosevelt | Republican | 336 | 7,628,461 |
|      |    | Alton B. Parker | Democrat | 140 | 5,084,223 |
|      |    | Eugene V. Debs | Socialist | -- | 402,283 |
|      |    | Silas C. Swallow | Prohibition | -- | 258,536 |
|      |    | Thomas E. Watson | People's | -- | 117,183 |
|      |    | Charles H. Corregan | Socialist Labor | -- | 31,249 |
| 1908 | 46 | William H. Taft | Republican | 321 | 7,675,320 |
|      |    | William J. Bryan | Democrat | 162 | 6,412,294 |

Table 3.1 (continued)

| Year | Number of States | Presidential Candidates | Party | Electoral Vote | Popular Vote |
|------|------|------|------|------|------|
| | | Eugene V. Debs | Socialist | -- | 420,793 |
| | | Eugene W. Chafin | Prohibition | -- | 253,840 |
| | | Thomas L. Hisgen | Independence | -- | 82,872 |
| | | Thomas E. Watson | People's | -- | 29,100 |
| | | August Gillhaus | Socialist Labor | -- | 14,021 |
| 1912 | 48 | Woodrow Wilson | Democrat | 435 | 6,296,547 |
| | | Theodore Roosevelt | Progressive | 88 | 4,118,571 |
| | | William H. Taft | Republican | 8 | 3,486,720 |
| | | Eugene V. Debs | Socialist | -- | 900,672 |
| | | Eugene W. Chafin | Prohibition | -- | 206,275 |
| | | Arthur E. Reimer | Socialist Labor | -- | 28,750 |
| 1916 | 48 | Woodrow Wilson | Democrat | 277 | 9,127,695 |
| | | Charles E. Hughes | Republican | 254 | 8,533,507 |
| | | Allan L. Benson | Socialist | -- | 585,113 |
| | | J. Frank Hanly | Prohibition | -- | 220,506 |
| | | Arthur E. Reimer | Socialist Labor | -- | 13,403 |
| 1920 | 48 | Warren G. Harding | Republican | 404 | 16,143,407 |
| | | James M. Cox | Democrat | 127 | 9,130,328 |
| | | Eugene V. Debs | Socialist | -- | 919,799 |
| | | Parley P. Christensen | Farmer-Labor | -- | 265,411 |
| | | Aaron S. Watkins | Prohibition | -- | 189,408 |
| | | James E. Ferguson | American | -- | 48,000 |
| | | William E. Cox | Socialist Labor | -- | 31,715 |
| 1924 | 48 | Calvin Coolidge | Republican | 382 | 15,718,211 |
| | | John W. Davis | Democrat | 136 | 8,385,283 |
| | | Robert M. LaFollette | Progresssive | 13 | 4,831,289 |
| | | Herman P. Faris | Prohibition | -- | 57,520 |
| | | Frank T. Johns | Socialist Labor | -- | 36,428 |
| | | William Z. Foster | Workers | -- | 36,386 |
| | | Gilbert O. Nations | American | -- | 23,967 |
| 1928 | 48 | Herbert C. Hoover | Republican | 444 | 21,391,993 |
| | | Alfred E. Smith | Democrat | 87 | 15,016,169 |
| | | Norman Thomas | Socialist | -- | 267,835 |
| | | Verne L. Reynolds | Socialist Labor | -- | 21,603 |
| | | William Z. Foster | Workers | -- | 21,181 |
| | | William F. Varney | Prohibition | -- | 20,106 |
| 1932 | 48 | Franklin D. Roosevelt | Democrat | 472 | 22,809,638 |
| | | Herbert C. Hoover | Republican | 59 | 15,758,901 |
| | | Norman Thomas | Socialist | -- | 881,951 |
| | | William Z. Foster | Communist | -- | 102,785 |
| | | William D. Upshaw | Prohibition | -- | 81,869 |
| | | Verne L. Reynolds | Socialist Labor | -- | 33,276 |
| | | William H. Harvey | Liberty | -- | 53,425 |
| 1936 | 48 | Franklin D. Roosevelt | Democrat | 523 | 27,752,869 |
| | | Alfred M. Landon | Republican | 8 | 16,674,665 |
| | | William Lemke | Union | -- | 882,479 |
| | | Norman Thomas | Socialist | -- | 187,720 |
| | | Earl Browder | Communist | -- | 80,159 |
| | | D. Leigh Colvin | Prohibition | -- | 37,847 |
| | | John W. Aiken | Socialist Labor | -- | 12,777 |

Table 3.1 (continued)

| Year | Number of States | Presidential Candidates | Party | Electoral Vote | Popular Vote |
|------|------|-------------------------|-------|----------------|--------------|
| 1940 | 48 | Franklin D. Roosevelt | Democrat | 449 | 27,307,819 |
|      |    | Wendell L. Willkie | Republican | 82 | 22,321,018 |
|      |    | Norman Thomas | Socialist | -- | 99,557 |
|      |    | Roger Q. Babson | Prohibition | -- | 57,812 |
|      |    | Earl Browder | Communist | -- | 46,251 |
|      |    | John W. Aiken | Socialist Labor | -- | 14,892 |
| 1944 | 48 | Franklin D. Roosevelt | Democrat | 432 | 25,606,585 |
|      |    | Thomas E. Dewey | Republican | 99 | 22,014,745 |
|      |    | Norman Thomas | Socialist | -- | 80,518 |
|      |    | Claude A. Watson | Prohibition | -- | 74,758 |
|      |    | Edward A. Teichert | Socialist Labor | -- | 45,336 |
| 1948 | 48 | Harry S. Truman | Democrat | 303 | 24,179,345 |
|      |    | Thomas E. Dewey | Republican | 189 | 21,991,291 |
|      |    | Strom Thurmond | States' Rights | 39 | 1,176,125 |
|      |    | Henry Wallace | Progressive | -- | 1,157,326 |
|      |    | Norman Thomas | Socialist | -- | 139,572 |
|      |    | Claude A. Watson | Prohibition | -- | 103,900 |
|      |    | Edward A. Teichert | Socialist Labor | -- | 29,241 |
|      |    | Farrell Dobbs | Socialist Workers | -- | 13,614 |
| 1952 | 48 | Dwight D. Eisenhower | Republican | 442 | 33,936,234 |
|      |    | Adlai E. Stevenson | Democrat | 89 | 27,314,992 |
|      |    | Vincent Hallinan | Progressive | -- | 140,023 |
|      |    | Stuart Hamblen | Prohibition | -- | 72,949 |
|      |    | Eric Hass | Socialist Labor | -- | 30,267 |
|      |    | Darlington Hoopes | Socialist | -- | 20,203 |
|      |    | Douglas A. MacArthur | Constitution | -- | 17,205 |
|      |    | Farrell Dobbs | Socialist Workers | -- | 10,312 |
| 1956 | 48 | Dwight D. Eisenhower | Republican | 457 | 35,590,472 |
|      |    | Adlai E. Stevenson | Democrat | 73 | 26,022,752 |
|      |    | T. Coleman Andrews | States' Rights | -- | 111,178 |
|      |    | Eric Hass | Socialist Labor | -- | 44,450 |
|      |    | Enoch A. Holtwick | Prohibition | -- | 41,937 |
|      |    | Walter Jones | Unknown | 1 | |
| 1960 | 50 | John F. Kennedy | Democrat | 303 | 34,226,731 |
|      |    | Richard M. Nixon | Republican | 219 | 34,108,157 |
|      |    | Eric Hass | Socialist Labor | -- | 47,522 |
|      |    | Rutherford L. Decker | Prohibition | -- | 46,203 |
|      |    | Orval E. Faubus | National States' Rights | -- | 44,977 |
|      |    | Farrell Dobbs | Socialist Workers | -- | 40,165 |
|      |    | Charles L. Sullivan | Constitution | -- | 18,162 |
|      |    | Harry F. Byrd | Democrat | 15 | |
| 1964 | 50 | Lyndon B. Johnson | Democrat | 486 | 43,129,566 |
|      |    | Barry M. Goldwater | Republican | 52 | 27,178,188 |
|      |    | Eric Hass | Socialist Labor | -- | 45,219 |
|      |    | Clifton DeBerry | Socialist Workers | -- | 32,720 |
|      |    | E. Harold Munn | Prohibition | -- | 23,267 |
| 1968 | 50 | Richard M. Nixon | Republican | 301 | 31,785,480 |
|      |    | Hubert H. Humphrey | Democrat | 191 | 31,275,166 |
|      |    | George C. Wallace | American Independent | 46 | 9,906,473 |
|      |    | Henning A. Blomen | Socialist Labor | -- | 52,588 |

99

Table 3.1 (continued)

| Year | Number of States | Presidential Candidates | Party | Electoral Vote | Popular Vote |
|------|------|------|------|------|------|
| | | Dick Gregory | Peace & Freedom | -- | 47,133 |
| | | Fred Halstead | Socialist Workers | -- | 41,388 |
| | | Eldridge Cleaver | Peace & Freedom | -- | 8,736 |
| | | Eugene J. McCarthy | Independent | -- | 25,552 |
| | | E. Harold Munn | Prohibition | -- | 15,123 |
| | | (No Presidential Candidate) | Peace & Freedom | | 27,887 |
| 1972 | 50 | Richard M. Nixon | Republican | 520 | 47,170,179 |
| | | George McGovern | Democrat | 17 | 29,171,791 |
| | | John Hospers | Libertarian | 1 | 3,671 |
| | | John G. Schmitz | American | -- | 1,090,673 |
| | | Benjamin Spock | People's | -- | 78,751 |
| | | Louis Fisher | Socialist Labor | -- | 53,811 |
| | | Linda Jenness | Socialist Workers | -- | 37,423 |
| | | Gus Hall | Communist | -- | 25,343 |
| | | E. Harold Munn | Prohibition | -- | 12,818 |
| 1976 | 50 | Jimmy Carter | Democrat | 297 | 40,827,394 |
| | | Gerald Ford | Republican | 241 | 39,145,977 |
| | | Ronald W. Reagan | Republican | 1 | -- |
| | | Eugene McCarthy | Independent | -- | 745,042 |
| | | Lester G. Maddox | American Independent | -- | 170,673 |
| | | Roger L. MacBride | Libertarian | -- | 173,011 |
| | | Thomas J. Anderson | American | -- | 160,773 |
| | | Peter Camejo | Socialist Workers | -- | 91,314 |
| | | Gus Hall | Communist | -- | 58,992 |
| | | Margaret Wright | People's | -- | 49,024 |
| | | Lyndon LaRouche | United States Labor | -- | 40,043 |
| | | Benjamin C. Bubar | Prohibition | -- | 15,934 |
| | | Julius Levin | Socialist Labor | -- | 9,616 |
| | | Frank P. Zeidler | Socialist | -- | 6,038 |
| | | Ernest L. Miller | Restoration | -- | 361 |
| | | Frank Taylor | United American | -- | 36 |
| 1980 | 50 | Ronald W. Reagan | Republican | 489 | 43,904,153 |
| | | Jimmy Carter | Democrat | 49 | 35,483,883 |
| | | John B. Anderson | Independent | -- | 5,720,060 |
| | | Edward E. Clark | Libertarian | -- | 921,299 |
| | | Barry Commoner | Citizens | -- | 234,294 |
| | | Gus Hall | Communist | -- | 45,023 |
| | | John R. Rarick | American Independent | -- | 41,268 |
| | | Clifton DeBerry | Socialist Workers | -- | 38,737 |
| | | Ellen McCormack | Right to Life | -- | 32,327 |
| | | Maureen Smith | Peace and Freedom | -- | 18,116 |
| | | Deirdre Griswold | Workers World | -- | 13,300 |
| | | Benjamin C. Bubar | Statesman | -- | 7,212 |
| | | David McReynolds | Socialist | -- | 6,898 |
| | | Percy L. Greaves | American | -- | 6,647 |
| | | Andrew Pulley | Socialist Workers | -- | 6,272 |
| | | Richard Congress | Socialist Workers | -- | 4,029 |
| | | Kurt Lynen | Middle Class | -- | 3,694 |
| | | Bill Gahres | Down with Lawyers | -- | 1,718 |
| | | Frank Shelton | American | -- | 1,555 |
| | | Martin Wendelken | Independent | -- | 923 |
| | | Harry McLain | Natural Peoples | -- | 296 |

Table 3.1 (continued)

| Year | Number of States | Presidential Candidates | Party | Electoral Vote | Popular Vote |
|------|------|------|------|------|------|
| 1984 | 50 | Ronald W. Reagan | Republican | 525 | 54,158,802 |
| | | Walter Mondale | Democrat | 13 | 37,443,559 |
| | | David Bergland | Libertarian | -- | 226,161 |
| | | Sonia Johnson | Citizens Party | -- | 72,093 |
| | | Bob Richards | Populist | -- | 66,241 |
| | | Lyndon H. LaRouche, Jr. | Independent | -- | 64,992 |
| | | Dennis L. Serrette | Independent Alliance | -- | 61,021 |
| | | Gus Hall | Communist | -- | 37,038 |
| | | Larry Holmes | Workers World | -- | 19,604 |
| | | Melvin T. Mason | Socialist Workers | -- | 23,719 |
| | | Ed Winn | Workers League | -- | 15,019 |
| | | Delmar D. Dennis | American Party | -- | 11,804 |
| | | Earl Dodge | Prohibition | -- | 4,238 |

[a]The Whig party endorsed three regional candidates and only one ran in each state. Harrison ran in 15 states, White in 9, and Webster in one.

[b]Horace Greenley died between the popular vote and the meeting of the presidential electors. Thus the Democratic electors were left to their own judgment, casting their votes for the politicians cited above.

Table 3.2

Electoral Vote Cast for President, by State,
1789-1984

1789 Electoral Vote for President[a]

| | WASHINGTON | ADAMS | JAY | HARRISON | RUTLEDGE | HANCOCK | CLINTON | HUNTINGTON | MILTON | ARMSTRONG | LINCOLN | TELFAIR |
|---|---|---|---|---|---|---|---|---|---|---|---|---|
| CONNECTICUT | 7 | 5 | -- | -- | -- | -- | -- | 2 | -- | -- | -- | -- |
| DELAWARE | 3 | -- | 3 | -- | -- | -- | -- | -- | -- | -- | -- | -- |
| GEORGIA | 5 | -- | -- | -- | -- | -- | -- | -- | 2 | 1 | 1 | 1 |
| MARYLAND | 6 | -- | -- | 6 | -- | -- | -- | -- | -- | -- | -- | -- |
| MASSACHUSETTS | 10 | 10 | -- | -- | -- | -- | -- | -- | -- | -- | -- | -- |
| NEW HAMPSHIRE | 5 | 5 | -- | -- | -- | -- | -- | -- | -- | -- | -- | -- |
| NEW JERSEY | 6 | 1 | 5 | -- | -- | -- | -- | -- | -- | -- | -- | -- |
| NEW YORK | -- | -- | -- | -- | -- | -- | -- | -- | -- | -- | -- | -- |
| NORTH CAROLINA | -- | -- | -- | -- | -- | -- | -- | -- | -- | -- | -- | -- |
| PENNSYLVANIA | 10 | 8 | -- | -- | -- | 2 | -- | -- | -- | -- | -- | -- |
| RHODE ISLAND | -- | -- | -- | -- | -- | 1 | -- | -- | -- | -- | -- | -- |
| SOUTH CAROLINA | 7 | -- | -- | -- | 6 | 1 | -- | -- | -- | -- | -- | -- |
| VIRGINIA | 10 | 5 | 1 | -- | -- | -- | 3 | -- | -- | -- | -- | -- |
| Total | 69 | 34 | 9 | 6 | 6 | 4 | 3 | 2 | 2 | 1 | 1 | 1 |

[a]Includes votes cast for Vice President (see description of early election procedures).

Table 3.2 (continued)

1792  Electoral Vote for President[a]

|  | WASHINGTON | ADAMS | CLINTON | JEFFERSON | BURR |
|---|---|---|---|---|---|
| CONNECTICUT | 9 | 9 | -- | -- | -- |
| DELAWARE | 3 | 3 | -- | -- | -- |
| GEORGIA | 4 | -- | 4 | -- | -- |
| KENTUCKY | 4 | -- | -- | 4 | -- |
| MARYLAND | 8 | 8 | -- | -- | -- |
| MASSACHUSETTS | 16 | 16 | -- | -- | -- |
| NEW HAMPSHIRE | 6 | 6 | -- | -- | -- |
| NEW JERSEY | 7 | 7 | -- | -- | -- |
| NEW YORK | 12 | -- | 12 | -- | -- |
| NORTH CAROLINA | 12 | -- | 12 | -- | -- |
| PENNSYLVANIA | 15 | 14 | 1 | -- | -- |
| RHODE ISLAND | 4 | 4 | -- | -- | -- |
| SOUTH CAROLINA | 8 | 7 | -- | -- | 1 |
| VERMONT | 3 | 3 | -- | -- | -- |
| VIRGINIA | 21 | -- | 21 | -- | -- |
| Total | 132 | 77 | 50 | 4 | 1 |

[a]Includes votes cast for Vice President (see description of early election procedures).

Table 3.2 (continued)

1796 Electoral Vote for President[a]

| | J. ADAMS | JEFFERSON | T. PINCKNEY | BURR | S. ADAMS | ELLSWORTH | CLINTON | JAY | IREDELL | HENRY | JOHNSTON | WASHINGTON | C. PINCKNEY |
|---|---|---|---|---|---|---|---|---|---|---|---|---|---|
| CONNECTICUT | 9 | -- | 4 | -- | -- | -- | -- | 5 | -- | -- | -- | -- | -- |
| DELAWARE | 3 | -- | 3 | -- | -- | -- | -- | -- | -- | -- | -- | -- | -- |
| GEORGIA | -- | 4 | -- | -- | -- | -- | 4 | -- | -- | -- | -- | -- | -- |
| KENTUCKY | -- | 4 | -- | 4 | -- | -- | -- | -- | -- | -- | -- | -- | -- |
| MARYLAND | 7 | 4 | 4 | 3 | -- | -- | -- | -- | -- | 2 | 2 | -- | -- |
| MASSACHUSETTS | 16 | -- | 13 | -- | -- | 1 | -- | -- | -- | -- | -- | -- | -- |
| NEW HAMPSHIRE | 6 | -- | -- | -- | -- | 6 | -- | -- | -- | -- | -- | -- | -- |
| NEW JERSEY | 7 | -- | 7 | -- | -- | -- | -- | -- | -- | -- | -- | -- | -- |
| NEW YORK | 12 | -- | 12 | -- | -- | -- | -- | -- | -- | -- | -- | -- | -- |
| NORTH CAROLINA | 1 | 11 | 1 | 6 | -- | -- | -- | -- | 3 | -- | -- | 1 | 1 |
| PENNSYLVANIA | 1 | 14 | 2 | 13 | -- | -- | -- | -- | -- | -- | -- | 1 | -- |
| RHODE ISLAND | 4 | -- | -- | -- | -- | 4 | -- | -- | -- | -- | -- | -- | -- |
| SOUTH CAROLINA | -- | 8 | 8 | -- | -- | -- | -- | -- | -- | -- | -- | -- | -- |
| TENNESSEE | -- | 3 | -- | 3 | -- | -- | -- | -- | -- | -- | -- | -- | -- |
| VERMONT | 4 | -- | 4 | -- | -- | -- | -- | -- | -- | -- | -- | -- | -- |
| VIRGINIA | 1 | 20 | 1 | 1 | 15 | -- | 3 | -- | -- | -- | -- | 1 | -- |
| Total | 71 | 68 | 59 | 30 | 15 | 11 | 7 | 5 | 3 | 2 | 2 | 2 | 1 |

[a]Includes votes cast for Vice President (See description of early election procedures).

Table 3.2 (continued)

### 1800 Electoral Vote for President[a]

|  | JEFFERSON | BURR | ADAMS | PINCKNEY | JAY |
|---|---|---|---|---|---|
| CONNECTICUT | -- | -- | 9 | 9 | -- |
| DELAWARE | -- | -- | 3 | 3 | -- |
| GEORGIA | 4 | 4 | -- | -- | -- |
| KENTUCKY | 4 | 4 | -- | -- | -- |
| MARYLAND | 5 | 5 | 5 | 5 | -- |
| MASSACHUSETTS | -- | -- | 16 | 15 | -- |
| NEW HAMPSHIRE | -- | -- | 6 | 6 | -- |
| NEW JERSEY | -- | -- | 7 | 7 | -- |
| NEW YORK | 12 | 12 | -- | -- | -- |
| NORTH CAROLINA | 8 | 8 | 4 | 4 | -- |
| PENNSYLVANIA | 8 | 8 | 7 | 7 | -- |
| RHODE ISLAND | -- | -- | 4 | 3 | 1 |
| SOUTH CAROLINA | 8 | 8 | -- | -- | -- |
| TENNESSEE | 3 | 3 | -- | -- | -- |
| VERMONT | -- | -- | 4 | 4 | -- |
| VIRGINIA | 21 | 21 | -- | -- | -- |
| Total | 73 | 73 | 65 | 64 | 1 |

[a]Includes votes cast for Vice President (see description of early election procedures).

### 1804 and 1808 Electoral Vote for President

|  | 1804 | | 1808 | | |
|---|---|---|---|---|---|
|  | JEFFERSON | PINCKNEY | MADISON | PINCKNEY | CLINTON |
| CONNECTICUT | -- | 9 | -- | 9 | -- |
| DELAWARE | -- | 3 | -- | 3 | -- |
| GEORGIA | 6 | -- | 6 | -- | -- |
| KENTUCKY | 8 | -- | 7 | -- | -- |
| MARYLAND | 9 | 2 | 9 | 2 | -- |
| MASSACHUSETTS | 19 | -- | -- | 19 | -- |
| NEW HAMPSHIRE | 7 | -- | -- | 7 | -- |
| NEW JERSEY | 8 | -- | 8 | -- | -- |
| NEW YORK | 19 | -- | 13 | -- | 6 |
| NORTH CAROLINA | 14 | -- | 11 | 3 | -- |
| OHIO | 3 | -- | 3 | -- | -- |
| PENNSYLVANIA | 20 | -- | 20 | -- | -- |
| RHODE ISLAND | 4 | -- | -- | 4 | -- |
| SOUTH CAROLINA | 10 | -- | 10 | -- | -- |
| TENNESSEE | 5 | -- | 5 | -- | -- |
| VERMONT | 6 | -- | 6 | -- | -- |
| VIRGINIA | 24 | -- | 24 | -- | -- |
| Total | 162 | 14 | 122 | 47 | 6 |

Table 3.2 (continued)

### 1812 and 1816 Electoral Vote for President

| | 1812 | | 1816 | |
|---|---|---|---|---|
| | MADISON | CLINTON | MONROE | KING |
| CONNECTICUT | -- | 9 | -- | 9 |
| DELAWARE | -- | 4 | -- | 3 |
| GEORGIA | 8 | -- | 8 | -- |
| INDIANA | -- | -- | 3 | -- |
| KENTUCKY | 12 | -- | 12 | -- |
| LOUISIANA | 3 | -- | 3 | -- |
| MARYLAND | 6 | 5 | 8 | -- |
| MASSACHUSETTS | -- | 22 | -- | 22 |
| NEW HAMPSHIRE | -- | 8 | 8 | -- |
| NEW JERSEY | -- | 8 | 8 | -- |
| NEW YORK | -- | 29 | 29 | -- |
| NORTH CAROLINA | 15 | -- | 15 | -- |
| OHIO | 7 | -- | 8 | -- |
| PENNSYLVANIA | 25 | -- | 25 | -- |
| RHODE ISLAND | -- | 4 | 4 | -- |
| SOUTH CAROLINA | 11 | -- | 11 | -- |
| TENNESSEE | 8 | -- | 8 | -- |
| VERMONT | 8 | -- | 8 | -- |
| VIRGINIA | 25 | -- | 25 | -- |
| Total | 128 | 89 | 183 | 34 |

Table 3.2 (continued)

## 1820 and 1824 Electoral Vote for President

|  | 1820 | | 1824 | | | |
|---|---|---|---|---|---|---|
|  | MONROE | ADAMS | JACKSON | ADAMS | CRAWFORD | CLAY |
| ALABAMA | 3 | -- | 5 | -- | -- | -- |
| CONNECTICUT | 9 | -- | -- | 8 | -- | -- |
| DELAWARE | 4 | -- | -- | 1 | 2 | -- |
| GEORGIA | 8 | -- | -- | -- | 9 | -- |
| ILLINOIS | 3 | -- | 2 | 1 | -- | -- |
| INDIANA | 3 | -- | 5 | -- | -- | -- |
| KENTUCKY | 12 | -- | -- | -- | -- | 14 |
| LOUISIANA | 3 | -- | 3 | 2 | -- | -- |
| MAINE | 9 | -- | -- | 9 | -- | -- |
| MARYLAND | 11 | -- | 7 | 3 | 1 | -- |
| MASSACHUSETTS | 15 | -- | -- | 15 | -- | -- |
| MISSISSIPPI | 2 | -- | 3 | -- | -- | -- |
| MISSOURI | 3 | -- | -- | -- | -- | 3 |
| NEW HAMPSHIRE | 7 | 1 | -- | 8 | -- | -- |
| NEW JERSEY | 8 | -- | 8 | -- | -- | -- |
| NEW YORK | 29 | -- | 1 | 26 | 5 | 4 |
| NORTH CAROLINA | 15 | -- | 15 | -- | -- | -- |
| OHIO | 8 | -- | -- | -- | -- | 16 |
| PENNSYLVANIA | 24 | -- | 28 | -- | -- | -- |
| RHODE ISLAND | 4 | -- | -- | 4 | -- | -- |
| SOUTH CAROLINA | 11 | -- | 11 | -- | -- | -- |
| TENNESSEE | 7 | -- | 11 | -- | -- | -- |
| VERMONT | 8 | -- | -- | 7 | -- | -- |
| VIRGINIA | 25 | -- | -- | -- | 24 | -- |
| Total | 231 | 1 | 99 | 84 | 41 | 37 |

Table 3.2 (continued)

1828 and 1832 Electoral Vote for President

| | 1828 | | 1832 | | | |
|---|---|---|---|---|---|---|
| | JACKSON | ADAMS | JACKSON | CLAY | FLOYD | WIRT |
| ALABAMA | 5 | -- | 7 | -- | -- | -- |
| CONNECTICUT | -- | 8 | -- | 8 | -- | -- |
| DELAWARE | -- | 3 | -- | 3 | -- | -- |
| GEORGIA | 9 | -- | 11 | -- | -- | -- |
| ILLINOIS | 3 | -- | 5 | -- | -- | -- |
| INDIANA | 5 | -- | 9 | -- | -- | -- |
| KENTUCKY | 14 | -- | -- | 15 | -- | -- |
| LOUISIANA | 5 | -- | 5 | -- | -- | -- |
| MAINE | 1 | 8 | 10 | -- | -- | -- |
| MARYLAND | 5 | 6 | 3 | 5 | -- | -- |
| MASSACHUSETTS | -- | 15 | -- | 14 | -- | -- |
| MISSISSIPPI | 3 | -- | 4 | -- | -- | -- |
| MISSOURI | 3 | -- | 4 | -- | -- | -- |
| NEW HAMPSHIRE | -- | 8 | 7 | -- | -- | -- |
| NEW JERSEY | -- | 8 | 8 | -- | -- | -- |
| NEW YORK | 20 | 16 | 42 | -- | -- | -- |
| NORTH CAROLINA | 15 | -- | 15 | -- | -- | -- |
| OHIO | 16 | -- | 21 | -- | -- | -- |
| PENNSYLVANIA | 28 | -- | 30 | -- | -- | -- |
| RHODE ISLAND | -- | 4 | -- | 4 | -- | -- |
| SOUTH CAROLINA | 11 | -- | -- | -- | 11 | -- |
| TENNESSEE | 11 | -- | 15 | -- | -- | -- |
| VERMONT | -- | 7 | -- | -- | -- | 7 |
| VIRGINIA | 24 | -- | 23 | -- | -- | -- |
| Total | 178 | 83 | 219 | 49 | 11 | 7 |

Table 3.2 (continued)

1836 and 1840 Electoral Vote for President

| | 1836 | | | | | 1840 | |
| | VAN BUREN | HARRISON | WHITE | WEBSTER | MANGUM | HARRISON | VAN BUREN |
|---|---|---|---|---|---|---|---|
| ALABAMA | 7 | -- | -- | -- | -- | -- | 7 |
| ARKANSAS | 3 | -- | -- | -- | -- | -- | 3 |
| CONNECTICUT | 8 | -- | -- | -- | -- | 8 | -- |
| DELAWARE | -- | 3 | -- | -- | -- | 3 | -- |
| GEORGIA | -- | -- | 11 | -- | -- | 11 | -- |
| ILLINOIS | 5 | -- | -- | -- | -- | -- | 5 |
| INDIANA | -- | 9 | -- | -- | -- | 9 | -- |
| KENTUCKY | -- | 15 | -- | -- | -- | 15 | -- |
| LOUISIANA | 5 | -- | -- | -- | -- | 5 | -- |
| MAINE | 10 | -- | -- | -- | -- | 10 | -- |
| MARYLAND | -- | 10 | -- | -- | -- | 10 | -- |
| MASSACHUSETTS | -- | -- | -- | 14 | -- | 14 | -- |
| MICHIGAN | 3 | -- | -- | -- | -- | 3 | -- |
| MISSISSIPPI | 4 | -- | -- | -- | -- | 4 | -- |
| MISSOURI | 4 | -- | -- | -- | -- | -- | 4 |
| NEW HAMPSHIRE | 7 | -- | -- | -- | -- | -- | 7 |
| NEW JERSEY | -- | 8 | -- | -- | -- | 8 | -- |
| NEW YORK | 42 | -- | -- | -- | -- | 42 | -- |
| NORTH CAROLINA | 15 | -- | -- | -- | -- | 15 | -- |
| OHIO | -- | 21 | -- | -- | -- | 21 | -- |
| PENNSYLVANIA | 20 | -- | -- | -- | -- | 30 | -- |
| RHODE ISLAND | 4 | -- | -- | -- | -- | 4 | -- |
| SOUTH CAROLINA | -- | -- | -- | -- | 11 | -- | 11 |
| TENNESSEE | -- | -- | 15 | -- | -- | 15 | -- |
| VERMONT | -- | 7 | -- | -- | -- | 7 | -- |
| VIRGINIA | 23 | -- | -- | -- | -- | -- | 23 |
| Total | 170 | 73 | 26 | 14 | 11 | 234 | 60 |

Table 3.2 (continued)

### 1844 and 1848 Electoral Vote for President

| | 1844 | | 1848 | |
|---|---|---|---|---|
| | POLK | CLAY | TAYLOR | CASS |
| ALABAMA | 9 | -- | -- | 9 |
| ARKANSAS | 3 | -- | -- | 3 |
| CONNECTICUT | -- | 6 | 6 | -- |
| DELAWARE | -- | 3 | 3 | -- |
| FLORIDA | -- | -- | 3 | -- |
| GEORGIA | 10 | -- | 10 | -- |
| ILLINOIS | 9 | -- | -- | 9 |
| INDIANA | 12 | -- | -- | 12 |
| IOWA | -- | -- | -- | 4 |
| KENTUCKY | -- | 12 | 12 | -- |
| LOUISIANA | 6 | -- | 6 | -- |
| MAINE | 9 | -- | -- | 9 |
| MARYLAND | -- | 8 | 8 | -- |
| MASSACHUSETTS | -- | 12 | 12 | -- |
| MICHIGAN | 5 | -- | -- | 5 |
| MISSISSIPPI | 6 | -- | -- | 6 |
| MISSOURI | 7 | -- | -- | 7 |
| NEW HAMPSHIRE | 6 | -- | -- | 6 |
| NEW JERSEY | -- | 7 | 7 | -- |
| NEW YORK | 36 | -- | 36 | -- |
| NORTH CAROLINA | -- | 11 | 11 | -- |
| OHIO | -- | 23 | -- | 23 |
| PENNSYLVANIA | 26 | -- | 26 | -- |
| RHODE ISLAND | -- | 4 | 4 | -- |
| SOUTH CAROLINA | 9 | -- | -- | 9 |
| TENNESSEE | -- | 13 | 13 | -- |
| TEXAS | -- | -- | -- | 4 |
| VERMONT | -- | 6 | 6 | -- |
| VIRGINIA | 17 | -- | -- | 17 |
| WISCONSIN | -- | -- | -- | 4 |
| Total | 170 | 105 | 163 | 127 |

Table 3.2 (continued)

1852 and 1856 Electoral Vote for President

| | 1852 | | 1856 | | |
|---|---|---|---|---|---|
| | PIERCE | SCOTT | BUCHANAN | FREMONT | FILLMORE |
| ALABAMA | 9 | -- | 9 | -- | -- |
| ARKANSAS | 4 | -- | 4 | -- | -- |
| CALIFORNIA | 4 | -- | 4 | -- | -- |
| CONNECTICUT | 6 | -- | -- | 6 | -- |
| DELAWARE | 3 | -- | 3 | -- | -- |
| FLORIDA | 3 | -- | 3 | -- | -- |
| GEORGIA | 10 | -- | 10 | -- | -- |
| ILLINOIS | 11 | -- | 11 | -- | -- |
| INDIANA | 13 | -- | 13 | -- | -- |
| IOWA | 4 | -- | -- | 4 | -- |
| KENTUCKY | -- | 12 | 12 | -- | -- |
| LOUISIANA | 6 | -- | 6 | -- | -- |
| MAINE | 8 | -- | -- | 8 | -- |
| MARYLAND | 8 | -- | -- | -- | 8 |
| MASSACHUSETTS | -- | 13 | -- | 13 | -- |
| MICHIGAN | 6 | -- | -- | 6 | -- |
| MISSISSIPPI | 7 | -- | 7 | -- | -- |
| MISSOURI | 9 | -- | 9 | -- | -- |
| NEW HAMPSHIRE | 5 | -- | -- | 5 | -- |
| NEW JERSEY | 7 | -- | 7 | -- | -- |
| NEW YORK | 35 | -- | -- | 35 | -- |
| NORTH CAROLINA | 10 | -- | 10 | -- | -- |
| OHIO | 23 | -- | -- | 23 | -- |
| PENNSYLVANIA | 27 | -- | 27 | -- | -- |
| RHODE ISLAND | 4 | -- | -- | 4 | -- |
| SOUTH CAROLINA | 8 | -- | 8 | -- | -- |
| TENNESSEE | -- | 12 | 12 | -- | -- |
| TEXAS | 4 | -- | 4 | -- | -- |
| VERMONT | -- | 5 | -- | 5 | -- |
| VIRGINIA | 15 | -- | 15 | -- | -- |
| WISCONSIN | 5 | -- | -- | 5 | -- |
| Total | 254 | 42 | 174 | 114 | 8 |

Table 3.2 (continued)

1860 Electoral Vote for President

| | LINCOLN | BRECKINRIDGE | BELL | DOUGLAS |
|---|---|---|---|---|
| ALABAMA | -- | 9 | -- | -- |
| ARKANSAS | -- | 4 | -- | -- |
| CALIFORNIA | 4 | -- | -- | -- |
| CONNECTICUT | 6 | -- | -- | -- |
| DELAWARE | -- | 3 | -- | -- |
| FLORIDA | -- | 3 | -- | -- |
| GEORGIA | -- | 10 | -- | -- |
| ILLINOIS | 11 | -- | -- | -- |
| INDIANA | 13 | -- | -- | -- |
| IOWA | 4 | -- | -- | -- |
| KENTUCKY | -- | -- | 12 | -- |
| LOUISIANA | -- | 6 | -- | -- |
| MAINE | 8 | -- | -- | -- |
| MARYLAND | -- | 8 | -- | -- |
| MASSACHUSETTS | 13 | -- | -- | -- |
| MICHIGAN | 6 | -- | -- | -- |
| MINNESOTA | 4 | -- | -- | -- |
| MISSISSIPPI | -- | 7 | -- | -- |
| MISSOURI | -- | -- | -- | 9 |
| NEW HAMPSHIRE | 5 | -- | -- | -- |
| NEW JERSEY | 4 | -- | -- | 3 |
| NEW YORK | 35 | -- | -- | -- |
| NORTH CAROLINA | -- | 10 | -- | -- |
| OHIO | 23 | -- | -- | -- |
| OREGON | 3 | -- | -- | -- |
| PENNSYLVANIA | 27 | -- | -- | -- |
| RHODE ISLAND | 4 | -- | -- | -- |
| SOUTH CAROLINA | -- | 8 | -- | -- |
| TENNESSEE | -- | -- | 12 | -- |
| TEXAS | -- | 4 | -- | -- |
| VERMONT | 5 | -- | -- | -- |
| VIRGINIA | -- | -- | 15 | -- |
| WISCONSIN | 5 | -- | -- | -- |
| Total | 180 | 72 | 39 | 12 |

Table 3.2 (continued)

1864 Electoral Vote for President

|  | LINCOLN | McCLELLAN |
|---|---|---|
| CALIFORNIA | 5 | -- |
| CONNECTICUT | 6 | -- |
| DELAWARE | -- | 3 |
| ILLINOIS | 16 | -- |
| INDIANA | 13 | -- |
| IOWA | 8 | -- |
| KANSAS | 3 | -- |
| KENTUCKY | -- | 11 |
| MAINE | 7 | -- |
| MARYLAND | 7 | -- |
| MASSACHUSETTS | 12 | -- |
| MICHIGAN | 8 | -- |
| MINNESOTA | 4 | -- |
| MISSOURI | 11 | -- |
| NEVADA | 2 | -- |
| NEW HAMPSHIRE | 5 | -- |
| NEW JERSEY | -- | 7 |
| NEW YORK | 33 | -- |
| OHIO | 21 | -- |
| OREGON | 3 | -- |
| PENNSYLVANIA | 26 | -- |
| RHODE ISLAND | 4 | -- |
| VERMONT | 5 | -- |
| WEST VIRGINIA | 5 | -- |
| WISCONSIN | 8 | -- |
| Total | 212 | 21 |

Table 3.2 (continued)

1868 and 1872 Electoral Vote for President

| | 1868 | | 1872 | | | | |
|---|---|---|---|---|---|---|---|
| | GRANT | SEYMOUR | GRANT | HENDRICKS | BROWN | JENKINS | DAVIS |
| ALABAMA | 8 | -- | 10 | -- | -- | -- | -- |
| ARKANSAS | 5 | -- | -- | -- | -- | -- | -- |
| CALIFORNIA | 5 | -- | 6 | -- | -- | -- | -- |
| CONNECTICUT | 6 | -- | 6 | -- | -- | -- | -- |
| DELAWARE | -- | 3 | 3 | -- | -- | -- | -- |
| FLORIDA | 3 | -- | 4 | -- | -- | -- | -- |
| GEORGIA | -- | 9 | -- | -- | 6 | 2 | -- |
| ILLINOIS | 16 | -- | 21 | -- | -- | -- | -- |
| INDIANA | 13 | -- | 15 | -- | -- | -- | -- |
| IOWA | 8 | -- | 11 | -- | -- | -- | -- |
| KANSAS | 3 | -- | 5 | -- | -- | -- | -- |
| KENTUCKY | -- | 11 | -- | 8 | 4 | -- | -- |
| LOUISIANA | -- | 7 | -- | -- | -- | -- | -- |
| MAINE | 7 | -- | 7 | -- | -- | -- | -- |
| MARYLAND | -- | 7 | -- | 8 | -- | -- | -- |
| MASSACHUSETTS | 12 | -- | 13 | -- | -- | -- | -- |
| MICHIGAN | 8 | -- | 11 | -- | -- | -- | -- |
| MINNESOTA | 4 | -- | 5 | -- | -- | -- | -- |
| MISSISSIPPI | -- | -- | 8 | -- | -- | -- | -- |
| MISSOURI | 11 | -- | -- | 6 | 8 | -- | 1 |
| NEBRASKA | 3 | -- | 3 | -- | -- | -- | -- |
| NEVADA | 3 | -- | 3 | -- | -- | -- | -- |
| NEW HAMPSHIRE | 5 | -- | 5 | -- | -- | -- | -- |
| NEW JERSEY | -- | 7 | 9 | -- | -- | -- | -- |
| NEW YORK | -- | 33 | 35 | -- | -- | -- | -- |
| NORTH CAROLINA | 9 | -- | 10 | -- | -- | -- | -- |
| OHIO | 21 | -- | 22 | -- | -- | -- | -- |
| OREGON | -- | 3 | 3 | -- | -- | -- | -- |
| PENNSYLVANIA | 26 | -- | 29 | -- | -- | -- | -- |
| RHODE ISLAND | 4 | -- | 4 | -- | -- | -- | -- |
| SOUTH CAROLINA | 6 | -- | 7 | -- | -- | -- | -- |
| TENNESSEE | 10 | -- | -- | 12 | -- | -- | -- |
| TEXAS | -- | -- | -- | 8 | -- | -- | -- |
| VERMONT | 5 | -- | 5 | -- | -- | -- | -- |
| VIRGINIA | -- | -- | 11 | -- | -- | -- | -- |
| WEST VIRGINIA | 5 | -- | 5 | -- | -- | -- | -- |
| WISCONSIN | 8 | -- | 10 | -- | -- | -- | -- |
| Total | 214 | 80 | 286 | 42 | 18 | 2 | 1 |

Table 3.2 (continued)

1876 and 1880 Electoral Vote for President

| | 1876 | | 1880 | |
|---|---|---|---|---|
| | HAYES | TILDEN | GARFIELD | HANCOCK |
| ALABAMA | -- | 10 | -- | 10 |
| ARKANSAS | -- | 6 | -- | 6 |
| CALIFORNIA | 6 | -- | 1 | 5 |
| COLORADO | 3 | -- | 3 | -- |
| CONNECTICUT | -- | 6 | 6 | -- |
| DELAWARE | -- | 3 | -- | 3 |
| FLORIDA | 4 | -- | -- | 4 |
| GEORGIA | -- | 11 | -- | 11 |
| ILLINOIS | 21 | -- | 21 | -- |
| INDIANA | -- | 15 | 15 | -- |
| IOWA | 11 | -- | 11 | -- |
| KANSAS | 5 | -- | 5 | -- |
| KENTUCKY | -- | 12 | -- | 12 |
| LOUISIANA | 8 | -- | -- | 8 |
| MAINE | 7 | -- | 7 | -- |
| MARYLAND | -- | 8 | -- | 8 |
| MASSACHUSETTS | 13 | -- | 13 | --' |
| MICHIGAN | 11 | -- | 11 | -- |
| MINNESOTA | 5 | -- | 5 | -- |
| MISSISSIPPI | -- | 8 | -- | 8 |
| MISSOURI | -- | 15 | -- | 15 |
| NEBRASKA | 3 | -- | 3 | -- |
| NEVADA | 3 | -- | -- | 3 |
| NEW HAMPSHIRE | 5 | -- | 5 | -- |
| NEW JERSEY | -- | 9 | -- | 9 |
| NEW YORK | -- | 35 | 35 | -- |
| NORTH CAROLINA | -- | 10 | -- | 10 |
| OHIO | 22 | -- | 22 | -- |
| OREGON | 3 | -- | 3 | -- |
| PENNSYLVANIA | 29 | -- | 29 | -- |
| RHODE ISLAND | 4 | -- | 4 | -- |
| SOUTH CAROLINA | 7 | -- | -- | 7 |
| TENNESSEE | -- | 12 | -- | 12 |
| TEXAS | -- | 8 | -- | 8 |
| VERMONT | 5 | -- | 5 | -- |
| VIRGINIA | -- | 11 | -- | 11 |
| WEST VIRGINIA | -- | 5 | -- | 5 |
| WISCONSIN | 10 | -- | 10 | -- |
| Total | 185 | 184 | 214 | 155 |

Table 3.2 (continued)

1884 and 1888 Electoral Vote For President

| | 1884 | | 1888 | |
| --- | --- | --- | --- | --- |
| | CLEVELAND | BLAINE | HARRISON | CLEVELAND |
| ALABAMA | 10 | -- | -- | 10 |
| ARKANSAS | 7 | -- | -- | 7 |
| CALIFORNIA | -- | 8 | 8 | -- |
| COLORADO | -- | 3 | 3 | -- |
| CONNECTICUT | 6 | -- | -- | 6 |
| DELAWARE | 3 | -- | -- | 3 |
| FLORIDA | 4 | -- | -- | 4 |
| GEORGIA | 12 | -- | -- | 12 |
| ILLINOIS | -- | 22 | 22 | -- |
| INDIANA | 15 | -- | 15 | -- |
| IOWA | -- | 13 | 13 | -- |
| KANSAS | -- | 9 | 9 | -- |
| KENTUCKY | 13 | -- | -- | 13 |
| LOUISIANA | 8 | -- | -- | 8 |
| MAINE | -- | 6 | 6 | -- |
| MARYLAND | 8 | -- | -- | 8 |
| MASSACHUSETTS | -- | 14 | 14 | -- |
| MICHIGAN | -- | 13 | 13 | -- |
| MINNESOTA | -- | 7 | 7 | -- |
| MISSISSIPPI | 9 | -- | -- | 9 |
| MISSOURI | 16 | -- | -- | 16 |
| NEBRASKA | -- | 5 | 5 | -- |
| NEVADA | -- | 3 | 3 | -- |
| NEW HAMPSHIRE | -- | 4 | 4 | -- |
| NEW JERSEY | 9 | -- | -- | 9 |
| NEW YORK | 36 | -- | 36 | -- |
| NORTH CAROLINA | 11 | -- | -- | 11 |
| OHIO | -- | 23 | 23 | -- |
| OREGON | -- | 3 | 3 | -- |
| PENNSYLVANIA | -- | 30 | 30 | -- |
| RHODE ISLAND | -- | 4 | 4 | -- |
| SOUTH CAROLINA | 9 | -- | -- | 9 |
| TENNESSEE | 12 | -- | -- | 12 |
| TEXAS | 13 | -- | -- | 13 |
| VERMONT | -- | 4 | 4 | -- |
| VIRGINIA | 12 | -- | -- | 12 |
| WEST VIRGINIA | 6 | -- | -- | 6 |
| WISCONSIN | -- | 11 | 11 | -- |
| Total | 219 | 182 | 233 | 168 |

Table 3.2 (continued)

## 1892 and 1896 Electoral Vote for President

| | 1892 | | | 1896 | |
|---|---|---|---|---|---|
| | CLEVELAND | HARRISON | WEAVER | McKINLEY | BRYAN |
| ALABAMA | 11 | -- | -- | -- | 11 |
| ARKANSAS | 8 | -- | -- | -- | 8 |
| CALIFORNIA | 8 | 1 | -- | 8 | 1 |
| COLORADO | -- | -- | 4 | -- | 4 |
| CONNECTICUT | 6 | -- | -- | 6 | -- |
| DELAWARE | 3 | -- | -- | 3 | -- |
| FLORIDA | 4 | -- | -- | -- | 4 |
| GEORGIA | 13 | -- | -- | -- | 13 |
| IDAHO | -- | -- | 3 | -- | 3 |
| ILLINOIS | 24 | -- | -- | 24 | -- |
| INDIANA | 15 | -- | -- | 15 | -- |
| IOWA | -- | 13 | -- | 13 | -- |
| KANSAS | -- | -- | 10 | -- | 10 |
| KENTUCKY | 13 | -- | -- | 12 | 1 |
| LOUISIANA | 8 | -- | -- | -- | 8 |
| MAINE | -- | 6 | -- | 6 | -- |
| MARYLAND | 8 | -- | -- | 8 | -- |
| MASSACHUSETTS | -- | 15 | -- | 15 | -- |
| MICHIGAN | 5 | 9 | -- | 14 | -- |
| MINNESOTA | -- | 9 | -- | 9 | -- |
| MISSISSIPPI | 9 | -- | -- | -- | 9 |
| MISSOURI | 17 | -- | -- | -- | 17 |
| MONTANA | -- | 3 | -- | -- | 3 |
| NEBRASKA | -- | 8 | -- | -- | 8 |
| NEVADA | -- | -- | 3 | -- | 3 |
| NEW HAMPSHIRE | -- | 4 | -- | 4 | -- |
| NEW JERSEY | 10 | -- | -- | 10 | -- |
| NEW YORK | 36 | -- | -- | 36 | -- |
| NORTH CAROLINA | 11 | -- | -- | -- | 11 |
| NORTH DAKOTA | 1 | 1 | 1 | 3 | -- |
| OHIO | 1 | 22 | -- | 23 | -- |
| OREGON | -- | 3 | 1 | 4 | -- |
| PENNSYLVANIA | -- | 32 | -- | 32 | -- |
| RHODE ISLAND | -- | 4 | -- | 4 | -- |
| SOUTH CAROLINA | 9 | -- | -- | -- | 9 |
| SOUTH DAKOTA | -- | 4 | -- | -- | 4 |
| TENNESSEE | 12 | -- | -- | -- | 12 |
| TEXAS | 15 | -- | -- | -- | 15 |
| UTAH | -- | -- | -- | -- | 3 |
| VERMONT | -- | 4 | -- | 4 | -- |
| VIRGINIA | 12 | -- | -- | -- | 12 |
| WASHINGTON | -- | 4 | -- | -- | 4 |
| WEST VIRGINIA | 6 | -- | -- | 6 | -- |
| WISCONSIN | 12 | -- | -- | 12 | -- |
| WYOMING | -- | 3 | -- | -- | 3 |
| Total | 277 | 145 | 22 | 271 | 176 |

Table 3.2 (continued)

1900 and 1904 Electoral Vote for President

| | 1900 | | 1904 | |
| | McKINLEY | BRYAN | ROOSEVELT | PARKER |
|---|---|---|---|---|
| ALABAMA | -- | 11 | -- | 11 |
| ARKANSAS | -- | 8 | -- | 9 |
| CALIFORNIA | 9 | -- | 10 | -- |
| COLORADO | -- | 4 | 5 | -- |
| CONNECTICUT | 6 | -- | 7 | -- |
| DELAWARE | 3 | -- | 3 | -- |
| FLORIDA | -- | 4 | -- | 5 |
| GEORGIA | -- | 13 | -- | 13 |
| IDAHO | -- | 3 | 3 | -- |
| ILLINOIS | 24 | -- | 27 | -- |
| INDIANA | 15 | -- | 15 | -- |
| IOWA | 13 | -- | 13 | -- |
| KANSAS | 10 | -- | 10 | -- |
| KENTUCKY | -- | 13 | -- | 13 |
| LOUISIANA | -- | 8 | -- | 9 |
| MAINE | 6 | -- | 6 | -- |
| MARYLAND | 8 | -- | 1 | 7 |
| MASSACHUSETTS | 15 | -- | 16 | -- |
| MICHIGAN | 14 | -- | 14 | -- |
| MINNESOTA | 9 | -- | 11 | -- |
| MISSISSIPPI | -- | 9 | -- | 10 |
| MISSOURI | -- | 17 | 18 | -- |
| MONTANA | -- | 3 | 3 | -- |
| NEBRASKA | 8 | -- | 8 | -- |
| NEVADA | -- | 3 | 3 | -- |
| NEW HAMPSHIRE | 4 | -- | 4 | -- |
| NEW JERSEY | 10 | -- | 12 | -- |
| NEW YORK | 36 | -- | 39 | -- |
| NORTH CAROLINA | -- | 11 | -- | 12 |
| NORTH DAKOTA | 3 | -- | 4 | -- |
| OHIO | 23 | -- | 23 | -- |
| OREGON | 4 | -- | 4 | -- |
| PENNSYLVANIA | 32 | -- | 34 | -- |
| RHODE ISLAND | 4 | -- | 4 | -- |
| SOUTH CAROLINA | -- | 9 | -- | 9 |
| SOUTH DAKOTA | 4 | -- | 4 | -- |
| TENNESSEE | -- | 12 | -- | 12 |
| TEXAS | -- | 15 | -- | 18 |
| UTAH | 3 | -- | 3 | -- |
| VERMONT | 4 | -- | 4 | -- |
| VIRGINIA | -- | 12 | -- | 12 |
| WASHINGTON | 4 | -- | 5 | -- |
| WEST VIRGINIA | 6 | -- | 7 | -- |
| WISCONSIN | 12 | -- | 13 | -- |
| WYOMING | 3 | -- | 3 | -- |
| Total | 292 | 155 | 336 | 140 |

Table 3.2 (continued)

1908 and 1912 Electoral Vote for President

| | 1908 | | 1912 | | |
|---|---|---|---|---|---|
| | TAFT | BRYAN | WILSON | ROOSEVELT | TAFT |
| ALABAMA | -- | 11 | 12 | -- | -- |
| ARIZONA | -- | -- | 3 | -- | -- |
| ARKANSAS | -- | 9 | 9 | -- | -- |
| CALIFORNIA | 10 | -- | 2 | 11 | -- |
| COLORADO | -- | 5 | 6 | -- | -- |
| CONNECTICUT | 7 | -- | 7 | -- | -- |
| DELAWARE | 3 | -- | 3 | -- | -- |
| FLORIDA | -- | 5 | 6 | -- | -- |
| GEORGIA | -- | 13 | 14 | -- | -- |
| IDAHO | 3 | -- | 4 | -- | -- |
| ILLINOIS | 27 | -- | 29 | -- | -- |
| INDIANA | 15 | -- | 15 | -- | -- |
| IOWA | 13 | -- | 13 | -- | -- |
| KANSAS | 10 | -- | 10 | -- | -- |
| KENTUCKY | -- | 13 | 13 | -- | -- |
| LOUISIANA | -- | 9 | 10 | -- | -- |
| MAINE | 6 | -- | 6 | -- | -- |
| MARYLAND | 2 | 6 | 8 | -- | -- |
| MASSACHUSETTS | 16 | -- | 18 | -- | -- |
| MICHIGAN | 14 | -- | -- | 15 | -- |
| MINNESOTA | 11 | -- | -- | 12 | -- |
| MISSISSIPPI | -- | 10 | 10 | -- | -- |
| MISSOURI | 18 | -- | 18 | -- | -- |
| MONTANA | 3 | -- | 4 | -- | -- |
| NEBRASKA | -- | 8 | 8 | -- | -- |
| NEVADA | -- | 3 | 3 | -- | -- |
| NEW HAMPSHIRE | 4 | -- | 4 | -- | -- |
| NEW JERSEY | 12 | -- | 14 | -- | -- |
| NEW MEXICO | -- | -- | 3 | -- | -- |
| NEW YORK | 39 | -- | 45 | -- | -- |
| NORTH CAROLINA | -- | 12 | 12 | -- | -- |
| NORTH DAKOTA | 4 | -- | 5 | -- | -- |
| OHIO | 23 | -- | 24 | -- | -- |
| OKLAHOMA | -- | 7 | 10 | -- | -- |
| OREGON | 4 | -- | 5 | -- | -- |
| PENNSYLVANIA | 34 | -- | -- | 38 | -- |
| RHODE ISLAND | 4 | -- | 5 | -- | -- |
| SOUTH CAROLINA | -- | 9 | 9 | -- | -- |
| SOUTH DAKOTA | 4 | -- | -- | 5 | -- |
| TENNESSEE | -- | 12 | 12 | -- | -- |
| TEXAS | -- | 18 | 20 | -- | -- |
| UTAH | 3 | -- | -- | -- | 4 |
| VERMONT | 4 | -- | -- | -- | 4 |
| VIRGINIA | -- | 12 | 12 | -- | -- |
| WASHINGTON | 5 | -- | -- | 7 | -- |
| WEST VIRGINIA | 7 | -- | 8 | -- | -- |
| WISCONSIN | 13 | -- | 13 | -- | -- |
| WYOMING | 3 | -- | 3 | -- | -- |
| Total | 321 | 162 | 435 | 88 | 8 |

Table 3.2 (continued)

1916 and 1920 Electoral Vote for President

|  | 1916 | | 1920 | |
|---|---|---|---|---|
|  | WILSON | HUGHES | HARDING | COX |
| ALABAMA | 12 | -- | -- | 12 |
| ARIZONA | 3 | -- | 3 | -- |
| ARKANSAS | 9 | -- | -- | 9 |
| CALIFORNIA | 13 | -- | 13 | -- |
| COLORADO | 6 | -- | 6 | -- |
| CONNECTICUT | -- | 7 | 7 | -- |
| DELAWARE | -- | 3 | 3 | -- |
| FLORIDA | 6 | -- | -- | 6 |
| GEORGIA | 14 | -- | -- | 14 |
| IDAHO | 4 | -- | 4 | -- |
| ILLINOIS | -- | 29 | 29 | -- |
| INDIANA | -- | 15 | 15 | -- |
| IOWA | -- | 13 | 13 | -- |
| KANSAS | 10 | -- | 10 | -- |
| KENTUCKY | 13 | -- | -- | 13 |
| LOUISIANA | 10 | -- | -- | 10 |
| MAINE | -- | 6 | 6 | -- |
| MARYLAND | 8 | -- | 8 | -- |
| MASSACHUSETTS | -- | 18 | 18 | -- |
| MICHIGAN | -- | 15 | 15 | -- |
| MINNESOTA | -- | 12 | 12 | -- |
| MISSISSIPPI | 10 | -- | -- | 10 |
| MISSOURI | 18 | -- | 18 | -- |
| MONTANA | 4 | -- | 4 | -- |
| NEBRASKA | 8 | -- | 8 | -- |
| NEVADA | 3 | -- | 3 | -- |
| NEW HAMPSHIRE | 4 | -- | 4 | -- |
| NEW JERSEY | -- | 14 | 14 | -- |
| NEW MEXICO | 3 | -- | 3 | -- |
| NEW YORK | -- | 45 | 45 | -- |
| NORTH CAROLINA | 12 | -- | -- | 12 |
| NORTH DAKOTA | 5 | -- | 5 | -- |
| OHIO | 24 | -- | 24 | -- |
| OKLAHOMA | 10 | -- | 10 | -- |
| OREGON | -- | 5 | 5 | -- |
| PENNSYLVANIA | -- | 38 | 38 | -- |
| RHODE ISLAND | -- | 5 | 5 | -- |
| SOUTH CAROLINA | 9 | -- | -- | 9 |
| SOUTH DAKOTA | -- | 5 | 5 | -- |
| TENNESSEE | 12 | -- | 12 | -- |
| TEXAS | 20 | -- | -- | 20 |
| UTAH | 4 | -- | 4 | -- |
| VERMONT | -- | 4 | 4 | -- |
| VIRGINIA | 12 | -- | -- | 12 |
| WASHINGTON | 7 | -- | 7 | -- |
| WEST VIRGINIA | 1 | 7 | 8 | -- |
| WISCONSIN | -- | 13 | 13 | -- |
| WYOMING | 3 | -- | 3 | -- |
| Total | 277 | 254 | 404 | 127 |

Table 3.2 (continued)

1924 and 1928 Electoral Vote for President

| | 1924 | | | 1928 | |
|---|---|---|---|---|---|
| | COOLIDGE | DAVIS | LAFOLLETTE | HOOVER | SMITH |
| ALABAMA | -- | 12 | -- | -- | 12 |
| ARIZONA | 3 | -- | -- | 3 | -- |
| ARKANSAS | -- | 9 | -- | -- | 9 |
| CALIFORNIA | 13 | -- | -- | 13 | -- |
| COLORADO | 6 | -- | -- | 6 | -- |
| CONNECTICUT | 7 | -- | -- | 7 | -- |
| DELAWARE | 3 | -- | -- | 3 | -- |
| FLORIDA | -- | 6 | -- | 6 | -- |
| GEORGIA | -- | 14 | -- | -- | 14 |
| IDAHO | 4 | -- | -- | 4 | -- |
| ILLINOIS | 29 | -- | -- | 29 | -- |
| INDIANA | 15 | -- | -- | 15 | -- |
| IOWA | 13 | -- | -- | 13 | -- |
| KANSAS | 10 | -- | -- | 10 | -- |
| KENTUCKY | 13 | -- | -- | 13 | -- |
| LOUISIANA | -- | 10 | -- | -- | 10 |
| MAINE | 6 | -- | -- | 6 | -- |
| MARYLAND | 8 | -- | -- | 8 | -- |
| MASSACHUSETTS | 18 | -- | -- | -- | 18 |
| MICHIGAN | 15 | -- | -- | 15 | -- |
| MINNESOTA | 12 | -- | -- | 12 | -- |
| MISSISSIPPI | -- | 10 | -- | -- | 10 |
| MISSOURI | 18 | -- | -- | 18 | -- |
| MONTANA | 4 | -- | -- | 4 | -- |
| NEBRASKA | 8 | -- | -- | 8 | -- |
| NEVADA | 3 | -- | -- | 3 | -- |
| NEW HAMPSHIRE | 4 | -- | -- | 4 | -- |
| NEW JERSEY | 14 | -- | -- | 14 | -- |
| NEW MEXICO | 3 | -- | -- | 3 | -- |
| NEW YORK | 45 | -- | -- | 45 | -- |
| NORTH CAROLINA | -- | 12 | -- | 12 | -- |
| NORTH DAKOTA | 5 | -- | -- | 5 | -- |
| OHIO | 24 | -- | -- | 24 | -- |
| OKLAHOMA | -- | 10 | -- | 10 | -- |
| OREGON | 5 | -- | -- | 5 | -- |
| PENNSYLVANIA | 38 | -- | -- | 38 | -- |
| RHODE ISLAND | 5 | -- | -- | -- | 5 |
| SOUTH CAROLINA | -- | 9 | -- | -- | 9 |
| SOUTH DAKOTA | 5 | -- | -- | 5 | -- |
| TENNESSEE | -- | 12 | -- | 12 | -- |
| TEXAS | -- | 20 | -- | 20 | -- |
| UTAH | 4 | -- | -- | 4 | -- |
| VERMONT | 4 | -- | -- | 4 | -- |
| VIRGINIA | -- | 12 | -- | 12 | -- |
| WASHINGTON | 7 | -- | -- | 7 | -- |
| WEST VIRGINIA | 8 | -- | -- | 8 | -- |
| WISCONSIN | -- | -- | 13 | 13 | -- |
| WYOMING | 3 | -- | -- | 3 | -- |
| Total | 382 | 136 | 13 | 444 | 87 |

# 121

Table 3.2 (continued)

1932 and 1936 Electoral Vote for President

| | 1932 | | 1936 | |
|---|---|---|---|---|
| | ROOSEVELT | HOOVER | ROOSEVELT | LANDON |
| ALABAMA | 11 | -- | 11 | -- |
| ARIZONA | 3 | -- | 3 | -- |
| ARKANSAS | 9 | -- | 9 | -- |
| CALIFORNIA | 22 | -- | 22 | -- |
| COLORADO | 6 | -- | 6 | -- |
| CONNECTICUT | -- | 8 | 8 | -- |
| DELAWARE | -- | 3 | 3 | -- |
| FLORIDA | 7 | -- | 7 | -- |
| GEORGIA | 12 | -- | 12 | -- |
| IDAHO | 4 | -- | 4 | -- |
| ILLINOIS | 29 | -- | 29 | -- |
| INDIANA | 14 | -- | 14 | -- |
| IOWA | 11 | -- | 11 | -- |
| KANSAS | 9 | -- | 9 | -- |
| KENTUCKY | 11 | -- | 11 | -- |
| LOUISIANA | 10 | -- | 10 | -- |
| MAINE | -- | 5 | -- | 5 |
| MARYLAND | 8 | -- | 8 | -- |
| MASSACHUSETTS | 17 | -- | 17 | -- |
| MICHIGAN | 19 | -- | 19 | -- |
| MINNESOTA | 11 | -- | 11 | -- |
| MISSISSIPPI | 9 | -- | 9 | -- |
| MISSOURI | 15 | -- | 15 | -- |
| MONTANA | 4 | -- | 4 | -- |
| NEBRASKA | 7 | -- | 7 | -- |
| NEVADA | 3 | -- | 3 | -- |
| NEW HAMPSHIRE | -- | 4 | 4 | -- |
| NEW JERSEY | 16 | -- | 16 | -- |
| NEW MEXICO | 3 | -- | 3 | -- |
| NEW YORK | 47 | -- | 47 | -- |
| NORTH CAROLINA | 13 | -- | 13 | -- |
| NORTH DAKOTA | 4 | -- | 4 | -- |
| OHIO | 26 | -- | 26 | -- |
| OKLAHOMA | 11 | -- | 11 | -- |
| OREGON | 5 | -- | 5 | -- |
| PENNSYLVANIA | -- | 36 | 36 | -- |
| RHODE ISLAND | 4 | -- | 4 | -- |
| SOUTH CAROLINA | 8 | -- | 8 | -- |
| SOUTH DAKOTA | 4 | -- | 4 | -- |
| TENNESSEE | 11 | -- | 11 | -- |
| TEXAS | 23 | -- | 23 | -- |
| UTAH | 4 | -- | 4 | -- |
| VERMONT | -- | 3 | -- | 3 |
| VIRGINIA | 11 | -- | 11 | -- |
| WASHINGTON | 8 | -- | 8 | -- |
| WEST VIRGINIA | 8 | -- | 8 | -- |
| WISCONSIN | 12 | -- | 12 | -- |
| WYOMING | 3 | -- | 3 | -- |
| Total | 472 | 59 | 523 | 8 |

Table 3.2 (continued)

### 1940 and 1944 Electoral Vote for President

| | 1940 | | 1944 | |
|---|---|---|---|---|
| | ROOSEVELT | WILLKIE | ROOSEVELT | DEWEY |
| ALABAMA | 11 | -- | 11 | -- |
| ARIZONA | 3 | -- | 4 | -- |
| ARKANSAS | 9 | -- | 9 | -- |
| CALIFORNIA | 22 | -- | 25 | -- |
| COLORADO | -- | 6 | -- | 6 |
| CONNECTICUT | 8 | -- | 8 | -- |
| DELAWARE | 3 | -- | 3 | -- |
| FLORIDA | 7 | -- | 8 | -- |
| GEORGIA | 12 | -- | 12 | -- |
| IDAHO | 4 | -- | 4 | -- |
| ILLINOIS | 29 | -- | 28 | -- |
| INDIANA | -- | 14 | -- | 13 |
| IOWA | -- | 11 | -- | 10 |
| KANSAS | | 9 | -- | 8 |
| KENTUCKY | 11 | -- | 11 | -- |
| LOUISIANA | 10 | -- | 10 | -- |
| MAINE | -- | 5 | -- | 5 |
| MARYLAND | 8 | -- | 8 | -- |
| MASSACHUSETTS | 17 | -- | 16 | -- |
| MICHIGAN | -- | 19 | 19 | -- |
| MINNESOTA | 11 | -- | 11 | -- |
| MISSISSIPPI | 9 | -- | 9 | -- |
| MISSOURI | 15 | -- | 15 | -- |
| MONTANA | 4 | -- | 4 | -- |
| NEBRASKA | -- | 7 | -- | 6 |
| NEVADA | 3 | -- | 3 | -- |
| NEW HAMPSHIRE | 4 | -- | 4 | -- |
| NEW JERSEY | 16 | -- | 16 | -- |
| NEW MEXICO | 3 | -- | 4 | -- |
| NEW YORK | 47 | -- | 47 | -- |
| NORTH CAROLINA | 13 | -- | 14 | -- |
| NORTH DAKOTA | -- | 4 | -- | 4 |
| OHIO | 26 | -- | -- | 25 |
| OKLAHOMA | 11 | -- | 10 | -- |
| OREGON | 5 | -- | 6 | -- |
| PENNSYLVANIA | 36 | -- | 35 | -- |
| RHODE ISLAND | 4 | -- | 4 | -- |
| SOUTH CAROLINA | 8 | -- | 8 | -- |
| SOUTH DAKOTA | -- | 4 | -- | 4 |
| TENNESSEE | 11 | -- | 12 | -- |
| TEXAS | 23 | -- | 23 | -- |
| UTAH | 4 | -- | 4 | -- |
| VERMONT | -- | 3 | -- | 3 |
| VIRGINIA | 11 | -- | 11 | -- |
| WASHINGTON | 8 | -- | 8 | -- |
| WEST VIRGINIA | 8 | -- | 8 | -- |
| WISCONSIN | 12 | -- | -- | 12 |
| WYOMING | 3 | -- | -- | 3 |
| Total | 449 | 82 | 432 | 99 |

Table 3.2 (continued)

1948 and 1952 Electoral Vote for President

| | 1948 | | | 1952 | |
|---|---|---|---|---|---|
| | TRUMAN | DEWEY | THURMOND | EISENHOWER | STEVENSON |
| ALABAMA | -- | -- | 11 | -- | 11 |
| ARIZONA | 4 | -- | -- | 4 | -- |
| ARKANSAS | 9 | -- | -- | -- | 8 |
| CALIFORNIA | 25 | -- | -- | 32 | -- |
| COLORADO | 6 | -- | -- | 6 | -- |
| CONNECTICUT | -- | 8 | -- | 8 | -- |
| DELAWARE | -- | 3 | -- | 3 | -- |
| FLORIDA | 8 | -- | -- | 10 | -- |
| GEORGIA | 12 | -- | -- | -- | 12 |
| IDAHO | 4 | -- | -- | 4 | -- |
| ILLINOIS | 28 | -- | -- | 27 | -- |
| INDIANA | -- | 13 | -- | 13 | -- |
| IOWA | 10 | -- | -- | 10 | -- |
| KANSAS | -- | 8 | -- | 8 | -- |
| KENTUCKY | 11 | -- | -- | -- | 10 |
| LOUISIANA | -- | -- | 10 | -- | 10 |
| MAINE | -- | 5 | -- | 5 | -- |
| MARYLAND | -- | 8 | -- | 9 | -- |
| MASSACHUSETTS | 16 | -- | -- | 16 | -- |
| MICHIGAN | -- | 19 | -- | 20 | -- |
| MINNESOTA | 11 | -- | -- | 11 | -- |
| MISSISSIPPI | -- | -- | 9 | -- | 8 |
| MISSOURI | 15 | -- | -- | 13 | -- |
| MONTANA | 4 | -- | -- | 4 | -- |
| NEBRASKA | -- | 6 | -- | 6 | -- |
| NEVADA | 3 | -- | -- | 3 | -- |
| NEW HAMPSHIRE | -- | 4 | -- | 4 | -- |
| NEW JERSEY | -- | 16 | -- | 16 | -- |
| NEW MEXICO | 4 | -- | -- | 4 | -- |
| NEW YORK | -- | 47 | -- | 45 | -- |
| NORTH CAROLINA | 14 | -- | -- | -- | 14 |
| NORTH DAKOTA | -- | 4 | -- | 4 | -- |
| OHIO | 25 | -- | -- | 25 | -- |
| OKLAHOMA | 10 | -- | -- | 8 | -- |
| OREGON | -- | 6 | -- | 6 | -- |
| PENNSYLVANIA | -- | 35 | -- | 32 | -- |
| RHODE ISLAND | 4 | -- | -- | 4 | -- |
| SOUTH CAROLINA | -- | -- | 8 | -- | 8 |
| SOUTH DAKOTA | -- | 4 | -- | 4 | -- |
| TENNESSEE | 11 | -- | 1 | 11 | -- |
| TEXAS | 23 | -- | -- | 24 | -- |
| UTAH | 4 | -- | -- | 4 | -- |
| VERMONT | -- | 3 | -- | 3 | -- |
| VIRGINIA | 11 | -- | -- | 12 | -- |
| WASHINGTON | 8 | -- | -- | 9 | -- |
| WEST VIRGINIA | 8 | -- | -- | -- | 8 |
| WISCONSIN | 12 | -- | -- | 12 | -- |
| WYOMING | 3 | -- | -- | 3 | -- |
| Total | 303 | 189 | 39 | 442 | 89 |

Table 3.2 (continued)

### 1956 and 1960 Electoral Vote for President

| | 1956 | | | 1960 | | |
|---|---|---|---|---|---|---|
| | EISENHOWER | STEVENSON | JONES | KENNEDY | NIXON | BYRD |
| ALABAMA | -- | 10 | 1 | 5 | -- | 6 |
| ALASKA | -- | -- | -- | -- | 3 | -- |
| ARIZONA | 4 | -- | -- | -- | 4 | -- |
| ARKANSAS | -- | 8 | -- | 8 | -- | -- |
| CALIFORNIA | 32 | -- | -- | -- | 32 | -- |
| COLORADO | 6 | -- | -- | -- | 6 | -- |
| CONNECTICUT | 8 | -- | -- | 8 | -- | -- |
| DELAWARE | 3 | -- | -- | 3 | -- | -- |
| FLORIDA | 10 | -- | -- | -- | 10 | -- |
| GEORGIA | -- | 12 | -- | 12 | -- | -- |
| HAWAII | -- | -- | -- | 3 | -- | -- |
| IDAHO | 4 | -- | -- | -- | 4 | -- |
| ILLINOIS | 27 | -- | -- | 27 | -- | -- |
| INDIANA | 13 | -- | -- | -- | 13 | -- |
| IOWA | 10 | -- | -- | -- | 10 | -- |
| KANSAS | 8 | -- | -- | -- | 8 | -- |
| KENTUCKY | 10 | -- | -- | -- | 10 | -- |
| LOUISIANA | 10 | -- | -- | 10 | -- | -- |
| MAINE | 5 | -- | -- | -- | 5 | -- |
| MARYLAND | 9 | -- | -- | 9 | -- | -- |
| MASSACHUSETTS | 16 | -- | -- | 16 | -- | -- |
| MICHIGAN | 20 | -- | -- | 20 | -- | -- |
| MINNESOTA | 11 | -- | -- | 11 | -- | -- |
| MISSISSIPPI | -- | 8 | -- | -- | -- | 8 |
| MISSOURI | -- | 13 | -- | 13 | -- | -- |
| MONTANA | 4 | -- | -- | -- | 4 | -- |
| NEBRASKA | 6 | -- | -- | -- | 6 | -- |
| NEVADA | 3 | -- | -- | 3 | -- | -- |
| NEW HAMPSHIRE | 4 | -- | -- | -- | 4 | -- |
| NEW JERSEY | 16 | -- | -- | 16 | -- | -- |
| NEW MEXICO | 4 | -- | -- | 4 | -- | -- |
| NEW YORK | 45 | -- | -- | 45 | -- | -- |
| NORTH CAROLINA | -- | 14 | -- | 14 | -- | -- |
| NORTH DAKOTA | 4 | -- | -- | -- | 4 | -- |
| OHIO | 25 | -- | -- | -- | 25 | -- |
| OKLAHOMA | 8 | -- | -- | -- | 7 | 1 |
| OREGON | 6 | -- | -- | -- | 6 | -- |
| PENNSYLVANIA | 32 | -- | -- | 32 | -- | -- |
| RHODE ISLAND | 4 | -- | -- | 4 | -- | -- |
| SOUTH CAROLINA | -- | 8 | -- | 8 | -- | -- |
| SOUTH DAKOTA | 4 | -- | -- | -- | 4 | -- |
| TENNESSEE | 11 | -- | -- | -- | 11 | -- |
| TEXAS | 24 | -- | -- | 24 | -- | -- |
| UTAH | 4 | -- | -- | -- | 4 | -- |
| VERMONT | 3 | -- | -- | -- | 3 | -- |
| VIRGINIA | 12 | -- | -- | -- | 12 | -- |
| WASHINGTON | 9 | -- | -- | -- | 9 | -- |
| WEST VIRGINIA | 8 | -- | -- | 8 | -- | -- |
| WISCONSIN | 12 | -- | -- | -- | 12 | -- |
| WYOMING | 3 | -- | -- | -- | 3 | -- |
| Total | 457 | 73 | 1 | 303 | 219 | 15 |

Table 3.2 (continued)

### 1964 and 1968 Electoral Vote for President

| | 1964 | | 1968 | | |
|---|---|---|---|---|---|
| | JOHNSON | GOLDWATER | NIXON | HUMPHREY | WALLACE |
| ALABAMA | -- | 10 | -- | -- | 10 |
| ALASKA | 3 | -- | 3 | -- | -- |
| ARIZONA | -- | 5 | 5 | -- | -- |
| ARKANSAS | 6 | -- | -- | -- | 6 |
| CALIFORNIA | 40 | -- | 40 | -- | -- |
| COLORADO | 6 | -- | 6 | -- | -- |
| CONNECTICUT | 8 | -- | -- | 8 | -- |
| DELAWARE | 3 | -- | 3 | -- | -- |
| DIST. OF COLUMBIA | 3 | -- | -- | 3 | -- |
| FLORIDA | 14 | -- | 14 | -- | -- |
| GEORGIA | -- | 12 | -- | -- | 12 |
| HAWAII | 4 | -- | -- | 4 | -- |
| IDAHO | 4 | -- | 4 | -- | -- |
| ILLINOIS | 26 | -- | 26 | -- | -- |
| INDIANA | 13 | -- | 13 | -- | -- |
| IOWA | 9 | -- | 9 | -- | -- |
| KANSAS | 7 | -- | 7 | -- | -- |
| KENTUCKY | 9 | -- | 9 | -- | -- |
| LOUISIANA | -- | 10 | -- | -- | 10 |
| MAINE | 4 | -- | -- | 4 | -- |
| MARYLAND | 10 | -- | -- | 10 | -- |
| MASSACHUSETTS | 14 | -- | -- | 14 | -- |
| MICHIGAN | 21 | -- | -- | 21 | -- |
| MINNESOTA | 10 | -- | -- | 10 | -- |
| MISSISSIPPI | -- | 7 | -- | -- | 7 |
| MISSOURI | 12 | -- | 12 | -- | -- |
| MONTANA | 4 | -- | 4 | -- | -- |
| NEBRASKA | 5 | -- | 5 | -- | -- |
| NEVADA | 3 | -- | 3 | -- | -- |
| NEW HAMPSHIRE | 4 | -- | 4 | -- | -- |
| NEW JERSEY | 17 | -- | 17 | -- | -- |
| NEW MEXICO | 4 | -- | 4 | -- | -- |
| NEW YORK | 43 | -- | -- | 43 | -- |
| NORTH CAROLINA | 13 | -- | 12 | -- | 1 |
| NORTH DAKOTA | 4 | -- | 4 | -- | -- |
| OHIO | 26 | -- | 26 | -- | -- |
| OKLAHOMA | 8 | -- | 8 | -- | -- |
| OREGON | 6 | -- | 6 | -- | -- |
| PENNSYLVANIA | 29 | -- | -- | 29 | -- |
| RHODE ISLAND | 4 | -- | -- | 4 | -- |
| SOUTH CAROLINA | -- | 8 | 8 | -- | -- |
| SOUTH DAKOTA | 4 | -- | 4 | -- | -- |
| TENNESSEE | 11 | -- | 11 | -- | -- |
| TEXAS | 25 | -- | -- | 25 | -- |
| UTAH | 4 | -- | 4 | -- | -- |
| VERMONT | 3 | -- | 3 | -- | -- |
| VIRGINIA | 12 | -- | 12 | -- | -- |
| WASHINGTON | 9 | -- | -- | 9 | -- |
| WEST VIRGINIA | 7 | -- | -- | 7 | -- |
| WISCONSIN | 12 | -- | 12 | -- | -- |
| WYOMING | 3 | -- | 3 | -- | -- |
| Total | 486 | 52 | 301 | 191 | 46 |

Table 3.2 (continued)

## 1972 and 1976 Electoral Vote for President

| | 1972[a] | | 1976[b] | |
|---|---|---|---|---|
| | NIXON | McGOVERN | FORD | CARTER |
| ALABAMA | 9 | -- | -- | 9 |
| ALASKA | 3 | -- | 3 | -- |
| ARIZONA | 6 | -- | 6 | -- |
| ARKANSAS | 6 | -- | -- | 6 |
| CALIFORNIA | 45 | -- | 45 | -- |
| COLORADO | 7 | -- | 7 | -- |
| CONNECTICUT | 8 | -- | 8 | -- |
| DELAWARE | 3 | -- | -- | 3 |
| DIST. OF COLUMBIA | -- | 3 | -- | 3 |
| FLORIDA | 17 | -- | -- | 17 |
| GEORGIA | 12 | -- | -- | 12 |
| HAWAII | 4 | -- | -- | 4 |
| IDAHO | 4 | -- | 4 | -- |
| ILLINOIS | 26 | -- | 26 | -- |
| INDIANA | 13 | -- | 13 | -- |
| IOWA | 8 | -- | 8 | -- |
| KANSAS | 7 | -- | 7 | -- |
| KENTUCKY | 9 | -- | -- | 9 |
| LOUISIANA | 10 | -- | -- | 10 |
| MAINE | 4 | -- | 4 | -- |
| MARYLAND | 10 | -- | -- | 10 |
| MASSACHUSETTS | -- | 14 | -- | 14 |
| MICHIGAN | 21 | -- | 21 | -- |
| MINNESOTA | 10 | -- | -- | 10 |
| MISSISSIPPI | 7 | -- | -- | 7 |
| MISSOURI | 12 | -- | -- | 12 |
| MONTANA | 4 | -- | 4 | -- |
| NEBRASKA | 5 | -- | 5 | -- |
| NEVADA | 3 | -- | 3 | -- |
| NEW HAMPSHIRE | 4 | -- | 4 | -- |
| NEW JERSEY | 17 | -- | 17 | -- |
| NEW MEXICO | 4 | -- | 4 | -- |
| NEW YORK | 41 | -- | -- | 41 |
| NORTH CAROLINA | 13 | -- | -- | 13 |
| NORTH DAKOTA | 3 | -- | 3 | -- |
| OHIO | 25 | -- | -- | 25 |
| OKLAHOMA | 8 | -- | 8 | -- |
| OREGON | 6 | -- | 6 | -- |
| PENNSYLVANIA | 27 | -- | -- | 27 |
| RHODE ISLAND | 4 | -- | -- | 4 |
| SOUTH CAROLINA | 8 | -- | -- | 8 |
| SOUTH DAKOTA | 4 | -- | 4 | -- |
| TENNESSEE | 10 | -- | -- | 10 |
| TEXAS | 26 | -- | -- | 26 |
| UTAH | 4 | -- | 4 | -- |
| VERMONT | 3 | -- | 3 | -- |
| VIRGINIA | 11 | -- | 12 | -- |
| WASHINGTON | 9 | -- | 8 | -- |
| WEST VIRGINIA | 6 | -- | -- | 6 |
| WISCONSIN | 11 | -- | -- | 11 |
| WYOMING | 3 | -- | 3 | -- |
| Total | 520 | 17 | 240 | 297 |

[a]John Hospers received one electoral vote from the State of Virginia.

[b]Ronald Reagan received one electoral vote from the State of Washington.

Table 3.2 (continued)

1980 and 1984 Electoral Vote for President

| | 1980 | | 1984 | |
|---|---|---|---|---|
| | REAGAN | CARTER | REAGAN | MONDALE |
| ALABAMA | 9 | -- | 9 | -- |
| ALASKA | 3 | -- | 3 | -- |
| ARIZONA | 6 | -- | 7 | -- |
| ARKANSAS | 6 | -- | 6 | -- |
| CALIFORNIA | 45 | -- | 47 | -- |
| COLORADO | 7 | -- | 8 | -- |
| CONNECTICUT | 8 | -- | 8 | -- |
| DELAWARE | 3 | -- | 3 | -- |
| DIST. OF COLUMBIA | 3 | -- | -- | 3 |
| FLORIDA | 17 | -- | 21 | -- |
| GEORGIA | -- | 12 | 12 | -- |
| HAWAII | -- | 4 | 4 | -- |
| IDAHO | 4 | -- | 4 | -- |
| ILLINOIS | 26 | -- | 24 | -- |
| INDIANA | 13 | -- | 12 | -- |
| IOWA | 8 | -- | 8 | -- |
| KANSAS | 7 | -- | 7 | -- |
| KENTUCKY | 9 | -- | 9 | -- |
| LOUISIANA | 10 | -- | 10 | -- |
| MAINE | 4 | -- | 4 | -- |
| MARYLAND | -- | 10 | 10 | -- |
| MASSACHUSETTS | 14 | -- | 13 | -- |
| MICHIGAN | 21 | -- | 20 | -- |
| MINNESOTA | -- | 10 | -- | 10 |
| MISSISSIPPI | 7 | -- | 7 | -- |
| MISSOURI | 12 | -- | 11 | -- |
| MONTANA | 4 | -- | 4 | -- |
| NEBRASKA | 5 | -- | 5 | -- |
| NEVADA | 3 | -- | 4 | -- |
| NEW HAMPSHIRE | 4 | -- | 4 | -- |
| NEW JERSEY | 17 | -- | 16 | -- |
| NEW MEXICO | 4 | -- | 5 | -- |
| NEW YORK | 41 | -- | 36 | -- |
| NORTH CAROLINA | 13 | -- | 13 | -- |
| NORTH DAKOTA | 3 | -- | 3 | -- |
| OHIO | 25 | -- | 23 | -- |
| OKLAHOMA | 8 | -- | 8 | -- |
| OREGON | 6 | -- | 7 | -- |
| PENNSYLVANIA | 27 | -- | 25 | -- |
| RHODE ISLAND | -- | 4 | 4 | -- |
| SOUTH CAROLINA | 8 | -- | 8 | -- |
| SOUTH DAKOTA | 4 | -- | 3 | -- |
| TENNESSEE | 10 | -- | 11 | -- |
| TEXAS | 26 | -- | 29 | -- |
| UTAH | 4 | -- | 5 | -- |
| VERMONT | 3 | -- | 3 | -- |
| VIRGINIA | 12 | -- | 12 | -- |
| WASHINGTON | 9 | -- | 10 | -- |
| WEST VIRGINIA | -- | 6 | 6 | -- |
| WISCONSIN | 11 | -- | 11 | -- |
| WYOMING | 3 | -- | 3 | -- |
| Total | 489 | 49 | 525 | 13 |

## TABLE 3.3

### POPULAR VOTE CAST FOR PRESIDENT,
### BY STATE, 1824–1984

| | 1824 PRESIDENTIAL ELECTION | | | |
|---|---|---|---|---|
| | JACKSON (DEM-REP) | ADAMS (DEM-REP) | (OTHER) | TOTAL VOTE CAST |
| ALABAMA | 9429 | 2422 | 1752 | 13603 |
| ALASKA | --- | --- | --- | --- |
| ARIZONA | --- | --- | --- | --- |
| ARKANSAS | --- | --- | --- | --- |
| CALIFORNIA | --- | --- | --- | --- |
| COLORADO | --- | --- | --- | --- |
| CONNECTICUT | 0 | 7494 | 3153 | 10647 |
| DELAWARE | --- | --- | --- | --- |
| DIST OF COLUMBIA | --- | --- | --- | --- |
| FLORIDA | --- | --- | --- | --- |
| GEORGIA | --- | --- | --- | --- |
| HAWAII | --- | --- | --- | --- |
| IDAHO | --- | --- | --- | --- |
| ILLINOIS | 1151 | 1516 | 1849 | 4516 |
| INDIANA | 7444 | 3071 | 5323 | 15838 |
| IOWA | --- | --- | --- | --- |
| KANSAS | --- | --- | --- | --- |
| KENTUCKY | 6356 | 0 | 16982 | 23338 |
| LOUISIANA | --- | --- | --- | --- |
| MAINE | --- | --- | --- | --- |
| MARYLAND | --- | --- | --- | --- |
| MASSACHUSETTS | 0 | 30687 | 11369 | 42056 |
| MICHIGAN | --- | --- | --- | --- |
| MINNESOTA | --- | --- | --- | --- |
| MISSISSIPPI | 3121 | 1654 | 119 | 4894 |
| MISSOURI | 1166 | 159 | 2107 | 3432 |
| MONTANA | --- | --- | --- | --- |
| NEBRASKA | --- | --- | --- | --- |
| NEVADA | --- | --- | --- | --- |
| NEW HAMPSHIRE | 0 | 9357 | 0 | 9357 |
| NEW JERSEY | 10332 | 8309 | 1196 | 19837 |
| NEW MEXICO | --- | --- | --- | --- |
| NEW YORK | --- | --- | --- | --- |
| NORTH CAROLINA | 20231 | 0 | 15878 | 36109 |
| NORTH DAKOTA | --- | --- | --- | --- |
| OHIO | 19277 | 12194 | 19215 | 50686 |
| OKLAHOMA | --- | --- | --- | --- |
| OREGON | --- | --- | --- | --- |
| PENNSYLVANIA | 35736 | 5441 | 5896 | 47073 |
| RHODE ISLAND | 0 | 2144 | 200 | 2344 |
| SOUTH CAROLINA | --- | --- | --- | --- |
| SOUTH DAKOTA | --- | --- | --- | --- |
| TENNESSEE | --- | --- | --- | --- |
| TEXAS | --- | --- | --- | --- |
| UTAH | --- | --- | --- | --- |
| VERMONT | --- | --- | --- | --- |
| VIRGINIA | 2975 | 3419 | 8977 | 15371 |
| WASHINGTON | --- | --- | --- | --- |
| WEST VIRGINIA | --- | --- | --- | --- |
| WISCONSIN | --- | --- | --- | --- |
| WYOMING | --- | --- | --- | --- |

TABLE 3.3 (CONTINUED)

## 1828 PRESIDENTIAL ELECTION

| JACKSON (DEMOCRAT) | ADAMS (NATL REPUB) | (OTHER) | TOTAL VOTE CAST |
|---|---|---|---|
| 16736 | 1878 | 4 | 18618 |
| --- | --- | --- | --- |
| --- | --- | --- | --- |
| --- | --- | --- | --- |
| --- | --- | --- | --- |
| --- | --- | --- | --- |
| 4448 | 13829 | 1101 | 19378 |
| --- | --- | --- | --- |
| --- | --- | --- | --- |
| --- | --- | --- | --- |
| --- | --- | --- | --- |
| --- | --- | --- | --- |
| --- | --- | --- | --- |
| 9560 | 4662 | 0 | 14222 |
| 22201 | 17009 | 0 | 39210 |
| --- | --- | --- | --- |
| --- | --- | --- | --- |
| 39308 | 31468 | 0 | 70776 |
| 4605 | 4082 | 0 | 8687 |
| 13927 | 20773 | 89 | 34789 |
| 22782 | 23014 | 0 | 45796 |
| 6012 | 29836 | 3226 | 39074 |
| --- | --- | --- | --- |
| --- | --- | --- | --- |
| 6763 | 1581 | 0 | 8344 |
| 8232 | 3422 | 0 | 11654 |
| --- | --- | --- | --- |
| --- | --- | --- | --- |
| --- | --- | --- | --- |
| 20212 | 23823 | 0 | 44035 |
| 21809 | 23753 | 8 | 45570 |
| --- | --- | --- | --- |
| 139412 | 131563 | 0 | 270975 |
| 37814 | 13918 | 15 | 51747 |
| --- | --- | --- | --- |
| 67596 | 63453 | 0 | 131049 |
| --- | --- | --- | --- |
| --- | --- | --- | --- |
| 101457 | 50763 | 0 | 152220 |
| 820 | 2755 | 5 | 3580 |
| --- | --- | --- | --- |
| --- | --- | --- | --- |
| --- | --- | --- | --- |
| --- | --- | --- | --- |
| --- | --- | --- | --- |
| 8350 | 24363 | 120 | 32833 |
| 26854 | 12070 | 0 | 38924 |
| --- | --- | --- | --- |
| --- | --- | --- | --- |
| --- | --- | --- | --- |
| --- | --- | --- | --- |

TABLE 3.3 (CONTINUED)

## 1832 PRESIDENTIAL ELECTION

| | JACKSON (DEMOCRAT) | CLAY (NATL REPUB) | (OTHER) | TOTAL VOTE CAST |
|---|---|---|---|---|
| ALABAMA | 14286 | 5 | 0 | 14291 |
| ALASKA | --- | --- | --- | --- |
| ARIZONA | --- | --- | --- | --- |
| ARKANSAS | --- | --- | --- | --- |
| CALIFORNIA | --- | --- | --- | --- |
| COLORADO | --- | --- | --- | --- |
| CONNECTICUT | 11269 | 18155 | 3409 | 32833 |
| DELAWARE | 4110 | 4276 | 0 | 8386 |
| DIST OF COLUMBIA | --- | --- | --- | --- |
| FLORIDA | --- | --- | --- | --- |
| GEORGIA | --- | --- | --- | --- |
| HAWAII | --- | --- | --- | --- |
| IDAHO | --- | --- | --- | --- |
| ILLINOIS | 14609 | 6745 | 127 | 21481 |
| INDIANA | 31652 | 25473 | 27 | 57152 |
| IOWA | --- | --- | --- | --- |
| KANSAS | --- | --- | --- | --- |
| KENTUCKY | 36292 | 43449 | 0 | 79741 |
| LOUISIANA | 3908 | 2429 | 0 | 6337 |
| MAINE | 33978 | 27331 | 844 | 62153 |
| MARYLAND | 19156 | 19160 | 0 | 38316 |
| MASSACHUSETTS | 13933 | 31963 | 21723 | 67619 |
| MICHIGAN | --- | --- | --- | --- |
| MINNESOTA | --- | --- | --- | --- |
| MISSISSIPPI | 5750 | 0 | 0 | 5750 |
| MISSOURI | --- | --- | --- | --- |
| MONTANA | --- | --- | --- | --- |
| NEBRASKA | --- | --- | --- | --- |
| NEVADA | --- | --- | --- | --- |
| NEW HAMPSHIRE | 24855 | 18938 | 0 | 43793 |
| NEW JERSEY | 23826 | 23466 | 468 | 47760 |
| NEW MEXICO | --- | --- | --- | --- |
| NEW YORK | 168497 | 154896 | 0 | 323393 |
| NORTH CAROLINA | 25261 | 4538 | 0 | 29799 |
| NORTH DAKOTA | --- | --- | --- | --- |
| OHIO | 81246 | 76566 | 538 | 158350 |
| OKLAHOMA | --- | --- | --- | --- |
| OREGON | --- | --- | --- | --- |
| PENNSYLVANIA | 90973 | 0 | 66706 | 157679 |
| RHODE ISLAND | 2051 | 2871 | 825 | 5747 |
| SOUTH CAROLINA | --- | --- | --- | --- |
| SOUTH DAKOTA | --- | --- | --- | --- |
| TENNESSEE | 28078 | 1347 | 0 | 29425 |
| TEXAS | --- | --- | --- | --- |
| UTAH | --- | --- | --- | --- |
| VERMONT | 7865 | 11161 | 13318 | 32344 |
| VIRGINIA | 34243 | 11436 | 3 | 45682 |
| WASHINGTON | --- | --- | --- | --- |
| WEST VIRGINIA | --- | --- | --- | --- |
| WISCONSIN | --- | --- | --- | --- |
| WYOMING | --- | --- | --- | --- |

TABLE 3.3 (CONTINUED)

## 1836 PRESIDENTIAL ELECTION

| VAN BUREN (DEMOCRAT) | HARRISON (WHIG) * | (OTHER) | TOTAL VOTE CAST |
|---|---|---|---|
| 20638 | 16658 | 0 | 37296 |
| --- | --- | --- | --- |
| --- | --- | --- | --- |
| 2380 | 1334 | 0 | 3714 |
| --- | --- | --- | --- |
| --- | --- | --- | --- |
| 19294 | 18799 | 0 | 38093 |
| 4154 | 4736 | 5 | 8895 |
| --- | --- | --- | --- |
| --- | --- | --- | --- |
| 22778 | 24481 | 0 | 47259 |
| --- | --- | --- | --- |
| --- | --- | --- | --- |
| 18369 | 15220 | 0 | 33589 |
| 33084 | 41339 | 0 | 74423 |
| --- | --- | --- | --- |
| --- | --- | --- | --- |
| 33229 | 36861 | 0 | 70090 |
| 3842 | 3583 | 0 | 7425 |
| 14803 | 22825 | 1112 | 38740 |
| 22267 | 25852 | 0 | 48119 |
| 33486 | 41201 | 45 | 74732 |
| --- | --- | --- | --- |
| --- | --- | --- | --- |
| 10297 | 9782 | 0 | 20079 |
| 11341 | 7377 | 0 | 18718 |
| --- | --- | --- | --- |
| --- | --- | --- | --- |
| --- | --- | --- | --- |
| 18697 | 6228 | 0 | 24925 |
| 25592 | 26137 | 0 | 51729 |
| --- | --- | --- | --- |
| 166795 | 138548 | 0 | 305343 |
| 26631 | 23521 | 1 | 50153 |
| --- | --- | --- | --- |
| 97122 | 105809 | 0 | 202931 |
| --- | --- | --- | --- |
| --- | --- | --- | --- |
| 91466 | 87235 | 0 | 178701 |
| 2962 | 2710 | 1 | 5673 |
| --- | --- | --- | --- |
| --- | --- | --- | --- |
| 26170 | 36027 | 0 | 62197 |
| --- | --- | --- | --- |
| --- | --- | --- | --- |
| 14040 | 20994 | 65 | 35099 |
| 30556 | 23384 | 5 | 53945 |
| --- | --- | --- | --- |
| --- | --- | --- | --- |
| --- | --- | --- | --- |
| --- | --- | --- | --- |

*FOR CONVENIENCE, THE DATA FOR ALL THREE WHIG CANDIDATES WHO CONTESTED THE 1836 ELECTION ARE LISTED IN THIS COLUMN. THE WHIG PARTY ENDORSED REGIONAL CANDIDATES, AND ONLY ONE WHIG CANDIDATE RAN IN EACH STATE. WILLIAM HENRY HARRISON RAN IN 15 STATES, HUGH L. WHITE IN 9, AND DANIEL WEBSTER IN 1.

TABLE 3.3 (CONTINUED)

## 1840 PRESIDENTIAL ELECTION

|  | VAN BUREN (DEMOCRAT) | HARRISON (WHIG) | (OTHER) | TOTAL VOTE CAST |
|---|---|---|---|---|
| ALABAMA | 33996 | 28515 | 0 | 62511 |
| ALASKA | --- | --- | --- | --- |
| ARIZONA | --- | --- | --- | --- |
| ARKANSAS | 6679 | 5160 | 0 | 11839 |
| CALIFORNIA | --- | --- | --- | --- |
| COLORADO | --- | --- | --- | --- |
| CONNECTICUT | 25281 | 31598 | 0 | 56879 |
| DELAWARE | 4872 | 5967 | 13 | 10852 |
| DIST OF COLUMBIA | --- | --- | --- | --- |
| FLORIDA | --- | --- | --- | --- |
| GEORGIA | 31983 | 40339 | 0 | 72322 |
| HAWAII | --- | --- | --- | --- |
| IDAHO | --- | --- | --- | --- |
| ILLINOIS | 47441 | 45574 | 160 | 93175 |
| INDIANA | 51696 | 65280 | 629 | 117605 |
| IOWA | --- | --- | --- | --- |
| KANSAS | --- | --- | --- | --- |
| KENTUCKY | 32616 | 58488 | 0 | 91104 |
| LOUISIANA | 7616 | 11296 | 0 | 18912 |
| MAINE | 46190 | 46612 | 0 | 92802 |
| MARYLAND | 28752 | 33528 | 0 | 62280 |
| MASSACHUSETTS | 52355 | 72852 | 1618 | 126825 |
| MICHIGAN | 21096 | 22933 | 0 | 44029 |
| MINNESOTA | --- | --- | --- | --- |
| MISSISSIPPI | 17010 | 19515 | 0 | 36525 |
| MISSOURI | 29969 | 22954 | 0 | 52923 |
| MONTANA | --- | --- | --- | --- |
| NEBRASKA | --- | --- | --- | --- |
| NEVADA | --- | --- | --- | --- |
| NEW HAMPSHIRE | 32774 | 26310 | 872 | 59956 |
| NEW JERSEY | 31034 | 33351 | 69 | 64454 |
| NEW MEXICO | --- | --- | --- | --- |
| NEW YORK | 212733 | 226001 | 2809 | 441543 |
| NORTH CAROLINA | 34168 | 46567 | 0 | 80735 |
| NORTH DAKOTA | --- | --- | --- | --- |
| OHIO | 123944 | 148043 | 903 | 272890 |
| OKLAHOMA | --- | --- | --- | --- |
| OREGON | --- | --- | --- | --- |
| PENNSYLVANIA | 143672 | 144023 | 0 | 287695 |
| RHODE ISLAND | 3263 | 5213 | 155 | 8631 |
| SOUTH CAROLINA | --- | --- | --- | --- |
| SOUTH DAKOTA | --- | --- | --- | --- |
| TENNESSEE | 47951 | 60194 | 0 | 108145 |
| TEXAS | --- | --- | --- | --- |
| UTAH | --- | --- | --- | --- |
| VERMONT | 18006 | 32440 | 336 | 50782 |
| VIRGINIA | 43757 | 42637 | 0 | 86394 |
| WASHINGTON | --- | --- | --- | --- |
| WEST VIRGINIA | --- | --- | --- | --- |
| WISCONSIN | --- | --- | --- | --- |
| WYOMING | --- | --- | --- | --- |

TABLE 3.3 (CONTINUED)

## 1844 PRESIDENTIAL ELECTION

|  | POLK (DEMOCRAT) | CLAY (WHIG) | BIRNEY (LIBERTY) | (OTHER) | TOTAL VOTE CAST |
|---|---|---|---|---|---|
| ALABAMA | 37401 | 26002 | 0 | 0 | 63403 |
| ALASKA | --- | --- | --- | --- | --- |
| ARIZONA | --- | --- | --- | --- | --- |
| ARKANSAS | 9546 | 5604 | 0 | 0 | 15150 |
| CALIFORNIA | --- | --- | --- | --- | --- |
| COLORADO | --- | --- | --- | --- | --- |
| CONNECTICUT | 29841 | 32832 | 1943 | 0 | 64616 |
| DELAWARE | 5970 | 6271 | 0 | 6 | 12247 |
| DIST OF COLUMBIA | --- | --- | --- | --- | --- |
| FLORIDA | --- | --- | --- | --- | --- |
| GEORGIA | 44147 | 42100 | 0 | 0 | 86247 |
| HAWAII | --- | --- | --- | --- | --- |
| IDAHO | --- | --- | --- | --- | --- |
| ILLINOIS | 58795 | 45854 | 3469 | 939 | 109057 |
| INDIANA | 70183 | 67866 | 2108 | 0 | 140157 |
| IOWA | --- | --- | --- | --- | --- |
| KANSAS | --- | --- | --- | --- | --- |
| KENTUCKY | 51988 | 61249 | 0 | 0 | 113237 |
| LOUISIANA | 13782 | 13083 | 0 | 0 | 26865 |
| MAINE | 45719 | 34378 | 4836 | 0 | 84933 |
| MARYLAND | 32706 | 35984 | 0 | 0 | 68690 |
| MASSACHUSETTS | 53039 | 67062 | 10830 | 1106 | 132037 |
| MICHIGAN | 27737 | 24185 | 3638 | 0 | 55560 |
| MINNESOTA | --- | --- | --- | --- | --- |
| MISSISSIPPI | 25846 | 19158 | 0 | 0 | 45004 |
| MISSOURI | 41322 | 31200 | 0 | 0 | 72522 |
| MONTANA | --- | --- | --- | --- | --- |
| NEBRASKA | --- | --- | --- | --- | --- |
| NEVADA | --- | --- | --- | --- | --- |
| NEW HAMPSHIRE | 27160 | 17866 | 4161 | 0 | 49187 |
| NEW JERSEY | 37495 | 38318 | 131 | 0 | 75944 |
| NEW MEXICO | --- | --- | --- | --- | --- |
| NEW YORK | 237588 | 232482 | 15812 | 0 | 485882 |
| NORTH CAROLINA | 39287 | 43232 | 0 | 2 | 82521 |
| NORTH DAKOTA | --- | --- | --- | --- | --- |
| OHIO | 149127 | 155091 | 8082 | 0 | 312300 |
| OKLAHOMA | --- | --- | --- | --- | --- |
| OREGON | --- | --- | --- | --- | --- |
| PENNSYLVANIA | 167311 | 161195 | 3139 | 0 | 331645 |
| RHODE ISLAND | 4867 | 7322 | 0 | 5 | 12194 |
| SOUTH CAROLINA | --- | --- | --- | --- | --- |
| SOUTH DAKOTA | --- | --- | --- | --- | --- |
| TENNESSEE | 59917 | 60040 | 0 | 0 | 119957 |
| TEXAS | --- | --- | --- | --- | --- |
| UTAH | --- | --- | --- | --- | --- |
| VERMONT | 18041 | 26770 | 3954 | 0 | 48765 |
| VIRGINIA | 50679 | 44860 | 0 | 0 | 95539 |
| WASHINGTON | --- | --- | --- | --- | --- |
| WEST VIRGINIA | --- | --- | --- | --- | --- |
| WISCONSIN | --- | --- | --- | --- | --- |
| WYOMING | --- | --- | --- | --- | --- |

TABLE 3.3 (CONTINUED)

## 1848 PRESIDENTIAL ELECTION

| | CASS (DEMOCRAT) | TAYLOR (WHIG) | VAN BUREN (FREE SOIL) | (OTHER) | TOTAL VOTE CAST |
|---|---|---|---|---|---|
| ALABAMA | 31173 | 30482 | 0 | 4 | 61659 |
| ALASKA | --- | --- | --- | --- | --- |
| ARIZONA | --- | --- | --- | --- | --- |
| ARKANSAS | 9301 | 7587 | 0 | 0 | 16888 |
| CALIFORNIA | --- | --- | --- | --- | --- |
| COLORADO | --- | --- | --- | --- | --- |
| CONNECTICUT | 27051 | 30318 | 5005 | 24 | 62398 |
| DELAWARE | 5910 | 6440 | 82 | 0 | 12432 |
| DIST OF COLUMBIA | --- | --- | --- | --- | --- |
| FLORIDA | 3083 | 4120 | 0 | 0 | 7203 |
| GEORGIA | 44785 | 47532 | 0 | 0 | 92317 |
| HAWAII | --- | --- | --- | --- | --- |
| IDAHO | --- | --- | --- | --- | --- |
| ILLINOIS | 55952 | 52853 | 15702 | 89 | 124596 |
| INDIANA | 74695 | 69668 | 8031 | 0 | 152394 |
| IOWA | 11238 | 9930 | 1103 | 0 | 22271 |
| KANSAS | --- | --- | --- | --- | --- |
| KENTUCKY | 49720 | 67145 | 0 | 0 | 116865 |
| LOUISIANA | 15379 | 18487 | 0 | 0 | 33866 |
| MAINE | 40195 | 35273 | 12157 | 0 | 87625 |
| MARYLAND | 34528 | 37702 | 129 | 0 | 72359 |
| MASSACHUSETTS | 35281 | 61072 | 38333 | 62 | 134748 |
| MICHIGAN | 30742 | 23947 | 10393 | 0 | 65082 |
| MINNESOTA | --- | --- | --- | --- | --- |
| MISSISSIPPI | 26545 | 25911 | 0 | 0 | 52456 |
| MISSOURI | 40077 | 32671 | 0 | 0 | 72748 |
| MONTANA | --- | --- | --- | --- | --- |
| NEBRASKA | --- | --- | --- | --- | --- |
| NEVADA | --- | --- | --- | --- | --- |
| NEW HAMPSHIRE | 27763 | 14781 | 7560 | 0 | 50104 |
| NEW JERSEY | 36901 | 40015 | 829 | 0 | 77745 |
| NEW MEXICO | --- | --- | --- | --- | --- |
| NEW YORK | 114319 | 218583 | 120497 | 2545 | 455944 |
| NORTH CAROLINA | 35772 | 44054 | 0 | 26 | 79852 |
| NORTH DAKOTA | --- | --- | --- | --- | --- |
| OHIO | 154782 | 138656 | 35523 | 0 | 328961 |
| OKLAHOMA | --- | --- | --- | --- | --- |
| OREGON | --- | --- | --- | --- | --- |
| PENNSYLVANIA | 172186 | 185730 | 11176 | 0 | 369092 |
| RHODE ISLAND | 3613 | 6705 | 726 | 5 | 11049 |
| SOUTH CAROLINA | --- | --- | --- | --- | --- |
| SOUTH DAKOTA | --- | --- | --- | --- | --- |
| TENNESSEE | 58142 | 64321 | 0 | 0 | 122463 |
| TEXAS | 11644 | 5281 | 0 | 75 | 17000 |
| UTAH | --- | --- | --- | --- | --- |
| VERMONT | 10943 | 23117 | 13837 | 0 | 47897 |
| VIRGINIA | 46739 | 45265 | 0 | 0 | 92004 |
| WASHINGTON | --- | --- | --- | --- | --- |
| WEST VIRGINIA | --- | --- | --- | --- | --- |
| WISCONSIN | 15001 | 13747 | 10418 | 0 | 39166 |
| WYOMING | --- | --- | --- | --- | --- |

TABLE 3.3 (CONTINUED)

## 1852 PRESIDENTIAL ELECTION

| | PIERCE (DEMOCRAT) | SCOTT (WHIG) | HALE (FREE SOIL) | (OTHER) | TOTAL VOTE CAST |
|---|---|---|---|---|---|
| ALABAMA | 26881 | 15061 | 0 | 2205 | 44147 |
| ALASKA | --- | --- | --- | --- | --- |
| ARIZONA | --- | --- | --- | --- | --- |
| ARKANSAS | 12173 | 7404 | 0 | 0 | 19577 |
| CALIFORNIA | 40721 | 35972 | 61 | 56 | 76810 |
| COLORADO | --- | --- | --- | --- | --- |
| CONNECTICUT | 33249 | 30359 | 3161 | 12 | 66781 |
| DELAWARE | 6318 | 6293 | 62 | 0 | 12673 |
| DIST OF COLUMBIA | --- | --- | --- | --- | --- |
| FLORIDA | 4318 | 2875 | 0 | 0 | 7193 |
| GEORGIA | 34705 | 16660 | 0 | 11135 | 62500 |
| HAWAII | --- | --- | --- | --- | --- |
| IDAHO | --- | --- | --- | --- | --- |
| ILLINOIS | 80378 | 64733 | 9863 | 0 | 154974 |
| INDIANA | 95340 | 80907 | 6929 | 0 | 183176 |
| IOWA | 17763 | 15856 | 1606 | 139 | 35364 |
| KANSAS | --- | --- | --- | --- | --- |
| KENTUCKY | 53949 | 57428 | 266 | 0 | 111643 |
| LOUISIANA | 18647 | 17255 | 0 | 0 | 35902 |
| MAINE | 41609 | 32543 | 8030 | 0 | 82182 |
| MARYLAND | 40022 | 35077 | 21 | 0 | 75120 |
| MASSACHUSETTS | 44569 | 52683 | 28023 | 1828 | 127103 |
| MICHIGAN | 41842 | 33860 | 7237 | 0 | 82939 |
| MINNESOTA | --- | --- | --- | --- | --- |
| MISSISSIPPI | 26896 | 17558 | 0 | 0 | 44454 |
| MISSOURI | 38817 | 29984 | 0 | 0 | 68801 |
| MONTANA | --- | --- | --- | --- | --- |
| NEBRASKA | --- | --- | --- | --- | --- |
| NEVADA | --- | --- | --- | --- | --- |
| NEW HAMPSHIRE | 28503 | 15486 | 6546 | 0 | 50535 |
| NEW JERSEY | 44301 | 38551 | 336 | 738 | 83926 |
| NEW MEXICO | --- | --- | --- | --- | --- |
| NEW YORK | 262083 | 234882 | 25329 | 0 | 522294 |
| NORTH CAROLINA | 39788 | 39043 | 0 | 60 | 78891 |
| NORTH DAKOTA | --- | --- | --- | --- | --- |
| OHIO | 169193 | 152577 | 31133 | 0 | 352903 |
| OKLAHOMA | --- | --- | --- | --- | --- |
| OREGON | --- | --- | --- | --- | --- |
| PENNSYLVANIA | 198568 | 179182 | 8500 | 1670 | 387920 |
| RHODE ISLAND | 8735 | 7626 | 644 | 0 | 17005 |
| SOUTH CAROLINA | --- | --- | --- | --- | --- |
| SOUTH DAKOTA | --- | --- | --- | --- | --- |
| TENNESSEE | 56900 | 58586 | 0 | 0 | 115486 |
| TEXAS | 14857 | 5356 | 0 | 10 | 20223 |
| UTAH | --- | --- | --- | --- | --- |
| VERMONT | 13044 | 22173 | 8621 | 0 | 43838 |
| VIRGINIA | 73872 | 58732 | 0 | 0 | 132604 |
| WASHINGTON | --- | --- | --- | --- | --- |
| WEST VIRGINIA | --- | --- | --- | --- | --- |
| WISCONSIN | 33658 | 22240 | 8842 | 0 | 64740 |
| WYOMING | --- | --- | --- | --- | --- |

TABLE 3.3 (CONTINUED)

## 1856 PRESIDENTIAL ELECTION

| | BUCHANAN (DEMOCRAT) | FREMONT (REPUBLICAN) | FILLMORE (WHIG) | (OTHER) | TOTAL VOTE CAST |
|---|---|---|---|---|---|
| ALABAMA | 46739 | 0 | 28552 | 0 | 75291 |
| ALASKA | --- | --- | --- | --- | --- |
| ARIZONA | --- | --- | --- | --- | --- |
| ARKANSAS | 21910 | --- | 10732 | --- | 32642 |
| CALIFORNIA | 53342 | 20704 | 36195 | 14 | 110255 |
| COLORADO | --- | --- | --- | --- | --- |
| CONNECTICUT | 35028 | 42717 | 2615 | 0 | 80360 |
| DELAWARE | 8004 | 310 | 6275 | 9 | 14598 |
| DIST OF COLUMBIA | --- | --- | --- | --- | --- |
| FLORIDA | 6358 | 0 | 4833 | 0 | 11191 |
| GEORGIA | 56581 | 0 | 42439 | 0 | 99020 |
| HAWAII | --- | --- | --- | --- | --- |
| IDAHO | --- | --- | --- | --- | --- |
| ILLINOIS | 105528 | 96275 | 37531 | 0 | 239334 |
| INDIANA | 118670 | 94375 | 22356 | 0 | 235401 |
| IOWA | 37568 | 45073 | 9669 | 0 | 92310 |
| KANSAS | --- | --- | --- | --- | --- |
| KENTUCKY | 74642 | 0 | 67416 | 0 | 142058 |
| LOUISIANA | 22164 | 0 | 20709 | 0 | 42873 |
| MAINE | 39140 | 67279 | 3270 | 0 | 109689 |
| MARYLAND | 39123 | 285 | 47452 | 0 | 86860 |
| MASSACHUSETTS | 39244 | 108172 | 19626 | 3006 | 170048 |
| MICHIGAN | 52136 | 71762 | 1660 | 0 | 125558 |
| MINNESOTA | --- | --- | --- | --- | --- |
| MISSISSIPPI | 35456 | 0 | 24191 | 0 | 59647 |
| MISSOURI | 57964 | 0 | 48522 | 0 | 106486 |
| MONTANA | --- | --- | --- | --- | --- |
| NEBRASKA | --- | --- | --- | --- | --- |
| NEVADA | --- | --- | --- | --- | --- |
| NEW HAMPSHIRE | 31891 | 37473 | 410 | 0 | 69774 |
| NEW JERSEY | 46943 | 28338 | 24115 | 0 | 99396 |
| NEW MEXICO | --- | --- | --- | --- | --- |
| NEW YORK | 195878 | 276004 | 124604 | 0 | 596486 |
| NORTH CAROLINA | 48243 | 0 | 36720 | 0 | 84963 |
| NORTH DAKOTA | --- | --- | --- | --- | --- |

| | | | | | |
|---|---|---|---|---|---|
| OHIO | 170874 | 187497 | 28121 | 148 | 386640 |
| OKLAHOMA | -- | -- | -- | -- | -- |
| OREGON | -- | -- | -- | -- | -- |
| PENNSYLVANIA | 230772 | 147963 | 82202 | -- | 460937 |
| RHODE ISLAND | 6680 | 11467 | 1675 | -- | 19822 |
| SOUTH CAROLINA | -- | -- | -- | -- | -- |
| SOUTH DAKOTA | 69704 | 0 | 63878 | 0 | 133582 |
| TENNESSEE | 31995 | 0 | 16010 | 0 | 48005 |
| TEXAS | -- | -- | -- | -- | -- |
| UTAH | 10569 | 39561 | 545 | -- | 50675 |
| VERMONT | 90083 | 0 | 60150 | 0 | 150233 |
| VIRGINIA | -- | -- | -- | -- | -- |
| WASHINGTON | -- | -- | -- | -- | -- |
| WEST VIRGINIA | 52843 | 67090 | 580 | 0 | 120513 |
| WISCONSIN | -- | -- | -- | -- | -- |
| WYOMING | -- | -- | -- | -- | -- |

## 1860 PRESIDENTIAL ELECTION

| | DOUGLAS (NORTH DEM) | LINCOLN (REPUBLICAN) | BRECKENRIDGE (SOUTH DEM) | BELL (CONST UNION) | (OTHER) | TOTAL VOTE CAST |
|---|---|---|---|---|---|---|
| ALABAMA | 13618 | 0 | 48669 | 27835 | 0 | 90122 |
| ALASKA | --- | --- | --- | --- | --- | --- |
| ARIZONA | --- | --- | --- | --- | --- | --- |
| ARKANSAS | 5357 | 0 | 28732 | 20063 | 0 | 54152 |
| CALIFORNIA | 37999 | 38733 | 33969 | 9111 | 15 | 119827 |
| COLORADO | --- | --- | --- | --- | --- | --- |
| CONNECTICUT | 15431 | 43488 | 14372 | 1528 | 0 | 74819 |
| DELAWARE | 1066 | 3822 | 7339 | 3888 | 0 | 16115 |
| DIST OF COLUMBIA | --- | --- | --- | --- | --- | --- |
| FLORIDA | 223 | 0 | 8277 | 4801 | 0 | 13301 |
| GEORGIA | 11581 | 0 | 52176 | 42960 | 0 | 106717 |
| HAWAII | --- | --- | --- | --- | --- | --- |
| IDAHO | --- | --- | --- | --- | --- | --- |
| ILLINOIS | 160215 | 172171 | 2331 | 4914 | 35 | 339666 |
| INDIANA | 115509 | 139033 | 12295 | 5306 | 0 | 272143 |
| IOWA | 55639 | 70302 | 1035 | 1763 | 0 | 128739 |
| KANSAS | --- | --- | --- | --- | --- | --- |
| KENTUCKY | 53163 | 1364 | 25638 | 66051 | 0 | 146216 |
| LOUISIANA | 7625 | 0 | 22681 | 2204 | 0 | 50510 |

TABLE 3.3 (CONTINUED)

### 1860 PRESIDENTIAL ELECTION

| | DOUGLAS (NORTH DEM) | LINCOLN (REPUBLICAN) | BRECKENRIDGE (SOUTH DEM) | BELL (CONST UNION) | (OTHER) | TOTAL VOTE CAST |
|---|---|---|---|---|---|---|
| MAINE | 29693 | 62811 | 6368 | 2046 | 0 | 100918 |
| MARYLAND | 5966 | 2294 | 42482 | 41760 | 0 | 92502 |
| MASSACHUSETTS | 34370 | 106684 | 6163 | 22331 | 328 | 169876 |
| MICHIGAN | 65057 | 88481 | 805 | 415 | 0 | 154758 |
| MINNESOTA | 11920 | 22069 | 748 | 50 | 17 | 34804 |
| MISSISSIPPI | 3282 | 0 | 40768 | 25045 | 0 | 69095 |
| MISSOURI | 58801 | 17028 | 31362 | 58372 | 0 | 165563 |
| MONTANA | --- | --- | --- | --- | --- | --- |
| NEBRASKA | --- | --- | --- | --- | --- | --- |
| NEVADA | --- | --- | --- | --- | --- | --- |
| NEW HAMPSHIRE | 25887 | 37519 | 2125 | 412 | 0 | 65943 |
| NEW JERSEY | 0 | 58324 | 62801 | 0 | 0 | 121125 |
| NEW MEXICO | --- | --- | --- | --- | --- | --- |
| NEW YORK | 312510 | 362646 | 0 | 0 | 0 | 675156 |
| NORTH CAROLINA | 2737 | 0 | 48846 | 45129 | 0 | 96712 |
| NORTH DAKOTA | --- | --- | --- | --- | --- | --- |
| OHIO | 187421 | 231709 | 11406 | 12194 | 136 | 442866 |
| OKLAHOMA | --- | --- | --- | --- | --- | --- |
| OREGON | 4136 | 5329 | 5075 | 218 | 0 | 14758 |
| PENNSYLVANIA | 16765 | 268030 | 178871 | 12776 | 0 | 476442 |
| RHODE ISLAND | 7707 | 12244 | 0 | 0 | 0 | 19951 |
| SOUTH CAROLINA | --- | --- | --- | --- | --- | --- |
| SOUTH DAKOTA | --- | --- | --- | --- | --- | --- |
| TENNESSEE | 11281 | 0 | 65097 | 69728 | 0 | 146106 |
| TEXAS | 18 | 0 | 15383 | 47454 | 0 | 62855 |
| UTAH | --- | --- | --- | --- | --- | --- |
| VERMONT | 8649 | 33808 | 218 | 1969 | 0 | 44644 |
| VIRGINIA | 16198 | 1887 | 74325 | 74481 | 0 | 166891 |
| WASHINGTON | --- | --- | --- | --- | --- | --- |
| WEST VIRGINIA | --- | --- | --- | --- | --- | --- |
| WISCONSIN | 65021 | 86110 | 887 | 161 | 0 | 152179 |
| WYOMING | --- | --- | --- | --- | --- | --- |

TABLE 3.3 (CONTINUED)

## 1864 PRESIDENTIAL ELECTION

| | MCCLELLAN (DEMOCRAT) | LINCOLN (REPUBLICAN) | (OTHER) | TOTAL VOTE CAST |
|---|---|---|---|---|
| ALABAMA * | --- | --- | --- | --- |
| ALASKA | --- | --- | --- | --- |
| ARIZONA | --- | --- | --- | --- |
| ARKANSAS * | --- | --- | --- | --- |
| CALIFORNIA | 43837 | 62053 | 0 | 105890 |
| COLORADO | --- | --- | --- | --- |
| CONNECTICUT | 42285 | 44673 | 0 | 86958 |
| DELAWARE | 8767 | 8155 | 0 | 16922 |
| DIST OF COLUMBIA | --- | --- | --- | --- |
| FLORIDA ** | --- | --- | --- | --- |
| GEORGIA * | --- | --- | --- | --- |
| HAWAII | --- | --- | --- | --- |
| IDAHO | --- | --- | --- | --- |
| ILLINOIS | 158724 | 189512 | 0 | 348236 |
| INDIANA | 130230 | 149887 | 0 | 280117 |
| IOWA | 49089 | 83858 | 0 | 132947 |
| KANSAS | 3836 | 17089 | 655 | 21580 |
| KENTUCKY | 64301 | 27787 | 0 | 92088 |
| LOUISIANA * | --- | --- | --- | --- |
| MAINE | 46992 | 67805 | 0 | 114797 |
| MARYLAND | 32739 | 40153 | 0 | 72892 |
| MASSACHUSETTS | 48745 | 126742 | 6 | 175493 |
| MICHIGAN | 74146 | 91133 | 0 | 165279 |
| MINNESOTA | 17376 | 25031 | 26 | 42433 |
| MISSISSIPPI ** | --- | --- | --- | --- |
| MISSOURI | 31596 | 72750 | 0 | 104346 |
| MONTANA | --- | --- | --- | --- |
| NEBRASKA | --- | --- | --- | --- |
| NEVADA | 6594 | 9826 | 0 | 16420 |
| NEW HAMPSHIRE | 33034 | 36596 | 0 | 69630 |
| NEW JERSEY | 68020 | 60724 | 0 | 128744 |
| NEW MEXICO | --- | --- | --- | --- |
| NEW YORK | 361986 | 368735 | 0 | 730721 |
| NORTH CAROLINA * | --- | --- | --- | --- |
| NORTH DAKOTA | --- | --- | --- | --- |
| OHIO | 205609 | 265674 | 0 | 471283 |
| OKLAHOMA | --- | --- | --- | --- |
| OREGON | 8457 | 9888 | 5 | 18350 |
| PENNSYLVANIA | 277443 | 296292 | 0 | 573735 |
| RHODE ISLAND | 8718 | 14349 | 0 | 23067 |
| SOUTH CAROLINA * | --- | --- | --- | --- |
| SOUTH DAKOTA | --- | --- | --- | --- |
| TENNESSEE * | --- | --- | --- | --- |
| TEXAS ** | --- | --- | --- | --- |
| UTAH | --- | --- | --- | --- |
| VERMONT | 13321 | 42419 | 0 | 55740 |
| VIRGINIA ** | --- | --- | --- | --- |
| WASHINGTON | --- | --- | --- | --- |
| WEST VIRGINIA | 11078 | 23799 | 0 | 34877 |
| WISCONSIN | 65884 | 83458 | 0 | 149342 |
| WYOMING | --- | --- | --- | --- |

* THESE SOUTHERN STATES SECEDED FROM THE UNION IN 1861, PRIOR TO THE CIVIL WAR, AND THERFORE DID NOT PARTICIPATE IN THE 1864 PRESIDENTIAL ELECTION.

** THESE SOUTHERN STATES WERE NOT IN THE UNION IN 1864 AND HAD NOT REJOINED THE UNION BY THE 1868 ELECTION.

TABLE 3.3 (CONTINUED)

## 1868 PRESIDENTIAL ELECTION

| SEYMOUR (DEMOCRAT) | GRANT (REPUBLICAN) | (OTHER) | TOTAL VOTE CAST) |
|---|---|---|---|
| 72921 | 76667 | 6 | 149594 |
| --- | --- | --- | --- |
| --- | --- | --- | --- |
| 19078 | 22112 | 0 | 41190 |
| 54068 | 54588 | 0 | 108656 |
| --- | --- | --- | --- |
| 47781 | 50789 | 0 | 98570 |
| 10957 | 7614 | 0 | 18571 |
| --- | --- | --- | --- |
| --- | --- | --- | --- |
| 102707 | 57109 | 0 | 159816 |
| --- | --- | --- | --- |
| --- | --- | --- | --- |
| 199116 | 250304 | 0 | 449420 |
| 166980 | 176548 | 0 | 343528 |
| 74040 | 120399 | 0 | 194439 |
| 13600 | 30027 | 3 | 43630 |
| 115889 | 39566 | 0 | 155455 |
| 80225 | 33263 | 0 | 113488 |
| 42460 | 70502 | 0 | 112962 |
| 62357 | 30438 | 0 | 92795 |
| 59103 | 136379 | 26 | 195508 |
| 97069 | 128563 | 0 | 225632 |
| 28075 | 43545 | 0 | 71620 |
| --- | --- | --- | --- |
| 65628 | 86860 | 0 | 152488 |
| --- | --- | --- | --- |
| 5519 | 9772 | 0 | 15291 |
| 5215 | 6474 | 0 | 11689 |
| 30575 | 37718 | 11 | 68304 |
| 83001 | 80132 | 0 | 163133 |
| --- | --- | --- | --- |
| 429883 | 419888 | 0 | 849771 |
| 84559 | 96939 | 0 | 181498 |
| --- | --- | --- | --- |
| 238506 | 280159 | 0 | 518665 |
| --- | --- | --- | --- |
| 11125 | 10961 | ' 0 | 22086 |
| 313382 | 342280 | 0 | 655662 |
| 6494 | 13017 | 0 | 19511 |
| 45237 | 62301 | 0 | 107538 |
| --- | --- | --- | --- |
| 26129 | 56628 | 0 | 82757 |
| --- | --- | --- | --- |
| --- | --- | --- | --- |
| 12051 | 44173 | 0 | 56224 |
| --- | --- | --- | --- |
| --- | --- | --- | --- |
| 20306 | 29015 | 0 | 49321 |
| 84708 | 108920 | 0 | 193628 |
| --- | --- | --- | --- |

TABLE 3.3 (CONTINUED)

## 1872 PRESIDENTIAL ELECTION

| | GREELEY (DEMOCRAT) | GRANT (REPUBLICAN) | (OTHER) | TOTAL VOTE CAST |
|---|---|---|---|---|
| ALABAMA | 79444 | 90272 | 0 | 169716 |
| ALASKA | --- | --- | --- | --- |
| ARIZONA | --- | --- | --- | --- |
| ARKANSAS | 37927 | 41373 | 0 | 79300 |
| CALIFORNIA | 41778 | 54007 | 0 | 95785 |
| COLORADO | --- | --- | --- | --- |
| CONNECTICUT | 45685 | 50307 | 0 | 95992 |
| DELAWARE | 10205 | 11129 | 488 | 21822 |
| DIST OF COLUMBIA | --- | --- | --- | --- |
| FLORIDA | 15427 | 17763 | 0 | 33190 |
| GEORGIA | 76356 | 62550 | 4004 | 142910 |
| HAWAII | --- | --- | --- | --- |
| IDAHO | --- | --- | --- | --- |
| ILLINOIS | 188035 | 241936 | 3058 | 433029 |
| INDIANA | 163632 | 186147 | 1417 | 351196 |
| IOWA | 71189 | 131566 | 13610 | 216365 |
| KANSAS | 32970 | 66805 | 737 | 100512 |
| KENTUCKY | 99995 | 88766 | 2374 | 191135 |
| LOUISIANA | 57029 | 71663 | 0 | 128692 |
| MAINE | 29097 | 61426 | 0 | 90523 |
| MARYLAND | 67687 | 66760 | 0 | 134447 |
| MASSACHUSETTS | 59195 | 133455 | 0 | 192650 |
| MICHIGAN | 81530 | 138768 | 4146 | 224444 |
| MINNESOTA | 35131 | 56040 | 168 | 91339 |
| MISSISSIPPI | 47282 | 82175 | 0 | 129457 |
| MISSOURI | 151434 | 119196 | 2429 | 273059 |
| MONTANA | --- | --- | --- | --- |
| NEBRASKA | 7603 | 18329 | 0 | 25932 |
| NEVADA | 6236 | 8413 | 0 | 14649 |
| NEW HAMPSHIRE | 31425 | 37168 | 313 | 68906 |
| NEW JERSEY | 76456 | 91656 | 606 | 168718 |
| NEW MEXICO | --- | --- | --- | --- |
| NEW YORK | 387282 | 440738 | 1655 | 829675 |
| NORTH CAROLINA | 70130 | 94772 | 261 | 165163 |
| NORTH DAKOTA | --- | --- | --- | --- |
| OHIO | 244320 | 281852 | 3263 | 529435 |
| OKLAHOMA | --- | --- | --- | --- |
| OREGON | 7742 | 11818 | 547 | 20107 |
| PENNSYLVANIA | 212040 | 349589 | 0 | 561629 |
| RHODE ISLAND | 5329 | 13665 | 0 | 18994 |
| SOUTH CAROLINA | 22699 | 72290 | 463 | 95452 |
| SOUTH DAKOTA | --- | --- | --- | --- |
| TENNESSEE | 93391 | 85655 | 0 | 179046 |
| TEXAS | 67675 | 47910 | 115 | 115700 |
| UTAH | --- | --- | --- | --- |
| VERMONT | 10927 | 41481 | 553 | 52961 |
| VIRGINIA | 91647 | 93463 | 85 | 185195 |
| WASHINGTON | --- | --- | --- | --- |
| WEST VIRGINIA | 29532 | 32320 | 615 | 62467 |
| WISCONSIN | 86390 | 105012 | 853 | 192255 |
| WYOMING | --- | --- | --- | --- |

TABLE 3.3 (CONTINUED)

## 1876 PRESIDENTIAL ELECTION

| TILDEN (DEMOCRAT) | HAYES (REPUBLICAN) | (OTHER) | TOTAL VOTE CAST |
|---|---|---|---|
| 102989 | 68708 | 2 | 171699 |
| --- | --- | --- | --- |
| --- | --- | --- | --- |
| 58086 | 38649 | 211 | 96946 |
| 76460 | 79258 | 66 | 155784 |
| --- | --- | --- | --- |
| 61927 | 59033 | 1174 | 122134 |
| 13381 | 10752 | 0 | 24133 |
| --- | --- | --- | --- |
| 22927 | 23849 | 0 | 46776 |
| 130157 | 50533 | 0 | 180690 |
| --- | --- | --- | --- |
| --- | --- | --- | --- |
| 258611 | 278232 | 17525 | 554368 |
| 213529 | 208011 | 9533 | 431073 |
| 112121 | 171326 | 9951 | 293398 |
| 37902 | 78324 | 7908 | 124134 |
| 160060 | 97568 | 2998 | 260626 |
| 70508 | 75315 | 0 | 145823 |
| 49917 | 66300 | 828 | 117045 |
| 91779 | 71980 | 0 | 163759 |
| 108777 | 150063 | 779 | 259619 |
| 141665 | 166901 | 9860 | 318426 |
| 48799 | 72962 | 2399 | 124160 |
| 112173 | 52603 | 0 | 164776 |
| 202086 | 145027 | 3497 | 350610 |
| --- | --- | --- | --- |
| 17343 | 31915 | 0 | 49258 |
| 9308 | 10383 | 0 | 19691 |
| 38510 | 41540 | 93 | 80143 |
| 115962 | 103517 | 714 | 220193 |
| --- | --- | --- | --- |
| 521949 | 489207 | 4347 | 1015503 |
| 125427 | 108484 | 0 | 233911 |
| --- | --- | --- | --- |
| 323182 | 330698 | 4770 | 658650 |
| --- | --- | --- | --- |
| 14157 | 15207 | 509 | 29873 |
| 366204 | 384157 | 8612 | 758973 |
| 10712 | 15787 | 0 | 26499 |
| 90897 | 91786 | 0 | 182683 |
| --- | --- | --- | --- |
| 133177 | 89566 | 0 | 222743 |
| 106372 | 45013 | 46 | 151431 |
| --- | --- | --- | --- |
| 20254 | 44092 | 114 | 64460 |
| 140770 | 95518 | 0 | 236288 |
| --- | --- | --- | --- |
| 56546 | 41997 | 1104 | 99647 |
| 123922 | 130050 | 3204 | 257176 |
| --- | --- | --- | --- |

TABLE 3.3 (CONTINUED)

## 1880 PRESIDENTIAL ELECTION

| | HANCOCK (DEMOCRAT) | GARFIELD (REPUBLICAN) | WEAVER (GREENBACK) | (OTHER) | TOTAL VOTE CAST |
|---|---|---|---|---|---|
| ALABAMA | 91130 | 56350 | 4422 | 0 | 151902 |
| ALASKA | --- | --- | --- | --- | --- |
| ARIZONA | --- | --- | --- | --- | --- |
| ARKANSAS | 60489 | 41661 | 4079 | 1543 | 107772 |
| CALIFORNIA | 80426 | 80282 | 3381 | 129 | 164218 |
| COLORADO | 24647 | 27450 | 1435 | 14 | 53546 |
| CONNECTICUT | 64411 | 67071 | 868 | 448 | 132798 |
| DELAWARE | 15181 | 14148 | 129 | 0 | 29458 |
| DIST OF COLUMBIA | --- | --- | --- | --- | --- |
| FLORIDA | 27964 | 23654 | 0 | 0 | 51618 |
| GEORGIA | 102981 | 54470 | 0 | 0 | 157451 |
| HAWAII | --- | --- | --- | --- | --- |
| IDAHO | --- | --- | --- | --- | --- |
| ILLINOIS | 277321 | 318036 | 26358 | 590 | 622305 |
| INDIANA | 225523 | 232169 | 13066 | 0 | 470758 |
| IOWA | 105845 | 183904 | 32327 | 1064 | 323140 |
| KANSAS | 59789 | 121520 | 19710 | 35 | 201054 |
| KENTUCKY | 148875 | 106490 | 11506 | 233 | 267104 |
| LOUISIANA | 65047 | 38978 | 437 | 0 | 104462 |
| MAINE | 65211 | 74052 | 4409 | 231 | 143903 |
| MARYLAND | 93706 | 78515 | 0 | 0 | 172221 |
| MASSACHUSETTS | 111960 | 165198 | 4548 | 799 | 282505 |
| MICHIGAN | 131596 | 185335 | 34895 | 1250 | 353076 |
| MINNESOTA | 53314 | 93939 | 3267 | 286 | 150806 |
| MISSISSIPPI | 75750 | 34844 | 5797 | 677 | 117068 |
| MISSOURI | 208600 | 153647 | 35042 | 0 | 397289 |
| MONTANA | --- | --- | --- | --- | --- |
| NEBRASKA | 28523 | 54979 | 3853 | 0 | 87355 |
| NEVADA | 9611 | 8732 | 0 | 0 | 18343 |
| NEW HAMPSHIRE | 40797 | 44856 | 528 | 180 | 86361 |
| NEW JERSEY | 122565 | 120555 | 2617 | 191 | 245928 |
| NEW MEXICO | --- | --- | --- | --- | --- |
| NEW YORK | 534511 | 555544 | 12373 | 1517 | 1103945 |

TABLE 3.3 (CONTINUED)

## 1880 PRESIDENTIAL ELECTION

| | HANCOCK (DEMOCRAT) | GARFIELD (REPUBLICAN) | WEAVER (GREENBACK) | (OTHER) | TOTAL VOTE CAST |
|---|---|---|---|---|---|
| NORTH CAROLINA | 124204 | 115616 | 1126 | 0 | 240946 |
| NORTH DAKOTA | --- | --- | --- | --- | --- |
| OHIO | 340867 | 375048 | 6456 | 2613 | 724984 |
| OKLAHOMA | --- | --- | --- | --- | --- |
| OREGON | 19955 | 20619 | 267 | 0 | 40841 |
| PENNSYLVANIA | 407428 | 444704 | 20667 | 1984 | 874783 |
| RHODE ISLAND | 10779 | 18195 | 236 | 25 | 29235 |
| SOUTH CAROLINA | 111236 | 57954 | 567 | 36 | 169793 |
| SOUTH DAKOTA | --- | --- | --- | --- | --- |
| TENNESSEE | 129569 | 107677 | 6017 | 0 | 243263 |
| TEXAS | 156010 | 50217 | 27405 | 0 | 233632 |
| UTAH | --- | --- | --- | --- | --- |
| VERMONT | 18316 | 45567 | 1215 | 0 | 65098 |
| VIRGINIA | 128083 | 83533 | 0 | 0 | 211616 |
| WASHINGTON | --- | --- | --- | --- | --- |
| WEST VIRGINIA | 57390 | 46243 | 9008 | 0 | 112641 |
| WISCONSIN | 114650 | 144406 | 7986 | 160 | 267202 |
| WYOMING | --- | --- | --- | --- | --- |

## 1884 PRESIDENTIAL ELECTION

| | CLEVELAND (DEMOCRAT) | BLAINE (REPUBLICAN) | SAINTJOHN (PROHIBITION) | BUTLER (GREENBACK) | (OTHER) | TOTAL VOTE CAST |
|---|---|---|---|---|---|---|
| ALABAMA | 92736 | 59444 | 610 | 762 | 72 | 153624 |
| ALASKA | --- | --- | --- | --- | --- | --- |
| ARIZONA | --- | --- | --- | --- | --- | --- |
| ARKANSAS | 72734 | 51198 | 0 | 1847 | 0 | 125779 |
| CALIFORNIA | 89288 | 102369 | 2965 | 2037 | 329 | 196988 |
| COLORADO | 27723 | 36084 | 756 | 1956 | 0 | 66519 |
| CONNECTICUT | 67167 | 65879 | 2493 | 1682 | 0 | 137221 |
| DELAWARE | 16957 | 12953 | 64 | 10 | 0 | 29984 |
| DIST OF COLUMBIA | --- | --- | --- | --- | --- | --- |
| FLORIDA | 31769 | 28031 | 72 | 0 | 118 | 59990 |
| GEORGIA | 94667 | 48603 | 195 | 145 | 0 | 143610 |

TABLE 3.3 (CONTINUED)

| | | | | | | |
|---|---|---|---|---|---|---|
| HAWAII | --- | --- | --- | --- | --- | --- |
| IDAHO | --- | --- | --- | --- | --- | --- |
| ILLINOIS | 312351 | 337469 | 12074 | 10776 | 0 | 672670 |
| INDIANA | 244989 | 238466 | 0 | 8194 | 0 | 491649 |
| IOWA | 177316 | 197089 | 1499 | | 1297 | 377201 |
| KANSAS | 90111 | 154410 | 4311 | 16341 | 468 | 265641 |
| KENTUCKY | 152961 | 118690 | 3139 | 1691 | 0 | 276481 |
| LOUISIANA | 62594 | 46347 | 338 | 120 | 0 | 109399 |
| MAINE | 52153 | 72217 | 2160 | 3955 | 6 | 130491 |
| MARYLAND | 96866 | 85748 | 2827 | 578 | 0 | 186019 |
| MASSACHUSETTS | 122352 | 146724 | 9923 | 24382 | 2 | 303383 |
| MICHIGAN | 149835 | 192669 | 18403 | 42252 | 0 | 403159 |
| MINNESOTA | 70065 | 111685 | 4684 | 3583 | 0 | 190017 |
| MISSISSIPPI | 77653 | 43035 | 0 | 0 | 0 | 120688 |
| MISSOURI | 236023 | 203081 | 2164 | 0 | 0 | 441268 |
| MONTANA | --- | --- | --- | --- | --- | --- |
| NEBRASKA | 54391 | 76912 | 2899 | 0 | 0 | 134202 |
| NEVADA | 5577 | 7176 | 0 | 26 | 0 | 12779 |
| NEW HAMPSHIRE | 39198 | 43254 | 1580 | 554 | 0 | 84586 |
| NEW JERSEY | 127747 | 123436 | 6156 | 3486 | 28 | 260853 |
| NEW MEXICO | --- | --- | --- | --- | --- | --- |
| NEW YORK | 563048 | 562001 | 24999 | 16955 | 0 | 1167003 |
| NORTH CAROLINA | 142905 | 125021 | 430 | 0 | 0 | 268356 |
| NORTH DAKOTA | --- | --- | --- | --- | --- | --- |
| OHIO | 368280 | 400092 | 11069 | 5179 | 0 | 784620 |
| OKLAHOMA | --- | --- | --- | --- | --- | --- |
| OREGON | 24598 | 26845 | 479 | 0 | 761 | 52683 |
| PENNSYLVANIA | 394772 | 472792 | 15154 | 16992 | 0 | 899710 |
| RHODE ISLAND | 12391 | 19030 | 928 | 422 | 0 | 32771 |
| SOUTH CAROLINA | 69845 | 21730 | 0 | 0 | 1237 | 92812 |
| SOUTH DAKOTA | --- | --- | --- | --- | --- | --- |
| TENNESSEE | 133770 | 124101 | 1150 | 957 | 0 | 259978 |
| TEXAS | 223209 | 91234 | 3489 | 3310 | 0 | 321242 |
| UTAH | --- | --- | --- | --- | --- | --- |
| VERMONT | 17331 | 39514 | 1752 | 785 | 27 | 59409 |
| VIRGINIA | 145491 | 139356 | 130 | 0 | 0 | 284977 |
| WASHINGTON | --- | --- | --- | --- | --- | --- |
| WEST VIRGINIA | 67311 | 63096 | 939 | 799 | 0 | 132145 |
| WISCONSIN | 146447 | 161155 | 7651 | 4594 | 0 | 319847 |
| WYOMING | --- | --- | --- | --- | --- | --- |

TABLE 3.3 (CONTINUED)

## 1888 PRESIDENTIAL ELECTION

| | CLEVELAND (DEMOCRAT) | HARRISON (REPUBLICAN) | FISK (PROHIBITION) | STREETER (UNION LABOR) | (OTHER) | TOTAL VOTE CAST |
|---|---|---|---|---|---|---|
| ALABAMA | 117314 | 57177 | 594 | 0 | 0 | 175085 |
| ALASKA | --- | --- | --- | --- | --- | --- |
| ARIZONA | --- | --- | --- | --- | --- | --- |
| ARKANSAS | 86062 | 59752 | 614 | 10630 | 0 | 157058 |
| CALIFORNIA | 117729 | 124816 | 5761 | 0 | 3033 | 251339 |
| COLORADO | 37549 | 50772 | 2182 | 1265 | 178 | 91946 |
| CONNECTICUT | 74920 | 74584 | 4234 | 240 | 0 | 153978 |
| DELAWARE | 16414 | 12950 | 399 | 0 | 1 | 29764 |
| DIST OF COLUMBIA | --- | --- | --- | --- | --- | --- |
| FLORIDA | 39557 | 26529 | 414 | 0 | 0 | 66500 |
| GEORGIA | 100493 | 40499 | 1808 | 136 | 0 | 142936 |
| HAWAII | --- | --- | --- | --- | --- | --- |
| IDAHO | --- | --- | --- | --- | --- | --- |
| ILLINOIS | 348351 | 370475 | 21703 | 7134 | 150 | 747813 |
| INDIANA | 260990 | 263366 | 9939 | 2693 | 0 | 536988 |
| IOWA | 179876 | 211607 | 3550 | 9105 | 556 | 404694 |
| KANSAS | 102739 | 182845 | 6774 | 37838 | 937 | 331133 |
| KENTUCKY | 183830 | 155138 | 5223 | 677 | 0 | 344868 |
| LOUISIANA | 85032 | 30660 | 160 | 39 | 0 | 115891 |
| MAINE | 50472 | 73730 | 2691 | 1344 | 16 | 128253 |
| MARYLAND | 106188 | 99986 | 4767 | 0 | 0 | 210941 |
| MASSACHUSETTS | 151590 | 183892 | 8701 | 0 | 60 | 344243 |
| MICHIGAN | 213469 | 236387 | 20945 | 4555 | 0 | 475356 |
| MINNESOTA | 104372 | 142492 | 15201 | 1097 | 0 | 263162 |
| MISSISSIPPI | 85451 | 30095 | 240 | 0 | 0 | 115786 |
| MISSOURI | 261943 | 236252 | 4539 | 18625 | 0 | 521359 |
| MONTANA | --- | --- | --- | --- | --- | --- |
| NEBRASKA | 80552 | 108417 | 9435 | 4226 | 0 | 202630 |
| NEVADA | 5303 | 7229 | 41 | 0 | 0 | 12573 |
| NEW HAMPSHIRE | 43382 | 45734 | 1596 | 0 | 58 | 90770 |
| NEW JERSEY | 151493 | 144347 | 7794 | 0 | 0 | 303634 |
| NEW MEXICO | --- | --- | --- | --- | --- | --- |
| NEW YORK | 635965 | 650338 | 30231 | 627 | 2587 | 1319748 |
| NORTH CAROLINA | 147902 | 134784 | 2840 | 0 | 37 | 285563 |
| NORTH DAKOTA | --- | --- | --- | --- | --- | --- |

TABLE 3.3 (CONTINUED)

### 1888 PRESIDENTIAL ELECTION

| | CLEVELAND (DEMOCRAT) | HARRISON (REPUBLICAN) | FISK (PROHIBITION) | STREETER (UNION LABOR) | (OTHER) | TOTAL VOTE CAST |
|---|---|---|---|---|---|---|
| OHIO | 395456 | 416054 | 24356 | 3491 | 0 | 839357 |
| OKLAHOMA | --- | --- | --- | --- | --- | --- |
| OREGON | 26518 | 33291 | 1676 | 0 | 404 | 61889 |
| PENNSYLVANIA | 446633 | 526091 | 20947 | 3873 | 24 | 997568 |
| RHODE ISLAND | 17530 | 21969 | 1251 | 18 | 7 | 40775 |
| SOUTH CAROLINA | 65824 | 13736 | 0 | 0 | 437 | 79997 |
| SOUTH DAKOTA | --- | --- | --- | --- | --- | --- |
| TENNESSEE | 158699 | 138978 | 5969 | 48 | 0 | 303694 |
| TEXAS | 232189 | 88604 | 4739 | 28880 | 0 | 354412 |
| UTAH | --- | --- | --- | --- | --- | --- |
| VERMONT | 16788 | 45193 | 1460 | 0 | 35 | 63476 |
| VIRGINIA | 152004 | 150399 | 1684 | 0 | 0 | 304087 |
| WASHINGTON | --- | --- | --- | --- | --- | --- |
| WEST VIRGINIA | 78677 | 78171 | 1084 | 1508 | 0 | 159440 |
| WISCONSIN | 155232 | 176553 | 14277 | 8552 | 0 | 354614 |
| WYOMING | --- | --- | --- | --- | --- | --- |

### 1892 PRESIDENTIAL ELECTION

| | CLEVELAND (DEMOCRAT) | HARRISON (REPUBLICAN) | BIDWELL (PROHIBITION) | WEAVER (POPULIST) | (OTHER) | TOTAL VOTE CAST |
|---|---|---|---|---|---|---|
| ALABAMA | 138135 | 9167 | 240 | 85178 | 0 | 232720 |
| ALASKA | --- | --- | --- | --- | --- | --- |
| ARIZONA | --- | --- | --- | --- | --- | --- |
| ARKANSAS | 87834 | 47072 | 113 | 11831 | 1267 | 148117 |
| CALIFORNIA | 118151 | 118027 | 8096 | 25311 | 0 | 269585 |
| COLORADO | 0 | 38620 | 1677 | 53584 | 0 | 93881 |
| CONNECTICUT | 82395 | 77030 | 4026 | 809 | 333 | 164593 |
| DELAWARE | 18581 | 18077 | 564 | 0 | 13 | 37235 |
| DIST OF COLUMBIA | --- | --- | --- | --- | --- | --- |
| FLORIDA | 30153 | 0 | 475 | 4843 | 0 | 35471 |
| GEORGIA | 129446 | 48408 | 988 | 41939 | 2345 | 223126 |
| HAWAII | --- | --- | --- | --- | --- | --- |
| IDAHO | 0 | 8599 | 288 | 10520 | 0 | 19407 |

| State | | | | | | |
|---|---|---|---|---|---|---|
| ILLINOIS | 426281 | 399308 | 25871 | 22207 | 0 | 873667 |
| INDIANA | 262740 | 255615 | 13050 | 22208 | 0 | 553613 |
| IOWA | 196367 | 219795 | 6402 | 20595 | 0 | 443159 |
| KANSAS | 0 | 156134 | 4569 | 162888 | 0 | 323591 |
| KENTUCKY | 175461 | 135462 | 6441 | 23500 | 0 | 340864 |
| LOUISIANA | 87926 | 26963 | 0 | 0 | 0 | 114889 |
| MAINE | 48049 | 62936 | 3066 | 2396 | 4 | 116451 |
| MARYLAND | 113866 | 92736 | 5877 | 796 | 0 | 213275 |
| MASSACHUSETTS | 176813 | 202814 | 7539 | 3210 | 652 | 391028 |
| MICHIGAN | 202396 | 222708 | 20857 | 20031 | 925 | 466917 |
| MINNESOTA | 100396 | 122736 | 14117 | 30399 | 0 | 268172 |
| MISSISSIPPI | 40030 | 1398 | 973 | 10118 | 0 | 52519 |
| MISSOURI | 268400 | 227646 | 4333 | 41204 | 0 | 541583 |
| MONTANA | 17690 | 18871 | 562 | 7338 | 0 | 44461 |
| NEBRASKA | 24956 | 87213 | 4902 | 83134 | 0 | 200205 |
| NEVADA | 703 | 2811 | 86 | 7226 | 0 | 10826 |
| NEW HAMPSHIRE | 42081 | 45658 | 1297 | 292 | 0 | 89328 |
| NEW JERSEY | 170987 | 156059 | 8133 | 969 | 1337 | 337485 |
| NEW MEXICO | --- | --- | --- | --- | --- | --- |
| NEW YORK | 654868 | 609350 | 38190 | 16429 | 17956 | 1336793 |
| NORTH CAROLINA | 132951 | 100346 | 2637 | 44336 | 0 | 280270 |
| NORTH DAKOTA | | 17472 | 853 | 17790 | 0 | 36115 |
| OHIO | 404115 | 405187 | 26012 | 14850 | 0 | 850164 |
| OKLAHOMA | --- | --- | --- | --- | --- | --- |
| OREGON | 14243 | 35002 | 2258 | 26875 | 0 | 78378 |
| PENNSYLVANIA | 452264 | 516011 | 25123 | 8714 | 888 | 1003000 |
| RHODE ISLAND | 24336 | 26975 | 1654 | 228 | 3 | 53196 |
| SOUTH CAROLINA | 54680 | 13345 | 0 | 2407 | 72 | 70504 |
| SOUTH DAKOTA | 8894 | 34714 | 4809 | 26552 | 0 | 70160 |
| TENNESSEE | 136468 | 100537 | 2164 | 23918 | 4086 | 265732 |
| TEXAS | 236979 | 70982 | | 96649 | 0 | 410860 |
| UTAH | --- | --- | --- | --- | --- | --- |
| VERMONT | 16325 | 37992 | 1424 | 42 | 10 | 55793 |
| VIRGINIA | 164136 | 113098 | 2729 | 12275 | 0 | 292238 |
| WASHINGTON | 29802 | 36459 | 2542 | 19165 | 0 | 87968 |
| WEST VIRGINIA | 84467 | 80292 | 2153 | 4167 | 0 | 171079 |
| WISCONSIN | 177325 | 171101 | 13136 | 9919 | 0 | 371481 |
| WYOMING | 0 | 8454 | 498 | 7722 | 29 | 16703 |

TABLE 3.3 (CONTINUED)

## 1896 PRESIDENTIAL ELECTION

| | BRYAN (DEMOCRAT) | MCKINLEY (REPUBLICAN) | (OTHER) | TOTAL VOTE CAST |
|---|---|---|---|---|
| ALABAMA | 130298 | 55673 | 8609 | 194580 |
| ALASKA | --- | --- | --- | --- |
| ARIZONA | --- | --- | --- | --- |
| ARKANSAS | 110103 | 37512 | 1781 | 149396 |
| CALIFORNIA | 144877 | 146756 | 6965 | 298598 |
| COLORADO | 161005 | 26271 | 2263 | 189539 |
| CONNECTICUT | 56740 | 110285 | 7369 | 174394 |
| DELAWARE | 16574 | 20450 | 1432 | 38456 |
| DIST OF COLUMBIA | --- | --- | --- | --- |
| FLORIDA | 32756 | 11298 | 2434 | 46488 |
| GEORGIA | 93885 | 59395 | 9200 | 162480 |
| HAWAII | --- | --- | --- | --- |
| IDAHO | 23135 | 6324 | 172 | 29631 |
| ILLINOIS | 465593 | 607130 | 18043 | 1090766 |
| INDIANA | 305538 | 323754 | 7797 | 637089 |
| IOWA | 223744 | 289293 | 8513 | 521550 |
| KANSAS | 173049 | 159484 | 3552 | 336085 |
| KENTUCKY | 217894 | 218171 | 9863 | 445928 |
| LOUISIANA | 77175 | 22037 | 1834 | 101046 |
| MAINE | 34587 | 80403 | 3429 | 118419 |
| MARYLAND | 104150 | 136959 | 9140 | 250249 |
| MASSACHUSETTS | 105474 | 278976 | 16879 | 401329 |
| MICHIGAN | 244087 | 293336 | 8160 | 545583 |
| MINNESOTA | 139735 | 193503 | 8524 | 341762 |
| MISSISSIPPI | 63355 | 4819 | 1417 | 69591 |
| MISSOURI | 363667 | 304940 | 5425 | 674032 |
| MONTANA | 42628 | 10509 | 193 | 53330 |
| NEBRASKA | 115804 | 103064 | 4313 | 223181 |
| NEVADA | 8348 | 1938 | 0 | 10286 |
| NEW HAMPSHIRE | 21650 | 57444 | 4576 | 83670 |
| NEW JERSEY | 133675 | 221367 | 15972 | 371014 |
| NEW MEXICO | --- | --- | --- | --- |
| NEW YORK | 551369 | 819838 | 52669 | 1423876 |
| NORTH CAROLINA | 174408 | 155122 | 1807 | 331337 |
| NORTH DAKOTA | 20686 | 26335 | 370 | 47391 |
| OHIO | 477497 | 525991 | 10807 | 1014295 |
| OKLAHOMA | --- | --- | --- | --- |
| OREGON | 46739 | 48700 | 1896 | 97335 |
| PENNSYLVANIA | 433228 | 728300 | 32827 | 1194355 |
| RHODE ISLAND | 14459 | 37437 | 2889 | 54785 |
| SOUTH CAROLINA | 58801 | 9313 | 824 | 68938 |
| SOUTH DAKOTA | 41225 | 41040 | 672 | 82937 |
| TENNESSEE | 167168 | 148683 | 5052 | 320903 |
| TEXAS | 370308 | 163894 | 6816 | 541018 |
| UTAH | 64607 | 13491 | 0 | 78098 |
| VERMONT | 10637 | 51127 | 2074 | 63838 |
| VIRGINIA | 154708 | 135379 | 4587 | 294674 |
| WASHINGTON | 53314 | 39153 | 1116 | 93583 |
| WEST VIRGINIA | 94480 | 105379 | 1898 | 201757 |
| WISCONSIN | 165523 | 268135 | 13751 | 447409 |
| WYOMING | 10862 | 10072 | 133 | 21067 |

TABLE 3.3 (CONTINUED)

### 1900 PRESIDENTIAL ELECTION

| | BRYAN (DEMOCRAT) | MCKINLEY (REPUBLICAN) | WOOLLEY (PROHIBITION) | (OTHER) | TOTAL VOTE CAST |
|---|---|---|---|---|---|
| ALABAMA | 97129 | 55612 | 2763 | 4188 | 159692 |
| ALASKA | --- | --- | --- | --- | --- |
| ARIZONA | --- | --- | --- | --- | --- |
| ARKANSAS | 81242 | 44800 | 584 | 1340 | 127966 |
| CALIFORNIA | 124985 | 164755 | 5024 | 7554 | 302318 |
| COLORADO | 122705 | 92701 | 3790 | 1699 | 220895 |
| CONNECTICUT | 74014 | 102572 | 1617 | 1992 | 180195 |
| DELAWARE | 18852 | 22535 | 546 | 56 | 41989 |
| DIST OF COLUMBIA | --- | --- | --- | --- | --- |
| FLORIDA | 28273 | 7355 | 2244 | 1777 | 39649 |
| GEORGIA | 81180 | 34260 | 1402 | 4568 | 121410 |
| HAWAII | --- | --- | --- | --- | --- |
| IDAHO | 29484 | 27198 | 857 | 445 | 57984 |
| ILLINOIS | 503061 | 597985 | 17626 | 13226 | 1131898 |
| INDIANA | 309584 | 336063 | 13718 | 4729 | 664094 |
| IOWA | 209261 | 307799 | 9502 | 3783 | 530345 |
| KANSAS | 60187 | 185952 | 3605 | 104023 | 353767 |
| KENTUCKY | 235126 | 227132 | 2890 | 3117 | 468265 |
| LOUISIANA | 53668 | 14234 | 0 | 4 | 67906 |
| MAINE | 36822 | 65412 | 2581 | 878 | 105693 |
| MARYLAND | 122237 | 136151 | 4574 | 1424 | 264386 |
| MASSACHUSETTS | 156997 | 238866 | 6202 | 12739 | 414804 |
| MICHIGAN | 211432 | 316014 | 11804 | 4539 | 543789 |
| MINNESOTA | 112901 | 190461 | 8555 | 4394 | 316311 |
| MISSISSIPPI | 51706 | 5707 | 0 | 1642 | 59055 |
| MISSOURI | 351922 | 314092 | 5965 | 11679 | 683658 |
| MONTANA | 37311 | 25409 | 306 | 830 | 63856 |
| NEBRASKA | 114013 | 121835 | 3655 | 1927 | 241430 |
| NEVADA | 6347 | 3849 | 0 | 0 | 10196 |
| NEW HAMPSHIRE | 35489 | 54799 | 1270 | 806 | 92364 |
| NEW JERSEY | 164808 | 221707 | 7183 | 7352 | 401050 |
| NEW MEXICO | --- | --- | --- | --- | --- |
| NEW YORK | 678462 | 822013 | 22077 | 25491 | 1548043 |
| NORTH CAROLINA | 157733 | 132997 | 990 | 798 | 292518 |

TABLE 3.3 (CONTINUED)

## 1900 PRESIDENTIAL ELECTION

| | BRYAN (DEMOCRAT) | MCKINLEY (REPUBLICAN) | WOOLLEY (PROHIBITION) | (OTHER) | TOTAL VOTE CAST |
|---|---|---|---|---|---|
| NORTH DAKOTA | 20524 | 35898 | 735 | 626 | 57783 |
| OHIO | 474882 | 543918 | 10203 | 11070 | 1040073 |
| OKLAHOMA | --- | --- | --- | --- | --- |
| OREGON | 32810 | 46172 | 2536 | 1733 | 83251 |
| PENNSYLVANIA | 424232 | 712665 | 27908 | 8405 | 1173210 |
| RHODE ISLAND | 19812 | 33784 | 1529 | 1423 | 56548 |
| SOUTH CAROLINA | 47173 | 3525 | 0 | 0 | 50698 |
| SOUTH DAKOTA | 39538 | 54574 | 1541 | 516 | 96169 |
| TENNESSEE | 145240 | 123108 | 3844 | 1668 | 273860 |
| TEXAS | 267945 | 131174 | 2642 | 22573 | 424334 |
| UTAH | 44949 | 47089 | 205 | 828 | 93071 |
| VERMONT | 12849 | 42569 | 383 | 411 | 56212 |
| VIRGINIA | 146079 | 115769 | 2130 | 230 | 264208 |
| WASHINGTON | 44833 | 57455 | 2363 | 2872 | 107523 |
| WEST VIRGINIA | 98807 | 119829 | 1628 | 532 | 220796 |
| WISCONSIN | 159163 | 265760 | 10027 | 7551 | 442501 |
| WYOMING | 10164 | 14482 | 0 | 62 | 24708 |

## 1904 PRESIDENTIAL ELECTION

| | PARKER (DEMOCRAT) | ROOSEVELT (REPUBLICAN) | SWALLOW (PROHIBITION) | DEBS (SOCIALIST) | (OTHER) | TOTAL VOTE CAST |
|---|---|---|---|---|---|---|
| ALABAMA | 79797 | 22472 | 612 | 853 | 5051 | 108785 |
| ALASKA | --- | --- | --- | --- | --- | --- |
| ARIZONA | --- | --- | --- | --- | --- | --- |
| ARKANSAS | 64434 | 46760 | 992 | 1816 | 2326 | 116328 |
| CALIFORNIA | 89294 | 205226 | 7380 | 29535 | 333 | 331768 |
| COLORADO | 100105 | 134661 | 3438 | 4304 | 1159 | 243667 |
| CONNECTICUT | 72909 | 111089 | 1506 | 4543 | 1089 | 191136 |
| DELAWARE | 19347 | 23705 | 607 | 146 | 51 | 43856 |
| DIST OF COLUMBIA | --- | --- | --- | --- | --- | --- |
| FLORIDA | 26449 | 8314 | 0 | 2337 | 1605 | 38705 |
| GEORGIA | 83466 | 24004 | 685 | 196 | 22635 | 130986 |

| | | | | | | |
|---|---:|---:|---:|---:|---:|---:|
| HAWAII | --- | --- | --- | --- | --- | --- |
| IDAHO | 18480 | 47783 | 1013 | 4949 | 352 | 72577 |
| ILLINOIS | 327606 | 632645 | 34770 | 69225 | 12249 | 1076495 |
| INDIANA | 274356 | 368289 | 23496 | 12023 | 4042 | 682206 |
| IOWA | 149141 | 307907 | 11601 | 14847 | 2207 | 485703 |
| KANSAS | 86164 | 213455 | 7306 | 15869 | 6253 | 329047 |
| KENTUCKY | 217170 | 205457 | 6603 | 995 | 3117 | 435946 |
| LOUISIANA | 47708 | 5205 | 0 | 2102 | 0 | 53908 |
| MAINE | 27642 | 65432 | 1510 | 2247 | 337 | 97023 |
| MARYLAND | 109446 | 109497 | 3034 | 13604 | 5 | 224229 |
| MASSACHUSETTS | 165746 | 257813 | 4279 | 8942 | 3658 | 445100 |
| MICHIGAN | 134163 | 361863 | 13312 | 11692 | 2163 | 520443 |
| MINNESOTA | 55187 | 216651 | 6253 | 462 | 3077 | 292860 |
| MISSISSIPPI | 53480 | 3280 | 7191 | 13009 | 1499 | 58721 |
| MISSOURI | 296312 | 321449 | 339 | 5675 | 5900 | 643861 |
| MONTANA | 21816 | 33994 | 6323 | 7412 | 1744 | 63568 |
| NEBRASKA | 52921 | 138558 | 750 | 925 | 20518 | 225732 |
| NEVADA | 3982 | 6864 | 6845 | 1090 | 344 | 12115 |
| NEW HAMPSHIRE | 34071 | 54157 | | 9587 | 83 | 90151 |
| NEW JERSEY | 164566 | 245164 | | | 6085 | 432247 |
| NEW MEXICO | --- | --- | --- | --- | --- | --- |
| NEW YORK | 683981 | 859533 | 20787 | 36883 | 16581 | 1617765 |
| NORTH CAROLINA | 124091 | 82442 | 342 | 124 | 819 | 207818 |
| NORTH DAKOTA | 14273 | 52595 | 1137 | 2009 | 0 | 70014 |
| OHIO | 344674 | 600095 | 19339 | 36260 | 4027 | 1004395 |
| OKLAHOMA | --- | --- | --- | --- | --- | --- |
| OREGON | 17327 | 60309 | 3795 | 7479 | 746 | 89656 |
| PENNSYLVANIA | 337998 | 840949 | 33717 | 21863 | 2211 | 1236738 |
| RHODE ISLAND | 24839 | 41605 | 768 | 956 | 488 | 68656 |
| SOUTH CAROLINA | 53320 | 2570 | 0 | 0 | 0 | 55890 |
| SOUTH DAKOTA | 21969 | 72083 | 2965 | 3138 | 1240 | 101395 |
| TENNESSEE | 131653 | 105363 | 1889 | 1354 | 2491 | 242750 |
| TEXAS | 167088 | 51307 | 3933 | 2788 | 8493 | 233609 |
| UTAH | 33413 | 62446 | 0 | 5767 | 0 | 101626 |
| VERMONT | 9777 | 40459 | 792 | 859 | 1 | 51888 |
| VIRGINIA | 80649 | 48180 | 1379 | 202 | 0 | 130410 |
| WASHINGTON | 28098 | 101540 | 3229 | 10023 | 2261 | 145151 |
| WEST VIRGINIA | 100855 | 132620 | 4599 | 1573 | 339 | 239986 |
| WISCONSIN | 124205 | 280314 | 9872 | 28240 | 809 | 443440 |
| WYOMING | 8930 | 20489 | 208 | 987 | 0 | 30614 |

TABLE 3.3 (CONTINUED)

1908 PRESIDENTIAL ELECTION

| | BRYAN (DEMOCRAT) | TAFT (REPUBLICAN) | CHAPIN (PROHIBITION) | DEBS (SOCIALIST) | (OTHER) | TOTAL VOTE CAST |
|---|---|---|---|---|---|---|
| ALABAMA | 74391 | 25561 | 690 | 1450 | 3060 | 105152 |
| ALASKA | --- | --- | --- | --- | --- | --- |
| ARIZONA | --- | --- | --- | --- | --- | --- |
| ARKANSAS | 87020 | 56684 | 1026 | 5842 | 1273 | 151845 |
| CALIFORNIA | 127492 | 214398 | 11770 | 28659 | 4306 | 386625 |
| COLORADO | 126644 | 123693 | 5559 | 7960 | 2 | 263858 |
| CONNECTICUT | 68255 | 112815 | 2380 | 5113 | 1340 | 189903 |
| DELAWARE | 22055 | 25014 | 670 | 239 | 29 | 48007 |
| DIST OF COLUMBIA | --- | --- | --- | --- | --- | --- |
| FLORIDA | 31104 | 10654 | 1356 | 3747 | 2499 | 49360 |
| GEORGIA | 72350 | 41355 | 1452 | 584 | 16763 | 132504 |
| HAWAII | --- | --- | --- | --- | --- | --- |
| IDAHO | 36162 | 52621 | 1986 | 6400 | 124 | 97293 |
| ILLINOIS | 450810 | 629932 | 29364 | 34711 | 10437 | 1155254 |
| INDIANA | 338262 | 348993 | 18036 | 13476 | 2350 | 721117 |
| IOWA | 200771 | 275210 | 9837 | 8287 | 665 | 494770 |
| KANSAS | 161209 | 197316 | 5030 | 12820 | 68 | 376043 |
| KENTUCKY | 244092 | 235711 | 5885 | 4093 | 938 | 490719 |
| LOUISIANA | 63568 | 8958 | 0 | 2514 | 77 | 75117 |
| MAINE | 35403 | 66987 | 1487 | 1758 | 700 | 106335 |
| MARYLAND | 115908 | 116513 | 3302 | 2323 | 485 | 238531 |
| MASSACHUSETTS | 155533 | 265966 | 4373 | 10778 | 20255 | 456905 |
| MICHIGAN | 174619 | 333313 | 16785 | 11527 | 1880 | 538124 |
| MINNESOTA | 109401 | 195843 | 10114 | 14472 | 424 | 330254 |
| MISSISSIPPI | 60287 | 4363 | 0 | 978 | 1276 | 66904 |
| MISSOURI | 346574 | 347203 | 4209 | 15431 | 2424 | 715841 |
| MONTANA | 29511 | 32471 | 838 | 5920 | 493 | 69233 |
| NEBRASKA | 131099 | 126997 | 5179 | 3524 | 0 | 266799 |
| NEVADA | 11212 | 10775 | 0 | 2103 | 436 | 24526 |
| NEW HAMPSHIRE | 33655 | 53144 | 905 | 1299 | 592 | 89595 |
| NEW JERSEY | 182522 | 265298 | 4930 | 10249 | 4112 | 467111 |
| NEW MEXICO | --- | --- | --- | --- | --- | --- |
| NEW YORK | 667468 | 870070 | 22667 | 38451 | 39694 | 1638350 |
| NORTH CAROLINA | 136928 | 114887 | 354 | 372 | 13 | 252554 |

154

## 1912 PRESIDENTIAL ELECTION

| | WILSON (DEMOCRAT) | TAFT (REPUBLICAN) | CHAPIN (PROHIBITION) | DEBS (SOCIALIST) | ROOSEVELT (PROGRESSIVE) | (OTHER) | TOTAL VOTE CAST |
|---|---|---|---|---|---|---|---|
| NORTH DAKOTA | 32884 | 57680 | 1496 | 2421 | | 43 | 94524 |
| OHIO | 502721 | 572312 | 11402 | 33795 | | 1322 | 1121552 |
| OKLAHOMA | 122362 | 110473 | 0 | 21425 | | 0 | 254260 |
| OREGON | 37792 | 62454 | 2682 | 7322 | | 289 | 110539 |
| PENNSYLVANIA | 448782 | 745779 | 36694 | 33914 | | 2281 | 1267450 |
| RHODE ISLAND | 24706 | 43942 | 1016 | 1365 | | 1288 | 72317 |
| SOUTH CAROLINA | 62288 | 3945 | 0 | 100 | | 46 | 66379 |
| SOUTH DAKOTA | 40266 | 67536 | 4039 | 2846 | | 88 | 114775 |
| TENNESSEE | 135608 | 117977 | 301 | 1870 | | 1424 | 257180 |
| TEXAS | 216662 | 65605 | 1626 | 7779 | | 1241 | 292913 |
| UTAH | 42610 | 61165 | 0 | 4890 | | 92 | 108757 |
| VERMONT | 11496 | 39552 | 799 | 0 | | 833 | 52680 |
| VIRGINIA | 82946 | 52572 | 1111 | 255 | | 181 | 137065 |
| WASHINGTON | 58383 | 106062 | 4700 | 14177 | | 248 | 183570 |
| WEST VIRGINIA | 111410 | 137869 | 5140 | 3679 | | 0 | 258098 |
| WISCONSIN | 166662 | 247744 | 11565 | 28147 | | 320 | 454438 |
| WYOMING | 14918 | 20846 | 66 | 1715 | | 63 | 37608 |
| ALABAMA | 82438 | 9807 | 0 | 3029 | 22685 | 0 | 117959 |
| ALASKA | --- | --- | --- | --- | --- | --- | --- |
| ARIZONA | 10324 | 2986 | 265 | 3163 | 6949 | 0 | 23687 |
| ARKANSAS | 68814 | 25585 | 908 | 8153 | 21644 | 0 | 125104 |
| CALIFORNIA | 283436 | 3847 | 23366 | 79201 | 283610 | 4417 | 677877 |
| COLORADO | 113912 | 58386 | 5063 | 16366 | 71752 | 475 | 265954 |
| CONNECTICUT | 74561 | 68324 | 2068 | 10056 | 34129 | 1266 | 190404 |
| DELAWARE | 22631 | 15997 | 620 | 556 | 8886 | --- | 48690 |
| DIST OF COLUMBIA | --- | --- | --- | --- | --- | --- | --- |
| FLORIDA | 35343 | 4279 | 1854 | 4806 | 4555 | 0 | 50837 |
| GEORGIA | 93087 | 5191 | 149 | 1058 | 21985 | 0 | 121470 |
| HAWAII | --- | --- | --- | --- | --- | --- | --- |
| IDAHO | 33921 | 32810 | 1536 | 11960 | 25527 | 0 | 105754 |
| ILLINOIS | 405048 | 253593 | 15710 | 81278 | 386478 | 4066 | 1146173 |
| INDIANA | 281890 | 151267 | 19249 | 36931 | 162007 | 3130 | 654474 |
| IOWA | 185322 | 119805 | 8440 | 16967 | 161819 | 0 | 492353 |
| KANSAS | 143663 | 74845 | 0 | 26779 | 120210 | 63 | 365560 |
| KENTUCKY | 219484 | 115510 | 3253 | 11646 | 107766 | 1055 | 452714 |

TABLE 3.3 (CONTINUED)

## 1912 PRESIDENTIAL ELECTION

| | WILSON (DEMOCRAT) | TAFT (REPUBLICAN) | CHAPIN (PROHIBITION) | DEBS (SOCIALIST) | ROOSEVELT (PROGRESSIVE) | (OTHER) | TOTAL VOTE CAST |
|---|---|---|---|---|---|---|---|
| LOUISIANA | 60871 | 3833 | 0 | 5261 | 9283 | 0 | 79248 |
| MAINE | 51113 | 26545 | 947 | 2541 | 48495 | 0 | 129641 |
| MARYLAND | 112674 | 54956 | 2244 | 3996 | 57789 | 322 | 231981 |
| MASSACHUSETTS | 173408 | 155948 | 2753 | 12616 | 142228 | 1103 | 488056 |
| MICHIGAN | 150201 | 151434 | 8794 | 23060 | 213243 | 1239 | 547971 |
| MINNESOTA | 106426 | 64334 | 7886 | 27505 | 125856 | 2212 | 334219 |
| MISSISSIPPI | 57324 | 1560 | 0 | 2050 | 3549 | 0 | 64483 |
| MISSOURI | 330746 | 207821 | 5380 | 28466 | 124375 | 1778 | 698566 |
| MONTANA | 28129 | 18575 | 32 | 10811 | 22709 | 0 | 80256 |
| NEBRASKA | 109008 | 54226 | 3383 | 10185 | 72681 | 0 | 249483 |
| NEVADA | 7986 | 3196 | 0 | 3313 | 5620 | 0 | 20115 |
| NEW HAMPSHIRE | 34724 | 32927 | 535 | 1981 | 17794 | 0 | 87961 |
| NEW JERSEY | 178638 | 89066 | 2936 | 15948 | 145679 | 1396 | 433663 |
| NEW MEXICO | 20437 | 17164 | 0 | 2859 | 8347 | 0 | 48807 |
| NEW YORK | 655573 | 455487 | 19455 | 63434 | 390093 | 4273 | 1588315 |
| NORTH CAROLINA | 144407 | 29129 | 118 | 987 | 69135 | 0 | 243776 |
| NORTH DAKOTA | 29549 | 22990 | 1243 | 6966 | 25726 | 0 | 86474 |
| OHIO | 424834 | 278168 | 11511 | 90164 | 229807 | 2630 | 1037114 |
| OKLAHOMA | 119143 | 90726 | 2195 | 41630 | 0 | 0 | 253694 |
| OREGON | 47064 | 34673 | 4360 | 13343 | 37600 | 0 | 137040 |
| PENNSYLVANIA | 395637 | 273360 | 19525 | 83614 | 444894 | 706 | 1217736 |
| RHODE ISLAND | 30412 | 27703 | 616 | 2049 | 16878 | 236 | 77894 |
| SOUTH CAROLINA | 48355 | 536 | 0 | 164 | 1293 | 55 | 50403 |
| SOUTH DAKOTA | 48942 | 0 | 3910 | 4664 | 58811 | 0 | 116327 |
| TENNESSEE | 133021 | 60475 | 832 | 3564 | 54041 | 0 | 251933 |
| TEXAS | 218921 | 28310 | 1701 | 24884 | 26715 | 430 | 300961 |
| UTAH | 36576 | 42013 | 0 | 8999 | 24174 | 510 | 112272 |
| VERMONT | 15350 | 23303 | 1094 | 928 | 22129 | 0 | 62804 |
| VIRGINIA | 90332 | 23288 | 709 | 820 | 21776 | 0 | 136975 |
| WASHINGTON | 86840 | 70445 | 9810 | 40134 | 113698 | 50 | 322799 |
| WEST VIRGINIA | 113097 | 56754 | 4517 | 15248 | 79112 | 1872 | 268728 |
| WISCONSIN | 164230 | 130596 | 8584 | 33476 | 63080 | 9 | 399975 |
| WYOMING | 15310 | 14560 | 421 | 2760 | 9232 | 0 | 42283 |

TABLE 3.3 (CONTINUED)

## 1916 PRESIDENTIAL ELECTION

| | WILSON (DEMOCRAT) | HUGHES (REPUBLICAN) | HANLY (PROHIBITION) | BENSON (SOCIALIST) | (OTHER) | TOTAL VOTE CAST |
|---|---|---|---|---|---|---|
| ALABAMA | 99116 | 28662 | 741 | 1916 | 0 | 130435 |
| ALASKA | --- | --- | --- | --- | --- | --- |
| ARIZONA | 33170 | 20522 | 1153 | 3174 | 0 | 58019 |
| ARKANSAS | 112211 | 48879 | 2015 | 6999 | 0 | 170104 |
| CALIFORNIA | 465936 | 462516 | 27713 | 42898 | 187 | 999250 |
| COLORADO | 177496 | 101388 | 2793 | 9951 | 409 | 292037 |
| CONNECTICUT | 99786 | 106514 | 1789 | 5179 | 606 | 213874 |
| DELAWARE | 24753 | 26011 | 566 | 480 | 0 | 51810 |
| DIST OF COLUMBIA | --- | --- | --- | --- | --- | --- |
| FLORIDA | 55984 | 14611 | 4786 | 5353 | 0 | 80734 |
| GEORGIA | 127754 | 11294 | 0 | 941 | 20692 | 160681 |
| HAWAII | --- | --- | --- | --- | --- | --- |
| IDAHO | 70054 | 55368 | 1127 | 8066 | 0 | 134615 |
| ILLINOIS | 950229 | 1152549 | 26047 | 61394 | 2488 | 2192707 |
| INDIANA | 334063 | 341005 | 16368 | 21860 | 5557 | 718853 |
| IOWA | 221699 | 280439 | 3371 | 10976 | 460 | 516945 |
| KANSAS | 314588 | 277658 | 12882 | 24685 | 0 | 629813 |
| KENTUCKY | 269990 | 241854 | 3039 | 4734 | 461 | 520078 |
| LOUISIANA | 79875 | 6466 | 0 | 284 | 6349 | 92974 |
| MAINE | 64033 | 69508 | 596 | 2177 | 0 | 136314 |
| MARYLAND | 138359 | 117347 | 2903 | 2674 | 756 | 262039 |
| MASSACHUSETTS | 247885 | 268784 | 2993 | 11058 | 1102 | 531822 |
| MICHIGAN | 283993 | 337952 | 8085 | 16012 | 831 | 646873 |
| MINNESOTA | 179155 | 179544 | 7793 | 20117 | 758 | 387367 |
| MISSISSIPPI | 80422 | 4253 | 0 | 1484 | 0 | 86159 |
| MISSOURI | 398032 | 369339 | 3887 | 14612 | 903 | 786773 |
| MONTANA | 101104 | 66933 | 0 | 9634 | 338 | 178009 |
| NEBRASKA | 158827 | 117771 | 2952 | 7141 | 624 | 287315 |
| NEVADA | 17776 | 12127 | 346 | 3065 | 0 | 33314 |
| NEW HAMPSHIRE | 43781 | 43725 | 303 | 1318 | 0 | 89127 |
| NEW JERSEY | 211018 | 268982 | 3182 | 10405 | 855 | 494442 |
| NEW MEXICO | 33693 | 31097 | 112 | 1977 | 0 | 66879 |
| NEW YORK | 759426 | 879238 | 19031 | 45944 | 2666 | 1706305 |
| NORTH CAROLINA | 168383 | 120890 | 55 | 509 | 0 | 289837 |

TABLE 3.3 (CONTINUED)

### 1916 PRESIDENTIAL ELECTION

| | WILSON (DEMOCRAT) | HUGHES (REPUBLICAN) | HANLY (PROHIBITION) | BENSON (SOCIALIST) | (OTHER) | TOTAL VOTE CAST |
|---|---|---|---|---|---|---|
| NORTH DAKOTA | 55206 | 53471 | 997 | 5716 | 0 | 115390 |
| OHIO | 604161 | 514753 | 8085 | 38092 | 0 | 1165091 |
| OKLAHOMA | 148123 | 97233 | 1646 | 45091 | 234 | 292327 |
| OREGON | 120087 | 126813 | 4729 | 9711 | 310 | 261650 |
| PENNSYLVANIA | 521784 | 703823 | 28525 | 42638 | 419 | 1297189 |
| RHODE ISLAND | 40394 | 44858 | 470 | 1914 | 180 | 87816 |
| SOUTH CAROLINA | 61845 | 1550 | 0 | 135 | 420 | 63950 |
| SOUTH DAKOTA | 59191 | 64217 | 1774 | 3760 | 0 | 128942 |
| TENNESSEE | 153280 | 116223 | 145 | 2542 | 0 | 272190 |
| TEXAS | 287415 | 64999 | 1936 | 18960 | 0 | 373310 |
| UTAH | 84145 | 54137 | 149 | 4460 | 254 | 143145 |
| VERMONT | 22708 | 40250 | 709 | 798 | 10 | 64475 |
| VIRGINIA | 101840 | 48384 | 678 | 1056 | 67 | 152025 |
| WASHINGTON | 183388 | 167208 | 6868 | 22800 | 730 | 380994 |
| WEST VIRGINIA | 140403 | 143124 | 0 | 6144 | 0 | 289671 |
| WISCONSIN | 191363 | 220822 | 7318 | 27631 | 0 | 447134 |
| WYOMING | 28376 | 21698 | 373 | 1459 | 0 | 51906 |

### 1920 PRESIDENTIAL ELECTION

| | COX (DEMOCRAT) | HARDING (REPUBLICAN) | DEBS (SOCIALIST) | (OTHER) | TOTAL VOTE CAST |
|---|---|---|---|---|---|
| ALABAMA | 156064 | 74719 | 2402 | 766 | 233951 |
| ALASKA | --- | --- | --- | --- | --- |
| ARIZONA | 29546 | 37016 | 0 | 0 | 66562 |
| ARKANSAS | 107406 | 71107 | 5108 | 0 | 183621 |
| CALIFORNIA | 229191 | 624992 | 64076 | 25672 | 943931 |
| COLORADO | 103721 | 171709 | 7860 | 5705 | 288995 |
| CONNECTICUT | 120721 | 229238 | 10350 | 5209 | 365518 |
| DELAWARE | 39911 | 52858 | 988 | 1107 | 94864 |
| DIST OF COLUMBIA | --- | --- | --- | --- | --- |
| FLORIDA | 89646 | 82261 | 5189 | 13059 | 190155 |
| GEORGIA | 106112 | 42981 | 558 | 0 | 149651 |

| | | | | | |
|---|---|---|---|---|---|
| | --- | --- | --- | --- | --- |
| HAWAII | 46579 | 88975 | 38 | 32 | 135624 |
| IDAHO | 534395 | 1420480 | 74747 | 65093 | 2094715 |
| ILLINOIS | 511364 | 696370 | 24713 | 30527 | 1262974 |
| INDIANA | 227924 | 634674 | 16981 | 15506 | 895085 |
| IOWA | 185464 | 369268 | 15511 | 75 | 570318 |
| KANSAS | 457203 | 451480 | 6409 | 3250 | 918342 |
| KENTUCKY | 87355 | 38539 | 0 | 342 | 126236 |
| LOUISIANA | 69306 | 136535 | 2210 | 310 | 208181 |
| MAINE | 180626 | 236117 | 8876 | 2831 | 428450 |
| MARYLAND | 276691 | 681153 | 32265 | 3607 | 993716 |
| MASSACHUSETTS | 231046 | 755941 | 28446 | 22548 | 1037981 |
| MICHIGAN | 142994 | 519421 | 56106 | 17317 | 735838 |
| MINNESOTA | 69252 | 11527 | 1639 | 0 | 82418 |
| MISSISSIPPI | 574799 | 727252 | 20342 | 9847 | 1332240 |
| MISSOURI | 57746 | 109680 | 0 | 12283 | 179709 |
| MONTANA | 119608 | 247498 | 9600 | 6037 | 382743 |
| NEBRASKA | 9851 | 15479 | 1864 | 0 | 27194 |
| NEVADA | 62662 | 95196 | 1234 | 0 | 159092 |
| NEW HAMPSHIRE | 256887 | 611541 | 27141 | 8314 | 903883 |
| NEW JERSEY | 46668 | 57634 | 0 | 1097 | 105399 |
| NEW MEXICO | 781238 | 1871167 | 203201 | 42907 | 2898513 |
| NEW YORK | 305367 | 232819 | 446 | 17 | 538649 |
| NORTH CAROLINA | 374409 | 158997 | 8273 | 0 | 204679 |
| NORTH DAKOTA | 780037 | 1182022 | 57147 | 2447 | 2021653 |
| OHIO | 215798 | 243465 | 25698 | 0 | 484961 |
| OKLAHOMA | 80019 | 143592 | 9801 | 5110 | 238522 |
| OREGON | 503843 | 1218216 | 70571 | 59987 | 1852617 |
| PENNSYLVANIA | 55062 | 107463 | 4351 | 1105 | 167981 |
| RHODE ISLAND | 64170 | 2244 | 28 | 366 | 66808 |
| SOUTH CAROLINA | 35938 | 109874 | 0 | 35306 | 181118 |
| SOUTH DAKOTA | 206558 | 219229 | 2249 | 0 | 428036 |
| TENNESSEE | 288933 | 114384 | 8122 | 75010 | 486449 |
| TEXAS | 56639 | 81555 | 3159 | 4475 | 145828 |
| UTAH | 20884 | 67964 | 0 | 818 | 89666 |
| VERMONT | 141670 | 87456 | 808 | 1066 | 231000 |
| VIRGINIA | 84298 | 223137 | 8913 | 82357 | 398705 |
| WASHINGTON | 220789 | 282010 | 5609 | 1526 | 509934 |
| WEST VIRGINIA | 113196 | 498576 | 80635 | 8648 | 701055 |
| WISCONSIN | 17429 | 35091 | 0 | 2180 | 54700 |
| WYOMING | | | | | |

TABLE 3.3 (CONTINUED)

## 1924 PRESIDENTIAL ELECTION

| | DAVIS (DEMOCRAT) | COOLIDGE (REPUBLICAN) | LAPOLLETTE (PROGRESSIVE) | (OTHER) | TOTAL VOTE CAST |
|---|---|---|---|---|---|
| ALABAMA | 113138 | 40615 | 8040 | 562 | 162355 |
| ALASKA | --- | --- | --- | --- | --- |
| ARIZONA | 26235 | 30516 | 17210 | 0 | 73961 |
| ARKANSAS | 84759 | 40518 | 13146 | 10 | 138433 |
| CALIFORNIA | 105514 | 733196 | 424649 | 18558 | 1281917 |
| COLORADO | 75238 | 193956 | 57368 | 0 | 326562 |
| CONNECTICUT | 110184 | 246322 | 42416 | 1373 | 402295 |
| DELAWARE | 33445 | 52441 | 4995 | 0 | 90881 |
| DIST OF COLUMBIA | --- | --- | --- | --- | --- |
| FLORIDA | 62083 | 30633 | 8625 | 7813 | 109154 |
| GEORGIA | 123260 | 30300 | 12687 | 0 | 166247 |
| HAWAII | --- | --- | --- | --- | --- |
| IDAHO | 24217 | 72084 | 53664 | 0 | 149965 |
| ILLINOIS | 576975 | 1453321 | 432027 | 7744 | 2470067 |
| INDIANA | 492245 | 703042 | 71700 | 5403 | 1272390 |
| IOWA | 160382 | 537458 | 274448 | 4482 | 976770 |
| KANSAS | 156320 | 407671 | 98462 | 3 | 662456 |
| KENTUCKY | 375543 | 396758 | 38465 | 3093 | 813859 |
| LOUISIANA | 93218 | 24670 | 0 | 4063 | 121951 |
| MAINE | 41964 | 138440 | 11382 | 406 | 192192 |
| MARYLAND | 148072 | 162414 | 48144 | 0 | 358630 |
| MASSACHUSETTS | 280817 | 703476 | 141225 | 4304 | 1129822 |
| MICHIGAN | 152359 | 874631 | 122014 | 11415 | 1160419 |
| MINNESOTA | 55913 | 420759 | 339192 | 6282 | 822146 |
| MISSISSIPPI | 100057 | 8384 | 3448 | 0 | 111889 |
| MISSOURI | 572962 | 648486 | 83996 | 2649 | 1308093 |
| MONTANA | 33867 | 74246 | 66251 | 370 | 174734 |
| NEBRASKA | 137299 | 218985 | 105681 | 1594 | 463559 |
| NEVADA | 5909 | 11243 | 9769 | 0 | 26921 |
| NEW HAMPSHIRE | 57201 | 98575 | 8993 | 0 | 164769 |
| NEW JERSEY | 297743 | 675162 | 109720 | 3454 | 1086079 |
| NEW MEXICO | 48542 | 54745 | 9543 | 0 | 112830 |
| NEW YORK | 950796 | 1820058 | 474913 | 18172 | 3263939 |
| NORTH CAROLINA | 284190 | 190754 | 6651 | 13 | 481608 |

1928 PRESIDENTIAL ELECTION

| STATE | SMITH (DEMOCRAT) | HOOVER (REPUBLICAN) | | (OTHER) | TOTAL VOTE CAST |
|---|---|---|---|---|---|
| NORTH DAKOTA | 13858 | 94931 | 89922 | 370 | 199081 |
| OHIO | 477888 | 1176130 | 358008 | 4271 | 2016297 |
| OKLAHOMA | 255798 | 225756 | 46276 | 0 | 527830 |
| OREGON | 67589 | 142579 | 68403 | 908 | 279479 |
| PENNSYLVANIA | 409192 | 1401481 | 307567 | 26479 | 2144719 |
| RHODE ISLAND | 76606 | 125286 | 7628 | 595 | 210115 |
| SOUTH CAROLINA | 49008 | 1123 | 623 | 1 | 50755 |
| SOUTH DAKOTA | 27214 | 101299 | 75200 | 0 | 203713 |
| TENNESSEE | 159339 | 130831 | 10666 | 194 | 301030 |
| TEXAS | 485443 | 130794 | 42879 | 0 | 659116 |
| UTAH | 46908 | 77327 | 32662 | 0 | 156897 |
| VERMONT | 16124 | 80498 | 5943 | 321 | 102886 |
| VIRGINIA | 139717 | 73328 | 10369 | 189 | 223603 |
| WASHINGTON | 42842 | 220224 | 150727 | 7709 | 421502 |
| WEST VIRGINIA | 257232 | 288635 | 36723 | 1072 | 583662 |
| WISCONSIN | 68096 | 311614 | 453678 | 7359 | 840747 |
| WYOMING | 12868 | 41858 | 25174 | 0 | 79900 |
| ALABAMA | 127796 | 120725 | | 460 | 248981 |
| ALASKA | ---- | ---- | | ---- | ---- |
| ARIZONA | 38537 | 52533 | | 184 | 91254 |
| ARKANSAS | 119195 | 77785 | | 751 | 197731 |
| CALIFORNIA | 614365 | 1147929 | | 34362 | 1796656 |
| COLORADO | 132747 | 252924 | | 4397 | 390068 |
| CONNECTICUT | 252040 | 296614 | | 4371 | 553025 |
| DELAWARE | 35354 | 68860 | | 387 | 104601 |
| DIST OF COLUMBIA | ---- | ---- | | ---- | ---- |
| FLORIDA | 100721 | 144168 | | 7740 | 252629 |
| GEORGIA | 129602 | 63498 | | 36058 | 229158 |
| HAWAII | ---- | ---- | | ---- | ---- |
| IDAHO | 52926 | 97322 | | 1293 | 151541 |
| ILLINOIS | 1312235 | 1770723 | | 24531 | 3107489 |
| INDIANA | 562691 | 848290 | | 10333 | 1421314 |
| IOWA | 379011 | 623570 | | 6608 | 1009189 |
| KANSAS | 193003 | 513672 | | 6524 | 713199 |
| KENTUCKY | 381060 | 558064 | | 1507 | 940631 |

TABLE 3.3 (CONTINUED)

## 1928 PRESIDENTIAL ELECTION

| | SMITH (DEMOCRAT) | HOOVER (REPUBLICAN) | (OTHER) | TOTAL VOTE CAST |
|---|---|---|---|---|
| LOUISIANA | 164655 | 51160 | 0 | 215815 |
| MAINE | 81179 | 179923 | 1065 | 262167 |
| MARYLAND | 223626 | 301479 | 3243 | 528348 |
| MASSACHUSETTS | 792758 | 775566 | 9499 | 1577823 |
| MICHIGAN | 396762 | 965396 | 9924 | 1372082 |
| MINNESOTA | 396451 | 560977 | 13548 | 970976 |
| MISSISSIPPI | 124445 | 26202 | 788 | 151435 |
| MISSOURI | 662684 | 834080 | 4081 | 1500845 |
| MONTANA | 78638 | 113472 | 2267 | 194377 |
| NEBRASKA | 197950 | 345745 | 3433 | 547128 |
| NEVADA | 14090 | 18327 | 0 | 32417 |
| NEW HAMPSHIRE | 80715 | 115404 | 638 | 196757 |
| NEW JERSEY | 616162 | 925285 | 6748 | 1548195 |
| NEW MEXICO | 48211 | 69708 | 158 | 118077 |
| NEW YORK | 2089863 | 2193344 | 122419 | 4405626 |
| NORTH CAROLINA | 286227 | 348923 | 0 | 635150 |
| NORTH DAKOTA | 106648 | 131419 | 1778 | 239845 |
| OHIO | 864210 | 1627546 | 16590 | 2508346 |
| OKLAHOMA | 219174 | 394046 | 5207 | 618427 |
| OREGON | 109223 | 205341 | 5378 | 319942 |
| PENNSYLVANIA | 1067586 | 2055382 | 27644 | 3150612 |
| RHODE ISLAND | 118973 | 117522 | 699 | 237194 |
| SOUTH CAROLINA | 62700 | 3188 | 2717 | 68605 |
| SOUTH DAKOTA | 102660 | 157603 | 1594 | 261857 |
| TENNESSEE | 156169 | 195195 | 660 | 352024 |
| TEXAS | 341458 | 367036 | 850 | 709344 |
| UTAH | 80985 | 94485 | 1000 | 176470 |
| VERMONT | 44440 | 90404 | 347 | 135191 |
| VIRGINIA | 140146 | 164609 | 609 | 305364 |
| WASHINGTON | 156772 | 335503 | 7766 | 500041 |
| WEST VIRGINIA | 263784 | 375551 | 3417 | 642752 |
| WISCONSIN | 450259 | 544205 | 22367 | 1016831 |
| WYOMING | 29299 | 52748 | 788 | 82835 |

## 1932 PRESIDENTIAL ELECTION

| | ROOSEVELT (DEMOCRAT) | HOOVER (REPUBLICAN) | THOMAS (SOCIALIST) | (OTHER) | TOTAL VOTE CAST |
|---|---|---|---|---|---|
| ALABAMA | 207732 | 34647 | 2060 | 689 | 245128 |
| ALASKA | --- | --- | --- | --- | --- |
| ARIZONA | 79264 | 36104 | 2618 | 265 | 118251 |
| ARKANSAS | 186829 | 27465 | 1166 | 1109 | 216569 |
| CALIFORNIA | 1324157 | 847902 | 63299 | 30464 | 2265822 |
| COLORADO | 250151 | 188364 | 13591 | 3582 | 455688 |
| CONNECTICUT | 281632 | 288420 | 20480 | 3651 | 594183 |
| DELAWARE | 54319 | 57073 | 1376 | 133 | 112901 |
| DIST OF COLUMBIA | --- | --- | --- | --- | --- |
| FLORIDA | 206307 | 69170 | 0 | 0 | 275477 |
| GEORGIA | 234118 | 19863 | 461 | 1148 | 255590 |
| HAWAII | --- | --- | --- | --- | --- |
| IDAHO | 109479 | 71312 | 526 | 5151 | 186468 |
| ILLINOIS | 1882304 | 1432756 | 67258 | 25608 | 3407926 |
| INDIANA | 862054 | 677184 | 21388 | 16271 | 1576897 |
| IOWA | 598019 | 414433 | 20467 | 3768 | 1036687 |
| KANSAS | 424204 | 349498 | 18276 | 0 | 791978 |
| KENTUCKY | 580574 | 394716 | 3858 | 3938 | 983086 |
| LOUISIANA | 249418 | 18853 | 533 | 0 | 268804 |
| MAINE | 128907 | 166631 | 2489 | 417 | 298444 |
| MARYLAND | 314314 | 184184 | 10489 | 2067 | 511054 |
| MASSACHUSETTS | 800148 | 736959 | 34305 | 8702 | 1580114 |
| MICHIGAN | 871700 | 739894 | 39205 | 13966 | 1664765 |
| MINNESOTA | 600806 | 363959 | 25476 | 12602 | 1002843 |
| MISSISSIPPI | 140168 | 0 | 675 | 5170 | 146013 |
| MISSOURI | 1025406 | 564713 | 16374 | 3401 | 1609894 |
| MONTANA | 127476 | 78134 | 7902 | 3262 | 216774 |
| NEBRASKA | 359082 | 201177 | 9876 | 0 | 570135 |
| NEVADA | 28756 | 12622 | 0 | 0 | 41378 |
| NEW HAMPSHIRE | 100680 | 103629 | 947 | 264 | 205520 |
| NEW JERSEY | 806394 | 775406 | 42981 | 4719 | 1629500 |
| NEW MEXICO | 95089 | 54146 | 1771 | 522 | 151528 |
| NEW YORK | 2534959 | 1937963 | 177397 | 38295 | 4688614 |
| NORTH CAROLINA | 497566 | 208344 | 5585 | 0 | 711495 |
| NORTH DAKOTA | 178350 | 71772 | 3521 | 2647 | 256290 |
| OHIO | 1301695 | 1227319 | 64094 | 16620 | 2609728 |
| OKLAHOMA | 516468 | 188165 | 0 | 0 | 704633 |
| OREGON | 213871 | 136019 | 15450 | 3411 | 368751 |

TABLE 3.3 (CONTINUED)

### 1932 PRESIDENTIAL ELECTION

| | ROOSEVELT (DEMOCRAT) | HOOVER (REPUBLICAN) | THOMAS (SOCIALIST) | (OTHER) | TOTAL VOTE CAST |
|---|---|---|---|---|---|
| PENNSYLVANIA | 1295948 | 1453540 | 91223 | 18466 | 2859177 |
| RHODE ISLAND | 146604 | 115266 | 3138 | 1162 | 266170 |
| SOUTH CAROLINA | 102347 | 1978 | 82 | 4 | 104411 |
| SOUTH DAKOTA | 183515 | 99212 | 463 | 3333 | 286523 |
| TENNESSEE | 259463 | 126752 | 1796 | 2252 | 390263 |
| TEXAS | 767585 | 97852 | 4416 | 591 | 870444 |
| UTAH | 116749 | 84513 | 4087 | 946 | 206295 |
| VERMONT | 56266 | 78984 | 1533 | 197 | 136980 |
| VIRGINIA | 203979 | 89634 | 2382 | 1944 | 297939 |
| WASHINGTON | 353260 | 208645 | 17080 | 35816 | 614801 |
| WEST VIRGINIA | 405124 | 330731 | 5133 | 2786 | 743774 |
| WISCONSIN | 707410 | 347741 | 53379 | 6270 | 1114800 |
| WYOMING | 54370 | 39583 | 2829 | 180 | 96962 |

### 1936 PRESIDENTIAL ELECTION

| | ROOSEVELT (DEMOCRAT) | LANDON (REPUBLICAN) | LEMKE (UNION) | (OTHER) | TOTAL VOTE CAST |
|---|---|---|---|---|---|
| ALABAMA | 238131 | 35358 | 543 | 1639 | 275671 |
| ALASKA | --- | --- | --- | --- | --- |
| ARIZONA | 86722 | 33433 | 3307 | 701 | 124163 |
| ARKANSAS | 146756 | 32049 | 0 | 613 | 179418 |
| CALIFORNIA | 1766836 | 836431 | 0 | 35119 | 2638386 |
| COLORADO | 294599 | 181267 | 9962 | 2418 | 488246 |
| CONNECTICUT | 382129 | 278685 | 21805 | 8104 | 690723 |
| DELAWARE | 69702 | 54014 | 442 | 3445 | 127603 |
| DIST OF COLUMBIA | --- | --- | --- | --- | --- |
| FLORIDA | 249117 | 78248 | 0 | 0 | 327365 |
| GEORGIA | 255364 | 36943 | 136 | 728 | 293171 |
| HAWAII | --- | --- | --- | --- | --- |
| IDAHO | 125683 | 66232 | 7677 | 0 | 199592 |
| ILLINOIS | 2282999 | 1570393 | 89430 | 12892 | 3955714 |
| INDIANA | 934974 | 691570 | 19407 | 4946 | 1650897 |

| | | | | | |
|---|---|---|---|---|---|
| IOWA | 621756 | 487977 | 29887 | 3317 | 1142937 |
| KANSAS | 464520 | 397727 | 497 | 2770 | 865514 |
| KENTUCKY | 541944 | 369702 | 12532 | 2121 | 926299 |
| LOUISIANA | 292802 | 36697 | 0 | 93 | 329592 |
| MAINE | 126333 | 168823 | 7581 | 1119 | 303856 |
| MARYLAND | 389612 | 231435 | | 3849 | 624896 |
| MASSACHUSETTS | 942716 | 768613 | 118639 | 10389 | 1840357 |
| MICHIGAN | 1016794 | 699733 | 75795 | 12776 | 1805098 |
| MINNESOTA | 698811 | 350461 | 74296 | 6407 | 1129975 |
| MISSISSIPPI | 157333 | | 0 | 4809 | 162142 |
| MISSOURI | 1111043 | 697891 | 14630 | 5071 | 1828635 |
| MONTANA | 159690 | 63598 | 5539 | 1675 | 230502 |
| NEBRASKA | 347445 | 247731 | 12847 | 0 | 608023 |
| NEVADA | 31925 | 11923 | 0 | 0 | 43848 |
| NEW HAMPSHIRE | 1084460 | 104642 | 4819 | 193 | 218114 |
| NEW JERSEY | 1083549 | 719421 | 9405 | 6752 | 1819127 |
| NEW MEXICO | 105848 | 61727 | 924 | 447 | 168946 |
| NEW YORK | 3293222 | 2180670 | 0 | 122506 | 5596398 |
| NORTH CAROLINA | 616141 | 223294 | 36708 | 1109 | 839435 |
| NORTH DAKOTA | 163148 | 72751 | 132212 | 5251 | 273716 |
| OHIO | 1747140 | 1127855 | 0 | 3539 | 3012458 |
| OKLAHOMA | 501069 | 245122 | 21831 | 2751 | 749730 |
| OREGON | 266733 | 122706 | 67478 | 26771 | 414021 |
| PENNSYLVANIA | 2353987 | 1690200 | 19569 | 1340 | 4138436 |
| RHODE ISLAND | 164338 | 125031 | | | 310278 |
| SOUTH CAROLINA | 113791 | 1646 | 10338 | | 115437 |
| SOUTH DAKOTA | 160137 | 125977 | 296 | | 296452 |
| TENNESSEE | 328083 | 146520 | 3193 | 1652 | 476551 |
| TEXAS | 730843 | 104728 | 1121 | 1839 | 840603 |
| UTAH | 150248 | 64555 | 0 | 755 | 216679 |
| VERMONT | 62124 | 81023 | 233 | 542 | 143689 |
| VIRGINIA | 234980 | 98336 | 17463 | 1041 | 334590 |
| WASHINGTON | 459579 | 206885 | 0 | 8404 | 692331 |
| WEST VIRGINIA | 502872 | 325486 | | 2005 | 830363 |
| WISCONSIN | 802984 | 380828 | 60297 | 14451 | 1258560 |
| WYOMING | 62624 | 38739 | 1653 | 366 | 103382 |

TABLE 3.3 (CONTINUED)

## 1940 PRESIDENTIAL ELECTION

| | ROOSEVELT (DEMOCRAT) | WILLKIE (REPUBLICAN) | (OTHER) | TOTAL VOTE CAST |
|---|---|---|---|---|
| ALABAMA | 250723 | 42167 | 1307 | 294197 |
| ALASKA | --- | --- | --- | --- |
| ARIZONA | 95267 | 54030 | 742 | 150039 |
| ARKANSAS | 157258 | 42122 | 1094 | 200474 |
| CALIFORNIA | 1877618 | 1351419 | 39754 | 3268791 |
| COLORADO | 265364 | 279022 | 3874 | 548260 |
| CONNECTICUT | 417621 | 361021 | 2860 | 781502 |
| DELAWARE | 74599 | 61440 | 297 | 136336 |
| DIST OF COLUMBIA | --- | --- | --- | --- |
| FLORIDA | 359334 | 126158 | 0 | 485492 |
| GEORGIA | 265194 | 23934 | 23558 | 312686 |
| HAWAII | --- | --- | --- | --- |
| IDAHO | 127842 | 106509 | 760 | 235111 |
| ILLINOIS | 2149934 | 2047240 | 20104 | 4217278 |
| INDIANA | 874063 | 899466 | 9218 | 1782747 |
| IOWA | 578802 | 632370 | 4260 | 1215432 |
| KANSAS | 364725 | 489169 | 6403 | 860297 |
| KENTUCKY | 557312 | 410384 | 2527 | 970223 |
| LOUISIANA | 319751 | 52446 | 108 | 372305 |
| MAINE | 156478 | 163951 | 411 | 320840 |
| MARYLAND | 384552 | 269534 | 6044 | 660130 |
| MASSACHUSETTS | 1076522 | 939700 | 10771 | 2026993 |
| MICHIGAN | 1032991 | 1039917 | 13021 | 2085929 |
| MINNESOTA | 644196 | 596274 | 10718 | 1251188 |
| MISSISSIPPI | 168267 | 2814 | 4742 | 175823 |
| MISSOURI | 958476 | 871009 | 4244 | 1833729 |
| MONTANA | 145698 | 99579 | 2596 | 247873 |
| NEBRASKA | 263677 | 352201 | 0 | 615878 |
| NEVADA | 31945 | 21229 | 0 | 53174 |
| NEW HAMPSHIRE | 125292 | 110127 | 0 | 235419 |
| NEW JERSEY | 1016404 | 944876 | 12935 | 1974215 |
| NEW MEXICO | 103699 | 79315 | 243 | 183257 |
| NEW YORK | 3251918 | 3027478 | 22200 | 6301596 |
| NORTH CAROLINA | 609015 | 213633 | 0 | 822648 |
| NORTH DAKOTA | 124036 | 154590 | 2149 | 280775 |
| OHIO | 1733139 | 1586773 | 0 | 3319912 |
| OKLAHOMA | 474313 | 348872 | 3027 | 826212 |
| OREGON | 258415 | 219555 | 3230 | 481200 |
| PENNSYLVANIA | 2171035 | 1889848 | 17831 | 4078714 |
| RHODE ISLAND | 182182 | 138653 | 313 | 321148 |
| SOUTH CAROLINA | 95470 | 1864 | 2496 | 99830 |
| SOUTH DAKOTA | 131362 | 177065 | 0 | 308427 |
| TENNESSEE | 351601 | 169153 | 2069 | 522823 |
| TEXAS | 861390 | 201866 | 1771 | 1065027 |
| UTAH | 153833 | 92973 | 389 | 247195 |
| VERMONT | 64269 | 78371 | 422 | 143062 |
| VIRGINIA | 235961 | 109363 | 1284 | 346608 |
| WASHINGTON | 462145 | 322123 | 9565 | 793833 |
| WEST VIRGINIA | 495662 | 372414 | 0 | 868076 |
| WISCONSIN | 704811 | 679206 | 21482 | 1405499 |
| WYOMING | 59287 | 52633 | 320 | 112240 |

TABLE 3.3 (CONTINUED)

## 1944 PRESIDENTIAL ELECTION

| ROOSEVELT (DEMOCRAT) | DEWEY (REPUBLICAN) | (OTHER) | TOTAL VOTE CAST |
|---|---|---|---|
| 198904 | 44478 | 1243 | 244625 |
| --- | --- | --- | --- |
| 80926 | 56287 | 421 | 137634 |
| 148965 | 63556 | 438 | 212959 |
| 1988564 | 1512965 | 19346 | 3520875 |
| 234331 | 268731 | 1977 | 505039 |
| 435146 | 390527 | 6317 | 831990 |
| 68166 | 56747 | 448 | 125361 |
| --- | --- | --- | --- |
| 339377 | 143215 | 0 | 482592 |
| 268187 | 56507 | 3415 | 328109 |
| --- | --- | --- | --- |
| 107399 | 100137 | 785 | 208321 |
| 2079479 | 1939314 | 17268 | 4036061 |
| 781803 | 875891 | 14797 | 1672091 |
| 499876 | 547267 | 5456 | 1052599 |
| 287458 | 442096 | 4222 | 733776 |
| 472589 | 392448 | 2875 | 867912 |
| 281564 | 67750 | 69 | 349383 |
| 140631 | 155434 | 335 | 296400 |
| 315983 | 292150 | 0 | 608133 |
| 1035296 | 921350 | 4019 | 1960665 |
| 1106899 | 1084423 | 13901 | 2205223 |
| 589864 | 527416 | 8224 | 1125504 |
| 150826 | 3739 | 17824 | 172389 |
| 807804 | 761524 | 3166 | 1572494 |
| 112566 | 93163 | 1636 | 207365 |
| 233246 | 329880 | 0 | 563126 |
| 29623 | 24611 | 0 | 54234 |
| 119663 | 109916 | 46 | 229625 |
| 987874 | 961335 | 14552 | 1963761 |
| 81338 | 70559 | 147 | 152044 |
| 3304238 | 2987647 | 24905 | 6316790 |
| 527408 | 263155 | 0 | 790563 |
| 100144 | 118535 | 1503 | 220182 |
| 1570763 | 1582293 | 0 | 3153056 |
| 401549 | 319424 | 1663 | 722636 |
| 248635 | 225365 | 6147 | 480147 |
| 1940481 | 1835054 | 19261 | 3794796 |
| 175356 | 123487 | 433 | 299276 |
| 90601 | 4617 | 8164 | 103382 |
| 96711 | 135365 | 0 | 232076 |
| 308707 | 200311 | 1674 | 510692 |
| 820048 | 191372 | 137266 | 1148686 |
| 150088 | 97833 | 340 | 248261 |
| 53806 | 71420 | 14 | 125240 |
| 242276 | 145243 | 966 | 388485 |
| 486774 | 361689 | 7865 | 856328 |
| 392777 | 322819 | 0 | 715596 |
| 650413 | 674532 | 14207 | 1339152 |
| 49419 | 51921 | 0 | 101340 |

TABLE 3.3 (CONTINUED)

1948 PRESIDENTIAL ELECTION

| | TRUMAN (DEMOCRAT) | DEWEY (REPUBLICAN) | WALLACE (PROGRESSIVE) | THURMOND (STATES RIGHTS) | (OTHER) | TOTAL VOTE CAST |
|---|---|---|---|---|---|---|
| ALABAMA | 0 | 40930 | 1522 | 171272 | 1026 | 214750 |
| ALASKA | -- | -- | -- | -- | -- | -- |
| ARIZONA | 95251 | 77597 | 3310 | 0 | 907 | 177065 |
| ARKANSAS | 149659 | 50959 | 751 | 40068 | 1038 | 242475 |
| CALIFORNIA | 1913134 | 1895269 | 190381 | 1228 | 21526 | 4021538 |
| COLORADO | 267288 | 239714 | 6115 | 0 | 2120 | 515237 |
| CONNECTICUT | 423297 | 437754 | 13713 | 0 | 8754 | 883518 |
| DELAWARE | 67813 | 69588 | 1050 | 0 | 622 | 139073 |
| DIST OF COLUMBIA | -- | -- | -- | -- | -- | -- |
| FLORIDA | 281988 | 194280 | 11620 | 89755 | 0 | 577643 |
| GEORGIA | 254646 | 76691 | 1636 | 85138 | 733 | 418844 |
| HAWAII | -- | -- | -- | -- | -- | -- |
| IDAHO | 107370 | 101514 | 4972 | 0 | 960 | 214816 |
| ILLINOIS | 1994715 | 1961103 | 0 | 0 | 28228 | 3984046 |
| INDIANA | 807833 | 821079 | 9649 | 0 | 17653 | 1656214 |
| IOWA | 522380 | 494018 | 12125 | 0 | 9749 | 1038272 |
| KANSAS | 351902 | 423039 | 4603 | 0 | 9275 | 788819 |
| KENTUCKY | 466756 | 341210 | 1567 | 10411 | 2714 | 822658 |
| LOUISIANA | 136344 | 72657 | 3035 | 204290 | 10 | 416336 |
| MAINE | 111916 | 150234 | 1884 | 0 | 0 | 264034 |
| MARYLAND | 286521 | 294814 | 9983 | 2467 | 5235 | 599020 |
| MASSACHUSETTS | 1151788 | 909370 | 38157 | 0 | 7832 | 2107147 |
| MICHIGAN | 1003448 | 1038595 | 46515 | 0 | 21051 | 2109609 |
| MINNESOTA | 692966 | 483617 | 27866 | 0 | 7777 | 1212226 |
| MISSISSIPPI | 19384 | 5043 | 225 | 167538 | 0 | 192190 |
| MISSOURI | 917315 | 655039 | 3998 | 1 | 2275 | 1578628 |
| MONTANA | 119071 | 96770 | 7307 | 0 | 1124 | 224272 |
| NEBRASKA | 224165 | 264774 | 0 | 0 | 0 | 488939 |
| NEVADA | 31290 | 29357 | 1469 | 0 | 0 | 62116 |
| NEW HAMPSHIRE | 107995 | 121299 | 1970 | 7 | 169 | 231440 |
| NEW JERSEY | 895455 | 981124 | 42683 | 0 | 30293 | 1949555 |
| NEW MEXICO | 105240 | 80303 | 1037 | 0 | 253 | 186833 |
| NEW YORK | 2780204 | 2841163 | 509559 | 0 | 46283 | 6177209 |
| NORTH CAROLINA | 459070 | 258572 | 3915 | 69652 | 0 | 791209 |

| | | | | | | |
|---|---|---|---|---|---|---|
| NORTH DAKOTA | 95812 | 115139 | 8391 | 374 | 1000 | 220716 |
| OHIO | 1452791 | 1445584 | 37487 | 0 | 0 | 2935962 |
| OKLAHOMA | 452782 | 268817 | 0 | 0 | 0 | 721599 |
| OREGON | 243147 | 260904 | 14978 | 0 | 5051 | 524080 |
| PENNSYLVANIA | 1752426 | 1902197 | 55161 | 0 | 25564 | 3735348 |
| RHODE ISLAND | 188736 | 135787 | 2619 | | 560 | 327702 |
| SOUTH CAROLINA | 34423 | 5386 | 154 | 102607 | 1 | 142571 |
| SOUTH DAKOTA | 117653 | 129651 | 2801 | 0 | 0 | 250105 |
| TENNESSEE | 270402 | 202914 | 1864 | 73815 | 1288 | 550283 |
| TEXAS | 750700 | 282240 | 3764 | 106909 | 3632 | 1147245 |
| UTAH | 149151 | 124402 | 2679 | 0 | 74 | 276306 |
| VERMONT | 45557 | 75926 | 1279 | 0 | 619 | 123381 |
| VIRGINIA | 200786 | 172070 | 2047 | 43393 | 960 | 419256 |
| WASHINGTON | 476165 | 386315 | 31692 | 0 | 10887 | 905059 |
| WEST VIRGINIA | 429188 | 316251 | 3311 | 0 | 0 | 748750 |
| WISCONSIN | 647310 | 590959 | 25282 | 0 | 13249 | 1276800 |
| WYOMING | 52354 | 47947 | 931 | 0 | 193 | 101425 |

TABLE 3.3 (CONTINUED)

1952 PRESIDENTIAL ELECTION

| | STEVENSON (DEMOCRAT) | EISENHOWER (REPUBLICAN) | (OTHER) | TOTAL VOTE CAST |
|---|---|---|---|---|
| ALABAMA | 275075 | 149231 | 1814 | 426120 |
| ALASKA | --- | --- | --- | --- |
| ARIZONA | 108528 | 152042 | 0 | 260570 |
| ARKANSAS | 226300 | 177155 | 1345 | 404800 |
| CALIFORNIA | 2197548 | 2897310 | 48370 | 5143228 |
| COLORADO | 245504 | 379782 | 4817 | 630103 |
| CONNECTICUT | 481649 | 611012 | 4245 | 1096906 |
| DELAWARE | 83315 | 90059 | 651 | 174025 |
| DIST OF COLUMBIA | --- | --- | --- | --- |
| FLORIDA | 444950 | 544036 | 0 | 988986 |
| GEORGIA | 456823 | 198961 | 1 | 655785 |
| HAWAII | --- | --- | --- | --- |
| IDAHO | 95081 | 180707 | 466 | 276254 |
| ILLINOIS | 2013920 | 2457327 | 9811 | 4481058 |
| INDIANA | 801530 | 1136259 | 17536 | 1955325 |
| IOWA | 451513 | 808906 | 8325 | 1268744 |
| KANSAS | 273296 | 616302 | 6568 | 896166 |
| KENTUCKY | 495729 | 495029 | 2390 | 993148 |
| LOUISIANA | 345027 | 306925 | 0 | 651952 |
| MAINE | 118806 | 232353 | 0 | 351159 |
| MARYLAND | 395337 | 499424 | 7313 | 902074 |
| MASSACHUSETTS | 1083525 | 1292325 | 7548 | 2383398 |
| MICHIGAN | 1230657 | 1551529 | 16406 | 2798592 |
| MINNESOTA | 608458 | 763211 | 7814 | 1379483 |
| MISSISSIPPI | 172553 | 112966 | 0 | 285519 |
| MISSOURI | 929830 | 959429 | 2803 | 1892062 |
| MONTANA | 106213 | 157394 | 1430 | 265037 |
| NEBRASKA | 188057 | 421603 | 0 | 609660 |
| NEVADA | 31688 | 50502 | 0 | 82190 |
| NEW HAMPSHIRE | 106663 | 166287 | 0 | 272950 |
| NEW JERSEY | 1015902 | 1373613 | 29039 | 2418554 |
| NEW MEXICO | 105435 | 132170 | 772 | 238377 |
| NEW YORK | 3104601 | 3952815 | 70825 | 7128241 |
| NORTH CAROLINA | 652803 | 558107 | 0 | 1210910 |
| NORTH DAKOTA | 76694 | 191712 | 1721 | 270127 |
| OHIO | 1600367 | 2100391 | 0 | 3700758 |
| OKLAHOMA | 430939 | 518045 | 0 | 948984 |
| OREGON | 270579 | 420815 | 3665 | 695059 |
| PENNSYLVANIA | 2146269 | 2415789 | 18911 | 4580969 |
| RHODE ISLAND | 203293 | 210935 | 270 | 414498 |
| SOUTH CAROLINA | 172957 | 168043 | 1 | 341001 |
| SOUTH DAKOTA | 90426 | 203857 | 0 | 294283 |
| TENNESSEE | 443710 | 446147 | 2698 | 892555 |
| TEXAS | 969227 | 1102818 | 3840 | 2075885 |
| UTAH | 135364 | 194190 | 0 | 329554 |
| VERMONT | 43299 | 109717 | 485 | 153501 |
| VIRGINIA | 268677 | 349037 | 1975 | 619689 |
| WASHINGTON | 492845 | 599107 | 10756 | 1102708 |
| WEST VIRGINIA | 453578 | 419970 | 0 | 873548 |
| WISCONSIN | 622175 | 979744 | 5451 | 1607370 |
| WYOMING | 47934 | 81049 | 270 | 129253 |

TABLE 3.3 (CONTINUED)

## 1956 PRESIDENTIAL ELECTION

| STEVENSON (DEMOCRAT) | EISENHOWER (REPUBLICAN) | (OTHER) | TOTAL VOTE CAST |
|---|---|---|---|
| 279542 | 195694 | 20333 | 495569 |
| --- | --- | --- | --- |
| 112880 | 176990 | 303 | 290173 |
| 213277 | 186287 | 7008 | 406572 |
| 2420135 | 3027668 | 18555 | 5466358 |
| 263997 | 394479 | 4598 | 663074 |
| 405079 | 711837 | 0 | 1116916 |
| 79421 | 98057 | 510 | 177988 |
| --- | --- | --- | --- |
| 480371 | 643849 | 1542 | 1125762 |
| 444688 | 222778 | 2189 | 669655 |
| --- | --- | --- | --- |
| 105868 | 166979 | 158 | 273005 |
| 1775682 | 2623327 | 8398 | 4407407 |
| 783908 | 1182811 | 7888 | 1974607 |
| 501858 | 729187 | 3519 | 1234564 |
| 296317 | 566878 | 3048 | 866243 |
| 476453 | 572192 | 5160 | 1053805 |
| 243977 | 329047 | 44520 | 617544 |
| 102468 | 249238 | 0 | 351706 |
| 372613 | 559738 | 0 | 932351 |
| 948190 | 1393197 | 7119 | 2348506 |
| 1359898 | 1713647 | 6923 | 3080468 |
| 617525 | 719302 | 3178 | 1340005 |
| 144453 | 60683 | 42961 | 248097 |
| 918273 | 914289 | 0 | 1832562 |
| 116238 | 154933 | 0 | 271171 |
| 199029 | 378108 | 0 | 577137 |
| 40640 | 56049 | 0 | 96689 |
| 90364 | 176519 | 111 | 266994 |
| 850337 | 1606942 | 27033 | 2484312 |
| 106098 | 146788 | 1040 | 253926 |
| 2750769 | 4340340 | 0 | 7091109 |
| 590530 | 575069 | 0 | 1165599 |
| 96742 | 156766 | 483 | 253991 |
| 1439655 | 2262610 | 0 | 3702265 |
| 385581 | 473769 | 0 | 859350 |
| 329204 | 406393 | 0 | 735597 |
| 1981769 | 2585252 | 9482 | 4576503 |
| 161790 | 225819 | 0 | 387609 |
| 136278 | 75634 | 88511 | 300423 |
| 122288 | 171569 | 0 | 293857 |
| 456507 | 462288 | 20609 | 939404 |
| 859958 | 1080619 | 14591 | 1955168 |
| 118364 | 215631 | 0 | 333995 |
| 42540 | 110390 | 39 | 152969 |
| 267760 | 386459 | 43759 | 697978 |
| 523002 | 620430 | 7457 | 1150889 |
| 381534 | 449297 | 0 | 830831 |
| 586768 | 954844 | 8946 | 1550558 |
| 49554 | 74573 | 0 | 124127 |

TABLE 3.3 (CONTINUED)

## 1960 PRÉSIDENTIAL ELECTION

| | KENNEDY (DEMOCRAT) | NIXON (REPUBLICAN) | (OTHER) | TOTAL VOTE CAST |
|---|---|---|---|---|
| ALABAMA | 318303 | 236110 | 6083 | 560496 |
| ALASKA | 29809 | 30953 | 0 | 60762 |
| ARIZONA | 176781 | 221241 | 469 | 398491 |
| ARKANSAS | 193775 | 165496 | 23725 | 382996 |
| CALIFORNIA | 3224099 | 3259722 | 22757 | 6506578 |
| COLORADO | 330629 | 402242 | 3366 | 736237 |
| CONNECTICUT | 657055 | 565813 | 0 | 1222868 |
| DELAWARE | 99590 | 96373 | 720 | 196683 |
| DIST OF COLUMBIA | --- | --- | --- | --- |
| FLORIDA | 748700 | 795476 | 0 | 1544176 |
| GEORGIA | 458638 | 274472 | 245 | 733355 |
| HAWAII | 92410 | 92295 | 0 | 184705 |
| IDAHO | 138853 | 161597 | 0 | 300450 |
| ILLINOIS | 2377846 | 2368988 | 10575 | 4757409 |
| INDIANA | 952358 | 1175120 | 7882 | 2135360 |
| IOWA | 550565 | 722381 | 864 | 1273810 |
| KANSAS | 363213 | 561474 | 4138 | 928825 |
| KENTUCKY | 521855 | 602607 | 0 | 1124462 |
| LOUISIANA | 407339 | 230980 | 169572 | 807891 |
| MAINE | 181159 | 240608 | 0 | 421767 |
| MARYLAND | 565808 | 489538 | 3 | 1055349 |
| MASSACHUSETTS | 1487174 | 976750 | 5556 | 2469480 |
| MICHIGAN | 1687269 | 1620428 | 10400 | 3318097 |
| MINNESOTA | 779933 | 757915 | 4039 | 1541887 |
| MISSISSIPPI | 108362 | 73561 | 116248 | 298171 |
| MISSOURI | 972201 | 962218 | 0 | 1934419 |
| MONTANA | 134891 | 141841 | 847 | 277579 |
| NEBRASKA | 232542 | 380553 | 0 | 613095 |
| NEVADA | 54880 | 52387 | 0 | 107267 |
| NEW HAMPSHIRE | 137772 | 157989 | 0 | 295761 |
| NEW JERSEY | 1385415 | 1363324 | 24372 | 2773111 |
| NEW MEXICO | 156027 | 153733 | 1347 | 311107 |
| NEW YORK | 3830085 | 3446419 | 14319 | 7290823 |
| NORTH CAROLINA | 713136 | 655420 | 0 | 1368556 |
| NORTH DAKOTA | 123963 | 154310 | 158 | 278431 |
| OHIO | 1944248 | 2217611 | 0 | 4161859 |
| OKLAHOMA | 370111 | 533039 | 0 | 903150 |
| OREGON | 367402 | 408065 | 959 | 776426 |
| PENNSYLVANIA | 2556282 | 2439956 | 10303 | 5006541 |
| RHODE ISLAND | 258032 | 147502 | 0 | 405534 |
| SOUTH CAROLINA | 198121 | 188558 | 1 | 386680 |
| SOUTH DAKOTA | 128070 | 178417 | 0 | 306487 |
| TENNESSEE | 481453 | 556577 | 13746 | 1051776 |
| TEXAS | 1167935 | 1121693 | 22213 | 2311841 |
| UTAH | 169248 | 205361 | 100 | 374709 |
| VERMONT | 69186 | 98131 | 7 | 167324 |
| VIRGINIA | 362327 | 404521 | 4601 | 771449 |
| WASHINGTON | 599298 | 629273 | 13001 | 1241572 |
| WEST VIRGINIA | 441786 | 395995 | 0 | 837781 |
| WISCONSIN | 830805 | 895175 | 3102 | 1729082 |
| WYOMING | 63331 | 77451 | 0 | 140782 |

TABLE 3.3 (CONTINUED)

### 1964 PRESIDENTIAL ELECTION

| JOHNSON (DEMOCRAT) | GOLDWATER (REPUBLICAN) | (OTHER) | TOTAL VOTE CAST |
|---|---|---|---|
| 0 | 479085 | 210733 | 689818 |
| 44329 | 22930 | 0 | 67259 |
| 237753 | 242535 | 482 | 480770 |
| 314197 | 243264 | 2965 | 560426 |
| 4171877 | 2879108 | 6592 | 7057577 |
| 476024 | 296767 | 4194 | 776985 |
| 826269 | 390996 | 1313 | 1218578 |
| 122704 | 78078 | 538 | 201320 |
| --- | --- | --- | --- |
| 948540 | 905941 | 0 | 1854481 |
| 522163 | 616584 | 195 | 1138942 |
| 163249 | 44022 | 0 | 207271 |
| 148920 | 143557 | 0 | 292477 |
| 2796833 | 1905946 | 62 | 4702841 |
| 1170848 | 911118 | 9640 | 2091606 |
| 733030 | 449148 | 2361 | 1184539 |
| 464028 | 386579 | 7294 | 857901 |
| 669659 | 372977 | 3469 | 1046105 |
| 387068 | 509225 | 0 | 896293 |
| 262264 | 118701 | 0 | 380965 |
| 730912 | 385495 | 0 | 1116407 |
| 1786422 | 549727 | 8649 | 2344798 |
| 2136615 | 1060152 | 6335 | 3203102 |
| 991117 | 559624 | 3721 | 1554462 |
| 52616 | 356512 | 0 | 409128 |
| 1164344 | 653535 | 0 | 1817879 |
| 164246 | 113032 | 1350 | 278628 |
| 307307 | 276847 | 0 | 584154 |
| 79339 | 56094 | 0 | 135433 |
| 182065 | 104029 | 0 | 286094 |
| 1867671 | 963843 | 15256 | 2846770 |
| 194015 | 132838 | 1760 | 328613 |
| 4913156 | 2243559 | 9565 | 7166280 |
| 800139 | 624841 | 0 | 1424980 |
| 149784 | 108207 | 398 | 258389 |
| 2498331 | 1470865 | 0 | 3969196 |
| 519834 | 412665 | 0 | 932499 |
| 501017 | 282779 | 2509 | 786305 |
| 3130954 | 1673657 | 18079 | 4822690 |
| 315463 | 74615 | 0 | 390078 |
| 215723 | 309048 | 8 | 524779 |
| 163010 | 130108 | 0 | 293118 |
| 635047 | 508965 | 34 | 1144046 |
| 1663185 | 958566 | 5060 | 2626811 |
| 219628 | 181785 | 0 | 401413 |
| 108127 | 54942 | 20 | 163089 |
| 558038 | 481334 | 2895 | 1042267 |
| 779699 | 470366 | 8309 | 1258374 |
| 538087 | 253953 | 0 | 792040 |
| 1050424 | 638495 | 2896 | 1691815 |
| 80718 | 61998 | 0 | 142716 |

TABLE 3.3 (CONTINUED)

## 1968 PRESIDENTIAL ELECTION

| | HUMPHREY (DEMOCRAT) | NIXON (REPUBLICAN) | WALLACE (AMER INDEP) | (OTHER) | TOTAL VOTE CAST |
|---|---|---|---|---|---|
| ALABAMA | 195918 | 146591 | 687664 | 14332 | 1044505 |
| ALASKA | 35411 | 37600 | 10024 | 0 | 83035 |
| ARIZONA | 170514 | 266721 | 46573 | 3128 | 486936 |
| ARKANSAS | 184809 | 189062 | 235627 | 0 | 609498 |
| CALIFORNIA | 3244318 | 3467664 | 487270 | 52335 | 7251587 |
| COLORADO | 335174 | 409345 | 60813 | 5867 | 811199 |
| CONNECTICUT | 621561 | 556721 | 76650 | 1300 | 1256232 |
| DELAWARE | 89194 | 96714 | 28459 | 0 | 214367 |
| DIST OF COLUMBIA | --- | --- | --- | --- | --- |
| FLORIDA | 676794 | 886804 | 624207 | 0 | 2187805 |
| GEORGIA | 334440 | 380111 | 535550 | 173 | 1250274 |
| HAWAII | 141324 | 91425 | 3469 | 0 | 236218 |
| IDAHO | 89273 | 165369 | 36541 | 0 | 291183 |
| ILLINOIS | 2039814 | 2174774 | 390958 | 14203 | 4619749 |
| INDIANA | 806659 | 1067885 | 243108 | 5909 | 2123561 |
| IOWA | 476699 | 619106 | 66422 | 5704 | 1167931 |
| KANSAS | 302996 | 478674 | 88921 | 2192 | 872783 |
| KENTUCKY | 397541 | 462411 | 193098 | 2843 | 1055893 |
| LOUISIANA | 309615 | 257535 | 530300 | 0 | 1097450 |
| MAINE | 217312 | 169254 | 6370 | 0 | 392936 |
| MARYLAND | 538310 | 517995 | 178734 | 0 | 1235039 |
| MASSACHUSETTS | 1469218 | 766844 | 87088 | 8602 | 2331752 |
| MICHIGAN | 1593082 | 1370665 | 331968 | 10535 | 3306250 |
| MINNESOTA | 857738 | 658643 | 68931 | 3194 | 1588506 |
| MISSISSIPPI | 150644 | 88516 | 415349 | 0 | 654509 |
| MISSOURI | 791444 | 811932 | 206126 | 0 | 1809502 |
| MONTANA | 114117 | 138835 | 20015 | 1437 | 274404 |
| NEBRASKA | 170784 | 321163 | 44904 | 0 | 536851 |
| NEVADA | 60598 | 73188 | 20432 | 0 | 154218 |
| NEW HAMPSHIRE | 130589 | 154903 | 11173 | 633 | 297298 |
| NEW JERSEY | 1264206 | 1325467 | 262187 | 23535 | 2875395 |
| NEW MEXICO | 130081 | 169692 | 25737 | 1771 | 327281 |
| NEW YORK | 3378470 | 3007932 | 358864 | 44800 | 6790066 |
| NORTH CAROLINA | 464113 | 627192 | 496188 | 0 | 1587493 |

| | | | | | |
|---|---|---|---|---|---|
| NORTH DAKOTA | 94769 | 138669 | 14278 | 166 | 247882 |
| OHIO | 1700586 | 1791014 | 467495 | 603 | 3959698 |
| OKLAHOMA | 301658 | 449697 | 191731 | 0 | 943086 |
| OREGON | 358866 | 408433 | 49683 | 2640 | 819622 |
| PENNSYLVANIA | 2259403 | 2090017 | 378582 | 19924 | 4747926 |
| RHODE ISLAND | 246518 | 122359 | 15678 | 383 | 384938 |
| SOUTH CAROLINA | 197486 | 254062 | 215430 | 0 | 666978 |
| SOUTH DAKOTA | 118023 | 149841 | 13400 | 0 | 281264 |
| TENNESSEE | 351233 | 472592 | 424792 | 0 | 1248617 |
| TEXAS | 1266804 | 1227844 | 584269 | 489 | 3079406 |
| UTAH | 156665 | 238728 | 26906 | 269 | 422568 |
| VERMONT | 70255 | 85142 | 5104 | 903 | 161404 |
| VIRGINIA | 442387 | 590319 | 320272 | 6952 | 1359930 |
| WASHINGTON | 620220 | 595553 | 98220 | 2810 | 1316803 |
| WEST VIRGINIA | 374091 | 307555 | 72560 | 0 | 754206 |
| WISCONSIN | 748804 | 809997 | 1338 | 2342 | 1562481 |
| WYOMING | 45173 | 70927 | 11105 | 0 | 127205 |

TABLE 3.3 (CONTINUED)

## 1972 PRESIDENTIAL ELECTION

| | MCGOVERN (DEMOCRAT) | NIXON (REPUBLICAN) | (OTHER) | TOTAL VOTE CAST |
|---|---|---|---|---|
| ALABAMA | 255668 | 727034 | 19227 | 1001929 |
| ALASKA | 32967 | 55349 | 6903 | 95219 |
| ARIZONA | 198540 | 402812 | 52153 | 653505 |
| ARKANSAS | 199892 | 448541 | 2887 | 651320 |
| CALIFORNIA | 3475847 | 4602096 | 289919 | 8367862 |
| COLORADO | 329980 | 597189 | 26715 | 953884 |
| CONNECTICUT | 555498 | 810763 | 18016 | 1384277 |
| DELAWARE | 92283 | 140357 | 2144 | 234784 |
| DIST OF COLUMBIA | 127627 | 35226 | 568 | 163421 |
| FLORIDA | 718117 | 1857759 | 7407 | 2583283 |
| GEORGIA | 289529 | 881490 | 0 | 1171019 |
| HAWAII | 101433 | 168933 | 0 | 270366 |
| IDAHO | 80826 | 199384 | 30169 | 310379 |
| ILLINOIS | 1913472 | 2788179 | 21585 | 4723236 |
| INDIANA | 708568 | 1405154 | 11807 | 2125529 |
| IOWA | 496206 | 706207 | 23531 | 1225944 |
| KANSAS | 270287 | 619812 | 25996 | 916095 |
| KENTUCKY | 371159 | 676446 | 19894 | 1067499 |
| LOUISIANA | 298142 | 647487 | 26296 | 971925 |
| MAINE | 160584 | 256458 | 0 | 417042 |
| MARYLAND | 505781 | 829305 | 18726 | 1353812 |
| MASSACHUSETTS | 1332540 | 1112078 | 14138 | 2458756 |
| MICHIGAN | 1459435 | 1961721 | 69169 | 3490325 |
| MINNESOTA | 802346 | 898269 | 41037 | 1741652 |
| MISSISSIPPI | 126782 | 505125 | 14056 | 645963 |
| MISSOURI | 698531 | 1154058 | 0 | 1852589 |
| MONTANA | 120197 | 183976 | 13430 | 317603 |
| NEBRASKA | 169991 | 406298 | 0 | 576289 |
| NEVADA | 66016 | 115750 | 0 | 181766 |
| NEW HAMPSHIRE | 116435 | 213724 | 3896 | 334055 |
| NEW JERSEY | 1102211 | 1845502 | 49516 | 2997229 |
| NEW MEXICO | 141084 | 235606 | 9241 | 385931 |
| NEW YORK | 2951084 | 4192778 | 179609 | 7323471 |
| NORTH CAROLINA | 438705 | 1054889 | 25018 | 1518612 |
| NORTH DAKOTA | 100384 | 174109 | 6021 | 280514 |
| OHIO | 1558889 | 2441827 | 94071 | 4094787 |
| OKLAHOMA | 247147 | 759025 | 23728 | 1029900 |
| OREGON | 392760 | 486686 | 48500 | 927946 |
| PENNSYLVANIA | 1796951 | 2714521 | 80633 | 4592105 |
| RHODE ISLAND | 194645 | 220383 | 729 | 415757 |
| SOUTH CAROLINA | 186824 | 477044 | 10092 | 673960 |
| SOUTH DAKOTA | 139945 | 166476 | 994 | 307415 |
| TENNESSEE | 357293 | 813147 | 30742 | 1201182 |
| TEXAS | 1154289 | 2298896 | 18096 | 3471281 |
| UTAH | 126284 | 323643 | 28549 | 478476 |
| VERMONT | 68174 | 117149 | 1010 | 186333 |
| VIRGINIA | 438887 | 988493 | 29639 | 1457019 |
| WASHINGTON | 568334 | 837135 | 65378 | 1470847 |
| WEST VIRGINIA | 277435 | 484964 | 0 | 762399 |
| WISCONSIN | 810174 | 989430 | 53286 | 1852890 |
| WYOMING | 44358 | 100464 | 748 | 145570 |

TABLE 3.3 (CONTINUED)

1976 PRESIDENTIAL ELECTION

| | CARTER (DEMOCRATIC) | FORD (REPUBLICAN) | (OTHER) | TOTAL VOTE CAST |
|---|---|---|---|---|
| ALABAMA | 659,170 | 504,070 | 19,719 | 1,182,959 |
| ALASKA | 44,055 | 71,555 | 6,773 | 122,383 |
| ARIZONA | 295,602 | 418,642 | 28,475 | 742,719 |
| ARKANSAS | 498,604 | 267,903 | 639 | 767,146 |
| CALIFORNIA | 3,743,284 | 3,882,244 | 237,654 | 7,862,182 |
| COLORADO | 460,801 | 584,456 | 37,709 | 1,082,966 |
| CONNECTICUT | 647,895 | 719,261 | 12,690 | 1,379,846 |
| DELAWARE | 122,559 | 109,780 | 2,403 | 235,742 |
| DIST. OF COLUMBIA | 137,818 | 27,873 | 6,127 | 171,818 |
| FLORIDA | 1,636,000 | 1,469,531 | 44,969 | 3,150,500 |
| GEORGIA | 979,427 | 483,753 | 3,434 | 1,468,614 |
| HAWAII | 147,375 | 140,003 | 3,923 | 291,301 |
| IDAHO | 126,649 | 204,151 | 10,232 | 340,932 |
| ILLINOIS | 2,271,295 | 2,364,269 | 93,289 | 4,728,853 |
| INDIANA | 1,014,714 | 1,185,958 | 21,690 | 2,222,362 |
| IOWA | 619,931 | 632,863 | 26,512 | 1,279,306 |
| KANSAS | 430,421 | 502,752 | 24,672 | 957,845 |
| KENTUCKY | 615,717 | 531,762 | 19,573 | 1,167,052 |
| LOUISIANA | 661,365 | 587,446 | 28,572 | 1,277,383 |
| MAINE | 232,279 | 236,320 | 14,342 | 482,968 |
| MARYLAND | 759,612 | 672,661 | 0 | 1,432,273 |
| MASSACHUSETTS | 1,429,475 | 1,030,276 | 86,252 | 2,546,003 |
| MICHIGAN | 1,696,714 | 1,893,742 | 73,434 | 3,663,890 |
| MINNESOTA | 1,070,440 | 819,395 | 59,722 | 1,949,557 |
| MISSISSIPPI | 381,329 | 366,846 | 21,205 | 769,380 |
| MISSOURI | 998,387 | 927,443 | 27,770 | 1,953,600 |
| MONTANA | 149,259 | 173,703 | 5,772 | 328,734 |
| NEBRASKA | 233,293 | 359,219 | 5,237 | 606,749 |
| NEVADA | 92,479 | 101,273 | 8,124 | 201,876 |
| NEW HAMPSHIRE | 147,645 | 185,935 | 5,444 | 339,024 |
| NEW JERSEY | 1,444,653 | 1,509,588 | 60,131 | 3,014,472 |
| NEW MEXICO | 201,148 | 211,419 | 4,023 | 416,590 |
| NEW YORK | 3,389,558 | 3,100,791 | 177,913 | 6,668,262 |
| NORTH CAROLINA | 927,365 | 741,960 | 9,582 | 1,678,907 |
| NORTH DAKOTA | 136,078 | 153,470 | 7,546 | 297,094 |
| OHIO | 2,011,621 | 2,000,505 | 99,747 | 4,111,873 |
| OKLAHOMA | 532,442 | 545,708 | 14,101 | 1,092,251 |
| OREGON | 490,350 | 491,909 | 47,410 | 1,029,669 |
| PENNSYLVANIA | 2,327,423 | 2,204,355 | 86,193 | 4,617,971 |
| RHODE ISLAND | 227,636 | 181,249 | 1,629 | 410,514 |
| SOUTH CAROLINA | 450,807 | 346,149 | 5,627 | 802,583 |
| SOUTH DAKOTA | 147,068 | 151,505 | 2,105 | 300,678 |
| TENNESSEE | 825,879 | 633,979 | 16,498 | 1,476,356 |
| TEXAS | 2,082,319 | 1,953,294 | 36,265 | 4,071,878 |
| UTAH | 182,110 | 337,908 | 21,200 | 541,218 |
| VERMONT | 78,789 | 100,387 | 4,726 | 183,902 |
| VIRGINIA | 813,896 | 836,554 | 46,644 | 1,697,094 |
| WASHINGTON | 717,323 | 777,732 | 60,428 | 1,555,537 |
| WEST VIRGINIA | 435,864 | 314,726 | 0 | 750,590 |
| WISCONSIN | 1,040,232 | 1,004,987 | 58,984 | 2,104,176 |
| WYOMING | 62,239 | 92,717 | 1,387 | 156,343 |

TABLE 3.3 (CONTINUED)

1980 PRESIDENTIAL ELECTION

|  | CARTER (DEMOCRATIC) | REAGAN (REPUBLICAN) | (OTHER) | TOTAL VOTE CAST |
|---|---|---|---|---|
| ALABAMA | 630,430 | 654,192 | 51,007 | 1,335,629 |
| ALASKA | 41,842 | 86,112 | 30,491 | 158,445 |
| ARIZONA | 246,843 | 529,688 | 97,414 | 873,945 |
| ARKANSAS | 398,041 | 403,164 | 36,377 | 837,582 |
| CALIFORNIA | 3,083,661 | 4,524,858 | 977,302 | 8,585,821 |
| COLORADO | 367,973 | 652,264 | 164,178 | 1,184,415 |
| CONNECTICUT | 541,732 | 677,210 | 186,507 | 1,405,449 |
| DELAWARE | 105,754 | 111,252 | 18,662 | 235,668 |
| DIST. OF COLUMBIA | 130,231 | 23,313 | 16,131 | 169,675 |
| FLORIDA | 1,419,475 | 2,046,951 | 220,501 | 3,686,927 |
| GEORGIA | 890,733 | 654,168 | 51,682 | 1,596,583 |
| HAWAII | 135,857 | 130,085 | 37,286 | 303,228 |
| IDAHO | 110,192 | 290,699 | 36,540 | 437,431 |
| ILLINOIS | 1,981,413 | 2,358,049 | 409,655 | 4,749,117 |
| INDIANA | 844,197 | 1,255,656 | 142,180 | 2,242,033 |
| IOWA | 508,672 | 676,026 | 132,963 | 1,317,661 |
| KANSAS | 326,150 | 566,812 | 86,833 | 979,795 |
| KENTUCKY | 616,417 | 635,274 | 42,936 | 1,294,627 |
| LOUISIANA | 708,453 | 792,853 | 47,285 | 1,548,591 |
| MAINE | 220,974 | 238,522 | 63,515 | 523,011 |
| MARYLAND | 726,161 | 680,606 | 133,729 | 1,540,496 |
| MASSACHUSETTS | 1,053,802 | 1,057,631 | 412,865 | 2,524,298 |
| MICHIGAN | 1,661,532 | 1,915,225 | 332,968 | 3,909,725 |
| MINNESOTA | 954,174 | 873,268 | 218,459 | 2,045,901 |
| MISSISSIPPI | 429,281 | 441,089 | 22,250 | 892,620 |
| MISSOURI | 932,182 | 1,074,181 | 94,059 | 2,100,422 |
| MONTANA | 118,032 | 206,814 | 39,106 | 363,952 |
| NEBRASKA | 166,424 | 419,214 | 53,895 | 639,533 |
| NEVADA | 66,666 | 155,017 | 26,202 | 247,885 |
| NEW HAMPSHIRE | 108,864 | 221,705 | 53,421 | 383,990 |
| NEW JERSEY | 1,147,364 | 1,546,557 | 281,763 | 2,975,684 |
| NEW MEXICO | 167,826 | 250,779 | 37,632 | 456,237 |
| NEW YORK | 2,728,372 | 2,647,700 | 835,887 | 6,211,959 |
| NORTH CAROLINA | 875,635 | 915,018 | 65,180 | 1,855,833 |
| NORTH DAKOTA | 79,189 | 193,695 | 28,661 | 301,545 |
| OHIO | 1,752,414 | 2,206,545 | 324,644 | 4,283,603 |
| OKLAHOMA | 402,026 | 695,570 | 52,112 | 1,149,708 |
| OREGON | 456,890 | 571,044 | 153,582 | 1,181,516 |
| PENNSYLVANIA | 1,937,540 | 2,261,872 | 362,089 | 4,561,501 |
| RHODE ISLAND | 198,342 | 154,793 | 62,832 | 415,967 |
| SOUTH CAROLINA | 430,385 | 441,841 | 21,469 | 893,695 |
| SOUTH DAKOTA | 103,855 | 198,343 | 25,505 | 327,703 |
| TENNESSEE | 783,051 | 787,761 | 46,805 | 1,617,617 |
| TEXAS | 1,881,147 | 2,510,705 | 149,785 | 4,541,637 |
| UTAH | 124,266 | 439,687 | 40,269 | 604,222 |
| VERMONT | 81,891 | 94,598 | 36,718 | 213,207 |
| VIRGINIA | 752,174 | 989,609 | 124,249 | 1,866,032 |
| WASHINGTON | 650,193 | 865,244 | 226,957 | 1,742,394 |
| WEST VIRGINIA | 367,462 | 334,206 | 36,047 | 737,715 |
| WISCONSIN | 981,584 | 1,088,845 | 202,792 | 2,273,221 |
| WYOMING | 49,427 | 110,700 | 16,586 | 176,713 |

TABLE 3.3 (CONTINUED)

1984 PRESIDENTIAL ELECTION

|  | MONDALE (DEMOCRATIC) | REAGAN (REPUBLICAN) | (OTHER) | TOTAL VOTE CAST |
|---|---|---|---|---|
| ALABAMA | 551,899 | 872,849 | 16,965 | 1,441,713 |
| ALASKA | 62,007 | 138,377 | 7,221 | 207,605 |
| ARIZONA | 333,854 | 681,416 | 10,627 | 1,025,897 |
| ARKANSAS | 338,646 | 534,774 | 10,986 | 884,406 |
| CALIFORNIA | 3,922,519 | 5,467,009 | 115,513 | 9,505,041 |
| COLORADO | 454,975 | 821,817 | 18,588 | 1,295,380 |
| CONNECTICUT | 569,597 | 890,877 | 6,200 | 1,466,674 |
| DELAWARE | 101,656 | 152,190 | 726 | 254,572 |
| DIST. OF COLUMBIA | 180,408 | 29,009 | 1,871 | 211,288 |
| FLORIDA | 1,448,816 | 2,730,350 | 885 | 4,180,051 |
| GEORGIA | 706,628 | 1,068,722 | 0 | 1,775,350 |
| HAWAII | 147,154 | 185,050 | 3,642 | 335,846 |
| IDAHO | 108,510 | 297,523 | 5,111 | 411,144 |
| ILLINOIS | 2,086,499 | 2,707,103 | 25,486 | 4,819,088 |
| INDIANA | 841,481 | 1,377,230 | 14,358 | 2,233,069 |
| IOWA | 605,620 | 703,088 | 11,097 | 1,319,805 |
| KANSAS | 333,149 | 677,296 | 11,546 | 1,021,991 |
| KENTUCKY | 539,539 | 821,702 | 8,104 | 1,369,345 |
| LOUISIANA | 651,586 | 1,037,299 | 17,937 | 1,706,822 |
| MAINE | 214,515 | 336,500 | 2,129 | 553,144 |
| MARYLAND | 787,935 | 879,918 | 8,020 | 1,675,873 |
| MASSACHUSETTS | 1,239,606 | 1,310,936 | 8,911 | 2,559,453 |
| MICHIGAN | 1,529,638 | 2,251,571 | 20,449 | 3,801,658 |
| MINNESOTA | 1,036,364 | 1,032,603 | 14,759 | 2,083,726 |
| MISSISSIPPI | 352,192 | 582,377 | 6,535 | 941,104 |
| MISSOURI | 848,583 | 1,274,188 | 0 | 2,122,771 |
| MONTANA | 146,742 | 232,450 | 5,185 | 384,377 |
| NEBRASKA | 187,475 | 459,135 | 4,166 | 650,776 |
| NEVADA | 91,655 | 188,770 | 6,242 | 286,667 |
| NEW HAMPSHIRE | 120,347 | 267,050 | 1,507 | 388,904 |
| NEW JERSEY | 1,261,323 | 1,933,630 | 22,909 | 3,217,862 |
| NEW MEXICO | 201,769 | 307,101 | 5,499 | 514,369 |
| NEW YORK | 3,001,285 | 3,376,519 | 623,024 | 7,000,828 |
| NORTH CAROLINA | 824,287 | 1,346,481 | 4,593 | 2,175,361 |
| NORTH DAKOTA | 104,429 | 200,336 | 4,206 | 308,971 |
| OHIO | 1,819,577 | 2,671,451 | 65,384 | 4,556,412 |
| OKLAHOMA | 385,080 | 861,530 | 9,066 | 1,255,676 |
| OREGON | 536,479 | 685,700 | 4,348 | 1,226,527 |
| PENNSYLVANIA | 2,228,131 | 2,584,323 | 32,449 | 4,844,903 |
| RHODE ISLAND | 197,106 | 212,080 | 1303 | 410,489 |
| SOUTH CAROLINA | 344,459 | 615,539 | 8,531 | 968,529 |
| SOUTH DAKOTA | 116,113 | 200,267 | 1,487 | 317,867 |
| TENNESSEE | 711,714 | 990,212 | 10,067 | 1,711,993 |
| TEXAS | 1,949,276 | 3,433,428 | 14,867 | 5,397,571 |
| UTAH | 155,369 | 469,105 | 5,182 | 629,656 |
| VERMONT | 95,730 | 135,865 | 5,033 | 236,628 |
| VIRGINIA | 796,250 | 1,337,078 | 13,307 | 2,146,635 |
| WASHINGTON | 798,352 | 1,051,670 | 24,888 | 1,874,910 |
| WEST VIRGINIA | 328,125 | 405,483 | 2,134 | 735,742 |
| WISCONSIN | 995,740 | 1,198,584 | 17,365 | 2,211,689 |
| WYOMING | 53,370 | 133,241 | 2,357 | 188,968 |

# The Vote for the United States Senate

One-third of the United States Senate seats are up for election every two years. Until the early twentieth century, U.S. Senators were chosen by the respective state legislatures. Popular and political agitation for direct popular election of Senators culminated in the ratification of the Seventeenth Amendment (1913) calling for direct and popular election of U.S. Senators. Table 3.4 contains national-level returns, and table 3.5 presents returns for regularly scheduled elections to the U.S. Senate in each state from 1908 to 1984 (special elections to fill vacancies could not be presented because of space considerations). As shown in table 3.5, a few states had begun holding popular elections for the U.S. Senate before this procedure was made mandatory in 1913. Included in both tables are the votes cast for candidates of the major parties as well as for the more significant "minor" parties which contested these elections as well. Votes for candidates of parties not specifically listed in each election have been aggregated into the "other" column. Two-thirds of the states elect Senators in any given year. Dashes (—) have been inserted in table 3.5 for those states which did not hold U.S. Senate elections in any year, as well as for states which were not in the union or ineligible to elect Senators (e.g., the District of Columbia).

When Alaska and Hawaii joined the union in 1959, special elections were held in those states for both U.S. Senate seats in each state. The returns for those elections are not recorded in table 3.5, but are presented here.

|  | Democratic | Republican | Other | Total Votes Cast |
|---|---|---|---|---|
| Alaska (1958, 1 seat) | 40,939 | 7,299 | 599 | 48,837 |
| Alaska (1958, 1 seat) | 26,063 | 23,462 | 0 | 49,525 |
| Hawaii (1959, 1 seat) | 83,700 | 79,123 | 1,052 | 163,875 |
| Hawaii (1959, 1 seat) | 77,647 | 87,161 | 0 | 164,808 |

Table 3.4

National Popular Vote Cast for United States Senators, 1908–1984

| YEAR | DEMOCRATIC | REPUBLICAN | PROHIBITION | SOCIALIST | PROGRESSIVE | INDEPENDENT | OTHER | TOTAL VOTES CAST |
|---|---|---|---|---|---|---|---|---|
| 1908 | 64,894 | 59,871 | 3,787 | 7,186 | -- | -- | -- | 135,738 |
| 1910 | 8,624 | 9,779 | -- | 1,959 | -- | -- | -- | 20,362 |
| 1912 | 588,552 | 532,021 | 12,796 | 77,579 | 91,893 | -- | 26,104 | 1,328,945 |
| 1914 | 4,341,983 | 4,426,757 | 161,178 | 494,640 | 1,367,259 | -- | 92,782 | 10,884,599 |
| 1916 | 4,708,738 | 5,313,030 | 234,756 | 413,008 | 21,601 | -- | 1,493,131 | 12,184,264 |
| 1918 | 2,949,345 | 3,021,493 | 10,052 | 92,781 | -- | 27,545 | 170,787 | 6,272,003 |
| 1920 | 7,279,874 | 10,573,946 | 381,509 | -- | -- | 1,089,577 | 72,956 | 19,397,862 |
| 1922 | 6,934,140 | 7,397,175 | 158,036 | -- | -- | 703,499 | 446,742 | 15,639,592 |
| 1924 | 5,991,166 | 7,645,318 | -- | -- | -- | 625,281 | 254,009 | 14,515,774 |
| 1926 | 7,178,256 | 7,962,203 | -- | -- | -- | 256,842 | 712,932 | 16,110,233 |
| 1928 | 10,646,998 | 14,266,051 | -- | -- | -- | -- | 1,132,823 | 26,045,872 |
| 1930 | 6,750,996 | 5,684,132 | -- | -- | -- | 304,142 | 260,910 | 13,000,180 |
| 1932 | 15,637,272 | 11,343,826 | -- | -- | -- | 523,719 | 974,735 | 28,479,552 |
| 1934 | 12,463,210 | 9,021,543 | -- | -- | -- | 933,645 | 2,690,630 | 25,109,028 |
| 1936 | 11,796,087 | 8,048,762 | -- | -- | -- | 408,617 | 1,080,286 | 21,333,752 |
| 1938 | 12,926,642 | 12,895,453 | -- | -- | -- | 135,173 | 1,875,456 | 27,832,724 |
| 1940 | 16,959,635 | 14,954,385 | -- | -- | -- | 94,674 | 3,794,047 | 35,802,741 |
| 1942 | 6,330,213 | 6,661,132 | -- | -- | -- | 17,209 | 542,613 | 13,551,167 |
| 1944 | 18,421,375 | 16,110,559 | -- | -- | -- | 2,818 | 230,504 | 34,765,256 |
| 1946 | 11,980,848 | 14,977,533 | -- | -- | -- | 55,488 | 218,187 | 27,232,056 |

Table 3.4 (continued)

| YEAR | DEMOCRATIC | REPUBLICAN | PROHIBITION | SOCIALIST | PROGRESSIVE | INDEPENDENT | OTHER | TOTAL VOTES CAST |
|---|---|---|---|---|---|---|---|---|
| 1948 | 12,750,654 | 9,660,279 | -- | -- | -- | 75,375 | 110,926 | 22,597,234 |
| 1950 | 15,610,127 | 16,166,666 | -- | -- | -- | 80,690 | 322,583 | 32,180,637[a] |
| 1952 | 20,048,330 | 19,750,914 | -- | -- | -- | 48,352 | 4,939,415 | 44,787,011 |
| 1954 | 11,319,483 | 8,838,877 | -- | -- | -- | 1,563 | 388,610 | 20,548,533 |
| 1956 | 22,499,347 | 21,248,822 | -- | -- | -- | -- | 103,247 | 43,851,416 |
| 1958 | 20,854,861 | 16,171,640 | -- | -- | -- | 200,163 | 197,881 | 37,424,545 |
| 1960 | 17,173,127 | 14,014,291 | -- | -- | -- | 8,064 | 210,509 | 31,405,991 |
| 1962 | 19,673,520 | 19,318,958 | -- | -- | -- | 5,501 | 188,214 | 39,186,193 |
| 1964 | 30,034,986 | 22,204,687 | -- | -- | -- | 36,172 | 298,256 | 52,574,101 |
| 1966 | 11,726,321 | 13,170,556 | -- | -- | -- | -- | 112,607 | 25,166,861[b] |
| 1968 | 25,384,106 | 23,608,286 | -- | -- | -- | -- | 276,715 | 50,587,981[c] |
| 1970 | 23,338,266 | 17,806,612 | -- | -- | -- | -- | 3,847,650 | 44,992,528 |
| 1972 | 17,199,567 | 19,821,203 | -- | -- | -- | -- | 788,800 | 37,809,570 |
| 1974 | 24,590,453 | 18,960,789 | -- | -- | -- | -- | 1,964,955 | 45,516,197 |
| 1976 | 32,002,771 | 24,878,982 | -- | -- | -- | -- | 1,980,723 | 58,862,476 |
| 1978 | 14,538,245 | 12,656,618 | -- | -- | -- | -- | 456,861 | 27,651,724 |
| 1980 | 30,374,682 | 26,589,489 | -- | -- | -- | -- | 2,511,685 | 59,475,856 |
| 1982 | 27,898,841 | 22,412,150 | -- | -- | -- | -- | 1,282,011 | 51,593,002 |
| 1984 | 23,057,724 | 22,904,079 | -- | -- | -- | -- | 479,328 | 46,441,131 |

[a] Includes 571 votes cast for States Rights Democrats.

[b] Includes 157,377 votes cast for the Conservative Party.

[c] Includes 1,318,874 votes cast for the American Party.

Table 3.5

Vote Cast for United States Senator,
by State, 1908-1984

## 1908 SENATE ELECTION

| | DEMOCRAT | REPUBLICAN | PROHIBITION | SOCIALIST | OTHER | TOTAL VOTES CAST |
|---|---|---|---|---|---|---|
| ALABAMA | --- | --- | --- | --- | --- | --- |
| ALASKA | --- | --- | --- | --- | --- | --- |
| ARIZONA | --- | --- | --- | --- | --- | --- |
| ARKANSAS | --- | --- | --- | --- | --- | --- |
| CALIFORNIA | --- | --- | --- | --- | --- | --- |
| COLORADO | --- | --- | --- | --- | --- | --- |
| CONNECTICUT | --- | --- | --- | --- | --- | --- |
| DELAWARE | --- | --- | --- | --- | --- | --- |
| DIST OF COLUMBIA | --- | --- | --- | --- | --- | --- |
| FLORIDA | --- | --- | --- | --- | --- | --- |
| GEORGIA | --- | --- | --- | --- | --- | --- |
| HAWAII | --- | --- | --- | --- | --- | --- |
| IDAHO | --- | --- | --- | --- | --- | --- |
| ILLINOIS | --- | --- | --- | --- | --- | --- |
| INDIANA | --- | --- | --- | --- | --- | --- |
| IOWA | --- | --- | --- | --- | --- | --- |
| KANSAS | --- | --- | --- | --- | --- | --- |
| KENTUCKY | --- | --- | --- | --- | --- | --- |
| LOUISIANA | --- | --- | --- | --- | --- | --- |
| MAINE | --- | --- | --- | --- | --- | --- |
| MARYLAND | --- | --- | --- | --- | --- | --- |
| MASSACHUSETTS | --- | --- | --- | --- | --- | --- |
| MICHIGAN | --- | --- | --- | --- | --- | --- |
| MINNESOTA | --- | --- | --- | --- | --- | --- |
| MISSISSIPPI | --- | --- | --- | --- | --- | --- |
| MISSOURI | --- | --- | --- | --- | --- | --- |
| MONTANA | --- | --- | --- | --- | --- | --- |

| | | | | | | |
|---|---|---|---|---|---|---|
| NEBRASKA | | | | | | |
| NEVADA | 12473 | 8972 | 0 | 1929 | 0 | 23374 |
| NEW HAMPSHIRE | | | | | | |
| NEW JERSEY | | | | | | |
| NEW MEXICO | | | | | | |
| NEW YORK | | | | | | |
| NORTH CAROLINA | | | | | | |
| NORTH DAKOTA | | | | | | |
| OHIO | | | | | | |
| OKLAHOMA | | | | | | |
| OREGON | 52421 | 50899 | 3787 | 5257 | 0 | 112364 |
| PENNSYLVANIA | | | | | | |
| RHODE ISLAND | | | | | | |
| SOUTH CAROLINA | | | | | | |
| SOUTH DAKOTA | | | | | | |
| TENNESSEE | | | | | | |
| TEXAS | | | | | | |
| UTAH | | | | | | |
| VERMONT | | | | | | |
| VIRGINIA | | | | | | |
| WASHINGTON | | | | | | |
| WEST VIRGINIA | | | | | | |
| WISCONSIN | | | | | | |
| WYOMING | | | | | | |

TABLE 3.5 (CONTINUED)

## 1910 SENATE ELECTION

| | DEMOCRAT | REPUBLICAN | SOCIALIST | TOTAL VOTES CAST |
|---|---|---|---|---|
| ALABAMA | --- | --- | --- | --- |
| ALASKA | --- | --- | --- | --- |
| ARIZONA | --- | --- | --- | --- |
| ARKANSAS | --- | --- | --- | --- |
| CALIFORNIA | --- | --- | --- | --- |
| COLORADO | --- | --- | --- | --- |
| CONNECTICUT | --- | --- | --- | --- |
| DELAWARE | --- | --- | --- | --- |
| DIST OF COLUMBIA | --- | --- | --- | --- |
| FLORIDA | --- | --- | --- | --- |
| GEORGIA | --- | --- | --- | --- |
| HAWAII | --- | --- | --- | --- |
| IDAHO | --- | --- | --- | --- |
| ILLINOIS | --- | --- | --- | --- |
| INDIANA | --- | --- | --- | --- |
| IOWA | --- | --- | --- | --- |
| KANSAS | --- | --- | --- | --- |
| KENTUCKY | --- | --- | --- | --- |
| LOUISIANA | --- | --- | --- | --- |
| MAINE | --- | --- | --- | --- |
| MARYLAND | --- | --- | --- | --- |
| MASSACHUSETTS | --- | --- | --- | --- |
| MICHIGAN | --- | --- | --- | --- |
| MINNESOTA | --- | --- | ---. | --- |
| MISSISSIPPI | --- | --- | --- | --- |
| MISSOURI | --- | --- | --- | --- |
| MONTANA | --- | --- | --- | --- |
| NEBRASKA | --- | --- | --- | --- |
| NEVADA | 8624 | 9779 | 1959 | 20362 |
| NEW HAMPSHIRE | --- | --- | --- | --- |
| NEW JERSEY | --- | --- | --- | --- |
| NEW MEXICO | --- | --- | --- | --- |
| NEW YORK | --- | --- | --- | --- |
| NORTH CAROLINA | --- | --- | --- | --- |
| NORTH DAKOTA | --- | --- | --- | --- |
| OHIO | --- | --- | --- | --- |
| OKLAHOMA | --- | --- | --- | --- |
| OREGON | --- | --- | --- | --- |
| PENNSYLVANIA | --- | --- | --- | --- |
| RHODE ISLAND | --- | --- | --- | --- |
| SOUTH CAROLINA | --- | --- | --- | --- |
| SOUTH DAKOTA | --- | --- | --- | --- |
| TENNESSEE | --- | --- | --- | --- |
| TEXAS | --- | --- | --- | --- |
| UTAH | --- | --- | --- | --- |
| VERMONT | --- | --- | --- | --- |
| VIRGINIA | --- | --- | --- | --- |
| WASHINGTON | --- | --- | --- | --- |
| WEST VIRGINIA | --- | --- | --- | --- |
| WISCONSIN | --- | --- | --- | --- |
| WYOMING | --- | --- | --- | --- |

TABLE 3.5 (CONTINUED)

## 1912 SENATE ELECTION

| | DEMOCRAT | REPUBLICAN | PROHIBITION | SOCIALIST | PROGRESSIVE | OTHER | TOTAL VOTES CAST |
|---|---|---|---|---|---|---|---|
| ALABAMA | --- | --- | --- | --- | --- | --- | --- |
| ALASKA | --- | --- | --- | --- | --- | --- | --- |
| ARIZONA | --- | --- | --- | --- | --- | --- | --- |
| ARKANSAS | --- | --- | --- | --- | --- | --- | --- |
| CALIFORNIA | --- | --- | --- | --- | --- | --- | --- |
| COLORADO | 118260 | 66949 | 5948 | 0 | 58649 | 0 | 249806 |
| CONNECTICUT | --- | --- | --- | --- | --- | --- | --- |
| DELAWARE | --- | --- | --- | --- | --- | --- | --- |
| DIST OF COLUMBIA | --- | --- | --- | --- | --- | --- | --- |
| FLORIDA | --- | --- | --- | --- | --- | --- | --- |
| GEORGIA | --- | --- | --- | --- | --- | --- | --- |
| HAWAII | --- | --- | --- | --- | --- | --- | --- |
| IDAHO | --- | --- | --- | --- | --- | --- | --- |
| ILLINOIS | --- | --- | --- | --- | --- | --- | --- |
| INDIANA | --- | --- | --- | --- | --- | --- | --- |
| IOWA | --- | --- | --- | --- | --- | --- | --- |
| KANSAS | 172601 | 151647 | 0 | 25610 | 0 | 175 | 350033 |
| KENTUCKY | --- | --- | --- | --- | --- | --- | --- |
| LOUISIANA | --- | --- | --- | --- | --- | --- | --- |
| MAINE | --- | --- | --- | --- | --- | --- | --- |
| MARYLAND | --- | --- | --- | --- | --- | --- | --- |
| MASSACHUSETTS | --- | --- | --- | --- | --- | --- | --- |
| MICHIGAN | --- | --- | --- | --- | --- | --- | --- |
| MINNESOTA | 102691 | 173074 | 0 | 0 | 0 | 0 | 275765 |
| MISSISSIPPI | --- | --- | --- | --- | --- | --- | --- |
| MISSOURI | --- | --- | --- | --- | --- | --- | --- |
| MONTANA | 28421 | 18450 | 0 | 0 | 22161 | 0 | 69032 |
| NEBRASKA | --- | --- | --- | --- | --- | --- | --- |
| NEVADA | --- | --- | --- | --- | --- | --- | --- |
| NEW HAMPSHIRE | --- | --- | --- | --- | --- | --- | --- |
| NEW JERSEY | --- | --- | --- | --- | --- | --- | --- |
| NEW MEXICO | --- | --- | --- | --- | --- | --- | --- |
| NEW YORK | --- | --- | --- | --- | --- | --- | --- |

TABLE 3.5 (CONTINUED)

## 1912 SENATE ELECTION

| | DEMOCRAT | REPUBLICAN | PROHIBITION | SOCIALIST | PROGRESSIVE | OTHER | TOTAL VOTES CAST |
|---|---|---|---|---|---|---|---|
| NORTH CAROLINA | --- | --- | --- | --- | --- | --- | --- |
| NORTH DAKOTA | --- | --- | --- | --- | --- | --- | --- |
| OHIO | --- | --- | --- | --- | --- | --- | --- |
| OKLAHOMA | 126407 | 83448 | 0 | 40876 | 0 | 0 | 250731 |
| OREGON | 40172 | 38453 | 6848 | 11093 | 11083 | 25929 | 133578 |
| PENNSYLVANIA | --- | --- | --- | --- | --- | --- | --- |
| RHODE ISLAND | --- | --- | --- | --- | --- | --- | --- |
| SOUTH CAROLINA | --- | --- | --- | --- | --- | --- | --- |
| SOUTH DAKOTA | --- | --- | --- | --- | --- | --- | --- |
| TENNESSEE | --- | --- | --- | --- | --- | --- | --- |
| TEXAS | --- | --- | --- | --- | --- | --- | --- |
| UTAH | --- | --- | --- | --- | --- | --- | --- |
| VERMONT | --- | --- | --- | --- | --- | --- | --- |
| VIRGINIA | --- | --- | --- | --- | --- | --- | --- |
| WASHINGTON | --- | --- | --- | --- | --- | --- | --- |
| WEST VIRGINIA | --- | --- | --- | --- | --- | --- | --- |
| WISCONSIN | --- | --- | --- | --- | --- | --- | --- |
| WYOMING | --- | --- | --- | --- | --- | --- | --- |

## 1914 SENATE ELECTION

| | DEMOCRAT | REPUBLICAN | PROHIBITION | SOCIALIST | PROGRESSIVE | OTHER | TOTAL VOTES CAST |
|---|---|---|---|---|---|---|---|
| ALABAMA | 63388 | 12320 | 0 | 1159 | 4263 | 2 | 81133 |
| ALASKA | --- | --- | --- | --- | --- | --- | --- |
| ARIZONA | 25800 | 9182 | 0 | 3582 | 2608 | 7293 | 48463 |
| ARKANSAS | 33449 | 11222 | 0 | --- | --- | 0 | 44671 |
| CALIFORNIA | 279896 | 254159 | 39921 | 56804 | 255232 | 43 | 886056 |
| COLORADO | 102037 | 98728 | 0 | 13943 | 27072 | 11433 | 253213 |
| CONNECTICUT | 76081 | 89983 | 1356 | 5890 | 6853 | 651 | 180814 |
| DELAWARE | --- | --- | --- | --- | --- | --- | --- |
| DIST OF COLUMBIA | --- | --- | --- | --- | --- | --- | --- |
| FLORIDA | 22761 | 0 | 0 | 0 | 0 | 110 | 22871 |

188

| STATE | | | | | | | |
|---|---|---|---|---|---|---|---|
| GEORGIA | 61489 | 47486 | 0 | 0 | 28435 | 0 | 89924 |
| HAWAII | ---- | ---- | ---- | ---- | ---- | ---- | ---- |
| IDAHO | 41266 | 390661 | 1237 | 7888 | 10321 | 0 | 108198 |
| ILLINOIS | 373403 | 226766 | 6750 | 39889 | 203027 | 2078 | 1015816 |
| INDIANA | 272249 | 205832 | 13860 | 21719 | 108581 | 2884 | 646059 |
| IOWA | 167251 | 180823 | 6009 | 8462 | 15058 | 24490 | 427102 |
| KANSAS | 176929 | 144758 | 9885 | 24502 | 116755 | 0 | 508894 |
| KENTUCKY | 175999 | ---- | 0 | 0 | 14108 | 4890 | 339755 |
| LOUISIANA | ---- | ---- | ---- | ---- | ---- | ---- | ---- |
| MAINE | ---- | ---- | ---- | ---- | ---- | ---- | ---- |
| MARYLAND | 110204 | 94864 | 3144 | 3255 | 3697 | 969 | 216133 |
| MASSACHUSETTS | ---- | ---- | ---- | ---- | ---- | ---- | ---- |
| MICHIGAN | ---- | ---- | ---- | ---- | ---- | ---- | ---- |
| MINNESOTA | ---- | ---- | ---- | ---- | ---- | ---- | ---- |
| MISSISSIPPI | 311616 | 257054 | 3636 | 17061 | 27609 | 1251 | 618225 |
| MISSOURI | ---- | ---- | ---- | ---- | ---- | ---- | ---- |
| MONTANA | ---- | ---- | ---- | ---- | ---- | ---- | ---- |
| NEBRASKA | 8078 | 8038 | 0 | 5451 | 0 | 0 | 21567 |
| NEVADA | 36382 | 42113 | 0 | 1089 | 1938 | 6 | 81528 |
| NEW HAMPSHIRE | ---- | ---- | ---- | ---- | ---- | ---- | ---- |
| NEW JERSEY | ---- | ---- | ---- | ---- | ---- | ---- | ---- |
| NEW MEXICO | 571010 | 639112 | 27813 | 55266 | 61977 | 3507 | 1358685 |
| NEW YORK | 121342 | 87101 | 0 | 0 | 0 | 425 | 208868 |
| NORTH CAROLINA | 29640 | 48732 | 0 | 6231 | 2707 | 0 | 87310 |
| NORTH DAKOTA | 423742 | 526115 | 0 | 52803 | 67509 | 0 | 1070171 |
| OHIO | 119443 | 73292 | 8649 | 52229 | 3966 | 65 | 248995 |
| OKLAHOMA | 111748 | 88297 | 17685 | 10666 | 26220 | ---- | 245580 |
| OREGON | 266415 | 490008 | ---- | 37950 | 269265 | 30503 | 1111862 |
| PENNSYLVANIA | ---- | ---- | ---- | ---- | ---- | ---- | ---- |
| RHODE ISLAND | 32950 | 44244 | 0 | 89 | 0 | 0 | 33029 |
| SOUTH CAROLINA | 47668 | ---- | 2406 | 2674 | 0 | 2104 | 99096 |
| SOUTH DAKOTA | ---- | ---- | ---- | ---- | ---- | ---- | ---- |
| TENNESSEE | ---- | ---- | ---- | ---- | ---- | ---- | ---- |
| TEXAS | 53128 | 56282 | 0 | 5257 | 0 | 0 | 114666 |
| UTAH | 0 | 35137 | 0 | 772 | 26776 | 20 | 62705 |
| VERMONT | ---- | ---- | ---- | ---- | ---- | ---- | ---- |
| VIRGINIA | 91733 | 130479 | 9551 | 30234 | 83282 | 0 | 345279 |
| WASHINGTON | ---- | ---- | ---- | ---- | ---- | ---- | ---- |
| WEST VIRGINIA | 134925 | 133969 | 9276 | 29774 | 9276 | 58 | 308002 |
| WISCONSIN | ---- | ---- | ---- | ---- | ---- | ---- | ---- |
| WYOMING | ---- | ---- | ---- | ---- | ---- | ---- | ---- |

TABLE 3.5 (CONTINUED)

## 1916 SENATE ELECTION

| | DEMOCRAT | REPUBLICAN | PROHIBITION | SOCIALIST | PROGRESSIVE | OTHER | TOTAL VOTES CAST |
|---|---|---|---|---|---|---|---|
| ALABAMA | --- | --- | --- | --- | --- | --- | --- |
| ALASKA | --- | --- | --- | --- | --- | --- | --- |
| ARIZONA | 29882 | 21261 | 0 | 2827 | 0 | 0 | 53970 |
| ARKANSAS | 110293 | 48922 | --- | --- | --- | --- | 159215 |
| CALIFORNIA | 277852 | 0 | 38797 | 49341 | 0 | 574966 | 940956 |
| COLORADO | --- | --- | --- | --- | --- | --- | --- |
| CONNECTICUT | 98649 | 107020 | 1768 | 5288 | 0 | 619 | 213344 |
| DELAWARE | 25434 | 22925 | 0 | 490 | 2361 | 0 | 51210 |
| DIST OF COLUMBIA | --- | --- | --- | --- | --- | --- | --- |
| FLORIDA | 58391 | 8774 | 0 | 3304 | 0 | 0 | 70469 |
| GEORGIA | --- | --- | --- | --- | --- | --- | --- |
| HAWAII | --- | --- | --- | --- | --- | --- | --- |
| IDAHO | --- | --- | --- | --- | --- | --- | --- |
| ILLINOIS | --- | --- | --- | --- | --- | --- | --- |
| INDIANA | 325588 | 337089 | 15598 | 21558 | 4272 | 1562 | 705667 |
| IOWA | --- | --- | --- | --- | --- | --- | --- |
| KANSAS | --- | --- | --- | --- | --- | --- | --- |
| KENTUCKY | --- | --- | --- | --- | --- | --- | --- |
| LOUISIANA | --- | --- | --- | --- | --- | --- | --- |
| MAINE | 69486 | 79841 | 279 | 1510 | 0 | 0 | 151116 |
| MARYLAND | 109740 | 113662 | 3325 | 2590 | 0 | 1143 | 230460 |
| MASSACHUSETTS | 234238 | 267177 | 0 | 15558 | 0 | 26 | 516999 |
| MICHIGAN | 257954 | 364657 | 7569 | 15614 | 0 | 1484 | 647278 |
| MINNESOTA | 117541 | 185159 | 78425 | 0 | 0 | 0 | 381125 |
| MISSISSIPPI | 74290 | 0 | 0 | 0 | 0 | 0 | 74290 |
| MISSOURI | 396166 | 371710 | 0 | 14654 | 0 | 962 | 783492 |
| MONTANA | 85585 | 72753 | 0 | 9292 | 0 | 0 | 167630 |
| NEBRASKA | 0 | 0 | 4429 | 7425 | 0 | 274441 | 286295 |
| NEVADA | 12765 | 10618 | 0 | 9507 | 0 | 0 | 32890 |
| NEW HAMPSHIRE | --- | --- | --- | --- | --- | --- | --- |
| NEW JERSEY | 170019 | 244715 | 7178 | 13358 | 0 | 1826 | 437096 |
| NEW MEXICO | 34142 | 30622 | 0 | 2033 | 0 | 0 | 66797 |
| NEW YORK | 0 | 839314 | 19302 | 61167 | 0 | 625406 | 1545189 |

| STATE | DEMOCRAT | REPUBLICAN | PROHIBITION | SOCIALIST | INDEPENDENT | OTHER | TOTAL VOTES CAST |
|---|---|---|---|---|---|---|---|
| NORTH CAROLINA | --- | --- | --- | --- | --- | --- | 107174 |
| NORTH DAKOTA | 40988 | 57714 | 0 | 8472 | 0 | 0 | 1160091 |
| OHIO | 571488 | 535391 | 12060 | 38187 | 0 | 2965 | --- |
| OKLAHOMA | --- | --- | --- | --- | --- | --- | 1208457 |
| OREGON | 450112 | 662218 | 30089 | 45377 | 13364 | 7297 | 88877 |
| PENNSYLVANIA | 47048 | 39211 | 454 | 1996 | 0 | 168 | --- |
| RHODE ISLAND | --- | --- | --- | --- | --- | --- | 264075 |
| SOUTH CAROLINA | 143718 | 118174 | 0 | 2183 | 0 | 0 | 372761 |
| SOUTH DAKOTA | 303035 | 48788 | 2313 | 18616 | 0 | 9 | 142416 |
| TENNESSEE | 80895 | 56862 | 0 | 4497 | 162 | 0 | 63798 |
| TEXAS | 14956 | 47362 | 0 | 1336 | 0 | 144 | 133203 |
| UTAH | 133091 | 0 | 0 | 0 | 0 | 112 | 365189 |
| VERMONT | 135339 | 202287 | 4411 | 21709 | 1442 | 1 | 287705 |
| VIRGINIA | 138585 | 144243 | 0 | 4877 | 0 | 0 | 423883 |
| WASHINGTON | 135144 | 251303 | 8528 | 28908 | 0 | 0 | 51147 |
| WEST VIRGINIA | 26324 | 23258 | 231 | 1334 | 0 | 0 | |
| WISCONSIN | | | | | | | |
| WYOMING | | | | | | | |

## 1918 SENATE ELECTION

| STATE | DEMOCRAT | REPUBLICAN | PROHIBITION | SOCIALIST | INDEPENDENT | OTHER | TOTAL VOTES CAST |
|---|---|---|---|---|---|---|---|
| ALABAMA | 54880 | 0 | 0 | 0 | 0 | 0 | 54880 |
| ALASKA | --- | --- | --- | --- | --- | --- | --- |
| ARIZONA | --- | 0 | --- | --- | --- | --- | --- |
| ARKANSAS | 78386 | 0 | 0 | 0 | 0 | 0 | 78386 |
| CALIFORNIA | 104347 | 107726 | 0 | 5606 | 0 | 0 | 217679 |
| COLORADO | --- | --- | --- | --- | --- | --- | --- |
| CONNECTICUT | 20113 | 21519 | 0 | 420 | 0 | 0 | 42052 |
| DELAWARE | --- | --- | --- | --- | --- | --- | --- |
| DIST OF COLUMBIA | --- | --- | --- | --- | --- | --- | --- |
| FLORIDA | 53731 | 7078 | 0 | 0 | 0 | 0 | 60809 |
| GEORGIA | --- | --- | --- | --- | --- | --- | --- |
| HAWAII | --- | --- | --- | --- | --- | --- | --- |
| IDAHO | 31018 | 63587 | 3151 | 0 | 0 | 3268 | 94605 |
| ILLINOIS | 426943 | 479957 | | 37167 | 0 | | 950486 |
| INDIANA | --- | --- | --- | --- | --- | --- | --- |

TABLE 3.5 (CONTINUED)

## 1918 SENATE ELECTION

| | DEMOCRAT | REPUBLICAN | PROHIBITION | SOCIALIST | INDEPENDENT | OTHER | TOTAL VOTES CAST |
|---|---|---|---|---|---|---|---|
| IOWA | 121830 | 230264 | 0 | 0 | 0 | 0 | 352094 |
| KANSAS | 149300 | 281931 | 0 | 11419 | 0 | 4 | 442654 |
| KENTUCKY | 184385 | 178797 | 0 | 0 | 0 | 0 | 363182 |
| LOUISIANA | 44224 | 0 | 0 | 0 | 0 | 0 | 44224 |
| MAINE | 53460 | 66858 | 0 | 0 | 0 | 0 | 120318 |
| MARYLAND | --- | --- | --- | --- | --- | --- | --- |
| MASSACHUSETTS | 207478 | 188287 | 0 | 0 | 21985 | 92 | 417842 |
| MICHIGAN | 212487 | 220054 | 1133 | 4763 | 0 | 15 | 438452 |
| MINNESOTA | 0 | 206687 | 0 | 0 | 0 | 137294 | 343981 |
| MISSISSIPPI | 30055 | 0 | 0 | 0 | 0 | 1569 | 31624 |
| MISSOURI | --- | --- | --- | --- | --- | --- | --- |
| MONTANA | 46160 | 40229 | 0 | 0 | 0 | 26013 | 112402 |
| NEBRASKA | 99696 | 119486 | 0 | 0 | 0 | 0 | 219182 |
| NEVADA | --- | --- | --- | --- | --- | --- | --- |
| NEW HAMPSHIRE | 32763 | 37787 | 0 | 0 | 0 | 0 | 70550 |
| NEW JERSEY | 153743 | 179022 | 5768 | 14723 | 0 | 2352 | 355608 |
| NEW MEXICO | 22470 | 24322 | 0 | 531 | 0 | 0 | 47323 |
| NEW YORK | --- | --- | --- | --- | --- | --- | --- |
| NORTH CAROLINA | 143519 | 93707 | 0 | 0 | 0 | 0 | 237226 |
| NORTH DAKOTA | --- | --- | --- | --- | --- | --- | --- |
| OHIO | --- | --- | --- | --- | --- | --- | --- |
| OKLAHOMA | 105050 | 77188 | 0 | 7259 | 0 | 0 | 189497 |
| OREGON | 64303 | 82360 | 0 | 5373 | 0 | 0 | 152036 |
| PENNSYLVANIA | --- | --- | --- | --- | --- | --- | --- |
| RHODE ISLAND | 37573 | 42055 | 0 | 1623 | 0 | 0 | 81251 |
| SOUTH CAROLINA | 25792 | 0 | 0 | 0 | 0 | 0 | 25792 |
| SOUTH DAKOTA | 36210 | 51198 | 0 | 0 | 5560 | 0 | 92968 |
| TENNESSEE | 98605 | 59989 | 0 | 0 | 0 | 0 | 158594 |
| TEXAS | 155178 | 22214 | 0 | 1609 | 0 | 49 | 179050 |
| UTAH | --- | --- | --- | --- | --- | --- | --- |
| VERMONT | --- | --- | --- | --- | --- | --- | --- |
| VIRGINIA | 40403 | 0 | 0 | 0 | 0 | 131 | 40534 |
| WASHINGTON | --- | --- | --- | --- | --- | --- | --- |
| WEST VIRGINIA | 97715 | 115216 | 0 | 2288 | 0 | 0 | 215219 |
| WISCONSIN | --- | --- | --- | --- | --- | --- | --- |
| WYOMING | 17528 | 23975 | 0 | 0 | 0 | 0 | 41503 |

## 1920 SENATE ELECTION

| | DEMOCRAT | REPUBLICAN | INDEPENDENT | PROHIBITION | OTHER | TOTAL VOTES CAST |
|---|---|---|---|---|---|---|
| ALABAMA | 155664 | 71334 | 1984 | 0 | 0 | 228982 |
| ALASKA | --- | --- | --- | --- | --- | --- |
| ARIZONA | 29169 | 35893 | 0 | 0 | 0 | 65062 |
| ARKANSAS | 126577 | 65381 | 0 | 0 | 0 | 191958 |
| CALIFORNIA | 371580 | 447835 | 36545 | 57768 | 41 | 913769 |
| COLORADO | 112890 | 156577 | 17706 | 0 | 27 | 287200 |
| CONNECTICUT | 131824 | 216792 | 12194 | 2892 | 1486 | 365188 |
| DELAWARE | --- | --- | --- | --- | --- | --- |
| DIST OF COLUMBIA | --- | --- | --- | --- | --- | --- |
| FLORIDA | 98966 | 27914 | 3525 | 0 | 2855 | 133260 |
| GEORGIA | 124630 | 0 | 6700 | 0 | 0 | 131330 |
| HAWAII | --- | --- | --- | --- | --- | --- |
| IDAHO | 64513 | 75985 | 0 | 0 | 0 | 140498 |
| ILLINOIS | 554372 | 1381384 | 117212 | 10186 | 3891 | 2067045 |
| INDIANA | 514191 | 681854 | 40199 | 13323 | 0 | 1249567 |
| IOWA | 322015 | 528499 | 9014 | 0 | 942 | 860470 |
| KANSAS | 170443 | 327072 | 13417 | 0 | 1 | 510933 |
| KENTUCKY | 449244 | 454226 | 0 | 0 | 0 | 903470 |
| LOUISIANA | --- | --- | --- | --- | --- | --- |
| MAINE | --- | --- | --- | --- | --- | --- |
| MARYLAND | 169200 | 184999 | 30473 | 0 | 1 | 384673 |
| MASSACHUSETTS | --- | --- | --- | --- | --- | --- |
| MICHIGAN | --- | --- | --- | --- | --- | --- |
| MINNESOTA | --- | --- | --- | --- | --- | --- |
| MISSISSIPPI | --- | --- | --- | --- | --- | --- |
| MISSOURI | 589498 | 711161 | 19995 | 0 | 4865 | 1325519 |
| MONTANA | --- | --- | --- | --- | --- | --- |
| NEBRASKA | --- | --- | --- | --- | --- | --- |
| NEVADA | 10402 | 11550 | 5475 | 0 | 0 | 27427 |
| NEW HAMPSHIRE | 65035 | 90173 | 1004 | 0 | 0 | 156212 |
| NEW JERSEY | --- | --- | --- | --- | --- | --- |
| NEW MEXICO | --- | --- | --- | --- | --- | --- |
| NEW YORK | 901310 | 1434393 | 236089 | 159623 | 7902 | 2739317 |
| NORTH CAROLINA | 310504 | 229343 | 0 | 0 | 0 | 539847 |
| NORTH DAKOTA | 87006 | 130098 | 0 | 0 | 0 | 217104 |

TABLE 3.5 (CONTINUED)

## 1920 SENATE ELECTION

| | DEMOCRAT | REPUBLICAN | INDEPENDENT | PROHIBITION | OTHER | TOTAL VOTES CAST |
|---|---|---|---|---|---|---|
| OHIO | 782650 | 1134953 | 0 | 0 | 2647 | 1920250 |
| OKLAHOMA | 218371 | 247721 | 23663 | 0 | 0 | 489755 |
| OREGON | 100124 | 116696 | 11405 | 0 | 1782 | 230007 |
| PENNSYLVANIA | 484862 | 1068985 | 94717 | 132610 | 2165 | 1783339 |
| RHODE ISLAND | --- | --- | --- | --- | --- | --- |
| SOUTH CAROLINA | 64388 | 0 | 0 | 0 | 1 | 64389 |
| SOUTH DAKOTA | 36833 | 92267 | 738 | 0 | 44309 | 174147 |
| TENNESSEE | --- | --- | --- | --- | --- | --- |
| TEXAS | --- | --- | --- | --- | --- | --- |
| UTAH | 56280 | 82566 | 7012 | 0 | 0 | 145858 |
| VERMONT | 19580 | 69650 | 0 | 0 | 41 | 89271 |
| VIRGINIA | --- | --- | --- | --- | --- | --- |
| WASHINGTON | 68488 | 217069 | 99309 | 0 | 0 | 384866 |
| WEST VIRGINIA | --- | --- | --- | --- | --- | --- |
| WISCONSIN | 89265 | 281576 | 301201 | 5107 | 0 | 677149 |
| WYOMING | --- | --- | --- | --- | --- | --- |

## 1922 SENATE ELECTION

| | DEMOCRAT | REPUBLICAN | INDEPENDENT | PROHIBITION | OTHER | TOTAL VOTES CAST |
|---|---|---|---|---|---|---|
| ALABAMA | --- | --- | --- | --- | --- | --- |
| ALASKA | --- | --- | --- | --- | --- | --- |
| ARIZONA | 39722 | 21358 | 0 | 0 | 0 | 61080 |
| ARKANSAS | --- | --- | --- | --- | --- | --- |
| CALIFORNIA | 215748 | 564422 | 56982 | 70748 | 195 | 908095 |
| COLORADO | --- | --- | --- | --- | --- | --- |
| CONNECTICUT | 147276 | 169524 | 6161 | 0 | 945 | 323906 |
| DELAWARE | 37304 | 36979 | 0 | 0 | 608 | 74891 |
| DIST OF COLUMBIA | --- | --- | --- | --- | --- | --- |
| FLORIDA | 45707 | 0 | 0 | 0 | 6243 | 51950 |
| GEORGIA | --- | --- | --- | --- | --- | --- |

| State | 1 | 2 | 3 | 4 | 5 | 6 |
|---|---|---|---|---|---|---|
| HAWAII | --- | --- | --- | --- | --- | --- |
| IDAHO | --- | --- | --- | --- | --- | --- |
| ILLINOIS | 558169 | 524558 | 14635 | 0 | 0 | 1097362 |
| INDIANA | --- | --- | --- | --- | --- | --- |
| IOWA | --- | --- | --- | --- | --- | --- |
| KANSAS | --- | --- | --- | --- | --- | --- |
| KENTUCKY | --- | --- | --- | --- | --- | --- |
| LOUISIANA | --- | --- | --- | --- | --- | --- |
| MAINE | 74659 | 101026 | 0 | 0 | 0 | 175685 |
| MARYLAND | 160947 | 139581 | 5387 | 0 | 0 | 305915 |
| MASSACHUSETTS | 406776 | 414130 | 24376 | 0 | 24875 | 870157 |
| MICHIGAN | 294932 | 281843 | 4249 | 1936 | 0 | 582970 |
| MINNESOTA | 123624 | 241833 | 325372 | 0 | 0 | 690829 |
| MISSISSIPPI | 63636 | 1273 | 3362 | 0 | 0 | 68271 |
| MISSOURI | 496406 | 462009 | 7119 | 0 | 969 | 966503 |
| MONTANA | 88205 | 69464 | 1545 | 0 | 0 | 159214 |
| NEBRASKA | 148265 | 220350 | 19076 | 0 | 0 | 387691 |
| NEVADA | 18201 | 10770 | 0 | 0 | 0 | 28971 |
| NEW HAMPSHIRE | --- | --- | --- | --- | --- | --- |
| NEW JERSEY | 451832 | 362699 | 5970 | 0 | 2937 | 823438 |
| NEW MEXICO | 60969 | 48721 | 818 | 0 | 0 | 110508 |
| NEW YORK | 1276667 | 995421 | 0 | 32124 | 123002 | 2427214 |
| NORTH CAROLINA | --- | --- | --- | --- | --- | --- |
| NORTH DAKOTA | 0 | 0 | --- | 0 | 193776 | 193776 |
| OHIO | 744558 | 794149 | 21514 | 0 | 0 | 1560221 |
| OKLAHOMA | --- | --- | --- | --- | --- | --- |
| OREGON | --- | --- | --- | --- | --- | --- |
| PENNSYLVANIA | 423583 | 802146 | 160184 | 41935 | 3637 | 1431485 |
| RHODE ISLAND | 82889 | 68930 | 0 | 0 | 7070 | 158889 |
| SOUTH CAROLINA | --- | --- | --- | --- | --- | --- |
| SOUTH DAKOTA | --- | --- | --- | --- | --- | --- |
| TENNESSEE | 151523 | 71199 | 0 | 0 | 0 | 222722 |
| TEXAS | 261063 | 130731 | 3875 | 0 | 0 | 391794 |
| UTAH | 58749 | 58188 | 0 | 39 | 11 | 120823 |
| VERMONT | 21375 | 45245 | 2627 | 0 | 0 | 66659 |
| VIRGINIA | 116393 | 42903 | 35352 | 0 | 0 | 161923 |
| WASHINGTON | 130375 | 126556 | 4895 | 0 | 2394 | 294677 |
| WEST VIRGINIA | 198853 | 185046 | 0 | 11254 | 0 | 388794 |
| WISCONSIN | 0 | 379494 | 0 | 0 | 80070 | 470818 |
| WYOMING | 35734 | 26627 | 0 | 0 | 0 | 62361 |

TABLE 3.5 (CONTINUED)

1924 SENATE ELECTION

| | DEMOCRAT | REPUBLICAN | INDEPENDENT | OTHER | TOTAL VOTES CAST |
|---|---|---|---|---|---|
| ALABAMA | 120017 | 39623 | 0 | 0 | 159640 |
| ALASKA | --- | --- | --- | --- | --- |
| ARIZONA | --- | --- | --- | --- | --- |
| ARKANSAS | 100408 | 36163 | 0 | 0 | 136571 |
| CALIFORNIA | --- | --- | --- | --- | --- |
| COLORADO | 139660 | 159698 | 17614 | 1197 | 318169 |
| CONNECTICUT | --- | --- | --- | --- | --- |
| DELAWARE | 0 | 52731 | 0 | 36085 | 88816 |
| DIST OF COLUMBIA | --- | --- | --- | --- | --- |
| FLORIDA | --- | --- | --- | --- | --- |
| GEORGIA | 145178 | 0 | 0 | 0 | 145178 |
| HAWAII | --- | --- | --- | --- | --- |
| IDAHO | 25199 | 99846 | 554 | 0 | 125599 |
| ILLINOIS | 806702 | 1449180 | 18708 | 6257 | 2280847 |
| INDIANA | --- | --- | --- | --- | --- |
| IOWA | 446840 | 447594 | 0 | 0 | 894434 |
| KANSAS | 154189 | 428494 | 28606 | 1 | 611290 |
| KENTUCKY | 381605 | 406123 | 0 | 0 | 787728 |
| LOUISIANA | 94939 | 0 | 0 | 0 | 94939 |
| MAINE | 97428 | 148783 | 0 | 0 | 246211 |
| MARYLAND | --- | --- | --- | --- | --- |
| MASSACHUSETTS | 547600 | 566188 | 0 | 12738 | 1126526 |
| MICHIGAN | 284609 | 858934 | 1619 | 11564 | 1156726 |
| MINNESOTA | 53709 | 388594 | 385640 | 8620 | 836563 |
| MISSISSIPPI | 97257 | 0 | 0 | 0 | 97257 |
| MISSOURI | --- | --- | --- | --- | --- |
| MONTANA | 89681 | 72005 | 8180 | 0 | 169866 |
| NEBRASKA | 0 | 274040 | 0 | 165370 | 440010 |
| NEVADA | --- | --- | --- | --- | --- |
| NEW HAMPSHIRE | 63596 | 94432 | 0 | 0 | 158028 |
| NEW JERSEY | 331034 | 608020 | 37795 | 6326 | 983175 |
| NEW MEXICO | 57355 | 54558 | 3128 | 0 | 115041 |
| NEW YORK | --- | --- | --- | --- | --- |
| NORTH CAROLINA | 295344 | 184493 | 0 | 0 | 479837 |
| NORTH DAKOTA | --- | --- | --- | --- | --- |

| | DEMOCRAT | REPUBLICAN | INDEPENDENT | OTHER | TOTAL VOTES CAST |
|---|---|---|---|---|---|
| OHIO | 196527 | 341720 | 15637 | --- | 553884 |
| OKLAHOMA | 65340 | 174672 | 20379 | 4412 | 264803 |
| OREGON | --- | --- | --- | --- | --- |
| PENNSYLVANIA | 87620 | 120815 | 0 | 1191 | 209626 |
| RHODE ISLAND | 49060 | 0 | 0 | 0 | 49060 |
| SOUTH CAROLINA | 63548 | 90006 | 29578 | 0 | 183132 |
| SOUTH DAKOTA | 147821 | 109863 | 0 | 247 | 257931 |
| TENNESSEE | 592057 | 101252 | 0 | 0 | 693309 |
| TEXAS | --- | --- | --- | --- | --- |
| UTAH | --- | --- | --- | --- | --- |
| VERMONT | --- | --- | --- | --- | --- |
| VIRGINIA | 151498 | 5594 | 50092 | 1 | 207185 |
| WASHINGTON | --- | --- | --- | --- | --- |
| WEST VIRGINIA | 271809 | 290004 | 7751 | 0 | 569564 |
| WISCONSIN | --- | --- | --- | --- | --- |
| WYOMING | 33536 | 41293 | 0 | 0 | 74829 |

1926 SENATE ELECTION

| | DEMOCRAT | REPUBLICAN | INDEPENDENT | OTHER | TOTAL VOTES CAST |
|---|---|---|---|---|---|
| ALABAMA | 91843 | 21722 | 0 | 0 | 113565 |
| ALASKA | --- | --- | --- | --- | --- |
| ARIZONA | 44591 | 31845 | --- | 0 | 76436 |
| ARKANSAS | 28064 | 5848 | 0 | 0 | 33912 |
| CALIFORNIA | 391599 | 670128 | 0 | 127 | 1061854 |
| COLORADO | 143842 | 149585 | 0 | 4168 | 297595 |
| CONNECTICUT | 107753 | 191401 | 3173 | --- | 302327 |
| DELAWARE | --- | --- | --- | --- | --- |
| DIST OF COLUMBIA | --- | --- | --- | --- | --- |
| FLORIDA | 51054 | 6133 | 0 | 8381 | 65568 |
| GEORGIA | 47446 | 0 | 0 | 0 | 47446 |
| HAWAII | --- | --- | --- | --- | --- |
| IDAHO | 31285 | 56847 | 37047 | 0 | 125179 |
| ILLINOIS | 774943 | 842273 | 10225 | 169918 | 1797359 |
| INDIANA | 511454 | 522737 | 5106 | 5420 | 1044717 |
| IOWA | 247869 | 323409 | 0 | 908 | 572186 |

TABLE 3.5 (CONTINUED)

## 1926 SENATE ELECTION

| | DEMOCRAT | REPUBLICAN | INDEPENDENT | OTHER | TOTAL VOTES CAST |
|---|---|---|---|---|---|
| KANSAS | 168446 | 308222 | 8208 | 2 | 484878 |
| KENTUCKY | 286997 | 266657 | 0 | 0 | 553654 |
| LOUISIANA | 54180 | 0 | 0 | 13 | 54193 |
| MAINE | --- | --- | --- | --- | --- |
| MARYLAND | 195410 | 139995 | 3659 | 0 | 339064 |
| MASSACHUSETTS | --- | --- | --- | --- | --- |
| MICHIGAN | --- | --- | --- | --- | --- |
| MINNESOTA | --- | --- | --- | --- | --- |
| MISSISSIPPI | --- | --- | --- | --- | --- |
| MISSOURI | 506015 | 470654 | 1812 | 8005 | 986486 |
| MONTANA | --- | --- | --- | --- | --- |
| NEBRASKA | --- | --- | --- | --- | --- |
| NEVADA | 13273 | 17430 | 543 | 0 | 31246 |
| NEW HAMPSHIRE | 47935 | 79279 | 0 | 0 | 127214 |
| NEW JERSEY | --- | --- | --- | --- | --- |
| NEW MEXICO | --- | --- | --- | --- | --- |
| NEW YORK | 1321463 | 1205246 | 73412 | 242709 | 2842830 |
| NORTH CAROLINA | 218934 | 142891 | 0 | 0 | 361825 |
| NORTH DAKOTA | 18496 | 18951 | 0 | 107921 | 145368 |
| OHIO | 623221 | 711359 | 0 | 2846 | 1337426 |
| OKLAHOMA | 196097 | 159287 | 1178 | 0 | 356562 |
| OREGON | 81301 | 89007 | 3145 | 0 | 173453 |
| PENNSYLVANIA | 615550 | 822187 | 43000 | 23961 | 1504698 |
| RHODE ISLAND | --- | --- | --- | --- | --- |
| SOUTH CAROLINA | 14560 | 0 | 0 | 0 | 14560 |
| SOUTH DAKOTA | 71925 | 105756 | 0 | 0 | 177681 |
| TENNESSEE | --- | --- | --- | --- | --- |
| TEXAS | --- | --- | --- | --- | --- |
| UTAH | 53809 | 88101 | 1310 | 5 | 143225 |
| VERMONT | 0 | 50364 | 0 | 20852 | 71216 |
| VIRGINIA | --- | --- | --- | --- | --- |
| WASHINGTON | 152229 | 164130 | 0 | 3513 | 319872 |
| WEST VIRGINIA | --- | --- | --- | --- | --- |
| WISCONSIN | 66672 | 300759 | 65024 | 114183 | 546638 |
| WYOMING | --- | --- | --- | --- | --- |

## 1928 SENATE ELECTION

| | DEMOCRAT | REPUBLICAN | OTHER | TOTAL VOTES CAST |
|---|---|---|---|---|
| ALABAMA | --- | --- | --- | --- |
| ALASKA | --- | --- | --- | --- |
| ARIZONA | 47013 | 39651 | 0 | 86664 |
| ARKANSAS | --- | --- | --- | --- |
| CALIFORNIA | 282411 | 1148397 | 118988 | 1549796 |
| COLORADO | --- | --- | --- | --- |
| CONNECTICUT | 251429 | 296958 | 3014 | 551401 |
| DELAWARE | 40828 | 63725 | 0 | 104553 |
| DIST OF COLUMBIA | --- | --- | --- | --- |
| FLORIDA | 153816 | 70633 | 2 | 224451 |
| GEORGIA | --- | --- | --- | --- |
| HAWAII | --- | --- | --- | --- |
| IDAHO | --- | --- | --- | --- |
| ILLINOIS | 623996 | 782144 | 8300 | 1414440 |
| INDIANA | --- | --- | --- | --- |
| IOWA | --- | --- | --- | --- |
| KANSAS | --- | --- | --- | --- |
| KENTUCKY | --- | --- | --- | --- |
| LOUISIANA | --- | --- | --- | --- |
| MAINE | 63429 | 145501 | 0 | 208930 |
| MARYLAND | 214447 | 256224 | 3396 | 474067 |
| MASSACHUSETTS | 818055 | 693563 | 13335 | 1524953 |
| MICHIGAN | 376592 | 977893 | 7663 | 1362148 |
| MINNESOTA | 0 | 342992 | 674549 | 1017541 |
| MISSISSIPPI | 111210 | 0 | 0 | 111210 |
| MISSOURI | 726322 | 787499 | 3102 | 1516923 |
| MONTANA | 103655 | 91185 | 0 | 194840 |
| NEBRASKA | 204737 | 324014 | 0 | 528751 |
| NEVADA | 19515 | 13414 | 0 | 32929 |
| NEW HAMPSHIRE | 49913 | 68070 | 4 | 117987 |
| NEW JERSEY | 608623 | 841752 | 4252 | 1454627 |
| NEW MEXICO | --- | --- | --- | --- |
| NEW YORK | 2084273 | 2034014 | 128711 | 4246998 |
| NORTH CAROLINA | --- | --- | --- | --- |
| NORTH DAKOTA | 38856 | 159940 | 2047 | 200843 |

TABLE 3.5 (CONTINUED)

## 1928 SENATE ELECTION

|  | DEMOCRAT | REPUBLICAN | OTHER | TOTAL VOTES CAST |
|---|---|---|---|---|
| OHIO | 908952 | 1412805 | 4448 | 2326205 |
| OKLAHOMA | --- | --- | --- | --- |
| OREGON | --- | --- | --- | --- |
| PENNSYLVANIA | 1029055 | 1948646 | 49168 | 3026869 |
| RHODE ISLAND | 116234 | 119228 | 313 | 235775 |
| SOUTH CAROLINA | --- | --- | --- | --- |
| SOUTH DAKOTA | --- | --- | --- | --- |
| TENNESSEE | 175431 | 120289 | 0 | 295720 |
| TEXAS | 566139 | 130172 | 804 | 697115 |
| UTAH | 97436 | 77073 | 998 | 175507 |
| VERMONT | 37030 | 93136 | 11 | 130177 |
| VIRGINIA | 275425 | 0 | 623 | 276048 |
| WASHINGTON | 261524 | 227415 | 666 | 489605 |
| WEST VIRGINIA | 317620 | 327266 | 919 | 645805 |
| WISCONSIN | 0 | 635376 | 107177 | 742553 |
| WYOMING | 43032 | 37076 | 333 | 80441 |

## 1930 SENATE ELECTION

|  | DEMOCRAT | REPUBLICAN | INDEPENDENT | OTHER | TOTAL VOTES CAST |
|---|---|---|---|---|---|
| ALABAMA | 150985 | 0 | 101862 | 0 | 252847 |
| ALASKA | --- | --- | --- | --- | --- |
| ARIZONA | --- | --- | --- | --- | --- |
| ARKANSAS | 141806 | 0 | 0 | 0 | 141806 |
| CALIFORNIA | --- | --- | --- | --- | --- |
| COLORADO | 180028 | 137487 | 1745 | 3088 | 322348 |
| CONNECTICUT | --- | --- | --- | --- | --- |
| DELAWARE | 39881 | 47909 | 0 | 135 | 87925 |
| DIST OF COLUMBIA | --- | --- | --- | --- | --- |
| FLORIDA | --- | --- | --- | --- | --- |

| | | | | | |
|---|---|---|---|---|---|
| GEORGIA | 55606 | 0 | 0 | 1 | 55607 |
| HAWAII | --- | --- | --- | --- | --- |
| IDAHO | 36162 | 94938 | 0 | 0 | 131100 |
| ILLINOIS | 1432216 | 687469 | 110677 | 6742 | 2237104 |
| INDIANA | 235186 | 307613 | 1045 | 2670 | 546514 |
| IOWA | 232161 | 364548 | 0 | 0 | 596709 |
| KANSAS | 336748 | 309180 | 0 | 0 | 645928 |
| KENTUCKY | 130536 | --- | 0 | 24 | 130560 |
| LOUISIANA | 56561 | 88262 | 0 | 0 | 144823 |
| MAINE | --- | --- | --- | --- | --- |
| MARYLAND | 651939 | 539226 | 7244 | 8627 | 1207036 |
| MASSACHUSETTS | 169757 | 634577 | 2419 | 5254 | 812007 |
| MICHIGAN | 282018 | 293626 | 20669 | 184316 | 780629 |
| MINNESOTA | 33953 | 0 | 0 | 0 | 33953 |
| MISSISSIPPI | --- | --- | --- | --- | --- |
| MISSOURI | 106274 | 66724 | 1006 | 2157 | 176161 |
| MONTANA | 172795 | 247118 | 0 | 14884 | 434797 |
| NEBRASKA | --- | --- | --- | --- | --- |
| NEVADA | 52284 | 72225 | 0 | 282 | 124791 |
| NEW HAMPSHIRE | 401007 | 601497 | 4519 | 21200 | 1028223 |
| NEW JERSEY | 69356 | 48699 | 0 | 254 | 118309 |
| NEW MEXICO | --- | --- | --- | --- | --- |
| NEW YORK | 324293 | 210761 | 0 | 0 | 535054 |
| NORTH CAROLINA | --- | --- | --- | --- | --- |
| NORTH DAKOTA | 255838 | 232589 | 614 | 0 | 489041 |
| OHIO | 66028 | 137231 | 17488 | 5056 | 225803 |
| OKLAHOMA | --- | --- | --- | --- | --- |
| OREGON | 109687 | 112202 | 0 | 1195 | 223084 |
| PENNSYLVANIA | 16213 | 0 | 0 | 0 | 16213 |
| RHODE ISLAND | 106317 | 99595 | 0 | 0 | 205912 |
| SOUTH CAROLINA | 154071 | 58550 | 0 | 3392 | 216013 |
| SOUTH DAKOTA | 266562 | 39053 | 809 | 291 | 306715 |
| TENNESSEE | --- | --- | --- | --- | --- |
| TEXAS | 112002 | 0 | 34045 | 49 | 146096 |
| UTAH | --- | --- | --- | --- | --- |
| VERMONT | 342467 | 209427 | 0 | 1293 | 553187 |
| VIRGINIA | --- | --- | --- | --- | --- |
| WASHINGTON | 30259 | 43626 | 0 | 0 | 73885 |
| WEST VIRGINIA | --- | --- | --- | --- | --- |
| WISCONSIN | --- | --- | --- | --- | --- |
| WYOMING | --- | --- | --- | --- | --- |

TABLE 3.5 (CONTINUED)

## 1932 SENATE ELECTION

| | DEMOCRAT | REPUBLICAN | INDEPENDENT | OTHER | TOTAL VOTES CAST |
|---|---|---|---|---|---|
| ALABAMA | 209614 | 33425 | 0 | 1 | 243040 |
| ALASKA | --- | --- | --- | --- | --- |
| ARIZONA | 74310 | 35737 | 1110 | 306 | 111463 |
| ARKANSAS | 183795 | 21597 | 0 | 0 | 205392 |
| CALIFORNIA | 943164 | 669676 | 0 | 560994 | 2173834 |
| COLORADO | 226516 | 198519 | 8632 | 2672 | 436339 |
| CONNECTICUT | 282327 | 278061 | 19774 | 2243 | 582405 |
| DELAWARE | --- | --- | --- | --- | --- |
| DIST OF COLUMBIA | | | | | |
| FLORIDA | 204651 | 0 | 0 | 459 | 205110 |
| GEORGIA | 234590 | 18151 | 0 | 0 | 252741 |
| HAWAII | | | | | |
| IDAHO | 103020 | 78225 | 0 | 3801 | 185046 |
| ILLINOIS | 1670466 | 1471841 | 39131 | 16697 | 3198135 |
| INDIANA | 870053 | 661750 | 18724 | 15223 | 1565750 |
| IOWA | 538422 | 399929 | 0 | 43174 | 981525 |
| KANSAS | 328992 | 302809 | 74057 | 0 | 705858 |
| KENTUCKY | 574977 | 393865 | 3291 | 0 | 972133 |
| LOUISIANA | 249189 | 0 | 0 | 3 | 249192 |
| MAINE | | | | | |
| MARYLAND | 293389 | 138266 | 8105 | 3308 | 443068 |
| MASSACHUSETTS | --- | --- | --- | --- | --- |
| MICHIGAN | --- | --- | --- | --- | --- |
| MINNESOTA | --- | --- | --- | --- | --- |
| MISSISSIPPI | --- | --- | --- | --- | --- |
| MISSOURI | 1017046 | 577184 | 11421 | 4097 | 1609748 |
| MONTANA | --- | --- | --- | --- | --- |
| NEBRASKA | --- | --- | --- | --- | --- |
| NEVADA | 21398 | 19706 | 0 | 0 | 41104 |
| NEW HAMPSHIRE | 98766 | 96649 | 533 | 228 | 196176 |
| NEW JERSEY | --- | --- | --- | --- | --- |
| NEW MEXICO | --- | --- | --- | --- | --- |
| NEW YORK | 2532905 | 1751186 | 143282 | 114007 | 4541380 |

| | DEMOCRAT | REPUBLICAN | INDEPENDENT | OTHER | TOTAL VOTES CAST |
|---|---|---|---|---|---|
| NORTH CAROLINA | 476048 | 221392 | 0 | 0 | 697440 |
| NORTH DAKOTA | 65575 | 172796 | 543 | 0 | 238914 |
| OHIO | 1290175 | 1126830 | 0 | 41987 | 2458992 |
| OKLAHOMA | 426130 | 218854 | 1395 | 0 | 646379 |
| OREGON | 137237 | 186210 | 24125 | 5567 | 353139 |
| PENNSYLVANIA | 1200767 | 1371844 | 91556 | 116864 | 2781031 |
| RHODE ISLAND | --- | --- | --- | --- | --- |
| SOUTH CAROLINA | 104472 | 1976 | 0 | 0 | 106448 |
| SOUTH DAKOTA | 125731 | 151845 | 405 | 3873 | 281854 |
| TENNESSEE | --- | --- | --- | --- | --- |
| TEXAS | 116909 | 86066 | 2464 | 883 | 206322 |
| UTAH | 60453 | 74319 | 0 | 21 | 134793 |
| VERMONT | --- | --- | --- | --- | --- |
| VIRGINIA | 365949 | 197450 | 9364 | 31042 | 603805 |
| WASHINGTON | --- | --- | --- | --- | --- |
| WEST VIRGINIA | 610236 | 387668 | 65807 | 7285 | 1070996 |
| WISCONSIN | --- | --- | --- | --- | --- |
| WYOMING | --- | --- | --- | --- | --- |

## 1934 SENATE ELECTION

| | DEMOCRAT | REPUBLICAN | INDEPENDENT | OTHER | TOTAL VOTES CAST |
|---|---|---|---|---|---|
| ALABAMA | --- | --- | --- | --- | --- |
| ALASKA | --- | --- | --- | --- | --- |
| ARIZONA | 67648 | 24075 | 1591 | 606 | 93920 |
| ARKANSAS | --- | --- | --- | --- | --- |
| CALIFORNIA | 0 | 0 | 108748 | 1950192 | 2058940 |
| COLORADO | --- | --- | --- | --- | --- |
| CONNECTICUT | 265552 | 247623 | 0 | 0 | 513175 |
| DELAWARE | 45771 | 52829 | 497 | 69 | 99166 |
| DIST OF COLUMBIA | --- | --- | --- | --- | --- |
| FLORIDA | 131780 | 0 | 0 | 0 | 131780 |
| GEORGIA | --- | --- | --- | --- | --- |
| HAWAII | --- | --- | --- | --- | --- |
| IDAHO | --- | --- | --- | --- | --- |
| ILLINOIS | --- | --- | --- | --- | --- |
| INDIANA | 758801 | 700103 | 9414 | 6294 | 1474612 |
| IOWA | --- | --- | --- | --- | --- |

TABLE 3.5 (CONTINUED)

## 1934 SENATE ELECTION

| | DEMOCRAT | REPUBLICAN | INDEPENDENT | OTHER | TOTAL VOTES CAST |
|---|---|---|---|---|---|
| KANSAS | --- | --- | --- | --- | --- |
| KENTUCKY | --- | --- | --- | --- | --- |
| LOUISIANA | --- | --- | --- | --- | --- |
| MAINE | 138573 | 139773 | 0 | 422 | 278768 |
| MARYLAND | 264279 | 197643 | 6067 | 3123 | 471112 |
| MASSACHUSETTS | 852776 | 536692 | 22092 | 24372 | 1435932 |
| MICHIGAN | 573574 | 626017 | 10644 | 9499 | 1219734 |
| MINNESOTA | 294757 | 200083 | 5618 | 508999 | 1009457 |
| MISSISSIPPI | 51709 | 0 | 0 | 0 | 51709 |
| MISSOURI | 787110 | 524954 | 9010 | 802 | 1321876 |
| MONTANA | 142823 | 58519 | 1381 | 903 | 203626 |
| NEBRASKA | 305858 | 237126 | 0 | 10171 | 553155 |
| NEVADA | 27581 | 14273 | 901 | 0 | 42755 |
| NEW HAMPSHIRE | --- | --- | --- | --- | --- |
| NEW JERSEY | 785971 | 554483 | 9721 | 7234 | 1357409 |
| NEW MEXICO | 74944 | 76228 | 0 | 690 | 151862 |
| NEW YORK | 2046377 | 1363440 | 194952 | 93049 | 3697818 |
| NORTH CAROLINA | --- | --- | --- | --- | --- |
| NORTH DAKOTA | 104477 | 151205 | 3269 | 0 | 258951 |
| OHIO | 1276206 | 839068 | 0 | 13569 | 2128843 |
| OKLAHOMA | --- | --- | --- | --- | --- |
| OREGON | --- | --- | --- | --- | --- |
| PENNSYLVANIA | 1494001 | 1366877 | 50444 | 30955 | 2942277 |
| RHODE ISLAND | 140700 | 105545 | 0 | 68 | 246313 |
| SOUTH CAROLINA | --- | --- | --- | --- | --- |
| SOUTH DAKOTA | --- | --- | --- | --- | --- |
| TENNESSEE | 195430 | 110401 | 0 | 2443 | 308274 |
| TEXAS | 437254 | 12859 | 1837 | 309 | 452259 |
| UTAH | 95931 | 82154 | 1497 | 1210 | 180792 |
| VERMONT | 63632 | 67146 | 771 | 3 | 131552 |
| VIRGINIA | 109963 | 30289 | 2630 | 1868 | 144750 |
| WASHINGTON | 302606 | 168994 | 7192 | 17896 | 496688 |
| WEST VIRGINIA | 349882 | 281756 | 2 | 2931 | 634571 |
| WISCONSIN | 223438 | 210569 | 484966 | 2953 | 921926 |
| WYOMING | 53806 | 40819 | 401 | 0 | 95026 |

1936 SENATE ELECTION

| | DEMOCRAT | REPUBLICAN | INDEPENDENT | OTHER | TOTAL VOTES CAST |
|---|---|---|---|---|---|
| ALABAMA | 239632 | 33698 | 0 | 2023 | 275353 |
| ALASKA | --- | --- | --- | --- | --- |
| ARIZONA | 155075 | 30997 | 0 | 3425 | 189497 |
| ARKANSAS | --- | --- | --- | --- | --- |
| CALIFORNIA | 299376 | 166308 | 0 | 6143 | 471827 |
| COLORADO | --- | --- | --- | --- | --- |
| CONNECTICUT | 67136 | 52460 | 0 | 7133 | 126729 |
| DELAWARE | --- | --- | --- | --- | --- |
| DIST OF COLUMBIA | --- | --- | --- | --- | --- |
| FLORIDA | 263468 | 0 | 0 | 0 | 263468 |
| GEORGIA | --- | --- | --- | --- | --- |
| HAWAII | --- | --- | --- | --- | --- |
| IDAHO | 74444 | 128723 | 0 | 0 | 203167 |
| ILLINOIS | 2142887 | 1545160 | 93639 | 12910 | 3794596 |
| INDIANA | 539555 | 503635 | 0 | 25567 | 1068757 |
| IOWA | 396685 | 417873 | 0 | 4810 | 819368 |
| KANSAS | 539968 | 365850 | 11699 | 810 | 918327 |
| KENTUCKY | 293256 | 0 | 0 | 7 | 293263 |
| LOUISIANA | --- | --- | --- | --- | --- |
| MAINE | 153420 | 158068 | 0 | 0 | 311488 |
| MARYLAND | --- | --- | --- | --- | --- |
| MASSACHUSETTS | 739751 | 875160 | 134245 | 54201 | 1803357 |
| MICHIGAN | 910937 | 714602 | 75680 | 8345 | 1709564 |
| MINNESOTA | 0 | 402404 | 0 | 663363 | 1065767 |
| MISSISSIPPI | 140570 | --- | 0 | 0 | 140570 |
| MISSOURI | 121769 | 60038 | 39655 | 0 | 221462 |
| MONTANA | --- | --- | --- | --- | --- |
| NEBRASKA | 108391 | 223276 | 0 | 258700 | 590367 |
| NEVADA | --- | --- | --- | --- | --- |
| NEW HAMPSHIRE | 99195 | 107923 | 0 | 989 | 208107 |
| NEW JERSEY | 916414 | 740088 | 0 | 12789 | 1669291 |
| NEW MEXICO | 104550 | 64817 | 0 | 76 | 169443 |
| NEW YORK | --- | --- | --- | --- | --- |
| NORTH CAROLINA | 564088 | 233000 | 0 | 0 | 797088 |
| NORTH DAKOTA | --- | --- | --- | --- | --- |

TABLE 3.5 (CONTINUED)

## 1936 SENATE ELECTION

| | DEMOCRAT | REPUBLICAN | INDEPENDENT | OTHER | TOTAL VOTES CAST |
|---|---|---|---|---|---|
| OHIO | --- | --- | --- | --- | --- |
| OKLAHOMA | 493407 | 229004 | 344 | 2870 | 725625 |
| OREGON | 193822 | 199332 | 1956 | 2887 | 397997 |
| PENNSYLVANIA | --- | --- | --- | --- | --- |
| RHODE ISLAND | 149157 | 136174 | 21501 | 0 | 306832 |
| SOUTH CAROLINA | 113696 | 1663 | 0 | 1 | 115360 |
| SOUTH DAKOTA | 141509 | 135461 | 12816 | 0 | 289786 |
| TENNESSEE | 273298 | 67238 | 14627 | 2516 | 357679 |
| TEXAS | 773574 | 59491 | 1773 | 958 | 835796 |
| UTAH | --- | --- | --- | --- | --- |
| VERMONT | --- | --- | --- | --- | --- |
| VIRGINIA | 244518 | 12473 | 0 | 9675 | 266666 |
| WASHINGTON | --- | --- | --- | --- | --- |
| WEST VIRGINIA | 488620 | 338363 | 0 | 0 | 826983 |
| WISCONSIN | --- | --- | --- | --- | --- |
| WYOMING | 53919 | 45483 | 682 | 88 | 100172 |

## 1938 SENATE ELECTION

| | DEMOCRAT | REPUBLICAN | INDEPENDENT | OTHER | TOTAL VOTES CAST |
|---|---|---|---|---|---|
| ALABAMA | --- | --- | --- | --- | --- |
| ALASKA | --- | --- | --- | --- | --- |
| ARIZONA | 82714 | 25378 | 0 | 0 | 108092 |
| ARKANSAS | 122871 | 14240 | 0 | 0 | 137111 |
| CALIFORNIA | 0 | 1126240 | 0 | 1395902 | 2522142 |
| COLORADO | 262806 | 181297 | 0 | 7126 | 451229 |
| CONNECTICUT | 250929 | 270413 | 1497 | 107594 | 630433 |
| DELAWARE | --- | --- | --- | --- | --- |
| DIST OF COLUMBIA | --- | --- | --- | --- | --- |
| FLORIDA | 145757 | 31035 | 0 | 0 | 176792 |

| | | | | | |
|---|---|---|---|---|---|
| GEORGIA | 66897 | 0 | 3442 | 0 | 70339 |
| HAWAII | --- | --- | --- | --- | --- |
| IDAHO | 99801 | 81939 | 0 | 845 | 182585 |
| ILLINOIS | 1638162 | 1542574 | 0 | 10707 | 3191443 |
| INDIANA | 788386 | 783189 | 0 | 10215 | 1581790 |
| IOWA | 413788 | 410983 | 0 | 7068 | 831839 |
| KANSAS | 326774 | 419532 | 0 | 99 | 746405 |
| KENTUCKY | 346735 | 212266 | 0 | 0 | 559001 |
| LOUISIANA | 151585 | 0 | 250 | 0 | 151835 |
| MAINE | --- | --- | --- | --- | --- |
| MARYLAND | 357245 | 153253 | 5784 | 6956 | 523238 |
| MASSACHUSETTS | --- | --- | --- | --- | --- |
| MICHIGAN | --- | --- | --- | --- | --- |
| MINNESOTA | --- | --- | --- | --- | --- |
| MISSISSIPPI | --- | --- | --- | --- | --- |
| MISSOURI | 757587 | 488687 | 0 | 2003 | 1248277 |
| MONTANA | --- | --- | --- | --- | --- |
| NEBRASKA | --- | --- | --- | --- | --- |
| NEVADA | 27406 | 19078 | 0 | 0 | 46484 |
| NEW HAMPSHIRE | 84920 | 100633 | 0 | 0 | 185553 |
| NEW JERSEY | --- | --- | --- | --- | --- |
| NEW MEXICO | --- | --- | --- | --- | --- |
| NEW YORK | 2497029 | 2046794 | 0 | 39236 | 4583059 |
| NORTH CAROLINA | 316685 | 179461 | 0 | 0 | 496146 |
| NORTH DAKOTA | 19244 | 131907 | 112007 | 0 | 263158 |
| OHIO | 1086815 | 1257412 | 0 | 0 | 2344227 |
| OKLAHOMA | 307936 | 159734 | 603 | 2220 | 470493 |
| OREGON | 167135 | 203120 | 0 | 6 | 370261 |
| PENNSYLVANIA | 1684083 | 2086932 | 10307 | 33697 | 3815019 |
| RHODE ISLAND | --- | --- | --- | --- | --- |
| SOUTH CAROLINA | 45751 | 508 | 0 | 2 | 46261 |
| SOUTH DAKOTA | 133064 | 146813 | 0 | 0 | 279877 |
| TENNESSEE | --- | --- | --- | --- | --- |
| TEXAS | --- | --- | --- | --- | --- |
| UTAH | 102353 | 81071 | 0 | 0 | 183424 |
| VERMONT | 38673 | 73990 | 0 | 4 | 112667 |
| VIRGINIA | --- | --- | --- | --- | --- |
| WASHINGTON | 371535 | 220204 | 0 | 1553 | 593292 |
| WEST VIRGINIA | --- | --- | --- | --- | --- |
| WISCONSIN | 231976 | 446770 | 1283 | 250223 | 930252 |
| WYOMING | --- | --- | --- | --- | --- |

TABLE 3.5 (CONTINUED)

## 1940 SENATE ELECTION

| | DEMOCRAT | REPUBLICAN | INDEPENDENT | OTHER | TOTAL VOTES CAST |
|---|---|---|---|---|---|
| ALABAMA | --- | --- | --- | --- | --- |
| ALASKA | --- | --- | --- | --- | --- |
| ARIZONA | 101495 | 39657 | 0 | 579 | 141731 |
| ARKANSAS | --- | --- | --- | --- | --- |
| CALIFORNIA | 0 | 0 | 0 | 2713865 | 2713865 |
| COLORADO | --- | --- | --- | --- | --- |
| CONNECTICUT | 416740 | 357574 | 739 | 9014 | 784067 |
| DELAWARE | 68294 | 63799 | 0 | 2786 | 134879 |
| DIST OF COLUMBIA | --- | --- | --- | --- | --- |
| FLORIDA | 323216 | 0 | 0 | 0 | 323216 |
| GEORGIA | --- | --- | --- | --- | --- |
| HAWAII | --- | --- | --- | --- | --- |
| IDAHO | --- | --- | --- | --- | --- |
| ILLINOIS | --- | --- | --- | --- | --- |
| INDIANA | 864803 | 888070 | 0 | 7372 | 1760245 |
| IOWA | --- | --- | --- | --- | --- |
| KANSAS | --- | --- | --- | --- | --- |
| KENTUCKY | --- | --- | --- | --- | --- |
| LOUISIANA | --- | --- | --- | --- | --- |
| MAINE | 105740 | 150149 | 0 | 305 | 256194 |
| MARYLAND | 394239 | 203912 | 0 | 10824 | 608975 |
| MASSACHUSETTS | 1088838 | 838122 | 0 | 30129 | 1957089 |
| MICHIGAN | 939740 | 1053104 | 0 | 7499 | 2000343 |
| MINNESOTA | 248658 | 641049 | 0 | 319892 | 1209599 |
| MISSISSIPPI | 143333 | 0 | 0 | 0 | 143333 |
| MISSOURI | 930775 | 886376 | 0 | 1865 | 1819016 |
| MONTANA | 176753 | 63941 | 0 | 0 | 240694 |
| NEBRASKA | 247659 | 340250 | 0 | 8982 | 596891 |
| NEVADA | 31351 | 20488 | 0 | 0 | 51839 |
| NEW HAMPSHIRE | --- | --- | --- | --- | --- |
| NEW JERSEY | 823893 | 1029331 | 0 | 14551 | 1867775 |
| NEW MEXICO | 103194 | 81257 | 0 | 0 | 184451 |
| NEW YORK | 3274766 | 2868852 | 0 | 4956 | 6148574 |

| | DEMOCRAT | REPUBLICAN | INDEPENDENT | OTHER | TOTAL VOTES CAST |
|---|---|---|---|---|---|
| NORTH CAROLINA | --- | --- | --- | --- | --- |
| NORTH DAKOTA | 69847 | 100647 | 92593 | 1014 | 264101 |
| OHIO | 1457359 | 1602567 | 0 | 0 | 3059926 |
| OKLAHOMA | --- | --- | --- | --- | --- |
| OREGON | --- | --- | --- | --- | --- |
| PENNSYLVANIA | 2069980 | 1893104 | 0 | 33936 | 3997020 |
| RHODE ISLAND | 173847 | 141312 | 0 | 0 | 315159 |
| SOUTH CAROLINA | --- | --- | --- | --- | --- |
| SOUTH DAKOTA | --- | --- | --- | --- | --- |
| TENNESSEE | 295440 | 121790 | 34 | 0 | 417264 |
| TEXAS | 993974 | 60051 | 0 | 406 | 1054431 |
| UTAH | 155499 | 91931 | 0 | 0 | 247430 |
| VERMONT | 47101 | 93283 | 0 | 4 | 140388 |
| VIRGINIA | 274260 | 0 | 0 | 19621 | 293881 |
| WASHINGTON | 404718 | 342589 | 0 | 0 | 747307 |
| WEST VIRGINIA | 492413 | 381806 | 0 | 0 | 874219 |
| WISCONSIN | 176688 | 553692 | 1308 | 606447 | 1338135 |
| WYOMING | 65022 | 45682 | 0 | 0 | 110704 |

1942 SENATE ELECTION

| | DEMOCRAT | REPUBLICAN | INDEPENDENT | OTHER | TOTAL VOTES CAST |
|---|---|---|---|---|---|
| ALABAMA | 69212 | 0 | 0 | 4 | 69216 |
| ALASKA | --- | --- | --- | --- | --- |
| ARIZONA | --- | --- | --- | --- | --- |
| ARKANSAS | 99126 | 0 | 0 | 0 | 99126 |
| CALIFORNIA | --- | --- | --- | --- | --- |
| COLORADO | 174612 | 170970 | 0 | 2014 | 347596 |
| CONNECTICUT | --- | --- | --- | --- | --- |
| DELAWARE | 38322 | 46210 | 0 | 776 | 85308 |
| DIST OF COLUMBIA | --- | --- | --- | --- | --- |
| FLORIDA | --- | --- | --- | --- | --- |
| GEORGIA | 59870 | 0 | 1892 | 0 | 61762 |
| HAWAII | --- | --- | --- | --- | --- |
| IDAHO | 68989 | 73353 | 0 | 0 | 142342 |
| ILLINOIS | 1380011 | 1582887 | 0 | 10331 | 2973229 |
| INDIANA | --- | --- | --- | --- | --- |
| IOWA | 295194 | 410333 | 0 | 2282 | 707809 |
| KANSAS | 200437 | 284059 | 0 | 12863 | 497359 |

TABLE 3.5 (CONTINUED)

## 1942 SENATE ELECTION

| | DEMOCRAT | REPUBLICAN | INDEPENDENT | OTHER | TOTAL VOTES CAST |
|---|---|---|---|---|---|
| KENTUCKY | 216958 | 175081 | 0 | 0 | 392039 |
| LOUISIANA | 85488 | 0 | 0 | 0 | 85488 |
| MAINE | 55754 | 111520 | --- | --- | 167274 |
| MARYLAND | --- | --- | --- | --- | --- |
| MASSACHUSETTS | 641042 | 721239 | 0 | 13163 | 1375444 |
| MICHIGAN | 561595 | 589652 | 0 | 38719 | 1189966 |
| MINNESOTA | 78959 | 356297 | 0 | 323196 | 758452 |
| MISSISSIPPI | 51355 | 0 | 0 | 0 | 51355 |
| MISSOURI | --- | --- | --- | --- | --- |
| MONTANA | 83673 | 82461 | 0 | 4380 | 170514 |
| NEBRASKA | 83763 | 186207 | 0 | 110199 | 380169 |
| NEVADA | --- | --- | --- | --- | --- |
| NEW HAMPSHIRE | 73656 | 88601 | 0 | 0 | 162257 |
| NEW JERSEY | 559851 | 648855 | 0 | 13426 | 1222132 |
| NEW MEXICO | 63301 | 43704 | 0 | 0 | 107005 |
| NEW YORK | --- | --- | --- | --- | --- |
| NORTH CAROLINA | 230427 | 119165 | 0 | 0 | 349592 |
| NORTH DAKOTA | --- | --- | --- | --- | --- |
| OHIO | --- | --- | --- | --- | --- |
| OKLAHOMA | 166653 | 204163 | 0 | 1549 | 372365 |
| OREGON | 63946 | 214755 | 0 | 3 | 278704 |
| PENNSYLVANIA | --- | --- | --- | --- | --- |
| RHODE ISLAND | 138239 | 100236 | 0 | 0 | 238475 |
| SOUTH CAROLINA | 23356 | 0 | 0 | 2 | 23358 |
| SOUTH DAKOTA | 74945 | 106704 | 0 | 0 | 181649 |
| TENNESSEE | 109881 | 34324 | 15317 | 0 | 159522 |
| TEXAS | 260629 | 12054 | 0 | 1975 | 274658 |
| UTAH | --- | --- | --- | --- | --- |
| VERMONT | --- | --- | --- | --- | --- |
| VIRGINIA | 79421 | 0 | 0 | 7731 | 87152 |
| WASHINGTON | --- | --- | --- | --- | --- |
| WEST VIRGINIA | 207045 | 256816 | 0 | 0 | 463861 |
| WISCONSIN | --- | --- | --- | --- | --- |
| WYOMING | 34503 | 41486 | 0 | 0 | 75989 |

1944 SENATE ELECTION

| | DEMOCRAT | REPUBLICAN | INDEPENDENT | OTHER | TOTAL VOTES CAST |
|---|---|---|---|---|---|
| ALABAMA | 202604 | 41983 | 0 | 3162 | 247749 |
| ALASKA | --- | --- | --- | --- | --- |
| ARIZONA | 90335 | 39891 | 0 | 0 | 130226 |
| ARKANSAS | 182529 | 31942 | 0 | 0 | 214471 |
| CALIFORNIA | 1728155 | 1576553 | 0 | 526 | 3305234 |
| COLORADO | 236086 | 259862 | 0 | 0 | 495948 |
| CONNECTICUT | 430716 | 391748 | 0 | 6033 | 828497 |
| DELAWARE | --- | --- | --- | --- | --- |
| DIST OF COLUMBIA | --- | --- | --- | --- | --- |
| FLORIDA | 335685 | 135258 | 0 | 0 | 470943 |
| GEORGIA | 272541 | 0 | 0 | 4 | 272545 |
| HAWAII | --- | --- | --- | --- | --- |
| IDAHO | 107096 | 102373 | 0 | 0 | 209469 |
| ILLINOIS | 2059023 | 1841793 | 0 | 13109 | 3913925 |
| INDIANA | 807766 | 829489 | 0 | 14130 | 1651385 |
| IOWA | 494229 | 523963 | 0 | 3505 | 1021697 |
| KANSAS | 272053 | 387090 | 0 | 10057 | 669200 |
| KENTUCKY | 464053 | 380425 | 0 | 2148 | 846626 |
| LOUISIANA | 286365 | 0 | 26 | 0 | 286391 |
| MAINE | --- | --- | --- | --- | --- |
| MARYLAND | 344725 | 213705 | 0 | 0 | 558430 |
| MASSACHUSETTS | --- | --- | --- | --- | --- |
| MICHIGAN | --- | --- | --- | --- | --- |
| MINNESOTA | --- | --- | --- | --- | --- |
| MISSISSIPPI | --- | --- | --- | --- | --- |
| MISSOURI | 777229 | 779029 | 0 | 1535 | 1557793 |
| MONTANA | --- | --- | --- | --- | --- |
| NEBRASKA | --- | --- | --- | --- | --- |
| NEVADA | 30595 | 21816 | 0 | 0 | 52411 |
| NEW HAMPSHIRE | 106508 | 110549 | 0 | 0 | 217057 |
| NEW JERSEY | --- | --- | --- | --- | --- |
| NEW MEXICO | --- | --- | --- | --- | --- |
| NEW YORK | 3294576 | 2899497 | 0 | 15244 | 6209317 |
| NORTH CAROLINA | 533813 | 226037 | 0 | 0 | 759850 |
| NORTH DAKOTA | 95102 | 69530 | 0 | 45790 | 210422 |

TABLE 3.5 (CONTINUED)

### 1944 SENATE ELECTION

|  | DEMOCRAT | REPUBLICAN | INDEPENDENT | OTHER | TOTAL VOTES CAST |
|---|---|---|---|---|---|
| OHIO | 1483069 | 1500809 | 0 | 0 | 2983878 |
| OKLAHOMA | 390851 | 309222 | 1128 | 0 | 701201 |
| OREGON | 174140 | 269095 | 0 | 0 | 443235 |
| PENNSYLVANIA | 1864735 | 1840943 | 0 | 24714 | 3730392 |
| RHODE ISLAND | --- | --- | --- | --- | --- |
| SOUTH CAROLINA | 94556 | 3214 | 0 | 3966 | 101736 |
| SOUTH DAKOTA | 82199 | 145248 | 0 | 0 | 227447 |
| TENNESSEE | --- | --- | --- | --- | --- |
| TEXAS | --- | --- | --- | --- | --- |
| UTAH | 148748 | 99532 | 0 | 0 | 248280 |
| VERMONT | 42136 | 81094 | 0 | 18 | 123248 |
| VIRGINIA | --- | --- | --- | --- | --- |
| WASHINGTON | 452013 | 364356 | 0 | 3510 | 819879 |
| WEST VIRGINIA | --- | --- | --- | --- | --- |
| WISCONSIN | 537144 | 634513 | 1664 | 83053 | 1256374 |
| WYOMING | --- | --- | --- | --- | --- |

### 1946 SENATE ELECTION

|  | DEMOCRAT | REPUBLICAN | INDEPENDENT | OTHER | TOTAL VOTES CAST |
|---|---|---|---|---|---|
| ALABAMA | --- | --- | --- | --- | --- |
| ALASKA | --- | --- | --- | --- | --- |
| ARIZONA | 80415 | 35022 | 0 | 802 | 116239 |
| ARKANSAS | --- | --- | --- | --- | --- |
| CALIFORNIA | 1167161 | 1428067 | 0 | 44237 | 2639465 |
| COLORADO | --- | --- | --- | --- | --- |
| CONNECTICUT | 276424 | 381328 | 0 | 22013 | 679765 |
| DELAWARE | 50910 | 62603 | 0 | 0 | 113513 |
| DIST OF COLUMBIA | --- | --- | --- | --- | --- |
| FLORIDA | 156232 | 42413 | 0 | 0 | 198645 |

| State | Col 1 | Col 2 | Col 3 | Col 4 | Col 5 |
|---|---|---|---|---|---|
| GEORGIA | — | — | | | |
| HAWAII | — | — | | | |
| IDAHO | — | — | | | |
| ILLINOIS | 584288 | 739809 | | | |
| INDIANA | — | — | 0 | 23337 | 1347434 |
| IOWA | — | — | | | |
| KANSAS | — | — | | | |
| KENTUCKY | — | — | | | |
| LOUISIANA | — | — | | | |
| MAINE | 63799 | 111215 | 0 | 0 | 175014 |
| MARYLAND | 229776 | 228162 | | | 457938 |
| MASSACHUSETTS | 660200 | 989736 | 0 | 12127 | 1662063 |
| MICHIGAN | 517923 | 1085570 | 0 | 15227 | 1618720 |
| MINNESOTA | 349520 | 517775 | 0 | 11436 | 878731 |
| MISSISSIPPI | 46747 | 0 | 0 | 0 | 46747 |
| MISSOURI | 511544 | 572556 | 0 | 2141 | 1086241 |
| MONTANA | 86476 | 101901 | 0 | 2189 | 190566 |
| NEBRASKA | 111751 | 271208 | 0 | 0 | 382959 |
| NEVADA | 22553 | 27801 | 0 | 0 | 50354 |
| NEW HAMPSHIRE | — | — | | | |
| NEW JERSEY | 548458 | 799808 | 0 | 18889 | 1367155 |
| NEW MEXICO | 68650 | 64632 | 0 | 0 | 133282 |
| NEW YORK | 2308112 | 2559365 | 0 | 0 | 4867477 |
| NORTH CAROLINA | — | — | 38804 | | |
| NORTH DAKOTA | 38368 | 88210 | 0 | 0 | 165382 |
| OHIO | 947610 | 1275774 | 0 | 13885 | 2237269 |
| OKLAHOMA | — | — | | | |
| OREGON | — | — | | | |
| PENNSYLVANIA | 1205338 | 1853458 | 0 | 29064 | 3127860 |
| RHODE ISLAND | 150748 | 122780 | 0 | 0 | 273528 |
| SOUTH CAROLINA | — | — | | | |
| SOUTH DAKOTA | — | — | | | |
| TENNESSEE | 145654 | 57237 | 11516 | 0 | 214407 |
| TEXAS | 336931 | 43619 | 0 | 0 | 380550 |
| UTAH | 96257 | 101142 | 0 | 0 | 197399 |
| VERMONT | 18594 | 54729 | 5168 | 17 | 73340 |
| VIRGINIA | 163960 | 358847 | 0 | 6709 | 252842 |
| WASHINGTON | 298683 | 269617 | 0 | 2812 | 660342 |
| WEST VIRGINIA | 273151 | — | | | 542768 |
| WISCONSIN | 378772 | 620430 | 0 | 13302 | 1012504 |
| WYOMING | 45843 | 35714 | 0 | 0 | 81557 |

TABLE 3.5 (CONTINUED)

## 1948 SENATE ELECTION

|  | DEMOCRAT | REPUBLICAN | INDEPENDENT | OTHER | TOTAL VOTES CAST |
|---|---|---|---|---|---|
| ALABAMA | 185534 | 35341 | 0 | 0 | 220875 |
| ALASKA | --- | --- | --- | --- | --- |
| ARIZONA | --- | --- | --- | --- | --- |
| ARKANSAS | 216401 | 0 | 15521 | 0 | 231922 |
| CALIFORNIA | --- | --- | --- | --- | --- |
| COLORADO | 340719 | 165069 | 2981 | 1352 | 510121 |
| CONNECTICUT | --- | --- | --- | --- | --- |
| DELAWARE | 71888 | 68246 | 681 | 547 | 141362 |
| DIST OF COLUMBIA | --- | --- | --- | --- | --- |
| FLORIDA | --- | --- | --- | --- | --- |
| GEORGIA | 362104 | 0 | 0 | 400 | 362504 |
| HAWAII | --- | --- | --- | --- | --- |
| IDAHO | 107000 | 103868 | 3154 | 166 | 214188 |
| ILLINOIS | 2147754 | 1740026 | 0 | 12505 | 3900285 |
| INDIANA | --- | --- | --- | --- | --- |
| IOWA | 578226 | 415778 | 3387 | 3021 | 1000412 |
| KANSAS | 305987 | 393412 | 0 | 16943 | 716342 |
| KENTUCKY | 408256 | 383776 | 923 | 1486 | 794441 |
| LOUISIANA | 330315 | 0 | 9 | 0 | 330324 |
| MAINE | 64074 | 159182 | 0 | 0 | 223256 |
| MARYLAND | --- | --- | --- | --- | --- |
| MASSACHUSETTS | 954398 | 1088475 | 0 | 12925 | 2055798 |
| MICHIGAN | 1000329 | 1045156 | 0 | 16612 | 2062097 |
| MINNESOTA | 729494 | 482801 | 0 | 4955 | 1217250 |
| MISSISSIPPI | 151478 | 0 | 0 | 0 | 151478 |
| MISSOURI | --- | --- | --- | --- | --- |
| MONTANA | 125193 | 94458 | 0 | 1352 | 221003 |
| NEBRASKA | 204320 | 267575 | 0 | 0 | 471895 |
| NEVADA | --- | --- | --- | --- | --- |
| NEW HAMPSHIRE | 91760 | 129600 | 1538 | 0 | 222898 |
| NEW JERSEY | 884414 | 934720 | 22658 | 28090 | 1869882 |
| NEW MEXICO | 108269 | 80226 | 705 | 0 | 189200 |
| NEW YORK | --- | --- | --- | --- | --- |

| | DEMOCRAT | REPUBLICAN | INDEPENDENT | STATES RIGHTS | OTHER | TOTAL VOTES CAST |
|---|---|---|---|---|---|---|
| NORTH CAROLINA | 540762 | 220307 | 3454 | 0 | 0 | 764523 |
| NORTH DAKOTA | --- | --- | --- | --- | --- | --- |
| OHIO | 441654 | 265169 | 2108 | 0 | 0 | 708931 |
| OKLAHOMA | 199275 | 299295 | 0 | 0 | 0 | 498570 |
| OREGON | --- | --- | --- | --- | --- | --- |
| PENNSYLVANIA | 190284 | 130668 | 0 | 0 | 0 | 320952 |
| RHODE ISLAND | 135998 | 5008 | 0 | 0 | 0 | 141006 |
| SOUTH CAROLINA | 98749 | 144084 | 0 | 0 | 0 | 242833 |
| SOUTH DAKOTA | 326062 | 166947 | 6103 | 0 | 26 | 499138 |
| TENNESSEE | 702785 | 349665 | 0 | 0 | 8913 | 1061363 |
| TEXAS | --- | --- | --- | --- | --- | --- |
| UTAH | --- | --- | --- | --- | --- | --- |
| VERMONT | --- | --- | --- | --- | --- | --- |
| VIRGINIA | 253865 | 119366 | 12153 | 0 | 1633 | 387017 |
| WASHINGTON | --- | --- | --- | --- | --- | --- |
| WEST VIRGINIA | 435354 | 328534 | 0 | 0 | 0 | 763888 |
| WISCONSIN | 57953 | 43527 | 0 | 0 | 0 | 101480 |
| WYOMING | --- | --- | --- | --- | --- | --- |

## 1950 SENATE ELECTION

| | DEMOCRAT | REPUBLICAN | INDEPENDENT | STATES RIGHTS | OTHER | TOTAL VOTES CAST |
|---|---|---|---|---|---|---|
| ALABAMA | 125534 | 0 | 38477 | 0 | 0 | 164011 |
| ALASKA | --- | --- | --- | --- | --- | --- |
| ARIZONA | 116246 | 68846 | 0 | 0 | 0 | 185092 |
| ARKANSAS | 302582 | 0 | 0 | 0 | 0 | 302582 |
| CALIFORNIA | 1502507 | 2183454 | 0 | 0 | 354 | 3686315 |
| COLORADO | 210442 | 239734 | 0 | 0 | 0 | 450176 |
| CONNECTICUT | 453646 | 409053 | 0 | 0 | 15128 | 877827 |
| DELAWARE | --- | --- | --- | --- | --- | --- |
| DIST OF COLUMBIA | --- | --- | --- | --- | --- | --- |
| FLORIDA | 238987 | 74228 | 0 | 0 | 272 | 313487 |
| GEORGIA | 261290 | 0 | 0 | 0 | 3 | 261293 |
| HAWAII | --- | --- | --- | --- | --- | --- |
| IDAHO | 77180 | 124237 | 0 | 0 | 0 | 201417 |
| ILLINOIS | 1657630 | 1951984 | 0 | 0 | 13059 | 3622673 |
| INDIANA | 741025 | 844303 | 0 | 0 | 13396 | 1598724 |
| IOWA | 383766 | 470613 | 0 | 571 | 3573 | 858523 |

TABLE 3.5 (CONTINUED)

## 1950 SENATE ELECTION

| | DEMOCRAT | REPUBLICAN | INDEPENDENT | STATES RIGHTS | OTHER | TOTAL VOTES CAST |
|---|---|---|---|---|---|---|
| KANSAS | 271365 | 335880 | 0 | 0 | 11859 | 619104 |
| KENTUCKY | 334249 | 278368 | 4496 | 0 | 0 | 617113 |
| LOUISIANA | 220907 | 30931 | 0 | 0 | 0 | 251838 |
| MAINE | --- | --- | --- | --- | --- | --- |
| MARYLAND | 283180 | 326291 | 6143 | 0 | 0 | 615614 |
| MASSACHUSETTS | --- | --- | --- | --- | --- | --- |
| MICHIGAN | --- | --- | --- | --- | --- | --- |
| MINNESOTA | --- | --- | --- | --- | --- | --- |
| MISSISSIPPI | --- | --- | --- | --- | --- | --- |
| MISSOURI | 685732 | 593139 | 0 | 0 | 760 | 1279631 |
| MONTANA | --- | --- | --- | --- | --- | --- |
| NEBRASKA | --- | --- | --- | --- | --- | --- |
| NEVADA | 35829 | 25933 | 0 | 0 | 0 | 61762 |
| NEW HAMPSHIRE | 72473 | 106142 | 11958 | 0 | 0 | 190573 |
| NEW JERSEY | --- | --- | --- | --- | --- | --- |
| NEW MEXICO | --- | --- | --- | --- | --- | --- |
| NEW YORK | 2632313 | 2367353 | 0 | 0 | 228737 | 5228403 |
| NORTH CAROLINA | 376473 | 171804 | 0 | 0 | 0 | 548277 |
| NORTH DAKOTA | 60507 | 126209 | 0 | 0 | 0 | 186716 |
| OHIO | 1214459 | 1645643 | 0 | 0 | 0 | 2860102 |
| OKLAHOMA | 345953 | 285224 | 0 | 0 | 0 | 631177 |
| OREGON | 116780 | 376510 | 10165 | 0 | 0 | 503455 |
| PENNSYLVANIA | 1694076 | 1820400 | 5516 | 0 | 28650 | 3548642 |
| RHODE ISLAND | --- | 0 | --- | --- | --- | --- |
| SOUTH CAROLINA | 50240 | 160670 | 0 | 0 | 37 | 50277 |
| SOUTH DAKOTA | 90692 | --- | 0 | 0 | 0 | 251362 |
| TENNESSEE | --- | --- | --- | --- | --- | --- |
| TEXAS | --- | --- | --- | --- | --- | --- |
| UTAH | 121198 | 142427 | 815 | 0 | 0 | 264440 |
| VERMONT | 19608 | 69543 | 0 | 0 | 20 | 89171 |
| VIRGINIA | --- | --- | --- | --- | --- | --- |
| WASHINGTON | 397719 | 342464 | 3120 | 0 | 1480 | 744783 |
| WEST VIRGINIA | --- | --- | --- | --- | --- | --- |
| WISCONSIN | 515539 | 595283 | 0 | 0 | 5255 | 1116077 |
| WYOMING | --- | --- | --- | --- | --- | --- |

1952 SENATE ELECTION

| | DEMOCRAT | REPUBLICAN | INDEPENDENT | OTHER | TOTAL VOTES CAST |
|---|---|---|---|---|---|
| ALABAMA | --- | --- | --- | --- | --- |
| ALASKA | --- | --- | --- | --- | --- |
| ARIZONA | 125338 | 132063 | 0 | 0 | 257401 |
| ARKANSAS | --- | --- | --- | --- | --- |
| CALIFORNIA | 0 | 0 | 0 | 4542548 | 4542548 |
| COLORADO | --- | --- | --- | --- | --- |
| CONNECTICUT | 485066 | 596122 | 0 | 12279 | 1093467 |
| DELAWARE | 77685 | 93020 | 0 | 0 | 170705 |
| DIST OF COLUMBIA | --- | --- | --- | --- | --- |
| FLORIDA | 616665 | 0 | 0 | 1135 | 617800 |
| GEORGIA | --- | --- | --- | --- | --- |
| HAWAII | --- | --- | --- | --- | --- |
| IDAHO | --- | --- | --- | --- | --- |
| ILLINOIS | --- | --- | --- | --- | --- |
| INDIANA | 911169 | 1020605 | 0 | 14344 | 1946118 |
| IOWA | --- | --- | --- | --- | --- |
| KANSAS | --- | --- | --- | --- | --- |
| KENTUCKY | --- | --- | --- | --- | --- |
| LOUISIANA | --- | --- | --- | --- | --- |
| MAINE | 82665 | 139205 | 0 | 0 | 221870 |
| MARYLAND | 406370 | 449823 | 0 | 0 | 856193 |
| MASSACHUSETTS | 1211984 | 1141247 | 0 | 7194 | 2360425 |
| MICHIGAN | 1383416 | 1428352 | 0 | 9363 | 2821131 |
| MINNESOTA | 590011 | 785649 | 0 | 11759 | 1387419 |
| MISSISSIPPI | 233919 | 0 | 0 | 0 | 233919 |
| MISSOURI | 1008523 | 858170 | 0 | 1408 | 1868101 |
| MONTANA | 133109 | 127360 | 0 | 1828 | 262297 |
| NEBRASKA | 164660 | 408971 | 0 | 18087 | 591718 |
| NEVADA | 39184 | 41906 | 0 | 0 | 81090 |
| NEW HAMPSHIRE | --- | --- | --- | --- | --- |
| NEW JERSEY | 1011187 | 1286782 | 0 | 20263 | 2318232 |
| NEW MEXICO | 122543 | 117168 | 0 | 0 | 239711 |
| NEW YORK | 3011511 | 3853934 | 0 | 114814 | 6980259 |
| NORTH CAROLINA | --- | --- | 24741 | --- | --- |
| NORTH DAKOTA | 55347 | 157907 | 0 | 0 | 237995 |

TABLE 3.5 (CONTINUED)

## 1952 SENATE ELECTION

| | DEMOCRAT | REPUBLICAN | INDEPENDENT | OTHER | TOTAL VOTES CAST |
|---|---|---|---|---|---|
| OHIO | 1563330 | 1878961 | 0 | 0 | 3442291 |
| OKLAHOMA | --- | --- | --- | --- | --- |
| OREGON | --- | --- | --- | --- | --- |
| PENNSYLVANIA | 2168546 | 2331034 | 0 | 20181 | 4519761 |
| RHODE ISLAND | 225128 | 185663 | 0 | 187 | 410978 |
| SOUTH CAROLINA | --- | --- | --- | --- | --- |
| SOUTH DAKOTA | --- | --- | --- | --- | --- |
| TENNESSEE | 545432 | 153479 | 22169 | 14139 | 735219 |
| TEXAS | 1425007 | 469594 | 0 | 589 | 1895190 |
| UTAH | 149598 | 177435 | 0 | 0 | 327033 |
| VERMONT | 42630 | 111406 | 0 | 16 | 154052 |
| VIRGINIA | 398677 | 0 | 0 | 144839 | 543516 |
| WASHINGTON | 595288 | 460884 | 0 | 2563 | 1058735 |
| WEST VIRGINIA | 470019 | 406554 | 0 | 0 | 876573 |
| WISCONSIN | 731402 | 870444 | 1442 | 1879 | 1605167 |
| WYOMING | 62921 | 67176 | 0 | 0 | 130097 |

## 1954 SENATE ELECTION

| | DEMOCRAT | INDEPENDENT | REPUBLICAN | OTHER | TOTAL VOTES CAST |
|---|---|---|---|---|---|
| ALABAMA | 259348 | 55110 | 0 | 1 | 314459 |
| ALASKA | --- | --- | --- | --- | --- |
| ARIZONA | --- | --- | --- | --- | --- |
| ARKANSAS | 291058 | 0 | 0 | 0 | 291058 |
| CALIFORNIA | --- | --- | --- | --- | --- |
| COLORADO | 235686 | 248502 | 0 | 0 | 484188 |
| CONNECTICUT | --- | --- | --- | --- | --- |
| DELAWARE | 82511 | 62389 | 0 | 0 | 144900 |
| DIST OF COLUMBIA | --- | --- | --- | --- | --- |
| FLORIDA | --- | --- | --- | --- | --- |

| State | Col 1 | Col 2 | Col 3 | Col 4 | Col 5 |
|---|---|---|---|---|---|
| GEORGIA | 333917 | 0 | 0 | 19 | 333936 |
| HAWAII | — | — | — | — | — |
| IDAHO | 84139 | 142269 | 0 | 0 | 226408 |
| ILLINOIS | 1804338 | 1563683 | 0 | 4 | 3368025 |
| INDIANA | — | — | — | — | — |
| IOWA | 402712 | 442409 | 0 | 2234 | 847355 |
| KANSAS | 258575 | 348144 | 0 | 11344 | 618063 |
| KENTUCKY | 434109 | 362948 | 0 | 0 | 797057 |
| LOUISIANA | 207115 | 0 | 0 | 0 | 207115 |
| MAINE | 102075 | 144530 | 0 | 0 | 246605 |
| MARYLAND | — | — | — | — | — |
| MASSACHUSETTS | 927899 | 956605 | 0 | 8206 | 1892710 |
| MICHIGAN | 1088550 | 1049420 | 0 | 6870 | 2144840 |
| MINNESOTA | 642193 | 479619 | 0 | 17140 | 1138952 |
| MISSISSIPPI | 100848 | 4678 | 0 | 0 | 105526 |
| MISSOURI | — | — | — | — | — |
| MONTANA | 114591 | 112863 | 0 | 0 | 227454 |
| NEBRASKA | 162990 | 255695 | 0 | 0 | 418685 |
| NEVADA | — | — | — | — | — |
| NEW HAMPSHIRE | 77386 | 117150 | 0 | 0 | 194536 |
| NEW JERSEY | 858158 | 861158 | 0 | 50871 | 1770557 |
| NEW MEXICO | 111351 | 83071 | 0 | 0 | 194422 |
| NEW YORK | — | — | — | — | — |
| NORTH CAROLINA | 408312 | 211322 | 0 | 0 | 619634 |
| NORTH DAKOTA | — | — | — | — | — |
| OHIO | 335127 | 262013 | 1563 | 0 | 598703 |
| OKLAHOMA | 285775 | 283313 | 0 | 0 | 569088 |
| OREGON | — | — | — | — | — |
| PENNSYLVANIA | 193654 | 132970 | 0 | 0 | 326624 |
| RHODE ISLAND | 0 | 0 | 0 | 227230 | 227230 |
| SOUTH CAROLINA | 100674 | 135071 | 0 | 0 | 235745 |
| SOUTH DAKOTA | 249121 | 106971 | 0 | 0 | 356092 |
| TENNESSEE | 539319 | 94131 | 0 | 3025 | 636475 |
| TEXAS | — | — | — | — | — |
| UTAH | 244844 | 0 | 0 | 61666 | 306510 |
| VERMONT | — | — | — | — | — |
| VIRGINIA | 325263 | 268066 | 0 | 0 | 593329 |
| WASHINGTON | — | — | — | — | — |
| WEST VIRGINIA | 57845 | 54407 | 0 | 0 | 112252 |
| WISCONSIN | | | | | |
| WYOMING | | | | | |

TABLE 3.5 (CONTINUED)

## 1956 SENATE ELECTION

| | DEMOCRAT | REPUBLICAN | OTHER | TOTAL VOTES CAST |
|---|---|---|---|---|
| ALABAMA | 330182 | 0 | 0 | 330182 |
| ALASKA | --- | --- | --- | --- |
| ARIZONA | 170816 | 107447 | 0 | 278263 |
| ARKANSAS | 331679 | 68016 | 0 | 399695 |
| CALIFORNIA | 2445816 | 2892918 | 22733 | 5361467 |
| COLORADO | 319872 | 317102 | 0 | 636974 |
| CONNECTICUT | 479460 | 610829 | 23497 | 1113786 |
| DELAWARE | --- | --- | --- | --- |
| DIST OF COLUMBIA | | | | |
| FLORIDA | 655418 | 0 | 0 | 655418 |
| GEORGIA | 541094 | 0 | 173 | 541267 |
| HAWAII | --- | --- | --- | --- |
| IDAHO | 149096 | 102781 | 13415 | 265292 |
| ILLINOIS | 1949883 | 2307352 | 7595 | 4264830 |
| INDIANA | 871781 | 1084262 | 7943 | 1963986 |
| IOWA | 543156 | 635499 | 0 | 1178655 |
| KANSAS | 333939 | 477822 | 13519 | 825280 |
| KENTUCKY | 499922 | 506903 | 0 | 1006825 |
| LOUISIANA | 335564 | 0 | 0 | 335564 |
| MAINE | --- | --- | --- | --- |
| MARYLAND | 419108 | 473059 | 0 | 892167 |
| MASSACHUSETTS | --- | --- | --- | --- |
| MICHIGAN | --- | --- | --- | --- |
| MINNESOTA | --- | --- | --- | --- |
| MISSISSIPPI | --- | --- | --- | --- |
| MISSOURI | 1015936 | 785048 | 0 | 1800984 |
| MONTANA | --- | --- | --- | --- |
| NEBRASKA | --- | --- | --- | --- |
| NEVADA | 50677 | 45712 | 0 | 96389 |
| NEW HAMPSHIRE | 90519 | 161424 | 0 | 251943 |
| NEW JERSEY | --- | --- | --- | --- |
| NEW MEXICO | --- | --- | --- | --- |
| NEW YORK | 3265159 | 3723933 | 0 | 6989092 |

| | DEMOCRAT | REPUBLICAN | INDEPENDENT | OTHER | TOTAL VOTES CAST |
|---|---|---|---|---|---|
| NORTH CAROLINA | 731353 | 367475 | --- | 0 | 1098828 |
| NORTH DAKOTA | 87919 | 155305 | --- | 937 | 244161 |
| OHIO | 1864589 | 1660910 | --- | 0 | 3525499 |
| OKLAHOMA | 459996 | 371146 | --- | 0 | 831142 |
| OREGON | 396849 | 335405 | --- | 0 | 732254 |
| PENNSYLVANIA | 2268641 | 2250671 | --- | 10562 | 4529874 |
| RHODE ISLAND | --- | --- | --- | --- | --- |
| SOUTH CAROLINA | 230150 | 49695 | --- | 124 | 279969 |
| SOUTH DAKOTA | 143001 | 147621 | --- | 0 | 290622 |
| TENNESSEE | --- | --- | --- | --- | --- |
| TEXAS | --- | --- | --- | --- | --- |
| UTAH | 152120 | 178261 | --- | 0 | 330381 |
| VERMONT | 52184 | 103101 | --- | 4 | 155289 |
| VIRGINIA | --- | --- | --- | --- | --- |
| WASHINGTON | 685565 | 436652 | --- | 0 | 1122217 |
| WEST VIRGINIA | --- | --- | --- | --- | --- |
| WISCONSIN | 627903 | 892473 | --- | 2745 | 1523121 |
| WYOMING | --- | --- | --- | --- | --- |

## 1958 SENATE ELECTION

| | DEMOCRAT | REPUBLICAN | INDEPENDENT | OTHER | TOTAL VOTES CAST |
|---|---|---|---|---|---|
| ALABAMA | --- | --- | --- | --- | --- |
| ALASKA | --- | --- | --- | --- | --- |
| ARIZONA | 129030 | 164593 | 0 | 0 | 293623 |
| ARKANSAS | --- | --- | --- | --- | --- |
| CALIFORNIA | 2927693 | 2204337 | 0 | 3191 | 5135221 |
| COLORADO | 554841 | 410622 | 0 | 0 | 965463 |
| CONNECTICUT | --- | --- | --- | --- | --- |
| DELAWARE | 72152 | 82280 | 0 | 0 | 154432 |
| DIST OF COLUMBIA | --- | --- | --- | --- | --- |
| FLORIDA | 386113 | 155956 | 0 | 0 | 542069 |
| GEORGIA | --- | --- | --- | --- | --- |
| HAWAII | --- | --- | --- | --- | --- |
| IDAHO | --- | --- | --- | --- | --- |
| ILLINOIS | --- | --- | --- | --- | --- |
| INDIANA | 973636 | 731635 | 0 | 19327 | 1724598 |
| IOWA | --- | --- | --- | --- | --- |

TABLE 3.5 (CONTINUED)

## 1958 SENATE ELECTION

| | DEMOCRAT | REPUBLICAN | INDEPENDENT | OTHER | TOTAL VOTES CAST |
|---|---|---|---|---|---|
| KANSAS | --- | --- | --- | --- | --- |
| KENTUCKY | --- | --- | --- | --- | --- |
| LOUISIANA | --- | --- | --- | --- | --- |
| MAINE | 172842 | 111522 | 0 | 0 | 284364 |
| MARYLAND | 367270 | 382021 | 0 | 0 | 749291 |
| MASSACHUSETTS | 1362926 | 488318 | 0 | 10797 | 1862041 |
| MICHIGAN | 1216966 | 1046963 | 0 | 7715 | 2271644 |
| MINNESOTA | 608847 | 536629 | 0 | 5407 | 1150883 |
| MISSISSIPPI | 61039 | 0 | 0 | 0 | 61039 |
| MISSOURI | 780083 | 393847 | 0 | 0 | 1173930 |
| MONTANA | 174910 | 54573 | 0 | 0 | 229483 |
| NEBRASKA | 185152 | 232227 | 0 | 0 | 417379 |
| NEVADA | 48732 | 35760 | 0 | 0 | 84492 |
| NEW HAMPSHIRE | --- | --- | --- | --- | --- |
| NEW JERSEY | 966832 | 882287 | 0 | 32210 | 1881329 |
| NEW MEXICO | 127496 | 75827 | 0 | 0 | 203323 |
| NEW YORK | 2709950 | 2842942 | 0 | 49087 | 5601979 |
| NORTH CAROLINA | --- | --- | --- | --- | --- |
| NORTH DAKOTA | 84892 | 117070 | 1700 | 0 | 203662 |
| OHIO | 1652211 | 1497199 | 0 | 0 | 3149410 |
| OKLAHOMA | --- | --- | --- | --- | --- |
| OREGON | --- | --- | --- | --- | --- |
| PENNSYLVANIA | 1929821 | 2042586 | 0 | 16215 | 3988622 |
| RHODE ISLAND | 222166 | 122353 | 0 | 0 | 344519 |
| SOUTH CAROLINA | --- | --- | --- | --- | --- |
| SOUTH DAKOTA | --- | --- | --- | --- | --- |
| TENNESSEE | 317324 | 76371 | 0 | 7971 | 401666 |
| TEXAS | 587030 | 185926 | 0 | 14172 | 787128 |
| UTAH | 112827 | 101471 | 77013 | 0 | 291311 |
| VERMONT | 59536 | 64900 | 0 | 6 | 124442 |
| VIRGINIA | 317221 | 0 | 120224 | 20195 | 457640 |
| WASHINGTON | 597040 | 278271 | 0 | 11511 | 886822 |
| WEST VIRGINIA | 381745 | 263172 | 0 | 0 | 644917 |
| WISCONSIN | 682440 | 510398 | 1226 | 77 | 1194141 |
| WYOMING | 58035 | 56122 | 0 | 0 | 114157 |

1960 SENATE ELECTION

| | DEMOCRAT | REPUBLICAN | INDEPENDENT | OTHER | TOTAL VOTES CAST |
|---|---|---|---|---|---|
| ALABAMA | 389196 | 164868 | 0 | 17 | 554081 |
| ALASKA | 38041 | 21937 | 0 | 0 | 59978 |
| ARIZONA | --- | --- | --- | --- | --- |
| ARKANSAS | --- | --- | --- | --- | --- |
| CALIFORNIA | 334854 | 389428 | 3351 | 0 | 727633 |
| COLORADO | --- | --- | --- | --- | --- |
| CONNECTICUT | 96090 | 98874 | 0 | 0 | 194964 |
| DELAWARE | --- | --- | --- | --- | --- |
| DIST OF COLUMBIA | --- | --- | --- | --- | --- |
| FLORIDA | 576140 | 0 | 0 | 355 | 576495 |
| GEORGIA | --- | --- | --- | --- | --- |
| HAWAII | --- | --- | --- | --- | --- |
| IDAHO | 139448 | 152648 | 0 | 0 | 292096 |
| ILLINOIS | 2530943 | 2093846 | 0 | 8007 | 4632796 |
| INDIANA | 595119 | 642463 | 0 | 0 | 1237582 |
| IOWA | 388895 | 485499 | 0 | 14198 | 888592 |
| KANSAS | 444290 | 644087 | 0 | 0 | 1088377 |
| KENTUCKY | 432228 | 109698 | 0 | 0 | 541926 |
| LOUISIANA | 159809 | 256890 | 0 | 0 | 416699 |
| MAINE | --- | --- | --- | --- | --- |
| MARYLAND | 1050725 | 1358556 | 0 | 8532 | 2417813 |
| MASSACHUSETTS | 1669179 | 1548873 | 0 | 8595 | 3226647 |
| MICHIGAN | 884168 | 648586 | 0 | 4085 | 1536839 |
| MINNESOTA | 244341 | 21807 | 0 | 0 | 266148 |
| MISSISSIPPI | --- | --- | --- | --- | --- |
| MISSOURI | 140331 | 136281 | 0 | 0 | 276612 |
| MONTANA | 245837 | 352748 | 0 | 0 | 598585 |
| NEBRASKA | --- | --- | --- | --- | --- |
| NEVADA | 114024 | 173521 | 0 | 0 | 287545 |
| NEW HAMPSHIRE | --- | --- | --- | --- | --- |
| NEW JERSEY | 1151385 | 1483832 | 0 | 29339 | 2664556 |
| NEW MEXICO | 190654 | 109897 | 0 | 0 | 300551 |
| NEW YORK | --- | --- | --- | --- | --- |
| NORTH CAROLINA | 793521 | 497964 | 0 | 0 | 1291485 |
| NORTH DAKOTA | --- | --- | --- | --- | --- |

TABLE 3.5 (CONTINUED)

## 1960 SENATE ELECTION

|  | DEMOCRAT | REPUBLICAN | INDEPENDENT | OTHER | TOTAL VOTES CAST |
|---|---|---|---|---|---|
| OHIO | --- | --- | --- | --- | --- |
| OKLAHOMA | 474116 | 385646 | 4713 | 0 | 864475 |
| OREGON | 412757 | 343009 | 0 | 109 | 755875 |
| PENNSYLVANIA | --- | --- | --- | --- | --- |
| RHODE ISLAND | 275575 | 124408 | 0 | 0 | 399983 |
| SOUTH CAROLINA | 330164 | 0 | 0 | 102 | 330266 |
| SOUTH DAKOTA | 145261 | 160181 | 0 | 0 | 305442 |
| TENNESSEE | 594460 | 234053 | 0 | 6 | 828519 |
| TEXAS | 1306605 | 926653 | 0 | 20511 | 2253769 |
| UTAH | --- | --- | --- | --- | --- |
| VERMONT | --- | --- | --- | --- | --- |
| VIRGINIA | 506169 | 0 | 0 | 116651 | 622820 |
| WASHINGTON | --- | --- | --- | --- | --- |
| WEST VIRGINIA | 458355 | 369935 | 0 | 2 | 828292 |
| WISCONSIN | --- | --- | --- | --- | --- |
| WYOMING | 60447 | 78103 | 0 | 0 | 138550 |

## 1962 SENATE ELECTION

|  | DEMOCRAT | REPUBLICAN | INDEPENDENT | OTHER | TOTAL VOTES CAST |
|---|---|---|---|---|---|
| ALABAMA | 201937 | 195134 | 0 | 8 | 397079 |
| ALASKA | 33827 | 24354 | 0 | 0 | 58181 |
| ARIZONA | 199217 | 163388 | 0 | 0 | 362605 |
| ARKANSAS | 214867 | 98013 | 0 | 0 | 312880 |
| CALIFORNIA | 2452839 | 3180483 | 0 | 14630 | 5647952 |
| COLORADO | 279586 | 328655 | 1217 | 3986 | 613444 |
| CONNECTICUT | 527522 | 501694 | 0 | 0 | 1029216 |
| DELAWARE | --- | --- | --- | --- | --- |
| DIST OF COLUMBIA | --- | --- | --- | --- | --- |
| FLORIDA | 657633 | 281381 | 0 | 193 | 939207 |

| State | | | | | |
|---|---|---|---|---|---|
| GEORGIA | 306250 | 0 | 0 | 0 | 306250 |
| HAWAII | 136294 | 60067 | 0 | 0 | 196361 |
| IDAHO | 141657 | 117129 | 0 | 0 | 258786 |
| ILLINOIS | 1748007 | 1961202 | 0 | 7 | 3709216 |
| INDIANA | 905491 | 894547 | 0 | 0 | 1800038 |
| IOWA | 376602 | 431364 | 0 | 10102 | 807966 |
| KANSAS | 223630 | 388500 | 0 | 0 | 622232 |
| KENTUCKY | 387440 | 432648 | 0 | 0 | 820088 |
| LOUISIANA | 318838 | 103066 | 0 | 0 | 421904 |
| MAINE | --- | --- | --- | --- | --- |
| MARYLAND | 439723 | 269131 | 0 | 1 | 708855 |
| MASSACHUSETTS | --- | --- | --- | --- | --- |
| MICHIGAN | --- | --- | --- | --- | --- |
| MINNESOTA | --- | --- | --- | --- | --- |
| MISSISSIPPI | 666929 | 555330 | 0 | 0 | 1222259 |
| MISSOURI | --- | --- | --- | --- | --- |
| MONTANA | --- | --- | --- | --- | --- |
| NEBRASKA | 63443 | 33749 | 0 | 0 | 97192 |
| NEVADA | 90444 | 134035 | 0 | 0 | 224479 |
| NEW HAMPSHIRE | --- | --- | --- | --- | --- |
| NEW JERSEY | --- | --- | --- | --- | --- |
| NEW MEXICO | --- | --- | --- | --- | --- |
| NEW YORK | 2289323 | 3272417 | 0 | 141377 | 5703117 |
| NORTH CAROLINA | 491520 | 321635 | 0 | 0 | 813155 |
| NORTH DAKOTA | 88032 | 135705 | 0 | 0 | 223737 |
| OHIO | 1843813 | 1155292 | 0 | 0 | 2995105 |
| OKLAHOMA | 353890 | 307966 | 2856 | 250 | 664712 |
| OREGON | 344716 | 291587 | 0 | 10443 | 636553 |
| PENNSYLVANIA | 2238383 | 2134649 | 0 | 0 | 4383475 |
| RHODE ISLAND | --- | --- | --- | --- | --- |
| SOUTH CAROLINA | 178712 | 133930 | 0 | 5 | 312647 |
| SOUTH DAKOTA | 127458 | 126861 | 0 | 0 | 254319 |
| TENNESSEE | --- | --- | --- | --- | --- |
| TEXAS | 151656 | 166755 | 0 | 0 | 318411 |
| UTAH | 40134 | 81241 | 0 | 0 | 121375 |
| VERMONT | --- | --- | --- | --- | --- |
| VIRGINIA | 491365 | 446204 | 0 | 5660 | 943229 |
| WASHINGTON | --- | --- | --- | --- | --- |
| WEST VIRGINIA | 662342 | 594846 | 1428 | 1552 | 1260168 |
| WISCONSIN | --- | --- | --- | --- | --- |
| WYOMING | --- | --- | --- | --- | --- |

TABLE 3.5 (CONTINUED)

## 1964 SENATE ELECTION

| | DEMOCRAT | REPUBLICAN | INDEPENDENT | OTHER | TOTAL VOTES CAST |
|---|---|---|---|---|---|
| ALABAMA | --- | --- | --- | --- | --- |
| ALASKA | --- | --- | --- | --- | --- |
| ARIZONA | 227704 | 241084 | 0 | 0 | 468788 |
| ARKANSAS | --- | --- | --- | --- | --- |
| CALIFORNIA | 3411912 | 3628555 | 0 | 1354 | 7041821 |
| COLORADO | 781008 | 426939 | 0 | 216 | 1208163 |
| CONNECTICUT | 96850 | 103782 | 0 | 71 | 200703 |
| DELAWARE | --- | --- | --- | --- | --- |
| DIST OF COLUMBIA | --- | --- | --- | --- | --- |
| FLORIDA | 997585 | 562212 | 0 | 540 | 1560337 |
| GEORGIA | --- | --- | --- | --- | --- |
| HAWAII | 96789 | 110747 | 0 | 1278 | 208814 |
| IDAHO | --- | --- | --- | --- | --- |
| ILLINOIS | 1128505 | 941519 | 0 | 6939 | 2076963 |
| INDIANA | --- | --- | --- | --- | --- |
| IOWA | --- | --- | --- | --- | --- |
| KANSAS | --- | --- | --- | --- | --- |
| KENTUCKY | --- | --- | --- | --- | --- |
| LOUISIANA | --- | --- | --- | --- | --- |
| MAINE | 253511 | 127040 | 0 | 0 | 380551 |
| MARYLAND | 678649 | 402393 | 0 | 7 | 1081049 |
| MASSACHUSETTS | 1716907 | 587663 | 0 | 7458 | 2312028 |
| MICHIGAN | 1996912 | 1096272 | 0 | 8483 | 3101667 |
| MINNESOTA | 931363 | 605933 | 0 | 6304 | 1543600 |
| MISSISSIPPI | 343364 | 0 | 0 | 0 | 343364 |
| MISSOURI | 1186666 | 596377 | 0 | 0 | 1783043 |
| MONTANA | 180643 | 99367 | 0 | 0 | 280010 |
| NEBRASKA | 217605 | 345772 | 0 | 24 | 563401 |
| NEVADA | 67336 | 67288 | 0 | 0 | 134624 |
| NEW HAMPSHIRE | --- | --- | 1 | --- | --- |
| NEW JERSEY | 1677515 | 1011280 | 0 | 20780 | 2709575 |
| NEW MEXICO | 178209 | 147562 | 0 | 0 | 325771 |
| NEW YORK | 3823749 | 3104056 | 0 | 223776 | 7151581 |

| | DEMOCRAT | REPUBLICAN | CONSERVATIVE | OTHER | TOTAL VOTES CAST |
|---|---|---|---|---|---|
| NORTH CAROLINA | --- | --- | --- | --- | --- |
| NORTH DAKOTA | 149264 | 109681 | 0 | 0 | 258945 |
| OHIO | 1923608 | 1906781 | 0 | 0 | 3830389 |
| OKLAHOMA | --- | --- | --- | --- | --- |
| OREGON | --- | --- | --- | --- | --- |
| PENNSYLVANIA | 2359223 | 2429858 | 0 | 14754 | 4803835 |
| RHODE ISLAND | 319607 | 66715 | 0 | 0 | 386322 |
| SOUTH CAROLINA | --- | --- | --- | --- | --- |
| SOUTH DAKOTA | --- | --- | --- | --- | --- |
| TENNESSEE | 570542 | 493475 | 0 | 1 | 1064018 |
| TEXAS | 1463958 | 1134337 | 0 | 5561 | 2603856 |
| UTAH | 227822 | 169562 | 0 | 0 | 397384 |
| VERMONT | 76457 | 83302 | 4516 | 75 | 164350 |
| VIRGINIA | 592260 | 176624 | 30594 | 50 | 799528 |
| WASHINGTON | 875950 | 337138 | 0 | 0 | 1213088 |
| WEST VIRGINIA | 515015 | 246072 | 0 | 0 | 761087 |
| WISCONSIN | 892013 | 780116 | 1062 | 585 | 1673776 |
| WYOMING | 76485 | 65185 | 0 | 0 | 141670 |

## 1966 SENATE ELECTION

| | DEMOCRAT | REPUBLICAN | CONSERVATIVE | OTHER | TOTAL VOTES CAST |
|---|---|---|---|---|---|
| ALABAMA | 482138 | 313018 | 7444 | 8 | 802608 |
| ALASKA | 49289 | 15961 | 0 | 0 | 65250 |
| ARIZONA | --- | --- | --- | --- | --- |
| ARKANSAS | --- | --- | --- | --- | --- |
| CALIFORNIA | --- | --- | --- | --- | --- |
| COLORADO | 266198 | 368307 | 332 | 0 | 634837 |
| CONNECTICUT | --- | --- | --- | --- | --- |
| DELAWARE | 67263 | 97268 | 0 | 0 | 164531 |
| DIST OF COLUMBIA | --- | --- | --- | --- | --- |
| FLORIDA | --- | --- | --- | --- | --- |
| GEORGIA | --- | --- | --- | --- | --- |
| HAWAII | --- | --- | --- | --- | --- |
| IDAHO | 112637 | 139819 | 0 | 0 | 252456 |
| ILLINOIS | 1678147 | 2100449 | 0 | 44128 | 3822724 |
| INDIANA | --- | --- | --- | --- | --- |
| IOWA | 324114 | 522339 | 0 | 11043 | 857496 |

TABLE 3.5 (CONTINUED)

1966 SENATE ELECTION

| | DEMOCRAT | REPUBLICAN | CONSERVATIVE | OTHER | TOTAL VOTES CAST |
|---|---|---|---|---|---|
| KANSAS | 303223 | 350077 | 7103 | 10942 | 671345 |
| KENTUCKY | 266079 | 483805 | 0 | 0 | 749884 |
| LOUISIANA | 437695 | 0 | 0 | 0 | 437695 |
| MAINE | 131136 | 188291 | 0 | 0 | 319427 |
| MARYLAND | --- | --- | --- | --- | --- |
| MASSACHUSETTS | 774761 | 1213473 | 0 | 11715 | 1999949 |
| MICHIGAN | 1069484 | 1363530 | 0 | 6351 | 2439365 |
| MINNESOTA | 685840 | 574868 | 0 | 10718 | 1271426 |
| MISSISSIPPI | 258248 | 105652 | 30641 | 0 | 394541 |
| MISSOURI | --- | --- | --- | --- | --- |
| MONTANA | 138166 | 121697 | 0 | 0 | 259863 |
| NEBRASKA | 187950 | 296116 | 0 | 0 | 484066 |
| NEVADA | --- | --- | --- | --- | --- |
| NEW HAMPSHIRE | 123888 | 105241 | 0 | 176 | 229305 |
| NEW JERSEY | 788021 | 1278843 | 53606 | 10218 | 2130688 |
| NEW MEXICO | 137205 | 120988 | 0 | 0 | 258193 |
| NEW YORK | --- | --- | --- | --- | --- |
| NORTH CAROLINA | 501440 | 400502 | 0 | 36 | 901978 |
| NORTH DAKOTA | --- | --- | --- | --- | --- |
| OHIO | --- | --- | --- | --- | --- |
| OKLAHOMA | 343157 | 295585 | 0 | 0 | 638742 |
| OREGON | 330374 | 354391 | 0 | 302 | 685067 |
| PENNSYLVANIA | --- | --- | --- | --- | --- |
| RHODE ISLAND | 219331 | 104838 | 0 | 0 | 324169 |
| SOUTH CAROLINA | 164955 | 271297 | 0 | 0 | 436252 |
| SOUTH DAKOTA | 76563 | 150517 | 0 | 0 | 227080 |
| TENNESSEE | 383843 | 483063 | 0 | 55 | 866961 |
| TEXAS | 643855 | 842501 | 0 | 6823 | 1493179 |
| UTAH | --- | --- | --- | --- | --- |
| VERMONT | --- | --- | --- | --- | --- |
| VIRGINIA | 429855 | 245681 | 58251 | 92 | 733879 |
| WASHINGTON | --- | --- | --- | --- | --- |
| WEST VIRGINIA | 292325 | 198891 | 0 | 0 | 491216 |
| WISCONSIN | --- | --- | --- | --- | --- |
| WYOMING | 59141 | 63548 | 0 | 0 | 122689 |

## 1968 SENATE ELECTION

| | DEMOCRAT | REPUBLICAN | AMERICAN | OTHER | TOTAL VOTES CAST |
|---|---|---|---|---|---|
| ALABAMA | 711473 | 201227 | 0 | 0 | 912700 |
| ALASKA | 36527 | 30286 | 0 | 14118 | 80931 |
| ARIZONA | 205338 | 274607 | 0 | 0 | 479945 |
| ARKANSAS | 349965 | 241739 | 0 | 0 | 591704 |
| CALIFORNIA | 3680352 | 3329148 | 0 | 92965 | 7102465 |
| COLORADO | 325584 | 459952 | 0 | 0 | 785536 |
| CONNECTICUT | 655043 | 551455 | 0 | 39 | 1206537 |
| DELAWARE | --- | --- | --- | --- | --- |
| DIST OF COLUMBIA | | | | | |
| FLORIDA | 892637 | 1131499 | 0 | 0 | 2024136 |
| GEORGIA | 885103 | 256796 | 0 | 0 | 1141899 |
| HAWAII | --- | --- | --- | --- | --- |
| IDAHO | 173482 | 114394 | 0 | 0 | 287876 |
| ILLINOIS | 2073242 | 2358947 | 0 | 17568 | 4449757 |
| INDIANA | 1060456 | 988571 | 0 | 4091 | 2053118 |
| IOWA | 574884 | 568469 | 0 | 733 | 1144086 |
| KANSAS | 315911 | 490911 | 0 | 10262 | 817084 |
| KENTUCKY | 448960 | 484260 | 9645 | 0 | 942865 |
| LOUISIANA | 518586 | 0 | 0 | 0 | 518586 |
| MAINE | --- | --- | --- | --- | --- |
| MARYLAND | 443367 | 541893 | 148467 | 0 | 1133727 |
| MASSACHUSETTS | --- | --- | --- | --- | --- |
| MICHIGAN | --- | --- | --- | --- | --- |
| MINNESOTA | --- | --- | --- | --- | --- |
| MISSISSIPPI | --- | --- | --- | --- | --- |
| MISSOURI | 880335 | 845144 | 0 | 0 | 1725479 |
| MONTANA | --- | --- | --- | --- | --- |
| NEBRASKA | --- | --- | --- | --- | --- |
| NEVADA | 83622 | 69068 | 0 | 0 | 152690 |
| NEW HAMPSHIRE | 116816 | 170163 | 0 | 10 | 286989 |
| NEW JERSEY | --- | --- | --- | --- | --- |
| NEW MEXICO | --- | --- | --- | --- | --- |
| NEW YORK | 2609631 | 2810836 | 1139402 | 21718 | 6581587 |
| NORTH CAROLINA | 870406 | 566934 | 0 | 0 | 1437340 |
| NORTH DAKOTA | 80815 | 154968 | 0 | 3993 | 239776 |

TABLE 3.5 (CONTINUED)

1968 SENATE ELECTION

| | DEMOCRAT | REPUBLICAN | AMERICAN | OTHER | TOTAL VOTES CAST |
|---|---|---|---|---|---|
| OHIO | 1814152 | 1928964 | 0 | 5 | 3743121 |
| OKLAHOMA | 419658 | 470120 | 19341 | 0 | 909119 |
| OREGON | 405380 | 408825 | 0 | 177 | 814382 |
| PENNSYLVANIA | 2117662 | 2399762 | 0 | 106794 | 4624218 |
| RHODE ISLAND | --- | --- | --- | --- | --- |
| SOUTH CAROLINA | 404060 | 248780 | 0 | 15 | 652855 |
| SOUTH DAKOTA | 158961 | 120951 | 0 | 0 | 279912 |
| TENNESSEE | --- | --- | --- | --- | --- |
| TEXAS | --- | --- | --- | --- | --- |
| UTAH | 192168 | 225075 | 2019 | 0 | 419262 |
| VERMONT | 62416 | 94738 | 0 | 221 | 157375 |
| VIRGINIA | --- | --- | --- | --- | --- |
| WASHINGTON | 796183 | 435894 | 0 | 3986 | 1236063 |
| WEST VIRGINIA | --- | --- | --- | --- | --- |
| WISCONSIN | 1020931 | 633910 | 0 | 20 | 1654861 |
| WYOMING | --- | --- | --- | --- | --- |

232

1970  SENATE  ELECTION

| | DEMOCRAT | REPUBLICAN | OTHER | TOTAL VOTES CAST |
|---|---|---|---|---|
| ALABAMA | --- | --- | --- | --- |
| ALASKA | --- | --- | --- | --- |
| ARIZONA | 179512 | 228284 | 0 | 407796 |
| ARKANSAS | --- | --- | --- | --- |
| CALIFORNIA | 3496558 | 2877617 | 117982 | 6492157 |
| COLORADO | --- | --- | --- | --- |
| CONNECTICUT | 368111 | 454721 | 266497 | 1089329 |
| DELAWARE | 64740 | 94979 | 1720 | 161439 |
| DIST OF COLUMBIA | --- | --- | --- | --- |
| FLORIDA | 902438 | 772817 | 123 | 1675378 |
| GEORGIA | --- | --- | --- | --- |
| HAWAII | 116597 | 124163 | 0 | 240760 |
| IDAHO | --- | --- | --- | --- |
| ILLINOIS | --- | --- | --- | --- |
| INDIANA | 870990 | 806707 | 0 | 1737697 |
| IOWA | --- | --- | --- | --- |
| KANSAS | --- | --- | --- | --- |
| KENTUCKY | --- | --- | --- | --- |
| LOUISIANA | --- | --- | --- | --- |
| MAINE | 199954 | 123906 | 0 | 323160 |
| MARYLAND | 460422 | 484960 | 10988 | 956370 |
| MASSACHUSETTS | 1202858 | 715978 | 16773 | 1935607 |
| MICHIGAN | 1744672 | 858438 | 7653 | 2610763 |
| MINNESOTA | 788256 | 568025 | 8606 | 1364687 |
| MISSISSIPPI | 286622 | 37593 | 0 | 324215 |
| MISSOURI | 654831 | 617903 | 10578 | 1283312 |
| MONTANA | 150060 | 97809 | 0 | 247869 |
| NEBRASKA | 217681 | 240894 | 391 | 458966 |
| NEVADA | 85187 | 60838 | 1743 | 147768 |
| NEW HAMPSHIRE | --- | --- | --- | --- |
| NEW JERSEY | 1157074 | 903026 | 82005 | 2142105 |
| NEW MEXICO | 1486 | 135004 | 3382 | 289872 |
| NEW YORK | 2171232 | 1178679 | 2551629 | 5901540 |
| NORTH CAROLINA | --- | --- | --- | --- |
| NORTH DAKOTA | 134519 | 82996 | 2045 | 219560 |
| OHIO | 1495262 | 1565682 | 90330 | 3151274 |
| OKLAHOMA | --- | --- | --- | --- |
| OREGON | --- | --- | --- | --- |
| PENNSYLVANIA | 1653774 | 1874106 | 116425 | 3644305 |
| RHODE ISLAND | 230469 | 107351 | 3402 | 341222 |
| SOUTH CAROLINA | --- | --- | --- | --- |
| SOUTH DAKOTA | --- | --- | --- | --- |
| TENNESSEE | 519858 | 562645 | 14538 | 1097041 |
| TEXAS | 1226568 | 1071234 | 1808 | 2299610 |
| UTAH | 210207 | 159004 | 5092 | 374303 |
| VERMONT | 62271 | 91198 | 1430 | 154899 |
| VIRGINIA | 295057 | 145031 | 506653 | 946741 |
| WASHINGTON | 879385 | 170790 | 16632 | 1066807 |
| WEST VIRGINIA | 345965 | 99658 | 0 | 445623 |
| WISCONSIN | 948445 | 381297 | 9225 | 1338967 |
| WYOMING | 67207 | 53279 | 0 | 120486 |

233

TABLE 3.5 (CONTINUED)

1972 SENATE ELECTION

| DEMOCRAT | REPUBLICAN | OTHER | TOTAL VOTES CAST |
|---|---|---|---|
| 654491 | 347523 | 49085 | 1051099 |
| 21791 | 74216 | 0 | 96007 |
| --- | --- | --- | --- |
| 386398 | 248238 | 0 | 634636 |
| --- | --- | --- | --- |
| 457545 | 447957 | 20591 | 926093 |
| --- | --- | --- | --- |
| 116006 | 112844 | 978 | 229828 |
| --- | --- | --- | --- |
| --- | --- | --- | --- |
| 635970 | 542331 | 0 | 1178301 |
| --- | --- | --- | --- |
| 140913 | 161804 | 6885 | 309602 |
| 1721031 | 2867078 | 20271 | 4608380 |
| --- | --- | --- | --- |
| 662637 | 530525 | 10171 | 1203333 |
| 200764 | 622591 | 48367 | 871722 |
| 528550 | 494337 | 14974 | 1037861 |
| 598987 | 206846 | 279071 | 1084904 |
| 224270 | 197040 | 0 | 421310 |
| --- | --- | --- | --- |
| 823278 | 1505932 | 41466 | 2370676 |
| 1577178 | 1781065 | 48715 | 3406958 |
| 981320 | 742121 | 8192 | 1731633 |
| 375102 | 249779 | 20865 | 645746 |
| --- | --- | --- | --- |
| 163609 | 151316 | 0 | 314925 |
| 265922 | 301841 | 817 | 568580 |
| --- | --- | --- | --- |
| 184495 | 139852 | 7 | 324354 |
| 963573 | 1743854 | 84480 | 2791907 |
| 173815 | 204253 | 0 | 378068 |
| --- | --- | --- | --- |
| 677293 | 795248 | 0 | 1472541 |
| --- | --- | --- | --- |
| --- | --- | --- | --- |
| 478212 | 516934 | 10002 | 1005148 |
| 425036 | 494671 | 1126 | 920833 |
| --- | --- | --- | --- |
| 221942 | 188990 | 2499 | 413431 |
| 241056 | 415806 | 172 | 657034 |
| 174773 | 131613 | 0 | 306386 |
| 440599 | 716539 | 7057 | 1164195 |
| 1511985 | 1822877 | 79041 | 3413903 |
| --- | --- | --- | --- |
| --- | --- | --- | --- |
| 643963 | 718337 | 33968 | 1396268 |
| --- | --- | --- | --- |
| 486310 | 245531 | 0 | 731841 |
| --- | --- | --- | --- |
| 40753 | 101314 | 0 | 142067 |

TABLE 3.5 (CONTINUED)

1974  SENATE ELECTIONS

| | DEMOCRATIC | REPUBLICAN | OTHER | TOTAL VOTES CAST |
|---|---|---|---|---|
| ALABAMA | 501,541 | 0 | 21,749 | 523,290 |
| ALASKA | 54,361 | 38,914 | 0 | 93,275 |
| ARIZONA | 229,523 | 320,396 | 0 | 549,919 |
| ARKANSAS | 461,056 | 82,026 | 0 | 543,082 |
| CALIFORNIA | 3,693,160 | 2,210,267 | 199,005 | 6,102,432 |
| COLORADO | 471,691 | 325,508 | 26,967 | 824,166 |
| CONNECTICUT | 690,820 | 372,055 | 22,043 | 1,084,918 |
| DELAWARE | — | — | — | — |
| FLORIDA | 781,031 | 736,674 | 282,834 | 1,800,539 |
| GEORGIA | 627,376 | 246,866 | 313 | 874,555 |
| HAWAII | 207,454 | 0 | 42,767 | 250,221 |
| IDAHO | 145,140 | 109,072 | 4,635 | 258,847 |
| ILLINOIS | 1,811,496 | 1,084,884 | 18,286 | 2,914,666 |
| INDIANA | 889,269 | 814,117 | 49,592 | 1,752,978 |
| IOWA | 462,947 | 420,546 | 6,068 | 889,561 |
| KANSAS | 390,451 | 403,983 | 3 | 794,437 |
| KENTUCKY | 399,406 | 328,982 | 17,606 | 745,994 |
| LOUISIANA | 434,643 | 0 | 0 | 434,643 |
| MAINE | — | — | — | — |
| MARYLAND | 374,563 | 503,223 | 0 | 877,786 |
| MASSACHUSETTS | — | — | — | — |
| MICHIGAN | — | — | — | — |
| MINNESOTA | — | — | — | — |
| MISSISSIPPI | — | — | — | — |
| MISSOURI | 735,433 | 480,900 | 7,970 | 1,224,303 |
| MONTANA | — | — | — | — |
| NEBRASKA | — | — | — | — |
| NEVADA | 78,981 | 79,605 | 10,887 | 169,473 |
| NEW HAMPSHIRE | 110,924 | 110,926 | 1,513 | 223,363 |
| NEW JERSEY | — | — | — | — |
| NEW MEXICO | — | — | — | — |
| NEW YORK | 1,973,781 | 2,340,188 | 849,631 | 5,163,600 |
| NORTH CAROLINA | 633,775 | 377,618 | 8,974 | 1,020,367 |
| NORTH DAKOTA | 113,931 | 114,117 | 7,613 | 235,661 |
| OHIO | 1,930,670 | 918,133 | 139,148 | 2,987,951 |
| OKLAHOMA | 387,162 | 390,997 | 13,650 | 791,809 |
| OREGON | 338,591 | 420,984 | 6,839 | 766,414 |
| PENNSYLVANIA | 1,596,121 | 1,843,317 | 38,374 | 3,477,812 |
| RHODE ISLAND | — | — | — | — |
| SOUTH CAROLINA | 356,126 | 146,645 | 9,626 | 512,397 |
| SOUTH DAKOTA | 147,929 | 130,955 | 0 | 278,884 |
| TENNESSEE | 440,599 | 716,539 | 7,057 | 1,164,195 |
| TEXAS | 1,511,985 | 1,822,877 | 79,041 | 3,413,903 |
| UTAH | 185,377 | 210,299 | 24,966 | 420,642 |
| VERMONT | 70,629 | 66,223 | 5,920 | 142,772 |
| VIRGINIA | — | — | — | — |
| WASHINGTON | 611,811 | 363,626 | 32,410 | 1,007,847 |
| WEST VIRGINIA | — | — | — | — |
| WISCONSIN | 740,700 | 429,327 | 29,468 | 1,199,495 |
| WYOMING | — | — | — | — |

TABLE 3.5 (CONTINUED)

1976 SENATE ELECTIONS

| | DEMOCRATIC | REPUBLICAN | OTHER | TOTAL VOTES CAST |
|---|---|---|---|---|
| ALABAMA | — | — | — | — |
| ALASKA | — | — | — | — |
| ARIZONA | 400,334 | 321,236 | 19,640 | 741,210 |
| ARKANSAS | — | — | — | — |
| CALIFORNIA | 3,502,862 | 3,748,973 | 220,433 | 7,472,268 |
| COLORADO | — | — | — | — |
| CONNECTICUT | 561,018 | 785,683 | 14,965 | 1,361,666 |
| DELAWARE | 98,055 | 125,502 | 1,302 | 244,859 |
| FLORIDA | 1,799,518 | 1,057,886 | 130 | 2,857,534 |
| GEORGIA | — | — | — | — |
| HAWAII | 162,305 | 122,724 | 17,063 | 302,092 |
| IDAHO | — | — | — | — |
| ILLINOIS | — | — | — | — |
| INDIANA | 878,522 | 1,275,833 | 16,832 | 2,171,187 |
| IOWA | — | — | — | — |
| KANSAS | — | — | — | — |
| KENTUCKY | — | — | — | — |
| LOUISIANA | — | — | — | — |
| MAINE | 292,704 | 193,489 | 61 | 486,254 |
| MARYLAND | 772,101 | 530,439 | 63,028 | 1,365,568 |
| MASSACHUSETTS | 1,726,657 | 722,641 | 41,957 | 2,491,255 |
| MICHIGAN | 1,831,031 | 1,635,087 | 24,546 | 3,490,664 |
| MINNESOTA | 1,290,736 | 478,611 | 142,721 | 1,912,068 |
| MISSISSIPPI | 554,433 | 0 | 0 | 554,433 |
| MISSOURI | 813,571 | 1,090,067 | 11,139 | 1,914,777 |
| MONTANA | 206,232 | 115,213 | 0 | 321,445 |
| NEBRASKA | 313,809 | 284,284 | 221 | 598,314 |
| NEVADA | 127,295 | 63,471 | 11,214 | 201,980 |
| NEW HAMPSHIRE | — | — | — | — |
| NEW JERSEY | 1,681,140 | 1,054,508 | 35,742 | 2,771,390 |
| NEW MEXICO | 176,382 | 234,681 | 2,078 | 413,141 |
| NEW YORK | 3,422,594 | 2,836,633 | 60,528 | 6,319,755 |
| NORTH CAROLINA | — | — | — | — |
| NORTH DAKOTA | 175,772 | 103,466 | 3,824 | 283,062 |
| OHIO | 1,941,113 | 1,823,774 | 155,726 | 3,920,613 |
| OKLAHOMA | — | — | — | — |
| OREGON | — | — | — | — |
| PENNSYLVANIA | 2,126,977 | 2,381,891 | 37,485 | 4,546,353 |
| RHODE ISLAND | 167,665 | 230,329 | 912 | 398,906 |
| SOUTH CAROLINA | — | — | — | — |
| SOUTH DAKOTA | — | — | — | — |
| TENNESSEE | 751,180 | 673,231 | 7,635 | 1,432,046 |
| TEXAS | 2,199,956 | 1,636,370 | 38,190 | 3,874,516 |
| UTAH | 241,948 | 290,221 | 7,939 | 540,108 |
| VERMONT | 85,682 | 94,481 | 8,897 | 189,060 |
| VIRGINIA | 596,009 | 0 | 961,491 | 1,557,500 |
| WASHINGTON | 1,071,219 | 361,546 | 58,346 | 1,491,111 |
| WEST VIRGINIA | 566,423 | — | 367 | 566,790 |
| WISCONSIN | 1,396,970 | 521,902 | 16,311 | 1,935,183 |
| WYOMING | 70,558 | 84,810 | 0 | 155,368 |

TABLE 3.5 (CONTINUED)

### 1978 SENATE ELECTIONS

| | DEMOCRATIC | REPUBLICAN | OTHER | TOTAL VOTES CAST |
|---|---|---|---|---|
| ALABAMA | 547,054 | 0 | 34,951 | 582,005 |
| ALASKA | 29,574 | 92,783 | 384 | 122,741 |
| ARIZONA | — | — | — | — |
| ARKANSAS | 399,916 | 84,722 | 37,601 | 522,239 |
| CALIFORNIA | — | — | — | — |
| COLORADO | 330,247 | 480,596 | 8,307 | 819,150 |
| CONNECTICUT | — | — | — | — |
| DELAWARE | 93,930 | 66,479 | 1,663 | 162,072 |
| FLORIDA | — | — | — | — |
| GEORGIA | 536,320 | 108,808 | 0 | 645,128 |
| HAWAII | — | — | — | — |
| IDAHO | — | — | — | — |
| ILLINOIS | 1,448,187 | 1,698,711 | 37,866 | 3,184,764 |
| INDIANA | — | — | — | — |
| IOWA | 395,066 | 421,598 | 7,990 | 824,654 |
| KANSAS | 317,602 | 403,354 | 27,883 | 748,839 |
| KENTUCKY | 290,730 | 175,766 | 10,287 | 476,783 |
| LOUISIANA | 839,669 | 0 | 0 | 839,669 |
| MAINE | 127,327 | 212,294 | 35,551 | 375,172 |
| MARYLAND | — | — | — | — |
| MASSACHUSETTS | 1,093,283 | 890,584 | 1,833 | 1,985,700 |
| MICHIGAN | 1,484,193 | 1,362,165 | 272 | 2,846,630 |
| MINNESOTA | 3,425 | 2,709 | 209 | 6,343 |
| MISSISSIPPI | 185,454 | 263,089 | 135,393 | 583,936 |
| MISSOURI | — | — | — | — |
| MONTANA | 160,353 | 127,589 | 0 | 287,942 |
| NEBRASKA | 334,276 | 159,806 | 286 | 494,368 |
| NEVADA | — | — | — | — |
| NEW HAMPSHIRE | 127,945 | 133,745 | 2,089 | 263,779 |
| NEW JERSEY | 1,082,960 | 844,200 | 30,355 | 1,957,515 |
| NEW MEXICO | 160,045 | 183,432 | 0 | 343,477 |
| NEW YORK | — | — | — | — |
| NORTH CAROLINA | 516,663 | 619,151 | 0 | 1,135,814 |
| NORTH DAKOTA | — | — | — | — |
| OHIO | — | — | — | — |
| OKLAHOMA | 493,953 | 247,857 | 12,454 | 754,264 |
| OREGON | 341,616 | 550,165 | 737 | 892,518 |
| PENNSYLVANIA | — | — | — | — |
| RHODE ISLAND | 229,557 | 76,061 | 0 | 305,618 |
| SOUTH CAROLINA | 281,119 | 351,733 | 0 | 632,852 |
| SOUTH DAKOTA | 84,767 | 170,832 | 0 | 255,599 |
| TENNESSEE | 466,229 | 642,644 | 48,222 | 1,157,095 |
| TEXAS | 1,139,149 | 1,151,376 | 22,015 | 2,312,540 |
| UTAH | — | — | — | — |
| VERMONT | — | — | — | — |
| VIRGINIA | 608,511 | 613,232 | 513 | 1,222,256 |
| WASHINGTON | — | — | — | — |
| WEST VIRGINIA | 249,034 | 244,317 | 0 | 493,351 |
| WISCONSIN | — | — | — | — |
| WYOMING | 50,456 | 82,908 | 0 | 133,364 |

TABLE 3.5 (CONTINUED)

1980 SENATE ELECTIONS

| | DEMOCRATIC | REPUBLICAN | OTHER | TOTAL VOTES CAST |
|---|---|---|---|---|
| ALABAMA | 610,175 | 650,362 | 36,220 | 1,296,757 |
| ALASKA | 72,007 | 84,159 | 596 | 156,762 |
| ARIZONA | 422,972 | 432,371 | 18,895 | 874,238 |
| ARKANSAS | 477,905 | 330,576 | 331 | 808,812 |
| CALIFORNIA | 4,705,399 | 3,093,426 | 528,483 | 8,327,308 |
| COLORADO | 590,501 | 571,295 | 11,346 | 1,173,142 |
| CONNECTICUT | 763,969 | 581,884 | 10,108 | 1,355,961 |
| DELAWARE | — | — | — | — |
| FLORIDA | 1,705,409 | 1,822,460 | 159 | 3,528,028 |
| GEORGIA | 776,143 | 803,686 | 0 | 1,579,829 |
| HAWAII | 224,450 | 53,056 | 10,448 | 287,954 |
| IDAHO | 214,439 | 218,701 | 6,507 | 439,647 |
| ILLINOIS | 2,565,302 | 1,946,296 | 68,431 | 4,580,029 |
| INDIANA | 1,015,962 | 1,182,414 | 0 | 2,198,376 |
| IOWA | 581,545 | 683,014 | 12,475 | 1,277,034 |
| KANSAS | 340,271 | 598,686 | 0 | 938,957 |
| KENTUCKY | 720,861 | 386,029 | 0 | 1,106,890 |
| LOUISIANA | 494,770 | 13,739 | 342,504 | 841,013 |
| MAINE | — | — | — | — |
| MARYLAND | 435,118 | 850,970 | 0 | 1,286,088 |
| MASSACHUSETTS | — | — | — | — |
| MICHIGAN | — | — | — | — |
| MINNESOTA | — | — | — | — |
| MISSISSIPPI | — | — | — | — |
| MISSOURI | 1,074,859 | 985,401 | 6,707 | 2,066,967 |
| MONTANA | — | — | — | — |
| NEBRASKA | — | — | — | — |
| NEVADA | 92,129 | 144,791 | 10,083 | 247,003 |
| NEW HAMPSHIRE | 179,455 | 195,559 | 46 | 375,060 |
| NEW JERSEY | — | — | — | — |
| NEW MEXICO | — | — | — | — |
| NEW YORK | 2,618,661 | 2,272,082 | 1,124,171 | 6,014,914 |
| NORTH CAROLINA | 887,653 | 898,064 | 11,948 | 1,797,665 |
| NORTH DAKOTA | 86,658 | 210,347 | 2,267 | 299,272 |
| OHIO | 2,770,786 | 1,137,695 | 118,822 | 4,027,303 |
| OKLAHOMA | 478,283 | 587,252 | 32,759 | 1,098, 294 |
| OREGON | 501,963 | 594,290 | 44,241 | 1,140,494 |
| PENNSYLVANIA | 2,122,391 | 2,230,404 | 65,247 | 4,418,042 |
| RHODE ISLAND | — | — | — | — |
| SOUTH CAROLINA | 612,554 | 257,946 | 0 | 870,500 |
| SOUTH DAKOTA | 129,018 | 190,594 | 7,866 | 327,478 |
| TENNESSEE | — | — | — | — |
| TEXAS | — | — | — | — |
| UTAH | 151,454 | 437,675 | 5,169 | 594,298 |
| VERMONT | 104,081 | 101,637 | 3,452 | 209,170 |
| VIRGINIA | — | — | — | — |
| WASHINGTON | 792,052 | 936,317 | 0 | 1,728,369 |
| WEST VIRGINIA | — | — | — | — |
| WISCONSIN | 1,065,487 | 1,106,311 | 32,404 | 2,204,202 |
| WYOMING | — | — | — | — |

TABLE 3.5 (CONTINUED)

1982 SENATE ELECTIONS

|  | DEMOCRATIC | REPUBLICAN | OTHER | TOTAL VOTES CAST |
|---|---|---|---|---|
| ALABAMA | — | — | — | — |
| ALASKA | — | — | — | — |
| ARIZONA | 411,970 | 291,749 | 20,166 | 723,885 |
| ARKANSAS | — | — | — | — |
| CALIFORNIA | 3,494,968 | 4,022,565 | 287,917 | 7,805,450 |
| COLORADO | — | — | — | — |
| CONNECTICUT | 499,146 | 545,987 | 38,375 | 1,083,508 |
| DELAWARE | 84,413 | 105,357 | 1,190 | 190,960 |
| FLORIDA | 1,636,857 | 1,014,551 | 0 | 2,651,408 |
| GEORGIA | — | — | — | — |
| HAWAII | 245,386 | 52,071 | 8,953 | 306,410 |
| IDAHO | — | — | — | — |
| ILLINOIS | — | — | — | — |
| INDIANA | 828,400 | 978,301 | 10,586 | 1,817,287 |
| IOWA | — | — | — | — |
| KANSAS | — | — | — | — |
| KENTUCKY | — | — | — | — |
| LOUISIANA | — | — | — | — |
| MAINE | 279,819 | 179,882 | 14 | 459,715 |
| MARYLAND | 707,356 | 407,334 | 0 | 1,114,690 |
| MASSACHUSETTS | 1,247,084 | 784,602 | 19,065 | 2,050,751 |
| MICHIGAN | 1,728,793 | 1,223,288 | 42,253 | 2,994,334 |
| MINNESOTA | 840,401 | 949,207 | 15,067 | 1,804,675 |
| MISSISSIPPI | 414,099 | 20,927 | 0 | 645,026 |
| MISSOURI | 758,629 | 784,876 | 16 | 1,543,521 |
| MONTANA | 174,861 | 133,789 | 12,412 | 321,062 |
| NEBRASKA | 363,350 | 155,760 | 26,537 | 545,647 |
| NEVADA | 114,720 | 120,377 | 5,297 | 240,394 |
| NEW HAMPSHIRE | — | — | — | — |
| NEW JERSEY | 1,117,549 | 1,047,626 | 28,770 | 2,193,945 |
| NEW MEXICO | 217,682 | 187,128 | 0 | 404,810 |
| NEW YORK | 3,089,871 | 1,415,749 | 461,867 | 4,967,487 |
| NORTH CAROLINA | — | — | — | — |
| NORTH DAKOTA | 14,873 | 89,304 | 8,288 | 262,465 |
| OHIO | 1,923,767 | 1,396,760 | 74,906 | 3,395,463 |
| OKLAHOMA | — | — | — | — |
| OREGON | — | — | — | — |
| PENNSYLVANIA | 1,412,965 | 2,136,418 | 54,725 | 3,604,108 |
| RHODE ISLAND | 167,283 | 175,495 | 0 | 342,778 |
| SOUTH CAROLINA | — | — | — | — |
| SOUTH DAKOTA | — | — | — | — |
| TENNESSEE | 780,113 | 479,642 | 0 | 1,259,755 |
| TEXAS | 1,818,223 | 1,256,759 | 28,097 | 3,103,079 |
| UTAH | 219,482 | 309,332 | 1,988 | 530,802 |
| VERMONT | 79,340 | 84,450 | 4,213 | 168,003 |
| VIRGINIA | 690,839 | 724,571 | 212 | 1,415,622 |
| WASHINGTON | 943,655 | 332,273 | 92,548 | 1,368,476 |
| WEST VIRGINIA | 387,170 | 173,910 | 4,234 | 565,314 |
| WISCONSIN | 983,311 | 527,355 | 34,315 | 1,544,981 |
| WYOMING | 72,466 | 94,725 | 0 | 167,191 |

TABLE 3.5 (CONTINUED)

1984 SENATE ELECTIONS

|  | DEMOCRATIC | REPUBLICAN | OTHER | TOTAL VOTES CAST |
|---|---|---|---|---|
| ALABAMA | 860,535 | 498,508 | 12,191 | 1,371,234 |
| ALASKA | 58,804 | 146,919 | 715 | 206,438 |
| ARIZONA | — | — | — | — |
| ARKANSAS | 502,341 | 373,615 | 0 | 875,956 |
| CALIFORNIA | — | — | — | — |
| COLORADO | 449,327 | 833,821 | 14,661 | 1,297,809 |
| CONNECTICUT | — | — | — | — |
| DELAWARE | 147,831 | 98,101 | 0 | 245,932 |
| FLORIDA | — | — | — | — |
| GEORGIA | 1,344,104 | 337,196 | 0 | 1,681,300 |
| HAWAII | — | — | — | — |
| IDAHO | 105,591 | 293,193 | 7,384 | 406,168 |
| ILLINOIS | 2,397,165 | 2,308,039 | 82,131 | 4,787,335 |
| INDIANA | — | — | — | — |
| IOWA | 716,883 | 564,381 | 11,436 | 1,292,700 |
| KANSAS | 211,664 | 757,402 | 27,663 | 996,729 |
| KENTUCKY | 639,721 | 644,990 | 7,696 | 1,292,407 |
| LOUISIANA | 838,181 | 52,746 | 86,546 | 4977,473 |
| MAINE | 142,626 | 404,414 | 4,366 | 551,406 |
| MARYLAND | — | — | — | — |
| MASSACHUSETTS | 1,392,981 | 1,136,806 | 408 | 2,530,195 |
| MICHIGAN | 1,915,831 | 1,745,302 | 39,805 | 3,700,938 |
| MINNESOTA | 852,844 | 1,199,926 | 13,133 | 2,065,903 |
| MISSISSIPPI | 371,926 | 580,314 | 0 | 952,240 |
| MISSOURI | — | — | — | — |
| MONTANA | 215,704 | 154,308 | 9,143 | 379,155 |
| NEBRASKA | 332,217 | 307,147 | 304 | 639,668 |
| NEVADA | — | — | — | — |
| NEW HAMPSHIRE | 157,447 | 225,828 | 1,131 | 384,406 |
| NEW JERSEY | 1,986,644 | 1,080,100 | 29,712 | 3,096,456 |
| NEW MEXICO | 141,253 | 361,371 | 10 | 502,634 |
| NEW YORK | — | — | — | — |
| NORTH CAROLINA | 1,070,488 | 1,156,768 | 11,795 | 2,239,051 |
| NORTH DAKOTA | — | — | — | — |
| OHIO | — | — | — | — |
| OKLAHOMA | 906,131 | 280,638 | 11,168 | 1,197,937 |
| OREGON | 406,122 | 808,152 | 461 | 1,214,735 |
| PENNSYLVANIA | — | — | — | — |
| RHODE ISLAND | 286,780 | 108,492 | 0 | 395,272 |
| SOUTH CAROLINA | 306,982 | 644,815 | 13,333 | 965,130 |
| SOUTH DAKOTA | 80,537 | 235,176 | 0 | 315,713 |
| TENNESSEE | 1,000,607 | 557,016 | 90,413 | 1,648,036 |
| TEXAS | 2,202,557 | 3,111,348 | 273 | 5,314,178 |
| UTAH | — | — | — | — |
| VERMONT | — | — | — | — |
| VIRGINIA | 601,142 | 1,406,194 | 151 | 2,007,487 |
| WASHINGTON | — | — | — | — |
| WEST VIRGINIA | 374,233 | 344,680 | 3,299 | 722,212 |
| WISCONSIN | — | — | — | — |
| WYOMING | 40,525 | 146,373 | 0 | 186,898 |

# The Vote for the United States
# House of Representatives

Popular voting for members of the United States House of Representatives was an early feature of the political scene in the United States. The following tables contain the returns for these elections from 1824 (when returns became available for nearly all states) to 1984. Table 3.6 presents votes cast for candidates of major and minor parties, reported by the partisan affiliation of the candidates and aggregated to the national level. Table 3.7 displays the votes cast in each state for U.S. Representative. All states for which returns are available are included in these totals, although because of scattered missing returns and the addition of new states to the union the number of states represented in each year during the nineteenth century varies from election to election.

Representation of all the states in the United States House of Representatives is determined by an apportionment of the available seats according to population. The Constitution provides for the apportionment of Representatives by means of an enumeration of the population of each state obtained from decennial censuses, which have been conducted since 1790. Table 3.8 contains the results of this apportionment of Representatives allowed each of the states, recorded by decade. The Constitution stipulates that there be one Representative for each 30,000 inhabitants; subsequent legislation changed both the total number of Representatives to be elected as well as the population per Representative. These summary totals are presented in the bottom two rows of table 3.8. Until the abolition of slavery in 1863, slaves were counted as a three-fifths fraction for purposes of apportionment. Dashes (—) have been inserted in the table for all decades before the state's entry into the union.

Table 3.6

National Popular Vote Cast for United States Representatives,
1824-1984

| YEAR | TOTAL VOTE CAST | DEMOCRATIC | REPUBLICAN | OTHER |
|------|-----------------|------------|------------|-------|
| 1824 | 570,360 | 23,586 | 36,983 | 509,791 |
| 1826 | 566,929 | 80,011 | 55,220 | 431,698 |
| 1828 | 521,216 | 81,629 | 80,682 | 358,905 |
| 1830 | 802,592 | 211,386 | 170,081 | 421,125 |
| 1832 | 1,467,518 | 410,448 | 310,682 | 746,388 |
| 1834 | 1,377,878 | 664,509 | 601,685 | 111,684 |
| 1836 | 1,071,964 | 482,037 | 438,754 | 151,173 |
| 1838 | 1,955,608 | 855,709 | 806,562 | 293,337 |
| 1840 | 1,820,874 | 794,454 | 1,017,501 | 8,919 |
| 1842 | 1,933,977 | 845,095 | 866,620 | 222,262 |
| 1844 | 2,027,862 | 949,209 | 905,473 | 173,180 |
| 1846 | 2,003,844 | 936,239 | 918,392 | 149,213 |
| 1848 | 2,518,063 | 1,050,192 | 1,100,167 | 367,704 |
| 1850 | 2,343,949 | 1,002,235 | 948,962 | 392,752 |
| 1852 | 2,694,317 | 1,262,617 | 1,180,416 | 251,284 |
| 1854 | 2,895,542 | 950,687 | 546,259 | 1,398,596 |
| 1856 | 3,730,004 | 1,627,580 | 1,184,881 | 917,543 |
| 1858 | 3,503,863 | 1,632,870 | 1,107,912 | 763,081 |
| 1860 | 3,814,497 | 1,500,505 | 1,960,642 | 353,350 |
| 1862 | 3,227,483 | 1,457,183 | 1,688,470 | 81,830 |
| 1864 | 3,984,113 | 1,576,645 | 2,077,496 | 329,972 |
| 1866 | 3,904,074 | 1,760,482 | 2,095,453 | 48,139 |
| 1868 | 5,605,908 | 2,551,018 | 2,931,201 | 123,689 |
| 1870 | 5,310,944 | 2,408,655 | 2,560,495 | 341,794 |
| 1872 | 6,663,763 | 2,903,521 | 3,401,847 | 358,395 |
| 1874 | 6,034,500 | 2,758,223 | 2,633,140 | 643,137 |
| 1876 | 8,310,364 | 4,175,350 | 3,887,508 | 247,506 |
| 1878 | 6,995,879 | 2,864,095 | 2,762,003 | 1,369,781 |
| 1880 | 9,061,910 | 4,106,940 | 4,097,190 | 857,780 |
| 1882 | 7,892,887 | 3,877,759 | 3,162,324 | 852,804 |
| 1884 | 9,891,409 | 4,836,334 | 4,425,348 | 629,727 |
| 1886 | 8,554,219 | 3,920,076 | 3,845,094 | 789,049 |
| 1888 | 11,469,328 | 5,297,025 | 5,381,407 | 790,896 |
| 1890 | 9,779,907 | 4,921,259 | 4,123,765 | 734,883 |
| 1892 | 11,815,832 | 5,447,346 | 4,872,422 | 1,496,064 |
| 1894 | 11,233,160 | 4,153,405 | 5,355,453 | 1,724,302 |
| 1896 | 13,620,730 | 5,825,838 | 6,515,078 | 1,279,814 |
| 1898 | 10,932,237 | 5,028,088 | 5,190,603 | 713,546 |
| 1900 | 13,724,473 | 6,282,577 | 6,944,437 | 497,459 |
| 1902 | 10,995,563 | 4,984,832 | 5,444,270 | 566,461 |
| 1904 | 13,147,301 | 5,255,392 | 7,156,241 | 735,668 |
| 1906 | 11,167,490 | 4,599,764 | 5,611,554 | 956,172 |
| 1908 | 14,397,183 | 6,531,634 | 7,182,430 | 683,119 |
| 1910 | 12,111,088 | 5,396,360 | 5,487,306 | 1,227,422 |
| 1912 | 14,207,655 | 6,196,032 | 4,440,431 | 3,571,192 |
| 1914 | 13,734,225 | 5,463,946 | 5,318,365 | 2,951,914 |
| 1916 | 16,644,913 | 7,058,113 | 7,032,611 | 2,554,189 |
| 1918 | 12,791,517 | 5,254,139 | 5,906,843 | 1,630,535 |
| 1920 | 25,572,313 | 9,085,413 | 13,645,677 | 2,841,223 |
| 1922 | 20,321,648 | 8,628,923 | 9,668,794 | 2,023,931 |
| 1924 | 26,695,022 | 11,068,196 | 13,613,021 | 2,013,805 |
| 1926 | 20,414,378 | 8,057,611 | 10,977,400 | 1,379,367 |
| 1928 | 34,743,966 | 14,699,249 | 18,399,200 | 1,645,517 |
| 1930 | 24,762,391 | 10,951,564 | 12,355,090 | 1,455,737 |

Table 3.6 (continued)

| YEAR | TOTAL VOTE CAST | DEMOCRATIC | REPUBLICAN | OTHER |
|------|-----------------|------------|------------|-------|
| 1932 | 37,297,876 | 20,175,502 | 15,247,923 | 1,874,451 |
| 1934 | 32,165,984 | 16,990,574 | 12,823,169 | 2,352,241 |
| 1936 | 42,974,793 | 23,676,107 | 16,637,251 | 2,661,435 |
| 1938 | 36,026,735 | 17,553,043 | 16,305,823 | 2,167,869 |
| 1940 | 46,547,884 | 23,583,384 | 20,340,107 | 2,624,393 |
| 1942 | 28,030,690 | 12,808,054 | 13,662,658 | 1,559,978 |
| 1944 | 45,013,459 | 23,176,524 | 20,774,534 | 1,062,401 |
| 1946 | 34,324,338 | 15,250,075 | 17,950,050 | 1,124,213 |
| 1948 | 45,838,975 | 23,184,940 | 19,701,272 | 2,952,763 |
| 1950 | 40,252,267 | 19,377,557 | 18,905,859 | 1,968,851 |
| 1952 | 57,846,855 | 27,824,786 | 27,883,325 | 2,138,744 |
| 1954 | 42,570,412 | 22,224,368 | 19,923,791 | 422,253 |
| 1956 | 58,186,272 | 29,542,364 | 28,106,624 | 537,284 |
| 1958 | 45,559,133 | 24,961,678 | 19,772,593 | 824,862 |
| 1960 | 64,000,763 | 34,996,730 | 28,708,772 | 295,261 |
| 1962 | 51,131,989 | 26,488,996 | 24,500,660 | 142,333 |
| 1964 | 65,627,094 | 37,752,513 | 27,549,040 | 325,541 |
| 1966 | 52,720,597 | 26,854,937 | 25,394,141 | 471,519 |
| 1968 | 66,100,295 | 33,397,797 | 31,704,567 | 997,931 |
| 1970 | 52,835,566 | 28,041,979 | 23,437,709 | 1,355,878 |
| 1972 | 71,318,949 | 36,817,347 | 33,178,253 | 1,323,349 |
| 1974 | 52,314,257 | 29,872,842 | 21,165,583 | 1,275,832 |
| 1976 | 74,114,914 | 41,241,509 | 31,302,910 | 1,570,495 |
| 1978 | 55,090,135 | 29,383,512 | 24,694,734 | 1,011,889 |
| 1980 | 77,717,583 | 39,045,259 | 36,954,452 | 1,717,872 |
| 1982 | 64,514,638 | 35,247,161 | 27,656,230 | 1,611,247 |
| 1984 | 82,775,697 | 42,961,006 | 38,679,827 | 1,134,864 |

## Table 3.7

## Vote Cast for United States Representative
## by State, 1824-1984

**1824-1825 HOUSE OF REPRESENTATIVES ELECTION**

| | DEM.-REP. | NATL. REPUE. | OTHER | TOTAL VOTES CAST |
|---|---|---|---|---|
| ALABAMA | 7328 | 342 | 942 | 8612 |
| ALASKA | --- | --- | --- | --- |
| ARIZONA | --- | --- | --- | --- |
| ARKANSAS | --- | --- | --- | --- |
| CALIFORNIA | --- | --- | --- | --- |
| COLORADO | --- | --- | --- | --- |
| CONNECTICUT | 0 | 0 | 8101 | 8101 |
| DELAWARE | 0 | 3163 | 3390 | 6553 |
| DIST OF COLUMBIA | --- | --- | --- | --- |
| FLORIDA | --- | --- | --- | --- |
| GEORGIA | 0 | 0 | 68799 | 68799 |
| HAWAII | --- | --- | --- | --- |
| IDAHO | --- | --- | --- | --- |
| ILLINOIS | 0 | 7425 | 4438 | 11863 |
| INDIANA | 4281 | 10214 | 11769 | 26264 |
| IOWA | --- | --- | --- | --- |
| KANSAS | --- | --- | --- | --- |
| KENTUCKY | --- | --- | --- | --- |
| LOUISIANA | --- | --- | --- | --- |
| MAINE | --- | --- | --- | --- |
| MARYLAND | 0 | 0 | 15113 | 15113 |
| MASSACHUSETTS | 1778 | 15839 | 19892 | 37509 |
| MICHIGAN | --- | --- | --- | --- |
| MINNESOTA | --- | --- | --- | --- |
| MISSISSIPPI | 5671 | 0 | 0 | 5671 |
| MISSOURI | 4528 | 0 | 6147 | 10675 |
| MONTANA | --- | --- | --- | --- |
| NEBRASKA | --- | --- | --- | --- |
| NEVADA | --- | --- | --- | --- |
| NEW HAMPSHIRE | 0 | 0 | 72066 | 72066 |
| NEW JERSEY | 0 | 0 | 105213 | 105213 |
| NEW MEXICO | --- | --- | --- | --- |
| NEW YORK | 0 | 0 | 183360 | 183360 |
| NORTH CAROLINA | --- | --- | --- | --- |
| NORTH DAKOTA | --- | --- | --- | --- |
| OHIO | --- | --- | --- | --- |
| OKLAHOMA | --- | --- | --- | --- |
| OREGON | --- | --- | --- | --- |
| PENNSYLVANIA | --- | --- | --- | --- |
| RHODE ISLAND | 0 | 0 | 10561 | 10561 |
| SOUTH CAROLINA | --- | --- | --- | --- |
| SOUTH DAKOTA | --- | --- | --- | --- |
| TENNESSEE | --- | --- | --- | --- |
| TEXAS | --- | --- | --- | --- |
| UTAH | --- | --- | --- | --- |
| VERMONT | --- | --- | --- | --- |
| VIRGINIA | --- | --- | --- | --- |
| WASHINGTON | --- | --- | --- | --- |
| WEST VIRGINIA | --- | --- | --- | --- |
| WISCONSIN | --- | --- | --- | --- |
| WYOMING | --- | --- | --- | --- |

TABLE 3.7 (CONTINUED)

1826-1827 HOUSE OF REPRESENTATIVES ELECTION

| | DEMOCRAT | NATL. REPUB. | OTHER | TOTAL VOTES CAST |
|---|---|---|---|---|
| ALABAMA | --- | --- | 1640 | --- |
| ALASKA | --- | --- | --- | --- |
| ARIZONA | --- | --- | --- | --- |
| ARKANSAS | --- | --- | --- | --- |
| CALIFORNIA | --- | --- | --- | --- |
| COLORADO | --- | --- | --- | --- |
| CONNECTICUT | 0 | 0 | 9933 | 9933 |
| DELAWARE | 0 | 3931 | 4630 | 8561 |
| DIST OF COLUMBIA | --- | --- | --- | --- |
| FLORIDA | --- | --- | --- | --- |
| GEORGIA | 0 | 0 | 33790 | 33790 |
| HAWAII | --- | --- | --- | --- |
| IDAHO | --- | --- | --- | --- |
| ILLINOIS | 6322 | 5669 | 839 | 12830 |
| INDIANA | 11217 | 10169 | 9679 | 31065 |
| IOWA | --- | --- | --- | --- |
| KANSAS | --- | --- | --- | --- |
| KENTUCKY | 34827 | 2070 | 34371 | 71268 |
| LOUISIANA | --- | --- | --- | --- |
| MAINE | 4751 | --- | --- | --- |
| MARYLAND | 0 | 0 | 16104 | 16104 |
| MASSACHUSETTS | 0 | 9657 | 16709 | 26366 |
| MICHIGAN | --- | --- | --- | --- |
| MINNESOTA | --- | --- | --- | --- |
| MISSISSIPPI | 1914 | 1096 | 2516 | 5526 |
| MISSOURI | 6636 | 4159 | 0 | 10795 |
| MONTANA | --- | --- | --- | --- |
| NEBRASKA | --- | --- | --- | --- |
| NEVADA | --- | --- | --- | --- |
| NEW HAMPSHIRE | --- | --- | --- | --- |
| NEW JERSEY | 9944 | 14697 | 25848 | 50489 |
| NEW MEXICO | --- | --- | --- | --- |
| NEW YORK | 0 | 0 | 181828 | 181828 |
| NORTH CAROLINA | --- | --- | --- | --- |
| NORTH DAKOTA | --- | --- | --- | --- |
| OHIO | --- | --- | 3787 | --- |
| OKLAHOMA | --- | --- | --- | --- |
| OREGON | --- | --- | --- | --- |
| PENNSYLVANIA | --- | --- | --- | --- |
| RHODE ISLAND | 0 | 2230 | 29 | 2259 |
| SOUTH CAROLINA | --- | --- | --- | --- |
| SOUTH DAKOTA | --- | --- | --- | --- |
| TENNESSEE | 0 | 0 | 78415 | 78415 |
| TEXAS | --- | --- | --- | --- |
| UTAH | --- | --- | --- | --- |
| VERMONT | 4400 | 1542 | 11580 | 17522 |
| VIRGINIA | --- | --- | --- | --- |
| WASHINGTON | --- | --- | --- | --- |
| WEST VIRGINIA | --- | --- | --- | --- |
| WISCONSIN | --- | --- | --- | --- |
| WYOMING | --- | --- | --- | --- |

TABLE 3.7 (CONTINUED)

1828-1829 HOUSE OF REPRESENTATIVES ELECTION

| | DEMOCRAT | NATL. REPUB. | OTHER | TOTAL VOTES CAST |
|---|---|---|---|---|
| ALABAMA | 8154 | 3960 | 11463 | 23577 |
| ALASKA | --- | --- | --- | --- |
| ARIZONA | --- | --- | --- | --- |
| ARKANSAS | --- | --- | --- | --- |
| CALIFORNIA | --- | --- | --- | --- |
| COLORADO | --- | --- | --- | --- |
| CONNECTICUT | 0 | 0 | 11634 | 11634 |
| DELAWARE | 0 | 4347 | 4797 | 9144 |
| DIST OF COLUMBIA | --- | --- | --- | --- |
| FLORIDA | --- | --- | --- | --- |
| GEORGIA | --- | --- | --- | --- |
| HAWAII | --- | --- | --- | --- |
| IDAHO | --- | --- | --- | --- |
| ILLINOIS | 10447 | 6158 | 2 | 16607 |
| INDIANA | 12705 | 13538 | 10447 | 36690 |
| IOWA | --- | --- | --- | --- |
| KANSAS | --- | --- | --- | --- |
| KENTUCKY | --- | 2519 | --- | --- |
| LOUISIANA | --- | --- | --- | --- |
| MAINE | 6776 | 0 | 15924 | 22700 |
| MARYLAND | 6085 | 0 | 6627 | 12712 |
| MASSACHUSETTS | 0 | 12268 | 23099 | 35367 |
| MICHIGAN | --- | --- | --- | --- |
| MINNESOTA | --- | --- | --- | --- |
| MISSISSIPPI | 4585 | 1920 | 0 | 6505 |
| MISSOURI | 7108 | 4539 | 0 | 11647 |
| MONTANA | --- | --- | --- | --- |
| NEBRASKA | --- | --- | --- | --- |
| NEVADA | --- | --- | --- | --- |
| NEW HAMPSHIRE | --- | --- | --- | --- |
| NEW JERSEY | 22003 | 23733 | 15 | 45751 |
| NEW MEXICO | --- | --- | --- | --- |
| NEW YORK | 0 | 0 | 195589 | 195589 |
| NORTH CAROLINA | --- | --- | --- | --- |
| NORTH DAKOTA | --- | --- | --- | --- |
| OHIO | --- | --- | 2632 | --- |

| | DEMOCRAT | NATL. REPUB | ANTI-MASON | OTHER | TOTAL VOTES CAST |
|---|---|---|---|---|---|
| OKLAHOMA | --- | --- | --- | --- | --- |
| OREGON | --- | --- | --- | --- | --- |
| PENNSYLVANIA | 0 | 4108 | 33 | --- | 4141 |
| RHODE ISLAND | --- | --- | --- | --- | --- |
| SOUTH CAROLINA | --- | --- | --- | --- | --- |
| SOUTH DAKOTA | --- | --- | --- | --- | --- |
| TENNESSEE | 0 | 0 | --- | 68940 | 68940 |
| TEXAS | --- | --- | --- | --- | --- |
| UTAH | --- | --- | --- | --- | --- |
| VERMONT | 3766 | 3592 | 7703 | --- | 15061 |
| VIRGINIA | --- | --- | --- | --- | --- |
| WASHINGTON | --- | --- | --- | --- | --- |
| WEST VIRGINIA | --- | --- | --- | --- | --- |
| WISCONSIN | --- | --- | --- | --- | --- |
| WYOMING | --- | --- | --- | --- | --- |

1830-1831 HOUSE OF REPRESENTATIVES ELECTION

| | DEMOCRAT | NATL. REPUB | ANTI-MASON | OTHER | TOTAL VOTES CAST |
|---|---|---|---|---|---|
| ALABAMA | 12440 | 4611 | 0 | 6268 | 23319 |
| ALASKA | --- | --- | --- | --- | --- |
| ARIZONA | --- | --- | --- | --- | --- |
| ARKANSAS | --- | --- | --- | --- | --- |
| CALIFORNIA | --- | --- | --- | --- | --- |
| COLORADO | --- | --- | --- | --- | --- |
| CONNECTICUT | 5784 | 11950 | 0 | 240 | 17974 |
| DELAWARE | 3833 | 4267 | 0 | 6 | 8106 |
| DIST OF COLUMBIA | --- | --- | --- | --- | --- |
| FLORIDA | --- | --- | --- | --- | --- |
| GEORGIA | 0 | 0 | 0 | 227900 | 49078 |
| HAWAII | --- | --- | --- | --- | --- |
| IDAHO | --- | --- | --- | --- | --- |
| ILLINOIS | 13052 | 0 | 0 | 11136 | 24188 |
| INDIANA | 22372 | 7712 | 0 | 2 | 30086 |
| IOWA | --- | --- | --- | --- | --- |
| KANSAS | --- | --- | --- | --- | --- |
| KENTUCKY | --- | --- | --- | --- | --- |

TABLE 3.7 (CONTINUED)

### 1830-1831 HOUSE OF REPRESENTATIVES ELECTION

| | DEMOCRAT | NATL. REPUB. | ANTI-MASON | OTHER | TOTAL VOTES CAST |
|---|---|---|---|---|---|
| LOUISIANA | --- | --- | --- | --- | --- |
| MAINE | --- | --- | --- | --- | --- |
| MARYLAND | 4906 | 1794 | 0 | 5464 | 40850 |
| MASSACHUSETTS | 352 | 27016 | 1088 | 14582 | 41950 |
| MICHIGAN | --- | --- | --- | --- | --- |
| MINNESOTA | --- | --- | --- | --- | --- |
| MISSISSIPPI | 2922 | 744 | 0 | 2074 | 5740 |
| MISSOURI | 8302 | 4775 | 0 | 0 | 13077 |
| MONTANA | --- | --- | --- | --- | --- |
| NEBRASKA | --- | --- | --- | --- | --- |
| NEVADA | --- | --- | --- | --- | --- |
| NEW HAMPSHIRE | 13915 | 14823 | 0 | 0 | 28738 |
| NEW JERSEY | --- | --- | --- | --- | --- |
| NEW MEXICO | --- | --- | --- | --- | --- |
| NEW YORK | 87269 | 53861 | 0 | 107948 | 249078 |
| NORTH CAROLINA | --- | --- | --- | --- | --- |
| NORTH DAKOTA | --- | --- | --- | --- | --- |
| OHIO | --- | --- | 3383 | --- | --- |
| OKLAHOMA | --- | --- | --- | --- | --- |
| OREGON | --- | --- | --- | --- | --- |
| PENNSYLVANIA | --- | --- | --- | --- | --- |
| RHODE ISLAND | 0 | 2931 | 0 | 519 | 3450 |
| SOUTH CAROLINA | --- | --- | --- | --- | --- |
| SOUTH DAKOTA | --- | --- | --- | --- | --- |
| TENNESSEE | 34756 | 32799 | 0 | 10638 | 78193 |
| TEXAS | --- | --- | --- | --- | --- |
| UTAH | --- | --- | --- | --- | --- |
| VERMONT | 1483 | 2798 | 4128 | 25749 | 30030 |
| VIRGINIA | --- | --- | --- | --- | --- |
| WASHINGTON | --- | --- | --- | --- | --- |
| WEST VIRGINIA | --- | --- | --- | --- | --- |
| WISCONSIN | --- | --- | --- | --- | --- |
| WYOMING | --- | --- | --- | --- | --- |

1832-1833 HOUSE OF REPRESENTATIVES ELECTION

| | DEMOCRAT | NATL. REPUB. | OTHER | TOTAL VOTES CAST |
|---|---|---|---|---|
| ALABAMA | --- | --- | --- | --- |
| ALASKA | --- | --- | --- | --- |
| ARIZONA | --- | --- | --- | --- |
| ARKANSAS | --- | --- | --- | --- |
| CALIFORNIA | --- | --- | --- | --- |
| COLORADO | --- | --- | --- | --- |
| CONNECTICUT | 0 | 3355 | 15796 | 19151 |
| DELAWARE | 4142 | 0 | 4257 | 8399 |
| DIST OF COLUMBIA | | | | |
| FLORIDA | --- | --- | --- | --- |
| GEORGIA | 0 | 0 | 415478 | 53189 |
| HAWAII | --- | --- | --- | --- |
| IDAHO | --- | --- | --- | --- |
| ILLINOIS | 13912 | 2078 | 9603 | 25593 |
| INDIANA | 29158 | 14022 | 18008 | 61188 |
| IOWA | --- | --- | --- | --- |
| KANSAS | --- | --- | --- | --- |
| KENTUCKY | 16814 | 16034 | --- | --- |
| LOUISIANA | --- | --- | --- | --- |
| MAINE | --- | 3542 | 567 | --- |
| MARYLAND | 22403 | 23591 | 1563 | 42519 |
| MASSACHUSETTS | 3176 | 26115 | 18334 | 47625 |
| MICHIGAN | --- | --- | --- | --- |
| MINNESOTA | --- | --- | --- | --- |
| MISSISSIPPI | 7682 | 4523 | 3466 | 15671 |
| MISSOURI | 3630 | 3671 | 20464 | 27765 |
| MONTANA | --- | --- | --- | --- |
| NEBRASKA | --- | --- | --- | --- |
| NEVADA | --- | --- | --- | --- |
| NEW HAMPSHIRE | 23903 | 23310 | 143289 | 48107 |
| NEW JERSEY | --- | --- | --- | --- |
| NEW MEXICO | --- | --- | --- | --- |
| NEW YORK | 165601 | 152102 | 0 | 317703 |
| NORTH CAROLINA | --- | --- | --- | --- |
| NORTH DAKOTA | --- | --- | --- | --- |
| OHIO | 91120 | 0 | 66956 | 158076 |

TABLE 3.7 (CONTINUED)

## 1832-1833 HOUSE OF REPRESENTATIVES ELECTION

| | DEMOCRAT | NATL. REPUB. | OTHER | TOTAL VOTES CAST |
|---|---|---|---|---|
| OKLAHOMA | --- | --- | --- | --- |
| OREGON | --- | --- | --- | --- |
| PENNSYLVANIA | --- | --- | --- | --- |
| RHODE ISLAND | 2078 | 3162 | 227 | 5467 |
| SOUTH CAROLINA | --- | 1282 | --- | --- |
| SOUTH DAKOTA | --- | --- | --- | --- |
| TENNESSEE | 26829 | 33895 | 28380 | 89104 |
| TEXAS | --- | --- | --- | --- |
| UTAH | --- | --- | --- | --- |
| VERMONT | --- | --- | --- | --- |
| VIRGINIA | --- | --- | --- | --- |
| WASHINGTON | --- | --- | --- | --- |
| WEST VIRGINIA | --- | --- | --- | --- |
| WISCONSIN | --- | --- | --- | --- |
| WYOMING | --- | --- | --- | --- |

## 1834-1835 HOUSE OF REPRESENTATIVES ELECTION

| | DEMOCRAT | WHIG | ANTI-MASON | OTHER | TOTAL VOTES CAST |
|---|---|---|---|---|---|
| ALABAMA | --- | 2969 | --- | --- | --- |
| ALASKA | --- | --- | --- | --- | --- |
| ARIZONA | --- | --- | --- | --- | --- |
| ARKANSAS | --- | --- | --- | --- | --- |
| CALIFORNIA | --- | --- | --- | --- | --- |
| COLORADO | --- | --- | --- | --- | --- |
| CONNECTICUT | 21262 | 18931 | 0 | 2099 | 42292 |
| DELAWARE | 4626 | 4779 | 0 | 0 | 9405 |
| DIST OF COLUMBIA | --- | --- | --- | --- | --- |
| FLORIDA | --- | --- | --- | --- | --- |

| State | | | | | |
|---|---|---|---|---|---|
| GEORGIA | 32581 | 27500 | 0 | 0 | 60081 |
| HAWAII | --- | --- | --- | --- | --- |
| IDAHO | 16198 | 0 | 0 | 11759 | 27957 |
| ILLINOIS | 33737 | 25235 | 0 | 7014 | 65986 |
| INDIANA | --- | --- | --- | --- | --- |
| IOWA | --- | --- | --- | --- | --- |
| KANSAS | --- | --- | --- | --- | --- |
| KENTUCKY | 1162 | 5306 | 0 | 3977 | 10445 |
| LOUISIANA | 35002 | 32098 | 0 | 2587 | 69687 |
| MAINE | 6111 | 8219 | 0 | 0 | 14330 |
| MARYLAND | --- | --- | --- | --- | --- |
| MASSACHUSETTS | 21254 | 36220 | 10962 | 13831 | 71305 |
| MICHIGAN | --- | --- | --- | --- | --- |
| MINNESOTA | 9387 | 7445 | 0 | 224 | 17056 |
| MISSISSIPPI | 10856 | 0 | 0 | 21668 | 32524 |
| MISSOURI | --- | --- | --- | --- | --- |
| MONTANA | --- | --- | --- | --- | --- |
| NEBRASKA | --- | --- | --- | --- | --- |
| NEVADA | --- | --- | --- | --- | --- |
| NEW HAMPSHIRE | 27404 | 26384 | 0 | 0 | 53788 |
| NEW JERSEY | 182366 | 167085 | 0 | 0 | 349451 |
| NEW MEXICO | --- | --- | --- | --- | --- |
| NEW YORK | --- | --- | --- | --- | --- |
| NORTH CAROLINA | 22683 | 69836 | 0 | 3078 | 136040 |
| NORTH DAKOTA | --- | --- | --- | --- | --- |
| OHIO | 65951 | 84534 | 0 | 253 | 184502 |
| OKLAHOMA | --- | --- | --- | --- | --- |
| OREGON | --- | --- | --- | --- | --- |
| PENNSYLVANIA | 99968 | 3776 | 0 | 0 | 7823 |
| RHODE ISLAND | 3901 | 44390 | 0 | 146 | 80865 |
| SOUTH CAROLINA | --- | --- | --- | --- | --- |
| SOUTH DAKOTA | --- | --- | --- | --- | --- |
| TENNESSEE | 27497 | 11177 | 0 | 8978 | 34420 |
| TEXAS | --- | --- | --- | --- | --- |
| UTAH | --- | --- | --- | --- | --- |
| VERMONT | 10210 | 25801 | 11733 | 13033 | 58496 |
| VIRGINIA | 32353 | --- | 0 | 342 | --- |
| WASHINGTON | --- | --- | --- | --- | --- |
| WEST VIRGINIA | --- | --- | --- | --- | --- |
| WISCONSIN | --- | --- | --- | --- | --- |
| WYOMING | --- | --- | --- | --- | --- |

TABLE 3.7 (CONTINUED)

## 1836-1837 HOUSE OF REPRESENTATIVES ELECTION

| | DEMOCRAT | WHIG | OTHER | TOTAL VOTES CAST |
|---|---|---|---|---|
| ALABAMA | 15372 | 12728 | --- | --- |
| ALASKA | --- | --- | --- | --- |
| ARIZONA | --- | --- | --- | --- |
| ARKANSAS | 5420 | 1967 | 0 | 7387 |
| CALIFORNIA | --- | --- | --- | --- |
| COLORADO | --- | --- | --- | --- |
| CONNECTICUT | 29369 | 26617 | 0 | 55986 |
| DELAWARE | 4297 | 4705 | 0 | 9002 |
| DIST OF COLUMBIA | --- | --- | --- | --- |
| FLORIDA | --- | --- | --- | --- |
| GEORGIA | 29580 | 28855 | 0 | 58435 |
| HAWAII | --- | --- | --- | --- |
| IDAHO | --- | --- | --- | --- |
| ILLINOIS | 27899 | 0 | 15982 | 43881 |
| INDIANA | 24756 | 49266 | 48 | 74070 |
| IOWA | --- | --- | --- | --- |
| KANSAS | --- | --- | --- | --- |
| KENTUCKY | 19183 | --- | 3249 | --- |
| LOUISIANA | --- | --- | --- | --- |
| MAINE | --- | --- | 10678 | --- |
| MARYLAND | 4801 | 6249 | 0 | 11050 |
| MASSACHUSETTS | 31364 | 41891 | 618 | 73873 |
| MICHIGAN | 11451 | 10329 | 5 | 21785 |
| MINNESOTA | --- | --- | --- | --- |
| MISSISSIPPI | 6206 | 13688 | 0 | 19894 |
| MISSOURI | 15129 | 0 | 17540 | 32669 |
| MONTANA | --- | --- | --- | --- |
| NEBRASKA | --- | --- | --- | --- |
| NEVADA | --- | --- | --- | --- |
| NEW HAMPSHIRE | --- | --- | --- | --- |
| NEW JERSEY | --- | --- | --- | --- |
| NEW MEXICO | --- | --- | --- | --- |
| NEW YORK | 135182 | 72565 | 91007 | 298754 |
| NORTH CAROLINA | --- | --- | --- | --- |
| NORTH DAKOTA | --- | --- | --- | --- |
| OHIO | 85179 | 91791 | 102 | 177072 |
| OKLAHOMA | --- | --- | --- | --- |
| OREGON | --- | --- | --- | --- |
| PENNSYLVANIA | --- | --- | --- | --- |
| RHODE ISLAND | 3261 | 4221 | 49 | 7531 |
| SOUTH CAROLINA | --- | --- | --- | --- |
| SOUTH DAKOTA | --- | --- | --- | --- |
| TENNESSEE | 29823 | 55151 | 0 | 84974 |
| TEXAS | --- | --- | --- | --- |
| UTAH | --- | --- | --- | --- |
| VERMONT | 3765 | 18731 | 11895 | 34391 |
| VIRGINIA | --- | --- | --- | --- |
| WASHINGTON | --- | --- | --- | --- |
| WEST VIRGINIA | --- | --- | --- | --- |
| WISCONSIN | --- | --- | --- | --- |
| WYOMING | --- | --- | --- | --- |

TABLE 3.7 (CONTINUED)

## 1838-1839 HOUSE OF REPRESENTATIVES ELECTION

| | DEMOCRAT | WHIG | OTHER | TOTAL VOTES CAST |
|---|---|---|---|---|
| ALABAMA | 20430 | 12838 | --- | --- |
| ALASKA | --- | --- | --- | --- |
| ARIZONA | --- | --- | --- | --- |
| ARKANSAS | 6771 | 4328 | 0 | 11099 |
| CALIFORNIA | --- | --- | --- | --- |
| COLORADO | --- | --- | --- | --- |
| CONNECTICUT | 27645 | 30724 | 496 | 58865 |
| DELAWARE | 4451 | 4399 | 0 | 8850 |
| DIST OF COLUMBIA | --- | --- | --- | --- |
| FLORIDA | --- | --- | --- | --- |
| GEORGIA | 30932 | 0 | 289644 | 63258 |
| HAWAII | --- | --- | --- | --- |
| IDAHO | --- | --- | --- | --- |
| ILLINOIS | 34609 | 23849 | 31 | 58489 |
| INDIANA | 51051 | 45675 | 0 | 96726 |
| IOWA | --- | --- | --- | --- |
| KANSAS | --- | --- | --- | --- |
| KENTUCKY | --- | --- | --- | --- |
| LOUISIANA | 3909 | --- | --- | --- |
| MAINE | 46091 | 42204 | 612 | 88907 |
| MARYLAND | 8367 | 9013 | 39 | 17419 |
| MASSACHUSETTS | 35848 | 50044 | 1983 | 87875 |
| MICHIGAN | 16360 | 16099 | 11 | 32470 |
| MINNESOTA | --- | --- | --- | --- |
| MISSISSIPPI | 16501 | 14094 | 0 | 30595 |
| MISSOURI | 23410 | 16706 | 0 | 40116 |
| MONTANA | --- | --- | --- | --- |
| NEBRASKA | --- | --- | --- | --- |
| NEVADA | --- | --- | --- | --- |
| NEW HAMPSHIRE | --- | --- | --- | --- |
| NEW JERSEY | 28453 | 28295 | 0 | 56748 |
| NEW MEXICO | --- | --- | --- | --- |
| NEW YORK | 181065 | 193137 | 0 | 374202 |
| NORTH CAROLINA | --- | --- | --- | --- |
| NORTH DAKOTA | --- | --- | --- | --- |
| OHIO | 103470 | 103242 | 24 | 206736 |
| OKLAHOMA | --- | --- | --- | --- |
| OREGON | --- | --- | --- | --- |
| PENNSYLVANIA | 115823 | 102307 | 0 | 218130 |
| RHODE ISLAND | 3595 | 3912 | 54 | 7561 |
| SOUTH CAROLINA | --- | 3339 | --- | --- |
| SOUTH DAKOTA | --- | --- | --- | --- |
| TENNESSEE | 45170 | 47966 | 7 | 93143 |
| TEXAS | --- | --- | --- | --- |
| UTAH | --- | --- | --- | --- |
| VERMONT | 19635 | 23746 | 436 | 43817 |
| VIRGINIA | 32123 | 30645 | 0 | 62768 |
| WASHINGTON | --- | --- | --- | --- |
| WEST VIRGINIA | --- | --- | --- | --- |
| WISCONSIN | --- | --- | --- | --- |
| WYOMING | --- | --- | --- | --- |

TABLE 3.7 (CONTINUED)

1840-1841 HOUSE OF REPRESENTATIVES ELECTION

| | DEMOCRAT | WHIG | LIBERTY | OTHER | TOTAL VOTES CAST |
|---|---|---|---|---|---|
| ALABAMA | 23376 | 16656 | 0 | 52 | 40084 |
| ALASKA | --- | --- | --- | --- | --- |
| ARIZONA | --- | --- | --- | --- | --- |
| ARKANSAS | 7876 | 5788 | 0 | 0 | 13664 |
| CALIFORNIA | --- | --- | --- | --- | --- |
| COLORADO | --- | --- | --- | --- | --- |
| CONNECTICUT | 21168 | 26800 | 0 | 0 | 47968 |
| DELAWARE | 4974 | 5896 | 0 | 3 | 10873 |
| DIST OF COLUMBIA | --- | --- | --- | --- | --- |
| FLORIDA | --- | --- | --- | --- | --- |
| GEORGIA | 35783 | 38980 | 0 | 0 | 74763 |
| HAWAII | --- | --- | --- | --- | --- |
| IDAHO | --- | --- | --- | --- | --- |
| ILLINOIS | 34557 | 34160 | 507 | 197 | 69421 |
| INDIANA | 38957 | 45268 | 0 | 250 | 84475 |
| IOWA | --- | --- | --- | --- | --- |
| KANSAS | --- | --- | --- | --- | --- |
| KENTUCKY | 7043 | 9149 | 0 | 2121 | 16192 |
| LOUISIANA | 40564 | 111988 | 0 | 0 | 93023 |
| MAINE | --- | --- | --- | 563 | --- |
| MARYLAND | 4130 | --- | --- | --- | --- |
| MASSACHUSETTS | 51485 | 71558 | 192 | 1338 | 124573 |
| MICHIGAN | 21464 | 22841 | 268 | 10 | 44583 |
| MINNESOTA | --- | --- | --- | --- | --- |
| MISSISSIPPI | 18988 | 16593 | 0 | 0 | 35581 |
| MISSOURI | 29594 | 21331 | 0 | 0 | 50925 |
| MONTANA | --- | --- | --- | --- | --- |
| NEBRASKA | --- | --- | --- | --- | --- |
| NEVADA | --- | --- | --- | --- | --- |
| NEW HAMPSHIRE | 28870 | 20833 | 0 | 0 | 49703 |
| NEW JERSEY | 31101 | 33315 | 65 | 2 | 64483 |
| NEW MEXICO | --- | --- | --- | --- | --- |
| NEW YORK | 214356 | 223879 | 1762 | 0 | 439997 |
| NORTH CAROLINA | --- | --- | --- | 111 | --- |

| STATE | DEMOCRAT | WHIG | LIBERTY | OTHER | TOTAL VOTES CAST |
|---|---|---|---|---|---|
| NORTH DAKOTA | --- | --- | --- | --- | --- |
| OHIO | 128284 | 145397 | 0 | 52 | 273733 |
| OKLAHOMA | --- | --- | --- | --- | --- |
| OREGON | --- | --- | --- | --- | --- |
| PENNSYLVANIA | --- | 92931 | --- | 246 | 2762 |
| RHODE ISLAND | 0 | 2516 | 0 | --- | --- |
| SOUTH CAROLINA | --- | 4530 | --- | --- | --- |
| SOUTH DAKOTA | --- | --- | --- | --- | --- |
| TENNESSEE | 30230 | 35085 | 0 | 766 | 66081 |
| TEXAS | --- | --- | --- | --- | --- |
| UTAH | --- | --- | --- | --- | --- |
| VERMONT | 21654 | 32007 | 0 | 414 | 54075 |
| VIRGINIA | --- | --- | --- | --- | --- |
| WASHINGTON | --- | --- | --- | --- | --- |
| WEST VIRGINIA | --- | --- | --- | --- | --- |
| WISCONSIN | --- | --- | --- | --- | --- |
| WYOMING | --- | --- | --- | --- | --- |

1842-1843 HOUSE OF REPRESENTATIVES ELECTION

| STATE | DEMOCRAT | WHIG | LIBERTY | OTHER | TOTAL VOTES CAST |
|---|---|---|---|---|---|
| ALABAMA | --- | 19559 | --- | --- | --- |
| ALASKA | --- | --- | --- | --- | --- |
| ARIZONA | --- | --- | --- | --- | --- |
| ARKANSAS | 9413 | 5315 | 0 | 1686 | 16414 |
| CALIFORNIA | --- | --- | --- | --- | --- |
| COLORADO | --- | --- | --- | --- | --- |
| CONNECTICUT | 27225 | 25729 | 1603 | 146 | 54703 |
| DELAWARE | 5458 | 5467 | 0 | 0 | 10925 |
| DIST OF COLUMBIA | --- | --- | --- | --- | --- |
| FLORIDA | --- | --- | --- | --- | --- |
| GEORGIA | 35181 | 33474 | 0 | 0 | 68655 |
| HAWAII | --- | --- | --- | --- | --- |
| IDAHO | --- | --- | --- | --- | --- |
| ILLINOIS | 49482 | 42288 | 1947 | 116 | 93833 |
| INDIANA | 57867 | 57793 | 0 | 4394 | 120054 |
| IOWA | --- | --- | --- | --- | --- |
| KANSAS | --- | --- | --- | --- | --- |

TABLE 3.7 (CONTINUED)

## 1842-1843 HOUSE OF REPRESENTATIVES ELECTION

| | DEMOCRAT | WHIG | LIBERTY | OTHER | TOTAL VOTES CAST |
|---|---|---|---|---|---|
| KENTUCKY | 42623 | 50761 | 0 | 0 | 93384 |
| LOUISIANA | --- | --- | --- | --- | --- |
| MAINE | 30733 | 11850 | 825 | 18890 | 62298 |
| MARYLAND | 22019 | 26660 | 0 | 215 | 48894 |
| MASSACHUSETTS | 35940 | 47557 | 1118 | 13035 | 97650 |
| MICHIGAN | 21242 | 14704 | 2824 | 81 | 38851 |
| MINNESOTA | --- | --- | --- | --- | --- |
| MISSISSIPPI | 0 | 0 | 0 | 132636 | 35384 |
| MISSOURI | --- | --- | --- | --- | --- |
| MONTANA | --- | --- | --- | --- | --- |
| NEBRASKA | --- | --- | --- | --- | --- |
| NEVADA | --- | --- | --- | --- | --- |
| NEW HAMPSHIRE | --- | --- | --- | --- | --- |
| NEW JERSEY | --- | 23091 | --- | 5313 | --- |
| NEW MEXICO | --- | --- | --- | --- | --- |
| NEW YORK | 195886 | 186469 | 7214 | 0 | 389569 |
| NORTH CAROLINA | 24188 | 28562 | 0 | 0 | 52750 |
| NORTH DAKOTA | --- | --- | --- | --- | --- |
| OHIO | 107249 | 97288 | 6141 | 7564 | 218242 |
| OKLAHOMA | --- | --- | --- | --- | --- |
| OREGON | --- | --- | --- | --- | --- |
| PENNSYLVANIA | 106632 | 89277 | 1060 | 4711 | 201680 |
| RHODE ISLAND | 4403 | 0 | 0 | 7018 | 11421 |
| SOUTH CAROLINA | --- | --- | --- | --- | --- |
| SOUTH DAKOTA | --- | --- | --- | --- | --- |
| TENNESSEE | 48883 | 55268 | 0 | 0 | 104151 |
| TEXAS | --- | --- | --- | --- | --- |
| UTAH | --- | --- | --- | --- | --- |
| VERMONT | 20671 | 23734 | 3026 | 516 | 47947 |
| VIRGINIA | --- | 21774 | --- | 183 | --- |
| WASHINGTON | --- | --- | --- | --- | --- |
| WEST VIRGINIA | --- | --- | --- | --- | --- |
| WISCONSIN | --- | --- | --- | --- | --- |
| WYOMING | --- | --- | --- | --- | --- |

1844-1845 HOUSE OF REPRESENTATIVES ELECTION

| | DEMOCRAT | WHIG | LIBERTY | OTHER | TOTAL VOTES CAST |
|---|---|---|---|---|---|
| ALABAMA | --- | --- | --- | --- | --- |
| ALASKA | --- | --- | --- | --- | --- |
| ARIZONA | --- | --- | --- | --- | --- |
| ARKANSAS | 11112 | 7576 | 0 | 113 | 18801 |
| CALIFORNIA | --- | --- | --- | --- | --- |
| COLORADO | --- | --- | --- | --- | --- |
| CONNECTICUT | 26002 | 29569 | 1973 | 30 | 57574 |
| DELAWARE | 6043 | 6221 | 0 | 0 | 12264 |
| DIST OF COLUMBIA | --- | --- | --- | --- | --- |
| FLORIDA | 2472 | 2523 | 0 | 0 | 4995 |
| GEORGIA | 40377 | 38111 | 0 | 0 | 78488 |
| HAWAII | --- | --- | --- | --- | --- |
| IDAHO | --- | --- | --- | --- | --- |
| ILLINOIS | 57735 | 33485 | 3000 | 4695 | 98915 |
| INDIANA | 64995 | 58816 | 1771 | 9 | 125591 |
| IOWA | --- | --- | --- | --- | --- |
| KANSAS | --- | --- | --- | --- | --- |
| KENTUCKY | 55115 | 51867 | 0 | 193 | 107175 |
| LOUISIANA | --- | --- | --- | --- | --- |
| MAINE | 6377 | 0 | 0 | 31201 | 37578 |
| MARYLAND | 30539 | 28504 | 0 | 1147 | 60190 |
| MASSACHUSETTS | 21313 | 63618 | 1014 | 29939 | 115884 |
| MICHIGAN | 27898 | 24611 | 3147 | 148 | 55804 |
| MINNESOTA | --- | --- | --- | --- | --- |
| MISSISSIPPI | 27193 | 17452 | 0 | 0 | 44645 |
| MISSOURI | 35128 | 28309 | 0 | 0 | 63437 |
| MONTANA | --- | --- | --- | --- | --- |
| NEBRASKA | --- | --- | --- | --- | --- |
| NEVADA | --- | --- | --- | --- | --- |
| NEW HAMPSHIRE | 23239 | 14677 | 0 | 11813 | 49729 |
| NEW JERSEY | 30361 | 39136 | 0 | 0 | 69497 |
| NEW MEXICO | --- | --- | --- | --- | --- |
| NEW YORK | 232430 | 260079 | 16862 | 33275 | 482646 |
| NORTH CAROLINA | 34107 | 33946 | 0 | 0 | 68053 |
| NORTH DAKOTA | --- | --- | --- | --- | --- |
| OHIO | 143950 | 138860 | 7691 | 11075 | 301576 |

TABLE 3.7 (CONTINUED)

1844-1845 HOUSE OF REPRESENTATIVES ELECTION

| | DEMOCRAT | WHIG | LIBERTY | OTHER | TOTAL VOTES CAST |
|---|---|---|---|---|---|
| OKLAHOMA | --- | --- | --- | --- | --- |
| OREGON | --- | --- | --- | --- | --- |
| PENNSYLVANIA | --- | --- | --- | --- | --- |
| RHODE ISLAND | 0 | 4900 | 0 | 6328 | 11228 |
| SOUTH CAROLINA | --- | 2902 | --- | --- | --- |
| SOUTH DAKOTA | --- | --- | --- | --- | --- |
| TENNESSEE | 53641 | 43445 | 0 | 2565 | 99651 |
| TEXAS | --- | --- | --- | --- | --- |
| UTAH | --- | --- | --- | --- | --- |
| VERMONT | 19182 | 26831 | 5034 | 157 | 51204 |
| VIRGINIA | --- | --- | --- | --- | --- |
| WASHINGTON | --- | --- | --- | --- | --- |
| WEST VIRGINIA | --- | --- | --- | --- | --- |
| WISCONSIN | --- | --- | --- | --- | --- |
| WYOMING | --- | --- | --- | --- | --- |

1846-1847 HOUSE OF REPRESENTATIVES ELECTION

| | DEMOCRAT | WHIG | LIBERTY | FREE SOIL | OTHER | TOTAL VOTES CAST |
|---|---|---|---|---|---|---|
| ALABAMA | --- | --- | --- | --- | 793 | --- |
| ALASKA | --- | --- | --- | --- | --- | --- |
| ARIZONA | --- | --- | --- | --- | --- | --- |
| ARKANSAS | --- | --- | --- | --- | --- | --- |
| CALIFORNIA | --- | --- | --- | --- | --- | --- |
| COLORADO | --- | --- | --- | --- | --- | --- |
| CONNECTICUT | 27394 | 30195 | 0 | 1802 | 0 | 59391 |
| DELAWARE | 6007 | 6154 | 0 | 0 | 0 | 12161 |
| DIST OF COLUMBIA | --- | --- | --- | --- | --- | --- |
| FLORIDA | --- | --- | --- | --- | --- | --- |

| State | | | | | | |
|---|---|---|---|---|---|---|
| GEORGIA | 30343 | 28613 | 0 | 0 | 121 | 59077 |
| HAWAII | --- | --- | --- | --- | --- | --- |
| IDAHO | --- | --- | --- | --- | --- | --- |
| ILLINOIS | 54293 | 27739 | 5122 | 0 | 12411 | 99565 |
| INDIANA | 64000 | 67657 | 0 | 0 | 4136 | 135793 |
| IOWA | 10690 | 9859 | 0 | 0 | 0 | 20549 |
| KANSAS | 53949 | 59246 | 0 | 0 | 3143 | 116338 |
| KENTUCKY | 14558 | 12826 | 0 | 0 | --- | 27384 |
| LOUISIANA | 32950 | 28095 | 0 | 537 | 8607 | 70189 |
| MAINE | --- | --- | --- | --- | --- | --- |
| MARYLAND | 30774 | 52113 | 8953 | 0 | 2003 | 93843 |
| MASSACHUSETTS | 23923 | 20934 | 2928 | 0 | 60 | 47845 |
| MICHIGAN | --- | --- | --- | --- | --- | --- |
| MINNESOTA | --- | --- | --- | --- | --- | --- |
| MISSISSIPPI | 20014 | 12526 | 0 | 0 | 6033 | 38573 |
| MISSOURI | 40325 | 25200 | 0 | 0 | 1755 | 67280 |
| MONTANA | --- | --- | --- | --- | --- | --- |
| NEBRASKA | --- | --- | --- | --- | --- | --- |
| NEVADA | 9111 | 5926 | 0 | 0 | 6247 | 54848 |
| NEW HAMPSHIRE | --- | --- | --- | --- | --- | --- |
| NEW JERSEY | --- | --- | --- | --- | --- | --- |
| NEW MEXICO | --- | --- | --- | --- | --- | --- |
| NEW YORK | 173862 | 176342 | 8020 | 0 | 50700 | 400904 |
| NORTH CAROLINA | 22799 | 30216 | 0 | 0 | 7454 | 60469 |
| NORTH DAKOTA | --- | --- | --- | --- | --- | --- |
| OHIO | 116527 | 109489 | 0 | 0 | 4555 | 238591 |
| OKLAHOMA | --- | --- | --- | --- | --- | --- |
| OREGON | --- | --- | --- | --- | --- | --- |
| PENNSYLVANIA | 94739 | 99860 | 0 | 0 | 0 | 194599 |
| RHODE ISLAND | 4357 | 5338 | 0 | 290 | 728 | 10713 |
| SOUTH CAROLINA | --- | --- | --- | --- | --- | --- |
| SOUTH DAKOTA | --- | --- | --- | --- | --- | --- |
| TENNESSEE | 54972 | 55611 | 0 | 0 | 58 | 110641 |
| TEXAS | 589 | 0 | 0 | 0 | 3519 | 4108 |
| UTAH | --- | --- | --- | --- | --- | --- |
| VERMONT | 15726 | 22787 | 4562 | 0 | 3446 | 46521 |
| VIRGINIA | 34337 | 31666 | 0 | 0 | 1230 | 67233 |
| WASHINGTON | --- | --- | --- | --- | --- | --- |
| WEST VIRGINIA | --- | --- | --- | --- | --- | --- |
| WISCONSIN | --- | --- | --- | --- | --- | --- |
| WYOMING | --- | --- | --- | --- | --- | --- |

TABLE 3.7 (CONTINUED)

## 1848-1849 HOUSE OF REPRESENTATIVES ELECTION

| | DEMOCRAT | WHIG | FREE SOIL | OTHER | TOTAL VOTES CAST |
|---|---|---|---|---|---|
| ALABAMA | 25347 | 23956 | 0 | 15485 | 64788 |
| ALASKA | --- | --- | --- | --- | --- |
| ARIZONA | --- | --- | --- | --- | --- |
| ARKANSAS | 14456 | 9328 | 0 | 0 | 23784 |
| CALIFORNIA | --- | --- | --- | --- | --- |
| COLORADO | --- | --- | --- | --- | --- |
| CONNECTICUT | 27284 | 28023 | 774 | 0 | 56081 |
| DELAWARE | 6026 | 6369 | 0 | 0 | 12395 |
| DIST OF COLUMBIA | --- | --- | --- | --- | --- |
| FLORIDA | 3805 | 4382 | 0 | 0 | 8187 |
| GEORGIA | 38908 | 38651 | 0 | 0 | 77559 |
| HAWAII | --- | --- | --- | --- | --- |
| IDAHO | --- | --- | --- | --- | --- |
| ILLINOIS | 64449 | 34387 | 4210 | 589 | 103635 |
| INDIANA | 65040 | 70504 | 4737 | 4935 | 145216 |
| IOWA | 12266 | 11489 | 488 | 8 | 24251 |
| KANSAS | --- | --- | --- | --- | --- |
| KENTUCKY | 41919 | 57248 | 0 | 4665 | 103832 |
| LOUISIANA | 15132 | 14284 | 0 | 0 | 29416 |
| MAINE | 27834 | 11856 | 0 | 42600 | 82290 |
| MARYLAND | --- | --- | --- | --- | --- |
| MASSACHUSETTS | 7133 | 54076 | 14259 | 29267 | 104735 |
| MICHIGAN | 31244 | 16549 | 4564 | 13588 | 65945 |
| MINNESOTA | --- | --- | --- | --- | --- |
| MISSISSIPPI | 31732 | 23625 | 0 | 0 | 55357 |
| MISSOURI | 50362 | 31427 | 0 | 0 | 81789 |
| MONTANA | --- | --- | --- | --- | --- |
| NEBRASKA | --- | --- | --- | --- | --- |
| NEVADA | --- | --- | --- | --- | --- |
| NEW HAMPSHIRE | 29969 | 0 | 22068 | 3685 | 55722 |
| NEW JERSEY | 36379 | 36668 | 741 | 718 | 74506 |
| NEW MEXICO | --- | --- | --- | --- | --- |
| NEW YORK | 107895 | 217679 | 118152 | 9246 | 452972 |
| NORTH CAROLINA | 32215 | 36243 | 0 | 1146 | 69604 |

|  | DEMOCRAT | WHIG | FREE SOIL | UNION | OTHER | TOTAL VOTES CAST |
|---|---|---|---|---|---|---|
| NORTH DAKOTA | --- | --- | --- | --- | --- | --- |
| OHIO | 142210 | 116111 | 3188 | 25001 | --- | 286510 |
| OKLAHOMA | --- | --- | --- | --- | --- | --- |
| OREGON | --- | --- | --- | --- | --- | --- |
| PENNSYLVANIA | 155169 | 149051 | 8666 | 16793 | --- | 329679 |
| RHODE ISLAND | 3267 | 4964 | 363 | 31 | --- | 8625 |
| SOUTH CAROLINA | 0 | 3369 | 0 | 5105 | --- | 8474 |
| SOUTH DAKOTA | --- | --- | --- | --- | --- | --- |
| TENNESSEE | 51215 | 55122 | --- | 0 | --- | 106337 |
| TEXAS | 13064 | 0 | --- | 3348 | --- | 16412 |
| UTAH | --- | --- | --- | --- | --- | --- |
| VERMONT | --- | --- | --- | --- | --- | --- |
| VIRGINIA | --- | 31573 | --- | --- | --- | --- |
| WASHINGTON | --- | --- | --- | --- | --- | --- |
| WEST VIRGINIA | --- | --- | --- | --- | --- | --- |
| WISCONSIN | 15872 | 13233 | 9284 | 0 | --- | 38389 |
| WYOMING | --- | --- | --- | --- | --- | --- |

## 1850-1851 HOUSE OF REPRESENTATIVES ELECTION

|  | DEMOCRAT | WHIG | FREE SOIL | UNION | OTHER | TOTAL VOTES CAST |
|---|---|---|---|---|---|---|
| ALABAMA | --- | --- | --- | --- | --- | --- |
| ALASKA | --- | --- | --- | --- | --- | --- |
| ARIZONA | --- | --- | --- | --- | --- | --- |
| ARKANSAS | 11970 | 8877 | 0 | 0 | 0 | 20847 |
| CALIFORNIA | 24315 | 21460 | 0 | 0 | 50 | 45825 |
| COLORADO | --- | --- | --- | --- | --- | --- |
| CONNECTICUT | 29984 | 28886 | 1566 | 0 | 5 | 60441 |
| DELAWARE | 6055 | 5926 | 0 | 0 | 453 | 12434 |
| DIST OF COLUMBIA | --- | --- | --- | --- | --- | --- |
| FLORIDA | 4050 | 4531 | 0 | 0 | 0 | 8581 |
| GEORGIA | 0 | 0 | 0 | 55988 | 37669 | 93657 |
| HAWAII | --- | --- | --- | --- | --- | --- |
| IDAHO | --- | --- | --- | --- | --- | --- |
| ILLINOIS | 59798 | 43204 | 1073 | 0 | 199 | 104274 |
| INDIANA | 74515 | 60717 | 4540 | 0 | 8822 | 148594 |
| IOWA | 13182 | 11710 | 408 | 0 | 67 | 25367 |

TABLE 3.7 (CONTINUED)

1050-1851 HOUSE OF REPRESENTATIVES ELECTION

| | DEMOCRAT | WHIG | FREE SOIL | UNION | OTHER | TOTAL VOTES CAST |
|---|---|---|---|---|---|---|
| KANSAS | ---- | ---- | ---- | ---- | ---- | ---- |
| KENTUCKY | 31730 | 45362 | 0 | ---- | 25620 | 102712 |
| LOUISIANA | 17653 | 18138 | 0 | 0 | 0 | 35791 |
| MAINE | 36955 | 31502 | 2701 | 0 | 6155 | 77313 |
| MARYLAND | ---- | ---- | ---- | ---- | ---- | ---- |
| MASSACHUSETTS | 10161 | 41305 | 20737 | ---- | 26009 | 98212 |
| MICHIGAN | 29270 | 0 | 0 | 0 | 31030 | 60300 |
| MINNESOTA | ---- | ---- | ---- | ---- | ---- | ---- |
| MISSISSIPPI | 0 | 0 | ---- | 29479 | 27607 | 57086 |
| MISSOURI | 5878 | 31784 | 0 | 0 | 40091 | 77753 |
| MONTANA | ---- | ---- | ---- | ---- | ---- | ---- |
| NEBRASKA | ---- | ---- | ---- | ---- | ---- | ---- |
| NEVADA | ---- | ---- | ---- | ---- | ---- | ---- |
| NEW HAMPSHIRE | 27340 | 6051 | 3078 | 0 | 16373 | 52842 |
| NEW JERSEY | 39368 | 33299 | 0 | 0 | 43 | 72710 |
| NEW MEXICO | ---- | ---- | ---- | ---- | ---- | ---- |
| NEW YORK | 207906 | 213082 | 0 | 0 | 273 | 421261 |
| NORTH CAROLINA | ---- | ---- | ---- | ---- | ---- | ---- |
| NORTH DAKOTA | ---- | ---- | ---- | ---- | ---- | ---- |
| OHIO | 132804 | 108914 | 2197 | 0 | 10032 | 253947 |
| OKLAHOMA | ---- | ---- | ---- | ---- | ---- | ---- |
| OREGON | ---- | ---- | ---- | ---- | ---- | ---- |
| PENNSYLVANIA | 140602 | 129687 | 0 | 0 | 5511 | 275800 |
| RHODE ISLAND | 6605 | 5636 | 128 | 0 | 39 | 12408 |
| SOUTH CAROLINA | ---- | ---- | ---- | ---- | 232 | ---- |
| SOUTH DAKOTA | ---- | ---- | ---- | ---- | ---- | ---- |
| TENNESSEE | 43362 | 52185 | 0 | 0 | 0 | 95547 |
| TEXAS | 13482 | 0 | 0 | 0 | 12865 | 26347 |
| UTAH | ---- | ---- | ---- | ---- | ---- | ---- |
| VERMONT | 17042 | 20737 | 0 | 0 | 3041 | 40820 |
| VIRGINIA | ---- | 20117 | ---- | ---- | ---- | ---- |
| WASHINGTON | ---- | ---- | ---- | ---- | ---- | ---- |
| WEST VIRGINIA | ---- | ---- | ---- | ---- | ---- | ---- |
| WISCONSIN | 18208 | 5852 | 18671 | 0 | 0 | 42731 |
| WYOMING | ---- | ---- | ---- | ---- | ---- | ---- |

1852-1853 HOUSE OF REPRESENTATIVES ELECTION

| | DEMOCRAT | WHIG | FREE SOIL | OTHER | TOTAL VOTES CAST |
|---|---|---|---|---|---|
| ALABAMA | 13604 | 2769 | 0 | 45895 | 62268 |
| ALASKA | --- | --- | --- | --- | --- |
| ARIZONA | --- | --- | --- | --- | --- |
| ARKANSAS | 39881 | 34299 | 0 | 11 | 74191 |
| CALIFORNIA | --- | --- | --- | --- | --- |
| COLORADO | --- | --- | --- | --- | --- |
| CONNECTICUT | 31605 | 24891 | 3239 | 0 | 59735 |
| DELAWARE | 6692 | 6630 | 0 | 0 | 13322 |
| DIST OF COLUMBIA | --- | --- | --- | --- | --- |
| FLORIDA | 4637 | 4587 | 0 | 0 | 9224 |
| GEORGIA | 42789 | 32713 | 0 | 0 | 75502 |
| HAWAII | --- | --- | --- | --- | --- |
| IDAHO | --- | --- | --- | --- | --- |
| ILLINOIS | 75797 | 62158 | 7287 | 6302 | 151544 |
| INDIANA | 89787 | 76957 | 0 | 0 | 166744 |
| IOWA | 16823 | 15651 | 0 | 0 | 32474 |
| KANSAS | --- | --- | --- | --- | --- |
| KENTUCKY | 56839 | 49203 | 6606 | 5598 | 118246 |
| LOUISIANA | 22454 | 18731 | 0 | 0 | 41185 |
| MAINE | 39951 | 40735 | 4661 | 678 | 86025 |
| MARYLAND | 19513 | 45504 | 23287 | 4414 | 92718 |
| MASSACHUSETTS | 41662 | 28287 | 2722 | 9448 | 82119 |
| MICHIGAN | --- | 21920 | --- | --- | --- |
| MINNESOTA | --- | --- | --- | --- | --- |
| MISSISSIPPI | --- | --- | --- | --- | --- |
| MISSOURI | 26268 | 46461 | 0 | 33137 | 105866 |
| MONTANA | --- | --- | --- | --- | --- |
| NEBRASKA | --- | --- | --- | --- | --- |
| NEVADA | --- | --- | --- | --- | --- |
| NEW HAMPSHIRE | 28853 | 20871 | 0 | 0 | 49724 |
| NEW JERSEY | 44323 | 38270 | 0 | 0 | 82593 |
| NEW MEXICO | --- | --- | --- | --- | --- |
| NEW YORK | 245703 | 229455 | 10660 | 17624 | 503442 |
| NORTH CAROLINA | 35524 | 32020 | 0 | 13554 | 81098 |
| NORTH DAKOTA | --- | --- | --- | --- | --- |
| OHIO | 141411 | 127544 | 25846 | 1027 | 295828 |

TABLE 3.7 (CONTINUED)

### 1852-1853 HOUSE OF REPRESENTATIVES ELECTION

|  | DEMOCRAT | WHIG | FREE SOIL | OTHER | TOTAL VOTES CAST |
|---|---|---|---|---|---|
| OKLAHOMA | --- | --- | --- | --- | --- |
| OREGON | --- | --- | --- | --- | --- |
| PENNSYLVANIA | 169723 | 144753 | 2007 | 8218 | 324701 |
| RHODE ISLAND | 9960 | 5392 | 403 | 18 | 15773 |
| SOUTH CAROLINA | --- | --- | --- | --- | --- |
| SOUTH DAKOTA | --- | --- | --- | --- | --- |
| TENNESSEE | --- | --- | --- | --- | --- |
| TEXAS | 18044 | 2126 | 0 | 168 | 20338 |
| UTAH | --- | --- | --- | --- | --- |
| VERMONT | 6943 | 22163 | 8023 | 239 | 37368 |
| VIRGINIA | --- | 25127 | --- | 807 | --- |
| WASHINGTON | --- | --- | --- | --- | --- |
| WEST VIRGINIA | --- | --- | --- | --- | --- |
| WISCONSIN | 33831 | 21199 | 9405 | 0 | 64435 |
| WYOMING | --- | --- | --- | --- | --- |

### 1854-1855 HOUSE OF REPRESENTATIVES ELECTION

|  | DEMOCRAT | REPUBLICAN | FREE SOIL | AMERICAN | OTHER | TOTAL VOTES CAST |
|---|---|---|---|---|---|---|
| ALABAMA | 33661 | 0 | 0 | 21916 | 15635 | 71212 |
| ALASKA | --- | --- | --- | --- | --- | --- |
| ARIZONA | --- | --- | --- | --- | --- | --- |
| ARKANSAS | 24267 | 0 | 4371 | 0 | 443 | 29081 |
| CALIFORNIA | 36681 | 34572 | 0 | 0 | 10435 | 81688 |
| COLORADO | --- | --- | --- | --- | --- | --- |
| CONNECTICUT | 27349 | 0 | 0 | 36151 | 0 | 63500 |
| DELAWARE | 6334 | 0 | 6820 | 0 | 0 | 13154 |
| DIST OF COLUMBIA | --- | --- | --- | --- | --- | --- |
| FLORIDA | 5642 | 0 | 4583 | 0 | 0 | 10225 |

| State | (1) | (2) | (3) | (4) | (5) | (6) |
|---|---|---|---|---|---|---|
| GEORGIA | 56905 | 0 | 0 | 45695 | 0 | 102600 |
| HAWAII | --- | --- | --- | --- | --- | --- |
| IDAHO | 60404 | 73210 | 2591 | 0 | 4202 | 140407 |
| ILLINOIS | 0 | 102424 | 0 | 0 | 87766 | 190190 |
| INDIANA | 21085 | 22466 | 0 | 0 | 174 | 43725 |
| IOWA | --- | --- | --- | --- | --- | --- |
| KANSAS | 65845 | 0 | 0 | 69687 | 0 | 135532 |
| KENTUCKY | 22106 | 0 | 0 | 19475 | 0 | 41581 |
| LOUISIANA | 31771 | 51370 | 5686 | 0 | 0 | 88827 |
| MAINE | 39864 | 0 | 0 | 41929 | 0 | 81793 |
| MARYLAND | 2503 | 0 | 109193 | 0 | 9901 | 121594 |
| MASSACHUSETTS | 38247 | 43660 | 0 | 0 | 32 | 81939 |
| MICHIGAN | --- | --- | --- | --- | --- | --- |
| MINNESOTA | 28305 | 0 | 0 | 14519 | 9374 | 52198 |
| MISSISSIPPI | 0 | 0 | 43074 | 0 | 57107 | 100181 |
| MISSOURI | --- | --- | --- | --- | --- | --- |
| MONTANA | --- | --- | --- | --- | --- | --- |
| NEBRASKA | --- | --- | --- | --- | --- | --- |
| NEVADA | 26188 | 0 | 0 | 36723 | 0 | 62911 |
| NEW HAMPSHIRE | 0 | 0 | 33996 | 0 | 44617 | 78613 |
| NEW JERSEY | 0 | 0 | 141682 | 0 | 305628 | 447310 |
| NEW MEXICO | 45318 | 0 | 0 | 42043 | 3756 | 91117 |
| NEW YORK | --- | --- | --- | --- | --- | --- |
| NORTH CAROLINA | 105584 | 186236 | 0 | 0 | 0 | 291820 |
| NORTH DAKOTA | --- | --- | --- | --- | --- | --- |
| OHIO | --- | --- | --- | --- | --- | --- |
| OKLAHOMA | --- | --- | --- | --- | --- | --- |
| OREGON | --- | --- | --- | --- | --- | --- |
| PENNSYLVANIA | 147079 | 0 | 0 | 0 | 0 | 147079 |
| RHODE ISLAND | 1576 | 0 | 0 | 9363 | 891 | 11830 |
| SOUTH CAROLINA | --- | --- | --- | --- | --- | --- |
| SOUTH DAKOTA | --- | --- | --- | --- | --- | --- |
| TENNESSEE | 61418 | 0 | 0 | 64857 | 0 | 126275 |
| TEXAS | 24690 | 0 | 0 | 19838 | 0 | 44528 |
| UTAH | --- | --- | --- | --- | --- | --- |
| VERMONT | 12920 | 0 | 24868 | 0 | 2680 | 40468 |
| VIRGINIA | 0 | 0 | 0 | 46895 | 0 | 46895 |
| WASHINGTON | --- | --- | --- | --- | --- | --- |
| WEST VIRGINIA | --- | --- | --- | --- | --- | --- |
| WISCONSIN | 24948 | 32321 | 0 | 0 | 0 | 57269 |
| WYOMING | --- | --- | --- | --- | --- | --- |

TABLE 3.7 (CONTINUED)

## 1856-1857 HOUSE OF REPRESENTATIVES ELECTION

| | DEMOCRAT | REPUBLICAN | AMERICAN | OTHER | TOTAL VOTES CAST |
|---|---|---|---|---|---|
| ALABAMA | 46551 | 0 | 13736 | 10499 | 70786 |
| ALASKA | --- | --- | --- | --- | --- |
| ARIZONA | --- | --- | --- | --- | --- |
| ARKANSAS | 27234 | 0 | 14862 | 0 | 42096 |
| CALIFORNIA | 50813 | 21975 | 36078 | 66 | 108932 |
| COLORADO | --- | --- | --- | --- | --- |
| CONNECTICUT | 30785 | 31785 | 0 | 0 | 62570 |
| DELAWARE | 8111 | 0 | 6360 | 0 | 14471 |
| DIST OF COLUMBIA | --- | --- | --- | --- | --- |
| FLORIDA | 6392 | 0 | 5650 | 0 | 12042 |
| GEORGIA | 54617 | 0 | 33096 | 12154 | 99867 |
| HAWAII | --- | --- | --- | --- | --- |
| IDAHO | --- | --- | --- | --- | --- |
| ILLINOIS | 110038 | 118011 | 257 | 2384 | 230690 |
| INDIANA | 117905 | 111673 | 0 | 0 | 229578 |
| IOWA | 32978 | 39953 | 828 | 50 | 73809 |
| KANSAS | --- | --- | --- | --- | --- |
| KENTUCKY | 72681 | 0 | 57539 | 68 | 130288 |
| LOUISIANA | 19808 | 0 | 15945 | 0 | 35753 |
| MAINE | 0 | 57125 | 0 | 50955 | 108080 |
| MARYLAND | 37819 | 0 | 46801 | 0 | 84620 |
| MASSACHUSETTS | 33530 | 92131 | 25070 | 11235 | 161966 |
| MICHIGAN | 54309 | 72810 | 0 | 30 | 127149 |
| MINNESOTA | --- | --- | --- | --- | --- |
| MISSISSIPPI | 23817 | 0 | 0 | 10916 | 34733 |
| MISSOURI | 51891 | 0 | 46671 | 12831 | 111393 |
| MONTANA | --- | --- | --- | --- | --- |
| NEBRASKA | --- | --- | --- | --- | --- |
| NEVADA | --- | --- | --- | --- | --- |
| NEW HAMPSHIRE | 30227 | 33910 | 0 | 0 | 64137 |
| NEW JERSEY | 47088 | 12356 | 7993 | 31164 | 98601 |
| NEW MEXICO | --- | --- | --- | --- | --- |
| NEW YORK | 174367 | 271484 | 111531 | 34609 | 591991 |
| NORTH CAROLINA | 52625 | 0 | 19385 | 6015 | 78025 |

| STATE | DEMOCRAT | REPUBLICAN | AMERICAN | OPPOSITION | OTHER | TOTAL VOTES CAST |
|---|---|---|---|---|---|---|
| NORTH DAKOTA | --- | --- | --- | --- | --- | --- |
| OHIO | 156654 | 178854 | --- | 19442 | --- | 354950 |
| OKLAHOMA | --- | --- | --- | --- | --- | --- |
| OREGON | --- | --- | --- | --- | --- | --- |
| PENNSYLVANIA | 211520 | 39240 | --- | 7826 | 162468 | 421054 |
| RHODE ISLAND | 5170 | 5442 | --- | 0 | 4035 | 14647 |
| SOUTH CAROLINA | --- | --- | --- | --- | 2274 | --- |
| SOUTH DAKOTA | --- | --- | --- | --- | --- | --- |
| TENNESSEE | 70280 | 0 | --- | 53153 | 0 | 123433 |
| TEXAS | 36941 | 0 | --- | 15098 | 0 | 52039 |
| UTAH | --- | --- | --- | --- | --- | --- |
| VERMONT | 10734 | 33209 | --- | 0 | 0 | 43943 |
| VIRGINIA | --- | --- | --- | 28469 | --- | --- |
| WASHINGTON | --- | --- | --- | --- | --- | --- |
| WEST VIRGINIA | --- | --- | --- | --- | --- | --- |
| WISCONSIN | 52695 | 64923 | --- | 0 | 117618 | --- |
| WYOMING | --- | --- | --- | --- | --- | --- |

1858-1859 HOUSE OF REPRESENTATIVES ELECTION

| STATE | DEMOCRAT | REPUBLICAN | AMERICAN | OPPOSITION | OTHER | TOTAL VOTES CAST |
|---|---|---|---|---|---|---|
| ALABAMA | 30217 | --- | --- | --- | --- | --- |
| ALASKA | --- | --- | --- | --- | --- | --- |
| ARIZONA | --- | --- | --- | --- | --- | --- |
| ARKANSAS | 35448 | 0 | 5970 | 0 | 3780 | 45198 |
| CALIFORNIA | 57665 | 41438 | 0 | 0 | 2969 | 102072 |
| COLORADO | --- | --- | --- | --- | --- | --- |
| CONNECTICUT | 38071 | 39731 | 0 | 0 | 499 | 78301 |
| DELAWARE | 7868 | 0 | 0 | 0 | 7452 | 15320 |
| DIST OF COLUMBIA | --- | --- | --- | --- | --- | --- |
| FLORIDA | 6465 | 0 | 0 | 0 | 4070 | 10535 |
| GEORGIA | 61140 | 0 | 0 | 36419 | 0 | 97559 |
| HAWAII | --- | --- | --- | --- | --- | --- |
| IDAHO | --- | --- | --- | --- | --- | --- |
| ILLINOIS | 122181 | 125668 | 0 | 0 | 4176 | 252025 |
| INDIANA | 103105 | 91909 | 0 | 0 | 19839 | 214853 |
| IOWA | 45693 | 49032 | 0 | 0 | 0 | 94725 |
| KANSAS | --- | --- | --- | --- | --- | --- |

TABLE 3.7 (CONTINUED)

## 1858-1859 HOUSE OF REPRESENTATIVES ELECTION

| | DEMOCRAT | REPUBLICAN | AMERICAN | OPPOSITION | OTHER | TOTAL VOTES CAST |
|---|---|---|---|---|---|---|
| KENTUCKY | 76542 | 0 | 15368 | 0 | 49302 | 141212 |
| LOUISIANA | 22815 | 0 | 0 | 10620 | 0 | 33435 |
| MAINE | 51896 | 60584 | 0 | --- | 233 | 112713 |
| MARYLAND | --- | --- | --- | --- | --- | --- |
| MASSACHUSETTS | 38511 | 70154 | 7769 | 0 | 585 | 117019 |
| MICHIGAN | 55819 | 65848 | 0 | 0 | 33 | 121700 |
| MINNESOTA | 17666 | 21360 | 0 | 0 | 0 | 39026 |
| MISSISSIPPI | 29647 | 0 | 0 | 288 | 2871 | 32806 |
| MISSOURI | --- | 6631 | 13610 | --- | 32584 | --- |
| MONTANA | --- | --- | --- | --- | --- | --- |
| NEBRASKA | --- | --- | --- | --- | --- | --- |
| NEVADA | --- | --- | --- | --- | --- | --- |
| NEW HAMPSHIRE | 32949 | 35844 | 0 | 0 | 0 | 68793 |
| NEW JERSEY | 41500 | 41218 | 3739 | 0 | 8837 | 95294 |
| NEW MEXICO | --- | --- | --- | --- | --- | --- |
| NEW YORK | 218409 | 173415 | 17290 | 0 | 127459 | 536573 |
| NORTH CAROLINA | 44453 | 0 | 0 | 0 | 37360 | 81813 |
| NORTH DAKOTA | --- | --- | --- | --- | --- | --- |
| OHIO | 159787 | 183962 | 0 | 0 | 851 | 344600 |
| OKLAHOMA | --- | --- | --- | --- | --- | --- |
| OREGON | 5646 | 5630 | 0 | 0 | 0 | 11276 |
| PENNSYLVANIA | 155291 | 0 | 0 | 0 | 214319 | 369915 |
| RHODE ISLAND | 3278 | 5523 | 305 | 0 | 3806 | 12607 |
| SOUTH CAROLINA | --- | --- | --- | --- | --- | --- |
| SOUTH DAKOTA | --- | --- | --- | --- | --- | --- |
| TENNESSEE | 67253 | 0 | 0 | 60921 | 6080 | 134254 |
| TEXAS | 36644 | 0 | 0 | 0 | 20062 | 56706 |
| UTAH | --- | --- | --- | --- | --- | --- |
| VERMONT | 11663 | 28609 | 0 | 0 | 0 | 40272 |
| VIRGINIA | --- | --- | --- | 18689 | 24926 | --- |
| WASHINGTON | --- | --- | --- | --- | --- | --- |
| WEST VIRGINIA | --- | --- | --- | --- | --- | --- |
| WISCONSIN | 55248 | 61356 | 0 | 0 | 0 | 116604 |
| WYOMING | --- | --- | --- | --- | --- | --- |

1860-1861 HOUSE OF REPRESENTATIVES ELECTION

| | DEMOCRAT | REPUBLICAN | SOUTHERN DEM. | OTHER | TOTAL VOTES CAST |
|---|---|---|---|---|---|
| ALABAMA | --- | --- | --- | 18194 | --- |
| ALASKA | --- | --- | --- | --- | --- |
| ARIZONA | | | | | |
| ARKANSAS | 33058 | 0 | 0 | 26268 | 59326 |
| CALIFORNIA | 35449 | 51651 | 31712 | 0 | 118812 |
| COLORADO | | | | | |
| CONNECTICUT | 41288 | 42466 | --- | 0 | 83754 |
| DELAWARE | 761 | 7732 | 7475 | 0 | 15968 |
| DIST OF COLUMBIA | | | | | |
| FLORIDA | 7722 | 0 | 0 | 5172 | 12894 |
| GEORGIA * | --- | --- | --- | --- | --- |
| HAWAII | | | | | |
| IDAHO | | | | | |
| ILLINOIS | 160832 | 173301 | 0 | 1385 | 335518 |
| INDIANA | 124252 | 137659 | 0 | 0 | 261911 |
| IOWA | 57446 | 70741 | 0 | 0 | 128187 |
| KANSAS | | | | | |
| KENTUCKY | 0 | 92365 | 0 | 37830 | 130195 |
| LOUISIANA * | --- | --- | --- | --- | --- |
| MAINE | 52958 | 69323 | 0 | 1267 | 123548 |
| MARYLAND | 0 | 103753 | 0 | 64052 | 167805 |
| MASSACHUSETTS | 66752 | 88450 | 0 | 406 | 155638 |
| MICHIGAN | 12168 | 22333 | 776 | 0 | 35277 |
| MINNESOTA | | | | | |
| MISSISSIPPI * | --- | --- | --- | --- | --- |
| MISSOURI | 83737 | 11453 | 0 | 58069 | 153259 |
| MONTANA | | | | | |
| NEBRASKA | | | | | |
| NEVADA | --- | --- | --- | --- | --- |
| NEW HAMPSHIRE | 31373 | 35596 | 0 | 0 | 66969 |
| NEW JERSEY | 61723 | 60376 | 0 | 0 | 122099 |
| NEW MEXICO | | | | | |
| NEW YORK | 253233 | 362391 | 38913 | 15594 | 670131 |
| NORTH CAROLINA * | --- | --- | --- | --- | --- |
| NORTH DAKOTA | | | | | |
| OHIO | 184931 | 218564 | 0 | 5872 | 409367 |

TABLE 3.7 (CONTINUED)

## 1860-1861 HOUSE OF REPRESENTATIVES ELECTION

| | DEMOCRAT | REPUBLICAN | SOUTHERN DEM. | OTHER | TOTAL VOTES CAST |
|---|---|---|---|---|---|
| OKLAHOMA | --- | --- | --- | --- | --- |
| OREGON | 6632 | 6529 | 0 | 1 | 13162 |
| PENNSYLVANIA | 211416 | 266467 | 0 | 470 | 478353 |
| RHODE ISLAND | 0 | 21921 | 0 | 24 | 21945 |
| SOUTH CAROLINA * | --- | --- | --- | --- | --- |
| SOUTH DAKOTA | --- | --- | --- | --- | --- |
| TENNESSEE | 0 | 0 | 0 | 39870 | 39870 |
| TEXAS * | --- | --- | --- | --- | --- |
| UTAH | --- | --- | --- | --- | --- |
| VERMONT | 9272 | 31149 | 0 | 0 | 40421 |
| VIRGINIA * | --- | --- | --- | --- | --- |
| WASHINGTON | --- | --- | --- | --- | --- |
| WEST VIRGINIA | --- | --- | --- | --- | --- |
| WISCONSIN | 65502 | 86422 | 0 | 0 | 151924 |
| WYOMING | --- | --- | --- | --- | --- |

* THESE SOUTHERN STATES HAD SECEDED FROM THE UNION AT THE BEGINNING OF THE AMERICAN CIVIL WAR AND DID NOT PARTICIPATE IN THIS ELECTION

## 1862-1863 HOUSE OF REPRESENTATIVES ELECTION

| | DEMOCRAT | REPUBLICAN | CONST. UNION | OTHER | TOTAL VOTES CAST |
|---|---|---|---|---|---|
| ALABAMA * | --- | --- | --- | --- | --- |
| ALASKA | --- | --- | --- | --- | --- |
| ARIZONA | --- | --- | --- | --- | --- |
| ARKANSAS | 0 | 0 | 0 | 607 | 607 |
| CALIFORNIA | 43567 | 64914 | 0 | 1 | 108482 |
| COLORADO | --- | --- | --- | --- | --- |
| CONNECTICUT | 38881 | 41039 | 0 | 0 | 79920 |
| DELAWARE | 8051 | 8014 | 0 | 0 | 16065 |
| DIST OF COLUMBIA | --- | --- | --- | --- | --- |
| FLORIDA * | --- | --- | --- | --- | --- |
| GEORGIA * | --- | --- | --- | --- | --- |

| | | | | | |
|---|---|---|---|---|---|
| HAWAII | --- | --- | --- | --- | --- |
| IDAHO | 136257 | 119819 | 0 | 55 | 256131 |
| ILLINOIS | 127371 | 117279 | 0 | 0 | 244650 |
| INDIANA | 49498 | 65842 | 0 | 23 | 115363 |
| IOWA | 930 | 14337 | 0 | 7 | 15274 |
| KANSAS | 15619 | 64837 | 0 | 221 | 80677 |
| KENTUCKY | 0 | 4911 | 0 | 436 | 5347 |
| LOUISIANA | 36238 | 47257 | 0 | 3605 | 87100 |
| MAINE | 10421 | 37492 | 2237 | 20 | 50170 |
| MARYLAND | 0 | 85053 | 0 | 48380 | 133433 |
| MASSACHUSETTS | 61137 | 68501 | 0 | 27 | 129665 |
| MICHIGAN | 11442 | 15754 | 0 | 0 | 27196 |
| MINNESOTA | --- | --- | --- | --- | --- |
| MISSISSIPPI * | --- | --- | --- | --- | --- |
| MISSOURI | 41866 | 40898 | 0 | 10454 | 93218 |
| MONTANA | --- | --- | --- | --- | --- |
| NEBRASKA | --- | --- | --- | --- | --- |
| NEVADA | --- | --- | --- | --- | --- |
| NEW HAMPSHIRE | 32629 | 33191 | 0 | 0 | 65820 |
| NEW JERSEY | 60421 | 47064 | 0 | 0 | 107485 |
| NEW MEXICO | --- | --- | --- | --- | --- |
| NEW YORK | 302142 | 296007 | 0 | 3572 | 601721 |
| NORTH CAROLINA * | --- | --- | --- | --- | --- |
| NORTH DAKOTA | --- | --- | --- | --- | --- |
| OHIO | 176693 | 174379 | 0 | 11036 | 362108 |
| OKLAHOMA | --- | --- | --- | --- | --- |
| OREGON | 3632 | 6809 | 0 | 0 | 10441 |
| PENNSYLVANIA | 217669 | 213900 | 0 | 639 | 432208 |
| RHODE ISLAND | 7737 | 10609 | 0 | 103 | 18449 |
| SOUTH CAROLINA * | --- | --- | --- | --- | --- |
| SOUTH DAKOTA | --- | --- | --- | --- | --- |
| TENNESSEE * | --- | --- | --- | --- | --- |
| TEXAS * | --- | --- | --- | --- | --- |
| UTAH | --- | --- | --- | --- | --- |
| VERMONT | 10944 | 27157 | 0 | 334 | 38435 |
| VIRGINIA * | --- | --- | --- | --- | --- |
| WASHINGTON | --- | --- | --- | --- | --- |
| WEST VIRGINIA | 0 | 14388 | 0 | 0 | 14388 |
| WISCONSIN | 64038 | 69019 | 0 | 73 | 133130 |
| WYOMING | --- | --- | --- | --- | --- |

* THESE SOUTHERN STATES HAD SECEDED FROM THE UNION AT THE BEGINNING OF THE AMERICAN CIVIL WAR AND DID NOT PARTICIPATE IN THIS ELECTION.

TABLE 3.7 (CONTINUED)

1864-1865 HOUSE OF REPRESENTATIVES ELECTION

| | DEMOCRAT | REPUBLICAN | OTHER | TOTAL VOTES CAST |
|---|---|---|---|---|
| ALABAMA * | 0 | 0 | 44574 | 44574 |
| ALASKA | --- | --- | --- | --- |
| ARIZONA | --- | --- | --- | --- |
| ARKANSAS * | --- | --- | --- | --- |
| CALIFORNIA | 43045 | 62039 | 0 | 105084 |
| COLORADO | --- | --- | --- | --- |
| CONNECTICUT | 31015 | 42168 | 314 | 73497 |
| DELAWARE | 8762 | 8253 | 0 | 17015 |
| DIST OF COLUMBIA | --- | --- | --- | --- |
| FLORIDA * | --- | --- | --- | --- |
| GEORGIA * | --- | --- | --- | --- |
| HAWAII | --- | --- | --- | --- |
| IDAHO | --- | --- | --- | --- |
| ILLINOIS | 158781 | 190216 | 0 | 348997 |
| INDIANA | 131904 | 149407 | 0 | 281311 |
| IOWA | 49363 | 88942 | 120 | 138425 |
| KANSAS | 0 | 10820 | 9712 | 20532 |
| KENTUCKY | 0 | 54008 | 57676 | 111684 |
| LOUISIANA * | --- | --- | --- | --- |
| MAINE | 46558 | 65721 | 0 | 112279 |
| MARYLAND | 40499 | 31913 | 0 | 72362 |
| MASSACHUSETTS | 48497 | 125923 | 48 | 174468 |
| MICHIGAN | 73257 | 91354 | 23 | 164634 |
| MINNESOTA | 17303 | 24839 | 0 | 42142 |
| MISSISSIPPI * | --- | --- | --- | --- |
| MISSOURI | 19129 | 0 | 73060 | 92189 |
| MONTANA | --- | --- | --- | --- |
| NEBRASKA | --- | --- | --- | --- |
| NEVADA | 6552 | 9776 | 0 | 16328 |
| NEW HAMPSHIRE | 28183 | 35577 | 0 | 63760 |
| NEW JERSEY | 67608 | 61745 | 0 | 129353 |
| NEW MEXICO | --- | --- | --- | --- |
| NEW YORK | 297120 | 365121 | 52288 | 714529 |
| NORTH CAROLINA * | 0 | 0 | 6963 | 6963 |
| NORTH DAKOTA | --- | --- | --- | --- |
| OHIO | 183524 | 235595 | 0 | 419119 |
| OKLAHOMA | --- | --- | --- | --- |
| OREGON | 5996 | 8759 | 0 | 14755 |
| PENNSYLVANIA | 243077 | 254761 | 0 | 497838 |
| RHODE ISLAND | 1286 | 8067 | 55 | 9408 |
| SOUTH CAROLINA * | --- | --- | --- | --- |
| SOUTH DAKOTA | --- | --- | --- | --- |
| TENNESSEE * | 0 | 25073 | 36650 | 61723 |
| TEXAS * | --- | --- | --- | --- |
| UTAH | --- | --- | --- | --- |
| VERMONT | 11700 | 30950 | 55 | 42705 |
| VIRGINIA * | 0 | 1583 | 41859 | 43442 |
| WASHINGTON | --- | --- | --- | --- |
| WEST VIRGINIA | 0 | 15307 | 6575 | 21882 |
| WISCONSIN | 63486 | 79579 | 0 | 143065 |
| WYOMING | --- | --- | --- | --- |

* THESE SOUTHERN STATES HAD SECEDED FROM THE UNION AT THE BEGINNING OF THE AMERICAN CIVIL WAR AND DID NOT PARTICIPATE IN ONE OR BOTH OF THESE ELECTIONS.

TABLE 3.7 (CONTINUED)

## 1866-1867 HOUSE OF REPRESENTATIVES ELECTION

| | DEMOCRAT | REPUBLICAN | OTHER | TOTAL VOTES CAST |
|---|---|---|---|---|
| ALABAMA * | --- | --- | --- | --- |
| ALASKA | --- | --- | --- | --- |
| ARIZONA | --- | --- | --- | --- |
| ARKANSAS * | --- | --- | --- | --- |
| CALIFORNIA | 48346 | 44436 | 0 | 92782 |
| COLORADO | --- | --- | --- | --- |
| CONNECTICUT | 47634 | 46240 | 23 | 93897 |
| DELAWARE | 9933 | 8553 | 0 | 18486 |
| DIST OF COLUMBIA | --- | --- | --- | --- |
| FLORIDA * | --- | --- | --- | --- |
| GEORGIA * | --- | --- | --- | --- |
| HAWAII | --- | --- | --- | --- |
| IDAHO | --- | --- | --- | --- |
| ILLINOIS | 147435 | 203045 | 2 | 350482 |
| INDIANA | 155757 | 168202 | 0 | 323959 |
| IOWA | 56435 | 90852 | 824 | 148111 |
| KANSAS | 0 | 19200 | 8211 | 27411 |
| KENTUCKY | 77621 | 28874 | 6366 | 112861 |
| LOUISIANA * | --- | --- | --- | --- |
| MAINE | 34429 | 68737 | 7701 | 110867 |
| MARYLAND | 43325 | 23396 | 26 | 66747 |
| MASSACHUSETTS | 26726 | 89752 | 720 | 117198 |
| MICHIGAN | 67347 | 97009 | 0 | 164356 |
| MINNESOTA | 15999 | 26832 | 0 | 42831 |
| MISSISSIPPI * | --- | --- | --- | --- |
| MISSOURI | --- | --- | --- | --- |
| MONTANA | --- | --- | --- | --- |
| NEBRASKA | --- | --- | --- | --- |
| NEVADA | 4196 | 5047 | 0 | 9243 |
| NEW HAMPSHIRE | 32798 | 35797 | 140 | 68735 |
| NEW JERSEY | 63947 | 65542 | 194 | 129683 |
| NEW MEXICO | --- | --- | --- | --- |
| NEW YORK | 325754 | 367555 | 19733 | 713042 |
| NORTH CAROLINA * | --- | --- | --- | --- |
| NORTH DAKOTA | --- | --- | --- | --- |
| OHIO | 214401 | 254043 | 0 | 468444 |
| OKLAHOMA | --- | --- | --- | --- |
| OREGON | 9808 | 10362 | 0 | 20170 |
| PENNSYLVANIA | 293124 | 303864 | 0 | 596988 |
| RHODE ISLAND | 1480 | 6980 | 112 | 8572 |
| SOUTH CAROLINA * | --- | --- | --- | --- |
| SOUTH DAKOTA | --- | --- | --- | --- |
| TENNESSEE * | --- | --- | --- | --- |
| TEXAS * | --- | --- | --- | --- |
| UTAH | --- | --- | --- | --- |
| VERMONT | 11482 | 28741 | 4087 | 44310 |
| VIRGINIA * | --- | --- | --- | --- |
| WASHINGTON | --- | --- | --- | --- |
| WEST VIRGINIA | 16885 | 23224 | 0 | 40109 |
| WISCONSIN | 55620 | 79170 | 0 | 134790 |
| WYOMING | --- | --- | --- | --- |

* THESE SOUTHERN STATES HAD SECEDED FROM THE UNION AT THE BEGINNING OF THE AMERICAN CIVIL WAR AND DID NOT PARTICIPATE IN ONE OR BOTH OF THESE ELECTIONS.

TABLE 3.7 (CONTINUED)

### 1868-1869 HOUSE OF REPRESENTATIVES ELECTION

| | DEMOCRAT | REPUBLICAN | OTHER | TOTAL VOTES CAST |
|---|---|---|---|---|
| ALABAMA | 0 | 57972 | 8372 | 66344 |
| ALASKA | --- | --- | --- | --- |
| ARIZONA | --- | --- | --- | --- |
| ARKANSAS | 19135 | 22030 | 0 | 41165 |
| CALIFORNIA | 54548 | 53872 | 2 | 108422 |
| COLORADO | --- | --- | --- | --- |
| CONNECTICUT | 43447 | 45846 | 0 | 89293 |
| DELAWARE | 10961 | 7636 | 0 | 18597 |
| DIST OF COLUMBIA | --- | --- | --- | --- |
| FLORIDA * | --- | --- | --- | --- |
| GEORGIA * | --- | --- | --- | --- |
| HAWAII | --- | --- | --- | --- |
| IDAHO | --- | --- | --- | --- |
| ILLINOIS | 199861 | 249422 | 0 | 449283 |
| INDIANA | 170880 | 170441 | 0 | 341321 |
| IOWA | 76242 | 117831 | 162 | 194235 |
| KANSAS | 13969 | 29324 | 1 | 43294 |
| KENTUCKY | 112066 | 35921 | 296 | 148283 |
| LOUISIANA | 71787 | 30201 | 0 | 101988 |
| MAINE | 56198 | 74921 | 191 | 131310 |
| MARYLAND | 60593 | 29898 | 0 | 90491 |
| MASSACHUSETTS | 54700 | 131693 | 5457 | 191850 |
| MICHIGAN | 99320 | 126178 | 0 | 225498 |
| MINNESOTA | 28152 | 32362 | 11265 | 71779 |
| MISSISSIPPI | 62410 | 54402 | 0 | 116812 |
| MISSOURI | 61874 | 80451 | 0 | 142325 |
| MONTANA | --- | --- | --- | --- |
| NEBRASKA | 6192 | 8715 | 0 | 14907 |
| NEVADA | 5349 | 6230 | 0 | 11579 |
| NEW HAMPSHIRE | 31933 | 35905 | 0 | 67838 |
| NEW JERSEY | 82917 | 79494 | 0 | 162411 |
| NEW MEXICO | --- | --- | --- | --- |
| NEW YORK | 423588 | 412175 | 4342 | 840105 |
| NORTH CAROLINA | 0 | 96436 | 84760 | 151196 |
| NORTH DAKOTA | --- | --- | --- | --- |
| OHIO | 251048 | 264032 | 0 | 515080 |
| OKLAHOMA | --- | --- | --- | --- |
| OREGON | 11754 | 10555 | 0 | 22309 |
| PENNSYLVANIA | 322281 | 329736 | 0 | 652017 |
| RHODE ISLAND | 6620 | 12128 | 87 | 18835 |
| SOUTH CAROLINA | 45185 | 61885 | 0 | 107070 |
| SOUTH DAKOTA | --- | --- | --- | --- |
| TENNESSEE | 14875 | 49550 | 8754 | 73179 |
| TEXAS | 31588 | 38705 | 0 | 70293 |
| UTAH | --- | --- | --- | --- |
| VERMONT | 13885 | 40511 | 0 | 54396 |
| VIRGINIA * | --- | --- | --- | --- |
| WASHINGTON | --- | --- | --- | --- |
| WEST VIRGINIA | 22052 | 26931 | 0 | 48983 |
| WISCONSIN | 85608 | 107812 | 0 | 193420 |
| WYOMING | --- | --- | --- | --- |

* THESE SOUTHERN STATES HAD SECEDED FROM THE UNION AT THE BEGINNING OF THE AMERICAN CIVIL WAR AND DID NOT PARTICIPATE IN ONE OR BOTH OF THESE ELECTIONS.

TABLE 3.7 (CONTINUED)

## 1870-1871 HOUSE OF REPRESENTATIVES ELECTION

|  | DEMOCRAT | REPUBLICAN | OTHER | TOTAL VOTES CAST |
|---|---|---|---|---|
| ALABAMA | 78457 | 74405 | 0 | 152862 |
| ALASKA | --- | --- | --- | --- |
| ARIZONA | --- | --- | --- | --- |
| ARKANSAS | 18479 | 18273 | 0 | 36752 |
| CALIFORNIA | 57065 | 62539 | 5 | 119609 |
| COLORADO | --- | --- | --- | --- |
| CONNECTICUT | 46622 | 47281 | 0 | 93903 |
| DELAWARE | 11446 | 9150 | 0 | 20596 |
| DIST OF COLUMBIA | --- | --- | --- | --- |
| FLORIDA | 11810 | 12439 | 0 | 24249 |
| GEORGIA | 94413 | 67643 | 2965 | 165021 |
| HAWAII | --- | --- | --- | --- |
| IDAHO | --- | --- | --- | --- |
| ILLINOIS | 145191 | 168801 | 3189 | 317181 |
| INDIANA | 148591 | 154580 | 9112 | 312283 |
| IOWA | 63636 | 98636 | 75 | 162347 |
| KANSAS | 20950 | 40368 | 0 | 61318 |
| KENTUCKY | 88945 | 57551 | 1432 | 147928 |
| LOUISIANA | 38586 | 65992 | 0 | 104578 |
| MAINE | 44476 | 54454 | 345 | 99275 |
| MARYLAND | 76608 | 57750 | 0 | 134358 |
| MASSACHUSETTS | 48487 | 87002 | 10924 | 146413 |
| MICHIGAN | 85733 | 96601 | 2403 | 184737 |
| MINNESOTA | 29395 | 36739 | 0 | 66134 |
| MISSISSIPPI | --- | --- | --- | --- |
| MISSOURI | 51890 | 0 | 112164 | 164054 |
| MONTANA | --- | --- | --- | --- |
| NEBRASKA | 7967 | 12375 | 0 | 20342 |
| NEVADA | 6821 | 6161 | 0 | 12982 |
| NEW HAMPSHIRE | 35098 | 33758 | 800 | 69656 |
| NEW JERSEY | 76373 | 80426 | 627 | 157426 |
| NEW MEXICO | --- | --- | --- | --- |
| NEW YORK | 375986 | 348068 | 31200 | 755254 |
| NORTH CAROLINA | 0 | 79830 | 82788 | 162618 |
| NORTH DAKOTA | --- | --- | --- | --- |
| OHIO | 205947 | 219341 | 1730 | 427018 |
| OKLAHOMA | --- | --- | --- | --- |
| OREGON | 11588 | 11245 | 0 | 22833 |
| PENNSYLVANIA | 267393 | 263549 | 1372 | 532314 |
| RHODE ISLAND | 2343 | 3434 | 451 | 6228 |
| SOUTH CAROLINA | 0 | 71742 | 0 | 71742 |
| SOUTH DAKOTA | --- | --- | --- | --- |
| TENNESSEE | 74492 | 36384 | 1432 | 112308 |
| TEXAS | 74841 | 50562 | 0 | 125403 |
| UTAH | --- | --- | --- | --- |
| VERMONT | 9928 | 30071 | 0 | 39999 |
| VIRGINIA | 0 | 0 | 78780 | 78780 |
| WASHINGTON | --- | --- | --- | --- |
| WEST VIRGINIA | 28460 | 26769 | 0 | 55229 |
| WISCONSIN | 70638 | 76576 | 0 | 147214 |
| WYOMING | --- | --- | --- | --- |

TABLE 3.7 (CONTINUED)

### 1872-1873 HOUSE OF REPRESENTATIVES ELECTION

|  | DEMOCRAT | REPUBLICAN | OTHER | TOTAL VOTES CAST |
|---|---|---|---|---|
| ALABAMA | 81311 | 89480 | 0 | 170791 |
| ALASKA | --- | --- | --- | --- |
| ARIZONA | --- | --- | --- | --- |
| ARKANSAS | 0 | 0 | 80114 | 80114 |
| CALIFORNIA | 46761 | 49247 | 406 | 96414 |
| COLORADO | --- | --- | --- | --- |
| CONNECTICUT | 41498 | 43352 | 0 | 84850 |
| DELAWARE | 11015 | 11377 | 0 | 22392 |
| DIST OF COLUMBIA | --- | --- | --- | --- |
| FLORIDA | 15811 | 17537 | 0 | 33348 |
| GEORGIA | 80140 | 61655 | 1293 | 143088 |
| HAWAII | --- | --- | --- | --- |
| IDAHO | --- | --- | --- | --- |
| ILLINOIS | 194217 | 240374 | 637 | 435228 |
| INDIANA | 188502 | 188664 | 0 | 377166 |
| IOWA | 79645 | 127094 | 216 | 206955 |
| KANSAS | 34450 | 67400 | 17 | 101867 |
| KENTUCKY | 104246 | 27147 | 29783 | 161176 |
| LOUISIANA | 59130 | 68947 | 0 | 128077 |
| MAINE | 54150 | 72094 | 151 | 126395 |
| MARYLAND | 67718 | 67024 | 0 | 134742 |
| MASSACHUSETTS | 61221 | 131745 | 669 | 193635 |
| MICHIGAN | 86160 | 135829 | 1048 | 223037 |
| MINNESOTA | 35281 | 56181 | 5 | 91467 |
| MISSISSIPPI | 40917 | 80545 | 6879 | 128341 |
| MISSOURI | 155029 | 117345 | 0 | 272374 |
| MONTANA | --- | --- | --- | --- |
| NEBRASKA | 10412 | 17124 | 0 | 27536 |
| NEVADA | 7847 | 0 | 7146 | 14993 |
| NEW HAMPSHIRE | 33131 | 33178 | 1204 | 67513 |
| NEW JERSEY | 76308 | 94431 | 0 | 170739 |
| NEW MEXICO | --- | --- | --- | --- |
| NEW YORK | 400797 | 438396 | 0 | 839193 |
| NORTH CAROLINA | 95726 | 98691 | 1 | 194418 |
| NORTH DAKOTA | --- | --- | --- | --- |
| OHIO | 251155 | 265512 | 1362 | 518029 |
| OKLAHOMA | --- | --- | --- | --- |
| OREGON | 12317 | 13168 | 0 | 25485 |
| PENNSYLVANIA | 322191 | 351949 | 0 | 674140 |
| RHODE ISLAND | 5643 | 13287 | 14 | 18944 |
| SOUTH CAROLINA | 0 | 68825 | 27798 | 96623 |
| SOUTH DAKOTA | --- | --- | --- | --- |
| TENNESSEE | 65188 | 80825 | 37900 | 183913 |
| TEXAS | 69085 | 47096 | 46252 | 116181 |
| UTAH | --- | --- | --- | --- |
| VERMONT | 9729 | 36604 | 2943 | 49276 |
| VIRGINIA | 0 | 78371 | 112281 | 190652 |
| WASHINGTON | --- | --- | --- | --- |
| WEST VIRGINIA | 18735 | 6210 | 276 | 25221 |
| WISCONSIN | 88055 | 105143 | 0 | 193198 |
| WYOMING | --- | --- | --- | --- |

TABLE 3.7 (CONTINUED)

### 1874-1875 HOUSE OF REPRESENTATIVES ELECTION

| | DEMOCRAT | REPUBLICAN | OTHER | TOTAL VOTES CAST |
|---|---|---|---|---|
| ALABAMA | 102994 | 94786 | 0 | 197780 |
| ALASKA | --- | --- | --- | --- |
| ARIZONA | --- | --- | --- | --- |
| ARKANSAS | 0 | 22787 | 40938 | 63725 |
| CALIFORNIA | 58863 | 39789 | 23716 | 122368 |
| COLORADO | --- | --- | --- | --- |
| CONNECTICUT | 51201 | 47425 | 2021 | 100647 |
| DELAWARE | 12602 | 11024 | 0 | 23626 |
| DIST OF COLUMBIA | --- | --- | --- | --- |
| FLORIDA | 17555 | 18609 | 0 | 36164 |
| GEORGIA | 85926 | 32258 | 8561 | 126745 |
| HAWAII | --- | --- | --- | --- |
| IDAHO | --- | --- | --- | --- |
| ILLINOIS | 182080 | 169874 | 15926 | 367880 |
| INDIANA | 183135 | 168670 | 9614 | 361419 |
| IOWA | 0 | 104815 | 79959 | 184774 |
| KANSAS | 11223 | 48908 | 27077 | 87208 |
| KENTUCKY | 76850 | 20420 | 28199 | 125469 |
| LOUISIANA | --- | --- | --- | --- |
| MAINE | 40992 | 53200 | 256 | 94448 |
| MARYLAND | 67458 | 53377 | 0 | 120835 |
| MASSACHUSETTS | 0 | 87599 | 94771 | 182370 |
| MICHIGAN | 87709 | 111965 | 16199 | 215873 |
| MINNESOTA | 43094 | 48637 | 0 | 91731 |
| MISSISSIPPI | 83966 | 54845 | 19250 | 158061 |
| MISSOURI | 165150 | 53137 | 25803 | 244090 |
| MONTANA | --- | --- | --- | --- |
| NEBRASKA | 8360 | 22532 | 5048 | 35940 |
| NEVADA | 8567 | 9317 | 0 | 17884 |
| NEW HAMPSHIRE | 39231 | 38950 | 713 | 78894 |
| NEW JERSEY | 95039 | 85456 | 0 | 180495 |
| NEW MEXICO | --- | --- | --- | --- |
| NEW YORK | 399287 | 335046 | 37930 | 772263 |
| NORTH CAROLINA | 102317 | 74271 | 14356 | 190944 |
| NORTH DAKOTA | --- | --- | --- | --- |
| OHIO | 238899 | 215123 | 9973 | 463995 |
| OKLAHOMA | --- | --- | --- | --- |
| OREGON | 9642 | 9340 | 6350 | 25332 |
| PENNSYLVANIA | 277251 | 239794 | 31503 | 548548 |
| RHODE ISLAND | 2059 | 4654 | 46 | 6759 |
| SOUTH CAROLINA | 27328 | 79199 | 34927 | 141454 |
| SOUTH DAKOTA | --- | --- | --- | --- |
| TENNESSEE | 102397 | 50787 | 1320 | 154504 |
| TEXAS | 31992 | 3615 | 4570 | 40177 |
| UTAH | --- | --- | --- | --- |
| VERMONT | 13281 | 24437 | 2614 | 40332 |
| VIRGINIA | 93956 | 76927 | 7427 | 178310 |
| WASHINGTON | --- | --- | --- | --- |
| WEST VIRGINIA | 37819 | 28440 | 466 | 66725 |
| WISCONSIN | 0 | 93127 | 93604 | 186731 |
| WYOMING | --- | --- | --- | --- |

TABLE 3.7 (CONTINUED)

### 1876—1877 HOUSE OF REPRESENTATIVES ELECTION

| | DEMOCRAT | REPUBLICAN | GREENBACK | OTHER | TOTAL VOTES CAST |
|---|---|---|---|---|---|
| ALABAMA | 95363 | 37198 | 0 | 24917 | 157478 |
| ALASKA | --- | --- | --- | --- | --- |
| ARIZONA | | | | | |
| ARKANSAS | 49688 | 26351 | 681 | 8872 | 85592 |
| CALIFORNIA | 74208 | 81043 | 0 | 55 | 155306 |
| COLORADO | 12541 | 13532 | 0 | 1 | 26074 |
| CONNECTICUT | 61797 | 58951 | 98 | 563 | 121409 |
| DELAWARE | 13169 | 10592 | 0 | 0 | 23761 |
| DIST OF COLUMBIA | | | | | |
| FLORIDA | 23239 | 23645 | 0 | 0 | 48854 |
| GEORGIA | 109913 | 49378 | 0 | 13269 | 172560 |
| HAWAII | | | | | |
| IDAHO | --- | --- | --- | --- | --- |
| ILLINOIS | 266341 | 267827 | 9175 | 6139 | 549482 |
| INDIANA | 209872 | 204593 | 15050 | 0 | 429515 |
| IOWA | 118356 | 168279 | 4351 | 1433 | 292419 |
| KANSAS | 15649 | 76611 | 85 | 29479 | 121824 |
| KENTUCKY | 150901 | 93754 | 0 | 8415 | 253070 |
| LOUISIANA | 84385 | 76385 | 0 | 0 | 160773 |
| MAINE | 60614 | 73625 | 550 | 74 | 134863 |
| MARYLAND | 89993 | 72627 | 0 | 0 | 162620 |
| MASSACHUSETTS | 109800 | 141821 | 0 | 2518 | 254139 |
| MICHIGAN | 99270 | 165626 | 3160 | 48432 | 316488 |
| MINNESOTA | 51771 | 68563 | 2879 | 0 | 123213 |
| MISSISSIPPI | 113684 | 51908 | 0 | 397 | 165989 |
| MISSOURI | 200853 | 129943 | 2246 | 6071 | 339113 |
| MONTANA | --- | --- | --- | --- | --- |
| NEBRASKA | 17206 | 30900 | 3589 | 87 | 51782 |
| NEVADA | 9330 | 10241 | 0 | 0 | 19571 |
| NEW HAMPSHIRE | 37868 | 39776 | 0 | 282 | 77926 |
| NEW JERSEY | 115168 | 90574 | 520 | 11900 | 218162 |
| NEW MEXICO | --- | --- | --- | --- | --- |
| NEW YORK | 495920 | 471350 | 0 | 26663 | 993933 |

| | DEMOCRAT | REPUBLICAN | GREENBACK | NATIONAL | OTHER | TOTAL VOTES CAST |
|---|---|---|---|---|---|---|
| NORTH CAROLINA | 121484 | 104513 | 0 | 0 | 0 | 225997 |
| NORTH DAKOTA | --- | --- | --- | --- | --- | --- |
| OHIO | 308437 | 314519 | 2446 | 4084 | 0 | 629486 |
| OKLAHOMA | --- | --- | --- | --- | --- | --- |
| OREGON | 14239 | 15347 | 0 | 8 | 0 | 29594 |
| PENNSYLVANIA | 369226 | 379475 | 2315 | 2038 | 0 | 753054 |
| RHODE ISLAND | 10358 | 15695 | 87 | 0 | 0 | 26140 |
| SOUTH CAROLINA | 91559 | 91143 | 0 | 5 | 0 | 182707 |
| SOUTH DAKOTA | --- | --- | --- | --- | --- | --- |
| TENNESSEE | 130202 | 83432 | 0 | 1841 | 0 | 215475 |
| TEXAS | 103664 | 41451 | 0 | 335 | 0 | 145450 |
| UTAH | --- | --- | --- | --- | --- | --- |
| VERMONT | 18163 | 40100 | 0 | 256 | 0 | 58519 |
| VIRGINIA | 139642 | 95440 | 0 | 502 | 0 | 235584 |
| WASHINGTON | --- | --- | --- | --- | --- | --- |
| WEST VIRGINIA | 56350 | 43069 | 0 | 10 | 0 | 99429 |
| WISCONSIN | 125157 | 128231 | 1429 | 199 | 0 | 255016 |
| WYOMING | --- | --- | --- | --- | --- | --- |

## 1878-1879 HOUSE OF REPRESENTATIVES ELECTION

| | DEMOCRAT | REPUBLICAN | GREENBACK | NATIONAL | OTHER | TOTAL VOTES CAST |
|---|---|---|---|---|---|---|
| ALABAMA | 54775 | 6545 | 12180 | 0 | 14793 | 88293 |
| ALASKA | --- | --- | --- | --- | --- | --- |
| ARIZONA | --- | --- | --- | --- | --- | --- |
| ARKANSAS | 32652 | 0 | 16227 | 0 | 2639 | 51518 |
| CALIFORNIA | 27896 | 74651 | 0 | 0 | 54267 | 156814 |
| COLORADO | 12003 | 14294 | 2329 | 0 | 0 | 28626 |
| CONNECTICUT | 48905 | 51763 | 0 | 2845 | 868 | 104381 |
| DELAWARE | 10576 | 0 | 2966 | 0 | 0 | 13542 |
| DIST OF COLUMBIA | --- | --- | --- | --- | --- | --- |
| FLORIDA | 21175 | 17928 | 0 | 0 | 0 | 39103 |
| GEORGIA | 70112 | 3643 | 13227 | 0 | 38725 | 125707 |
| HAWAII | --- | --- | --- | --- | --- | --- |
| IDAHO | --- | --- | --- | --- | --- | --- |
| ILLINOIS | 169737 | 211989 | 57687 | 0 | 10662 | 450075 |
| INDIANA | 175513 | 171017 | 32415 | 0 | 28432 | 407377 |
| IOWA | 42985 | 131790 | 40384 | 0 | 45317 | 260476 |

TABLE 3.7 (CONTINUED)

## 1878-1879 HOUSE OF REPRESENTATIVES ELECTION

| | DEMOCRAT | REPUBLICAN | GREENBACK | NATIONAL | OTHER | TOTAL VOTES CAST |
|---|---|---|---|---|---|---|
| KANSAS | 36355 | 74714 | 26733 | 0 | 21 | 137823 |
| KENTUCKY | 86525 | 38780 | 10022 | 0 | 17569 | 152896 |
| LOUISIANA | 78661 | 21997 | 0 | 6076 | 10821 | 117555 |
| MAINE | 20889 | 56644 | 47445 | 0 | 228 | 125206 |
| MARYLAND | 67980 | 40836 | 1268 | 627 | 8904 | 119615 |
| MASSACHUSETTS | 81289 | 136116 | 0 | 25150 | 10618 | 253173 |
| MICHIGAN | 77642 | 126461 | 74014 | 0 | 3070 | 281187 |
| MINNESOTA | 45250 | 53310 | 0 | 0 | 0 | 98560 |
| MISSISSIPPI | 37128 | 2056 | 6939 | 5969 | 121 | 52213 |
| MISSOURI | 167846 | 64962 | 76686 | 0 | 3590 | 313084 |
| MONTANA | 0 | --- | --- | --- | --- | --- |
| NEBRASKA | 9047 | 28347 | 0 | 0 | 21876 | 50223 |
| NEVADA | 9047 | 9727 | 0 | 0 | 0 | 18774 |
| NEW HAMPSHIRE | 31549 | 38199 | 5857 | 0 | 170 | 75775 |
| NEW JERSEY | 65328 | 90514 | 24631 | 0 | 15364 | 195837 |
| NEW MEXICO | --- | --- | --- | --- | --- | --- |
| NEW YORK | 220839 | 370296 | 80561 | 0 | 157851 | 829547 |
| NORTH CAROLINA | 68263 | 41935 | 584 | 0 | 19284 | 130066 |
| NORTH DAKOTA | --- | --- | --- | --- | --- | --- |
| OHIO | 252302 | 277875 | 33308 | 0 | 22897 | 586382 |
| OKLAHOMA | --- | --- | --- | --- | --- | --- |
| OREGON | 16744 | 15593 | 1184 | 0 | 4 | 33525 |
| PENNSYLVANIA | 264766 | 287509 | 99816 | 25756 | 14273 | 692120 |
| RHODE ISLAND | 5770 | 11400 | 934 | 0 | 97 | 18201 |
| SOUTH CAROLINA | 116919 | 45031 | 0 | 0 | 152 | 162102 |
| SOUTH DAKOTA | --- | --- | --- | --- | --- | --- |
| TENNESSEE | 75524 | 34413 | 16720 | 0 | 11588 | 138245 |
| TEXAS | 148559 | 18956 | 9617 | 0 | 39123 | 216255 |
| UTAH | --- | --- | --- | --- | --- | --- |
| VERMONT | 11879 | 29210 | 0 | 8367 | 117 | 49573 |
| VIRGINIA | 67141 | 27217 | 4172 | 0 | 22276 | 120806 |
| WASHINGTON | --- | --- | --- | --- | --- | --- |
| WEST VIRGINIA | 50318 | 36248 | 0 | 8317 | 23 | 94906 |
| WISCONSIN | 93253 | 100037 | 13028 | 0 | 0 | 206318 |
| WYOMING | --- | --- | --- | --- | --- | --- |

1880 HOUSE OF REPRESENTATIVES ELECTION

| | DEMOCRAT | REPUBLICAN | GREENBACK | OTHER | TOTAL VOTES CAST |
|---|---|---|---|---|---|
| ALABAMA | 80876 | 32433 | 0 | 23649 | 136958 |
| ALASKA | --- | --- | --- | --- | --- |
| ARIZONA | --- | --- | --- | --- | --- |
| ARKANSAS | 55438 | 40597 | 3920 | 5731 | 105686 |
| CALIFORNIA | 39320 | 79796 | 688 | 43895 | 163699 |
| COLORADO | 24476 | 27069 | 1692 | 6 | 53243 |
| CONNECTICUT | 63505 | 67383 | 954 | 0 | 131842 |
| DELAWARE | 14966 | 14336 | 0 | 0 | 29302 |
| DIST OF COLUMBIA | | | | | |
| FLORIDA | 28076 | 23035 | 0 | 0 | 51111 |
| GEORGIA | 92151 | 25060 | 0 | 30620 | 147831 |
| HAWAII | --- | --- | --- | --- | --- |
| IDAHO | --- | --- | --- | --- | --- |
| ILLINOIS | 279242 | 317962 | 21746 | 1479 | 620429 |
| INDIANA | 224680 | 229630 | 15170 | 0 | 469480 |
| IOWA | 83914 | 181737 | 18503 | 36435 | 320589 |
| KANSAS | 39703 | 120451 | 40451 | 41 | 200646 |
| KENTUCKY | 140552 | 96537 | 10857 | 194 | 248140 |
| LOUISIANA | 66044 | 35691 | 0 | 0 | 101735 |
| MAINE | 0 | 73639 | 364 | 73069 | 147072 |
| MARYLAND | 91131 | 80313 | 451 | 0 | 171895 |
| MASSACHUSETTS | 111833 | 164280 | 0 | 4867 | 280980 |
| MICHIGAN | 131122 | 183796 | 37196 | 196 | 352310 |
| MINNESOTA | 56279 | 83328 | 0 | 7656 | 147263 |
| MISSISSIPPI | 76125 | 24319 | 7433 | 5878 | 113755 |
| MISSOURI | 205676 | 38254 | 1133 | 123289 | 368352 |
| MONTANA | --- | --- | --- | --- | --- |
| NEBRASKA | 23634 | 52648 | 4067 | 3917 | 84266 |
| NEVADA | 9815 | 8578 | 0 | 0 | 18393 |
| NEW HAMPSHIRE | 40943 | 44651 | 0 | 739 | 86333 |
| NEW JERSEY | 122169 | 120114 | 3017 | 0 | 245300 |
| NEW MEXICO | --- | --- | --- | --- | --- |
| NEW YORK | 459514 | 548535 | 6585 | 68077 | 1082711 |
| NORTH CAROLINA | 120479 | 100179 | 1207 | 7684 | 229549 |
| NORTH DAKOTA | --- | --- | --- | --- | --- |
| OHIO | 340562 | 362040 | 8628 | 84 | 711314 |

TABLE 3.7 (CONTINUED)

## 1880 HOUSE OF REPRESENTATIVES ELECTION

| | DEMOCRAT | REPUBLICAN | GREENBACK | OTHER | TOTAL VOTES CAST |
|---|---|---|---|---|---|
| OKLAHOMA | --- | --- | --- | --- | --- |
| OREGON | 18181 | 19578 | 300 | 11 | 38070 |
| PENNSYLVANIA | 358116 | 428710 | 20133 | 59825 | 866784 |
| RHODE ISLAND | 10477 | 18156 | 0 | 322 | 28955 |
| SOUTH CAROLINA | 116884 | 60796 | 414 | 2 | 178096 |
| SOUTH DAKOTA | --- | --- | --- | --- | --- |
| TENNESSEE | 115487 | 104315 | 4230 | 8308 | 232340 |
| TEXAS | 176172 | 0 | 72874 | 144 | 249190 |
| UTAH | --- | --- | --- | --- | --- |
| VERMONT | 19660 | 43858 | 2025 | 172 | 65715 |
| VIRGINIA | 96532 | 52709 | 0 | 56797 | 206038 |
| WASHINGTON | --- | --- | --- | --- | --- |
| WEST VIRGINIA | 57144 | 49012 | 4871 | 396 | 111423 |
| WISCONSIN | 116062 | 143665 | 5277 | 111 | 265115 |
| WYOMING | --- | --- | --- | --- | --- |

## 1882 HOUSE OF REPRESENTATIVES ELECTION

| | DEMOCRAT | REPUBLICAN | GREENBACK | OTHER | TOTAL VOTES CAST |
|---|---|---|---|---|---|
| ALABAMA | 76725 | 24094 | 2406 | 17470 | 120695 |
| ALASKA | --- | --- | --- | --- | --- |
| ARIZONA | --- | --- | --- | --- | --- |
| ARKANSAS | 43619 | 0 | 21422 | 466 | 65507 |
| CALIFORNIA | 87233 | 73647 | 3915 | 17 | 164812 |
| COLORADO | 29380 | 30847 | 1195 | 49 | 61471 |
| CONNECTICUT | 57995 | 55722 | 955 | 635 | 115307 |
| DELAWARE | 16563 | 14640 | 0 | 41 | 31244 |
| DIST OF COLUMBIA | --- | --- | --- | --- | --- |

| | | | | | |
|---|---|---|---|---|---|
| FLORIDA | 24067 | 20139 | 0 | 3553 | 47759 |
| GEORGIA | 79540 | 24645 | 0 | 0 | 104185 |
| HAWAII | --- | --- | --- | --- | --- |
| IDAHO | | | | | |
| ILLINOIS | 235153 | 233799 | 23023 | 34269 | 526244 |
| INDIANA | 220929 | 207173 | 11186 | 22 | 439310 |
| IOWA | 115463 | 141795 | 31921 | 199 | 289378 |
| KANSAS | 58079 | 99866 | 22243 | 354 | 180542 |
| KENTUCKY | 102096 | 77555 | 335 | 10755 | 190741 |
| LOUISIANA | 48827 | 22922 | 0 | 6146 | 77895 |
| MAINE | 63304 | 72811 | 1614 | 1084 | 138813 |
| MARYLAND | 80723 | 74521 | 257 | 1576 | 157077 |
| MASSACHUSETTS | 94858 | 130308 | 4833 | 26721 | 256720 |
| MICHIGAN | 148242 | 157519 | 343 | 6427 | 312531 |
| MINNESOTA | 46654 | 75846 | 6470 | 16956 | 145926 |
| MISSISSIPPI | 47977 | 20498 | 0 | 10793 | 79268 |
| MISSOURI | 193872 | 97297 | 13779 | 47569 | 352517 |
| MONTANA | --- | --- | --- | --- | --- |
| NEBRASKA | 25692 | 41277 | 0 | 21061 | 88030 |
| NEVADA | 7720 | 6462 | 0 | 0 | 14182 |
| NEW HAMPSHIRE | 35059 | 40672 | 0 | 673 | 76404 |
| NEW JERSEY | 99962 | 97869 | 7814 | 368 | 206013 |
| NEW MEXICO | --- | --- | --- | --- | --- |
| NEW YORK | 453275 | 371809 | 14719 | 29725 | 869528 |
| NORTH CAROLINA | 111763 | 0 | 0 | 111320 | 223083 |
| NORTH DAKOTA | --- | --- | --- | --- | --- |
| OHIO | 316975 | 296514 | 13974 | 1943 | 629406 |
| OKLAHOMA | --- | --- | --- | --- | --- |
| OREGON | 19152 | 22517 | 0 | 2 | 41671 |
| PENNSYLVANIA | 352855 | 323255 | 24962 | 41585 | 742657 |
| RHODE ISLAND | 3322 | 6864 | 0 | 21 | 10207 |
| SOUTH CAROLINA | 61301 | 27458 | 6851 | 25789 | 121399 |
| SOUTH DAKOTA | --- | --- | --- | --- | --- |
| TENNESSEE | 112426 | 79041 | 1479 | 26547 | 219493 |
| TEXAS | 151591 | 28125 | 40615 | 23188 | 243519 |
| UTAH | --- | --- | --- | --- | --- |
| VERMONT | 12372 | 28433 | 1255 | 277 | 42337 |
| VIRGINIA | 94184 | 4342 | 0 | 100021 | 198547 |
| WASHINGTON | --- | --- | --- | --- | --- |
| WEST VIRGINIA | 45171 | 41227 | 5023 | 114 | 91535 |
| WISCONSIN | 103640 | 90815 | 16710 | 5769 | 216934 |
| WYOMING | --- | --- | --- | --- | --- |

TABLE 3.7 (CONTINUED)

## 1884 HOUSE OF REPRESENTATIVES ELECTION

| | DEMOCRAT | REPUBLICAN | PROHIBITION | GREENBACK | OTHER | TOTAL VOTES CAST |
|---|---|---|---|---|---|---|
| ALABAMA | 93398 | 34709 | 0 | 0 | 13209 | 141316 |
| ALASKA | --- | --- | --- | --- | --- | --- |
| ARIZONA | --- | --- | --- | --- | --- | --- |
| ARKANSAS | 71703 | 51738 | 0 | 0 | 0 | 123441 |
| CALIFORNIA | 90952 | 101572 | 2315 | 571 | 117 | 195527 |
| COLORADO | 28720 | 35446 | 0 | 2485 | 18 | 66669 |
| CONNECTICUT | 66658 | 67235 | 1978 | 1263 | 0 | 137134 |
| DELAWARE | 17054 | 12978 | 0 | 0 | 33 | 30065 |
| DIST OF COLUMBIA | --- | --- | --- | --- | --- | --- |
| FLORIDA | 31867 | 27750 | 0 | 0 | 219 | 59836 |
| GEORGIA | 76069 | 43260 | 0 | 0 | 6644 | 125973 |
| HAWAII | --- | --- | --- | --- | --- | --- |
| IDAHO | --- | --- | --- | --- | --- | --- |
| ILLINOIS | 300109 | 296746 | 6515 | 2322 | 64238 | 669930 |
| INDIANA | 248521 | 238233 | 285 | 3541 | 1568 | 492148 |
| IOWA | 147199 | 196980 | 0 | 0 | 31720 | 375899 |
| KANSAS | 96624 | 155148 | 0 | 7766 | 127 | 259665 |
| KENTUCKY | 147635 | 97104 | 0 | 0 | 8113 | 252852 |
| LOUISIANA | 60978 | 35509 | 0 | 0 | 9971 | 106458 |
| MAINE | 59706 | 78115 | 0 | 1407 | 2685 | 141913 |
| MARYLAND | 96749 | 86360 | 1184 | 0 | 37 | 184330 |
| MASSACHUSETTS | 109110 | 164220 | 5902 | 18730 | 4489 | 302451 |
| MICHIGAN | 191614 | 189282 | 16208 | 2298 | 4 | 399406 |
| MINNESOTA | 77310 | 108412 | 3219 | 0 | 0 | 188941 |
| MISSISSIPPI | 81878 | 38405 | 0 | 0 | 322 | 120605 |
| MISSOURI | 234673 | 15854 | 0 | 3635 | 182673 | 436835 |
| MONTANA | --- | --- | --- | --- | --- | --- |
| NEBRASKA | 59990 | 69511 | 2772 | 0 | 0 | 132273 |
| NEVADA | 6002 | 6797 | 0 | 0 | 0 | 12799 |
| NEW HAMPSHIRE | 38809 | 43424 | 0 | 0 | 1893 | 84126 |
| NEW JERSEY | 127614 | 124800 | 5692 | 2028 | 0 | 260134 |
| NEW MEXICO | --- | --- | --- | --- | --- | --- |
| NEW YORK | 494981 | 520619 | 20712 | 4904 | 92396 | 1133612 |
| NORTH CAROLINA | 140894 | 118890 | 0 | 0 | 97 | 259881 |

| | DEMOCRAT | REPUBLICAN | PROHIBITION | GREENBACK | OTHER | TOTAL VOTES CAST |
|---|---|---|---|---|---|---|
| NORTH DAKOTA | --- | --- | --- | --- | --- | --- |
| OHIO | 374934 | 394578 | 6867 | 4332 | 225 | 780936 |
| OKLAHOMA | --- | --- | --- | --- | --- | --- |
| OREGON | 23652 | 25699 | 0 | 0 | 0 | 49351 |
| PENNSYLVANIA | 401042 | 478240 | 10473 | 9674 | 0 | 899429 |
| RHODE ISLAND | 11971 | 17892 | 2040 | 274 | 94 | 32271 |
| SOUTH CAROLINA | 68804 | 20369 | 0 | 0 | 0 | 89173 |
| SOUTH DAKOTA | --- | --- | --- | --- | --- | --- |
| TENNESSEE | 131458 | 115999 | 0 | 0 | 2304 | 249761 |
| TEXAS | 251133 | 40292 | 0 | 0 | 14346 | 305771 |
| UTAH | --- | --- | --- | --- | --- | --- |
| VERMONT | 15070 | 38925 | 0 | 0 | 478 | 54473 |
| VIRGINIA | 145106 | 134344 | 0 | 0 | 6502 | 285952 |
| WASHINGTON | --- | --- | --- | --- | --- | --- |
| WEST VIRGINIA | 67481 | 63884 | 0 | 0 | 20 | 131385 |
| WISCONSIN | 148866 | 136029 | 8180 | 271 | 25342 | 318688 |
| WYOMING | --- | --- | --- | --- | --- | --- |

## 1886 HOUSE OF REPRESENTATIVES ELECTION

| | DEMOCRAT | REPUBLICAN | PROHIBITION | GREENBACK | OTHER | TOTAL VOTES CAST |
|---|---|---|---|---|---|---|
| ALABAMA | 62211 | 21917 | 0 | 0 | 2563 | 86691 |
| ALASKA | --- | --- | --- | --- | --- | --- |
| ARIZONA | --- | --- | --- | --- | --- | --- |
| ARKANSAS | 36673 | 8549 | 0 | 7420 | 2846 | 55488 |
| CALIFORNIA | 91710 | 93921 | 5261 | 2184 | 1091 | 194167 |
| COLORADO | 26929 | 27732 | 3597 | 0 | 34 | 58292 |
| CONNECTICUT | 58581 | 57234 | 4472 | 2718 | 59 | 123064 |
| DELAWARE | 13837 | 0 | 0 | 0 | 8393 | 22230 |
| DIST OF COLUMBIA | --- | --- | --- | --- | --- | --- |
| FLORIDA | 33383 | 23153 | 0 | 0 | 243 | 56779 |
| GEORGIA | 25470 | 33 | 0 | 0 | 2050 | 27553 |
| HAWAII | --- | --- | --- | --- | --- | --- |
| IDAHO | --- | --- | --- | --- | --- | --- |
| ILLINOIS | 207078 | 276581 | 19797 | 25605 | 35435 | 564496 |
| INDIANA | 221680 | 222890 | 7760 | 2725 | 14199 | 469194 |
| IOWA | 0 | 172023 | 0 | 8946 | 164340 | 345309 |
| KANSAS | 110009 | 150338 | 6382 | 0 | 6455 | 273184 |

TABLE 3.7 (CONTINUED)

## 1886 HOUSE OF REPRESENTATIVES ELECTION

| | DEMOCRAT | REPUBLICAN | PROHIBITION | GREENBACK | OTHER | TOTAL VOTES CAST |
|---|---|---|---|---|---|---|
| KENTUCKY | 111203 | 83258 | 0 | 5651 | 8653 | 208765 |
| LOUISIANA | 63103 | 20793 | 0 | 0 | 799 | 84695 |
| MAINE | 52654 | 68987 | 2202 | 328 | 4559 | 128730 |
| MARYLAND | 83208 | 49272 | 5546 | 0 | 10747 | 148773 |
| MASSACHUSETTS | 114155 | 119100 | 7204 | 0 | 3045 | 243504 |
| MICHIGAN | 173376 | 183134 | 21921 | 0 | 0 | 378431 |
| MINNESOTA | 68313 | 126000 | 7789 | 0 | 13260 | 215362 |
| MISSISSIPPI | 35559 | 10998 | 0 | 0 | 176 | 46733 |
| MISSOURI | 217973 | 162095 | 243 | 8814 | 29528 | 418653 |
| MONTANA | --- | --- | --- | --- | --- | --- |
| NEBRASKA | 60644 | 66427 | 9040 | 0 | 0 | 136111 |
| NEVADA | 5670 | 6700 | 0 | 0 | 0 | 12370 |
| NEW HAMPSHIRE | 36919 | 37880 | 0 | 2071 | 123 | 76993 |
| NEW JERSEY | 98562 | 105468 | 17340 | 6331 | 3668 | 231369 |
| NEW MEXICO | --- | --- | --- | --- | --- | --- |
| NEW YORK | 431332 | 440918 | 40782 | 0 | 19758 | 932790 |
| NORTH CAROLINA | 115788 | 42765 | 1959 | 0 | 52057 | 212569 |
| NORTH DAKOTA | --- | --- | --- | --- | --- | --- |
| OHIO | 325639 | 336063 | 26655 | 3900 | 779 | 693036 |
| OKLAHOMA | --- | --- | --- | --- | --- | --- |
| OREGON | 25221 | 26918 | 2753 | 0 | 0 | 54892 |
| PENNSYLVANIA | 367551 | 415166 | 30475 | 4473 | 0 | 817665 |
| RHODE ISLAND | 7763 | 8306 | 1598 | 0 | 9 | 17676 |
| SOUTH CAROLINA | 32969 | 5961 | 0 | 0 | 94 | 39024 |
| SOUTH DAKOTA | --- | --- | --- | --- | --- | --- |
| TENNESSEE | 125357 | 106956 | 0 | 0 | 25 | 232338 |
| TEXAS | 183541 | 22110 | 0 | 0 | 53410 | 259061 |
| UTAH | --- | --- | --- | --- | --- | --- |
| VERMONT | 13831 | 34317 | 0 | 56 | 269 | 48473 |
| VIRGINIA | 102490 | 102145 | 0 | 9470 | 10993 | 225098 |
| WASHINGTON | --- | --- | --- | --- | --- | --- |
| WEST VIRGINIA | 65184 | 64279 | 1492 | 0 | 55 | 131010 |
| WISCONSIN | 114510 | 144707 | 10672 | 13355 | 407 | 283651 |
| WYOMING | --- | --- | --- | --- | --- | --- |

## 1888-1889 HOUSE OF REPRESENTATIVES ELECTION

| | DEMOCRAT | REPUBLICAN | PROHIBITION | LABOR | OTHER | TOTAL VOTES CAST |
|---|---|---|---|---|---|---|
| ALABAMA | 118585 | 54547 | 0 | 0 | 997 | 174129 |
| ALASKA | --- | --- | --- | --- | --- | --- |
| ARIZONA | --- | --- | --- | --- | --- | --- |
| ARKANSAS | 89576 | 19086 | 0 | 0 | 47957 | 156619 |
| CALIFORNIA | 116069 | 126646 | 3032 | 0 | 3405 | 249152 |
| COLORADO | 37725 | 50620 | 2355 | 1309 | 6 | 92015 |
| CONNECTICUT | 74340 | 75129 | 4073 | 81 | 7 | 153630 |
| DELAWARE | 16396 | 12935 | 387 | 0 | 2 | 29720 |
| DIST OF COLUMBIA | --- | --- | --- | --- | --- | --- |
| FLORIDA | 39334 | 27144 | 0 | 0 | 0 | 66478 |
| GEORGIA | 95823 | 23478 | 0 | 0 | 10324 | 129625 |
| HAWAII | --- | --- | --- | --- | --- | --- |
| IDAHO | --- | --- | --- | --- | --- | --- |
| ILLINOIS | 347562 | 372138 | 21618 | 4340 | 84 | 745742 |
| INDIANA | 238422 | 264365 | 9252 | 1994 | 21565 | 535598 |
| IOWA | 148991 | 196248 | 2819 | 1943 | 52941 | 402942 |
| KANSAS | 103629 | 182375 | 3476 | 37240 | 22 | 326742 |
| KENTUCKY | 182037 | 152710 | 3635 | 193 | 335 | 338910 |
| LOUISIANA | 86435 | 26817 | 0 | 0 | 262 | 113514 |
| MAINE | 60970 | 79744 | 3070 | 1134 | 34 | 144952 |
| MARYLAND | 106095 | 99975 | 4214 | 0 | 0 | 210284 |
| MASSACHUSETTS | 150917 | 179841 | 7807 | 0 | 193 | 338758 |
| MICHIGAN | 196994 | 236898 | 18603 | 3255 | 18096 | 473846 |
| MINNESOTA | 108012 | 139466 | 14310 | 0 | 0 | 261788 |
| MISSISSIPPI | 88614 | 26603 | 0 | 0 | 0 | 115217 |
| MISSOURI | 261196 | 235668 | 987 | 16390 | 2606 | 516847 |
| MONTANA | 18435 | 19915 | 0 | 0 | 0 | 38350 |
| NEBRASKA | 81838 | 106073 | 10071 | 3852 | 0 | 201834 |
| NEVADA | 5682 | 6921 | 0 | 0 | 0 | 12603 |
| NEW HAMPSHIRE | 43935 | 45271 | 1417 | 0 | 90 | 90713 |
| NEW JERSEY | 144160 | 146035 | 8076 | 0 | 5079 | 303350 |
| NEW MEXICO | --- | --- | --- | --- | --- | --- |
| NEW YORK | 424377 | 605855 | 36212 | 0 | 205911 | 1272355 |
| NORTH CAROLINA | 148344 | 130680 | 1303 | 0 | 41 | 280368 |
| NORTH DAKOTA | 12006 | 26077 | 0 | 0 | 0 | 38083 |
| OHIO | 395654 | 416520 | 22880 | 2377 | 531 | 837962 |

TABLE 3.7 (CONTINUED)

288

## 1888-1889 HOUSE OF REPRESENTATIVES ELECTION

| | DEMOCRAT | REPUBLICAN | PROHIBITION | LABOR | OTHER | TOTAL VOTES CAST |
|---|---|---|---|---|---|---|
| OKLAHOMA | --- | --- | --- | --- | --- | --- |
| OREGON | 25413 | 32820 | 1974 | 0 | 2 | 60209 |
| PENNSYLVANIA | 430764 | 503221 | 17191 | 2438 | 28794 | 982408 |
| RHODE ISLAND | 17051 | 22032 | 1286 | 0 | 0 | 40369 |
| SOUTH CAROLINA | 65915 | 10031 | 0 | 0 | 431 | 76377 |
| SOUTH DAKOTA | 23229 | 54983 | 0 | 0 | 60 | 78272 |
| TENNESSEE | 159506 | 136914 | 3240 | 0 | 0 | 299660 |
| TEXAS | 242814 | 52655 | 0 | 19631 | 30993 | 346093 |
| UTAH | --- | --- | --- | --- | --- | --- |
| VERMONT | 19351 | 48111 | 782 | 0 | 7 | 68251 |
| VIRGINIA | 151889 | 147372 | 0 | 0 | 3926 | 303187 |
| WASHINGTON | 24492 | 34039 | 0 | 0 | 12 | 58543 |
| WEST VIRGINIA | 75043 | 73848 | 727 | 96 | 417 | 150131 |
| WISCONSIN | 119405 | 179601 | 14032 | 2649 | 38015 | 353702 |
| WYOMING | --- | --- | --- | --- | --- | --- |

## 1890 HOUSE OF REPRESENTATIVES ELECTION

| | DEMOCRAT | REPUBLICAN | PROHIBITION | LABOR | OTHER | TOTAL VOTES CAST |
|---|---|---|---|---|---|---|
| ALABAMA | 82150 | 7379 | 0 | 0 | 28903 | 118432 |
| ALASKA | --- | --- | --- | --- | --- | --- |
| ARIZONA | --- | --- | --- | --- | --- | --- |
| ARKANSAS | 69768 | 7488 | 0 | 34775 | 675 | 112706 |
| CALIFORNIA | 114869 | 128025 | 6199 | 0 | 2833 | 251926 |
| COLORADO | 34736 | 43118 | 1054 | 0 | 5221 | 84129 |
| CONNECTICUT | 67888 | 63701 | 3250 | 3 | 30 | 134872 |
| DELAWARE | 17848 | 17150 | 257 | 0 | 0 | 35255 |
| DIST OF COLUMBIA | --- | --- | --- | --- | --- | --- |

| | | | | | |
|---|---|---|---|---|---|
| FLORIDA | 28466 | 15148 | 0 | 0 | 0 | 43614 |
| GEORGIA | 77668 | 16737 | 0 | 0 | 4087 | 98492 |
| HAWAII | --- | --- | --- | --- | --- | --- |
| IDAHO | 7985 | 10171 | 0 | 0 | 0 | 18156 |
| ILLINOIS | 342042 | 311320 | 15458 | 0 | 6968 | 675788 |
| INDIANA | 238911 | 216114 | 10711 | 6991 | 0 | 472727 |
| IOWA | 194912 | 185785 | 1427 | 7011 | 96 | 389231 |
| KANSAS | 27010 | 122672 | 245 | 0 | 140802 | 290729 |
| KENTUCKY | 116684 | 63528 | 2037 | 0 | 10719 | 194968 |
| LOUISIANA | 59801 | 12873 | 0 | 277 | 1304 | 74255 |
| MAINE | 45313 | 63486 | 3259 | 51 | 218 | 112327 |
| MARYLAND | 99848 | 77200 | 3925 | 0 | 55 | 181028 |
| MASSACHUSETTS | 137083 | 129650 | 9764 | 0 | 3570 | 280067 |
| MICHIGAN | 186649 | 177021 | 24102 | 0 | 7129 | 394901 |
| MINNESOTA | 86943 | 98317 | 5500 | 0 | 44874 | 235634 |
| MISSISSIPPI | 49154 | 13553 | 0 | 0 | 0 | 62707 |
| MISSOURI | 253736 | 184337 | 561 | 23143 | 1345 | 463122 |
| MONTANA | 15411 | 15128 | 389 | 162 | 2 | 31092 |
| NEBRASKA | 54729 | 72879 | 3851 | 0 | 80901 | 212360 |
| NEVADA | 5736 | 6610 | 0 | 0 | 34 | 12380 |
| NEW HAMPSHIRE | 42870 | 41375 | 1235 | 0 | 0 | 85480 |
| NEW JERSEY | 128417 | 114808 | 8425 | 0 | 0 | 251650 |
| NEW MEXICO | --- | --- | --- | --- | --- | --- |
| NEW YORK | 494880 | 423663 | 33399 | 0 | 13542 | 965484 |
| NORTH CAROLINA | 139266 | 92181 | 197 | 0 | 13894 | 245538 |
| NORTH DAKOTA | 14830 | 21365 | 0 | 0 | 0 | 36195 |
| OHIO | 351528 | 362624 | 21891 | 2068 | 1427 | 739538 |
| OKLAHOMA | --- | --- | --- | --- | --- | --- |
| OREGON | 30263 | 40176 | 0 | 0 | 2883 | 73322 |
| PENNSYLVANIA | 431082 | 457988 | 13611 | 0 | 11282 | 913963 |
| RHODE ISLAND | 18723 | 16941 | 1537 | 0 | 0 | 37201 |
| SOUTH CAROLINA | 58805 | 13069 | 0 | 0 | 1688 | 73562 |
| SOUTH DAKOTA | 17527 | 34553 | 0 | 0 | 49715 | 101795 |
| TENNESSEE | 104316 | 68913 | 8570 | 0 | 12507 | 194306 |
| TEXAS | 257393 | 59026 | 0 | 0 | 3408 | 319827 |
| UTAH | --- | --- | --- | --- | --- | --- |
| VERMONT | 17565 | 35228 | 0 | 0 | 44 | 52837 |
| VIRGINIA | 126254 | 46435 | 2126 | 0 | 14097 | 188912 |
| WASHINGTON | 22861 | 29133 | 0 | 0 | 0 | 51994 |
| WEST VIRGINIA | 78918 | 69631 | 964 | 0 | 103 | 149616 |
| WISCONSIN | 161901 | 128179 | 10301 | 1605 | 196 | 302182 |
| WYOMING | 6520 | 9087 | 0 | 0 | 0 | 15607 |

TABLE 3.7 (CONTINUED)

## 1892 HOUSE OF REPRESENTATIVES ELECTION

| | DEMOCRAT | REPUBLICAN | PROHIBITION | INDEPENDENT | OTHER | TOTAL VOTES CAST |
|---|---|---|---|---|---|---|
| ALABAMA | 136503 | 11818 | 0 | 20925 | 63025 | 232271 |
| ALASKA | --- | --- | --- | --- | --- | --- |
| ARIZONA | --- | --- | --- | --- | --- | --- |
| ARKANSAS | 94603 | 9541 | 0 | 33108 | 437 | 137689 |
| CALIFORNIA | 107608 | 101080 | 7009 | 23768 | 979 | 240444 |
| COLORADO | 2240 | 37181 | 1521 | 51591 | 0 | 92533 |
| CONNECTICUT | 82004 | 77031 | 3946 | 640 | 497 | 164418 |
| DELAWARE | 18554 | 18080 | 548 | 0 | 13 | 37195 |
| DIST OF COLUMBIA | --- | --- | --- | --- | --- | --- |
| FLORIDA | 14668 | 0 | 0 | 20750 | 172 | 35590 |
| GEORGIA | 137087 | 5386 | 0 | 74245 | 0 | 216718 |
| HAWAII | --- | --- | --- | --- | --- | --- |
| IDAHO | 6029 | 8549 | 222 | 4567 | 0 | 19367 |
| ILLINOIS | 425336 | 399096 | 2596 | 21707 | 0 | 871735 |
| INDIANA | 259190 | 253588 | 12530 | 24308 | 0 | 549616 |
| IOWA | 181218 | 219214 | 4974 | 36029 | 30 | 441465 |
| KANSAS | 0 | 155791 | 4055 | 164624 | 107 | 324577 |
| KENTUCKY | 174359 | 121960 | 1559 | 23635 | 8 | 321521 |
| LOUISIANA | 85060 | 0 | 0 | 0 | 28714 | 113774 |
| MAINE | 54142 | 65637 | 3561 | 2626 | 1776 | 127742 |
| MARYLAND | 113931 | 91762 | 5480 | 569 | 0 | 211742 |
| MASSACHUSETTS | 164782 | 187046 | 7713 | 3201 | 9558 | 372300 |
| MICHIGAN | 121753 | 222837 | 19590 | 101674 | 59 | 465913 |
| MINNESOTA | 96421 | 115637 | 13646 | 34025 | 0 | 259729 |
| MISSISSIPPI | 38200 | 547 | 0 | 12694 | 0 | 51441 |
| MISSOURI | 266865 | 227652 | 1557 | 36312 | 383 | 532769 |
| MONTANA | 17762 | 17934 | 601 | 7027 | 0 | 43324 |
| NEBRASKA | 47992 | 82842 | 4928 | 60501 | 0 | 196263 |
| NEVADA | 345 | 2295 | 77 | 0 | 7171 | 9888 |
| NEW HAMPSHIRE | 41408 | 42456 | 1394 | 295 | 86 | 85639 |
| NEW JERSEY | 164428 | 158191 | 8136 | 940 | 889 | 332584 |
| NEW MEXICO | --- | --- | --- | --- | --- | --- |
| NEW YORK | 633638 | 605007 | 37750 | 14041 | 8081 | 1298517 |

| | | | | | |
|---|---|---|---|---|---|
| NORTH CAROLINA | 132844 | 70177 | 0 | 66141 | 1773 | 270935 |
| NORTH DAKOTA | 11021 | 17715 | 0 | 7439 | 0 | 36175 |
| OHIO | 407156 | 397200 | 24373 | 12480 | 85 | 841294 |
| OKLAHOMA | --- | --- | | --- | --- | --- |
| OREGON | 25139 | 34586 | 2463 | 13458 | 0 | 75646 |
| PENNSYLVANIA | 448714 | 512557 | 23677 | 7466 | 1299 | 993713 |
| RHODE ISLAND | 23642 | 25168 | 906 | 1233 | 0 | 50949 |
| SOUTH CAROLINA | 56140 | 12377 | 0 | 171 | 113 | 68801 |
| SOUTH DAKOTA | 736 | 33769 | 0 | 24539 | 0 | 59044 |
| TENNESSEE | 132019 | 86646 | 3289 | 12092 | 22139 | 256185 |
| TEXAS | 238958 | 71620 | 0 | 93894 | 9936 | 414408 |
| UTAH | --- | --- | --- | --- | --- | --- |
| VERMONT | 18045 | 37995 | 1281 | 0 | 7 | 57328 |
| VIRGINIA | 165628 | 38600 | 0 | 61242 | 18891 | 284361 |
| WASHINGTON | 30659 | 35434 | 2412 | 20083 | 0 | 86588 |
| WEST VIRGINIA | 85823 | 80484 | 1331 | 2705 | 1 | 170344 |
| WISCONSIN | 175841 | 171542 | 10356 | 9557 | 40 | 367336 |
| WYOMING | 8855 | 8394 | 0 | 0 | 12 | 17261 |

1894 HOUSE OF REPRESENTATIVES ELECTION

| | DEMOCRAT | REPUBLICAN | PROHIBITION | INDEPENDENT | OTHER | TOTAL VOTES CAST |
|---|---|---|---|---|---|---|
| ALABAMA | 73299 | 15473 | 0 | 38772 | 2 | 127546 |
| ALASKA | --- | --- | --- | --- | --- | --- |
| ARIZONA | --- | --- | --- | --- | --- | --- |
| ARKANSAS | 37584 | 10389 | 0 | 3703 | 756 | 52432 |
| CALIFORNIA | 89341 | 110542 | 7336 | 55289 | 6817 | 269325 |
| COLORADO | 1849 | 90079 | 4506 | 34223 | 47860 | 178517 |
| CONNECTICUT | 64542 | 85178 | 2149 | 1586 | 895 | 154350 |
| DELAWARE | 18492 | 19699 | 587 | 0 | 67 | 38845 |
| DIST OF COLUMBIA | --- | --- | --- | --- | --- | --- |
| FLORIDA | 21626 | 0 | 0 | 4469 | 68 | 26163 |
| GEORGIA | 128531 | 0 | 0 | 80514 | 0 | 209045 |
| HAWAII | --- | --- | --- | --- | --- | --- |
| IDAHO | 5834 | 10383 | 173 | 7547 | 0 | 23937 |
| ILLINOIS | 312840 | 448075 | 16057 | 73780 | 645 | 851397 |
| INDIANA | 238874 | 284447 | 9469 | 26257 | 0 | 559047 |

TABLE 3.7 (CONTINUED)

## 1894 HOUSE OF REPRESENTATIVES ELECTION

| | DEMOCRAT | REPUBLICAN | PROHIBITION | INDEPENDENT | OTHER | TOTAL VOTES CAST |
|---|---|---|---|---|---|---|
| IOWA | 84787 | 230702 | 3599 | 100442 | 6 | 419536 |
| KANSAS | 26093 | 147858 | 4898 | 114429 | 3 | 293281 |
| KENTUCKY | 160407 | 153022 | 2822 | 18287 | 5217 | 339755 |
| LOUISIANA | 77650 | 22507 | 0 | 13352 | 559 | 114068 |
| MAINE | 30502 | 69457 | 2643 | 5316 | 27 | 107945 |
| MARYLAND | 96628 | 99244 | 7465 | 3390 | 0 | 206727 |
| MASSACHUSETTS | 113939 | 188142 | 3280 | 10583 | 11357 | 327301 |
| MICHIGAN | 112076 | 234329 | 15537 | 42380 | 4276 | 408598 |
| MINNESOTA | 73590 | 149973 | 8036 | 56006 | 0 | 287605 |
| MISSISSIPPI | 26736 | 165 | 422 | 11713 | 0 | 39036 |
| MISSOURI | 220227 | 231693 | 1733 | 43742 | 1345 | 498740 |
| MONTANA | 10369 | 23140 | 519 | 15240 | 0 | 49268 |
| NEBRASKA | 18946 | 98101 | 4769 | 0 | 76829 | 198645 |
| NEVADA | 217 | 2774 | 0 | 2751 | 4581 | 10323 |
| NEW HAMPSHIRE | 33629 | 46146 | 1500 | 673 | 22 | 81970 |
| NEW JERSEY | 115345 | 163823 | 7246 | 4155 | 5647 | 296216 |
| NEW MEXICO | --- | --- | --- | --- | --- | --- |
| NEW YORK | 482736 | 664024 | 18960 | 10660 | 42505 | 1218885 |
| NORTH CAROLINA | 126692 | 50182 | | 55103 | 45309 | 277286 |
| NORTH DAKOTA | 0 | 21615 | 439 | 15660 | 0 | 37714 |
| OHIO | 274628 | 409245 | 19564 | 51474 | 415 | 755326 |
| OKLAHOMA | --- | --- | --- | --- | --- | --- |
| OREGON | 19803 | 41139 | 1855 | 23369 | 0 | 86166 |
| PENNSYLVANIA | 328677 | 571085 | 23481 | 17820 | 3083 | 944146 |
| RHODE ISLAND | 13866 | 22681 | 1159 | 267 | 813 | 38786 |
| SOUTH CAROLINA | 47465 | 14322 | 0 | 361 | 1517 | 63665 |
| SOUTH DAKOTA | 8102 | 40683 | 872 | 27379 | 0 | 77036 |
| TENNESSEE | 95750 | 87549 | 3076 | 27914 | 13528 | 227817 |
| TEXAS | 217880 | 30775 | 0 | 177107 | 6490 | 432252 |
| UTAH | --- | --- | --- | --- | --- | --- |
| VERMONT | 13645 | 41883 | 0 | 0 | 71 | 55599 |
| VIRGINIA | 113439 | 88846 | 1049 | 10711 | 709 | 214754 |
| WASHINGTON | 14602 | 35981 | 210 | 26238 | 405 | 77436 |
| WEST VIRGINIA | 76077 | 89517 | 0 | 3190 | 135 | 168919 |
| WISCONSIN | 119938 | 200517 | 8936 | 39094 | 144 | 368629 |
| WYOMING | 6152 | 10068 | 0 | 2906 | 0 | 19126 |

## 1896 HOUSE OF REPRESENTATIVES ELECTION

| | DEMOCRAT | REPUBLICAN | PROHIBITION | INDEPENDENT | OTHER | TOTAL VOTES CAST |
|---|---|---|---|---|---|---|
| ALABAMA | 128422 | 20893 | 0 | 0 | 36008 | 185323 |
| ALASKA | --- | --- | --- | --- | --- | --- |
| ARIZONA | --- | --- | --- | --- | --- | --- |
| ARKANSAS | 109644 | 41745 | 0 | 0 | 0 | 151389 |
| CALIFORNIA | 37144 | 128941 | 4251 | 80672 | 27099 | 278107 |
| COLORADO | 151839 | 24010 | 2095 | 181 | 1261 | 179386 |
| CONNECTICUT | 56564 | 109494 | 1821 | 0 | 6483 | 174362 |
| DELAWARE | 15407 | 0 | 462 | 0 | 19176 | 35045 |
| DIST OF COLUMBIA | --- | --- | --- | --- | --- | --- |
| FLORIDA | 31360 | 9372 | 396 | 0 | 1214 | 42342 |
| GEORGIA | 99816 | 32812 | 0 | 38019 | 0 | 170647 |
| HAWAII | --- | --- | --- | --- | --- | --- |
| IDAHO | 0 | 6054 | 0 | 0 | 22221 | 28275 |
| ILLINOIS | 422295 | 600667 | 9530 | 0 | 47715 | 1080657 |
| INDIANA | 307706 | 321250 | 868 | 450 | 828 | 630652 |
| IOWA | 39752 | 287951 | 2071 | 187132 | 236 | 517142 |
| KANSAS | 168420 | 158147 | 1497 | 0 | 4 | 328068 |
| KENTUCKY | 213833 | 187793 | 317 | 4547 | 19822 | 426312 |
| LOUISIANA | 75338 | 2547 | 0 | 0 | 19452 | 97337 |
| MAINE | 37731 | 83947 | 2543 | 0 | 23 | 124244 |
| MARYLAND | 107232 | 135423 | 5710 | 0 | 526 | 248891 |
| MASSACHUSETTS | 117202 | 246269 | 993 | 0 | 9595 | 374059 |
| MICHIGAN | 241322 | 291697 | 1695 | 0 | 334 | 535048 |
| MINNESOTA | 146584 | 187566 | 4306 | 0 | 0 | 338456 |
| MISSISSIPPI | 61232 | 3112 | 964 | 0 | 1395 | 65739 |
| MISSOURI | 334430 | 304101 | 0 | 24676 | 543 | 664774 |
| MONTANA | 0 | 9492 | 0 | 0 | 33932 | 43424 |
| NEBRASKA | 0 | 100076 | 2279 | 917 | 113265 | 216537 |
| NEVADA | 8377 | 1319 | 0 | 0 | 0 | 9696 |
| NEW HAMPSHIRE | 28425 | 52350 | 1158 | 0 | 324 | 82257 |
| NEW JERSEY | 133318 | 199977 | 0 | 5433 | 30342 | 369070 |
| NEW MEXICO | --- | --- | --- | --- | --- | --- |
| NEW YORK | 496761 | 731201 | 12185 | 200 | 101233 | 1341580 |
| NORTH CAROLINA | 171193 | 37971 | 0 | 0 | 118755 | 327919 |
| NORTH DAKOTA | 21172 | 25233 | 349 | 0 | 0 | 46754 |
| OHIO | 475692 | 523772 | 2585 | 0 | 1720 | 1003769 |

TABLE 3.7 (CONTINUED)

## 1896 HOUSE OF REPRESENTATIVES ELECTION

| | DEMOCRAT | REPUBLICAN | PROHIBITION | INDEPENDENT | OTHER | TOTAL VOTES CAST |
|---|---|---|---|---|---|---|
| OKLAHOMA | --- | --- | --- | --- | --- | --- |
| OREGON | 46544 | 31972 | 2131 | 0 | 8807 | 89454 |
| PENNSYLVANIA | 416408 | 711346 | 18336 | 7482 | 9442 | 1163014 |
| RHODE ISLAND | 16630 | 33990 | 1891 | 0 | 918 | 53429 |
| SOUTH CAROLINA | 59930 | 8435 | 0 | 22 | 213 | 68600 |
| SOUTH DAKOTA | 41122 | 40943 | 683 | 0 | 0 | 82748 |
| TENNESSEE | 174675 | 116135 | 694 | 0 | 23758 | 315357 |
| TEXAS | 288036 | 111133 | 0 | 95 | 745 | 535167 |
| UTAH | 49735 | 0 | 0 | 135253 | 27813 | 77548 |
| VERMONT | 14467 | 52464 | 0 | 0 | 24 | 66955 |
| VIRGINIA | 157532 | 123061 | 969 | 0 | 20150 | 301712 |
| WASHINGTON | 51544 | 38196 | 1011 | 0 | 154 | 90905 |
| WEST VIRGINIA | 94739 | 104951 | 0 | 0 | 287 | 199977 |
| WISCONSIN | 165327 | 267226 | 4539 | 0 | 589 | 437681 |
| WYOMING | 10938 | 10044 | 0 | 0 | 0 | 20982 |

## 1898 HOUSE OF REPRESENTATIVES ELECTION

| | DEMOCRAT | REPUBLICAN | PROHIBITION | INDEPENDENT | OTHER | TOTAL VOTES CAST |
|---|---|---|---|---|---|---|
| ALABAMA | 66556 | 17656 | 209 | 0 | 1707 | 86128 |
| ALASKA | --- | --- | --- | --- | --- | --- |
| ARIZONA | --- | --- | --- | --- | --- | --- |
| ARKANSAS | 24814 | 2706 | 0 | 0 | 81 | 27601 |
| CALIFORNIA | 128106 | 139382 | 0 | 0 | 5653 | 273141 |
| COLORADO | 95483 | 46163 | 1410 | 0 | 1429 | 144485 |
| CONNECTICUT | 63337 | 81747 | 1409 | 0 | 2755 | 149248 |
| DELAWARE | 15053 | 17566 | 454 | 0 | 0 | 33073 |
| DIST OF COLUMBIA | --- | --- | --- | --- | --- | --- |
| FLORIDA | 25656 | 7316 | 0 | 0 | 3 | 32975 |

| State | | | | | | |
|---|---|---|---|---|---|---|
| GEORGIA | 62636 | 7280 | 0 | 0 | 70 | 69986 |
| HAWAII | --- | --- | --- | --- | --- | --- |
| IDAHO | 7428 | 13056 | 914 | 0 | 17694 | 39092 |
| ILLINOIS | 399505 | 463298 | 7976 | 0 | 2968 | 873747 |
| INDIANA | 275054 | 283306 | 7445 | 82 | 237 | 566042 |
| IOWA | 180226 | 233456 | 5838 | 1652 | 396 | 419998 |
| KANSAS | 0 | 147691 | 2021 | 0 | 131432 | 281144 |
| KENTUCKY | 138434 | 130785 | 0 | 0 | 3029 | 273900 |
| LOUISIANA | 29355 | 3920 | 2021 | 0 | 20 | 33295 |
| MAINE | 29664 | 54981 | 7527 | 0 | 130 | 86796 |
| MARYLAND | 100874 | 106927 | 0 | 0 | 1185 | 216513 |
| MASSACHUSETTS | 123640 | 176262 | 3423 | 0 | 12665 | 312567 |
| MICHIGAN | 612 | 232525 | 5392 | 399 | 179299 | 415859 |
| MINNESOTA | 104288 | 136797 | 0 | 0 | 2797 | 249673 |
| MISSISSIPPI | 24778 | 782 | 434 | 0 | 1759 | 27319 |
| MISSOURI | 292556 | 255796 | 0 | 0 | 2489 | 551275 |
| MONTANA | 23351 | 14829 | 0 | 0 | 11607 | 49787 |
| NEBRASKA | 94884 | 93509 | 0 | 0 | 50 | 18443 |
| NEVADA | 8877 | 0 | 1130 | 0 | 0 | 8877 |
| NEW HAMPSHIRE | 35840 | 43768 | 6962 | 0 | 611 | 81349 |
| NEW JERSEY | 154658 | 165120 | | 0 | 5338 | 332078 |
| NEW MEXICO | --- | --- | --- | --- | --- | --- |
| NEW YORK | 622322 | 658934 | 17169 | 70 | 25542 | 1324037 |
| NORTH CAROLINA | 187711 | 17560 | 70 | 0 | 126228 | 331569 |
| NORTH DAKOTA | 17844 | 27776 | 950 | 0 | 0 | 45620 |
| OHIO | 356169 | 404659 | | 0 | 8824 | 770602 |
| OKLAHOMA | --- | --- | --- | --- | --- | --- |
| OREGON | 38027 | 42615 | 2233 | 0 | 0 | 82875 |
| PENNSYLVANIA | 354208 | 532898 | 48600 | 0 | 10506 | 946212 |
| RHODE ISLAND | 12827 | 21176 | 951 | 0 | 2554 | 37508 |
| SOUTH CAROLINA | 28967 | 2804 | 882 | 0 | 20 | 31791 |
| SOUTH DAKOTA | 32240 | 38780 | 1382 | 0 | 0 | 71902 |
| TENNESSEE | 106884 | 67888 | 0 | 0 | 656 | 176810 |
| TEXAS | 344724 | 59513 | 0 | 0 | 2767 | 407004 |
| UTAH | 35646 | 29603 | 559 | 0 | 0 | 65249 |
| VERMONT | 13993 | 38078 | 1169 | 678 | 65 | 52136 |
| VIRGINIA | 107879 | 52593 | 330 | 0 | 8276 | 169985 |
| WASHINGTON | 36385 | 39809 | 6792 | 0 | 897 | 78260 |
| WEST VIRGINIA | 85809 | 88019 | | 0 | 326 | 174484 |
| WISCONSIN | 131879 | 180512 | | 0 | 2948 | 322131 |
| WYOMING | 8909 | 10762 | 0 | 0 | 0 | 19671 |

TABLE 3.7 (CONTINUED)

## 1900 HOUSE OF REPRESENTATIVES ELECTION

| | DEMOCRAT | REPUBLICAN | PROHIBITION | INDEPENDENT | OTHER | TOTAL VOTES CAST |
|---|---|---|---|---|---|---|
| ALABAMA | 104626 | 33031 | 0 | 0 | 3576 | 141233 |
| ALASKA | --- | --- | --- | --- | --- | --- |
| ARIZONA | --- | --- | --- | --- | --- | --- |
| ARKANSAS | 84319 | 42650 | 0 | 0 | 0 | 126969 |
| CALIFORNIA | 120420 | 157441 | 4130 | 1116 | 8971 | 292078 |
| COLORADO | 121272 | 92805 | 1924 | 0 | 1219 | 217220 |
| CONNECTICUT | 74989 | 102559 | 1554 | 0 | 1938 | 181040 |
| DELAWARE | 19157 | 22353 | 548 | 0 | 54 | 42112 |
| DIST OF COLUMBIA | --- | --- | --- | --- | --- | --- |
| FLORIDA | 26451 | 5264 | 0 | 0 | 0 | 31715 |
| GEORGIA | 90814 | 11605 | 0 | 2685 | 684 | 105788 |
| HAWAII | --- | --- | --- | --- | --- | --- |
| IDAHO | 0 | 26860 | 0 | 0 | 28079 | 54939 |
| ILLINOIS | 502746 | 591886 | 16716 | 0 | 7413 | 1118761 |
| INDIANA | 313700 | 330813 | 10700 | 0 | 316 | 655529 |
| IOWA | 212724 | 304302 | 5956 | 54 | 1996 | 525032 |
| KANSAS | 0 | 180162 | 2401 | 0 | 162106 | 344669 |
| KENTUCKY | 233140 | 228676 | 0 | 642 | 722 | 463180 |
| LOUISIANA | 52725 | 14554 | 0 | 0 | 30 | 67309 |
| MAINE | 40485 | 72901 | 3502 | 0 | 625 | 117513 |
| MARYLAND | 122778 | 135474 | 4161 | 2 | 1199 | 263614 |
| MASSACHUSETTS | 151603 | 222299 | 1677 | 2858 | 13726 | 392163 |
| MICHIGAN | 216824 | 312911 | 9986 | 0 | 1568 | 541289 |
| MINNESOTA | 129050 | 180356 | 4804 | 0 | 3726 | 317936 |
| MISSISSIPPI | 48959 | 2579 | 0 | 0 | 0 | 51538 |
| MISSOURI | 354180 | 313563 | 0 | 0 | 5838 | 673581 |
| MONTANA | 28130 | 23207 | 0 | 0 | 10057 | 61394 |
| NEBRASKA | 111339 | 113191 | 2941 | 0 | 402 | 227873 |
| NEVADA | 5975 | 4190 | 0 | 0 | 0 | 10165 |
| NEW HAMPSHIRE | 34918 | 53512 | 1121 | 0 | 723 | 90274 |
| NEW JERSEY | 165370 | 220350 | 6999 | 0 | 6678 | 399397 |
| NEW MEXICO | --- | --- | --- | --- | --- | --- |
| NEW YORK | 668002 | 814575 | 19280 | 0 | 20839 | 1522696 |

|  |  |  |  |  |  |  |
|---|---|---|---|---|---|---|
| NORTH CAROLINA | 175748 | 111247 | 218 | 0 | 4627 | 291840 |
| NORTH DAKOTA | 21297 | 34887 | 585 | 0 | 412 | 57181 |
| OHIO | 479188 | 537026 | 1859 | 0 | 11075 | 1029148 |
| OKLAHOMA | --- | --- | --- | --- | --- | --- |
| OREGON | 35972 | 43300 | 3675 | 0 | 0 | 82947 |
| PENNSYLVANIA | 412347 | 683941 | 24531 | 0 | 13665 | 1134484 |
| RHODE ISLAND | 18368 | 30566 | 1625 | 0 | 1512 | 52071 |
| SOUTH CAROLINA | 46929 | 3168 | 0 | 0 | 2 | 50099 |
| SOUTH DAKOTA | 40865 | 53583 | 1323 | 0 | 0 | 95771 |
| TENNESSEE | 142931 | 109248 | 1051 | 10697 | 994 | 264921 |
| TEXAS | 327195 | 82821 | 0 | 581 | 1345 | 411942 |
| UTAH | 45939 | 46180 | 0 | 0 | 0 | 92119 |
| VERMONT | 16732 | 46118 | 1032 | 0 | 289 | 64171 |
| VIRGINIA | 165075 | 98728 | 487 | 3081 | 669 | 268040 |
| WASHINGTON | 44882 | 55268 | 2239 | 0 | 5670 | 108059 |
| WEST VIRGINIA | 100577 | 118221 | 1426 | 0 | 125 | 220349 |
| WISCONSIN | 163819 | 261527 | 8932 | 0 | 5490 | 439768 |
| WYOMING | 10017 | 14539 | 0 | 0 | 0 | 24556 |

## 1902 HOUSE OF REPRESENTATIVES ELECTION

|  | DEMOCRAT | REPUBLICAN | PROHIBITION | OTHER | TOTAL VOTES CAST |
|---|---|---|---|---|---|
| ALABAMA | 68074 | 22378 | 0 | 4 | 90456 |
| ALASKA | --- | --- | --- | --- | --- |
| ARIZONA | --- | --- | --- | --- | --- |
| ARKANSAS | 32821 | 6587 | 0 | 9 | 39417 |
| CALIFORNIA | 87432 | 152373 | 3840 | 47382 | 291027 |
| COLORADO | 87205 | 85217 | 3845 | 8781 | 185048 |
| CONNECTICUT | 70590 | 83666 | 1454 | 3478 | 159188 |
| DELAWARE | 16396 | 8028 | 569 | 13214 | 38207 |
| DIST OF COLUMBIA | --- | --- | --- | --- | --- |
| FLORIDA | 16334 | 0 | 0 | 0 | 16334 |
| GEORGIA | 40876 | 0 | 0 | 0 | 40876 |
| HAWAII | --- | --- | --- | --- | --- |
| IDAHO | 24878 | 32384 | 636 | 1738 | 59636 |
| ILLINOIS | 373659 | 406582 | 19101 | 16079 | 815421 |
| INDIANA | 269180 | 295565 | 14880 | 5984 | 585609 |
| IOWA | 158849 | 223021 | 7024 | 4779 | 393673 |
| KANSAS | 115946 | 158307 | 3744 | 3984 | 281981 |

TABLE 3.7 (CONTINUED)

## 1902 HOUSE OF REPRESENTATIVES ELECTION

|  | DEMOCRAT | REPUBLICAN | PROHIBITION | OTHER | TOTAL VOTES CAST |
|---|---|---|---|---|---|
| KENTUCKY | 157471 | 124953 | 5618 | 3807 | 291849 |
| LOUISIANA | 22218 | 4047 | 0 | 0 | 26265 |
| MAINE | 38631 | 65491 | 1080 | 2018 | 107220 |
| MARYLAND | 91546 | 100054 | 5069 | 514 | 197183 |
| MASSACHUSETTS | 139703 | 191770 | 5232 | 53011 | 389716 |
| MICHIGAN | 155732 | 228399 | 5904 | 2856 | 392891 |
| MINNESOTA | 103472 | 158962 | 935 | 1600 | 264969 |
| MISSISSIPPI | 18058 | 0 | 0 | 0 | 18058 |
| MISSOURI | 274220 | 230649 | 1070 | 4096 | 510035 |
| MONTANA | 19560 | 24626 | 0 | 9138 | 53324 |
| NEBRASKA | 89234 | 98367 | 3106 | 2209 | 192916 |
| NEVADA | 0 | 5073 | 0 | 5848 | 10921 |
| NEW HAMPSHIRE | 30204 | 44629 | 1187 | 967 | 76987 |
| NEW JERSEY | 164199 | 183576 | 6518 | 6389 | 360682 |
| NEW MEXICO | --- | --- | --- | --- | --- |
| NEW YORK | 651067 | 661243 | 16690 | 35835 | 1364835 |
| NORTH CAROLINA | 135277 | 59166 | 0 | 2328 | 196771 |
| NORTH DAKOTA | 14392 | 32976 | 0 | 1195 | 48563 |
| OHIO | 337758 | 439765 | 11298 | 21167 | 809988 |
| OKLAHOMA | --- | --- | --- | --- | --- |
| OREGON | 31811 | 46982 | 4142 | 5329 | 88264 |
| PENNSYLVANIA | 288232 | 601903 | 20178 | 92170 | 1002483 |
| RHODE ISLAND | 27855 | 28215 | 1291 | 894 | 58255 |
| SOUTH CAROLINA | 31343 | 742 | 0 | 5 | 32090 |
| SOUTH DAKOTA | 21113 | 48310 | 2319 | 5316 | 77058 |
| TENNESSEE | 98787 | 53565 | 0 | 99 | 152451 |
| TEXAS | 283196 | 57440 | 0 | 2177 | 342813 |
| UTAH | 38196 | 43710 | 0 | 2938 | 84844 |
| VERMONT | 8544 | 33539 | 2027 | 15 | 44125 |
| VIRGINIA | 82526 | 33387 | 1418 | 5601 | 122932 |
| WASHINGTON | 33435 | 58453 | 1708 | 16169 | 109765 |
| WEST VIRGINIA | 89061 | 99266 | 2683 | 1 | 191011 |
| WISCONSIN | 136859 | 195096 | 9004 | 13767 | 354726 |
| WYOMING | 8892 | 15808 | 0 | 0 | 24700 |

1904 HOUSE OF REPRESENTATIVES ELECTION

| | DEMOCRAT | REPUBLICAN | PROHIBITION | SOCIALIST | OTHER | TOTAL VOTES CAST |
|---|---|---|---|---|---|---|
| ALABAMA | 82826 | 19551 | 0 | 0 | 426 | 102806 |
| ALASKA | --- | --- | --- | --- | --- | --- |
| ARIZONA | --- | --- | --- | --- | --- | --- |
| ARKANSAS | 77460 | 32517 | 0 | 0 | 102 | 110079 |
| CALIFORNIA | 99775 | 186427 | 6547 | 21642 | 13735 | 328126 |
| COLORADO | 112373 | 121236 | 3631 | 3698 | 594 | 241532 |
| CONNECTICUT | 75212 | 108918 | 1508 | 4247 | 1039 | 190924 |
| DELAWARE | 19552 | 23512 | 615 | 135 | 0 | 43814 |
| DIST OF COLUMBIA | --- | --- | --- | --- | --- | --- |
| FLORIDA | 25592 | 6010 | 0 | 1156 | 1 | 32759 |
| GEORGIA | 80774 | 15736 | 0 | 0 | 1738 | 98248 |
| HAWAII | --- | --- | --- | --- | --- | --- |
| IDAHO | 20146 | 44813 | 1008 | 4209 | 219 | 70395 |
| ILLINOIS | 343125 | 608691 | 40685 | 59542 | 7205 | 1059248 |
| INDIANA | 288706 | 353087 | 18979 | 9155 | 1235 | 671162 |
| IOWA | 161801 | 295258 | 7731 | 12350 | 140 | 477280 |
| KANSAS | 105479 | 187983 | 6210 | 11956 | 0 | 311628 |
| KENTUCKY | 219749 | 204484 | 2551 | 174 | 2662 | 429620 |
| LOUISIANA | 47388 | 4632 | 0 | 412 | 74 | 52506 |
| MAINE | 50383 | 76519 | 737 | 1405 | 50 | 129094 |
| MARYLAND | 99180 | 103992 | 3412 | 1063 | 443 | 208090 |
| MASSACHUSETTS | 152142 | 235365 | 2101 | 21423 | 601 | 411632 |
| MICHIGAN | 158146 | 344043 | 9877 | 2106 | 694 | 514866 |
| MINNESOTA | 72919 | 205639 | 1754 | 0 | 3184 | 283496 |
| MISSISSIPPI | 52796 | 91 | 1218 | 449 | 0 | 53336 |
| MISSOURI | 304391 | 317003 | 0 | 7979 | 658 | 631249 |
| MONTANA | 0 | 32957 | 0 | 4025 | 26729 | 63711 |
| NEBRASKA | 0 | 123986 | 5839 | 4494 | 90012 | 224331 |
| NEVADA | 5525 | 5301 | 0 | 0 | 572 | 11398 |
| NEW HAMPSHIRE | 33328 | 52112 | 769 | 921 | 15 | 87145 |
| NEW JERSEY | 173217 | 236218 | 6614 | 8917 | 5820 | 430786 |
| NEW MEXICO | --- | --- | --- | --- | --- | --- |
| NEW YORK | 661896 | 841418 | 20474 | 35318 | 7789 | 1566895 |
| NORTH CAROLINA | 130038 | 78693 | 0 | 0 | 120 | 208851 |
| NORTH DAKOTA | 15622 | 49111 | 967 | 1734 | 20 | 67454 |
| OHIO | 354803 | 581376 | 18637 | 28686 | 2096 | 985598 |

TABLE 3.7 (CONTINUED)

## 1904 HOUSE OF REPRESENTATIVES ELECTION

|  | DEMOCRAT | REPUBLICAN | PROHIBITION | SOCIALIST | OTHER | TOTAL VOTES CAST |
|---|---|---|---|---|---|---|
| OKLAHOMA | --- | --- | --- | --- | --- | --- |
| OREGON | 29930 | 51096 | 6402 | 6478 | 0 | 93906 |
| PENNSYLVANIA | 316741 | 729760 | 30449 | 11030 | 17584 | 1105564 |
| RHODE ISLAND | 28861 | 33662 | 1072 | 0 | 0 | 63595 |
| SOUTH CAROLINA | 54666 | 2132 | 0 | 0 | 17 | 56815 |
| SOUTH DAKOTA | 22640 | 69936 | 3012 | 3115 | 2391 | 101094 |
| TENNESSEE | 128452 | 99439 | 0 | 557 | 124 | 228572 |
| TEXAS | 204772 | 42441 | 0 | 0 | 2616 | 249829 |
| UTAH | 37445 | 52675 | 0 | 4823 | 6796 | 101739 |
| VERMONT | 15934 | 46989 | 1122 | 740 | 4 | 64789 |
| VIRGINIA | 86361 | 44100 | 0 | 243 | 1316 | 132020 |
| WASHINGTON | 35636 | 92436 | 3059 | 9005 | 3936 | 144072 |
| WEST VIRGINIA | 109331 | 124425 | 3562 | 1382 | 801 | 239501 |
| WISCONSIN | 150376 | 250609 | 8955 | 26950 | 118 | 437008 |
| WYOMING | 9903 | 19862 | 154 | 822 | 0 | 30741 |

## 1906-7 HOUSE OF REPRESENTATIVES ELECTION

|  | DEMOCRAT | REPUBLICAN | PROHIBITION | SOCIALIST | OTHER | TOTAL VOTES CAST |
|---|---|---|---|---|---|---|
| ALABAMA | 59548 | 5982 | 0 | 0 | 11 | 65541 |
| ALASKA | --- | --- | --- | --- | --- | --- |
| ARIZONA | --- | --- | --- | --- | --- | --- |
| ARKANSAS | 38472 | 12511 | 0 | 0 | 31 | 51014 |
| CALIFORNIA | 100960 | 155897 | 4027 | 17461 | 3625 | 281970 |
| COLORADO | 76792 | 102426 | 4326 | 12668 | 0 | 196212 |
| CONNECTICUT | 67747 | 88115 | 1689 | 2940 | 408 | 160899 |
| DELAWARE | 17118 | 20210 | 767 | 149 | 0 | 38244 |
| DIST OF COLUMBIA | --- | --- | --- | --- | --- | --- |
| FLORIDA | 20419 | 0 | 0 | 2530 | 5 | 22954 |
| GEORGIA | 32912 | 429 | 0 | 0 | 3 | 33344 |

| | | | | | | |
|---|---:|---:|---:|---:|---:|---:|
| HAWAII | --- | --- | --- | --- | --- | --- |
| IDAHO | 23818 | 42134 | 1129 | 4834 | 0 | 71915 |
| ILLINOIS | 312082 | 435985 | 27585 | 37567 | 12267 | 825486 |
| INDIANA | 276163 | 282827 | 17100 | 6918 | 60 | 583068 |
| IOWA | 168844 | 224341 | 5227 | 7675 | 49 | 406136 |
| KANSAS | 127715 | 165210 | 3493 | 8066 | 904 | 305388 |
| KENTUCKY | 155835 | 123954 | 6910 | 1674 | 141 | 288514 |
| LOUISIANA | 32701 | 3962 | 0 | 603 | 0 | 37266 |
| MAINE | 61196 | 69572 | 814 | 1373 | 110 | 133065 |
| MARYLAND | 92366 | 99266 | 4417 | 3106 | 0 | 199155 |
| MASSACHUSETTS | 153881 | 228536 | 0 | 20699 | 41 | 403157 |
| MICHIGAN | 83432 | 232662 | 7002 | 4296 | 288 | 327680 |
| MINNESOTA | 64944 | 171349 | 1968 | 14445 | 0 | 252706 |
| MISSISSIPPI | 20092 | 0 | 0 | 173 | 0 | 20265 |
| MISSOURI | 291276 | 286132 | 0 | 7743 | 225 | 585376 |
| MONTANA | 0 | 0 | 1816 | 4638 | 51523 | 56161 |
| NEBRASKA | 11644 | 98903 | 0 | 2306 | 72878 | 187547 |
| NEVADA | 7320 | 5665 | 1083 | 1251 | 0 | 14236 |
| NEW HAMPSHIRE | 31270 | 45774 | 4264 | 896 | 11 | 79034 |
| NEW JERSEY | 149860 | 172261 | | 7766 | 24205 | 358356 |
| NEW MEXICO | --- | --- | --- | --- | --- | --- |
| NEW YORK | 493694 | 700000 | 15076 | 25948 | 215556 | 1450274 |
| NORTH CAROLINA | 124696 | 77747 | 0 | 0 | 188 | 202631 |
| NORTH DAKOTA | 21050 | 38923 | 0 | 1151 | 5 | 61129 |
| OHIO | 330644 | 407698 | 10738 | 16872 | 5660 | 771612 |
| OKLAHOMA | 136096 | 101648 | 0 | 0 | 0 | 242827 |
| OREGON | 31491 | 51435 | 4209 | 6326 | 0 | 93461 |
| PENNSYLVANIA | 308667 | 506598 | 21570 | 18252 | 104065 | 959152 |
| RHODE ISLAND | 31439 | 33009 | 643 | 409 | 0 | 65500 |
| SOUTH CAROLINA | 28874 | 436 | 0 | 19 | 1 | 29330 |
| SOUTH DAKOTA | 19976 | 48096 | 3392 | 2439 | 0 | 73903 |
| TENNESSEE | 111480 | 80343 | 0 | 1552 | 0 | 206093 |
| TEXAS | 151402 | 20609 | 0 | 0 | 6718 | 174170 |
| UTAH | 28031 | 42620 | 643 | 3019 | 2159 | 85081 |
| VERMONT | 17114 | 41398 | 0 | 364 | 11411 | 59529 |
| VIRGINIA | 55259 | 30558 | 2582 | 0 | 10 | 86057 |
| WASHINGTON | 31811 | 71353 | 4170 | 8367 | 240 | 114113 |
| WEST VIRGINIA | 77117 | 98339 | 2864 | 3165 | 0 | 182791 |
| WISCONSIN | 113572 | 169828 | 0 | 24027 | 127 | 310418 |
| WYOMING | 8944 | 16813 | | 0 | 56 | 25813 |

TABLE 3.7 (CONTINUED)

## 1908 HOUSE OF REPRESENTATIVES ELECTION

| | DEMOCRAT | REPUBLICAN | PROHIBITION | SOCIALIST | OTHER | TOTAL VOTES CAST |
|---|---|---|---|---|---|---|
| ALABAMA | 81629 | 12415 | 0 | 0 | 7067 | 101111 |
| ALASKA | --- | --- | --- | --- | --- | --- |
| ARIZONA | --- | --- | --- | --- | --- | --- |
| ARKANSAS | 104861 | 48081 | 0 | 0 | 0 | 152942 |
| CALIFORNIA | 134699 | 202309 | 7776 | 25037 | 1746 | 371567 |
| COLORADO | 126934 | 121265 | 6188 | 8151 | 10 | 262548 |
| CONNECTICUT | 70029 | 111557 | 2313 | 5067 | 1282 | 190248 |
| DELAWARE | 22515 | 24314 | 930 | 228 | 10 | 47997 |
| DIST OF COLUMBIA | --- | --- | --- | --- | --- | --- |
| FLORIDA | 30011 | 6254 | 0 | 2561 | 191 | 39017 |
| GEORGIA | 96226 | 38 | 0 | 0 | 0 | 96264 |
| HAWAII | --- | --- | --- | --- | --- | --- |
| IDAHO | 37605 | 49983 | 2094 | 6248 | 109 | 96039 |
| ILLINOIS | 458117 | 614396 | 31004 | 32732 | 4969 | 1141218 |
| INDIANA | 351658 | 334224 | 14766 | 10702 | 481 | 711831 |
| IOWA | 198031 | 253826 | 6685 | 5884 | 19 | 464445 |
| KANSAS | 160900 | 195113 | 3467 | 12337 | 1 | 371818 |
| KENTUCKY | 241364 | 228607 | 1899 | 3367 | 0 | 475237 |
| LOUISIANA | 63891 | 4693 | 0 | 1521 | 648 | 70753 |
| MAINE | 64493 | 75307 | 1383 | 1404 | 14 | 142601 |
| MARYLAND | 106792 | 100661 | 3605 | 1261 | 1 | 212320 |
| MASSACHUSETTS | 135868 | 249206 | 0 | 6671 | 30673 | 422418 |
| MICHIGAN | 192437 | 323403 | 9644 | 4735 | 601 | 530820 |
| MINNESOTA | 87868 | 195812 | 0 | 12783 | 15010 | 311473 |
| MISSISSIPPI | 59317 | 384 | 0 | 0 | 0 | 59701 |
| MISSOURI | 349047 | 347362 | 215 | 12513 | 1968 | 711105 |
| MONTANA | 29032 | 32819 | 0 | 5318 | 0 | 67169 |
| NEBRASKA | 131027 | 128866 | 1660 | 2501 | 0 | 264054 |
| NEVADA | 11253 | 7552 | 0 | 1965 | 3031 | 23801 |
| NEW HAMPSHIRE | 34066 | 50420 | 758 | 1069 | 490 | 86803 |
| NEW JERSEY | 206808 | 241619 | 4549 | 8966 | 309 | 462251 |
| NEW MEXICO | --- | --- | --- | --- | --- | --- |
| NEW YORK | 707542 | 827619 | 15961 | 38759 | 41647 | 1631528 |

| | DEMOCRAT | REPUBLICAN | PROHIBITION | SOCIALIST | OTHER | TOTAL VOTES CAST |
|---|---|---|---|---|---|---|
| NORTH CAROLINA | 143840 | 108592 | 0 | 0 | 422 | 252854 |
| NORTH DAKOTA | 29426 | 57357 | 0 | 0 | 1124 | 87907 |
| OHIO | 523406 | 532914 | 11267 | 29730 | 20016 | 1117333 |
| OKLAHOMA | 122804 | 90264 | 0 | 20766 | 0 | 233834 |
| OREGON | 28706 | 67468 | 5874 | 8204 | 0 | 110252 |
| PENNSYLVANIA | 402079 | 636926 | 39330 | 21715 | 5742 | 1105792 |
| RHODE ISLAND | 30775 | 39596 | 1056 | 1214 | 0 | 72641 |
| SOUTH CAROLINA | 63732 | 1687 | 0 | 0 | 0 | 65419 |
| SOUTH DAKOTA | 38758 | 67400 | 3785 | 2676 | 110 | 112729 |
| TENNESSEE | 126142 | 90363 | 0 | 1208 | 122 | 217835 |
| TEXAS | 235846 | 45710 | 0 | 0 | 5315 | 286871 |
| UTAH | 35981 | 57544 | 0 | 4374 | 13553 | 111452 |
| VERMONT | 14942 | 45058 | 842 | 323 | 247 | 61412 |
| VIRGINIA | 90356 | 48284 | 0 | 89 | 1235 | 139964 |
| WASHINGTON | 56322 | 107862 | 26 | 3640 | 0 | 167850 |
| WEST VIRGINIA | 113579 | 135674 | 4888 | 3332 | 0 | 257473 |
| WISCONSIN | 167277 | 240195 | 3345 | 27814 | 295 | 438926 |
| WYOMING | 13643 | 21431 | 0 | 2486 | 0 | 37560 |

## 1910-11 HOUSE OF REPRESENTATIVES ELECTION

| | DEMOCRAT | REPUBLICAN | PROHIBITION | SOCIALIST | OTHER | TOTAL VOTES CAST |
|---|---|---|---|---|---|---|
| ALABAMA | 82272 | 14976 | 0 | 0 | 77 | 97325 |
| ALASKA | --- | --- | --- | --- | --- | --- |
| ARIZONA | --- | --- | --- | --- | --- | --- |
| ARKANSAS | 31828 | 9235 | 0 | 0 | 0 | 41063 |
| CALIFORNIA | 111620 | 169723 | 6208 | 40936 | 34461 | 362948 |
| COLORADO | 105700 | 101722 | 4689 | 8620 | 0 | 220731 |
| CONNECTICUT | 73221 | 79585 | 1874 | 10304 | 1169 | 166153 |
| DELAWARE | 20281 | 22410 | 775 | 556 | 0 | 44022 |
| DIST OF COLUMBIA | --- | --- | --- | --- | --- | --- |
| FLORIDA | 30995 | 1372 | 0 | 5182 | 3 | 37552 |
| GEORGIA | 43454 | 2285 | 0 | 0 | 10053 | 55792 |
| HAWAII | --- | --- | --- | --- | --- | --- |
| IDAHO | 31832 | 46401 | 0 | 5463 | 0 | 83696 |
| ILLINOIS | 412333 | 413569 | 19026 | 47748 | 3 | 892679 |
| INDIANA | 312153 | 277636 | 13386 | 18458 | 0 | 621633 |
| IOWA | 157504 | 207272 | 1822 | 8095 | 0 | 374693 |

TABLE 3.7 (CONTINUED)

1910–11 HOUSE OF REPRESENTATIVES ELECTION

| | DEMOCRAT | REPUBLICAN | PROHIBITION | SOCIALIST | OTHER | TOTAL VOTES CAST |
|---|---|---|---|---|---|---|
| KANSAS | 116225 | 162880 | 555 | 15489 | 0 | 295149 |
| KENTUCKY | 175574 | 147372 | 595 | 5239 | 212 | 328992 |
| LOUISIANA | 46283 | 3874 | 0 | 706 | 229 | 51092 |
| MAINE | 70542 | 67563 | 1257 | 1287 | 25 | 140674 |
| MARYLAND | 101663 | 95230 | 3720 | 3924 | 3 | 204540 |
| MASSACHUSETTS | 203619 | 203136 | 0 | 7567 | 11915 | 426237 |
| MICHIGAN | 146701 | 212663 | 7605 | 7808 | 110 | 374887 |
| MINNESOTA | 67474 | 180124 | 0 | 17607 | 0 | 265205 |
| MISSISSIPPI | 23865 | 0 | 0 | 0 | 23 | 23888 |
| MISSOURI | 328216 | 318587 | 4954 | 18665 | 332 | 670754 |
| MONTANA | 28071 | 32519 | 0 | 5184 | 0 | 65774 |
| NEBRASKA | 113505 | 115065 | 1560 | 4335 | 0 | 234465 |
| NEVADA | 7688 | 10066 | 0 | 2409 | 0 | 20163 |
| NEW HAMPSHIRE | 37006 | 42580 | 188 | 974 | 13 | 80761 |
| NEW JERSEY | 225817 | 187842 | 2830 | 9951 | 4120 | 430560 |
| NEW MEXICO | --- | --- | --- | --- | --- | --- |
| NEW YORK | 483153 | 552077 | 22683 | 47344 | 316522 | 1421779 |
| NORTH CAROLINA | 141049 | 94430 | 0 | 0 | 443 | 235922 |
| NORTH DAKOTA | 25880 | 51556 | 0 | 3225 | 0 | 80661 |
| OHIO | 453735 | 384234 | 6000 | 58239 | 233 | 902441 |
| OKLAHOMA | 118348 | 93206 | 0 | 22900 | 0 | 234454 |
| OREGON | 37709 | 56898 | 8049 | 10554 | 0 | 113210 |
| PENNSYLVANIA | 230148 | 481564 | 31773 | 59630 | 138658 | 941773 |
| RHODE ISLAND | 31236 | 34664 | 923 | 529 | 0 | 67352 |
| SOUTH CAROLINA | 30787 | 372 | 0 | 19 | 5 | 31183 |
| SOUTH DAKOTA | 32655 | 64777 | 4139 | 0 | 1641 | 103212 |
| TENNESSEE | 142718 | 56939 | 0 | 4489 | 6562 | 210708 |
| TEXAS | 182382 | 17313 | 564 | 6626 | 602 | 207487 |
| UTAH | 32730 | 50614 | 0 | 4857 | 14042 | 102243 |
| VERMONT | 14441 | 37136 | 0 | 834 | 3 | 52414 |
| VIRGINIA | 67570 | 31610 | 0 | 0 | 1631 | 100811 |
| WASHINGTON | 44827 | 78291 | 2061 | 13064 | 0 | 138243 |
| WEST VIRGINIA | 102933 | 94457 | 3675 | 8156 | 7 | 209228 |
| WISCONSIN | 103958 | 161169 | 3476 | 40714 | 96 | 309413 |
| WYOMING | 14659 | 20312 | 0 | 2155 | 0 | 37126 |

## 1912 HOUSE OF REPRESENTATIVES ELECTION

| | DEMOCRAT | REPUBLICAN | PROHIBITION | SOCIALIST | PROGRESSIVE | OTHER | TOTAL VOTES CAST |
|---|---|---|---|---|---|---|---|
| ALABAMA | 87519 | 9589 | 0 | 2533 | 0 | 0 | 99641 |
| ALASKA | --- | --- | --- | --- | --- | --- | --- |
| ARIZONA | 11389 | 3110 | 193 | 3034 | 5819 | 0 | 23545 |
| ARKANSAS | 89718 | 26453 | 0 | 0 | 0 | 0 | 116171 |
| CALIFORNIA | 196610 | 287222 | 14347 | 104122 | 20341 | 136 | 622778 |
| COLORADO | 117775 | 65877 | 2642 | 16748 | 58096 | 0 | 261138 |
| CONNECTICUT | 76148 | 70048 | 2014 | 10536 | 29737 | 1009 | 189492 |
| DELAWARE | 22485 | 16740 | 597 | 563 | 2825 | 5497 | 48707 |
| DIST OF COLUMBIA | --- | --- | --- | --- | --- | --- | --- |
| FLORIDA | 34324 | 2942 | 777 | 3636 | 2680 | 0 | 44359 |
| GEORGIA | 116092 | 356 | 0 | 0 | 0 | 0 | 116448 |
| HAWAII | --- | --- | --- | --- | --- | --- | --- |
| IDAHO | 30172 | 43571 | 1169 | 11393 | 12066 | 0 | 98371 |
| ILLINOIS | 415386 | 313608 | 15721 | 84352 | 304072 | 8130 | 1141269 |
| INDIANA | 291288 | 166698 | 17344 | 38458 | 127039 | 0 | 640827 |
| IOWA | 182969 | 184776 | 4311 | 14240 | 43621 | 0 | 429917 |
| KANSAS | 163926 | 159248 | 900 | 26577 | 0 | 1 | 350652 |
| KENTUCKY | 210685 | 86975 | 0 | 11010 | 91384 | 505 | 400559 |
| LOUISIANA | 62776 | 0 | 0 | 2841 | 3 | 0 | 65620 |
| MAINE | 66894 | 71850 | 1115 | 1805 | 0 | 5 | 141669 |
| MARYLAND | 107476 | 62382 | 3339 | 4426 | 2303 | 2 | 179928 |
| MASSACHUSETTS | 188633 | 179557 | 0 | 11899 | 89497 | 79 | 469665 |
| MICHIGAN | 152188 | 185657 | 8624 | 19789 | 0 | 175492 | 541750 |
| MINNESOTA | 69652 | 154308 | 25863 | 30042 | 0 | 0 | 279865 |
| MISSISSIPPI | 48797 | 0 | 0 | 302 | 0 | 0 | 49099 |
| MISSOURI | 337702 | 198275 | 1410 | 23824 | 98713 | 26223 | 686147 |
| MONTANA | 25891 | 23505 | 0 | 10271 | 16644 | 0 | 76311 |
| NEBRASKA | 114044 | 24766 | 7182 | 10055 | 84 | 94164 | 250295 |
| NEVADA | 7311 | 7380 | 0 | 3011 | 2072 | 0 | 19774 |
| NEW HAMPSHIRE | 40682 | 35324 | 381 | 1580 | 4307 | 2 | 82276 |
| NEW JERSEY | 169540 | 94883 | 4494 | 9585 | 54373 | 25269 | 358144 |
| NEW MEXICO | 22139 | 17892 | 0 | 5882 | 2644 | 0 | 48557 |
| NEW YORK | 629362 | 450613 | 17421 | 66090 | 404 | 381729 | 1545619 |
| NORTH CAROLINA | 149569 | 67980 | 0 | 469 | 7869 | 225 | 226112 |
| NORTH DAKOTA | 24341 | 47003 | 0 | 8486 | 0 | 66 | 79896 |

TABLE 3.7 (CONTINUED)

## 1912 HOUSE OF REPRESENTATIVES ELECTION

|  | DEMOCRAT | REPUBLICAN | PROHIBITION | SOCIALIST | PROGRESSIVE | OTHER | TOTAL VOTES CAST |
|---|---|---|---|---|---|---|---|
| OHIO | 423301 | 297355 | 11862 | 91201 | 192809 | 0 | 1016528 |
| OKLAHOMA | 122974 | 87494 | 321 | 40908 | 397 | 0 | 252094 |
| OREGON | 35285 | 42046 | 7554 | 13283 | 14959 | 16783 | 129910 |
| PENNSYLVANIA | 357562 | 269872 | 21074 | 81785 | 348665 | 22680 | 1101638 |
| RHODE ISLAND | 33626 | 31716 | 702 | 0 | 8844 | 0 | 74888 |
| SOUTH CAROLINA | 49292 | 190 | 0 | 0 | 0 | 50 | 49532 |
| SOUTH DAKOTA | 44487 | 63809 | 2839 | 3974 | 0 | 0 | 115109 |
| TENNESSEE | 118527 | 59649 | 0 | 2209 | 27263 | 1 | 207649 |
| TEXAS | 235065 | 22656 | 1195 | 24466 | 16422 | 0 | 299804 |
| UTAH | 36640 | 43133 | 0 | 8953 | 22358 | 0 | 111778 |
| VERMONT | 17422 | 28785 | 1329 | 1210 | 1 | 694 | 48853 |
| VIRGINIA | 99053 | 23856 | 0 | 3867 | 7273 | 106 | 134813 |
| WASHINGTON | 73133 | 86300 | 8185 | 39772 | 90348 | 764 | 297738 |
| WEST VIRGINIA | 114485 | 128467 | 4168 | 13944 | 0 | 0 | 261064 |
| WISCONSIN | 156977 | 177385 | 8351 | 37404 | 0 | 335 | 380452 |
| WYOMING | 14720 | 19130 | 296 | 2230 | 4828 | 0 | 41204 |

## 1914 HOUSE OF REPRESENTATIVES ELECTION

|  | DEMOCRAT | REPUBLICAN | PROHIBITION | SOCIALIST | PROGRESSIVE | OTHER | TOTAL VOTES CAST |
|---|---|---|---|---|---|---|---|
| ALABAMA | 62830 | 12832 | 0 | 1143 | 3742 | 0 | 80547 |
| ALASKA | --- | --- | --- | --- | --- | --- | --- |
| ARIZONA | 33306 | 7586 | 0 | 3773 | 0 | 0 | 44665 |
| ARKANSAS | 37266 | 4087 | 0 | 0 | 1747 | 0 | 43100 |
| CALIFORNIA | 78736 | 203824 | 43492 | 68215 | 107865 | 354537 | 856669 |
| COLORADO | 118212 | 52318 | 1333 | 6965 | 10985 | 53027 | 241507 |
| CONNECTICUT | 78110 | 89000 | 0 | 5718 | 6734 | 460 | 181355 |
| DELAWARE | 20681 | 22922 | 0 | 463 | 0 | 1653 | 45719 |
| DIST OF COLUMBIA | --- | --- | --- | --- | --- | --- | --- |
| FLORIDA | 23951 | 0 | 0 | 0 | 0 | 125 | 24076 |

| | | | | | | |
|---|---|---|---|---|---|---|
| GEORGIA | 80832 | 0 | 0 | 0 | 640 | 0 | 81472 |
| HAWAII | --- | --- | --- | --- | --- | --- | --- |
| IDAHO | 39736 | 43918 | 1329 | 8061 | 0 | 15694 | 108738 |
| ILLINOIS | 375465 | 388896 | 7644 | 42841 | 105088 | 2060 | 921994 |
| INDIANA | 275891 | 233140 | 14882 | 19580 | 86849 | 0 | 630342 |
| IOWA | 162982 | 212865 | 4508 | 7964 | 19937 | 280 | 408536 |
| KANSAS | 195830 | 188056 | 11345 | 14001 | 74401 | 0 | 483633 |
| KENTUCKY | 173374 | 123518 | 150 | 4231 | 21911 | 71 | 323255 |
| LOUISIANA | 40545 | 0 | 0 | 1344 | 9017 | 189 | 51095 |
| MAINE | 60649 | 60264 | 257 | 1830 | 17883 | 16 | 140899 |
| MARYLAND | 111410 | 95586 | 3518 | 2421 | 3188 | 746 | 216869 |
| MASSACHUSETTS | 177945 | 207623 | 0 | 5524 | 30118 | 26490 | 447700 |
| MICHIGAN | 149762 | 218445 | 3624 | 10177 | 47700 | 153 | 429861 |
| MINNESOTA | 87305 | 181482 | 0 | 29296 | 24737 | 0 | 322820 |
| MISSISSIPPI | 35830 | 0 | 0 | 1124 | 0 | 0 | 36954 |
| MISSOURI | 318587 | 240897 | 602 | 17149 | 22747 | 607 | 600589 |
| MONTANA | 37011 | 26046 | 0 | 12282 | 6166 | 0 | 81505 |
| NEBRASKA | 112309 | 24441 | 1238 | 5044 | 3141 | 87454 | 233627 |
| NEVADA | 8031 | 8915 | 0 | 4294 | 0 | 0 | 21240 |
| NEW HAMPSHIRE | 35241 | 42450 | 0 | 1054 | 2371 | 9 | 81125 |
| NEW JERSEY | 167511 | 179930 | 0 | 14581 | 14584 | 7701 | 384307 |
| NEW MEXICO | 19805 | 23812 | 0 | 1101 | 1695 | 9 | 46422 |
| NEW YORK | 408392 | 477172 | 29013 | 61415 | 61459 | 312242 | 1349693 |
| NORTH CAROLINA | 122129 | 79842 | 0 | 352 | 341 | 80 | 202744 |
| NORTH DAKOTA | 26684 | 50792 | 0 | 6156 | 0 | 499 | 84131 |
| OHIO | 484348 | 480482 | 1779 | 50020 | 50911 | 0 | 1067540 |
| OKLAHOMA | 121411 | 87468 | 0 | 41235 | 0 | 0 | 250114 |
| OREGON | 67349 | 77931 | 32150 | 9596 | 2751 | 46595 | 236372 |
| PENNSYLVANIA | 281154 | 486988 | 27561 | 43148 | 189220 | 129969 | 1158040 |
| RHODE ISLAND | 35076 | 39001 | 575 | 1666 | 1321 | 114 | 77753 |
| SOUTH CAROLINA | 33076 | 273 | 0 | 71 | 0 | 0 | 33420 |
| SOUTH DAKOTA | 37942 | 52844 | 1850 | 2688 | 1501 | 0 | 96825 |
| TENNESSEE | 149248 | 47932 | 0 | 3530 | 7753 | 6353 | 214816 |
| TEXAS | 173803 | 10489 | 0 | 24276 | 1542 | 549 | 210659 |
| UTAH | 44270 | 54940 | 0 | 5673 | 8603 | 184 | 113670 |
| VERMONT | 13685 | 36451 | 1470 | 1073 | | | 61466 |
| VIRGINIA | 58770 | 23654 | 0 | 1812 | 641 | 423 | 85300 |
| WASHINGTON | 96652 | 128001 | 10230 | 32512 | 66666 | 1129 | 335190 |
| WEST VIRGINIA | 102223 | 110520 | 1931 | 11944 | 8733 | 0 | 235351 |
| WISCONSIN | 115501 | 159370 | 5247 | 28763 | 30 | 0 | 308911 |
| WYOMING | 17246 | 21362 | 0 | 1693 | 1308 | 0 | 41609 |

TABLE 3.7 (CONTINUED)

## 1916 HOUSE OF REPRESENTATIVES ELECTION

| | DEMOCRAT | REPUBLICAN | PROHIBITION | SOCIALIST | PROGRESSIVE | OTHER | TOTAL VOTES CAST |
|---|---|---|---|---|---|---|---|
| ALABAMA | 98780 | 23515 | 0 | 790 | 0 | 0 | 123085 |
| ALASKA | --- | --- | --- | --- | --- | --- | --- |
| ARIZONA | 34377 | 14907 | 0 | 3060 | 0 | 0 | 52344 |
| ARKANSAS | 143288 | 29626 | 0 | 0 | 0 | 0 | 172914 |
| CALIFORNIA | 194126 | 266566 | 40843 | 59886 | 47575 | 273603 | 882599 |
| COLORADO | 130589 | 113320 | 1833 | 11622 | 956 | 3734 | 260221 |
| CONNECTICUT | 98652 | 106930 | 0 | 5268 | 2130 | 626 | 213309 |
| DELAWARE | 24395 | 24202 | 0 | 484 | 0 | 0 | 51211 |
| DIST OF COLUMBIA | --- | --- | --- | --- | --- | --- | --- |
| FLORIDA | 52389 | 10995 | 1156 | 2750 | 0 | 0 | 67290 |
| GEORGIA | 126555 | 0 | 0 | 0 | 0 | 7691 | 134246 |
| HAWAII | --- | --- | --- | --- | --- | --- | --- |
| IDAHO | 55807 | 64648 | 0 | 8079 | 0 | 0 | 128534 |
| ILLINOIS | 546471 | 707958 | 9366 | 49842 | 0 | 3529 | 1317166 |
| INDIANA | 321751 | 342806 | 12985 | 18335 | 10505 | 0 | 706382 |
| IOWA | 186358 | 282179 | 868 | 7731 | 1119 | 0 | 478255 |
| KANSAS | 261589 | 261622 | 18121 | 21814 | 5144 | 78 | 568368 |
| KENTUCKY | 266717 | 240478 | 2502 | 3743 | 6481 | 0 | 513440 |
| LOUISIANA | 78607 | 359 | 0 | 1030 | 0 | 5 | 86482 |
| MAINE | 68569 | 80998 | 145 | 1444 | 0 | 0 | 151156 |
| MARYLAND | 109138 | 105627 | 6674 | 3149 | 0 | 0 | 224588 |
| MASSACHUSETTS | 197772 | 281546 | 1205 | 7113 | 17079 | 27 | 504742 |
| MICHIGAN | 257483 | 355298 | 3296 | 13693 | 0 | 13205 | 642975 |
| MINNESOTA | 94095 | 209611 | 30252 | 26543 | 19696 | 0 | 380197 |
| MISSISSIPPI | | | | | | | |
| MISSOURI | 396617 | 368832 | 1149 | 12110 | 69 | 582 | 779359 |
| MONTANA | 84499 | 66974 | 0 | 9002 | 0 | 0 | 160475 |
| NEBRASKA | 111681 | 35871 | 0 | 8276 | 0 | 127335 | 283163 |
| NEVADA | 13100 | 14106 | 0 | 5125 | 0 | 0 | 32331 |
| NEW HAMPSHIRE | 39951 | 44122 | 270 | 1162 | 30 | 0 | 85535 |
| NEW JERSEY | 186792 | 225858 | 9758 | 16479 | 0 | 1113 | 440000 |
| NEW MEXICO | 32731 | 32056 | 0 | 2052 | 0 | 0 | 66839 |
| NEW YORK | 238148 | 194650 | 24300 | 69163 | 0 | 1000560 | 1526821 |
| NORTH CAROLINA | 165954 | 120246 | 0 | 0 | 0 | 258 | 286458 |

| | DEMOCRAT | REPUBLICAN | PROHIBITION | SOCIALIST | PROGRESSIVE | OTHER | TOTAL VOTES CAST |
|---|---|---|---|---|---|---|---|
| NORTH DAKOTA | 29167 | 63329 | 0 | 4359 | 0 | 0 | 96855 |
| OHIO | 545975 | 543941 | 283 | 28811 | 0 | 7 | 1119017 |
| OKLAHOMA | 142031 | 98594 | 816 | 47389 | 0 | 0 | 288830 |
| OREGON | 9824 | 35832 | 0 | 15308 | 0 | 163886 | 224850 |
| PENNSYLVANIA | 471308 | 668581 | 29937 | 46896 | 31588 | 1679 | 1249989 |
| RHODE ISLAND | 41630 | 43259 | 0 | 2041 | 0 | 1 | 86930 |
| SOUTH CAROLINA | 61869 | 1204 | 0 | 0 | 0 | 0 | 63074 |
| SOUTH DAKOTA | 52769 | 69243 | 862 | 3472 | 0 | 0 | 126346 |
| TENNESSEE | 131538 | 97144 | 0 | 2675 | 0 | 2677 | 234034 |
| TEXAS | 298966 | 46467 | 1525 | 18583 | 0 | 0 | 365541 |
| UTAH | 79728 | 57680 | 0 | 4574 | 154 | 0 | 142136 |
| VERMONT | 15955 | 44244 | 1087 | 1152 | 0 | 10 | 62448 |
| VIRGINIA | 105646 | 47652 | 0 | 2238 | 234 | 251 | 156021 |
| WASHINGTON | 152410 | 184117 | 0 | 21422 | 2 | 0 | 357951 |
| WEST VIRGINIA | 140769 | 142188 | 0 | 0 | 0 | 0 | 282957 |
| WISCONSIN | 137391 | 238537 | 5298 | 35800 | 0 | 53 | 417079 |
| WYOMING | 24156 | 24693 | 219 | 1302 | 0 | 0 | 50370 |

## 1918 HOUSE OF REPRESENTATIVES ELECTION

| | DEMOCRAT | REPUBLICAN | PROHIBITION | SOCIALIST | PROGRESSIVE | OTHER | TOTAL VOTES CAST |
|---|---|---|---|---|---|---|---|
| ALABAMA | 53489 | 8856 | 0 | 0 | 0 | 0 | 62345 |
| ALASKA | --- | --- | --- | --- | --- | --- | --- |
| ARIZONA | 26805 | 16822 | 0 | 754 | 0 | 0 | 44381 |
| ARKANSAS | 78573 | 0 | 0 | 0 | 0 | 0 | 78573 |
| CALIFORNIA | 61912 | 92806 | 17642 | 36855 | 0 | 417695 | 626910 |
| COLORADO | 93906 | 112787 | 0 | 2492 | 6112 | 22 | 215319 |
| CONNECTICUT | 78373 | 82983 | 1007 | 3998 | 0 | 633 | 166994 |
| DELAWARE | 19652 | 21226 | 0 | 420 | 0 | 0 | 41298 |
| DIST OF COLUMBIA | --- | --- | --- | --- | --- | --- | --- |
| FLORIDA | 31813 | 0 | 0 | 0 | 0 | 0 | 31813 |
| GEORGIA | 57274 | 2831 | 0 | 0 | 0 | 0 | 60105 |
| HAWAII | --- | --- | --- | --- | --- | --- | --- |
| IDAHO | 34499 | 59358 | 0 | 0 | 0 | 0 | 93857 |
| ILLINOIS | 361505 | 501974 | 3110 | 33835 | 0 | 5746 | 906170 |
| INDIANA | 251331 | 306807 | 568 | 8705 | 0 | 0 | 567411 |
| IOWA | 121994 | 223381 | 0 | 3405 | 0 | 36 | 348816 |
| KANSAS | 171897 | 244374 | 0 | 11392 | 1445 | 0 | 429108 |

TABLE 3.7 (CONTINUED)

1918 HOUSE OF REPRESENTATIVES ELECTION

| | DEMOCRAT | REPUBLICAN | PROHIBITION | SOCIALIST | PROGRESSIVE | OTHER | TOTAL VOTES CAST |
|---|---|---|---|---|---|---|---|
| KENTUCKY | 186214 | 170218 | 0 | 0 | 0 | 0 | 356432 |
| LOUISIANA | 44794 | 0 | 0 | 0 | 0 | 1 | 44795 |
| MAINE | 53775 | 68061 | 0 | 0 | 0 | 0 | 121836 |
| MARYLAND | 81485 | 76057 | 0 | 2512 | 0 | 1 | 160055 |
| MASSACHUSETTS | 150774 | 233809 | 0 | 2648 | 7003 | 193 | 394427 |
| MICHIGAN | 135987 | 265334 | 0 | 5450 | 0 | 90 | 406861 |
| MINNESOTA | 82533 | 216594 | 0 | 0 | 0 | 33853 | 332980 |
| MISSISSIPPI | 31599 | 0 | 0 | 712 | 0 | 0 | 32311 |
| MISSOURI | 287840 | 256474 | 0 | 6386 | 0 | 423 | 551123 |
| MONTANA | 48356 | 47358 | 0 | 0 | 0 | 8121 | 103835 |
| NEBRASKA | 94538 | 121476 | 1012 | 0 | 0 | 0 | 217026 |
| NEVADA | 12670 | 10660 | 0 | 1377 | 0 | 0 | 24707 |
| NEW HAMPSHIRE | 32045 | 38001 | 0 | 0 | 0 | 0 | 70046 |
| NEW JERSEY | 158899 | 173228 | 4841 | 11349 | 171 | 649 | 349137 |
| NEW MEXICO | 22627 | 23862 | 0 | 564 | 0 | 0 | 47053 |
| NEW YORK | 737386 | 604151 | 23102 | 148176 | 0 | 526796 | 2039611 |
| NORTH CAROLINA | 141807 | 91245 | 0 | 0 | 0 | 0 | 233052 |
| NORTH DAKOTA | 29405 | 54508 | 0 | 0 | 0 | 0 | 83913 |
| OHIO | 392581 | 495616 | 0 | 17344 | 0 | 0 | 905541 |
| OKLAHOMA | 103702 | 78244 | 0 | 6972 | 73 | 0 | 188991 |
| OREGON | 26189 | 41589 | 0 | 9207 | 0 | 64906 | 141891 |
| PENNSYLVANIA | 276836 | 546373 | 29309 | 23273 | 5117 | 22663 | 903571 |
| RHODE ISLAND | 34646 | 43225 | 0 | 1737 | 0 | 0 | 79608 |
| SOUTH CAROLINA | 25280 | 176 | 0 | 0 | 0 | 0 | 25456 |
| SOUTH DAKOTA | 34165 | 48905 | 0 | 255 | 2864 | 0 | 86189 |
| TENNESSEE | 92890 | 27620 | 0 | 0 | 0 | 178 | 120688 |
| TEXAS | 159032 | 6113 | 0 | 0 | 0 | 0 | 165145 |
| UTAH | 25327 | 36612 | 0 | 1067 | 0 | 23931 | 86937 |
| VERMONT | 10697 | 31788 | 658 | 0 | 0 | 15 | 43158 |
| VIRGINIA | 33902 | 8555 | 0 | 0 | 0 | 50 | 42507 |
| WASHINGTON | 81350 | 112166 | 0 | 7870 | 0 | 9 | 201395 |
| WEST VIRGINIA | 99917 | 112022 | 0 | 1864 | 0 | 0 | 213803 |
| WISCONSIN | 67229 | 166354 | 819 | 53605 | 15229 | 218 | 303454 |
| WYOMING | 14639 | 26244 | 0 | 0 | 0 | 0 | 40883 |

1920 HOUSE OF REPRESENTATIVES ELECTION

| | DEMOCRAT | REPUBLICAN | SOCIALIST | PROHIBITION | OTHER | TOTAL VOTES CAST |
|---|---|---|---|---|---|---|
| ALABAMA | 161243 | 62095 | 917 | 0 | 0 | 224255 |
| ALASKA | --- | --- | --- | --- | --- | --- |
| ARIZONA | 35397 | 25841 | 0 | 0 | 0 | 61238 |
| ARKANSAS | 128265 | 61924 | 0 | 0 | 0 | 190189 |
| CALIFORNIA | 37108 | 299794 | 95072 | 0 | 379949 | 811923 |
| COLORADO | 109605 | 167587 | 0 | 0 | 0 | 277192 |
| CONNECTICUT | 122019 | 227635 | 11754 | 1365 | 270 | 363043 |
| DELAWARE | 40206 | 52145 | 0 | 0 | 1259 | 93610 |
| DIST OF COLUMBIA | --- | --- | --- | --- | --- | --- |
| FLORIDA | 97082 | 21024 | 3405 | 0 | 1608 | 123119 |
| GEORGIA | 118904 | 15614 | 0 | 0 | 0 | 134518 |
| HAWAII | --- | --- | --- | --- | --- | --- |
| IDAHO | 44348 | 84296 | 8605 | 0 | 0 | 137249 |
| ILLINOIS | 579799 | 1369673 | 66385 | 19123 | 53488 | 2088468 |
| INDIANA | 515085 | 695031 | 40549 | 0 | 0 | 1250665 |
| IOWA | 88857 | 605532 | 22714 | 0 | 200 | 717303 |
| KANSAS | 192262 | 325686 | 9483 | 0 | 1 | 527432 |
| KENTUCKY | 431913 | 409165 | 11274 | 0 | 0 | 852352 |
| LOUISIANA | 92037 | 0 | 0 | 0 | 15 | 92052 |
| MAINE | 67515 | 135230 | 0 | 0 | 0 | 202745 |
| MARYLAND | 163920 | 189937 | 23659 | 0 | 0 | 377516 |
| MASSACHUSETTS | 276217 | 618132 | 16815 | 5121 | 20398 | 936683 |
| MICHIGAN | 228583 | 761334 | 17379 | 506 | 1957 | 1009759 |
| MINNESOTA | 104458 | 447297 | 195315 | 0 | 0 | 747070 |
| MISSISSIPPI | 66306 | 1577 | 2079 | 0 | 0 | 69962 |
| MISSOURI | 583378 | 713264 | 17189 | 0 | 5632 | 1319463 |
| MONTANA | 66792 | 108215 | 0 | 0 | 0 | 175007 |
| NEBRASKA | 116512 | 222060 | 21738 | 0 | 14 | 360324 |
| NEVADA | 9167 | 13149 | 4554 | 0 | 0 | 26870 |
| NEW HAMPSHIRE | 60730 | 93326 | 588 | 4464 | 0 | 154644 |
| NEW JERSEY | 295260 | 517659 | 18233 | 0 | 1447 | 837063 |
| NEW MEXICO | 49426 | 54672 | 1290 | 0 | 0 | 105388 |
| NEW YORK | 881565 | 800400 | 231818 | 10500 | 783689 | 2707972 |
| NORTH CAROLINA | 306919 | 225368 | 0 | 0 | 0 | 532287 |
| NORTH DAKOTA | 0 | 78379 | 0 | 0 | 130559 | 208938 |

TABLE 3.7 (CONTINUED)

### 1920 HOUSE OF REPRESENTATIVES ELECTION

|  | DEMOCRAT | REPUBLICAN | SOCIALIST | PROHIBITION | OTHER | TOTAL VOTES CAST |
|---|---|---|---|---|---|---|
| OHIO | 798981 | 1125574 | 13676 | 0 | 0 | 1938231 |
| OKLAHOMA | 227557 | 232202 | 25144 | 0 | 0 | 484903 |
| OREGON | 13049 | 67539 | 8258 | 31853 | 78849 | 199548 |
| PENNSYLVANIA | 666583 | 1134013 | 67596 | 89683 | 28252 | 1786108 |
| RHODE ISLAND | 58927 | 105692 | 2222 | 0 | 195 | 167036 |
| SOUTH CAROLINA | 64400 | 1336 | 0 | 0 | 1 | 65737 |
| SOUTH DAKOTA | 39799 | 103325 | 38932 | 0 | 0 | 182056 |
| TENNESSEE | 190153 | 198400 | 7394 | 0 | 0 | 395947 |
| TEXAS | 311566 | 86856 | 0 | 0 | 7496 | 405918 |
| UTAH | 56175 | 80984 | 7214 | 0 | 0 | 144373 |
| VERMONT | 20587 | 66958 | 0 | 933 | 68 | 88546 |
| VIRGINIA | 154402 | 84300 | 0 | 0 | 3605 | 242307 |
| WASHINGTON | 63390 | 218655 | 93111 | 0 | 0 | 375156 |
| WEST VIRGINIA | 226017 | 273288 | 0 | 0 | 1 | 499306 |
| WISCONSIN | 107997 | 428825 | 87297 | 0 | 283 | 624402 |
| WYOMING | 14952 | 34689 | 6780 | 0 | 0 | 56421 |

### 1922 HOUSE OF REPRESENTATIVES ELECTION

|  | DEMOCRAT | REPUBLICAN | SOCIALIST | PROHIBITION | OTHER | TOTAL VOTES CAST |
|---|---|---|---|---|---|---|
| ALABAMA | 114610 | --- | 0 | - | 26660 | 141270 |
| ALASKA | --- | --- | --- | - | --- | --- |
| ARIZONA | 37262 | 14601 | 0 | 0 | 0 | 51863 |
| ARKANSAS | 30674 | 0 | 0 | 0 | 4306 | 34980 |
| CALIFORNIA | 22711 | 126123 | 31190 | 0 | 602500 | 782524 |
| COLORADO | 127751 | 136926 | 959 | 0 | 0 | 265636 |
| CONNECTICUT | 147760 | 170194 | 5636 | 0 | 0 | 323590 |
| DELAWARE | 39126 | 32577 | 0 | 0 | 908 | 72611 |
| DIST OF COLUMBIA | --- | --- | --- | - | --- | --- |
| FLORIDA | 44544 | 6323 | 0 | 0 | 16 | 50883 |

| State | | | | | | |
|---|---:|---:|---:|---:|---:|---:|
| GEORGIA | 74762 | 964 | 0 | 0 | 644 | 76370 |
| HAWAII | --- | --- | --- | --- | --- | --- |
| IDAHO | 33647 | 57373 | 30123 | 0 | 0 | 121143 |
| ILLINOIS | 666583 | 943684 | 36311 | 0 | 32595 | 1679173 |
| INDIANA | 524183 | 546595 | 11310 | 0 | 0 | 1082088 |
| IOWA | 225821 | 357174 | 2588 | 0 | 7 | 585590 |
| KANSAS | 233706 | 284687 | 6461 | 0 | 4 | 524858 |
| KENTUCKY | 196480 | 138239 | 10281 | 0 | 9197 | 354197 |
| LOUISIANA | 44337 | 0 | 0 | 0 | 40 | 44377 |
| MAINE | 74287 | 101064 | 0 | 0 | 0 | 175351 |
| MARYLAND | 151408 | 145314 | 6122 | 0 | 1015 | 303859 |
| MASSACHUSETTS | 347203 | 475942 | 0 | 0 | 1568 | 824713 |
| MICHIGAN | 178633 | 365970 | 1699 | 0 | 31 | 546333 |
| MINNESOTA | 146325 | 385030 | 105541 | 0 | 0 | 636896 |
| MISSISSIPPI | 66482 | 1620 | 49 | 0 | 1 | 68152 |
| MISSOURI | 494376 | 476109 | 5671 | 0 | 373 | 976529 |
| MONTANA | 75736 | 73183 | 876 | 0 | 0 | 149795 |
| NEBRASKA | 173384 | 179070 | 21863 | 1224 | 0 | 375541 |
| NEVADA | 15991 | 12084 | 0 | 0 | 0 | 28075 |
| NEW HAMPSHIRE | 64773 | 62264 | 0 | 0 | 0 | 127037 |
| NEW JERSEY | 352971 | 393269 | 5339 | 0 | 40692 | 792271 |
| NEW MEXICO | 59254 | 49698 | 871 | 0 | 0 | 109823 |
| NEW YORK | 1026100 | 727481 | 32417 | 16778 | 625173 | 2427949 |
| NORTH CAROLINA | 226921 | 138522 | 0 | 0 | 0 | 365443 |
| NORTH DAKOTA | 0 | 115986 | 15834 | 0 | 18672 | 150492 |
| OHIO | 715974 | 855378 | 19983 | 34 | 1015 | 1592384 |
| OKLAHOMA | 279983 | 180203 | 4045 | 0 | 0 | 464231 |
| OREGON | 52479 | 123124 | 2530 | 0 | 2159 | 180292 |
| PENNSYLVANIA | 524104 | 827256 | 46793 | 32773 | 15278 | 1446204 |
| RHODE ISLAND | 81762 | 73688 | 0 | 0 | 0 | 155450 |
| SOUTH CAROLINA | 34391 | 679 | 0 | 0 | 0 | 35070 |
| SOUTH DAKOTA | 31229 | 87277 | 41270 | 0 | 0 | 159776 |
| TENNESSEE | 142033 | 76182 | 1279 | 0 | 0 | 219494 |
| TEXAS | 265317 | 45945 | 0 | 0 | 0 | 311262 |
| UTAH | 53946 | 61779 | 3888 | 0 | 0 | 119613 |
| VERMONT | 24989 | 42637 | 0 | 2703 | 22 | 70351 |
| VIRGINIA | 112906 | 52923 | 0 | 0 | 430 | 166259 |
| WASHINGTON | 58882 | 161646 | 39557 | 0 | 0 | 260085 |
| WEST VIRGINIA | 194585 | 185030 | 1832 | 0 | 43 | 381490 |
| WISCONSIN | 11585 | 346036 | 51216 | 0 | 43536 | 452373 |
| WYOMING | 27017 | 30885 | 0 | 0 | 0 | 57902 |

TABLE 3.7 (CONTINUED)

## 1924 HOUSE OF REPRESENTATIVES ELECTION

| | DEMOCRAT | REPUBLICAN | SOCIALIST | OTHER | TOTAL VOTES CAST |
|---|---|---|---|---|---|
| ALABAMA | 120221 | 31357 | 0 | 11 | 151589 |
| ALASKA | --- | --- | --- | --- | --- |
| ARIZONA | 40329 | 8628 | 0 | 0 | 48957 |
| ARKANSAS | 99426 | 36929 | 0 | 0 | 136355 |
| CALIFORNIA | 80870 | 322320 | 87931 | 506776 | 997897 |
| COLORADO | 139135 | 169546 | 2686 | 7909 | 319276 |
| CONNECTICUT | 120243 | 245089 | 7918 | 105 | 373355 |
| DELAWARE | 35943 | 51536 | 0 | 519 | 87998 |
| DIST OF COLUMBIA | --- | --- | --- | --- | --- |
| FLORIDA | 72243 | 21525 | 0 | 2995 | 96763 |
| GEORGIA | 154915 | 0 | 0 | 3516 | 158431 |
| HAWAII | --- | --- | --- | --- | --- |
| IDAHO | 33704 | 77712 | 23257 | 479 | 135152 |
| ILLINOIS | 1519021 | 669555 | 17580 | 5820 | 2211976 |
| INDIANA | 544259 | 690066 | 4971 | 7476 | 1246772 |
| IOWA | 258125 | 566918 | 0 | 0 | 825043 |
| KANSAS | 198626 | 236351 | 0 | 0 | 434977 |
| KENTUCKY | 389168 | 289123 | 16062 | 0 | 694353 |
| LOUISIANA | 93311 | 0 | 0 | 0 | 93311 |
| MAINE | 97855 | 148345 | 0 | 0 | 246200 |
| MARYLAND | 158272 | 149226 | 4025 | 0 | 311523 |
| MASSACHUSETTS | 415710 | 647535 | 770 | 12465 | 1076480 |
| MICHIGAN | 232180 | 882709 | 335 | 326 | 1115550 |
| MINNESOTA | 53388 | 422182 | 337035 | 0 | 812605 |
| MISSISSIPPI | 98548 | 579 | 0 | 0 | 99127 |
| MISSOURI | 620546 | 644762 | 12216 | 258 | 1277782 |
| MONTANA | 72847 | 79202 | 6847 | 0 | 158896 |
| NEBRASKA | 85993 | 219470 | 10622 | 122003 | 438088 |
| NEVADA | 12880 | 13107 | 0 | 0 | 25987 |
| NEW HAMPSHIRE | 66186 | 92346 | 0 | 0 | 158532 |
| NEW JERSEY | 353700 | 600352 | 15292 | 3691 | 973035 |
| NEW MEXICO | 57802 | 53960 | 1126 | 0 | 112888 |
| NEW YORK | 1246391 | 1533374 | 144507 | 153880 | 3078152 |
| NORTH CAROLINA | 289754 | 179607 | 0 | 0 | 469361 |

314

| | DEMOCRAT | REPUBLICAN | SOCIALIST | OTHER | TOTAL VOTES CAST |
|---|---|---|---|---|---|
| NORTH DAKOTA | 28241 | 113710 | 28193 | 562 | 170706 |
| OHIO | 769711 | 1055987 | 32650 | 3252 | 1861600 |
| OKLAHOMA | 283432 | 203869 | 17124 | 0 | 504425 |
| OREGON | 43945 | 153681 | 13494 | 45240 | 256360 |
| PENNSYLVANIA | 481400 | 1322681 | 131676 | 73139 | 2008896 |
| RHODE ISLAND | 84543 | 122775 | 0 | 0 | 207318 |
| SOUTH CAROLINA | 49238 | 253 | 0 | 0 | 49491 |
| SOUTH DAKOTA | 37973 | 112157 | 44130 | 0 | 194260 |
| TENNESSEE | 144534 | 75113 | 0 | 5578 | 225225 |
| TEXAS | 587437 | 89026 | 0 | 33 | 676496 |
| UTAH | 65689 | 82771 | 0 | 0 | 148460 |
| VERMONT | 19936 | 74495 | 0 | 2969 | 97400 |
| VIRGINIA | 165016 | 63051 | 1692 | 18 | 229777 |
| WASHINGTON | 90308 | 223793 | 33683 | 0 | 347784 |
| WEST VIRGINIA | 270683 | 287992 | 3120 | 0 | 561795 |
| WISCONSIN | 155982 | 505230 | 54113 | 1730 | 717055 |
| WYOMING | 28537 | 43026 | 0 | 0 | 71563 |

## 1926 HOUSE OF REPRESENTATIVES ELECTION

| | DEMOCRAT | REPUBLICAN | SOCIALIST | OTHER | TOTAL VOTES CAST |
|---|---|---|---|---|---|
| ALABAMA | 90366 | 16729 | 0 | 0 | 107095 |
| ALASKA | --- | --- | --- | --- | --- |
| ARIZONA | 43725 | 24502 | 0 | 0 | 68227 |
| ARKANSAS | 28911 | 4801 | 0 | 0 | 33712 |
| CALIFORNIA | 47046 | 324266 | 32900 | 550402 | 954614 |
| COLORADO | 130377 | 158396 | 2502 | 0 | 291275 |
| CONNECTICUT | 106571 | 192082 | 2805 | 0 | 301458 |
| DELAWARE | 29424 | 38909 | 0 | 0 | 68333 |
| DIST OF COLUMBIA | --- | --- | --- | --- | --- |
| FLORIDA | 49495 | 4947 | 0 | 10247 | 64689 |
| GEORGIA | 46992 | 0 | 0 | 375 | 47367 |
| HAWAII | --- | --- | --- | --- | --- |
| IDAHO | 20934 | 72210 | 21596 | 0 | 114740 |
| ILLINOIS | 631708 | 987968 | 2662 | 8272 | 1630610 |
| INDIANA | 480579 | 546605 | 223 | 0 | 1027407 |
| IOWA | 154625 | 348727 | 0 | 1672 | 505024 |
| KANSAS | 196084 | 283890 | 0 | 187 | 480161 |

TABLE 3.7 (CONTINUED)

1926 HOUSE OF REPRESENTATIVES ELECTION

| | DEMOCRAT | REPUBLICAN | SOCIALIST | OTHER | TOTAL VOTES CAST |
|---|---|---|---|---|---|
| KENTUCKY | 263307 | 239909 | 0 | 0 | 503215 |
| LOUISIANA | 53320 | 869 | 0 | 3 | 54192 |
| MAINE | 66332 | 106707 | 0 | 0 | 173039 |
| MARYLAND | 186890 | 132375 | 2549 | 0 | 321814 |
| MASSACHUSETTS | 379424 | 504684 | 0 | 48983 | 933091 |
| MICHIGAN | 122395 | 438653 | 157 | 508 | 561713 |
| MINNESOTA | 37807 | 386448 | 214688 | 19833 | 658776 |
| MISSISSIPPI | 26917 | 0 | 0 | 0 | 26917 |
| MISSOURI | 499807 | 487173 | 734 | 117 | 987831 |
| MONTANA | 75833 | 74515 | 3104 | 0 | 153452 |
| NEBRASKA | 157249 | 187963 | 747 | 43441 | 389400 |
| NEVADA | 12910 | 17598 | 0 | 0 | 30508 |
| NEW HAMPSHIRE | 46867 | 77164 | 0 | 0 | 124031 |
| NEW JERSEY | 339937 | 448038 | 3628 | 0 | 791603 |
| NEW MEXICO | 55433 | 52075 | 0 | 297 | 107805 |
| NEW YORK | 1332580 | 1237954 | 82410 | 136643 | 2789587 |
| NORTH CAROLINA | 220155 | 138762 | 0 | 0 | 358917 |
| NORTH DAKOTA | 25831 | 113856 | 6596 | 0 | 146283 |
| OHIO | 561206 | 722876 | 1286 | 1110 | 1286478 |
| OKLAHOMA | 204335 | 157345 | 694 | 0 | 362374 |
| OREGON | 39621 | 148266 | 0 | 20372 | 208259 |
| PENNSYLVANIA | 352355 | 1033944 | 33768 | 48758 | 1468825 |
| RHODE ISLAND | 68713 | 95367 | 0 | 0 | 164080 |
| SOUTH CAROLINA | 14322 | 0 | 0 | 0 | 14322 |
| SOUTH DAKOTA | 68590 | 99045 | 2737 | 0 | 170372 |
| TENNESSEE | 71851 | 30828 | 0 | 0 | 102679 |
| TEXAS | 230463 | 33513 | 0 | 0 | 263976 |
| UTAH | 54204 | 86080 | 1261 | 1 | 141546 |
| VERMONT | 17282 | 55130 | 0 | 14 | 72426 |
| VIRGINIA | 74365 | 32536 | 727 | 316 | 107944 |
| WASHINGTON | 79434 | 190797 | 526 | 0 | 270757 |
| WEST VIRGINIA | 206284 | 221016 | 163 | 0 | 427463 |
| WISCONSIN | 29673 | 382490 | 41288 | 27765 | 481216 |
| WYOMING | 25082 | 39392 | 0 | 300 | 64774 |

## 1928 HOUSE OF REPRESENTATIVES ELECTION

| | DEMOCRAT | REPUBLICAN | SOCIALIST | OTHER | TOTAL VOTES CAST |
|---|---|---|---|---|---|
| ALABAMA | 165023 | 35613 | 0 | 0 | 200636 |
| ALASKA | --- | | --- | --- | --- |
| ARIZONA | 50231 | 31382 | 0 | 0 | 81613 |
| ARKANSAS | 157907 | 43670 | 194 | 0 | 201771 |
| CALIFORNIA | 96210 | 353080 | 44587 | 832673 | 1326550 |
| COLORADO | 141005 | 210838 | 0 | 949 | 352792 |
| CONNECTICUT | 250526 | 297651 | 2710 | 507 | 551394 |
| DELAWARE | 38045 | 66361 | 0 | 0 | 104406 |
| DIST OF COLUMBIA | --- | | --- | --- | --- |
| FLORIDA | 148528 | 69469 | 0 | 17 | 218014 |
| GEORGIA | 200188 | 0 | 0 | 0 | 200188 |
| HAWAII | --- | | --- | --- | --- |
| IDAHO | 48486 | 97006 | 1039 | 0 | 146531 |
| ILLINOIS | 1711520 | 1711651 | 11958 | 4282 | 3439411 |
| INDIANA | 641498 | 770317 | 2078 | 0 | 1413893 |
| IOWA | 235427 | 576061 | 0 | 0 | 811488 |
| KANSAS | 218182 | 375500 | 0 | 0 | 593682 |
| KENTUCKY | 412421 | 526194 | 113 | 0 | 938728 |
| LOUISIANA | 152816 | 14661 | 0 | 0 | 167477 |
| MAINE | 61890 | 145955 | 0 | 0 | 207845 |
| MARYLAND | 226116 | 234848 | 2314 | 0 | 463278 |
| MASSACHUSETTS | 625003 | 753391 | 5115 | 61734 | 1445243 |
| MICHIGAN | 357065 | 979071 | 1169 | 1283 | 1338588 |
| MINNESOTA | 174383 | 52551 | 15365 | 256498 | 971757 |
| MISSISSIPPI | 112546 | 0 | 0 | 0 | 112546 |
| MISSOURI | 726050 | 790062 | 169 | 18 | 1516299 |
| MONTANA | 77651 | 103478 | 826 | 0 | 181955 |
| NEBRASKA | 233094 | 289899 | 0 | 0 | 522993 |
| NEVADA | 13287 | 18815 | 0 | 0 | 32102 |
| NEW HAMPSHIRE | 75843 | 108284 | 186 | 0 | 184313 |
| NEW JERSEY | 564621 | 870883 | 812 | 102 | 1436418 |
| NEW MEXICO | 56045 | 61208 | 0 | 0 | 117253 |
| NEW YORK | 1987677 | 1994064 | 146671 | 84269 | 4212681 |
| NORTH CAROLINA | 355360 | 289333 | 0 | 0 | 644693 |
| NORTH DAKOTA | 51547 | 149005 | 0 | 0 | 200552 |
| OHIO | 931103 | 1442859 | 1430 | 860 | 2376252 |

TABLE 3.7 (CONTINUED)

### 1928 HOUSE OF REPRESENTATIVES ELECTION

|  | DEMOCRAT | REPUBLICAN | SOCIALIST | OTHER | TOTAL VOTES CAST |
|---|---|---|---|---|---|
| OKLAHOMA | 296574 | 293876 | 2244 | 199 | 592893 |
| OREGON | 55880 | 196539 | 3020 | 38128 | 293567 |
| PENNSYLVANIA | 1003910 | 1955641 | 15346 | 30723 | 3005620 |
| RHODE ISLAND | 114454 | 120361 | 0 | 0 | 234815 |
| SOUTH CAROLINA | 61347 | 0 | 0 | 0 | 61347 |
| SOUTH DAKOTA | 104437 | 142664 | 0 | 1780 | 248881 |
| TENNESSEE | 178476 | 116447 | 0 | 0 | 294923 |
| TEXAS | 568457 | 81283 | 0 | 0 | 649740 |
| UTAH | 77914 | 97140 | 847 | 0 | 175901 |
| VERMONT | 36451 | 91223 | 0 | 1688 | 129362 |
| VIRGINIA | 206513 | 91832 | 5854 | 445 | 304644 |
| WASHINGTON | 134910 | 291977 | 823 | 0 | 427710 |
| WEST VIRGINIA | 292061 | 347085 | 115 | 0 | 639261 |
| WISCONSIN | 234599 | 598077 | 59421 | 4623 | 896720 |
| WYOMING | 35972 | 38935 | 333 | 0 | 75240 |

### 1930 HOUSE OF REPRESENTATIVES ELECTION

|  | DEMOCRAT | REPUBLICAN | SOCIALIST | OTHER | TOTAL VOTES CAST |
|---|---|---|---|---|---|
| ALABAMA | 165403 | 20071 | 12959 | 0 | 198433 |
| ALASKA | --- | --- | --- | --- | --- |
| ARIZONA | 52342 | 0 | 0 | 0 | 52342 |
| ARKANSAS | 144171 | 0 | 0 | 0 | 144171 |
| CALIFORNIA | 54231 | 344678 | 0 | 698162 | 1097071 |
| COLORADO | 146192 | 167227 | 0 | 1224 | 314643 |
| CONNECTICUT | 208502 | 216518 | 2914 | 645 | 428579 |
| DELAWARE | 38891 | 48493 | 0 | 127 | 87511 |
| DIST OF COLUMBIA | --- | --- | --- | --- | --- |
| FLORIDA | 84070 | 11819 | 0 | 54 | 95943 |

| State | Col 1 | Col 2 | Col 3 | Col 4 | Col 5 |
|---|---|---|---|---|---|
| GEORGIA | 54563 | 0 | 0 | 1898 | 56461 |
| HAWAII | 45659 | 80869 | 0 | 0 | 126528 |
| IDAHO | 1062606 | 991083 | 9526 | 2221 | 2065436 |
| ILLINOIS | 641206 | 572082 | 602 | 293 | 1214183 |
| INDIANA | 207584 | 321706 | 0 | 858 | 530148 |
| IOWA | 242477 | 322775 | 0 | 0 | 565252 |
| KANSAS | 288354 | 253903 | 4945 | 1380 | 548582 |
| KENTUCKY | 130086 | 2207 | 0 | 1 | 132294 |
| LOUISIANA | 55471 | 88070 | 0 | 0 | 143541 |
| MAINE | 275461 | 189815 | 780 | 0 | 466056 |
| MARYLAND | 529268 | 629821 | 17467 | 29 | 1176585 |
| MASSACHUSETTS | 171402 | 567205 | 1401 | 4421 | 744429 |
| MICHIGAN | 65490 | 412888 | 0 | 281385 | 759763 |
| MINNESOTA | 34897 | 0 | 0 | 0 | 34897 |
| MISSISSIPPI | 477467 | 468853 | 462 | 281 | 947063 |
| MISSOURI | 84604 | 82736 | 872 | 1935 | 170147 |
| MONTANA | 216405 | 199196 | 0 | 0 | 415601 |
| NEBRASKA | 15343 | 18279 | 0 | 0 | 33622 |
| NEVADA | 52323 | 71823 | 0 | 0 | 124146 |
| NEW HAMPSHIRE | 425352 | 558925 | 3949 | 2608 | 990034 |
| NEW JERSEY | 65228 | 47955 | 0 | 296 | 113479 |
| NEW MEXICO | 1493073 | 1304010 | 164405 | 63694 | 3025182 |
| NEW YORK | 334916 | 198310 | 0 | 0 | 533226 |
| NORTH CAROLINA | 52284 | 127378 | 3538 | 0 | 183200 |
| NORTH DAKOTA | 910931 | 955686 | 13468 | 0 | 1880085 |
| OHIO | 282620 | 173944 | 166 | 0 | 456730 |
| OKLAHOMA | 107187 | 116642 | 0 | 4696 | 228525 |
| OREGON | | | | | |
| PENNSYLVANIA | 566594 | 1421712 | 15868 | 15287 | 2019461 |
| RHODE ISLAND | 105968 | 113354 | 0 | 0 | 219322 |
| SOUTH CAROLINA | 16163 | 0 | 0 | 0 | 16163 |
| SOUTH DAKOTA | 55718 | 106429 | 7926 | 0 | 170073 |
| TENNESSEE | 108869 | 38099 | 990 | 35172 | 183130 |
| TEXAS | 248450 | 45281 | | | 265102 |
| UTAH | 62828 | 80981 | 641 | 10304 | 154754 |
| VERMONT | 23741 | 49074 | 0 | 7 | 72822 |
| VIRGINIA | 108308 | 54161 | 0 | 2461 | 164930 |
| WASHINGTON | 75424 | 205937 | 1350 | 6667 | 289378 |
| WEST VIRGINIA | 271793 | 265857 | 0 | 0 | 537650 |
| WISCONSIN | 68130 | 364348 | 47520 | 7880 | 487878 |
| WYOMING | 23519 | 44890 | 0 | 0 | 68409 |

TABLE 3.7 (CONTINUED)

## 1932 HOUSE OF REPRESENTATIVES ELECTION

| | DEMOCRAT | REPUBLICAN | SOCIALIST | OTHER | TOTAL VOTES CAST |
|---|---|---|---|---|---|
| ALABAMA | 207489 | 22669 | 1123 | 353 | 231634 |
| ALASKA | --- | --- | --- | --- | --- |
| ARIZONA | 75469 | 29710 | 1112 | 293 | 106584 |
| ARKANSAS | 213189 | 4996 | 0 | 0 | 218185 |
| CALIFORNIA | 775870 | 688220 | 42769 | 368170 | 1875029 |
| COLORADO | 234843 | 191903 | 1962 | 807 | 429515 |
| CONNECTICUT | 282557 | 284438 | 19349 | 0 | 586344 |
| DELAWARE | 51698 | 48841 | 887 | 10670 | 112096 |
| DIST OF COLUMBIA | --- | --- | --- | --- | --- |
| FLORIDA | 186284 | 61300 | 0 | 12 | 247596 |
| GEORGIA | 233915 | 8556 | 4365 | 0 | 246836 |
| HAWAII | --- | --- | --- | --- | --- |
| IDAHO | 100922 | 78838 | 0 | 3815 | 183575 |
| ILLINOIS | 1675274 | 1421221 | 38486 | 15152 | 3150133 |
| INDIANA | 850181 | 683517 | 9146 | 3928 | 1546772 |
| IOWA | 495782 | 439793 | 0 | 0 | 935575 |
| KANSAS | 357154 | 350332 | 11485 | 124 | 719095 |
| KENTUCKY | 575289 | 390370 | 3273 | 477 | 969409 |
| LOUISIANA | 244681 | 0 | 0 | 0 | 244681 |
| MAINE | 118391 | 115963 | 891 | 0 | 235245 |
| MARYLAND | 299954 | 150552 | 2852 | 478 | 453836 |
| MASSACHUSETTS | 716971 | 769317 | 12980 | 1436 | 1500704 |
| MICHIGAN | 769088 | 758768 | 17789 | 15867 | 1561512 |
| MINNESOTA | 237881 | 312198 | 0 | 460849 | 1010928 |
| MISSISSIPPI | 129954 | 0 | 0 | 4814 | 134768 |
| MISSOURI | 997642 | 588246 | 11573 | 627 | 1598088 |
| MONTANA | 115262 | 87223 | 3525 | 2861 | 208871 |
| NEBRASKA | 296256 | 208954 | 7525 | 33466 | 546201 |
| NEVADA | 24979 | 16133 | 0 | 0 | 41112 |
| NEW HAMPSHIRE | 94765 | 97802 | 286 | 230 | 193083 |
| NEW JERSEY | 724572 | 751130 | 21774 | 4294 | 1501770 |
| NEW MEXICO | 95363 | 52905 | 1349 | 550 | 150167 |
| NEW YORK | 2363627 | 1756343 | 166781 | 86982 | 4373733 |
| NORTH CAROLINA | 492100 | 214022 | 0 | 0 | 706122 |

| | | | | |
|---|---|---|---|---|
| NORTH DAKOTA | 72659 | 135339 | 690 | 0 | 208688 |
| OHIO | 1206631 | 1109562 | 0 | 31675 | 2347868 |
| OKLAHOMA | 467644 | 174415 | 1016 | 0 | 640075 |
| OREGON | 164682 | 148262 | 31655 | 5159 | 349758 |
| PENNSYLVANIA | 1197640 | 1412756 | 93215 | 81759 | 2785370 |
| RHODE ISLAND | 143652 | 116306 | 0 | 626 | 260584 |
| SOUTH CAROLINA | 104646 | 1987 | 0 | 0 | 106633 |
| SOUTH DAKOTA | 146886 | 121128 | 1718 | 3332 | 273064 |
| TENNESSEE | 217905 | 88656 | 27888 | 6121 | 340570 |
| TEXAS | 790024 | 62957 | 2424 | 258 | 855663 |
| UTAH | 110176 | 91746 | 2751 | 922 | 205595 |
| VERMONT | 47591 | 86194 | 0 | 16 | 133801 |
| VIRGINIA | 204372 | 78622 | 47984 | 17587 | 348565 |
| WASHINGTON | 327702 | 186571 | 2505 | 36760 | 553538 |
| WEST VIRGINIA | 392924 | 341170 | 1678 | 16 | 735788 |
| WISCONSIN | 499910 | 466176 | 71132 | 5708 | 1042926 |
| WYOMING | 43056 | 44816 | 1428 | 891 | 90191 |

## 1934 HOUSE OF REPRESENTATIVES ELECTION

| | DEMOCRAT | REPUBLICAN | SOCIALIST | OTHER | TOTAL VOTES CAST |
|---|---|---|---|---|---|
| ALABAMA | 149104 | 10200 | 5547 | 39 | 164890 |
| ALASKA | --- | --- | --- | --- | --- |
| ARIZONA | 65914 | 28283 | 1478 | 369 | 96044 |
| ARKANSAS | 130459 | 9436 | 0 | 0 | 139895 |
| CALIFORNIA | 668282 | 483496 | 18890 | 858862 | 2029530 |
| COLORADO | 237491 | 140202 | 6126 | 11879 | 395698 |
| CONNECTICUT | 263794 | 249146 | 0 | 0 | 512940 |
| DELAWARE | 45927 | 52468 | 404 | 58 | 98857 |
| DIST OF COLUMBIA | --- | --- | --- | --- | --- |
| FLORIDA | 125263 | 0 | 0 | 0 | 125263 |
| GEORGIA | 52443 | 240 | 0 | 0 | 52683 |
| HAWAII | --- | --- | --- | --- | --- |
| IDAHO | 99770 | 63169 | 437 | 0 | 163376 |
| ILLINOIS | 1507714 | 1201373 | 13586 | 27653 | 2750326 |
| INDIANA | 759795 | 686598 | 8247 | 1661 | 1456301 |
| IOWA | 443565 | 385862 | 0 | 0 | 829427 |
| KANSAS | 367747 | 380037 | 4675 | 4775 | 757234 |

TABLE 3.7 (CONTINUED)

## 1934 HOUSE OF REPRESENTATIVES ELECTION

| | DEMOCRAT | REPUBLICAN | SOCIALIST | OTHER | TOTAL VOTES CAST |
|---|---|---|---|---|---|
| KENTUCKY | 254584 | 206118 | 3377 | 5391 | 469470 |
| LOUISIANA | 186063 | 0 | 0 | 49 | 186112 |
| MAINE | 142436 | 136859 | 0 | 0 | 279295 |
| MARYLAND | 267204 | 180493 | 5791 | 2142 | 455630 |
| MASSACHUSETTS | 641349 | 636017 | 10936 | 85192 | 1373494 |
| MICHIGAN | 590620 | 605047 | 8419 | 8440 | 1212526 |
| MINNESOTA | 256001 | 323189 | 35883 | 380532 | 995605 |
| MISSISSIPPI | 57327 | 0 | 0 | 0 | 57327 |
| MISSOURI | 797975 | 515268 | 6693 | 407 | 1320343 |
| MONTANA | 135733 | 59270 | 1471 | 265 | 196739 |
| NEBRASKA | 278378 | 249882 | 0 | 9692 | 537952 |
| NEVADA | 29691 | 11992 | 0 | 0 | 41683 |
| NEW HAMPSHIRE | 85690 | 84131 | 167 | 225 | 170213 |
| NEW JERSEY | 676016 | 638424 | 9937 | 4030 | 1328407 |
| NEW MEXICO | 76833 | 70659 | 0 | 776 | 148268 |
| NEW YORK | 1978670 | 1417271 | 141799 | 76233 | 3613973 |
| NORTH CAROLINA | 320256 | 173447 | 0 | 0 | 493703 |
| NORTH DAKOTA | 79338 | 114841 | 1299 | 0 | 195478 |
| OHIO | 1061857 | 905233 | 0 | 13999 | 1981089 |
| OKLAHOMA | 354542 | 162991 | 12823 | 0 | 530356 |
| OREGON | 121816 | 132441 | 22850 | 3345 | 280452 |
| PENNSYLVANIA | 1455248 | 1365650 | 63678 | 41104 | 2925680 |
| RHODE ISLAND | 140281 | 104278 | 0 | 1 | 244560 |
| SOUTH CAROLINA | 21921 | 235 | 0 | 0 | 22156 |
| SOUTH DAKOTA | 158399 | 116935 | 2259 | 0 | 277593 |
| TENNESSEE | 194312 | 69454 | 7081 | 4395 | 275242 |
| TEXAS | 439685 | 5067 | 0 | 1165 | 445917 |
| UTAH | 113975 | 63885 | 1049 | 1068 | 179977 |
| VERMONT | 54967 | 73809 | 942 | 7 | 129725 |
| VIRGINIA | 108655 | 33010 | 5046 | 1460 | 148171 |
| WASHINGTON | 314685 | 151655 | 3642 | 9383 | 479365 |
| WEST VIRGINIA | 345144 | 272011 | 1 | 2791 | 619947 |
| WISCONSIN | 280367 | 215605 | 54243 | 335474 | 885689 |
| WYOMING | 53288 | 37492 | 437 | 166 | 91383 |

## 1936 HOUSE OF REPRESENTATIVES ELECTION

| | DEMOCRAT | REPUBLICAN | INDEPENDENT | OTHER | TOTAL VOTES CAST |
|---|---|---|---|---|---|
| ALABAMA | 238558 | 26044 | 150 | 300 | 255052 |
| ALASKA | ---- | ---- | ---- | ---- | ----- |
| ARIZONA | 84403 | 20383 | 3729 | 295 | 108810 |
| ARKANSAS | 167161 | 13994 | 0 | 0 | 181155 |
| CALIFORNIA | 745118 | 645330 | 0 | 851751 | 2242199 |
| COLORADO | 283147 | 169765 | 0 | 4847 | 457759 |
| CONNECTICUT | 371202 | 280615 | 19782 | 11671 | 683270 |
| DELAWARE | 65485 | 55664 | 0 | 5514 | 126663 |
| DIST OF COLUMBIA | ---- | ---- | ---- | ---- | ----- |
| FLORIDA | 233405 | 51532 | 0 | 0 | 284937 |
| GEORGIA | 260509 | 15765 | 0 | 0 | 276274 |
| HAWAII | ---- | ---- | ---- | ---- | ----- |
| IDAHO | 126179 | 68793 | 0 | 0 | 194972 |
| ILLINOIS | 2062886 | 1568552 | 0 | 97412 | 3728850 |
| INDIANA | 910851 | 706988 | 7390 | 3887 | 1629116 |
| IOWA | 519085 | 510875 | 0 | 14088 | 1044048 |
| KANSAS | 377432 | 412041 | 9926 | 451 | 799850 |
| KENTUCKY | 539598 | 368576 | 9303 | 170 | 917647 |
| LOUISIANA | 291930 | 0 | 0 | 33 | 291963 |
| MAINE | 119195 | 170431 | 3225 | 8197 | 301048 |
| MARYLAND | 321447 | 215236 | 3165 | 3533 | 543381 |
| MASSACHUSETTS | 779959 | 848416 | 30118 | 124116 | 1782609 |
| MICHIGAN | 887874 | 765887 | 32143 | 12040 | 1697944 |
| MINNESOTA | 190367 | 420321 | 12408 | 468099 | 1091195 |
| MISSISSIPPI | 146242 | 1929 | 0 | 0 | 148171 |
| MISSOURI | 1093138 | 715403 | 0 | 2434 | 1810975 |
| MONTANA | 134006 | 73685 | 0 | 776 | 208467 |
| NEBRASKA | 289381 | 262155 | 10958 | 6842 | 569336 |
| NEVADA | 25575 | 11785 | 6444 | 0 | 43804 |
| NEW HAMPSHIRE | 96807 | 105626 | 322 | 1079 | 203834 |
| NEW JERSEY | 901234 | 766595 | 0 | 20412 | 1688241 |
| NEW MEXICO | 106951 | 62375 | 0 | 57 | 169383 |
| NEW YORK | 3013931 | 2078803 | 0 | 171469 | 5264203 |
| NORTH CAROLINA | 568482 | 230402 | 0 | 0 | 798884 |
| NORTH DAKOTA | 100609 | 115913 | 2697 | 0 | 219219 |
| OHIO | 1553059 | 1226247 | 0 | 8945 | 2788251 |

TABLE 3.7 (CONTINUED)

### 1936 HOUSE OF REPRESENTATIVES ELECTION

| | DEMOCRAT | REPUBLICAN | INDEPENDENT | OTHER | TOTAL VOTES CAST |
|---|---|---|---|---|---|
| OKLAHOMA | 475567 | 193487 | 0 | 3306 | 672360 |
| OREGON | 184824 | 181758 | 21848 | 798 | 389228 |
| PENNSYLVANIA | 2215961 | 1708551 | 0 | 146087 | 4070599 |
| RHODE ISLAND | 149957 | 134180 | 20662 | 603 | 305402 |
| SOUTH CAROLINA | 113651 | 1598 | 0 | 6 | 115255 |
| SOUTH DAKOTA | 143378 | 143071 | 0 | 0 | 286449 |
| TENNESSEE | 281664 | 105819 | 0 | 5070 | 392553 |
| TEXAS | 765362 | 52201 | 1911 | 216 | 819690 |
| UTAH | 149996 | 65270 | 0 | 520 | 215786 |
| VERMONT | 56334 | 83091 | 0 | 970 | 140395 |
| VIRGINIA | 233462 | 86840 | 0 | 1974 | 322276 |
| WASHINGTON | 425985 | 219024 | 0 | 1847 | 646856 |
| WEST VIRGINIA | 495633 | 329833 | 0 | 0 | 825466 |
| WISCONSIN | 322923 | 315040 | 5429 | 479263 | 1122655 |
| WYOMING | 56204 | 41362 | 661 | 86 | 98313 |

### 1938 HOUSE OF REPRESENTATIVES ELECTION

| | DEMOCRAT | REPUBLICAN | INDEPENDENT | OTHER | TOTAL VOTES CAST |
|---|---|---|---|---|---|
| ALABAMA | 114253 | 9573 | 49 | 1 | 123876 |
| ALASKA | --- | --- | --- | --- | --- |
| ARIZONA | 83556 | 20502 | 0 | 0 | 104058 |
| ARKANSAS | 144356 | 0 | 0 | 0 | 144356 |
| CALIFORNIA | 751190 | 530468 | 0 | 1109480 | 2391138 |
| COLORADO | 265297 | 181829 | 0 | 2411 | 449537 |
| CONNECTICUT | 250013 | 271329 | 0 | 108790 | 630132 |
| DELAWARE | 46989 | 60661 | 0 | 921 | 108571 |
| DIST OF COLUMBIA | --- | --- | --- | --- | --- |
| FLORIDA | 146356 | 6705 | 0 | 0 | 153061 |

| | | | | |
|---|---|---|---|---|
| GEORGIA | 67252 | 0 | 197 | 616 | 68065 |
| HAWAII | 95517 | 83167 | 0 | 0 | 178684 |
| IDAHO | 1572870 | 1456535 | 0 | 9339 | 3038744 |
| ILLINOIS | 773121 | 799455 | 0 | 73 | 1572649 |
| INDIANA | 352516 | 445939 | 0 | 4182 | 802637 |
| IOWA | 302329 | 434692 | 0 | 0 | 737021 |
| KANSAS | 315427 | 218331 | 210 | 0 | 533968 |
| KENTUCKY | 152366 | 0 | 44 | 0 | 152410 |
| LOUISIANA | 116774 | 117324 | 3225 | 0 | 237323 |
| MAINE | 290342 | 192168 | 957 | 3006 | 486473 |
| MARYLAND | 792848 | 925853 | 0 | 976 | 1719677 |
| MASSACHUSETTS | 714017 | 830394 | 0 | 2805 | 1547216 |
| MICHIGAN | 190036 | 537465 | 0 | 343426 | 1070927 |
| MINNESOTA | 35439 | 0 | 0 | 0 | 35439 |
| MISSISSIPPI | 737851 | 505605 | 0 | 1578 | 1245034 |
| MISSOURI | 104825 | 103885 | 0 | 0 | 208710 |
| MONTANA | 218116 | 247996 | 0 | 11603 | 477715 |
| NEBRASKA | 30156 | 15285 | 0 | 0 | 45441 |
| NEVADA | 79133 | 102140 | 0 | 0 | 181273 |
| NEW HAMPSHIRE | 719301 | 794609 | 3999 | 13212 | 1531121 |
| NEW JERSEY | 90608 | 64281 | 0 | 268 | 155157 |
| NEW MEXICO | 2363463 | 2000814 | 0 | 135975 | 4500252 |
| NEW YORK | 313621 | 160458 | 0 | 0 | 474079 |
| NORTH CAROLINA | 44691 | 149047 | 8109 | 0 | 201847 |
| NORTH DAKOTA | 1068916 | 1177982 | 0 | 0 | 2246898 |
| OHIO | 306241 | 137733 | 0 | 1850 | 445824 |
| OKLAHOMA | 151364 | 214571 | 0 | 8 | 365943 |
| OREGON | 1752592 | 2001068 | 0 | 20441 | 3774101 |
| PENNSYLVANIA | 138892 | 161016 | 0 | 310 | 300218 |
| RHODE ISLAND | 45806 | 298 | 0 | 92 | 46196 |
| SOUTH CAROLINA | 121285 | 153140 | 0 | 0 | 274425 |
| SOUTH DAKOTA | 170473 | 64152 | 20494 | 9355 | 264474 |
| TENNESSEE | 361689 | 3288 | 0 | 0 | 364977 |
| TEXAS | 111383 | 71149 | 0 | 0 | 182532 |
| UTAH | 40483 | 71901 | 0 | 13 | 112397 |
| VERMONT | 97531 | 26144 | 0 | 2368 | 126043 |
| VIRGINIA | 357686 | 227958 | 0 | 849 | 586493 |
| WASHINGTON | 343334 | 279487 | 0 | 0 | 622821 |
| WEST VIRGINIA | 166214 | 399451 | 11508 | 335129 | 912302 |
| WISCONSIN | 44525 | 49975 | 0 | 0 | 94500 |
| WYOMING | | | | | |

TABLE 3.7 (CONTINUED)

## 1940 HOUSE OF REPRESENTATIVES ELECTION

| | DEMOCRAT | REPUBLICAN | INDEPENDENT | OTHER | TOTAL VOTES CAST |
|---|---|---|---|---|---|
| ALABAMA | 254425 | 14796 | 342 | 0 | 269563 |
| ALASKA | --- | --- | --- | --- | --- |
| ARIZONA | 99424 | 40360 | 0 | 0 | 139784 |
| ARKANSAS | 199937 | 8566 | 0 | 0 | 208503 |
| CALIFORNIA | 630582 | 473268 | 0 | 1668104 | 2771954 |
| COLORADO | 286104 | 237254 | 0 | 1668 | 525026 |
| CONNECTICUT | 407868 | 365851 | 851 | 8023 | 782593 |
| DELAWARE | 68205 | 64384 | 0 | 2189 | 134778 |
| DIST OF COLUMBIA | --- | --- | --- | --- | --- |
| FLORIDA | 327837 | 52411 | 0 | 0 | 380248 |
| GEORGIA | 240399 | 10012 | 1495 | 121 | 252027 |
| HAWAII | --- | --- | --- | --- | --- |
| IDAHO | 123833 | 107803 | 0 | 0 | 231636 |
| ILLINOIS | 1968143 | 2050493 | 0 | 27975 | 4046611 |
| INDIANA | 864526 | 896841 | 0 | 200 | 1761567 |
| IOWA | 504371 | 610378 | 0 | 220 | 1114969 |
| KANSAS | 333796 | 454866 | 0 | 0 | 788662 |
| KENTUCKY | 557992 | 335241 | 0 | 0 | 893233 |
| LOUISIANA | 307102 | 13933 | 9 | 0 | 321044 |
| MAINE | 87286 | 159387 | 0 | 0 | 246673 |
| MARYLAND | 356667 | 228745 | 0 | 6 | 585418 |
| MASSACHUSETTS | 925462 | 1024746 | 0 | 4530 | 1954738 |
| MICHIGAN | 969328 | 1013774 | 0 | 4256 | 1987358 |
| MINNESOTA | 262895 | 640120 | 0 | 302738 | 1205753 |
| MISSISSIPPI | 148812 | 0 | 0 | 0 | 148812 |
| MISSOURI | 951656 | 864919 | 0 | 154 | 1816729 |
| MONTANA | 130453 | 106326 | 0 | 1196 | 237975 |
| NEBRASKA | 231873 | 320175 | 0 | 23268 | 575316 |
| NEVADA | 32714 | 18032 | 0 | 0 | 50746 |
| NEW HAMPSHIRE | 104694 | 113512 | 0 | 0 | 218206 |
| NEW JERSEY | 870406 | 979158 | 312 | 12564 | 1862440 |
| NEW MEXICO | 106972 | 75085 | 0 | 0 | 182057 |
| NEW YORK | 3199019 | 2830517 | 0 | 5679 | 6035215 |
| NORTH CAROLINA | 601972 | 195683 | 0 | 0 | 797655 |

| | DEMOCRAT | REPUBLICAN | INDEPENDENT | OTHER | TOTAL VOTES CAST |
|---|---|---|---|---|---|
| NORTH DAKOTA | 63662 | 148227 | 23399 | 0 | 235288 |
| OHIO | 1384800 | 1519628 | 0 | 0 | 2904428 |
| OKLAHOMA | 479433 | 245384 | 1639 | 3267 | 729723 |
| OREGON | 189702 | 263479 | 2642 | 6079 | 461902 |
| PENNSYLVANIA | 1993546 | 1834084 | 845 | 19139 | 3847614 |
| RHODE ISLAND | 174862 | 139526 | 0 | 0 | 314388 |
| SOUTH CAROLINA | 98176 | 1564 | 0 | 4 | 99744 |
| SOUTH DAKOTA | 116144 | 182457 | 0 | 0 | 298601 |
| TENNESSEE | 282337 | 105186 | 24565 | 5069 | 417757 |
| TEXAS | 986071 | 33271 | 0 | 76 | 1019418 |
| UTAH | 147528 | 97353 | 0 | 0 | 244881 |
| VERMONT | 50804 | 89637 | 0 | 36 | 140477 |
| VIRGINIA | 253562 | 60731 | 0 | 2283 | 316576 |
| WASHINGTON | 430442 | 313614 | 0 | 230 | 744286 |
| WEST VIRGINIA | 500012 | 370103 | 0 | 0 | 870115 |
| WISCONSIN | 220520 | 579526 | 0 | 469063 | 1269109 |
| WYOMING | 57030 | 49701 | 0 | 157 | 106888 |

## 1942 HOUSE OF REPRESENTATIVES ELECTION

| | DEMOCRAT | REPUBLICAN | INDEPENDENT | OTHER | TOTAL VOTES CAST |
|---|---|---|---|---|---|
| ALABAMA | 68724 | 378 | 0 | 29 | 69131 |
| ALASKA | --- | --- | --- | --- | --- |
| ARIZONA | 56357 | 23015 | 0 | 375 | 79747 |
| ARKANSAS | 98346 | 0 | 0 | 0 | 98346 |
| CALIFORNIA | 487700 | 430774 | 0 | 983062 | 1901536 |
| COLORADO | 141761 | 199365 | 0 | 1270 | 342396 |
| CONNECTICUT | 257941 | 283280 | 0 | 27784 | 569005 |
| DELAWARE | 38791 | 45376 | 0 | 559 | 84726 |
| DIST OF COLUMBIA | --- | --- | --- | --- | --- |
| FLORIDA | 91120 | 0 | 0 | 0 | 91120 |
| GEORGIA | 58352 | 0 | 3527 | 0 | 61879 |
| HAWAII | --- | --- | --- | --- | --- |
| IDAHO | 67920 | 71367 | 0 | 0 | 139287 |
| ILLINOIS | 1395053 | 1481419 | 0 | 11161 | 2887633 |
| INDIANA | 572903 | 713831 | 0 | 0 | 1286734 |
| IOWA | 252570 | 410472 | 0 | 1705 | 664747 |
| KANSAS | 194677 | 299015 | 0 | 0 | 493692 |

TABLE 3.7 (CONTINUED)

## 1942 HOUSE OF REPRESENTATIVES ELECTION

| | DEMOCRAT | REPUBLICAN | INDEPENDENT | OTHER | TOTAL VOTES CAST |
|---|---|---|---|---|---|
| KENTUCKY | 193181 | 110951 | 3806 | 0 | 307938 |
| LOUISIANA | 84987 | 0 | 0 | 0 | 84987 |
| MAINE | 48923 | 111918 | 0 | 0 | 160841 |
| MARYLAND | 189808 | 147628 | 0 | 0 | 337436 |
| MASSACHUSETTS | 611714 | 713423 | 0 | 2160 | 1327297 |
| MICHIGAN | 534682 | 629679 | 0 | 6333 | 1170694 |
| MINNESOTA | 151302 | 452192 | 0 | 152634 | 756128 |
| MISSISSIPPI | 51698 | 0 | 0 | 0 | 51698 |
| MISSOURI | 448078 | 476994 | 0 | 247 | 925319 |
| MONTANA | 93243 | 73654 | 0 | 2611 | 169508 |
| NEBRASKA | 122279 | 228024 | 0 | 7266 | 357569 |
| NEVADA | 21100 | 18289 | 0 | 0 | 39389 |
| NEW HAMPSHIRE | 70216 | 85999 | 0 | 0 | 156215 |
| NEW JERSEY | 546134 | 648359 | 0 | 8962 | 1203455 |
| NEW MEXICO | 57474 | 43371 | 0 | 0 | 100545 |
| NEW YORK | 1909706 | 1965794 | 0 | 74363 | 3949863 |
| NORTH CAROLINA | 228980 | 85847 | 0 | 0 | 314827 |
| NORTH DAKOTA | 47972 | 85936 | 0 | 48472 | 182380 |
| OHIO | 717692 | 945995 | 0 | 0 | 1663687 |
| OKLAHOMA | 202284 | 147764 | 896 | 783 | 351727 |
| OREGON | 115519 | 160904 | 0 | 2 | 276425 |
| PENNSYLVANIA | 1105992 | 1360664 | 0 | 22726 | 2489382 |
| RHODE ISLAND | 137653 | 98951 | 0 | 0 | 236604 |
| SOUTH CAROLINA | 23356 | 0 | 0 | 0 | 23356 |
| SOUTH DAKOTA | 66349 | 111762 | 0 | 0 | 178111 |
| TENNESSEE | 102143 | 52367 | 1701 | 0 | 156211 |
| TEXAS | 275101 | 2698 | 369 | 274 | 278442 |
| UTAH | 79879 | 70614 | 0 | 0 | 150493 |
| VERMONT | 17304 | 40751 | 0 | 15 | 58070 |
| VIRGINIA | 77087 | 11291 | 0 | 1689 | 90067 |
| WASHINGTON | 225025 | 202332 | 0 | 829 | 428186 |
| WEST VIRGINIA | 228549 | 231738 | 0 | 0 | 460287 |
| WISCONSIN | 203537 | 350812 | 0 | 194368 | 748717 |
| WYOMING | 36892 | 37965 | 0 | 0 | 74857 |

1944 HOUSE OF REPRESENTATIVES ELECTION

| | DEMOCRAT | REPUBLICAN | INDEPENDENT | OTHER | TOTAL VOTES CAST |
|---|---|---|---|---|---|
| ALABAMA | 200462 | 21876 | 0 | 0 | 222338 |
| ALASKA | --- | --- | --- | --- | --- |
| ARIZONA | 86691 | 39035 | 0 | 469 | 126195 |
| ARKANSAS | 200700 | 16515 | 0 | 0 | 217215 |
| CALIFORNIA | 1137504 | 1080205 | 0 | 789790 | 3007499 |
| COLORADO | 210275 | 281578 | 749 | 1260 | 493862 |
| CONNECTICUT | 424146 | 397725 | 0 | 5874 | 827745 |
| DELAWARE | 63649 | 62378 | 0 | 413 | 126440 |
| DIST OF COLUMBIA | --- | --- | --- | --- | --- |
| FLORIDA | 349570 | 63183 | 0 | 0 | 412753 |
| GEORGIA | 272454 | 0 | 2929 | 0 | 275383 |
| HAWAII | --- | --- | --- | --- | --- |
| IDAHO | 105830 | 99749 | 0 | 0 | 205579 |
| ILLINOIS | 2030755 | 1839518 | 0 | 12386 | 3882659 |
| INDIANA | 767157 | 872721 | 0 | 11339 | 1651217 |
| IOWA | 420340 | 552046 | 0 | 373 | 972759 |
| KANSAS | 245860 | 418332 | 0 | 0 | 664192 |
| KENTUCKY | 459936 | 381552 | 0 | 2355 | 843843 |
| LOUISIANA | 282569 | 0 | 0 | 0 | 282569 |
| MAINE | 53861 | 129910 | 0 | 0 | 183771 |
| MARYLAND | 310811 | 240129 | 0 | 0 | 550940 |
| MASSACHUSETTS | 887957 | 1001682 | 0 | 111 | 1889750 |
| MICHIGAN | 1028171 | 1126956 | 0 | 8381 | 2163508 |
| MINNESOTA | 452945 | 653150 | 0 | 3014 | 1109109 |
| MISSISSIPPI | 147869 | 5133 | 0 | 0 | 153002 |
| MISSOURI | 798374 | 722889 | 0 | 136 | 1521399 |
| MONTANA | 118131 | 77513 | 0 | 1573 | 197217 |
| NEBRASKA | 165689 | 336400 | 0 | 12777 | 514866 |
| NEVADA | 32648 | 19096 | 0 | 0 | 51744 |
| NEW HAMPSHIRE | 102364 | 113448 | 0 | 35 | 215847 |
| NEW JERSEY | 860326 | 988108 | 0 | 11044 | 1859478 |
| NEW MEXICO | 85244 | 66309 | 0 | 0 | 151553 |
| NEW YORK | 3172862 | 2827282 | 0 | 24453 | 6024597 |
| NORTH CAROLINA | 524274 | 230384 | 0 | 0 | 754658 |
| NORTH DAKOTA | 56699 | 101007 | 0 | 45330 | 203036 |
| OHIO | 1362843 | 1542422 | 0 | 0 | 2905265 |

330

TABLE 3.7 (CONTINUED)

## 1944 HOUSE OF REPRESENTATIVES ELECTION

| | DEMOCRAT | REPUBLICAN | INDEPENDENT | OTHER | TOTAL VOTES CAST |
|---|---|---|---|---|---|
| OKLAHOMA | 401232 | 282279 | 618 | 431 | 684560 |
| OREGON | 170264 | 272212 | 0 | 0 | 442476 |
| PENNSYLVANIA | 1880691 | 1827055 | 86 | 4798 | 3712630 |
| RHODE ISLAND | 175368 | 118011 | 102 | 0 | 293481 |
| SOUTH CAROLINA | 97360 | 3495 | 0 | 7 | 100862 |
| SOUTH DAKOTA | 78850 | 146888 | 0 | 0 | 225738 |
| TENNESSEE | 260694 | 131714 | 6224 | 0 | 398632 |
| TEXAS | 1000260 | 62626 | 0 | 763 | 1063649 |
| UTAH | 149599 | 98082 | 0 | 0 | 247681 |
| VERMONT | 46230 | 76800 | 0 | 6 | 123036 |
| VIRGINIA | 239347 | 71604 | 10811 | 0 | 342980 |
| WASHINGTON | 426036 | 375554 | 0 | 21218 | 803093 |
| WEST VIRGINIA | 389738 | 328771 | 0 | 1503 | 718509 |
| WISCONSIN | 399320 | 617679 | 0 | 81043 | 1098942 |
| WYOMING | 42569 | 53533 | 0 | 0 | 96102 |

## 1946 HOUSE OF REPRESENTATIVES ELECTION

| | DEMOCRAT | REPUBLICAN | INDEPENDENT | OTHER | TOTAL VOTES CAST |
|---|---|---|---|---|---|
| ALABAMA | 165383 | 14105 | 0 | 0 | 179488 |
| ALASKA | -- | -- | -- | -- | -- |
| ARIZONA | 71836 | 37033 | 0 | 831 | 109700 |
| ARKANSAS | 143252 | 3776 | 4305 | 0 | 151333 |
| CALIFORNIA | 638387 | 772916 | 0 | 923959 | 2335262 |
| COLORADO | 145692 | 184429 | 710 | 1151 | 331982 |
| CONNECTICUT | 277872 | 377972 | 0 | 23922 | 679766 |
| DELAWARE | 49105 | 63516 | 0 | 0 | 112621 |
| DIST OF COLUMBIA | -- | -- | -- | -- | -- |
| FLORIDA | 151123 | 35640 | 0 | 0 | 186763 |
| GEORGIA | 141961 | 0 | 31 | 29 | 142021 |

| State | | | | | |
|---|---|---|---|---|---|
| HAWAII | --- | --- | --- | --- | --- |
| IDAHO | 77740 | 101018 | 0 | 0 | 178758 |
| ILLINOIS | 1539248 | 1906717 | 0 | 12924 | 3458889 |
| INDIANA | 588639 | 725622 | 0 | 18373 | 1332634 |
| IOWA | 228039 | 364992 | 0 | 0 | 599031 |
| KANSAS | 223173 | 328642 | 0 | 3045 | 554860 |
| KENTUCKY | 271480 | 257196 | 1 | 320 | 528996 |
| LOUISIANA | 100357 | 5651 | 0 | 0 | 106009 |
| MAINE | 63860 | 110388 | 0 | 0 | 174248 |
| MARYLAND | 232498 | 212457 | 0 | 0 | 444955 |
| MASSACHUSETTS | 744765 | 863274 | 0 | 9275 | 1617314 |
| MICHIGAN | 619318 | 975363 | 0 | 10051 | 1604732 |
| MINNESOTA | 357758 | 514784 | 0 | 2463 | 875005 |
| MISSISSIPPI | 50037 | 0 | 0 | 0 | 50037 |
| MISSOURI | 517980 | 566296 | 0 | 0 | 1084276 |
| MONTANA | 95982 | 93265 | 0 | 841 | 190088 |
| NEBRASKA | 118800 | 248724 | 0 | 4516 | 372040 |
| NEVADA | 20187 | 28859 | 0 | 0 | 49046 |
| NEW HAMPSHIRE | 61220 | 99872 | 0 | 0 | 161092 |
| NEW JERSEY | 553964 | 815261 | 0 | 12768 | 1381993 |
| NEW MEXICO | 65242 | 60519 | 0 | 0 | 125761 |
| NEW YORK | 2176040 | 2522927 | 0 | 13443 | 4712410 |
| NORTH CAROLINA | 277277 | 174945 | 0 | 0 | 452222 |
| NORTH DAKOTA | 29865 | 103205 | 0 | 0 | 133070 |
| OHIO | 871660 | 1281864 | 0 | 0 | 2153524 |
| OKLAHOMA | 287978 | 204163 | 0 | 0 | 492141 |
| OREGON | 117665 | 217005 | 0 | 0 | 334670 |
| PENNSYLVANIA | 1306723 | 1795552 | 0 | 9712 | 3111987 |
| RHODE ISLAND | 148673 | 122887 | 890 | 0 | 272450 |
| SOUTH CAROLINA | 26067 | 243 | 0 | 48 | 26358 |
| SOUTH DAKOTA | 58073 | 104731 | 0 | 0 | 162804 |
| TENNESSEE | 126530 | 58704 | 8210 | 4 | 193448 |
| TEXAS | 335437 | 17175 | 0 | 29 | 352641 |
| UTAH | 95486 | 101186 | 0 | 0 | 196672 |
| VERMONT | 26056 | 46985 | 0 | 25 | 73066 |
| VIRGINIA | 167919 | 81626 | 2026 | 2293 | 253864 |
| WASHINGTON | 267187 | 375715 | 2028 | 0 | 644930 |
| WEST VIRGINIA | 269306 | 268051 | 0 | 0 | 537357 |
| WISCONSIN | 312289 | 615287 | 41475 | 14515 | 983566 |
| WYOMING | 34946 | 44512 | 0 | 0 | 79458 |

TABLE 3.7 (CONTINUED)

1948 HOUSE OF REPRESENTATIVES ELECTION

| | DEMOCRAT | REPUBLICAN | INDEPENDENT | OTHER | TOTAL VOTES CAST |
|---|---|---|---|---|---|
| ALABAMA | 183519 | 13564 | 0 | 0 | 197083 |
| ALASKA | --- | --- | --- | --- | --- |
| ARIZONA | 96631 | 60004 | 1478 | 862 | 158975 |
| ARKANSAS | 230927 | 22027 | 0 | 0 | 252954 |
| CALIFORNIA | 588615 | 781647 | 229193 | 1961935 | 3561390 |
| COLORADO | 272484 | 224927 | 0 | 0 | 497411 |
| CONNECTICUT | 429348 | 433311 | 10329 | 6363 | 879351 |
| DELAWARE | 68909 | 71127 | 0 | 499 | 140535 |
| DIST OF COLUMBIA | --- | --- | --- | --- | --- |
| FLORIDA | 295330 | 55803 | 0 | 0 | 351133 |
| GEORGIA | 365176 | 0 | 4 | 230 | 365410 |
| HAWAII | --- | --- | --- | --- | --- |
| IDAHO | 105852 | 103094 | 3130 | 93 | 212169 |
| ILLINOIS | 2001650 | 1823266 | 23721 | 3 | 3848640 |
| INDIANA | 836852 | 782346 | 1076 | 13127 | 1633401 |
| IOWA | 429048 | 517207 | 2167 | 1322 | 949744 |
| KANSAS | 299478 | 404432 | 0 | 0 | 703910 |
| KENTUCKY | 416014 | 260382 | 686 | 3140 | 680222 |
| LOUISIANA | 308239 | 13437 | 0 | 0 | 321676 |
| MAINE | 72114 | 141780 | 0 | 0 | 213894 |
| MARYLAND | 291011 | 231003 | 12172 | 0 | 534186 |
| MASSACHUSETTS | 976241 | 970179 | 0 | 55 | 1946475 |
| MICHIGAN | 1022761 | 1024507 | 1608 | 15660 | 2064536 |
| MINNESOTA | 588628 | 593088 | 0 | 10 | 1181726 |
| MISSISSIPPI | 152285 | 252 | 0 | 0 | 152537 |
| MISSOURI | 914886 | 641851 | 3039 | 336 | 1560112 |
| MONTANA | 122987 | 91061 | 0 | 501 | 214549 |
| NEBRASKA | 191831 | 268620 | 0 | 0 | 460451 |
| NEVADA | 29733 | 28972 | 0 | 0 | 58705 |
| NEW HAMPSHIRE | 94551 | 124299 | 1513 | 0 | 220363 |
| NEW JERSEY | 880881 | 937820 | 24780 | 10032 | 1853513 |
| NEW MEXICO | 108529 | 76695 | 805 | 0 | 186029 |
| NEW YORK | 2827421 | 2657769 | 512148 | 109 | 5997447 |

| | DEMOCRAT | REPUBLICAN | INDEPENDENT | STATE RIGHTS | OTHER | TOTAL VOTES CAST |
|---|---|---|---|---|---|---|
| NORTH CAROLINA | 540873 | 219295 | 3345 | 0 | 0 | 763513 |
| NORTH DAKOTA | 56702 | 128454 | 0 | 1758 | 0 | 186914 |
| OHIO | 1455972 | 1342409 | 0 | 0 | 0 | 2798381 |
| OKLAHOMA | 457371 | 222390 | 0 | 0 | 0 | 679761 |
| OREGON | 143083 | 296387 | 18741 | 32931 | 0 | 491142 |
| PENNSYLVANIA | 1782985 | 1864161 | 6969 | 2914 | 0 | 3657029 |
| RHODE ISLAND | 193631 | 124881 | 0 | 0 | 0 | 318512 |
| SOUTH CAROLINA | 133732 | 6907 | 0 | 19 | 0 | 140658 |
| SOUTH DAKOTA | 104945 | 135775 | 0 | 0 | 0 | 240720 |
| TENNESSEE | 261294 | 186191 | 0 | 1488 | 0 | 448973 |
| TEXAS | 983944 | 65350 | 1449 | 0 | 0 | 1050743 |
| UTAH | 159411 | 114922 | 0 | 0 | 0 | 274333 |
| VERMONT | 47767 | 74076 | 0 | 125 | 0 | 121968 |
| VIRGINIA | 255176 | 121474 | 4205 | 2305 | 0 | 383160 |
| WASHINGTON | 402505 | 401334 | 13739 | 0 | 0 | 817578 |
| WEST VIRGINIA | 442554 | 316077 | 0 | 0 | 0 | 758631 |
| WISCONSIN | 513818 | 676501 | 10382 | 10267 | 0 | 1210968 |
| WYOMING | 47246 | 50218 | 0 | 0 | 0 | 97464 |

## 1950 HOUSE OF REPRESENTATIVES ELECTION

| | DEMOCRAT | REPUBLICAN | INDEPENDENT | STATE RIGHTS | OTHER | TOTAL VOTES CAST |
|---|---|---|---|---|---|---|
| ALABAMA | 151212 | 980 | 0 | 0 | 0 | 152192 |
| ALASKA | --- | --- | --- | --- | --- | --- |
| ARIZONA | 115517 | 62150 | 0 | 0 | 0 | 177667 |
| ARKANSAS | 295802 | 0 | 0 | 0 | 0 | 295802 |
| CALIFORNIA | 845655 | 886713 | 112725 | 0 | 1513549 | 3358642 |
| COLORADO | 214385 | 225986 | 1287 | 0 | 1234 | 442892 |
| CONNECTICUT | 426485 | 433912 | 2353 | 0 | 15638 | 878388 |
| DELAWARE | 56091 | 73313 | 0 | 0 | 0 | 129404 |
| DIST OF COLUMBIA | --- | --- | --- | --- | --- | --- |
| FLORIDA | 228786 | 24263 | 0 | 0 | 0 | 253049 |
| GEORGIA | 260155 | 0 | 0 | 0 | 14 | 260169 |
| HAWAII | --- | --- | --- | --- | --- | --- |
| IDAHO | 91295 | 108789 | 0 | 0 | 0 | 200084 |
| ILLINOIS | 1616550 | 1891277 | 1135 | 0 | 424 | 3509386 |
| INDIANA | 727467 | 850357 | 0 | 0 | 9485 | 1587309 |
| IOWA | 317222 | 500426 | 0 | 147 | 2164 | 819959 |
| KANSAS | 248897 | 355849 | 0 | 0 | 0 | 604746 |

TABLE 3.7 (CONTINUED)

## 1950 HOUSE OF REPRESENTATIVES ELECTION

| | DEMOCRAT | REPUBLICAN | INDEPENDENT | STATE RIGHTS | OTHER | TOTAL VOTES CAST |
|---|---|---|---|---|---|---|
| KENTUCKY | 307836 | 180778 | 0 | 0 | 0 | 488614 |
| LOUISIANA | 227075 | 0 | 0 | 0 | 0 | 227075 |
| MAINE | 100731 | 136901 | 0 | 0 | 0 | 237632 |
| MARYLAND | 283727 | 285957 | 3243 | 0 | 0 | 572927 |
| MASSACHUSETTS | 920988 | 930280 | 2205 | 0 | 5923 | 1859396 |
| MICHIGAN | 838752 | 956447 | 2563 | 0 | 6916 | 1804678 |
| MINNESOTA | 473710 | 538973 | 4255 | 0 | 1329 | 1018267 |
| MISSISSIPPI | 82696 | 2861 | 2199 | 0 | 0 | 87756 |
| MISSOURI | 697542 | 552014 | 0 | 0 | 594 | 1250150 |
| MONTANA | 108248 | 99948 | 1389 | 0 | 942 | 210527 |
| NEBRASKA | 164490 | 271840 | 0 | 0 | 0 | 436330 |
| NEVADA | 31843 | 28485 | 0 | 0 | 0 | 60328 |
| NEW HAMPSHIRE | 72760 | 112487 | 0 | 0 | 0 | 185247 |
| NEW JERSEY | 689814 | 859145 | 13973 | 0 | 8331 | 1571263 |
| NEW MEXICO | 97187 | 75447 | 0 | 0 | 0 | 172634 |
| NEW YORK | 2442119 | 2384402 | 225368 | 0 | 0 | 5051889 |
| NORTH CAROLINA | 365598 | 156602 | 0 | 0 | 0 | 522200 |
| NORTH DAKOTA | 32946 | 119047 | 0 | 0 | 0 | 151993 |
| OHIO | 1237409 | 1447154 | 0 | 0 | 0 | 2684563 |
| OKLAHOMA | 363452 | 243334 | 0 | 0 | 0 | 606786 |
| OREGON | 201096 | 288355 | 10038 | 0 | 0 | 499489 |
| PENNSYLVANIA | 1672788 | 1834128 | 3024 | 0 | 1949 | 3511889 |
| RHODE ISLAND | 183104 | 112589 | 0 | 0 | 0 | 295693 |
| SOUTH CAROLINA | 50381 | 0 | 0 | 0 | 19 | 50400 |
| SOUTH DAKOTA | 97720 | 150706 | 0 | 0 | 0 | 248426 |
| TENNESSEE | 165405 | 92014 | 5189 | 0 | 2 | 262610 |
| TEXAS | 326231 | 34314 | 0 | 0 | 0 | 360545 |
| UTAH | 138444 | 125403 | 0 | 0 | 0 | 263847 |
| VERMONT | 22709 | 65248 | 0 | 0 | 894 | 88851 |
| VIRGINIA | 155396 | 51493 | 2973 | 0 | 1968 | 211830 |
| WASHINGTON | 342162 | 378419 | 2750 | 0 | 274 | 723605 |
| WEST VIRGINIA | 374921 | 287915 | 0 | 0 | 0 | 662836 |
| WISCONSIN | 470275 | 639293 | 0 | 0 | 386 | 1109954 |
| WYOMING | 42483 | 50865 | 0 | 0 | 0 | 93348 |

1952 HOUSE OF REPRESENTATIVES ELECTION

| | DEMOCRAT | REPUBLICAN | INDEPENDENT | OTHER | TOTAL VOTES CAST |
|---|---|---|---|---|---|
| ALABAMA | 324153 | 18673 | 0 | 0 | 342826 |
| ALASKA | --- | | --- | --- | |
| ARIZONA | 127867 | 120533 | 0 | 0 | 248400 |
| ARKANSAS | 308838 | 51889 | 1196 | 0 | 361923 |
| CALIFORNIA | 1219448 | 1474818 | 4959 | 1864435 | 4563660 |
| COLORADO | 269865 | 335394 | 0 | 1307 | 606566 |
| CONNECTICUT | 489645 | 601238 | 0 | 3065 | 1093948 |
| DELAWARE | 81730 | 88285 | 0 | 0 | 170015 |
| DIST OF COLUMBIA | --- | | --- | --- | |
| FLORIDA | 550013 | 191582 | 0 | 0 | 741595 |
| GEORGIA | 547095 | 0 | 0 | 179 | 547274 |
| HAWAII | --- | | --- | --- | |
| IDAHO | 107417 | 157181 | 0 | 4 | 264602 |
| ILLINOIS | 2004628 | 2348725 | 0 | 5 | 4353358 |
| INDIANA | 830758 | 1093589 | 0 | 11216 | 1935563 |
| IOWA | 378763 | 762310 | 0 | 1989 | 1143062 |
| KANSAS | 334278 | 489661 | 0 | 0 | 823939 |
| KENTUCKY | 495420 | 454802 | 573 | 0 | 950795 |
| LOUISIANA | 380242 | 36161 | 0 | 0 | 416403 |
| MAINE | 76708 | 156727 | 0 | 0 | 233435 |
| MARYLAND | 405225 | 436113 | 0 | 0 | 841338 |
| MASSACHUSETTS | 1064454 | 1209742 | 0 | 14519 | 2288715 |
| MICHIGAN | 1316374 | 1457342 | 0 | 8218 | 2781934 |
| MINNESOTA | 638773 | 749415 | 0 | 0 | 1388188 |
| MISSISSIPPI | 234728 | 6024 | 0 | 0 | 240752 |
| MISSOURI | 971199 | 890237 | 0 | 0 | 1861436 |
| MONTANA | 110882 | 144296 | 0 | 888 | 256066 |
| NEBRASKA | 179849 | 386432 | 0 | 0 | 566281 |
| NEVADA | 39912 | 40683 | 0 | 0 | 80595 |
| NEW HAMPSHIRE | 95119 | 162750 | 0 | 0 | 257869 |
| NEW JERSEY | 977914 | 1317404 | 0 | 20259 | 2315577 |
| NEW MEXICO | 121477 | 112297 | 0 | 0 | 233774 |
| NEW YORK | 3193711 | 3618645 | 0 | 98031 | 6910387 |
| NORTH CAROLINA | 763388 | 358810 | 0 | 0 | 1122198 |
| NORTH DAKOTA | 49829 | 181218 | 0 | 0 | 231047 |
| OHIO | 1471110 | 1836354 | 74821 | 0 | 3382285 |

TABLE 3.7 (CONTINUED)

## 1952 HOUSE OF REPRESENTATIVES ELECTION

|  | DEMOCRAT | REPUBLICAN | INDEPENDENT | OTHER | TOTAL VOTES CAST |
|---|---|---|---|---|---|
| OKLAHOMA | 545713 | 383859 | 1573 | 0 | 931145 |
| OREGON | 257743 | 408349 | 0 | 0 | 666092 |
| PENNSYLVANIA | 2151247 | 2363167 | 0 | 3311 | 4517725 |
| RHODE ISLAND | 220461 | 186828 | 0 | 0 | 407289 |
| SOUTH CAROLINA | 278180 | 5577 | 0 | 95 | 283852 |
| SOUTH DAKOTA | 90338 | 197137 | 0 | 0 | 287475 |
| TENNESSEE | 479641 | 203766 | 16972 | 16 | 700395 |
| TEXAS | 1514776 | 465035 | 0 | 596 | 1980407 |
| UTAH | 144982 | 181841 | 0 | 0 | 326823 |
| VERMONT | 43187 | 109871 | 0 | 2 | 153060 |
| VIRGINIA | 298238 | 138604 | 9495 | 503 | 446840 |
| WASHINGTON | 515213 | 504783 | 0 | 517 | 1020513 |
| WEST VIRGINIA | 471175 | 403427 | 0 | 0 | 874602 |
| WISCONSIN | 602521 | 965590 | 0 | 0 | 1568111 |
| WYOMING | 50559 | 76161 | 0 | 0 | 126720 |

## 1954 HOUSE OF REPRESENTATIVES ELECTION

|  | DEMOCRAT | REPUBLICAN | INDEPENDENT | OTHER | TOTAL VOTES CAST |
|---|---|---|---|---|---|
| ALABAMA | 268552 | 11236 | 0 | 1 | 279789 |
| ALASKA | --- | --- | --- | --- | --- |
| ARIZONA | 121392 | 102010 | 0 | 0 | 223402 |
| ARKANSAS | 280264 | 4 | 0 | 6 | 280274 |
| CALIFORNIA | 1791637 | 1876626 | 0 | 205063 | 3873326 |
| COLORADO | 239565 | 240074 | 0 | 415 | 480054 |
| CONNECTICUT | 455887 | 474585 | 0 | 5413 | 930472 |
| DELAWARE | 79201 | 65035 | 0 | 0 | 144236 |
| DIST OF COLUMBIA | --- | --- | --- | --- | --- |
| FLORIDA | 255150 | 71137 | 0 | 0 | 326287 |
| GEORGIA | 317703 | 29911 | 0 | 5129 | 352743 |

| State | | | | | |
|---|---|---|---|---|---|
| HAWAII | 102895 | 123117 | 0 | 0 | 226012 |
| IDAHO | 1636443 | 1621278 | 0 | 1 | 3257722 |
| ILLINOIS | 747800 | 833304 | 0 | 5527 | 1586631 |
| INDIANA | 338931 | 478322 | 0 | 0 | 817253 |
| IOWA | 267531 | 347458 | 0 | 0 | 614989 |
| KANSAS | 431992 | 236194 | 302 | 0 | 668488 |
| KENTUCKY | 208111 | 8212 | 0 | 0 | 216323 |
| LOUISIANA | 108548 | 132895 | 0 | 0 | 241443 |
| MAINE | 342115 | 295426 | 0 | 1334 | 638875 |
| MARYLAND | 844835 | 834665 | 0 | 102722 | 1782222 |
| MASSACHUSETTS | 1100939 | 1028093 | 0 | 4358 | 2133390 |
| MICHIGAN | 600116 | 531376 | 0 | 0 | 1131492 |
| MINNESOTA | 101298 | 0 | 0 | 0 | 101298 |
| MISSISSIPPI | 665722 | 519091 | 0 | 0 | 1184813 |
| MISSOURI | 117109 | 107478 | 0 | 0 | 224587 |
| MONTANA | 156343 | 250347 | 0 | 0 | 406690 |
| NEBRASKA | 35318 | 42321 | 0 | 0 | 77639 |
| NEVADA | 86999 | 105062 | 0 | 0 | 192061 |
| NEW HAMPSHIRE | 862382 | 907839 | 18904 | 474 | 1789599 |
| NEW JERSEY | 111713 | 76528 | 0 | 0 | 188241 |
| NEW MEXICO | 2478502 | 2505228 | 0 | 14560 | 4998290 |
| NEW YORK | 390167 | 214012 | 0 | 0 | 604179 |
| NORTH CAROLINA | 64089 | 106341 | 0 | 0 | 170430 |
| NORTH DAKOTA | 1113334 | 1340847 | 44656 | 0 | 2498837 |
| OHIO | 354339 | 191450 | 0 | 0 | 545789 |
| OKLAHOMA | 257108 | 307386 | 0 | 0 | 564494 |
| OREGON | 1871625 | 1824186 | 0 | 99 | 3695910 |
| PENNSYLVANIA | 195200 | 130859 | 0 | 0 | 326059 |
| RHODE ISLAND | 210624 | 2711 | 0 | 31 | 213366 |
| SOUTH CAROLINA | 93894 | 137273 | 0 | 0 | 231167 |
| SOUTH DAKOTA | 204911 | 139885 | 0 | 1 | 344797 |
| TENNESSEE | 555446 | 75472 | 0 | 0 | 630918 |
| TEXAS | 116625 | 146406 | 0 | 0 | 263031 |
| UTAH | 44141 | 70143 | 0 | 0 | 114284 |
| VERMONT | 204433 | 128315 | 9370 | 226 | 342344 |
| VIRGINIA | 464045 | 342089 | 0 | 3661 | 809795 |
| WASHINGTON | 339958 | 251534 | 0 | 0 | 591492 |
| WEST VIRGINIA | 541776 | 598919 | 0 | 0 | 1140695 |
| WISCONSIN | 47660 | 61111 | 0 | 0 | 108771 |
| WYOMING | | | 0 | 0 | |

TABLE 3.7 (CONTINUED)

## 1956 HOUSE OF REPRESENTATIVES ELECTION

| | DEMOCRAT | REPUBLICAN | INDEPENDENT | OTHER | TOTAL VOTES CAST |
|---|---|---|---|---|---|
| ALABAMA | 334146 | 53022 | 0 | 4 | 387172 |
| ALASKA | --- | --- | --- | --- | --- |
| ARIZONA | 146915 | 133594 | 0 | 0 | 280509 |
| ARKANSAS | 235645 | 34318 | 0 | 0 | 269963 |
| CALIFORNIA | 2225027 | 2466620 | 0 | 486236 | 5177883 |
| COLORADO | 332051 | 296502 | 0 | 1 | 628554 |
| CONNECTICUT | 428709 | 683387 | 0 | 0 | 1112096 |
| DELAWARE | 84644 | 91538 | 0 | 0 | 176182 |
| DIST OF COLUMBIA | --- | --- | --- | --- | --- |
| FLORIDA | 589574 | 352149 | 0 | 0 | 941723 |
| GEORGIA | 522072 | 59234 | 10938 | 13 | 592257 |
| HAWAII | --- | --- | --- | --- | --- |
| IDAHO | 120722 | 139712 | 0 | 0 | 260434 |
| ILLINOIS | 1967104 | 2272995 | 0 | 1 | 4240100 |
| INDIANA | 864351 | 1092427 | 0 | 4603 | 1961381 |
| IOWA | 533641 | 636573 | 0 | 0 | 1170214 |
| KANSAS | 387096 | 438868 | 0 | 1417 | 827381 |
| KENTUCKY | 505482 | 461644 | 0 | 113 | 967239 |
| LOUISIANA | 330270 | 57385 | 0 | 0 | 387655 |
| MAINE | 142041 | 150415 | 0 | 0 | 292456 |
| MARYLAND | 444418 | 421382 | 0 | 0 | 865800 |
| MASSACHUSETTS | 1092697 | 1156137 | 0 | 672 | 2249506 |
| MICHIGAN | 1490834 | 1500172 | 0 | 3668 | 2994674 |
| MINNESOTA | 712406 | 676104 | 0 | 0 | 1388510 |
| MISSISSIPPI | 205532 | 0 | 0 | 0 | 205532 |
| MISSOURI | 1011057 | 681724 | 0 | 0 | 1692781 |
| MONTANA | 146449 | 116755 | 0 | 0 | 263204 |
| NEBRASKA | 220372 | 323641 | 0 | 2389 | 546402 |
| NEVADA | 51100 | 43154 | 0 | 0 | 94254 |
| NEW HAMPSHIRE | 97830 | 155315 | 0 | 0 | 253145 |
| NEW JERSEY | 972620 | 1391535 | 0 | 23447 | 2387602 |
| NEW MEXICO | 128330 | 114719 | 0 | 0 | 243049 |
| NEW YORK | 3140990 | 3745059 | 0 | 762 | 6886811 |

| | DEMOCRAT | REPUBLICAN | INDEPENDENT | OTHER | TOTAL VOTES CAST |
|---|---|---|---|---|---|
| NORTH CAROLINA | 716201 | 309071 | 0 | 0 | 1025272 |
| NORTH DAKOTA | 85743 | 143514 | 0 | 0 | 229257 |
| OHIO | 1444705 | 1936662 | 0 | 0 | 3381367 |
| OKLAHOMA | 485321 | 326993 | 401 | 0 | 812715 |
| OREGON | 380391 | 338303 | 0 | 0 | 718694 |
| PENNSYLVANIA | 2131833 | 2386657 | 0 | 289 | 4518779 |
| RHODE ISLAND | 202228 | 173282 | 0 | 0 | 375510 |
| SOUTH CAROLINA | 249591 | 12278 | 0 | 135 | 262004 |
| SOUTH DAKOTA | 145500 | 142516 | 0 | 0 | 288016 |
| TENNESSEE | 401385 | 278980 | 0 | 942 | 681307 |
| TEXAS | 1436831 | 21868 | 0 | 0 | 1458699 |
| UTAH | 135503 | 193790 | 0 | 0 | 329293 |
| VERMONT | 50797 | 103736 | 0 | 0 | 154533 |
| VIRGINIA | 415872 | 279660 | 828 | 425 | 696785 |
| WASHINGTON | 621118 | 439896 | 0 | 0 | 1061014 |
| WEST VIRGINIA | 428264 | 378130 | 0 | 0 | 806394 |
| WISCONSIN | 696731 | 825305 | 0 | 0 | 1522036 |
| WYOMING | 50225 | 69903 | 0 | 0 | 120128 |

## 1958 HOUSE OF REPRESENTATIVES ELECTION

| | DEMOCRAT | REPUBLICAN | INDEPENDENT | OTHER | TOTAL VOTES CAST |
|---|---|---|---|---|---|
| ALABAMA | 231112 | 6050 | 0 | 0 | 237162 |
| ALASKA | 27945 | 20699 | 0 | 0 | 48644 |
| ARIZONA | 139467 | 138099 | 0 | 0 | 277566 |
| ARKANSAS | --- | --- | --- | 30739 | --- |
| CALIFORNIA | 2260362 | 1981276 | 0 | 712127 | 4953765 |
| COLORADO | 309873 | 222971 | 0 | 1175 | 534019 |
| CONNECTICUT | 542315 | 425452 | 0 | 0 | 967767 |
| DELAWARE | 76797 | 76099 | 0 | 0 | 152896 |
| DIST OF COLUMBIA | --- | --- | --- | --- | --- |
| FLORIDA | 354942 | 139419 | 0 | 0 | 494361 |
| GEORGIA | 158636 | 1 | 0 | 1 | 158638 |
| HAWAII | --- | --- | --- | --- | --- |
| IDAHO | 124297 | 114731 | 0 | 0 | 239028 |
| ILLINOIS | 1754248 | 1411178 | 7026 | 0 | 3172452 |
| INDIANA | 921795 | 798850 | 0 | 819 | 1721464 |

TABLE 3.7 (CONTINUED)

## 1958 HOUSE OF REPRESENTATIVES ELECTION

| | DEMOCRAT | REPUBLICAN | INDEPENDENT | OTHER | TOTAL VOTES CAST |
|---|---|---|---|---|---|
| IOWA | 417118 | 412798 | 0 | 0 | 829916 |
| KANSAS | 359763 | 354732 | 0 | 3199 | 717694 |
| KENTUCKY | 309771 | 164425 | 0 | 1622 | 475818 |
| LOUISIANA | 177963 | 4160 | 1 | 0 | 182124 |
| MAINE | 146356 | 128606 | 0 | 0 | 274962 |
| MARYLAND | 463888 | 248238 | 0 | 0 | 712126 |
| MASSACHUSETTS | 1021174 | 754373 | 0 | 671 | 1776218 |
| MICHIGAN | 1193696 | 1054854 | 0 | 5260 | 2253810 |
| MINNESOTA | 596257 | 534870 | 0 | 0 | 1131127 |
| MISSISSIPPI | 61464 | 0 | 0 | 0 | 61464 |
| MISSOURI | 736877 | 42994C | 0 | 0 | 1166817 |
| MONTANA | 147726 | 80744 | 0 | 0 | 228470 |
| NEBRASKA | 195450 | 220140 | 0 | 0 | 415590 |
| NEVADA | 55053 | 27275 | 0 | 0 | 82328 |
| NEW HAMPSHIRE | 81263 | 115370 | 0 | 868 | 197501 |
| NEW JERSEY | 938603 | 944349 | 2817 | 20683 | 1906452 |
| NEW MEXICO | 124924 | 70925 | 0 | 0 | 195849 |
| NEW YORK | 2822815 | 2699291 | 0 | 810 | 5522916 |
| NORTH CAROLINA | 431202 | 177651 | 0 | 0 | 608853 |
| NORTH DAKOTA | 99562 | 92124 | 0 | 0 | 191686 |
| OHIO | 1581014 | 1529565 | 0 | 0 | 3110579 |
| OKLAHOMA | 369271 | 159168 | 1336 | 0 | 529775 |
| OREGON | 338858 | 257028 | 0 | 41 | 595927 |
| PENNSYLVANIA | 2019994 | 1940666 | 0 | 538 | 3961198 |
| RHODE ISLAND | 214931 | 125523 | 0 | 188 | 340642 |
| SOUTH CAROLINA | 76632 | 0 | 0 | 15 | 76647 |
| SOUTH DAKOTA | 132693 | 125296 | 0 | 0 | 257989 |
| TENNESSEE | 276870 | 92999 | 0 | 1936 | 371805 |
| TEXAS | 673773 | 91287 | 0 | 3789 | 768849 |
| UTAH | 140948 | 145375 | 0 | 0 | 286323 |
| VERMONT | 63131 | 59536 | 0 | 0 | 122667 |
| VIRGINIA | 318633 | 86211 | 26350 | 415 | 431609 |
| WASHINGTON | 406195 | 467678 | 0 | 2436 | 876309 |
| WEST VIRGINIA | 380983 | 234804 | 0 | 0 | 615787 |
| WISCONSIN | 633152 | 547873 | 0 | 0 | 1181025 |
| WYOMING | 51886 | 59894 | 0 | 0 | 111780 |

1960 HOUSE OF REPRESENTATIVES ELECTION

| | DEMOCRAT | REPUBLICAN | INDEPENDENT | OTHER | TOTAL VOTES CAST |
|---|---|---|---|---|---|
| ALABAMA | 389567 | 48117 | 0 | 29 | 437713 |
| ALASKA | 33546 | 25517 | 0 | 0 | 59063 |
| ARIZONA | 179188 | 197374 | 0 | 0 | 376562 |
| ARKANSAS | 57617 | 12054 | 0 | 0 | 69671 |
| CALIFORNIA | 3194735 | 2855115 | 0 | 142698 | 6192548 |
| COLORADO | 370487 | 344792 | 0 | 0 | 715279 |
| CONNECTICUT | 657680 | 560803 | 0 | 2350 | 1218483 |
| DELAWARE | 98227 | 96337 | 0 | 0 | 194564 |
| DIST OF COLUMBIA | --- | --- | --- | --- | --- |
| FLORIDA | 861261 | 386513 | 0 | 0 | 1247774 |
| GEORGIA | 549405 | 24551 | 1 | 315 | 574272 |
| HAWAII | 135827 | 46812 | 0 | 0 | 182639 |
| IDAHO | 159024 | 131266 | 0 | 0 | 290290 |
| ILLINOIS | 2299523 | 2235048 | 0 | 2 | 4534573 |
| INDIANA | 1032679 | 1087952 | 0 | 1707 | 2122338 |
| IOWA | 563358 | 662864 | 0 | 0 | 1226222 |
| KANSAS | 398892 | 471995 | 0 | 0 | 870887 |
| KENTUCKY | 539253 | 373773 | 0 | 0 | 913026 |
| LOUISIANA | 441533 | 78478 | 0 | 0 | 520011 |
| MAINE | 177442 | 230834 | 0 | 0 | 408276 |
| MARYLAND | 582315 | 398490 | 0 | 0 | 980805 |
| MASSACHUSETTS | 1378332 | 880079 | 0 | 551 | 2258962 |
| MICHIGAN | 1638588 | 1567845 | 0 | 5112 | 3211545 |
| MINNESOTA | 759893 | 749770 | 5459 | 0 | 1515122 |
| MISSISSIPPI | 252741 | 5036 | 0 | 0 | 257777 |
| MISSOURI | 1062939 | 780432 | 0 | 0 | 1843371 |
| MONTANA | 138588 | 133624 | 0 | 0 | 272212 |
| NEBRASKA | 251931 | 327246 | 0 | 0 | 579177 |
| NEVADA | 59616 | 43986 | 0 | 0 | 103602 |
| NEW HAMPSHIRE | 118862 | 165819 | 0 | 0 | 284681 |
| NEW JERSEY | 1275882 | 1361844 | 1394 | 19905 | 2659025 |
| NEW MEXICO | 172577 | 124101 | 0 | 807 | 297485 |
| NEW YORK | 3756044 | 3263706 | 0 | 0 | 7019750 |
| NORTH CAROLINA | 786983 | 515488 | 0 | 0 | 1302471 |
| NORTH DAKOTA | 109207 | 127118 | 0 | 0 | 236325 |
| OHIO | 1766362 | 2080270 | 0 | 0 | 3846632 |

TABLE 3.7 (CONTINUED)

### 1960 HOUSE OF REPRESENTATIVES ELECTION

|  | DEMOCRAT | REPUBLICAN | INDEPENDENT | OTHER | TOTAL VOTES CAST |
|---|---|---|---|---|---|
| OKLAHOMA | 459463 | 378131 | 0 | 0 | 837594 |
| OREGON | 389569 | 372187 | 0 | 81 | 761837 |
| PENNSYLVANIA | 2554885 | 2396322 | 0 | 2888 | 4954095 |
| RHODE ISLAND | 268706 | 123532 | 0 | 0 | 392238 |
| SOUTH CAROLINA | 328326 | 0 | 0 | 0 | 328438 |
| SOUTH DAKOTA | 132421 | 168583 | 0 | 112 | 301004 |
| TENNESSEE | 440103 | 202711 | 0 | 0 | 642819 |
| TEXAS | 1680675 | 279839 | 0 | 5 | 2039138 |
| UTAH | 186710 | 182752 | 0 | 78624 | 369462 |
| VERMONT | 71111 | 94905 | 0 | 0 | 166035 |
| VIRGINIA | 411015 | 199656 | 0 | 19 | 639991 |
| WASHINGTON | 478208 | 646517 | 0 | 29320 | 1124725 |
| WEST VIRGINIA | 468127 | 353353 | 0 | 0 | 820480 |
| WISCONSIN | 813217 | 845994 | 0 | 3882 | 1663093 |
| WYOMING | 64090 | 70241 | 0 | 0 | 134331 |

### 1962 HOUSE OF REPRESENTATIVES ELECTION

|  | DEMOCRAT | REPUBLICAN | INDEPENDENT | OTHER | TOTAL VOTES CAST |
|---|---|---|---|---|---|
| ALABAMA | 293182 | 138963 | 0 | 32446 | 464591 |
| ALASKA | 31953 | 26638 | 0 | 0 | 58591 |
| ARIZONA | 169632 | 179392 | 0 | 0 | 349024 |
| ARKANSAS | --- | 47805 | --- | 29 | --- |
| CALIFORNIA | 2891518 | 2679662 | 0 | 2166 | 5573346 |
| COLORADO | 282474 | 314122 | 0 | 0 | 596596 |
| CONNECTICUT | 543424 | 487575 | -0 | 1677 | 1030999 |
| DELAWARE | 81166 | 71934 | 0 | 256 | 153356 |
| DIST OF COLUMBIA | --- | --- | --- | --- | --- |
| FLORIDA | 588719 | 351954 | 0 | 162 | 940835 |
| GEORGIA | 272494 | 59559 | 94 | 1224 | 333371 |

| | | | | | |
|---|---|---|---|---|---|
| HAWAII | 123649 | 70880 | 0 | 0 | 194529 |
| IDAHO | 134574 | 119755 | 0 | 0 | 254329 |
| ILLINOIS | 1802063 | 1820824 | 0 | 2422 | 3625309 |
| INDIANA | 878311 | 911596 | 0 | 802 | 1790709 |
| IOWA | 370362 | 432483 | 0 | 0 | 802845 |
| KANSAS | 249556 | 375726 | 860 | 0 | 625282 |
| KENTUCKY | 372388 | 258182 | 0 | 0 | 631430 |
| LOUISIANA | 303813 | 42419 | 0 | 0 | 346232 |
| MAINE | 127288 | 158213 | 0 | 0 | 285501 |
| MARYLAND | 388107 | 308792 | 0 | 0 | 696899 |
| MASSACHUSETTS | 1146884 | 808240 | 0 | 15358 | 1970482 |
| MICHIGAN | 1392221 | 1282082 | 0 | 4950 | 2679253 |
| MINNESOTA | 599124 | 605054 | 0 | 0 | 1204178 |
| MISSISSIPPI | 157153 | 0 | 4461 | 0 | 161614 |
| MISSOURI | 683877 | 528447 | 0 | 0 | 1212324 |
| MONTANA | 119366 | 129075 | 0 | 8794 | 248441 |
| NEBRASKA | 164403 | 271777 | 0 | 0 | 444974 |
| NEVADA | 66866 | 26458 | 0 | 0 | 9324 |
| NEW HAMPSHIRE | 99449 | 121803 | 4455 | 9716 | 221252 |
| NEW JERSEY | 980509 | 964280 | 0 | 0 | 1958960 |
| NEW MEXICO | 128651 | 116262 | 0 | 1359 | 244913 |
| NEW YORK | 2872313 | 2686099 | 0 | 0 | 5559771 |
| NORTH CAROLINA | 482146 | 336383 | 0 | 0 | 818529 |
| NORTH DAKOTA | 98749 | 117533 | 0 | 0 | 216282 |
| OHIO | 1164776 | 1786018 | 0 | 0 | 2950794 |
| OKLAHOMA | 381827 | 242876 | 0 | 85 | 624703 |
| OREGON | 342209 | 288571 | 0 | 1059 | 630865 |
| PENNSYLVANIA | 2135717 | 2217431 | 0 | 0 | 4354207 |
| RHODE ISLAND | 207517 | 111141 | 0 | 0 | 318658 |
| SOUTH CAROLINA | 225714 | 36808 | 0 | 32 | 262554 |
| SOUTH DAKOTA | 101664 | 151067 | 0 | 0 | 252731 |
| TENNESSEE | 345066 | 212362 | 17185 | 31294 | 605907 |
| TEXAS | 870860 | 680839 | 0 | 0 | 1551699 |
| UTAH | 149620 | 167387 | 0 | 0 | 317007 |
| VERMONT | 52535 | 68822 | 0 | 0 | 121357 |
| VIRGINIA | 268699 | 178913 | 800 | 540 | 448952 |
| WASHINGTON | 337832 | 543318 | 0 | 0 | 881150 |
| WEST VIRGINIA | 343274 | 269744 | 0 | 107 | 613018 |
| WISCONSIN | 620317 | 623907 | 0 | 0 | 1244331 |
| WYOMING | 44985 | 71489 | 0 | 0 | 116474 |

TABLE 3.7 (CONTINUED)

1964 HOUSE OF REPRESENTATIVES ELECTION

| | DEMOCRAT | REPUBLICAN | INDEPENDENT | OTHER | TOTAL VOTES CAST |
|---|---|---|---|---|---|
| ALABAMA | 297951 | 317160 | 0 | 2018 | 617129 |
| ALASKA | 34605 | 32566 | 0 | 0 | 67171 |
| ARIZONA | 230733 | 230091 | 0 | 0 | 460824 |
| ARKANSAS | --- | 58884 | --- | --- | --- |
| CALIFORNIA | 3609315 | 3213798 | 0 | 586 | 6823699 |
| COLORADO | 440090 | 316322 | 0 | 1183 | 757595 |
| CONNECTICUT | 752983 | 456233 | 0 | 163 | 1209379 |
| DELAWARE | 112361 | 86254 | 0 | 76 | 198691 |
| DIST OF COLUMBIA | --- | --- | --- | --- | --- |
| FLORIDA | 991897 | 420856 | 0 | 2600 | 1415353 |
| GEORGIA | 562422 | 248024 | 25006 | 72 | 835524 |
| HAWAII | 140224 | 89425 | 0 | 0 | 229649 |
| IDAHO | 140225 | 144306 | 0 | 0 | 284531 |
| ILLINOIS | 2492433 | 2082167 | 0 | 7 | 4574607 |
| INDIANA | 1094999 | 977548 | 0 | 734 | 2073281 |
| IOWA | 622844 | 516929 | 0 | 1798 | 1141571 |
| KANSAS | 362162 | 451526 | 0 | 0 | 813688 |
| KENTUCKY | 618489 | 336696 | 0 | 0 | 955185 |
| LOUISIANA | 429567 | 171137 | 0 | 0 | 600704 |
| MAINE | 206126 | 163376 | 0 | 0 | 369502 |
| MARYLAND | 683143 | 301250 | 0 | 0 | 984393 |
| MASSACHUSETTS | 1313448 | 647789 | 7440 | 139657 | 2108334 |
| MICHIGAN | 1767716 | 1289291 | 0 | 2631 | 3059638 |
| MINNESOTA | 826879 | 691118 | 0 | 1311 | 1519308 |
| MISSISSIPPI | 325950 | 35277 | 0 | 0 | 361227 |
| MISSOURI | 1107512 | 664563 | 201 | 0 | 1772276 |
| MONTANA | 136308 | 139658 | 0 | 644 | 276610 |
| NEBRASKA | 272922 | 288153 | 0 | 0 | 561075 |
| NEVADA | 82748 | 47989 | 0 | 0 | 130737 |
| NEW HAMPSHIRE | 141479 | 137619 | 0 | 4 | 279102 |
| NEW JERSEY | 1482674 | 1227600 | 0 | 9398 | 2719672 |
| NEW MEXICO | 194407 | 120349 | 0 | 0 | 314756 |
| NEW YORK | 4009673 | 2698888 | 0 | 45212 | 6753773 |
| NORTH CAROLINA | 787902 | 516340 | 0 | 0 | 1304242 |

| | DEMOCRAT | REPUBLICAN | INDEPENDENT | OTHER | TOTAL VOTES CAST |
|---|---|---|---|---|---|
| NORTH DAKOTA | 123959 | 124453 | 232 | 0 | 248644 |
| OHIO | 1872351 | 1716480 | 0 | 0 | 3588831 |
| OKLAHOMA | 529728 | 310563 | 0 | 0 | 840291 |
| OREGON | 461690 | 305682 | 0 | 385 | 767757 |
| PENNSYLVANIA | 2613413 | 2062907 | 0 | 0 | 4676320 |
| RHODE ISLAND | 278430 | 94657 | 0 | 0 | 373087 |
| SOUTH CAROLINA | 395390 | 48970 | 0 | 2501 | 446861 |
| SOUTH DAKOTA | 123265 | 164448 | 0 | 0 | 287713 |
| TENNESSEE | 581011 | 416750 | 11441 | 24496 | 1033698 |
| TEXAS | 1690674 | 826991 | 0 | 9223 | 2526888 |
| UTAH | 209522 | 186498 | 0 | 0 | 396020 |
| VERMONT | 71193 | 86650 | 5575 | 34 | 163452 |
| VIRGINIA | 536527 | 322570 | 30387 | 25 | 889509 |
| WASHINGTON | 613420 | 583765 | 0 | 337 | 1197522 |
| WEST VIRGINIA | 450202 | 320183 | 0 | 0 | 770385 |
| WISCONSIN | 858858 | 789809 | 0 | 164 | 1648831 |
| WYOMING | 70693 | 68482 | 0 | 0 | 139175 |

1966 HOUSE OF REPRESENTATIVES ELECTION

| | DEMOCRAT | REPUBLICAN | INDEPENDENT | OTHER | TOTAL VOTES CAST |
|---|---|---|---|---|---|
| ALABAMA | 432422 | 278088 | 0 | 0 | 710519 |
| ALASKA | 31867 | 34040 | 0 | 0 | 65907 |
| ARIZONA | 159945 | 204478 | 0 | 0 | 364423 |
| ARKANSAS | --- | 130742 | --- | --- | --- |
| CALIFORNIA | 2937862 | 3336943 | 0 | 3796 | 6278601 |
| COLORADO | 339750 | 298472 | 0 | 2263 | 640485 |
| CONNECTICUT | 543149 | 443319 | 14461 | 2688 | 1003617 |
| DELAWARE | 72132 | 90961 | 0 | 0 | 163093 |
| DIST OF COLUMBIA | --- | --- | --- | --- | --- |
| FLORIDA | 680466 | 368976 | 0 | 4333 | 1053775 |
| GEORGIA | 557883 | 292150 | 0 | 755 | 850788 |
| HAWAII | 140880 | 67281 | 0 | 0 | 208161 |
| IDAHO | 98794 | 149434 | 0 | 0 | 248228 |
| ILLINOIS | 1707576 | 2027714 | 0 | 20 | 3735310 |
| INDIANA | 779588 | 897086 | 1363 | 0 | 1678037 |
| IOWA | 417740 | 458948 | 0 | 2280 | 878968 |
| KANSAS | 241571 | 416610 | 2349 | 0 | 660530 |

TABLE 3.7 (CONTINUED)

1966 HOUSE OF REPRESENTATIVES ELECTION

| | DEMOCRAT | REPUBLICAN | INDEPENDENT | OTHER | TOTAL VOTES CAST |
|---|---|---|---|---|---|
| KENTUCKY | 357345 | 319636 | 0 | 143 | 677124 |
| LOUISIANA | 447006 | 99252 | 0 | 0 | 546258 |
| MAINE | 167258 | 138460 | 7098 | 0 | 312816 |
| MARYLAND | 429380 | 336043 | 0 | 0 | 765423 |
| MASSACHUSETTS | 1098362 | 713144 | 0 | 78 | 1811584 |
| MICHIGAN | 1150400 | 1216202 | 0 | 0 | 2366602 |
| MINNESOTA | 590327 | 630049 | 0 | 0 | 1220376 |
| MISSISSIPPI | 282574 | 61514 | 31654 | 0 | 375742 |
| MISSOURI | 561112 | 484098 | 0 | 0 | 1045210 |
| MONTANA | 117431 | 140940 | 0 | 0 | 258371 |
| NEBRASKA | 178518 | 292603 | 0 | 0 | 471121 |
| NEVADA | 86467 | 41383 | 0 | 0 | 127850 |
| NEW HAMPSHIRE | 89588 | 139085 | 0 | 142 | 228815 |
| NEW JERSEY | 1020779 | 1045641 | 22832 | 8739 | 2097991 |
| NEW MEXICO | 140057 | 110441 | 0 | 0 | 250498 |
| NEW YORK | 2860394 | 2375909 | 255487 | 21569 | 5513059 |
| NORTH CAROLINA | 484413 | 432036 | 0 | 0 | 916449 |
| NORTH DAKOTA | 80687 | 116812 | 0 | 0 | 197499 |
| OHIO | 1196149 | 1599492 | 0 | 0 | 2795641 |
| OKLAHOMA | 333597 | 302792 | 0 | 0 | 636389 |
| OREGON | 314881 | 349902 | 0 | 96 | 664879 |
| PENNSYLVANIA | 1895621 | 2070037 | 0 | 0 | 3965658 |
| RHODE ISLAND | 196957 | 124531 | 0 | 534 | 322022 |
| SOUTH CAROLINA | 257153 | 106775 | 0 | 345 | 364273 |
| SOUTH DAKOTA | 81391 | 143655 | 0 | 0 | 225046 |
| TENNESSEE | 382296 | 382824 | 34739 | 12 | 799871 |
| TEXAS | 1037344 | 206419 | 5773 | 8935 | 1258471 |
| UTAH | 111261 | 196176 | 0 | 0 | 307437 |
| VERMONT | 46643 | 89097 | 0 | 8 | 135748 |
| VIRGINIA | 391538 | 268094 | 14827 | 8278 | 682737 |
| WASHINGTON | 474021 | 449765 | 12576 | 3079 | 939441 |
| WEST VIRGINIA | 262023 | 232322 | 0 | 0 | 494345 |
| WISCONSIN | 532897 | 620786 | 235 | 23 | 1153941 |
| WYOMING | 57442 | 62984 | 0 | 0 | 120426 |

## 1968 HOUSE OF REPRESENTATIVES ELECTION

| | DEMOCRAT | REPUBLICAN | INDEPENDENT | OTHER | TOTAL VOTES CAST |
|---|---|---|---|---|---|
| ALABAMA | 638844 | 247438 | 23422 | 0 | 909704 |
| ALASKA | 36785 | 43577 | 0 | 0 | 80362 |
| ARIZONA | 202967 | 260663 | 0 | 0 | 463630 |
| ARKANSAS | --- | 158055 | 56647 | --- | --- |
| CALIFORNIA | 3089104 | 3665712 | 56647 | 190523 | 7001986 |
| COLORADO | 362164 | 392779 | 7917 | 25499 | 780442 |
| CONNECTICUT | 625278 | 569957 | 0 | 3406 | 1206558 |
| DELAWARE | 82993 | 117827 | 0 | 0 | 200820 |
| DIST OF COLUMBIA | --- | --- | --- | --- | --- |
| FLORIDA | 1011749 | 757907 | 0 | 28 | 1769684 |
| GEORGIA | 750538 | 194129 | 0 | 166 | 944833 |
| HAWAII | 161954 | 78733 | 4377 | 4458 | 245145 |
| IDAHO | 116258 | 155899 | 0 | 0 | 276534 |
| ILLINOIS | 2053892 | 2368310 | 0 | 21 | 4422223 |
| INDIANA | 943806 | 1094964 | 0 | 366 | 2039136 |
| IOWA | 513529 | 608875 | 0 | 7 | 1122411 |
| KANSAS | 309551 | 507733 | 0 | 0 | 817284 |
| KENTUCKY | 440974 | 421010 | 1535 | 1721 | 865240 |
| LOUISIANA | 511355 | 117626 | 0 | 0 | 628981 |
| MAINE | 215870 | 168347 | 0 | 0 | 384217 |
| MARYLAND | 535819 | 483829 | 53047 | 0 | 1019648 |
| MASSACHUSETTS | 1032731 | 971190 | 0 | 477 | 2057445 |
| MICHIGAN | 1532693 | 1506972 | 0 | 4014 | 3043679 |
| MINNESOTA | 731536 | 801209 | 0 | 1299 | 1534044 |
| MISSISSIPPI | 415021 | 33683 | 953 | 0 | 448704 |
| MISSOURI | 959354 | 760123 | 0 | 0 | 1720430 |
| MONTANA | 114726 | 148750 | 0 | 0 | 263476 |
| NEBRASKA | 208356 | 309218 | 0 | 4597 | 522171 |
| NEVADA | 104136 | 40209 | 0 | 0 | 144345 |
| NEW HAMPSHIRE | 93901 | 188878 | 17438 | 4 | 282783 |
| NEW JERSEY | 1274653 | 1378203 | 1487 | 27746 | 2698040 |
| NEW MEXICO | 147975 | 160374 | 406457 | 0 | 309836 |
| NEW YORK | 3110178 | 2567251 | 0 | 10557 | 6094443 |
| NORTH CAROLINA | 765065 | 635396 | 0 | 0 | 1400461 |
| NORTH DAKOTA | 94347 | 140076 | 0 | 3692 | 238115 |

TABLE 3.7 (CONTINUED)

## 1968 HOUSE OF REPRESENTATIVES ELECTION

| | DEMOCRAT | REPUBLICAN | INDEPENDENT | OTHER | TOTAL VOTES CAST |
|---|---|---|---|---|---|
| OHIO | 1428021 | 2207658 | 0 | 599 | 3636278 |
| OKLAHOMA | 444995 | 364866 | 0 | 0 | 809861 |
| OREGON | 370036 | 417107 | 0 | 81 | 787224 |
| PENNSYLVANIA | 2286363 | 2229184 | 0 | 61826 | 4577373 |
| RHODE ISLAND | 221989 | 140896 | 1684 | 209 | 364778 |
| SOUTH CAROLINA | 416131 | 203902 | 7749 | 6 | 627788 |
| SOUTH DAKOTA | 112421 | 159219 | 0 | 0 | 271640 |
| TENNESSEE | 485833 | 507996 | 18552 | 22 | 1012403 |
| TEXAS | 1720408 | 675574 | 0 | 0 | 2395982 |
| UTAH | 195392 | 220404 | 0 | 0 | 415796 |
| VERMONT | 61720 | 95236 | 0 | 177 | 157133 |
| VIRGINIA | 621065 | 600893 | 46255 | 661 | 1268874 |
| WASHINGTON | 623630 | 576072 | 1736 | 2643 | 1204081 |
| WEST VIRGINIA | 434080 | 277925 | 0 | 0 | 712005 |
| WISCONSIN | 741661 | 895370 | 877 | 2993 | 1640901 |
| WYOMING | 45950 | 77363 | 0 | 0 | 123313 |

## 1970 HOUSE OF REPRESENTATIVES ELECTION

| | DEMOCRAT | REPUBLICAN | OTHER | TOTAL VOTES CAST |
|---|---|---|---|---|
| ALABAMA | 475095 | 189050 | 77927 | 742072 |
| ALASKA | 44137 | 35947 | 0 | 80084 |
| ARIZONA | 182256 | 218506 | 1357 | 402119 |
| ARKANSAS | --- | --- | --- | --- |
| CALIFORNIA | 3169817 | 3047735 | 101842 | 6319394 |
| COLORADO | 310027 | 317696 | 9335 | 637058 |
| CONNECTICUT | 531523 | 524953 | -14028 | 1070504 |
| DELAWARE | 71429 | 86125 | 2759 | 160313 |
| DIST OF COLUMBIA | --- | --- | --- | --- |

| | --- | --- | --- | --- |
|---|---|---|---|---|
| FLORIDA | 653513 | 225632 | 96 | 879241 |
| GEORGIA | 176449 | 31764 | 0 | 208213 |
| HAWAII | 87615 | 143943 | 2625 | 234183 |
| IDAHO | 1814064 | 1670861 | 53 | 3484978 |
| ILLINOIS | 878841 | 848785 | 0 | 1727626 |
| INDIANA | 387510 | 388428 | 3753 | 779691 |
| IOWA | 303988 | 407264 | 8419 | 719671 |
| KANSAS | 247585 | 222813 | 3265 | 473663 |
| KENTUCKY | 330464 | 19703 | 12881 | 363048 |
| LOUISIANA | 195718 | 122313 | 0 | 318031 |
| MAINE | 452549 | 430300 | 2695 | 885544 |
| MARYLAND | 1019657 | 718052 | 62789 | 1800498 |
| MASSACHUSETTS | 1314448 | 1241474 | 6476 | 2562398 |
| MICHIGAN | 709635 | 623583 | 2408 | 1335626 |
| MINNESOTA | 269193 | 28847 | 14317 | 312357 |
| MISSISSIPPI | 692026 | 493557 | 11824 | 1197407 |
| MISSOURI | 141257 | 108140 | 0 | 249397 |
| MONTANA | 164558 | 242507 | 41034 | 448099 |
| NEBRASKA | 113496 | 24147 | 0 | 137643 |
| NEVADA | 67256 | 146389 | 0 | 213645 |
| NEW HAMPSHIRE | 1100262 | 986242 | 14151 | 2100655 |
| NEW JERSEY | 129116 | 152261 | 0 | 281377 |
| NEW MEXICO | 2422171 | 2216721 | 806980 | 5445872 |
| NEW YORK | 513905 | 410742 | 5301 | 929948 |
| NORTH CAROLINA | 88104 | 122056 | 0 | 210160 |
| NORTH DAKOTA | 1323271 | 1706205 | 12535 | 3042011 |
| OHIO | 428706 | 245216 | 1534 | 675456 |
| OKLAHOMA | 337998 | 314724 | 268 | 652990 |
| OREGON | 1945360 | 1611619 | 56084 | 3613063 |
| PENNSYLVANIA | 207987 | 114781 | 2845 | 325613 |
| RHODE ISLAND | 309487 | 115531 | 1947 | 426965 |
| SOUTH CAROLINA | 127561 | 107422 | 0 | 234983 |
| SOUTH DAKOTA | 579783 | 403233 | 4938 | 987954 |
| TENNESSEE | 1339012 | 476824 | 17388 | 1833224 |
| TEXAS | 182499 | 186818 | 3583 | 372900 |
| UTAH | 44415 | 103806 | 4336 | 152557 |
| VERMONT | 464781 | 413748 | 25471 | 904000 |
| VIRGINIA | 608508 | 403946 | 9670 | 1022124 |
| WASHINGTON | 286006 | 152877 | 0 | 438883 |
| WEST VIRGINIA | 740485 | 576575 | 8964 | 1326024 |
| WISCONSIN | 58456 | 57848 | 0 | 116304 |
| WYOMING | | | | |

TABLE 3.7 (CONTINUED)

1972 HOUSE OF REPRESENTATIVES ELECTION

| | DEMOCRAT | REPUBLICAN | OTHER | TOTAL VOTES CAST |
|---|---|---|---|---|
| ALABAMA | 581688 | 383623 | 7318 | 972629 |
| ALASKA | 53651 | 41750 | 0 | 95401 |
| ARIZONA | 284045 | 309862 | 0 | 593907 |
| ARKANSAS | 42481 | 144571 | --- | --- |
| CALIFORNIA | 4209741 | 3779472 | 173728 | 8162941 |
| COLORADO | 428259 | 480059 | 4562 | 912880 |
| CONNECTICUT | 657265 | 690839 | 2897 | 1351001 |
| DELAWARE | 83230 | 141237 | 1384 | 225851 |
| DIST OF COLUMBIA | 95300 | 39487 | 24825 | 159612 |
| FLORIDA | 1030817 | 900683 | 10 | --- |
| GEORGIA | 638826 | 252901 | 79 | 891806 |
| HAWAII | 153682 | 121181 | 0 | 274863 |
| IDAHO | 108187 | 187807 | 5560 | 301554 |
| ILLINOIS | 2146823 | 2223260 | 14895 | 4384978 |
| INDIANA | 973706 | 1133646 | 2884 | 2110236 |
| IOWA | 616378 | 577425 | 1933 | 1195736 |
| KANSAS | 280653 | 581900 | 15812 | 878365 |
| KENTUCKY | 493795 | 487820 | 4362 | 985977 |
| LOUISIANA | 573977 | 86607 | 17844 | 678428 |
| MAINE | 218543 | 194868 | 0 | 413411 |
| MARYLAND | 634087 | 584859 | 0 | 1218946 |
| MASSACHUSETTS | 1245430 | 806717 | 106853 | 2159000 |
| MICHIGAN | 1535707 | 1710177 | 27290 | 3273174 |
| MINNESOTA | 896854 | 760620 | 32312 | 1689786 |
| MISSISSIPPI | 387389 | 184598 | 16086 | 588073 |
| MISSOURI | 1092405 | 737377 | 2846 | 1832628 |
| MONTANA | 190597 | 124436 | 0 | 315033 |
| NEBRASKA | 193644 | 375065 | 61 | 568770 |
| NEVADA | 86349 | 94113 | 0 | 180462 |
| NEW HAMPSHIRE | 94255 | 222753 | 26 | 317034 |
| NEW JERSEY | 1390819 | 1416485 | 24605 | 2831909 |
| NEW MEXICO | 210391 | 163187 | 0 | 373578 |
| NEW YORK | 3049560 | 2924748 | 634616 | 6608888 |
| NORTH CAROLINA | 734627 | 609926 | 6194 | 1350747 |

| | DEMOCRATIC | REPUBLICAN | OTHER | TOTAL VOTES CAST |
|---|---|---|---|---|
| NORTH DAKOTA | 72850 | 195360 | 511 | 268721 |
| OHIO | 1684303 | 2071040 | 80200 | 3835543 |
| OKLAHOMA | 496657 | 310180 | 10244 | 817081 |
| OREGON | 479024 | 390138 | 568 | 869730 |
| PENNSYLVANIA | 2172844 | 2281484 | 8461 | 4462789 |
| RHODE ISLAND | 243444 | 138786 | 5762 | 367992 |
| SOUTH CAROLINA | 328860 | 301695 | 102 | 630657 |
| SOUTH DAKOTA | 159857 | 141135 | 0 | 300992 |
| TENNESSEE | 504782 | 589272 | 8341 | 1102395 |
| TEXAS | 2032183 | 835185 | 18581 | 2885949 |
| UTAH | 259859 | 203481 | 9728 | 473068 |
| VERMONT | 65062 | 120924 | 42 | 186028 |
| VIRGINIA | 627298 | 589573 | 54117 | 1270988 |
| WASHINGTON | 857621 | 442811 | 1401 | 1301833 |
| WEST VIRGINIA | 426389 | 294811 | 0 | 721200 |
| WISCONSIN | 1012821 | 767139 | 21134 | 1801094 |
| WYOMING | 75632 | 70667 | 0 | 146299 |

1974 HOUSE OF REPRESENTATIVES ELECTION

| | DEMOCRATIC | REPUBLICAN | OTHER | TOTAL VOTES CAST |
|---|---|---|---|---|
| ALABAMA | 375,976 | 169,304 | 16,120 | 561,400 |
| ALASKA | 44,280 | 51,641 | — | 95,921 |
| ARIZONA | 269,489 | 266,117 | 8,217 | 543,823 |
| ARKANSAS | 267,573 | 156,183 | — | 423,756 |
| CALIFORNIA | 3,265,153 | 2,334,870 | 145,735 | 5,745,758 |
| COLORADO | 413,533 | 364,470 | 6,735 | 784,738 |
| CONNECTICUT | 620,029 | 440,207 | 18,297 | 1,078,533 |
| DELAWARE | 63,490 | 93,826 | 3,012 | 160,328 |
| FLORIDA | 477,121 | 580,975 | 3,524 | 1,061,620 |
| GEORGIA | 588,538 | 233,769 | 116 | 822,423 |
| HAWAII | 158,468 | 101,049 | — | 259,517 |
| IDAHO | 107,600 | 142,678 | — | 250,278 |
| ILLINOIS | 1,601,152 | 1,218,921 | 22,036 | 2,842,109 |
| INDIANA | 956,675 | 770,154 | 4,005 | 1,730,834 |
| IOWA | 488,214 | 413,230 | 2,025 | 903,469 |
| KANSAS | 325,400 | 417,956 | 32,202 | 775,558 |
| KENTUCKY | 425,272 | 238,637 | 15,316 | 679,225 |

352

TABLE 3.7 (CONTINUED)

1974 HOUSE OF REPRESENTATIVES ELECTION

| | DEMOCRATIC | REPUBLICAN | OTHER | TOTAL VOTES CAST |
|---|---|---|---|---|
| LOUISIANA | 396,581 | 140,008 | 9,453 | 546,042 |
| MAINE | 140,923 | 212,357 | — | 353,280 |
| MARYLAND | 526,809 | 347,280 | — | 874,089 |
| MASSACHUSETTS | 1,168,252 | 401,300 | 129,149 | 1,698,701 |
| MICHIGAN | 1,467,038 | 1,017,785 | 34,581 | 2,519,404 |
| MINNESOTA | 705,139 | 491,912 | 21,806 | 1,218,857 |
| MISSISSIPPI | 156,119 | 130,999 | 18,791 | 305,909 |
| MISSOURI | 809,719 | 396,617 | 2,706 | 1,209,042 |
| MONTANA | 148,984 | 236,076 | 119 | 254,146 |
| NEBRASKA | 211,496 | 105,162 | — | 447,691 |
| NEVADA | 93,665 | 61,182 | 13,119 | 167,966 |
| NEW HAMPSHIRE | 96,851 | 122,678 | — | 219,529 |
| NEW JERSEY | 1,240,933 | 794,698 | 47,926 | 2,083,557 |
| NEW MEXICO | 162,095 | 149,313 | 4,929 | 316,337 |
| NEW YORK | 2,573,185 | 1,846,094 | 297,428 | 4,894,349 |
| NORTH CAROLINA | 637,833 | 347,603 | 2,904 | 988,340 |
| NORTH DAKOTA | 103,504 | 130,184 | — | 233,688 |
| OHIO | 1,396,530 | 1,458,222 | 90,163 | 2,944,925 |
| OKLAHOMA | 294,704 | 208,243 | 3,365 | 506,312 |
| OREGON | 482,462 | 270,319 | 414 | 753,195 |
| PENNSYLVANIA | 1,937,154 | 1,421,944 | 18,179 | 3,377,277 |
| RHODE ISLAND | 230,047 | 73,824 | — | 303,871 |
| SOUTH CAROLINA | 301,516 | 212,893 | 2,803 | 517,212 |
| SOUTH DAKOTA | 105,458 | 167,012 | — | 272,470 |
| TENNESSEE | 533,402 | 363,502 | 4,925 | 901,829 |
| TEXAS | 1,074,982 | 406,744 | 6,524 | 1,488,250 |
| UTAH | 230,532 | 163,066 | 19,364 | 412,962 |
| VERMONT | 53,701 | 74,561 | 12,637 | 140,899 |
| VIRGINIA | 506,838 | 361,302 | 56,046 | 924,186 |
| WASHINGTON | 574,055 | 400,557 | 6,313 | 980,925 |
| WEST VIRGINIA | 290,146 | 125,368 | — | 415,514 |
| WISCONSIN | 703,992 | 475,292 | 17,286 | 1,196,570 |
| WYOMING | 69,434 | 57,499 | — | 126,933 |

TABLE 3.7 (CONTINUED)

1976 HOUSE OF REPRESENTATIVES ELECTION

| | DEMOCRATIC | REPUBLICAN | OTHER | TOTAL VOTES CAST |
|---|---|---|---|---|
| ALABAMA | 667,032 | 314,970 | 2,179 | 984,181 |
| ALASKA | 34,194 | 83,722 | 292 | 118,208 |
| ARIZONA | 355,747 | 340,478 | 32,777 | 729,002 |
| ARKANSAS | 260,997 | 75,384 | 8 | 336,389 |
| CALIFORNIA | 4,144,324 | 3,220,448 | 77,729 | 7,442,501 |
| COLORADO | 454,741 | 536,879 | 29,369 | 1,020,989 |
| CONNECTICUT | 681,730 | 651,250 | 15,492 | 1,348,472 |
| DELAWARE | 102,411 | 110,636 | 2,038 | 215,085 |
| FLORIDA | 1,125,762 | 937,257 | 19,511 | 2,082,530 |
| GEORGIA | 929,929 | 321,891 | 478 | 1,252,298 |
| HAWAII | 184,166 | 77,662 | 31,873 | 293,701 |
| IDAHO | 161,899 | 180,008 | —— | 341,907 |
| ILLINOIS | 2,246,614 | 2,112,868 | 6,569 | 4,366,051 |
| INDIANA | 1,166,368 | 932,002 | 4,718 | 2,103,188 |
| IOWA | 709,435 | 526,677 | 5,990 | 1,242,102 |
| KANSAS | 348,621 | 545,240 | 15,430 | 909,291 |
| KENTUCKY | 605,680 | 374,086 | 9,182 | 988,948 |
| LOUISIANA | 624,098 | 364,582 | 25,657 | 1,014,337 |
| MAINE | 151,255 | 314,815 | 7,0005 | 473,175 |
| MARYLAND | 789,029 | 473,316 | 53,526 | 1,315,871 |
| MASSACHUSETTS | 1,509,521 | 723,119 | 361,622 | 2,594,262 |
| MICHIGAN | 1,898,241 | 1,503,114 | 30,543 | 3,431,898 |
| MINNESOTA | 1,039,999 | 729,577 | 24,751 | 1,794,327 |
| MISSISSIPPI | 355,328 | 256,608 | 24,602 | 636,538 |
| MISSOURI | 1,080,807 | 812,238 | 11,764 | 1,904,809 |
| MONTANA | 180,459 | 140,446 | —— | 320,905 |
| NEBRASKA | 210,977 | 385,630 | 5,201 | 601,808 |
| NEVADA | 153,996 | 24,124 | 21,743 | 199,863 |
| NEW HAMPSHIRE | 173,598 | 148,998 | 2,349 | 324,945 |
| NEW JERSEY | 1,538,658 | 1,217,932 | 54,123 | 2,810,713 |
| NEW MEXICO | 185,363 | 214,718 | 1,159 | 401,240 |
| NEW YORK | 3,501,443 | 2,341,880 | 147,373 | 5,990,696 |
| NORTH CAROLINA | 1,010,630 | 549,410 | 11,387 | 1,571,427 |
| NORTH DAKOTA | 104,263 | 181,018 | 4,600 | 289,881 |
| OHIO | 1,817,529 | 1,917,322 | 108,903 | 3,843,754 |
| OKLAHOMA | 683,293 | 372,221 | 12,410 | 1,067,924 |
| OREGON | 599,135 | 262,514 | 65,015 | 926,664 |
| PENNSYLVANIA | 2,410,367 | 2,006,856 | 5,832 | 4,422,955 |
| RHODE ISLAND | 271,127 | 113,518 | 4,269 | 388,914 |
| SOUTH CAROLINA | 501,943 | 279,390 | 2,191 | 783,524 |
| SOUTH DAKOTA | 72,501 | 221,188 | 1,282 | 294,971 |
| TENNESSEE | 774,879 | 452,877 | 23,086 | 1,250,842 |
| TEXAS | 2,368,543 | 1,277,165 | 17,210 | 3,662,918 |
| UTAH | 266,562 | 251,403 | 5,358 | 523,323 |
| VERMONT | 60,202 | 124,458 | 123 | 184,783 |
| VIRGINIA | 666,082 | 670,400 | 71,225 | 1,407,707 |
| WASHINGTON | 817,948 | 585,719 | 21,935 | 1,425,602 |
| WEST VIRGINIA | 455,172 | 159,189 | 59,067 | 673,428 |
| WISCONSIN | 1,190,287 | 760,740 | 11,228 | 1,962,255 |
| WYOMING | 85,721 | 66,147 | —— | 151,868 |

1978 HOUSE OF REPRESENTATIVES ELECTION

| | DEMOCRATIC | REPUBLICAN | OTHER | TOTAL VOTES CAST |
|---|---|---|---|---|
| ALABAMA | 439,564 | 197,176 | 5,539 | 642,279 |
| ALASKA | 55,176 | 68,811 | 200 | 124,187 |
| ARIZONA | 261,567 | 230,573 | 22,435 | 514,575 |
| ARKANSAS | 97,888 | 195,371 | 0 | 293,259 |
| CALIFORNIA | 3,335,332 | 3,105,933 | 84,376 | 6,525,641 |
| COLORADO | 369,455 | 402,274 | 13,446 | 785,175 |
| CONNECTICUT | 592,396 | 423,474 | 5,033 | 1,020,903 |
| DELAWARE | 64,863 | 91,689 | 1,014 | 157,566 |
| FLORIDA | 948,045 | 671,942 | 0 | 1,619,987 |
| GEORGIA | 472,210 | 116,301 | 92 | 588,603 |
| HAWAII | 202,824 | 40,167 | 10,378 | 253,369 |
| IDAHO | 118,012 | 167,271 | 0 | 285,283 |
| ILLINOIS | 1,464,688 | 1,576,522 | 2,373 | 3,043,583 |
| INDIANA | 751,940 | 680,513 | 16,410 | 1,448,863 |
| IOWA | 403,365 | 406,248 | 1,942 | 811,555 |
| KANSAS | 233,001 | 440,586 | 2,353 | 675,940 |
| KENTUCKY | 264,798 | 207,568 | 5,095 | 477,461 |
| LOUISIANA | 442,651 | 314,510 | 8,411 | 765,572 |
| MAINE | 141,039 | 208,730 | 19,783 | 369,552 |
| MARYLAND | 604,457 | 312,974 | 6,626 | 924,057 |
| MASSACHUSETTS | 1,249,311 | 471,755 | 88,328 | 1,809,394 |
| MICHIGAN | 1,538,922 | 1,150,495 | 18,297 | 2,707,714 |
| MINNESOTA | 712,270 | 779,286 | 34,110 | 1,525,666 |
| MISSISSIPPI | 251,558 | 236,274 | 31,129 | 518,961 |
| MISSOURI | 966,553 | 575,578 | 3,696 | 1,545,827 |
| MONTANA | 143,496 | 139,859 | 0 | 283,355 |
| NEBRASKA | 183,817 | 310,919 | 102 | 494,838 |
| NEVADA | 132,513 | 44,425 | 13,705 | 190,643 |
| NEW HAMPSHIRE | 122,243 | 133,546 | 2,407 | 258,196 |
| NEW JERSEY | 1,043,747 | 837,783 | 52,393 | 1,933,923 |
| NEW MEXICO | 166,470 | 118,075 | 0 | 284,545 |
| NEW YORK | 2,200,810 | 1,796,078 | 382,140 | 4,379,028 |
| NORTH CAROLINA | 607,324 | 406,076 | 6,556 | 1,019,956 |
| NORTH DAKOTA | 68,016 | 147,746 | 4,586 | 220,348 |
| OHIO | 1,278,151 | 1,471,860 | 15,848 | 2,765,859 |
| OKLAHOMA | 330,952 | 258,160 | 0 | 589,112 |
| OREGON | 587,445 | 258,140 | 28,038 | 873,623 |
| PENNSYLVANIA | 1,822,336 | 1,711,318 | 25,742 | 3,559,396 |
| RHODE ISLAND | 174,165 | 133,637 | 0 | 307,802 |
| SOUTH CAROLINA | 378,885 | 183,369 | 14,944 | 577,198 |
| SOUTH DAKOTA | 120,199 | 135,324 | 0 | 255,523 |
| TENNESSEE | 512,009 | 401,537 | 15,041 | 928,587 |
| TEXAS | 1,285,348 | 888,215 | 8,817 | 2,182,380 |
| UTAH | 162,791 | 206,470 | 9,849 | 379,110 |
| VERMONT | 23,228 | 90,688 | 6,586 | 120,502 |
| VIRGINIA | 444,049 | 594,915 | 17,601 | 1,056,565 |
| WASHINGTON | 507,252 | 450,847 | 20,475 | 978,574 |
| WEST VIRGINIA | 284,323 | 151,918 | 0 | 436,241 |
| WISCONSIN | 768,536 | 675,953 | 5,993 | 1,450,482 |
| WYOMING | 53,522 | 75,855 | 0 | 129,377 |

TABLE 3.7 (CONTINUED)

1980 HOUSE OF REPRESENTATIVES ELECTION

| | DEMOCRATIC | REPUBLICAN | OTHER | TOTAL VOTES CAST |
|---|---|---|---|---|
| ALABAMA | 628,133 | 354,224 | 29,317 | 1,011,674 |
| ALASKA | 39,922 | 114,089 | 607 | 154,618 |
| ARIZONA | 394,275 | 434,024 | 25,653 | 853,952 |
| ARKANSAS | 42,278 | 159,148 | 0 | 201,426 |
| CALIFORNIA | 3,665,518 | 4,178,626 | 334,675 | 8,178,819 |
| COLORADO | 505,654 | 619,461 | 24,975 | 1,150,090 |
| CONNECTICUT | 695,255 | 640,177 | 3,706 | 1,339,138 |
| DELAWARE | 81,227 | 133,842 | 1,506 | 216,575 |
| FLORIDA | 1,813,164 | 1,239,031 | 5,480 | 3,057,675 |
| GEORGIA | 973,540 | 381,174 | 0 | 1,354,714 |
| HAWAII | 239,706 | 19,805 | 21,000 | 280,511 |
| IDAHO | 182,061 | 233,041 | 0 | 415,102 |
| ILLINOIS | 2,048,658 | 2,417,747 | 6,196 | 4,472,601 |
| INDIANA | 1,087,115 | 1,099,991 | 2,354 | 2,189,460 |
| IOWA | 642,763 | 609,478 | 4,795 | 1,257,036 |
| KANSAS | 404,549 | 519,874 | 8,691 | 933,114 |
| KENTUCKY | 610,411 | 442,309 | 3,372 | 1,056,092 |
| LOUISIANA | 418,549 | 253,654 | 96,842 | 769,045 |
| MAINE | 137,845 | 375,073 | 21 | 512,939 |
| MARYLAND | 865,969 | 537,078 | 0 | 1,403,047 |
| MASSACHUSETTS | 1,473,289 | 757,828 | 25,165 | 2,256,282 |
| MICHIGAN | 1,877,335 | 1,659,101 | 51,718 | 3,588,154 |
| MINNESOTA | 905,793 | 987,147 | 11,973 | 1,904,913 |
| MISSISSIPPI | 427,773 | 304,472 | 56,272 | 788,517 |
| MISSOURI | 1,110,060 | 940,510 | 0 | 2,050,570 |
| MONTANA | 176,236 | 162,305 | 0 | 338,541 |
| NEBRASKA | 167,415 | 451,328 | 6,518 | 625,261 |
| NEVADA | 165,099 | 63,163 | 16,317 | 244,579 |
| NEW HAMPSHIRE | 177,421 | 186,869 | 45 | 364,335 |
| NEW JERSEY | 1,316,100 | 1,368,981 | 56,314 | 2,741,395 |
| NEW MEXICO | 175,988 | 125,910 | 0 | 301,898 |
| NEW YORK | 2,596,006 | 2,458,365 | 562,995 | 5,617,366 |
| NORTH CAROLINA | 964,493 | 769,144 | 3,160 | 1,736,797 |
| NORTH DAKOTA | 166,437 | 124,707 | 1,932 | 293,076 |
| OHIO | 1,788,410 | 2,124,566 | 27,600 | 3,940,576 |
| OKLAHOMA | 439,651 | 391,209 | 4,722 | 835,582 |
| OREGON | 656,737 | 438,728 | 10,965 | 1,106,430 |
| PENNSYLVANIA | 2,055,590 | 2,161,638 | 103,528 | 4,320,756 |
| RHODE ISLAND | 213,726 | 172,901 | 0 | 386,627 |
| SOUTH CAROLINA | 408,296 | 399,039 | 22,354 | 829,689 |
| SOUTH DAKOTA | 173,357 | 146,146 | 0 | 319,503 |
| TENNESSEE | 663,796 | 618,876 | 20,816 | 1,303,488 |
| TEXAS | 2,405,026 | 1,608,636 | 54,532 | 4,068,194 |
| UTAH | 232,426 | 351,996 | 7,913 | 592,335 |
| VERMONT | 0 | 154,274 | 40,945 | 195,219 |
| VIRGINIA | 499,772 | 1,005,272 | 47,791 | 1,552,835 |
| WASHINGTON | 816,133 | 792,816 | 8,229 | 1,617,178 |
| WEST VIRGINIA | 390,986 | 294,846 | 0 | 685,832 |
| WISCONSIN | 1,071,978 | 1,055,472 | 6,878 | 2,134,328 |
| WYOMING | 53,338 | 116,361 | 0 | 169,699 |

TABLE 3.7 (CONTINUED)

1982 HOUSE OF REPRESENTATIVES ELECTION

|  | DEMOCRATIC | REPUBLICAN | OTHER | TOTAL VOTES CAST |
|---|---|---|---|---|
| ALABAMA | 676,584 | 276,568 | 7,855 | 961,007 |
| ALASKA | 52,011 | 128,274 | 799 | 181,084 |
| ARIZONA | 300,493 | 394,872 | 15,646 | 711,011 |
| ARKANSAS | 397,466 | 361,772 | 0 | 759,238 |
| CALIFORNIA | 3,797,795 | 3,494,525 | 237,398 | 7,529,718 |
| COLORADO | 448,295 | 484,947 | 13,181 | 946,423 |
| CONNECTICUT | 577,340 | 485,491 | 7,773 | 1,070,604 |
| DELAWARE | 98,533 | 87,153 | 2,378 | 188,064 |
| FLORIDA | 1,310,634 | 899,590 | 48 | 2,210,272 |
| GEORGIA | 670,110 | 225,215 | 9,049 | 904,374 |
| HAWAII | 266,851 | 0 | 31,064 | 297,915 |
| IDAHO | 150,996 | 170,150 | 0 | 321,146 |
| ILLINOIS | 2,093,272 | 1,671,309 | 11,441 | 3,776,022 |
| INDIANA | 882,378 | 909,731 | 3,951 | 1,796,060 |
| IOWA | 528,726 | 475,366 | 679 | 1,004,771 |
| KANSAS | 345,507 | 400,837 | 10,001 | 756,345 |
| KENTUCKY | 413,286 | 280,652 | 6,680 | 700,618 |
| LOUISIANA | 184,874 | 142,371 | 189,712 | 516,957 |
| MAINE | 186,970 | 260,925 | 4,246 | 452,141 |
| MARYLAND | 742,600 | 348,561 | 0 | 1,091,161 |
| MASSACHUSETTS | 1,300,344 | 415,674 | 174,348 | 1,890,366 |
| MICHIGAN | 1,669,522 | 1,093,425 | 45,469 | 2,808,416 |
| MINNESOTA | 956,321 | 777,584 | 16,026 | 1,749,931 |
| MISSISSIPPI | 368,403 | 259,580 | 13,176 | 641,159 |
| MISSOURI | 871,682 | 653,468 | 3,266 | 1,528,416 |
| MONTANA | 165,902 | 142,370 | 8,267 | 316,539 |
| NEBRASKA | 116,107 | 402,167 | 807 | 519,081 |
| NEVADA | 114,166 | 115,863 | 4,043 | 234,072 |
| NEW HAMPSHIRE | 114,187 | 153,974 | 763 | 268,924 |
| NEW JERSEY | 1,206,416 | 915,472 | 24,202 | 2,146,090 |
| NEW MEXICO | 202,802 | 191,946 | 0 | 394,748 |
| NEW YORK | 2,461,350 | 1,836,065 | 383,962 | 4,681,377 |
| NORTH CAROLINA | 708,279 | 579,817 | 32,984 | 1,321,080 |
| NORTH DAKOTA | 186,534 | 72,241 | 1,724 | 260,499 |
| OHIO | 1,807,305 | 1,456,712 | 62,075 | 3,326,092 |
| OKLAHOMA | 539,413 | 310,186 | 6,725 | 856,324 |
| OREGON | 577,949 | 436,754 | 169 | 1,014,872 |
| PENNSYLVANIA | 1,910,988 | 1,651,922 | 65,808 | 3,628,718 |
| RHODE ISLAND | 174,023 | 157,535 | 1,624 | 333,182 |
| SOUTH CAROLINA | 353,111 | 295,160 | 9,185 | 657,456 |
| SOUTH DAKOTA | 142,122 | 133,530 | 0 | 275,652 |
| TENNESSEE | 697,823 | 469,527 | 47,230 | 1,214,580 |
| TEXAS | 1,817,048 | 934,863 | 67,123 | 2,819,034 |
| UTAH | 144,987 | 312,003 | 32,661 | 489,651 |
| VERMONT | 38,296 | 114,191 | 12,464 | 164,951 |
| VIRGINIA | 629,656 | 690,167 | 15,563 | 1,335,386 |
| WASHINGTON | 689,811 | 603,916 | 13,772 | 1,307,499 |
| WEST VIRGINIA | 343,236 | 202,380 | 787 | 546,403 |
| WISCONSIN | 768,616 | 666,193 | 15,123 | 1,449,932 |
| WYOMING | 46,041 | 113,236 | 0 | 159,277 |

TABLE 3.7 (CONTINUED)

1984 HOUSE OF REPRESENTATIVES ELECTION

|  | DEMOCRATIC | REPUBLICAN | OTHER | TOTAL VOTES CAST |
|---|---|---|---|---|
| ALABAMA | 821,773 | 308,182 | 18,619 | 1,148,574 |
| ALASKA | 86,052 | 113,582 | 6,803 | 206,437 |
| ARIZONA | 319,560 | 602,737 | 20,826 | 943,123 |
| ARKANSAS[a] | 341,335 | 90,841 | 31,070 | 463,246 |
| CALIFORNIA | 4,327,237 | 4,423,734 | 202,363 | 8,953,334 |
| COLORADO | 436,041 | 779,700 | 31,897 | 1,247,638 |
| CONNECTICUT | 667,668 | 761,647 | 2,973 | 1,432,288 |
| DELAWARE[a] | 142,070 | 100,650 | 294 | 243,014 |
| FLORIDA | 1,194,553 | 1,241,973 | 1,188 | 2,437,714 |
| GEORGIA | 1,090,682 | 430,143 | 0 | 1,520,825 |
| HAWAII | 227,261 | 40,608 | 7,737 | 275,606 |
| IDAHO | 164,878 | 240,202 | 0 | 405,080 |
| ILLINOIS | 2,367,383 | 2,203,506 | 8,192 | 4,579,081 |
| INDIANA[b] | 1,019,666 | 1,144,293 | 11,114 | 2,175,073 |
| IOWA | 595,265 | 673,343 | 151 | 1,268,759 |
| KANSAS | 435,071 | 541,986 | 17,268 | 994,325 |
| KENTUCKY | 656,661 | 528,862 | 2,199 | 1,187,722 |
| LOUISIANA[a] | 332,468 | 238,794 | 70,588 | 641,850 |
| MAINE | 162,319 | 374,951 | 4,268 | 541,538 |
| MARYLAND | 954,873 | 535,915 | 4,492 | 1,495,280 |
| MASSACHUSETTS | 1,618,131 | 719,755 | 8,161 | 2,346,047 |
| MICHIGAN | 1,861,442 | 1,577,579 | 13,344 | 3,452,365 |
| MINNESOTA | 1,060,800 | 902,268 | 12,204 | 1,975,272 |
| MISSISSIPPI | 523,161 | 326,826 | 18,865 | 868,852 |
| MISSOURI | 1,129,689 | 802,917 | 6,851 | 1,939,457 |
| MONTANA | 187,443 | 178,726 | 4,660 | 370,829 |
| NEBRASKA | 167,617 | 482,121 | 323 | 650,061 |
| NEVADA | 109,372 | 155,166 | 6,086 | 270,624 |
| NEW HAMPSHIRE | 119,111 | 250,602 | 3,215 | 372,928 |
| NEW JERSEY | 1,508,320 | 1,470,836 | 12,502 | 2,991,658 |
| NEW MEXICO | 201,131 | 294,165 | 4,324 | 499,620 |
| NEW YORK | 3,072,707 | 2,722,637 | 422,570 | 6,217,914 |
| NORTH CAROLINA | 1,130,979 | 1,026,391 | 285 | 2,157,655 |
| NORTH DAKOTA | 242,968 | 65,761 | 0 | 308,729 |
| OHIO | 1,974,973 | 2,142,405 | 40,732 | 4,158,110 |
| OKLAHOMA | 645,537 | 458,053 | 7,294 | 1,110,884 |
| OREGON | 655,092 | 548,201 | 198 | 1,203,491 |
| PENNSYLVANIA | 2,513,946 | 2,111,851 | 17,160 | 4,642,957 |
| RHODE ISLAND | 194,942 | 195,077 | 0 | 390,019 |
| SOUTH CAROLINA | 470,567 | 441,256 | 15,779 | 927,602 |
| SOUTH DAKOTA | 181,401 | 134,821 | 0 | 316,222 |
| TENNESSEE | 726,462 | 589,118 | 155 | 1,315,735 |
| TEXAS | 2,753,758 | 1,923,093 | 3,534 | 4,680,385 |
| UTAH | 208,223 | 387,410 | 5,449 | 601,082 |
| VERMONT | 60,360 | 148,025 | 25,018 | 233,403 |
| VIRGINIA | 795,009 | 1,003,211 | 39,385 | 1,837,605 |
| WASHINGTON | 966,950 | 799,565 | 11,518 | 1,808,033 |
| WEST VIRGINIA | 429,209 | 275,160 | 0 | 704,369 |
| WISCONSIN | 1,033,033 | 1,032,948 | 9,397 | 2,075,378 |
| WYOMING | 45,857 | 138,234 | 3,813 | 187,904 |

[a]States not recording vote totals for uncontested districts.

[b]Congressional recount figures.

Table 3.8

Apportionment to the United States Congress, 1787-1980[a]

| State | Con- stitu- tion, 1787 | 1790 | 1800 | 1810 | 1820 | 1830 | 1840 | 1850 | 1860 |
|---|---|---|---|---|---|---|---|---|---|
| Alabama | -- | -- | -- | 1 | 3 | 5 | 7 | 7 | 6 |
| Alaska | -- | -- | -- | -- | -- | -- | -- | -- | -- |
| Arizona | -- | -- | -- | -- | -- | -- | -- | -- | -- |
| Arkansas | -- | -- | -- | -- | -- | -- | 1 | 2 | 3 |
| California | -- | -- | -- | -- | -- | -- | -- | 2 | 3 |
| Colorado | -- | -- | -- | -- | -- | -- | -- | -- | -- |
| Connecticut | 5 | 7 | 7 | 7 | 6 | 6 | 4 | 4 | 4 |
| Delaware | 1 | 1 | 1 | 2 | 1 | 1 | 1 | 1 | 1 |
| Florida | -- | -- | -- | -- | -- | -- | 1 | 1 | 1 |
| Georgia | 3 | 2 | 4 | 6 | 7 | 9 | 8 | 8 | 7 |
| Hawaii | -- | -- | -- | -- | -- | -- | -- | -- | -- |
| Idaho | -- | -- | -- | -- | -- | -- | -- | -- | -- |
| Illinois | -- | -- | -- | 1 | 1 | 3 | 7 | 9 | 14 |
| Indiana | -- | -- | -- | 1 | 3 | 7 | 10 | 11 | 11 |
| Iowa | -- | -- | -- | -- | -- | -- | 2 | 2 | 6 |
| Kansas | -- | -- | -- | -- | -- | -- | -- | -- | 1 |
| Kentucky | -- | 2 | 6 | 10 | 12 | 13 | 10 | 10 | 9 |
| Louisiana | -- | -- | -- | 1 | 3 | 3 | 4 | 4 | 5 |
| Maine | -- | -- | -- | 7 | 7 | 8 | 7 | 6 | 5 |
| Maryland | 6 | 8 | 9 | 9 | 9 | 8 | 6 | 6 | 5 |
| Massachusetts | 8 | 14 | 17 | 13 | 13 | 12 | 10 | 11 | 10 |
| Michigan | -- | -- | -- | -- | -- | 1 | 3 | 4 | 6 |
| Minnesota | -- | -- | -- | -- | -- | -- | -- | 2 | 2 |
| Mississippi | -- | -- | -- | 1 | 1 | 2 | 4 | 5 | 5 |
| Missouri | -- | -- | -- | -- | 1 | 2 | 5 | 7 | 9 |
| Montana | -- | -- | -- | -- | -- | -- | -- | -- | -- |
| Nebraska | -- | -- | -- | -- | -- | -- | -- | -- | -- |
| Nevada | -- | -- | -- | -- | -- | -- | -- | -- | 1 |

Table 3.8 (continued)

| State | Con-stitu-tion, 1787 | 1790 | 1800 | 1810 | 1820 | 1830 | 1840 | 1850 | 1860 |
|---|---|---|---|---|---|---|---|---|---|
| New Hampshire | 3 | 4 | 5 | 6 | 6 | 5 | 4 | 3 | 3 |
| New Jersey | 4 | 5 | 6 | 6 | 6 | 6 | 5 | 5 | 5 |
| New Mexico | -- | -- | -- | -- | -- | -- | -- | -- | -- |
| New York | 6 | 10 | 17 | 27 | 34 | 40 | 34 | 33 | 31 |
| North Carolina | 5 | 10 | 12 | 13 | 13 | 13 | 9 | 8 | 7 |
| North Dakota | -- | -- | -- | -- | -- | -- | -- | -- | -- |
| Ohio | -- | -- | 1 | 6 | 14 | 19 | 21 | 21 | 19 |
| Oklahoma | -- | -- | -- | -- | -- | -- | -- | -- | -- |
| Oregon | -- | -- | -- | -- | -- | -- | -- | 1 | 1 |
| Pennsylvania | 8 | 13 | 18 | 23 | 26 | 28 | 24 | 25 | 24 |
| Rhode Island | 1 | 2 | 2 | 2 | 2 | 2 | 2 | 2 | 2 |
| South Carolina | 5 | 6 | 8 | 9 | 9 | 9 | 7 | 6 | 4 |
| South Dakota | -- | -- | -- | -- | -- | -- | -- | -- | -- |
| Tennessee | -- | 1 | 3 | 6 | 9 | 13 | 11 | 10 | 8 |
| Texas | -- | -- | -- | -- | -- | -- | 2 | 2 | 4 |
| Utah | -- | -- | -- | -- | -- | -- | -- | -- | -- |
| Vermont | -- | 2 | 4 | 6 | 5 | 5 | 4 | 3 | 3 |
| Virginia | 10 | 19 | 22 | 23 | 22 | 21 | 15 | 13 | 11 |
| Washington | -- | -- | -- | -- | -- | -- | -- | -- | -- |
| West Virginia | -- | -- | -- | -- | -- | -- | -- | -- | -- |
| Wisconsin | -- | -- | -- | -- | -- | -- | 2 | 3 | 6 |
| Wyoming | -- | -- | -- | -- | -- | -- | -- | -- | -- |
| Total number of Representatives | 65 | 106 | 142 | 186 | 213 | 242 | 232 | 237 | 243 |
| Apportionment Population per Representative | 30,000 | 34,436 | 34,609 | 36,377 | 42,124 | 49,712 | 71,338 | 93,020 | 122,614 |

Table 3.8 (continued)

| State | 1870 | 1880 | 1890 | 1900 | 1910 | 1930 | 1940 | 1950 | 1960 | 1970 | 1980 |
|---|---|---|---|---|---|---|---|---|---|---|---|
| Alabama | 8 | 8 | 9 | 9 | 10 | 9 | 9 | 9 | 8 | 7 | 7 |
| Alaska | – | – | – | – | – | 1 | – | 1 | 1 | 1 | 1 |
| Arizona | – | – | – | – | 1 | 1 | 2 | 2 | 3 | 4 | 5 |
| Arkansas | 4 | 5 | 6 | 7 | 7 | 7 | 7 | 6 | 4 | 4 | 4 |
| California | 4 | 6 | 7 | 8 | 11 | 20 | 23 | 30 | 38 | 43 | 45 |
| Colorado | 1 | 1 | 2 | 3 | 4 | 4 | 4 | 4 | 4 | 5 | 6 |
| Connecticut | 4 | 4 | 4 | 5 | 5 | 6 | 6 | 6 | 6 | 6 | 6 |
| Delaware | 1 | 1 | 1 | 1 | 1 | 1 | 1 | 1 | 1 | 1 | 1 |
| Florida | 2 | 2 | 2 | 3 | 4 | 5 | 6 | 8 | 12 | 15 | 19 |
| Georgia | 9 | 10 | 11 | 11 | 12 | 10 | 10 | 10 | 10 | 10 | 10 |
| Hawaii | – | – | – | – | – | – | – | 1 | 2 | 2 | 2 |
| Idaho | – | 1 | 1 | 1 | 2 | 2 | 2 | 2 | 2 | 2 | 2 |
| Illinois | 19 | 20 | 22 | 25 | 27 | 27 | 26 | 25 | 24 | 24 | 22 |
| Indiana | 13 | 13 | 13 | 13 | 13 | 12 | 11 | 11 | 11 | 11 | 10 |
| Iowa | 9 | 11 | 11 | 11 | 11 | 9 | 8 | 8 | 7 | 6 | 6 |
| Kansas | 3 | 7 | 8 | 8 | 8 | 7 | 6 | 6 | 5 | 5 | 5 |
| Kentucky | 10 | 11 | 11 | 11 | 11 | 9 | 9 | 8 | 7 | 7 | 7 |
| Louisiana | 6 | 6 | 6 | 7 | 8 | 8 | 8 | 8 | 8 | 8 | 8 |
| Maine | 5 | 4 | 4 | 4 | 4 | 3 | 3 | 3 | 2 | 2 | 2 |
| Maryland | 6 | 6 | 6 | 6 | 6 | 6 | 6 | 7 | 8 | 8 | 8 |
| Massachusetts | 11 | 12 | 13 | 14 | 16 | 15 | 14 | 14 | 12 | 12 | 11 |
| Michigan | 9 | 11 | 12 | 12 | 13 | 17 | 17 | 18 | 19 | 19 | 18 |
| Minnesota | 3 | 5 | 7 | 9 | 10 | 9 | 9 | 9 | 8 | 8 | 8 |
| Mississippi | 6 | 7 | 7 | 8 | 8 | 7 | 7 | 6 | 5 | 5 | 5 |
| Missouri | 13 | 14 | 15 | 16 | 16 | 13 | 13 | 11 | 10 | 10 | 9 |
| Montana | – | 1 | 1 | 1 | 2 | 2 | 2 | 2 | 2 | 2 | 2 |
| Nebraska | 1 | 3 | 6 | 6 | 6 | 5 | 4 | 4 | 3 | 3 | 3 |
| Nevada | 1 | 1 | 1 | 1 | 1 | 1 | 1 | 1 | 1 | 1 | 2 |
| New Hampshire | 3 | 2 | 2 | 2 | 2 | 2 | 2 | 2 | 2 | 2 | 2 |
| New Jersey | 7 | 7 | 8 | 10 | 12 | 14 | 14 | 14 | 15 | 15 | 14 |
| New Mexico | – | – | – | – | 1 | 1 | 2 | 2 | 2 | 2 | 3 |
| New York | 33 | 34 | 34 | 37 | 43 | 45 | 45 | 43 | 41 | 39 | 34 |

Table 3.8 (continued)

| State | 1870 | 1880 | 1890 | 1900 | 1910 | 1930 | 1940 | 1950 | 1960 | 1970 | 1980 |
|---|---|---|---|---|---|---|---|---|---|---|---|
| North Carolina | 8 | 9 | 9 | 10 | 10 | 11 | 12 | 12 | 11 | 11 | 11 |
| North Dakota | — | 1 | 1 | 2 | 3 | 2 | 2 | 2 | 2 | 1 | 1 |
| Ohio | 20 | 21 | 21 | 21 | 22 | 24 | 23 | 23 | 24 | 23 | 21 |
| Oklahoma | — | — | — | 5 | 8 | 9 | 8 | 6 | 6 | 6 | 6 |
| Oregon | 1 | 1 | 2 | 2 | 3 | 3 | 4 | 4 | 4 | 4 | 5 |
| Pennsylvania | 27 | 28 | 30 | 32 | 36 | 34 | 33 | 30 | 27 | 25 | 23 |
| Rhode Island | 2 | 2 | 2 | 2 | 3 | 2 | 2 | 2 | 2 | 2 | 2 |
| South Carolina | 5 | 7 | 7 | 7 | 7 | 6 | 6 | 6 | 6 | 6 | 6 |
| South Dakota | — | 2 | 2 | 2 | 3 | 2 | 2 | 2 | 2 | 2 | 1 |
| Tennessee | 10 | 10 | 10 | 10 | 10 | 9 | 10 | 9 | 9 | 8 | 9 |
| Texas | 6 | 11 | 13 | 16 | 18 | 21 | 21 | 22 | 23 | 24 | 27 |
| Utah | — | — | 1 | 1 | 2 | 2 | 2 | 2 | 2 | 2 | 3 |
| Vermont | 3 | 2 | 2 | 2 | 2 | 2 | 2 | 2 | 1 | 1 | 1 |
| Virginia | 9 | 10 | 10 | 10 | 10 | 9 | 9 | 10 | 10 | 10 | 10 |
| Washington | — | 1 | 2 | 3 | 5 | 6 | 6 | 7 | 7 | 7 | 8 |
| West Virginia | 3 | 4 | 4 | 5 | 6 | 6 | 6 | 6 | 5 | 4 | 4 |
| Wisconsin | 8 | 9 | 10 | 11 | 11 | 10 | 10 | 10 | 10 | 9 | 9 |
| Wyoming | — | 1 | 1 | 1 | 1 | 1 | 1 | 1 | 1 | 1 | 1 |
| Total number of Representatives | 293 | 332 | 357 | 391 | 435 | 435 | 435 | 437 | 435 | 435 | 435 |
| Apportionment Population per Representative | 130,533 | 151,912 | 173,901 | 193,167 | 210,583 | 280,675 | 301,164 | 334,587 | 410,481 | 469,088 | 510,818 |

[a] No re-apportionment based on 1920 population census.

# Campaign Costs

The costs of conducting Presidential campaigns have risen dramatically over time. Table 3.9 contains estimated expenditures by all national committees established by the major (and some minor) parties to mount the quadrennial campaigns for President. The figures given here do not include money spent by the candidates themselves. The expenditures reported in Table 3.9 are estimated for the elections of 1860 to 1912. Reporting practices mandated by various laws after 1912 improve the reliability of the expenditure amounts presented for those elections. It is certain that all figures reported in this table underestimate the total amount of money spent. Table 3.10 contains information about Presidential nominating conventions held by the Whig/Republican and Democratic parties from 1832 to 1984.

Table 3.9

Presidential Election Campaign Costs,
1860-1984

| Year | Republicans | Democrats |
|------|-------------|-----------|
| 1860 | $100,000 | $50,000 |
| 1864 | 125,000 | 50,000 |
| 1868 | 150,000 | 75,000 |
| 1872 | 250,000 | 50,000 |
| 1876 | 950,000 | 900,000 |
| 1880 | 1,100,000 | 355,000 |
| 1884 | 1,300,000 | 1,400,000 |
| 1888 | 1,350,000 | 855,000 |
| 1892 | 1,700,000 | 2,350,000 |
| 1896 | 3,350,000 | 675,000 |
| 1900 | 3,000,000 | 425,000 |
| 1904 | 2,096,000 | 700,000 |
| 1908 | 1,665,518 | 629,341 |
| 1912[a] | 1,071,549 | 1,134,848 |
| 1916 | 2,441,565 | 2,284,590 |
| 1920 | 5,417,501 | 1,470,371 |
| 1924[b] | 4,020,478 | 1,108,836 |
| 1928 | 6,256,111 | 5,342,350 |
| 1932 | 2,900,052 | 2,245,975 |
| 1936 | 8,892,972 | 5,194,741 |
| 1940 | 3,451,310 | 2,783,654 |
| 1944 | 2,828,652 | 2,169,077 |
| 1948[c] | 2,127,296 | 2,736,334 |
| 1952 | 6,608,623 | 5,032,926 |
| 1956 | 7,778,702 | 5,106,651 |
| 1960 | 10,128,000 | 9,797,000 |
| 1964 | 16,026,000 | 8,757,000 |
| 1968[d] | 25,402,000 | 11,594,000 |
| 1972[e] | 37,624,278 | 13,041,661 |
| 1976[f] | 21,820,000 | 21,820,000 |
| 1980[g] | 29,400,000 | 29,400,000 |
| 1984[h] | 40,400,000 | 40,400,000 |

[a]Progressive Party, with T. Roosevelt as candidate, spent $665,420.

[b]Progressive Party, with R. M. LaFollette as candidate, spent $236,963.

[c]Progressive Party, with Henry Wallace as candidate, spent $1,133,863; States' Rights, with Strom Thurmond as candidate, spent $163,442.

[d]American Independent Party, with George Wallace as candidate, spent $7,223,000.

[e]American Independent Party, with John G. Schmitz as candidate, spent $195,152.

[f]Due to a new campaign spending law, each candidate was allocated $21,820,000 in federal funds and no private contributions were allowed.

[g]The campaign spending law allocation was increased to $29,400,000.

[h]The campaign spending law allocation was increased to $40,400,000.

Table 3.10

American Presidential Conventions, 1832–1984

| Year | Party | City | Dates | Nominees | Number of Ballots |
|---|---|---|---|---|---|
| 1832 | Dem. | Baltimore | May 21–23 | Andrew Jackson, Martin Van Buren | 1 |
| 1835 | Dem. | Baltimore | May 20–23 | Martin Van Buren, Richard M. Johnson | 1 |
| 1840 | Dem. | Baltimore | May 5–6 | Martin Van Buren[a] | 1 |
| 1844 | Dem. | Baltimore | May 27–29 | James K. Polk, George M. Dallas | 9 |
| 1848 | Dem. | Baltimore | May 22–25 | Lewis Cass, William O. Butler | 4 |
| 1852 | Dem. | Baltimore | June 1–5 | Franklin Pierce, William R. King | 49 |
| 1856 | Dem. | Cincinnati | June 2–6 | James Buchanan, John C. Breckinridge | 17 |
| 1856 | Rep. | Philadelphia | June 17–19 | John C. Fremont, William L. Dayton | 2 |
| 1860 | Dem. | Charleston | Apr. 23–May 3 | Deadlocked | 57 |
| 1860 | Dem. | Baltimore | June 18–23 | Stephen A. Douglas, Benjamin Fitzpatrick, Herschel V. Johnson[b] | 2 |
| 1860 | Rep. | Chicago | May 16–18 | Abraham Lincoln, Hannibal Hamlin | 3 |
| 1864 | Dem. | Chicago | Aug. 29–31 | George B. McClellan, George H. Pendleton | 1 |
| 1864 | Rep. | Baltimore | June 7–8 | Abraham Lincoln, Andrew Johnson | 1 |
| 1868 | Dem. | New York | July 4–9 | Horatio Seymour, Francis P. Blair | 22 |
| 1868 | Rep. | Chicago | May 20–21 | Ulysses S. Grant, Henry Wilson | 1 |
| 1872 | Dem. | Baltimore | July 9–10 | Horace Greeley, Benjamin G. Brown | 1 |
| 1872 | Rep. | Philadelphia | June 5–6 | Ulysses S. Grant, Henry Wilson | 1 |
| 1876 | Dem. | St. Louis | June 27–29 | Stephen J. Tilden, Thomas A. Hendricks | 2 |
| 1876 | Rep. | Cincinnati | June 14–16 | Rutherford B. Hayes, William A. Wheeler | 7 |

Table 3.10 (continued)

| Year | Party | City | Dates | Nominees | Number of Ballots |
|---|---|---|---|---|---|
| 1880 | Dem. | Cincinnati | June 22-24 | Winfield S. Hancock, William H. English | 2 |
| 1880 | Rep. | Chicago | June 2-8 | James A. Garfield, Chester A. Arthur | 36 |
| 1884 | Dem. | Chicago | July 8-11 | Grover Cleveland, Thomas A. Hendricks | 2 |
| 1884 | Rep. | Chicago | June 3-6 | James G. Blaine, John A. Logan | 4 |
| 1888 | Dem. | St. Louis | June 5-7 | Grover Cleveland, Allen G. Thurman | 1 |
| 1888 | Rep. | Chicago | June 19-25 | Benjamin Harrison, Levi P. Morton | 8 |
| 1892 | Dem. | Chicago | June 21-23 | Grover Cleveland, Adlai E. Stevenson | 1 |
| 1892 | Rep. | Minneapolis | June 7-10 | Benjamin Harrison, Whitelaw Reid | 1 |
| 1896 | Dem. | Chicago | July 7-11 | William J. Bryan, Arthur Sewall | 5 |
| 1896 | Rep. | St. Louis | June 16-18 | William McKinley, Garret A. Hobart | 1 |
| 1900 | Dem. | Kansas City | July 4-6 | William J. Bryan, Adlai E. Stevenson | 1 |
| 1900 | Rep. | Philadelphia | June 5-6 | William McKinley, Theodore Roosevelt | 1 |
| 1904 | Dem. | St. Louis | July 6-9 | Alton S. Parker, Henry G. Davis | 1 |
| 1904 | Rep. | Chicago | June 21-23 | Theodore Roosevelt, Charles W. Fairbanks | 1 |
| 1908 | Dem. | Denver | July 7-10 | William J. Bryan, John W. Kern | 1 |
| 1908 | Rep. | Chicago | June 16-19 | William H. Taft, James S. Sherman | 1 |
| 1912 | Dem. | Baltimore | June 25-July 2 | Woodrow Wilson, Thomas R. Marshall | 46 |
| 1912 | Rep. | Chicago | June 18-22 | William H. Taft, James S. Sherman, Nicholas M. Butler[c] | 1 |

Table 3.10 (continued)

| Year | Party | City | Dates | Nominees | Number of Ballots |
|------|-------|------|-------|----------|-------------------|
| 1916 | Dem. | St. Louis | June 14-16 | Woodrow Wilson, Thomas R. Marshall | 1 |
| 1916 | Rep. | Chicago | June 18-22 | Charles E. Hughes, Charles W. Fairbanks | 3 |
| 1920 | Dem. | San Francisco | June 28-July 6 | James M. Cox, Franklin D. Roosevelt | 43 |
| 1920 | Rep. | Chicago | June 8-12 | Warren G. Harding, Calvin Coolidge | 10 |
| 1924 | Dem. | New York | June 24-July 9 | John W. Davis, Charles W. Bryan | 103 |
| 1924 | Rep. | Cleveland | June 10-12 | Calvin Coolidge, Charles G. Dawes | 1 |
| 1928 | Dem. | Houston | June 26-29 | Alfred E. Smith, Joseph T. Robinson | 1 |
| 1928 | Rep. | Kansas City | June 12-15 | Herbert Hoover, Charles Curtis | 1 |
| 1932 | Dem. | Chicago | June 27-July 2 | Franklin D. Roosevelt, John N. Garner | 4 |
| 1932 | Rep. | Chicago | June 14-16 | Herbert Hoover, Charles Curtin | 1 |
| 1936 | Dem. | Philadelphia | June 23-27 | Franklin D. Roosevelt, John N. Garner | ACC |
| 1936 | Rep. | Cleveland | June 9-12 | Alfred M. Landon, Frank Knox | 1 |
| 1940 | Dem. | Chicago | July 15-18 | Franklin D. Roosevelt, Henry A. Wallace | 1 |
| 1940 | Rep. | Philadelphia | June 24-28 | Wendell L. Willkie, Charles L. McNary | 6 |
| 1944 | Dem. | Chicago | July 19-21 | Franklin D. Roosevelt, Harry S Truman | 1 |
| 1944 | Rep. | Chicago | June 26-28 | Thomas E. Dewey, John W. Bricker | 1 |
| 1948 | Dep. | Philadelphia | July 12-14 | Harry S Truman, Alben W. Barkley | 1 |
| 1948 | Rep. | Philadelphia | June 21-25 | Thomas E. Dewey, Earl Warren | 3 |
| 1952 | Dep. | Chicago | July 21-26 | Adlai E. Stevenson, John J. Sparkman | 3 |
| 1952 | Rep. | Chicago | July 7-11 | Dwight D. Eisenhower, Richard M. Nixon | 1 |

Table 3.10 (continued)

| Year | Party | City | Dates | Nominees | Number of Ballots |
|------|-------|------|-------|----------|-------------------|
| 1956 | Dem. | Chicago | Aug. 13-17 | Adlai E. Stevenson, Estes Kefauver | 1 |
| 1956 | Rep. | San Francisco | Aug. 23-26 | Dwight D. Eisenhower, Richard M. Nixon | 1 |
| 1960 | Dem. | Los Angeles | July 11-15 | John F. Kennedy, Lyndon B. Johnson | 1 |
| 1960 | Rep. | Chicago | July 25-28 | Richard M. Nixon, Henry C. Lodge | 1 |
| 1964 | Dem. | Atlantic City | Aug. 24-27 | Lyndon B. Johnson, Hubert H. Humphrey | ACC |
| 1964 | Rep. | San Francisco | July 13-16 | Barry Goldwater, William E. Miller | 1 |
| 1968 | Dem. | Chicago | Aug. 26-29 | Hubert H. Humphrey, Edmund S. Muskie | 1 |
| 1968 | Rep. | Miami Beach | Aug. 5-8 | Richard M. Nixon, Spiro T. Agnew | 1 |
| 1972 | Dem. | Miami Beach | July 10-13 | George McGovern, Thomas F. Eagleton, R. Sargent Shriver[d] | 1 |
| 1972 | Rep. | Miami Beach | Aug. 21-23 | Richard M. Nixon, Spiro T. Agnew | 1 |
| 1976 | Dem. | New York | July 12-15 | Jimmy Carter, Walter F. Mondale | 1 |
| 1976 | Rep. | Kansas City | Aug. 16-19 | Gerald R. Ford, Robert Dole | 1 |
| 1980 | Dem. | New York | Aug. 11-14 | Jimmy Carter, Walter F. Mondale | 1 |
| 1980 | Rep. | Detroit | July 14-17 | Ronald Reagan, George Bush | 1 |
| 1984 | Dem. | San Francisco | July 16-19 | Walter F. Mondale, Geraldine Ferraro | 1 |
| 1984 | Rep. | Dallas | Aug. 20-23 | Ronald Reagan, George Bush | 1 |

Table 3.10 (continued)

ACC = By acclamation.

[a]The 1840 Democratic convention did not nominate a candidate for Vice President.

[b]The 1860 Democratic convention nominated Benjamin Fitzpatrick, who declined the nomination shortly after the convention adjourned. On June 25th, the Democratic National Committee selected Herschel V. Johnson as the party's nominee.

[c]The 1912 Republican Convention nominated James S. Sherman, who died on Oct. 30th. The Republican National Committee subsequently selected Nicholas M. Butler to receive the Republican electoral votes for Vice President.

[d]The 1972 Democratic convention nominated Thomas F. Eagleton, who withdrew from the ticket on July 31st. On Aug. 8, the Democratic National Committee selected R. Sargent Shriver as the party's candidate for Vice President.

# Voting Qualifications

The qualifications for voting in the United States are set by the respective states and have varied considerably over time and across states. Table 3.11 details the most significant qualifications required of individuals to become voters, recorded for selected years. In most instances, the requirements listed in these tables were those specified in state constitutions and statutes. Enforcement of these and other rules for qualification as voters varied even within each state.

Age and sex qualifications have been the most persistent suffrage requirements. In nearly all states, eligible voters were required to be at least 21 from colonial times to the 1940s and 1950s. Several states lowered their voting age to 18 or 19 beginning in 1944, and in 1971 the Twenty-Sixth Amendment set 18 as the eligible voting age for all elections. Only men were permitted to vote until the late nineteenth century, and not until 1919, with the ratification of the Nineteenth Amendment, were women given the vote in all states.

In the table which follows, dashes (—) have been used to indicate that state laws made no mention of a particular voter qualification.

Table 3.11

Qualifications for Suffrage, 1776-1981

| | Qualifications in 1776 | | |
| State | Race | Residence | Other Requirements |
| Connecticut[a] | | | |
| Delaware | White | 2 years | Taxpayer |
| Georgia | White | 1/2 year | Property owner or tradesman |
| Maryland | White | 1 year | 50 acres or £30 valued property |
| Massachusetts | --- | 1 year | Property owner or poll tax |
| New Hampshire | --- | Town | Poll tax |
| New Jersey | --- | 1 year | Estate of £50 |
| New York | --- | 1/2 year | Estate of £20 or rent of £40 |
| North Carolina | --- | 1 year | 50 acres |
| Pennsylvania | --- | 1 year | Taxpayer |
| Rhode Island | --- | Town | Estate of £40 |
| South Carolina | White | 1 year | 50 acres |
| Vermont[a] | | | |

[a]Connecticut and Vermont were still governed by charters and had no suffrage requirements.

Table 3.11 (continued)

| State | Qualifications in 1830 | | | |
| | Race | Residence | Citizenship | Other Requirements |
|---|---|---|---|---|
| Alabama | White | 1 year | U.S. | |
| Connecticut | White | 1/2 year | U.S. | |
| Delaware | White | 1 year | State | Taxpayer |
| Georgia | White | 1/2 year | --- | Taxpayer |
| Illinois | White | 1/2 year | State | |
| Indiana | White | 1 year | U.S. | |
| Kentucky | White | 2 years | --- | |
| Louisiana | White | 1 year | U.S. | Taxpayer or buyer of government land |
| Maine | --- | 1/4 year | U.S. | |
| Maryland | White | 1 year | --- | |
| Massachusetts | --- | 1 year | State | Taxpayer |
| Mississippi | White | 1 year | U.S. | Taxpayer or in militia |
| Missouri | White | 1 year | U.S. | |
| New Hampshire | --- | Town | Inhabitant | |
| New Jersey | White | 1 year | U.S. | |
| New York | --- | 1 year | State | |
| North Carolina | --- | 1 year | --- | 50 acres |
| Ohio | White | 1 year | --- | Taxpayer |
| Pennsylvania | --- | 2 years | --- | Taxpayer |
| Rhode Island | --- | Town | --- | Estate of Ł40 |
| South Carolina | White | 2 years | --- | 50 acres or town lot or 1/2 year additional residence |
| Tennessee | --- | 1/2 year | --- | Landowner |
| Vermont | --- | 1 year | U.S. | |
| Virginia | White | "Resident" | State | $25 landowner, $20 renter |

Table 3.11 (continued)

| State | Qualifications in 1860 | | |
| --- | --- | --- | --- |
| | Race | Residence | Citizenship |
| Alabama | White | 1 year | U.S. |
| Arkansas | White | 1/2 year | U.S. |
| California | White | 1/2 year | U.S. |
| Connecticut | White | 1/2 year | U.S. |
| Delaware | White | 1 year | State |
| Florida | White | 1 year | U.S. |
| Georgia | White | 1/2 year | U.S. |
| Illinois | White | 1 year | State |
| Indiana | White | --- | Declarant[a] |
| Iowa | White | 1/2 year | U.S. |
| Kansas | White | 1/2 year | Declarant |
| Kentucky | White | 2 years | State |
| Louisiana | White | 1 year | U.S. |
| Maine | --- | 1/4 year | U.S. |
| Maryland | White | 1 year | U.S. |
| Massachusetts | --- | 1 year | U.S. + 2 years |
| Michigan | White | 1/2 year | Declarant |
| Minnesota | White | 1/2 year | Declarant |
| Mississippi | White | 1 year | U.S. |
| Missouri | White | 1 year | U.S. |
| New Hampshire | --- | --- | State |
| New Jersey | White | 1 year | U.S. |
| New York | --- | 1 year | State |
| North Carolina | White | 1 year | U.S. |
| Ohio | White | 1 year | U.S. |
| Oregon | White | 1/2 year | Declarant |
| Pennsylvania | White | 1 year | U.S. |
| Rhode Island | --- | 1 year | U.S. |
| South Carolina | White | 2 years | U.S. |
| Tennessee | White | 1/2 years | U.S. |
| Texas | White | 1 year | U.S. or State |
| Vermont | --- | 1 year | U.S. |
| Virginia | White | 2 years | State |
| Wisconsin | White | 1 year | Declarant |

[a]"Declarant" defined as person "declaring" U.S. citizenship or intention to become a citizen.

Table 3.11 (continued)

| State | Sex | Residency | Citizenship | Property | Education |
|-------|-----|-----------|-------------|----------|-----------|
| | | | Qualifications in 1890 | | |
| Alabama | Male | 1 year | Declarant[a] | --- | --- |
| Arkansas | Male | 1 year | Declarant | --- | --- |
| California | Male | 1 year | Citizen | --- | --- |
| Colorado | Male | 1/2 year | Declarant | --- | --- |
| Connecticut | Male | 1 year | Citizen | --- | Read |
| Delaware | Male | 1 year | Citizen | --- | --- |
| Florida | Male | 1 year | Declarant | --- | --- |
| Georgia | Male | 1 year | Citizen | Taxpayer | --- |
| Idaho | --- | 1/2 year | Citizen | --- | --- |
| Illinois | Male | 1 year | Citizen | --- | --- |
| Indiana | Male | 1/2 year | Declarant | --- | --- |
| Iowa | Male | 1/2 year | Citizen | --- | --- |
| Kansas | Male | 1/2 year | Declarant | --- | --- |
| Kentucky | Male | 2 years | Citizen | --- | --- |
| Louisiana | Male | 1 year | Declarant | --- | --- |
| Maine | Male | 1/4 year | Citizen | --- | --- |
| Maryland | Male | 1 year | Citizen | --- | --- |
| Massachusetts | Male | 1 year | Citizen | --- | --- |
| Michigan | Male | 1/4 year | Declarant | --- | --- |
| Minnesota | Male | 1/3 year | Declarant | --- | --- |
| Mississippi | Male | 2 years | Citizen | Taxpayer and poll tax | Read and understand Constitution |
| Missouri | Male | --- | Declarant | --- | --- |
| Montana | Male | 1 year | Citizen | --- | --- |
| Nebraska | Male | 1/2 year | Declarant | --- | --- |
| Nevada | Male | 1/2 year | Citizen | --- | --- |
| New Hampshire | Male | --- | --- | --- | --- |
| New Jersey | Male | 1 year | Citizen | --- | --- |
| New York | Male | 1 year | Citizen | --- | --- |
| North Carolina | Male | 1 year | Citizen | Poll tax | --- |
| North Dakota | Male | 1 year | Declarant | --- | --- |
| Ohio | Male | 1 year | Citizen | --- | --- |
| Oregon | Male | 1/2 year | Declarant | --- | --- |
| Pennsylvania | Male | 1 year | Citizen | Taxpayer | --- |
| Rhode Island | Male | 2 years | Citizen | Poll tax or militia or taxpayer | --- |
| South Carolina | Male | 1 year | Citizen | --- | --- |
| South Dakota | Male | 1/2 year | Declarant | --- | --- |
| Tennessee | Male | 1 year | Citizen | Poll tax | --- |
| Texas | Male | 1 year | Declarant | --- | --- |
| Vermont | Male | 1 year | Citizen | --- | --- |
| Virginia | Male | 1 year | Citizen | Poll tax | --- |
| Washington | Male | 1 year | Citizen | --- | --- |
| West Virginia | Male | 1 year | Citizen | --- | --- |
| Wisconsin | Male | 1 year | Declarant | --- | --- |
| Wyoming | --- | 1 year | Citizen | --- | Read Constitution |

[a]"Declarant" defined as person "declaring" U. S. citizenship or intending to become a citizen.

Table 3.11 (continued)

|  | | | Qualifications in 1930 | | |
| State | Residence | Education | Property | Use of Voting Machines | Registration Required |
|---|---|---|---|---|---|
| Alabama | 2 years | Read & write English | Poll tax, 40 acres | | --- |
| Arizona | 1 year | Read & write English | --- | Yes | --- |
| Arkansas | 1 year | --- | Poll tax | Yes | --- |
| California[a] | 1 year | Read & write English | --- | Yes | --- |
| Colorado | 1 year | --- | --- | | --- |
| Connecticut | 1 year | Read English | --- | Yes | --- |
| Delaware | 1 year | Read & write English | --- | | --- |
| Florida | 1 year | --- | Poll tax | Yes | --- |
| Georgia | 1 year | Read & write English | Taxpayer and 40 acres or $500 | Yes | --- |
| Idaho | 1/2 year | --- | --- | | --- |
| Illinois | 1 year | --- | --- | Yes | Yes |
| Indiana | 1/2 year | --- | --- | Yes | --- |
| Iowa | 1/2 year | --- | --- | Yes | Yes |
| Kansas | 1/2 year | --- | --- | Yes | --- |
| Kentucky | 1 year | --- | --- | | --- |
| Louisiana | 2 years | Read & write English | Poll tax and $300 property | | --- |
| Maine | 1/4 year | Read & write English | --- | Yes | --- |
| Maryland | 1 year | --- | --- | Yes | --- |
| Massachusetts | 1 year | Read & write English | Poll tax | Yes | --- |
| Michigan | 1/2 year | --- | --- | Yes | Yes |
| Minnesota | 1/2 year | --- | --- | Yes | Yes |
| Mississippi | 2 years | Read or explain Constitution | Poll tax | | --- |
| Missouri | 1 year | --- | --- | | --- |
| Montana | 1 year | --- | --- | Yes | --- |
| Nebraska | 1/2 year | --- | --- | | --- |
| Nevada[a] | 1/2 year | --- | --- | | --- |
| New Hampshire | 1/2 year | Read & write English | --- | | --- |
| New Jersey | 1 year | --- | --- | | --- |
| New Mexico | 1 year | --- | --- | | --- |
| New York | 1 year | Read & write English | --- | Yes | Yes |
| North Carolina | 1 year | Read & write English | Poll tax | | --- |
| North Dakota | 1 year | --- | --- | | --- |
| Ohio | 1 year | --- | --- | Yes | --- |
| Oklahoma | 1 year | Read & write Constitution | --- | Yes | --- |
| Oregon[a] | 1/2 year | Read & write English | --- | Yes | Yes |
| Pennsylvania | 1 year | --- | Taxpayer | Yes | Yes |
| Rhode Island | 2 years | --- | Militia or poll tax | | --- |
| South Carolina | 2 years | Read & write English | Poll tax | | --- |
| South Dakota | 1 year | --- | --- | | --- |
| Tennessee | 1 year | --- | Poll tax | | --- |
| Texas | 1 year | --- | Poll tax | | --- |
| Utah | 1 year | --- | --- | | --- |
| Vermont | 1 year | --- | --- | | --- |
| Virginia | 2 years | Read Constitution | Poll tax and $300 property | Yes | --- |
| Washington | 1 year | Read & write English | --- | Yes | --- |
| West Virginia | 1 year | --- | --- | | --- |
| Wisconsin | 1 year | --- | --- | Yes | Yes |
| Wyoming | 1 year | Read Constitution | --- | | --- |

[a]Chinese excluded.

Table 3.11 (continued)

| State or Jurisdiction | Qualifications in 1981 | | |
|---|---|---|---|
| | Residence Requirements | Registration Deadline | Mail Registration |
| Alabama | Close of registration | 10 days before election | No |
| Alaska | 30 days before election | 30 days | Yes |
| Arizona | 50 days | 50 days | No |
| Arkansas | None[a] | 20 days | No |
| California | None | 29 days | Yes |
| Colorado | 32 days | 32 days | No |
| Connecticut | Resident | 21 days | No |
| Delaware | Resident | 3rd Sat. in October | Yes |
| Florida | None | 30 days | No |
| Georgia | Resident | 30 days | No |
| Hawaii | Resident | 30 days | No |
| Idaho | Resident | 17/10[b] | No |
| Illinois | 30 days | 28 days | No |
| Indiana | 30 (in precinct) | 29 days | No |
| Iowa | None | 10 days | Yes |
| Kansas | Close of registration | 20 days | Yes |
| Kentucky | 30 days | 30 days | Yes |
| Louisiana | Resident | 30 days | No |
| Maine | Resident | Election Day | No |
| Maryland | Resident | 29 days | Yes |
| Massachusetts | Close of Registration | 28 days | No |
| Michigan | 30 days | 30 days | Yes |
| Minnesota | 20 days | 20[c] | Yes |
| Mississippi | 30 days | 30 days | No |
| Missouri | None | 4th Wed. before election | Yes |
| Montana | 30 days | 30 days | Yes |
| Nebraska | None | 2nd Fri. before election | No |
| Nevada | 30 days | 5th Sat. before election | No |
| New Hampshire | 10 days | 10 days | No |
| New Jersey | 30 days | 29 days | Yes |
| New Mexico | Resident | 42 days | No |
| New York | 30 days | [d] | Yes |
| North Carolina | 30 days | 21 days | No |
| North Dakota | 30 days | No registration | No |
| Ohio | 30 days | 30 days | Yes |
| Oklahoma | Resident | 10 days | No |
| Oregon | 20 days | 8 p.m. Election Day | Yes |

Table 3.11 (continued)

| State or Jurisdiction | Residence Requirements | Registration Deadline | Mail Regis- tration |
|---|---|---|---|
| Pennsylvania | 30 days | 30 days | Yes |
| Rhode Island | 30 days | 30 days | No |
| South Carolina | Resident | 30 days | No |
| South Dakota | None | 15 days | No |
| Tennessee | 20 days | 29 days | Yes |
| Texas | 30 days | 30 days | Yes |
| Utah | 30 days | 10 days | Yes |
| Vermont | None | 17 days | No |
| Virginia | Resident | 31 days | No |
| Washington | 30 days | 30 days | No |
| West Virginia | 29 days | 30 days | No |
| Wisconsin | 10 days | 2nd Wed. before election[c] | Yes |
| Wyoming | Resident | 30 days | No |
| Dist. of Columbia | None | 30 days | Yes |
| American Samoa | e | 30 days | n.a. |
| Guam | None | 30 days | n.a. |
| Puerto Rico | 50 days | 50 days | No |

n.a. Information not available.

[a] When law specifies no residence requirement, "None" is listed; when law states only that the voter must be a bona fide resident, "Resident" is listed.

[b] With precinct registrar 17 days before; with county clerk 10 days.

[c] Registration at polls with identification.

[d] Varies according to date set for local registration day.

[e] Two years in territory; 12 months in election district preceding next election.

# Voter Turnout

Voter turnout (defined as the percentage of eligible voters who actually vote in an election) has been seen as one indicator of citizen interest in political affairs. Tables 3.12 and 3.13 present estimated voter turnout figures for elections from 1824 to 1984. National voter turnout in all elections for President, United States Senator, and Representative is displayed in table 3.12. Turnout in this table is computed by summing the total votes cast for all candidates in all states participating in an election, and dividing that sum by the estimated number of eligible voters in the same states at the time of that election. Eligible voter estimates have been calculated from decennial census population figures and interpolations of those population totals for intercensal years. Table 3.13 contains voter turnout estimates for presidential elections, reported for each of the states. The state-level turnout figures in table 3.13 were calculated in the same manner as those presented in table 3.12. Dashes (—) are used in table 3.13 to indicate that a particular state was not in the Union at the time of the election.

Table 3.12

National Voter Turnout, 1824-1984
(in percent)

| Year | President | U.S. Representative | U.S. Senator[a] |
|------|-----------|--------------------|------------------|
| 1824 | 16.2 | 62.2 | --- |
| 1826 |      | 39.5 | --- |
| 1828 | 51.7 | 59.3 | --- |
| 1830 |      | 45.8 | --- |
| 1832 | 53.3 | 64.7 | --- |
| 1834 |      | 59.6 | --- |
| 1836 | 54.1 | 50.8 | --- |
| 1838 |      | 65.2 | --- |
| | | | |
| 1840 | 77.5 | 69.4 | --- |
| 1842 |      | 60.5 | --- |
| 1844 | 74.4 | 69.9 | --- |
| 1846 |      | 56.4 | --- |
| 1848 | 66.7 | 62.9 | --- |
| 1850 |      | 53.4 | --- |
| 1852 | 63.2 | 60.0 | --- |
| 1854 |      | 59.3 | --- |
| 1856 | 70.9 | 68.8 | --- |
| 1858 |      | 62.7 | --- |
| | | | |
| 1860 | 72.1 | 68.9 | --- |
| 1862 |      | 57.5 | --- |
| 1864 | 56.0 | 60.8 | --- |
| 1866 |      | 63.1 | --- |
| 1868 | 67.7 | 70.2 | --- |
| 1870 |      | 64.9 | --- |
| 1872 | 72.4 | 73.9 | --- |
| 1874 |      | 64.4 | --- |
| 1876 | 82.4 | 81.4 | --- |
| 1878 |      | 64.6 | --- |
| | | | |
| 1880 | 80.5 | 79.2 | --- |
| 1882 |      | 65.3 | --- |
| 1884 | 78.8 | 77.6 | --- |
| 1886 |      | 63.8 | --- |
| 1888 | 80.9 | 81.5 | --- |
| 1890 |      | 64.8 | --- |
| 1892 | 76.1 | 74.8 | --- |
| 1894 |      | 67.4 | --- |
| 1896 | 79.6 | 77.8 | --- |
| 1898 |      | 60.0 | --- |
| | | | |
| 1900 | 73.6 | 72.3 | --- |
| 1902 |      | 55.5 | --- |
| 1904 | 65.4 | 63.6 | --- |
| 1906 |      | 52.0 | --- |
| 1908 | 65.5 | 63.4 | --- |
| 1910 |      | 51.3 | --- |
| 1912 | 59.0 | 55.7 | --- |
| 1914 |      | 50.4 | 54.4 |
| 1916 | 65.3 | 59.5 | 59.5 |
| 1918 |      | 40.1 | 37.8 |

Table 3.12 (continued)

| Year | President | U.S. Representative | U.S. Senator[a] |
|------|-----------|---------------------|-----------------|
| 1920 | 49.3 | 46.7 | 50.2 |
| 1922 |      | 35.7 | 37.6 |
| 1924 | 48.8 | 44.8 | 42.2 |
| 1926 |      | 32.8 | 35.7 |
| 1928 | 56.7 | 53.5 | 56.1 |
| 1930 |      | 36.6 | 34.5 |
| 1932 | 57.0 | 53.4 | 53.9 |
| 1934 |      | 44.6 | 48.4 |
| 1936 | 61.4 | 57.8 | 51.7 |
| 1938 |      | 46.8 | 50.2 |
| 1940 | 62.8 | 58.6 | 62.3 |
| 1942 |      | 34.0 | 30.0 |
| 1944 | 56.0 | 52.6 | 53.7 |
| 1946 |      | 38.6 | 42.2 |
| 1948 | 53.0 | 49.8 | 45.4 |
| 1950 |      | 41.9 | 46.7 |
| 1952 | 63.1 | 59.3 | 61.6 |
| 1954 |      | 42.6 | 38.7 |
| 1956 | 60.4 | 56.7 | 58.8 |
| 1958 |      | 53.4 | 47.6 |
| 1960 | 63.7 | 59.2 | 57.0[b] |
| 1962 |      | 46.4 | 48.4 |
| 1964 | 61.7 | 58.0 | 61.2 |
| 1966 |      | 45.5 | 41.7 |
| 1968 | 60.1 | 55.6 | 58.4[c] |
| 1970 |      | 44.4 | 47.8 |
| 1972 | 55.5 | 51.8 | 52.2 |
| 1974 |      | 37.1 | 45.1 |
| 1976 | 54.4 | 49.6 | 51.2 |
| 1978 |      | 34.9 | 33.7[d] |
| 1980 | 52.6 | 47.0 | 49.8 |
| 1982 |      | 38.2 | 40.6 |
| 1984 | 53.4 | 47.7 | 51.5 |

[a]As stipulated in Article 1, Section 3, of the Constitution, only one-third of the Senate is elected every two years. Senators are categorized into Class 1, 2, or 3, depending upon their year of election. Consequently, the turnout figures represent only those states which are electing a Senator. This will usually result in only two-thirds of the states having a senatorial election in any election year. Before the adoption of the Twenty-Second Amendment (April 8, 1913), U.S. Senators were selected by the state legislators in most states, so turnout data are inappropriate.

[b]Arkansas state law does not require the tabulation of votes in elections where the candidate is unopposed, so Arkansas is excluded from this calculation.

[c]No adequate census for Alaska exists, so this state is excluded from the calculation.

[d]Figures for Louisiana represent primary elections where no general election was held. Figures for Representatives do not include the 3d district of the State of Louisiana. Figures for Senator from the State of Louisiana represent a primary election between two Democrats.

380

Table 3.12 (continued)

Class of Senators

| | | | |
|---|---|---|---|
| Alabama | 1, 2 | Montana | 1, 3 |
| Alaska | 1, 2 | Nebraska | 1, 3 |
| Arizona | 2, 3 | Nevada | 2, 3 |
| Arkansas | 1, 2 | New Hampshire | 1, 2 |
| California | 2, 3 | New Jersey | 1, 3 |
| Colorado | 1, 2 | New Mexico | 1, 3 |
| Connecticut | 2, 3 | New York | 2, 3 |
| Delaware | 1, 3 | North Carolina | 1, 2 |
| Florida | 2, 3 | North Dakota | 2, 3 |
| Georgia | 1, 2 | Ohio | 2, 3 |
| Hawaii | 2, 3 | Oklahoma | 1, 2 |
| Idaho | 1, 2 | Oregon | 1, 2 |
| Illinois | 1, 2 | Pennsylvania | 2, 3 |
| Indiana | 2, 3 | Rhode Island | 1, 3 |
| Iowa | 1, 2 | South Carolina | 1, 2 |
| Kansas | 1, 2 | South Dakota | 1, 2 |
| Kentucky | 1, 2 | Tennessee | 1, 3 |
| Louisiana | 1, 2 | Texas | 1, 3 |
| Maine | 1, 3 | Utah | 2, 3 |
| Maryland | 2, 3 | Vermont | 2, 3 |
| Massachusetts | 1, 3 | Virginia | 1, 3 |
| Michigan | 1, 3 | Washington | 2, 3 |
| Minnesota | 1, 3 | West Virginia | 1, 3 |
| Mississippi | 1, 3 | Wisconsin | 2, 3 |
| Missouri | 2, 3 | Wyoming | 1, 3 |

Class 1 Senatorial Elections: 1918, 1924, 1930, 1936, 1942, 1948, 1954, 1960, 1966, 1972, 1978, 1984

Class 2 Senatorial Elections: 1914, 1920, 1926, 1932, 1938, 1944. 1950, 1956, 1962, 1968, 1974, 1980

Class 3 Senatorial Elections: 1916, 1922, 1928, 1934, 1940, 1946, 1952, 1958, 1964, 1970, 1976, 1982

Table 3.13

Voter Turnout for Presidential Elections,
1824-1984
(in percent)

| State | 1824 | 1828 | 1832 | 1836 | 1840 | 1844 | 1848 | 1852 |
|---|---|---|---|---|---|---|---|---|
| Alabama | 49.0 | 52.6 | 31.5 | 64.9 | 89.7 | 81.3 | 71.5 | 46.5 |
| Arkansas | -- | -- | -- | 28.8 | 67.7 | 62.3 | 54.2 | 46.8 |
| California | -- | -- | -- | -- | -- | -- | -- | 84.7 |
| Connecticut | 16.6 | 28.7 | 46.6 | 52.3 | 75.6 | 76.3 | 66.2 | 64.3 |
| Delaware | a | a | 67.1 | 69.5 | 82.8 | 84.7 | 78.7 | 72.4 |
| Florida | -- | -- | -- | -- | -- | -- | 63.5 | 54.6 |
| Georgia | a | a | a | 64.3 | 88.2 | 93.2 | 89.6 | 55.7 |
| Illinois | 23.3 | 52.2 | 46.1 | 43.3 | 86.0 | 76.6 | 70.7 | 64.8 |
| Indiana | 37.1 | 68.9 | 72.8 | 69.4 | 86.4 | 84.7 | 78.3 | 80.2 |
| Iowa | -- | -- | -- | -- | -- | -- | 61.0 | 53.7 |
| Kentucky | 25.3 | 70.7 | 74.0 | 60.8 | 74.3 | 80.4 | 73.6 | 63.4 |
| Louisiana | a | 36.3 | 21.5 | 19.2 | 39.4 | 44.9 | 47.3 | 44.4 |
| Maine | a | 42.6 | 67.5 | 37.7 | 81.8 | 67.3 | 63.1 | 55.3 |
| Maryland | a | 69.7 | 55.7 | 67.6 | 84.5 | 80.4 | 74.4 | 70.0 |
| Massachusetts | 32.2 | 27.7 | 43.4 | 42.8 | 65.6 | 59.0 | 53.0 | 45.1 |
| Michigan | -- | -- | -- | -- | 84.9 | 79.4 | 73.8 | 71.3 |
| Mississippi | 40.0 | 56.5 | 27.2 | 64.2 | 88.2 | 88.1 | 86.3 | 64.9 |
| Missouri | 19.8 | 53.5 | a | 35.7 | 74.1 | 74.3 | 58.8 | 42.8 |
| New Hampshire | 16.7 | 74.5 | 70.3 | 38.1 | 87.4 | 65.5 | 61.4 | 59.0 |
| New Jersey | 33.1 | 70.8 | 68.9 | 69.2 | 80.5 | 81.4 | 73.0 | 68.3 |
| New York | a | 67.4 | 70.3 | 58.7 | 76.0 | 72.2 | 59.7 | 61.5 |
| North Carolina | 40.3 | 54.7 | 30.5 | 52.7 | 83.7 | 79.2 | 71.3 | 65.6 |
| Ohio | 35.2 | 75.9 | 73.9 | 75.5 | 84.5 | 83.6 | 77.6 | 75.4 |
| Pennsylvania | 18.8 | 54.6 | 50.7 | 51.5 | 77.5 | 75.6 | 73.2 | 68.6 |
| Rhode Island | 12.4 | 17.5 | 26.0 | 23.7 | 33.6 | 38.7 | 30.3 | 42.1 |
| South Carolina | a | a | a | a | a | a | a | a |
| Tennessee | a | a | 27.9 | 55.3 | 89.7 | 90.0 | 83.8 | 73.0 |
| Texas | -- | -- | -- | -- | -- | -- | -- | 39.1 |
| Vermont | a | 54.0 | 50.2 | 52.7 | 73.7 | 65.5 | 59.9 | 52.7 |
| Virginia | 11.5 | 27.8 | 31.1 | 35.4 | 54.7 | 54.6 | 48.0 | 63.9 |
| Wisconsin | -- | -- | -- | -- | -- | -- | 58.4 | 62.6 |

Table 3.13 (continued)

| State | 1856 | 1860 | 1864 | 1868 | 1872 | 1876 | 1880 | 1884 |
|---|---|---|---|---|---|---|---|---|
| Alabama | 72.1 | 79.2 | b | 80.6 | 79.6 | 72.9 | 58.9 | 54.2 |
| Arkansas | 58.1 | 76.7 | b | 42.3 | 68.1 | 65.6 | 60.2 | 60.0 |
| California | 85.8 | 72.1 | 60.7 | 59.5 | 59.6 | 81.6 | 73.4 | 74.4 |
| Connecticut | 70.6 | 60.4 | 65.2 | 69.0 | 72.6 | 86.1 | 87.7 | 83.3 |
| Delaware | 74.7 | 74.6 | 74.0 | 76.8 | 73.3 | 73.3 | 81.7 | 75.7 |
| Florida | 71.9 | 74.1 | b | a | 76.9 | 90.9 | 86.3 | 82.8 |
| Georgia | 82.5 | 83.5 | b | 74.1 | 56.7 | 63.3 | 49.3 | 41.1 |
| Illinois | 72.4 | 80.5 | 69.6 | 77.7 | 75.5 | 87.3 | 89.4 | 85.4 |
| Indiana | 88.4 | 89.4 | 83.5 | 93.7 | 87.7 | 97.2 | 96.8 | 93.8 |
| Iowa | 82.2 | 81.2 | 63.1 | 73.6 | 77.5 | 90.1 | 86.8 | 91.5 |
| Kansas | -- | -- | 37.0 | 50.1 | 76.7 | 64.6 | 79.4 | 89.1 |
| Kentucky | 73.7 | 69.8 | 41.2 | 65.3 | 63.8 | 78.1 | 72.5 | 69.5 |
| Louisiana | 48.9 | 53.4 | b | 71.3 | 76.6 | 78.4 | 50.9 | 49.9 |
| Maine | 70.4 | 62.0 | 69.4 | 67.1 | 57.9 | 71.9 | 85.1 | 74.9 |
| Maryland | 75.1 | 74.6 | 55.0 | 65.7 | 74.9 | 82.3 | 78.8 | 79.9 |
| Massachusetts | 55.6 | 51.4 | 49.1 | 50.8 | 58.5 | 71.7 | 71.6 | 68.2 |
| Michigan | 81.1 | 80.1 | 68.7 | 78.3 | 72.5 | 87.9 | 85.5 | 87.0 |
| Minnesota | -- | 75.0 | 57.7 | 70.8 | 87.1 | 89.4 | 87.2 | 81.8 |
| Mississippi | 80.5 | 86.6 | b | a | 70.8 | 78.8 | 49.7 | 48.5 |
| Missouri | 51.0 | 64.5 | 33.9 | 42.5 | 66.8 | 76.1 | 77.6 | 76.7 |
| Nebraska | -- | -- | -- | 46.5 | 48.5 | 56.8 | 72.9 | 73.6 |
| Nevada | -- | -- | -- | 57.1 | 76.1 | 96.1 | 84.5 | 65.8 |
| New Hampshire | 79.7 | 73.8 | 77.3 | 75.3 | 80.5 | 89.1 | 91.6 | 86.8 |
| New Jersey | 69.8 | 74.9 | 69.0 | 77.1 | 81.8 | 95.4 | 96.4 | 88.3 |
| New York | 64.3 | 67.1 | 68.5 | 75.3 | 81.0 | 91.6 | 92.5 | 88.6 |
| North Carolina | 65.8 | 70.2 | b | 89.4 | 71.9 | 89.7 | 82.6 | 86.1 |
| Ohio | 76.5 | 81.7 | 81.9 | 85.2 | 84.2 | 93.9 | 93.6 | 92.8 |
| Oregon | -- | 86.8 | 89.7 | 92.4 | 66.6 | 74.2 | 81.2 | 77.4 |
| Pennsylvania | 74.1 | 70.3 | 76.9 | 80.5 | 67.8 | 81.5 | 84.6 | 79.6 |
| Rhode Island | 46.0 | 43.5 | 45.2 | 34.7 | 40.7 | 50.8 | 50.7 | 50.6 |
| South Carolina | a | a | b | 81.5 | 60.4 | a | 83.1 | 42.9 |
| Tennessee | 78.6 | 80.5 | a | 42.3 | 65.7 | 74.3 | 74.4 | 73.2 |
| Texas | 62.5 | 61.7 | b | a | 56.2 | 53.8 | 65.8 | 77.3 |
| Vermont | 60.2 | 52.5 | 63.8 | 62.7 | 69.4 | 81.3 | 79.1 | 69.2 |
| Virginia | 67.6 | 70.5 | b | a | 66.2 | 77.2 | 63.7 | 81.7 |
| West Virginia | -- | -- | a | a | 61.2 | 83.6 | 82.5 | 86.3 |
| Wisconsin | 81.5 | 79.1 | 68.8 | 80.0 | 81.6 | 96.4 | 89.7 | 94.0 |

Table 3.13 (continued)

| State | 1888 | 1892 | 1896 | 1900 | 1904 | 1908 | 1912 | 1916 |
|---|---|---|---|---|---|---|---|---|
| Alabama | 56.6 | 68.5 | 51.8 | 38.8 | 24.2 | 21.6 | 22.7 | 24.0 |
| Arizona | -- | -- | -- | -- | -- | -- | 39.6 | 47.7 |
| Arkansas | 65.5 | 55.6 | 51.8 | 41.2 | 33.9 | 40.4 | 31.0 | 39.9 |
| California | 81.4 | 76.8 | 76.1 | 69.8 | 58.8 | 55.6 | 44.7 | 56.9 |
| Colorado | 68.2 | 61.6 | 69.7 | 74.0 | 70.0 | 65.0 | 58.8 | 60.0 |
| Connecticut | 86.6 | 85.4 | 83.3 | 79.7 | 80.4 | 76.2 | 71.5 | 74.2 |
| Delaware | 69.0 | 80.6 | 78.9 | 81.8 | 82.0 | 86.2 | 83.5 | 84.5 |
| Florida | 78.2 | 35.5 | 40.0 | 29.8 | 24.0 | 26.1 | 23.6 | 33.4 |
| Georgia | 37.6 | 53.7 | 35.6 | 24.4 | 24.0 | 22.4 | 19.2 | 24.0 |
| Idaho | -- | 63.7 | 76.2 | 75.0 | 64.6 | 66.0 | 60.0 | 67.6 |
| Illinois | 85.1 | 88.1 | 97.0 | 89.9 | 80.5 | 81.6 | 75.6 | 68.3 |
| Indiana | 95.6 | 91.5 | 97.6 | 94.7 | 92.5 | 93.4 | 81.0 | 84.9 |
| Iowa | 89.5 | 89.3 | 95.6 | 89.2 | 81.0 | 81.8 | 78.7 | 77.9 |
| Kansas | 96.5 | 87.1 | 87.6 | 89.5 | 76.7 | 81.3 | 75.0 | 65.9 |
| Kentucky | 80.7 | 73.9 | 89.3 | 87.1 | 77.7 | 84.0 | 74.6 | 82.6 |
| Louisiana | 49.7 | 45.1 | 35.6 | 21.7 | 15.5 | 19.7 | 19.4 | 21.5 |
| Maine | 71.5 | 63.3 | 63.0 | 55.0 | 49.5 | 53.1 | 63.6 | 65.8 |
| Maryland | 85.3 | 80.4 | 87.4 | 85.9 | 69.6 | 70.8 | 64.9 | 68.3 |
| Massachusetts | 69.5 | 71.7 | 67.3 | 64.1 | 64.4 | 62.2 | 62.2 | 63.3 |
| Michigan | 92.7 | 83.7 | 95.3 | 89.0 | 78.7 | 75.7 | 69.7 | 73.0 |
| Minnesota | 90.2 | 77.4 | 86.0 | 76.7 | 64.1 | 65.9 | 60.9 | 64.7 |
| Mississippi | 44.1 | 18.5 | 22.0 | 17.0 | 15.5 | 16.4 | 15.1 | 19.9 |
| Missouri | 81.7 | 77.2 | 88.2 | 82.6 | 74.2 | 78.9 | 74.0 | 80.4 |
| Montana | -- | 77.7 | 75.2 | 75.5 | 63.5 | 59.9 | 61.0 | 70.0 |
| Nebraska | 82.8 | 72.5 | 80.4 | 86.7 | 75.8 | 84.2 | 74.3 | 81.0 |
| Nevada | 73.3 | 69.1 | 68.7 | 71.4 | 55.8 | 84.1 | 63.4 | 70.7 |
| New Hampshire | 90.2 | 86.1 | 78.2 | 83.9 | 81.6 | 80.8 | 78.4 | 78.1 |
| New Jersey | 90.4 | 89.2 | 87.8 | 85.9 | 83.5 | 82.2 | 69.2 | 71.4 |
| New Mexico | -- | -- | -- | -- | -- | -- | 55.7 | 74.2 |
| New York | 91.7 | 85.4 | 83.9 | 84.6 | 83.2 | 79.5 | 72.1 | 72.0 |
| North Carolina | 86.1 | 78.5 | 85.7 | 70.2 | 46.0 | 51.9 | 46.6 | 51.5 |
| North Dakota | -- | 69.3 | 71.0 | 81.5 | 70.8 | 74.5 | 59.8 | 75.9 |
| Ohio | 91.6 | 85.9 | 95.1 | 91.0 | 82.8 | 87.4 | 75.0 | 77.1 |
| Oklahoma | -- | -- | -- | -- | -- | 68.8 | 55.6 | 58.8 |
| Oregon | 72.0 | 77.4 | 85.1 | 65.4 | 53.2 | 52.7 | 58.2 | 61.2 |
| Pennsylvania | 81.3 | 75.2 | 82.4 | 75.0 | 74.3 | 71.8 | 64.6 | 64.1 |
| Rhode Island | 56.7 | 66.1 | 60.5 | 56.2 | 63.3 | 62.3 | 62.9 | 66.6 |
| South Carolina | 35.0 | 28.9 | 26.2 | 18.0 | 18.5 | 20.6 | 14.7 | 17.5 |
| South Dakota | -- | 77.2 | 86.1 | 94.5 | 80.0 | 75.7 | 69.4 | 74.0 |
| Tennessee | 79.2 | 64.0 | 71.4 | 56.6 | 47.7 | 48.1 | 45.0 | 46.7 |
| Texas | 74.5 | 75.4 | 86.6 | 60.3 | 29.2 | 32.8 | 30.4 | 34.4 |
| Utah | -- | -- | 79.6 | 84.2 | 77.6 | 71.8 | 65.5 | 75.2 |
| Vermont | 71.0 | 60.4 | 67.4 | 57.9 | 52.7 | 52.8 | 62.6 | 64.5 |
| Virginia | 83.1 | 75.3 | 70.9 | 59.6 | 27.6 | 27.4 | 25.7 | 26.7 |
| Washington | -- | 68.7 | 63.7 | 64.9 | 59.3 | 56.7 | 49.8 | 54.1 |
| West Virginia | 94.0 | 89.7 | 93.4 | 91.4 | 89.1 | 86.9 | 83.1 | 83.1 |
| Wisconsin | 92.7 | 87.3 | 95.5 | 86.5 | 80.8 | 77.5 | 68.5 | 70.3 |
| Wyoming | -- | 46.4 | 50.6 | 51.0 | 50.5 | 51.7 | 50.4 | 55.0 |

Table 3.13 (continued)

| State | 1920 | 1924 | 1928 | 1932 | 1936 | 1940 | 1944 | 1948 |
|---|---|---|---|---|---|---|---|---|
| Alabama | 20.6 | 13.3 | 19.1 | 17.7 | 18.8 | 18.9 | 15.0 | 22.6 |
| Arizona | 46.7 | 40.8 | 41.6 | 48.5 | 49.0 | 57.0 | 42.0 | 45.1 |
| Arkansas | 21.3 | 15.3 | 20.9 | 21.8 | 17.2 | 18.2 | 19.3 | 21.9 |
| California | 47.3 | 49.1 | 55.8 | 61.0 | 64.6 | 73.4 | 64.7 | 62.6 |
| Colorado | 55.4 | 59.2 | 67.0 | 74.0 | 74.9 | 79.7 | 67.7 | 64.2 |
| Connecticut | 57.8 | 57.3 | 72.3 | 70.7 | 74.6 | 77.3 | 73.3 | 70.2 |
| Delaware | 75.1 | 68.5 | 75.3 | 76.3 | 79.8 | 79.3 | 67.2 | 69.1 |
| Florida | 37.0 | 16.9 | 32.6 | 30.3 | 31.2 | 40.9 | 33.7 | 34.4 |
| Georgia | 10.6 | 11.5 | 15.5 | 16.5 | 17.7 | 17.7 | 17.6 | 19.6 |
| Idaho | 61.2 | 65.6 | 64.4 | 74.0 | 71.6 | 77.0 | 64.8 | 63.6 |
| Illinois | 60.4 | 64.0 | 73.1 | 74.4 | 81.5 | 82.4 | 74.5 | 69.7 |
| Indiana | 73.1 | 70.6 | 74.7 | 78.8 | 78.6 | 81.1 | 71.6 | 67.0 |
| Iowa | 65.5 | 69.3 | 69.5 | 69.1 | 73.5 | 75.5 | 64.2 | 62.2 |
| Kansas | 58.0 | 63.9 | 65.5 | 70.7 | 76.4 | 75.2 | 62.1 | 64.8 |
| Kentucky | 71.8 | 61.0 | 67.7 | 67.4 | 60.0 | 59.5 | 51.8 | 47.9 |
| Louisiana | 14.1 | 12.4 | 20.1 | 23.0 | 26.0 | 27.3 | 24.1 | 27.1 |
| Maine | 49.4 | 44.9 | 60.2 | 66.3 | 64.4 | 65.0 | 57.1 | 48.5 |
| Maryland | 52.3 | 41.0 | 56.7 | 51.2 | 58.1 | 57.2 | 47.0 | 41.7 |
| Massachusetts | 53.3 | 56.5 | 73.8 | 69.3 | 75.8 | 78.7 | 70.6 | 70.7 |
| Michigan | 55.1 | 53.6 | 56.1 | 61.8 | 62.0 | 66.6 | 63.3 | 55.1 |
| Minnesota | 59.5 | 61.9 | 68.5 | 66.1 | 69.6 | 72.3 | 62.7 | 65.2 |
| Mississippi | 9.5 | 12.0 | 15.2 | 13.8 | 14.4 | 14.7 | 14.4 | 16.0 |
| Missouri | 67.1 | 63.2 | 69.1 | 70.9 | 77.2 | 74.4 | 62.1 | 60.8 |
| Montana | 61.7 | 59.1 | 64.9 | 70.0 | 70.6 | 72.2 | 58.7 | 61.8 |
| Nebraska | 55.7 | 63.7 | 71.3 | 71.8 | 75.5 | 75.4 | 67.7 | 57.7 |
| Nevada | 61.0 | 54.9 | 60.6 | 70.6 | 68.0 | 75.6 | 64.5 | 63.6 |
| New Hampshire | 67.5 | 67.4 | 77.7 | 77.5 | 77.6 | 79.6 | 73.1 | 69.6 |
| New Jersey | 59.2 | 60.7 | 75.4 | 71.9 | 74.9 | 76.1 | 68.7 | 62.5 |
| New Mexico | 62.3 | 60.3 | 57.6 | 66.9 | 67.4 | 66.6 | 48.6 | 53.3 |
| New York | 56.4 | 56.1 | 67.8 | 65.7 | 72.4 | 75.7 | 70.4 | 64.2 |
| North Carolina | 44.6 | 35.9 | 43.1 | 44.0 | 47.4 | 42.7 | 38.0 | 35.5 |
| North Dakota | 69.8 | 63.7 | 72.3 | 74.4 | 77.9 | 78.4 | 61.1 | 60.9 |
| Ohio | 62.6 | 57.7 | 66.8 | 65.4 | 71.8 | 75.4 | 66.7 | 58.1 |
| Oklahoma | 48.3 | 47.3 | 50.5 | 54.3 | 56.4 | 60.6 | 52.8 | 52.5 |
| Oregon | 52.4 | 55.1 | 57.3 | 60.4 | 62.4 | 67.1 | 58.2 | 56.2 |
| Pennsylvania | 42.8 | 45.8 | 62.5 | 53.1 | 72.5 | 67.6 | 59.5 | 55.6 |
| Rhode Island | 57.9 | 66.2 | 68.8 | 71.6 | 77.9 | 75.6 | 64.3 | 65.4 |
| South Carolina | 8.6 | 6.4 | 8.5 | 12.3 | 12.5 | 10.1 | 9.8 | 12.8 |
| South Dakota | 56.3 | 59.4 | 71.9 | 76.3 | 78.7 | 81.5 | 60.0 | 63.4 |
| Tennessee | 35.4 | 23.3 | 25.7 | 26.5 | 30.0 | 30.7 | 28.2 | 28.7 |
| Texas | 21.7 | 25.2 | 23.6 | 26.4 | 24.0 | 28.7 | 28.2 | 25.9 |
| Utah | 69.6 | 69.2 | 72.4 | 78.9 | 77.4 | 82.9 | 74.7 | 75.4 |
| Vermont | 45.1 | 51.3 | 66.8 | 66.6 | 68.5 | 66.8 | 56.7 | 54.2 |
| Virginia | 19.4 | 18.1 | 24.0 | 22.1 | 23.0 | 22.1 | 22.2 | 21.8 |
| Washington | 52.4 | 51.0 | 55.9 | 63.6 | 66.2 | 70.6 | 66.7 | 62.7 |
| West Virginia | 71.7 | 75.2 | 76.4 | 81.9 | 85.0 | 83.0 | 65.5 | 65.7 |
| Wisconsin | 52.2 | 57.3 | 63.8 | 65.1 | 68.9 | 72.4 | 65.5 | 59.4 |
| Wyoming | 52.3 | 70.3 | 67.5 | 73.6 | 73.4 | 74.8 | 63.1 | 59.3 |

Table 3.13 (continued)

| State | 1952 | 1956 | 1960 | 1964 | 1968 | 1972 | 1976 | 1980 | 1984 |
|---|---|---|---|---|---|---|---|---|---|
| Alabama | 24.2 | 27.5 | 30.5 | 36.1 | 52.7 | 44.1 | 47.3 | 48.6 | 50.1 |
| Alaska | -- | -- | 45.4 | 44.7 | 49.6 | 47.6 | 53.0 | 57.8 | 60.2 |
| Arizona | 53.6 | 47.7 | 54.5 | 56.5 | 50.2 | 52.7 | 47.8 | 44.7 | 46.6 |
| Arkansas | 36.9 | 38.0 | 36.7 | 51.3 | 53.3 | 49.7 | 51.1 | 51.4 | 52.2 |
| California | 68.9 | 63.8 | 67.3 | 66.0 | 61.8 | 60.0 | 51.4 | 49.0 | 49.9 |
| Colorado | 72.3 | 69.7 | 71.4 | 68.2 | 65.0 | 61.2 | 61.1 | 56.0 | 54.8 |
| Connecticut | 79.8 | 75.3 | 76.8 | 71.6 | 69.3 | 65.7 | 62.4 | 60.9 | 61.0 |
| Delaware | 79.0 | 73.0 | 73.6 | 69.6 | 68.8 | 63.5 | 58.5 | 54.6 | 55.7 |
| Dist. of Col. | -- | -- | -- | -- | -- | 31.5 | 33.4 | 35.5 | 43.8 |
| Florida | 48.1 | 43.7 | 50.0 | 51.6 | 53.4 | 50.6 | 49.8 | 48.6 | 49.0 |
| Georgia | 29.3 | 28.4 | 29.6 | 42.8 | 43.9 | 37.8 | 43.4 | 41.3 | 42.2 |
| Hawaii | -- | -- | 50.9 | 51.3 | 53.0 | 50.9 | 48.6 | 43.6 | 44.5 |
| Idaho | 78.7 | 75.5 | 80.7 | 75.5 | 72.3 | 64.8 | 60.1 | 68.0 | 60.4 |
| Illinois | 75.3 | 72.1 | 75.8 | 72.7 | 69.4 | 62.6 | 61.3 | 57.7 | 57.3 |
| Indiana | 75.6 | 73.6 | 76.8 | 72.2 | 70.5 | 60.6 | 61.1 | 57.7 | 54.1 |
| Iowa | 75.5 | 73.8 | 76.5 | 70.6 | 69.0 | 64.2 | 63.6 | 63.0 | 56.3 |
| Kansas | 71.5 | 67.3 | 70.2 | 63.9 | 64.1 | 59.4 | 59.5 | 56.8 | 57.0 |
| Kentucky | 56.9 | 55.5 | 58.8 | 52.6 | 51.1 | 48.4 | 49.2 | 50.0 | 50.7 |
| Louisiana | 40.1 | 36.0 | 44.8 | 47.2 | 55.1 | 44.5 | 50.4 | 53.1 | 54.2 |
| Maine | 62.5 | 61.6 | 72.6 | 64.9 | 66.3 | 62.6 | 65.2 | 64.6 | 65.2 |
| Maryland | 57.3 | 54.5 | 57.2 | 54.6 | 55.1 | 50.4 | 50.0 | 50.0 | 51.4 |
| Massachusetts | 76.5 | 73.9 | 76.1 | 70.0 | 67.5 | 62.1 | 61.0 | 59.0 | 57.9 |
| Michigan | 67.9 | 70.8 | 72.5 | 66.7 | 65.7 | 59.4 | 58.5 | 59.9 | 58.2 |
| Minnesota | 72.1 | 68.5 | 77.1 | 74.4 | 73.0 | 68.0 | 71.6 | 69.9 | 67.9 |
| Mississippi | 23.8 | 21.0 | 25.5 | 34.1 | 53.3 | 46.0 | 49.8 | 52.0 | 52.0 |
| Missouri | 71.6 | 68.6 | 71.8 | 65.6 | 63.6 | 56.7 | 58.4 | 58.7 | 57.7 |
| Montana | 71.2 | 71.3 | 71.4 | 70.5 | 68.3 | 69.0 | 63.5 | 65.1 | 65.0 |
| Nebraska | 71.3 | 67.4 | 71.5 | 67.0 | 60.5 | 56.4 | 56.2 | 56.7 | 56.0 |
| Nevada | 69.2 | 65.7 | 61.1 | 60.4 | 56.5 | 52.2 | 47.6 | 41.2 | 41.6 |
| New Hampshire | 78.5 | 74.1 | 79.4 | 71.4 | 69.3 | 64.1 | 59.1 | 57.2 | 53.9 |
| New Jersey | 71.7 | 68.7 | 71.9 | 69.4 | 66.3 | 59.6 | 58.5 | 54.9 | 56.9 |
| New Mexico | 60.3 | 56.7 | 62.2 | 63.0 | 60.2 | 60.7 | 54.0 | 50.9 | 51.6 |
| New York | 70.4 | 67.5 | 67.0 | 64.5 | 59.8 | 56.1 | 51.7 | 48.0 | 52.5 |
| North Carolina | 51.4 | 47.5 | 53.5 | 52.1 | 54.5 | 43.9 | 43.6 | 43.5 | 47.7 |
| North Dakota | 74.7 | 70.9 | 78.5 | 72.6 | 69.7 | 69.8 | 68.8 | 64.8 | 63.0 |
| Ohio | 69.3 | 66.2 | 71.2 | 65.6 | 63.3 | 57.0 | 55.1 | 55.4 | 58.1 |
| Oklahoma | 68.5 | 61.4 | 63.8 | 62.9 | 60.9 | 56.8 | 56.4 | 52.3 | 51.2 |
| Oregon | 69.2 | 70.8 | 72.3 | 67.9 | 66.0 | 61.9 | 62.3 | 61.5 | 62.5 |
| Pennsylvania | 66.1 | 65.2 | 70.5 | 67.0 | 65.0 | 56.3 | 54.7 | 51.9 | 53.9 |
| Rhode Island | 79.1 | 72.9 | 75.1 | 69.6 | 66.3 | 61.8 | 63.4 | 58.6 | 56.0 |
| South Carolina | 29.1 | 24.7 | 30.6 | 39.0 | 46.7 | 39.5 | 41.5 | 40.5 | 40.6 |
| South Dakota | 74.1 | 74.5 | 78.3 | 75.3 | 72.6 | 70.8 | 64.1 | 67.6 | 63.8 |
| Tennessee | 44.7 | 45.9 | 50.2 | 51.8 | 53.8 | 44.3 | 49.6 | 48.8 | 49.3 |
| Texas | 43.3 | 37.9 | 41.8 | 44.2 | 48.4 | 45.2 | 47.9 | 44.9 | 47.0 |
| Utah | 82.3 | 77.0 | 80.1 | 78.9 | 76.7 | 69.4 | 69.1 | 64.6 | 60.5 |
| Vermont | 66.4 | 66.2 | 72.5 | 67.2 | 63.4 | 60.3 | 56.2 | 57.8 | 60.5 |
| Virginia | 29.9 | 31.8 | 33.4 | 41.6 | 50.5 | 45.6 | 48.1 | 47.6 | 51.1 |
| Washington | 70.6 | 70.2 | 72.3 | 67.9 | 66.2 | 62.0 | 61.3 | 57.5 | 58.6 |
| West Virginia | 76.1 | 74.5 | 77.4 | 73.6 | 70.4 | 64.5 | 58.6 | 52.9 | 51.3 |
| Wisconsin | 72.0 | 67.6 | 73.4 | 69.0 | 61.4 | 62.7 | 65.5 | 67.2 | 63.4 |
| Wyoming | 72.1 | 67.2 | 73.9 | 74.2 | 65.5 | 64.7 | 58.8 | 53.2 | 51.8 |

--Not yet a state.

[a]Data not available.

[b]No election held.

# Party Identification

The partisan political identification of voters in the United States has been obtained from sample surveys (often called "public opinion polls") of the eligible electorate since 1940. Table 3.14 reports the distribution of the electorate's partisan preferences from 1940 to 1984. Except where indicated, the data in this table were obtained from the election surveys conducted by the Survey Research Center/ Center for Political Studies, Institute for Social Research, University of Michigan. In most of the surveys whose findings are reported here, the persons interviewed were asked, "Generally speaking, do you usually think of yourself as a Democrat, a Republican, an Independent, or what?"

Table 3.14

Party Identification of the
Electorate, 1937-1984
(in percent)

| Year | Democrat | Republican | Independent or Other | Apolitical Don't Know |
|------|----------|------------|----------------------|-----------------------|
| 1937[a] | 50 | 34 | 16 | * |
| 1940[a] | 41 | 38 | 20 | 1 |
| 1944[a] | 41 | 39 | 20 | * |
| 1947[b] | 46 | 27 | 21 | 7 |
| 1952 | 47 | 28 | 23 | 3 |
| 1954 | 48 | 27 | 22 | 4 |
| 1956 | 44 | 29 | 23 | 4 |
| 1958 | 49 | 28 | 19 | 4 |
| 1960 | 45 | 30 | 23 | 3 |
| 1962 | 46 | 28 | 21 | 4 |
| 1964 | 52 | 25 | 23 | 1 |
| 1966 | 46 | 25 | 28 | 1 |
| 1968 | 45 | 25 | 30 | 1 |
| 1970 | 44 | 24 | 31 | 1 |
| 1972 | 41 | 23 | 35 | 1 |
| 1974 | 39 | 22 | 37 | 3 |
| 1976 | 40 | 23 | 37 | 1 |
| 1978 | 39 | 21 | 38 | 3 |
| 1980 | 41 | 23 | 34 | 2 |
| 1982 | 44 | 24 | 30 | 2 |
| 1984 | 37 | 27 | 34 | 2 |

Note: Except where indicated, all data are from the University of Michigan's American National Election Study (see Sources for complete citations).

[a]Data were collected by the American Institute of Public Opinion (the Gallup Organization), Princeton, New Jersey.

[b]Data were collected by the National Opinion Research Center, Chicago, Illinois.

*Less than one percent.

# Voting Devices

As indicated earlier, the means by which voters in the United States have cast their ballots in elections have changed considerably, from voice voting in the eighteenth century, through the paper ballots which predominated until the mid-twentieth century. In the contemporary era the voting process has become largely automated. Table 3.15 describes the types of automated voting devices in use in each of the states in 1982; included are indicators of the frequency of use of the various types of devices. "Mechanical" devices include automatic vote tabulating machines containing levers over the names of each candidate which, when pulled, record votes for the candidates thus selected. Punch card voting schemes require the voter to indicate choice of candidates by pushing a stylus through a punch card in a selected location; the punched cards and the voters choices contained on them are then tabulated by computer. Optical scanning voting systems employ printed ballots which the voters mark with a pen or pencil; the marks are then "sensed" when the ballots are passed through an optical scanning device and the vote totals for each candidate accumulated in this manner.

Table 3.15

Use of Voting Devices, 1982

| State | Use of Voting Devices | Type of Device in Use | | | |
| | | Mechanical | Punch Card | Optical Scanning | Straight Party Vote[1] |
|---|---|---|---|---|---|
| Alabama | m | r | o | o | m |
| Alaska | f | o | r | o | o |
| Arizona | m | o | r | f | o |
| Arkansas | f | f | f | f | o |
| California | m | f | m | f | o |
| Colorado | m | m | m[2] | m | o |
| Connecticut | r | r | o | o | m |
| Delaware | r | r | o | o | o |
| Dist. of Columbia | r | o | r | o | o |
| Florida | m | m | f | o | o |
| Georgia | f | f | f | o | f[3] |
| Hawaii | r | o | r | o | o |
| Idaho | f | f | m | o | o |
| Illinois | m | f | m | f | m |
| Indiana | m | m | f | o | m |
| Iowa | m | r | o | o | m |
| Kansas | f | f | o | o | o |
| Kentucky | r | r | o | o | m |
| Louisiana | r | r | o | o | f[4] |
| Maine | f | f | f | o | o |
| Maryland | r | m | f | o | o |
| Massachusetts | f | m | f | f | o |
| Michigan | m | m | f | o | m |
| Minnesota | f | m | f | o | o |
| Mississippi | f | f | f | o | o |
| Missouri | f | f | f | f | m |
| Montana | f | f | f | o | o |
| Nebraska | f | f | f | m | o |
| Nevada | m | o | r | o | o |
| New Hampshire | f | m | f | o | m |
| New Jersey | m | m | f | f | o |
| New Mexico | r | r | o | o | m |
| New York | r[5] | r | o | o | o |
| North Carolina | f | m | f | f | f[6] |
| North Dakota | f | m | m | o | o |
| Ohio | f | m | m | o | o |

Table 3.15 (continued)

| State | Use of Voting Devices | Type of Device in Use | | | Straight Party Vote[1] |
| | | Mechanical | Punch Card | Optical Scanning | |
|---|---|---|---|---|---|
| Oklahoma | f | m | o | m | f[7] |
| Oregon | m | o | r | o | o |
| Pennsylvania | m | m | f | o | m |
| Rhode Island | r | r | o | o | m |
| South Carolina | f | f | f | o | m |
| South Dakota | f | f | f | o | m |
| Tennessee | m | m | f | o | o |
| Texas | m | m | m | f | m |
| Utah | f | o | f | f | m |
| Vermont | f | m | f | o | o |
| Virginia | m[8] | r | o | o | o |
| Washington | m | f | m | o | o |
| West Virginia | f | f | f | o | m |
| Wisconsin | m[9] | m | f | o | m |
| Wyoming | m | m | f | o | o |

Note:  Symbols used in table:
   r = required
   m = used in many areas
   f = used in few areas
   o = not used at all

1. The ballot or voting device allows the citizen to vote for all candidates of the same party by marking one box or pulling a single lever.

2. Used for absentee voting only.

3. Except in Presidential elections where candidates for the office of Presidential electors are on a separate straight party ticket.

4. Open elections preclude straight party voting.

5. Optional in primaries.  Mandatory with some exceptions in general elections.

6. Straight party vote used in primary only, crossover voting used in general elections.

7. Straight party ticket can be cast only for each level of government.

8. All precincts having 750 or more registered voters must have voting machines.

9. Mandatory for municipalities of 10,000 or more population; optional for smaller communities.

# CHAPTER FOUR
## *Foreign Affairs*

☆           ☆

The conduct of foreign affairs has in recent years taken on an importance in the United States which it did not have throughout much of the nation's history. During much of the nineteenth and early twentieth centuries, the country's preoccupation with economic development and domestic issues far overshadowed developments in international relations and diplomacy. In this chapter are recorded some basic data on the foreign affairs of the United States since 1789. Table 4.1 contains the dates of recognition by the United States of present-day countries of the world. Ambassadors of the United States sent to selected major nations are documented in table 4.2, while table 4.3 provides the names of the current U.S. ambassadors to most nations in existence as of late 1984. Table 4.4 details the economic assistance (often referred to as "foreign aid") provided by the United States to selected countries in the post-World War II period.

Table 4.1

United States Recognition of Foreign Nations

| Nation | Date of Recognition | Nation | Date of Recognition |
|---|---|---|---|
| Afghanistan | January 22, 1935 | Ethiopia | July 20, 1908 |
| Albania | September 22, 1922 | Fiji | February 15, 1972 |
| Algeria | November 29, 1962 | Finland | March 13, 1920 |
| Argentina | January 27, 1832 | France | September 14, 1778 |
| Australia | January 12, 1940 | Gabon | December 12, 1960 |
| Austria | February 8, 1838 | Gambia | May 18, 1965 |
| Bahamas | July 10, 1973 | Germany[a] | June 1, 1797 |
| Bahrain | December 9, 1971 | Ghana | February 28, 1957 |
| Bangladesh | September 11, 1972 | Greece | March 11, 1868 |
| Barbados | September 13, 1967 | Grenada | February 7, 1974 |
| Belgium | April 14, 1832 | Guatemala | March 7, 1825 |
| Benin | October 14, 1960 | Guinea | June 18, 1959 |
| Bolivia | March 30, 1848 | Guinea-Bissau | September 12, 1974 |
| Botswana | June 9, 1971 | Guyana | June 16, 1966 |
| Brazil | March 9, 1825 | Haiti | July 12, 1862 |
| Bulgaria | April 24, 1901 | Honduras | March 29, 1853 |
| Burma | October 17, 1947 | Hungary | December 27, 1921 |
| Burundi | October 25, 1962 | Iceland | August 8, 1941 |
| Cambodia | June 29, 1950 | India | April 10, 1947 |
| Cameroon | April 20, 1960, | Indonesia | December 28, 1949 |
| Canada | February 17, 1927 | Iran | January 29, 1883 |
| Cape Verde Is. | July 14, 1975 | Iraq | March 30, 1931 |
| Central Afr. Rep. | December 12, 1960 | Ireland | February 19, 1927 |
| Chad | December 12, 1960 | Israel[b] | March 18, 1949 |
| Chile | January 27, 1823 | Italy | June 5, 1840 |
| China | March 3, 1843 | Ivory Coast | October 14, 1960 |
| Colombia | January 27, 1823 | Jamaica | October 23, 1962 |
| Congo | November 9, 1960 | Japan | January 19, 1859 |
| Costa Rica | March 29, 1853 | Jordan | February 2, 1950 |
| Cuba | May 20, 1902 | Kenya | February 20, 1964 |
| Cyprus | August 27, 1960 | Korea | February 27, 1883 |
| Czechoslovakia | April 29, 1919 | Kuwait | October 2, 1961 |
| Denmark | March 3, 1827 | Laos | June 29, 1950 |
| Dominican Republic | November 12, 1883 | Lebanon | October 9, 1942 |
| Ecuador | April 10, 1848 | Lesotho | June 9, 1971 |
| Egypt | August 14, 1848 | Liberia | March 11, 1863 |
| El Salvador | March 29, 1853 | Libya | February 7, 1952 |
| Equatorial Guinea | October 28, 1968 | Luxembourg | June 5, 1903 |

Table 4.1 (continued)

| Nation | Date of Recognition | Nation | Date of Recognition |
|--------|---------------------|--------|---------------------|
| Madagascar | August 27, 1960 | Seychelles | June 26, 1976 |
| Malawi | July 1, 1964 | Sierra Leone | May 11, 1961 |
| Malaysia | August 31, 1957 | Singapore | October 13, 1966 |
| Maldives | November 10, 1965 | Somalia | July 5, 1960 |
| Mali | July 18, 1960 | South Africa | May 31, 1961 |
| Malta | July 22, 1965 | Spain | September 28, 1779 |
| Mauritania | November 28, 1960 | Sri Lanka | April 8, 1948 |
| Mauritius | June 24, 1968 | Sudan | March 2, 1956 |
| Mexico | January 27, 1823 | Surinam | November 26, 1975 |
| Morocco | March 8, 1905 | Swaziland | June 9, 1971 |
| Mozambique | June 26, 1975 | Sweden | September 28, 1782 |
| Nepal | February 26, 1948 | Switzerland | March 16, 1853 |
| Netherlands | August 16, 1781 | Syria | October 9, 1942 |
| New Zealand | February 14, 1942 | Tanzania | August 22, 1962 |
| Nicaragua | March 12, 1851 | Thailand | July 13, 1882 |
| Niger | October 14, 1960 | Togo | June 23, 1960 |
| Nigeria | September 23, 1960 | Tonga | October 2, 1972 |
| Norway | March 8, 1905 | Trinidad & Tobago | October 23, 1962 |
| Oman | February 29, 1972 | Tunisia | June 5, 1956 |
| Pakistan | September 20, 1947 | Turkey | April 15, 1831 |
| Panama | December 17, 1963 | U.S.S.R. | December 19, 1780 |
| Papua New Guinea | September 16, 1975 | Uganda | January 7, 1963 |
| Paraguay | June 8, 1861 | United Arab Emir. | February 29, 1972 |
| Peru | May 2, 1826 | United Kingdom | February 24, 1785 |
| Philippines | June 21, 1946 | Upper Volta | October 17, 1960 |
| Poland | April 16, 1919 | Uruguay | April 5, 1867 |
| Portugal | February 21, 1791 | Venezuela | March 3, 1835 |
| Qatar | December 9, 1971 | Vietnam | June 29, 1950 |
| Romania | June 11, 1880 | Western Samoa | February 10, 1971 |
| Rwanda | March 9, 1963 | Yemen | August 22, 1946 |
| Sao Tome & Principe | July 12, 1975 | Yugoslavia[c] | July 7, 1882 |
| Saudi Arabia | August 7, 1939 | Zaire | July 5, 1966 |
| Senegal | October 8, 1960 | Zambia | March 11, 1965 |

[a]Ambassador commissioned to Prussia.

[b]Ambassador commissioned to Kingdom of Sardinia.

[c]Ambassador commissioned to Serbia.

Table 4.2

United States Ambassadors to
Selected Nations

| Name | Home State | Dates of Service From | To |
|------|------------|----------------------|-----|
| | | Argentina | |
| Caesar A. Rodney | Delaware | Dec. 27, 1823 | June 10, 1824 |
| John M. Forbes | Massachusetts | Aug. 20, 1825 | June 14, 1831 |
| Francis Baylies | Massachusetts | June 15, 1832 | Sept. 26, 1832 |
| William Brent, Jr. | Wash., D.C. | Nov. 15, 1844 | July 7, 1846 |
| William A. Harris | Virginia | July 7, 1846 | Sept. 12, 1851 |
| John S. Pendleton | Virginia | Sept. 12, 1851 | Mar. 31, 1854 |
| James A. Peden | Florida | Jan. 22, 1855 | May 1, 1857 |
| Benjamin C. Yancey | Georgia | Dec. 1, 1858 | Sept. 30, 1859 |
| John F. Cushman | Mississippi | Dec. 22, 1859 | Feb. 17, 1861 |
| Robert M. Palmer | Pennsylvania | Oct. 5, 1861 | Apr. 12, 1862 |
| Robert C. Kirk | Ohio | June 21, 1862 | July 26, 1866 |
| Alexander Asboth | Misssouri | Oct. 20, 1866 | Jan. 21, 1868 |
| H. G. Worthington | Nevada | Sept. 11, 1868 | July 8, 1869 |
| Robert C. Kirk | Ohio | July 8, 1869 | Nov. 4, 1871 |
| Julius White | Illinois | May 6, 1873 | Nov. 14, 1873 |
| Thomas O. Osborn | Illinois | May 21, 1874 | Oct. 15, 1885 |
| Bayless W. Hanna | Indiana | Oct. 15, 1885 | July 8, 1889 |
| John R. G. Pitkin | Louisiana | Oct. 31, 1889 | Aug. 15, 1893 |
| William I. Buchanan | Iowa | May 19, 1894 | July 11, 1899 |
| William P. Lord | Oregon | Feb. 14, 1900 | Mar. 27, 1903 |
| John Barrett | Oregon | Dec. 21, 1903 | Apr. 27, 1904 |
| Arthur M. Beaupré | Illinois | June 17, 1904 | May 2, 1908 |
| Spencer F. Eddy | Illinois | Aug. 27, 1908 | Jan. 2, 1909 |
| Charles H. Sherrill | New York | June 30, 1909 | Sept. 16, 1910 |
| John W. Garrett | Maryland | Feb. 29, 1912 | Nov. 22, 1913 |
| Frederic Jessup Stimson | Massachusetts | Jan. 8, 1915 | Apr. 21, 1921 |
| John W. Riddle | Connecticut | Mar. 8, 1922 | May 28, 1925 |
| Peter Augustus Jay | Rhode Island | Sept. 24, 1925 | Dec. 30, 1926 |
| Robert Woods Bliss | New York | Sept. 9, 1927 | Apr. 29, 1933 |
| Alexander W. Weddell | Virginia | Sept. 18, 1933 | Oct. 29, 1938 |
| Norman Armour | New Jersey | June 19, 1939 | June 29, 1944 |
| Spruille Braden | New York | May 21, 1945 | Sept. 23, 1945 |
| George S. Messersmith | Delaware | May 23, 1946 | June 21, 1947 |
| James Bruce | Maryland | Aug. 21, 1947 | Aug. 20, 1949 |
| Stanton Griffis | Connecticut | Nov. 17, 1949 | Sept. 23, 1950 |
| Ellsworth Bunker | New York | May 8, 1951 | Mar. 21, 1952 |
| Albert F. Nufer | New York | Aug. 14, 1952 | May 12, 1956 |
| Willard L. Beaulac | Rhode Island | June 1, 1956 | Aug. 2, 1960 |
| Roy Richard Rubottom, Jr. | Texas | Oct.20,1960 | Oct.19, 1961 |
| Robert McClintock | California | Feb. 14, 1962 | May 10, 1964 |
| Edwin M. Martin | Ohio | June 11, 1964 | Jan. 5, 1968 |
| Carter L. Burgess | New York | Aug. 21, 1968 | Mar. 14, 1969 |
| John Davis Lodge | Connecticut | July 23, 1969 | Nov. 10, 1973 |
| Robert C. Hill | New Hampshire | Feb. 15, 1974 | May 10, 1977 |
| Raul H. Castro | Arizona | Nov. 16, 1977 | July 30, 1980 |
| Harry W. Shlaudeman | California | Nov. 4, 1981 | n.a. |
| Frank Ortiz, Jr. | New Mexico | Nov. 17, 1983 | |

Table 4.2 (continued)

| Name | Home State | Dates of Service | |
|---|---|---|---|
| | | From | To |

## Australia

| Name | Home State | From | To |
|---|---|---|---|
| Clarence E. Gauss | Connecticut | July 17, 1940 | Mar. 5, 1941 |
| Nelson T. Johnson | Oklahoma | Sept. 12, 1941 | Apr. 20, 1945 |
| Robert Butler | Minnesota | Sept. 25, 1946 | Mar. 31, 1948 |
| Myron Melvin Cowen | New York | Aug. 20, 1948 | Mar. 17, 1949 |
| Pete Jarman | Alabama | Sept. 7, 1949 | July 31, 1953 |
| Amos J. Peaslee | New Jersey | Aug. 12, 1953 | Feb. 16, 1956 |
| Douglas Maxwell Moffat | New York | Mar. 27, 1956 | Aug. 30, 1956 |
| William J. Sebald | Wash., D.C. | June 7, 1957 | Oct. 31, 1961 |
| William C. Battle | Virginia | July 13, 1962 | Aug. 31, 1964 |
| Edward Clark | Texas | Aug. 23, 1965 | Dec. 31, 1967 |
| William H. Crook | Texas | July 22, 1968 | Apr. 18, 1969 |
| Walter L. Rice | Virginia | Sept. 11, 1969 | May 26, 1973 |
| Marshall Green | Wash., D.C. | June 8, 1973 | July 31, 1975 |
| James W. Hargrove | Texas | Feb. 19, 1976 | Mar. 8, 1977 |
| Philip H. Alston, Jr. | Georgia | May 23, 1977 | Jan. 23, 1981 |
| Robert Dean Nesen | California | May 19, 1981 | |

## Austria

| Name | Home State | From | To |
|---|---|---|---|
| Henry A. Muhlenberg | Pennsylvania | Nov. 7, 1838 | Sept. 18, 1840 |
| Daniel Jenifer | Maryland | Mar. 30, 1842 | July 7, 1845 |
| William H. Stiles | Georgia | Aug. 5, 1845 | Aug. 1, 1849 |
| James Watson Webb | New York | Feb. 6, 1850 | May 8, 1850 |
| Charles J. McCurdy | Connecticut | Mar. 14, 1851 | Oct. 12, 1852 |
| Thomas M. Foote | New York | Dec. 14, 1852 | June 25, 1853 |
| Henry R. Jackson | Georgia | Sept. 16, 1853 | June 1, 1858 |
| J. Glancy Jones | Pennsylvania | Feb. 14, 1859 | Nov. 14, 1861 |
| J. Lothrop Motley | Massachusetts | Nov. 14, 1861 | June 14, 1867 |
| Henry M. Watts | Pennsylvania | Sept. 25, 1868 | June 1, 1869 |
| John Jay | New York | June 1, 1869 | March 31, 1875 |
| Godlove S. Orth | Indiana | May 24, 1875 | March 10, 1876 |
| Edward F. Beale | Wash., D.C. | Aug. 10, 1876 | Apr. 20, 1877 |
| John A. Kasson | Iowa | Aug. 30, 1877 | MAr. 25, 1881 |
| William Walter Phelps | New Jersey | June 20, 1881 | June 30, 1882 |
| Alphonso Taft | Ohio | June 30, 1882 | Aug. 25, 1884 |
| John M. Francis | New York | Sept. 11, 1884 | Aug. 3, 1885 |
| Alexander R. Lawton | Georgia | Aug. 25, 1887 | May 15, 1889 |
| Frederick D. Grant | New York | May 15, 1889 | June 8, 1893 |
| Bartlett Tripp | South Dakota | June 8, 1893 | June 18, 1897 |
| Charlemagne Tower | Pennsylvania | June 18, 1897 | Feb. 9, 1899 |
| Addison C. Harris | Indiana | Apr. 13, 1899 | Apr. 29, 1901 |
| Robert S. McCormick | Illinois | Apr. 29, 1901 | Dec. 29, 1902 |
| Ballamy Storer | Ohio | Jan. 3, 1903 | Feb. 8, 1906 |
| Charles S. Francis | New York | May 29, 1906 | Apr. 1, 1910 |
| Richard C. Kerens | Missouri | Apr. 12, 1910 | June 28, 1913 |
| Frederic C. Penfield | Pennsylvania | Sept. 26, 1913 | Apr. 7, 1917 |
| Arthur Hugh Frazier | Pennsylvania | Nov. 26, 1921 | May 21, 1922 |
| Albert Henry Washburn | Massachusetts | June 19, 1922 | Apr. 29, 1930 |
| Gilchrist Baker Stockton | Florida | May 15, 1930 | Sept. 21, 1933 |
| George H. Earle III | Pennsylvania | Sept. 27, 1933 | Mar. 25, 1934 |
| George S. Messersmith | Delaware | May 23, 1934 | July 11, 1937 |
| Grenville T. Emmet | New York | Sept. 14, 1937 | Sept. 26, 1937 |
| John G. Erhardt | New York | Sept. 7, 1946 | June 27, 1950 |
| Walter J. Donnelly | Wash., D.C. | Oct. 25, 1950 | July 19, 1952 |
| Llewellyn E. Thompson, Jr. | Colorado | Sept. 4, 1952 | July 9, 1957 |
| H. Freeman Matthews | Wash., D.C. | Sept. 4, 1957 | May 25, 1962 |

Table 4.2 (continued)

| Name | Home State | Dates of Service | |
|------|------------|------|----|
| | | From | To |

## Austria

| James W. Riddleberger | Virginia | Dec. 12, 1962 | May 10, 1967 |
| Douglas MacArthur II | Wash., D.C. | May 24, 1967 | Sept. 16, 1969 |
| John P. Humes | New York | Oct. 29, 1969 | Mar. 6, 1975 |
| Wiley T. Buchanan | Wash., D.C. | Apr. 2, 1975 | Mar. 31, 1977 |
| Milton A. Wolf | Ohio | Sept. 5, 1977 | Mar. 2, 1980 |
| Philip M. Kaiser | New York | Mar. 25, 1980 | Mar. 2, 1981 |
| Theodore E. Cummings | California | Sept. 2, 1981 | Mar. 30, 1982 |
| Helene A. von Damm | New Jersey | May 3, 1983 | |

## Brazil

| Condy Raguet | Pennsylvania | Oct. 29, 1825 | Apr. 16, 1827 |
| William Tudor | Massachusetts | June 25, 1828 | May 9, 1830 |
| Ethan A. Brown | Ohio | Feb. 18, 1831 | Apr. 11, 1834 |
| William Hunter | Rhode Island | Jan. 7, 1835 | Dec. 9, 1843 |
| George H. Proffit | Indiana | Dec. 11, 1843 | Aug. 10, 1844 |
| Henry A. Wise | Virginia | Aug. 10, 1844 | Aug. 28, 1847 |
| David Tod | Ohio | Aug. 28, 1847 | Aug. 9, 1851 |
| Robert C. Schenck | Ohio | Aug. 9, 1851 | Oct. 8, 1853 |
| William Trousdale | Tennessee | Oct. 8, 1853 | Dec. 5, 1857 |
| Richard K. Meade | Virginia | Dec. 5, 1857 | July 9, 1861 |
| James Watson Webb | New York | Oct. 21, 1861 | May 26, 1869 |
| Henry T. Blow | Missouri | Aug. 28, 1869 | Nov. 6, 1870 |
| James R. Partridge | Maryland | July 31, 1871 | June 11, 1877 |
| Henry W. Hilliard | Georgia | Oct. 23, 1877 | June 15, 1881 |
| Thomas A. Osborn | Kansas | Dec. 17, 1881 | July 11, 1885 |
| Thomas J. Jarvis | North Carolina | July 11, 1885 | Nov. 18, 1888 |
| Robert Adams, Jr. | Pennsylvania | July 20, 1889 | Mar. 1, 1890 |
| Edwin H. Conger | Iowa | Dec. 19, 1890 | Sept. 9, 1893 |
| Thomas L. Thompson | California | Sept. 9, 1893 | July 17, 1897 |
| Edwin H. Conger | Iowa | Aug. 9, 1897 | Feb. 6, 1898 |
| Charles Page Bryan | Illinois | Apr. 11, 1898 | Dec. 3, 1902 |
| David E. Thompson | Nebraska | Apr. 1, 1903 | Nov. 3, 1905 |
| LLoyd C. Griscom | Pennsylvania | June 6, 1906 | Jan. 2, 1907 |
| Irving B. Dudley | California | April 1, 1907 | Sept. 16, 1911 |
| Edwin V. Morgan | New York | June 4, 1912 | Apr. 23, 1933 |
| Hugh S. Gibson | California | Aug. 8, 1933 | Dec. 3, 1936 |
| Jefferson Caffery | Louisiana | Aug. 17, 1937 | Sept. 17, 1944 |
| Adolph A. Berle, Jr. | New York | Jan. 30, 1945 | Feb. 27, 1946 |
| William D. Pawley | Florida | June 13, 1946 | Mar. 26, 1948 |
| Herschel V. Johnson | North Carolina | July 22, 1948 | May 27, 1953 |
| James S. Kemper | Illinois | Aug. 18, 1953 | Jan. 26, 1955 |
| James Clement Dunn | New York | Mar. 11, 1955 | July 4, 1956 |
| Ellis O. Briggs | Maine | July 24, 1956 | May 2, 1959 |
| John M. Cabot | Wash., D.C. | July 22, 1959 | Aug. 17, 1961 |
| Lincoln Gordon | Massachusetts | Oct. 19, 1961 | Feb. 25, 1966 |
| John W. Tuthill | Illinois | June 30, 1966 | Jan. 9, 1969 |
| C. Burke Elbrick | Kentucky | July 14, 1969 | May 7, 1970 |
| William M. Roundtree | Florida | Nov. 16, 1970 | May 30, 1973 |
| John H. Crimmins | Maryland | Aug. 13, 1973 | Feb. 25, 1978 |
| Robert Marion Sayre | Virginia | June 8, 1978 | Sept. 19, 1981 |
| Langhorne A. Motley | Alaska | Oct. 6, 1981 | n.a. |
| Diego Ascencio | n.a. | Nov. 9, 1983 | |

Table 4.2 (continued)

| Name | Home State | Dates of Service | |
|------|------------|------|-----|
| | | From | To |

### Canada

| Name | Home State | From | To |
|------|------------|------|-----|
| William Phillips | Massachusetts | June 1, 1927 | Dec. 14, 1929 |
| Hanford MacNider | Iowa | Aug. 29, 1930 | Aug. 15, 1932 |
| Warren Delano Robbins | New York | May 16, 1933 | Mar. 28, 1935 |
| Norman Armour | New Jersey | Aug. 7, 1935 | Jan. 15, 1938 |
| Daniel C. Roper | Wash., D.C. | May 19, 1939 | Aug. 20, 1940 |
| ames H. R. Cromwell | New Jersey | Jan. 24, 1940 | May 16, 1940 |
| Jay Pierrepont Moffat | New Hampshire | June 13, 1940 | Jan. 24, 1943 |
| Ray Atherton | Illinois | Aug. 3, 1943 | Aug. 30, 1948 |
| Lawrence A. Steinhardt | New York | Nov. 1, 1948 | Mar. 28, 1950 |
| Stanley Woodward | Pennsylvania | June 22, 1950 | Jan. 14, 1953 |
| R. Douglas Stuart | Illinois | July 15, 1953 | May 4, 1956 |
| Livingstpn T. Merchant | Wash., D.C. | May 23, 1956 | Nov. 6, 1958 |
| Richard B. Wigglesworth | Massachusetts | Dec. 15, 1958 | Oct. 19, 1960 |
| Livingston T. Merchant | Wash., D.C. | Mar. 15, 1961 | May 26, 1962 |
| W. Walton Butterworth | Louisiana | Dec. 11, 1962 | Sept. 10, 1968 |
| Harold Francis Linder | New York | Sept. 10, 1968 | July 9, 1969 |
| Adolph W. Schmidt | Pennsylvania | Sept. 11, 1969 | Jan. 29, 1974 |
| William J. Porter | Massachusetts | Mar. 13, 1974 | Dec. 20, 1975 |
| Thomas O. Enders | Connecticut | Feb. 17, 1976 | Sept. 14, 1979 |
| Kenneth M. Curtis | Maine | Oct. 5, 1979 | Jan. 20, 1981 |
| Paul Heron Robinson, Jr. | Illinois | July 15, 1981 | |

### China, National Republic of[a]

| Name | Home State | From | To |
|------|------------|------|-----|
| Caleb Cushing | Massachusetts | June 12, 1844 | Aug. 27, 1844 |
| Alexander H. Everett | Massachusetts | Oct. 26, 1846 | June 28, 1847 |
| John W. Davis | Indiana | Oct. 6, 1848 | May 25, 1850 |
| Humphrey Marshall | Kentucky | July 4, 1853 | Jan. 27, 1854 |
| Robert M. McLane | Maryland | Nov. 3, 1854 | Dec. 12, 1854 |
| Peter Parker | Massachusetts | July 15, 1856 | Aug. 25, 1857 |
| William B. Reed | Pennsylvania | May 3, 1858 | Nov. 11, 1858 |
| John E. Ward | Georgia | Aug. 10, 1859 | Dec. 15, 1860 |
| Anson Burlingame | Massachusetts | Aug. 20, 1862 | Nov. 21, 1867 |
| J. Ross Browne | California | Sept. 29, 1868 | July 5, 1869 |
| Frederick F. Low | California | Apr. 27, 1870 | July 24, 1873 |
| Benjamin P. Avery | California | Nov. 29, 1874 | Nov. 8, 1875 |
| Goerge F. Seward | California | Apr. 24, 1876 | Aug. 16, 1880 |
| James B. Angell | Michigan | Aug. 16, 1880 | Oct. 4, 1881 |
| John Russell Young | New York | Aug. 17, 1882 | Apr. 7, 1885 |
| Charles Denby | Indiana | Oct. 1, 1885 | July 8, 1898 |
| Edwin H. Conger | Iowa | July 8, 1898 | Apr. 4, 1905 |
| William Woodville Rockhill | Wash., D.C. | June 17, 1905 | June 1, 1909 |
| William James Calhoun | Illinois | Apr. 21, 1910 | Feb. 26, 1913 |
| Paul S. Reinsch | Wisconsin | Nov. 15, 1913 | Sept. 15, 1919 |
| Charles R. Crane | Illinois | June 12, 1920 | July 2, 1921 |
| Jacob Gould Schurman | New York | Sept. 12, 1921 | Apr. 15, 1925 |
| John Van A. MacMurray | New Jersey | July 15, 1925 | Nov. 22, 1929 |
| Nelson T. Johnson | Oklahoma | Feb. 1, 1930 | May 14, 1941 |
| Clarence E. Gauss | Connecticut | May 26, 1941 | Nov. 14, 1944 |
| Patrick J. Hurley | New Mexico | Jan. 8, 1945 | Sept. 22, 1945 |
| J. Leighton Stuart | New York | July 19, 1946 | Aug. 2, 1949 |
| Karl L. Rankin | Maine | Apr. 2, 1953 | Dec. 30, 1957 |
| Everett F. Drumright | Oklahoma | Mar. 8, 1958 | Mar. 8, 1962 |

Table 4.2 (continued)

|  |  | Dates of Service | |
|  | Home | | |
| Name | State | From | To |

### China, National Republic of[a]

| Alan G. Kirk | New York | July 5, 1962 | Jan. 18, 1963 |
| Jerauld Wright | Wash., D.C. | June 29, 1963 | July 25, 1965 |
| Walter P. McConaughy | Alabama | June 28, 1966 | Apr. 4, 1974 |
| Leonard Unger | Maryland | May 25, 1974 | Jan. 19, 1979 |

### China, People's Republic of[b]

| David K. E. Bruce | Virginia | Mar. 15, 1973 | Sept. 25, 1974 |
| George Bush | Texas | Sept. 26, 1974 | Dec. 7, 1975 |
| Thomas S. Gates, Jr. | Pennsylvania | Apr. 14, 1976 | May 8, 1977 |
| Leonard Woodcock | Michigan | July 11, 1977 | Mar. 1, 1979 |
| Leonard Woodcock | Michigan | Mar. 1, 1979 | n.a. 1981 |
| Arthur W. Hummel, Jr. | Maryland | n.a. 1981 | n.a. 1981 |

### France

| Benjamin Franklin | Pennsylvania | Mar. 23, 1779 | May 17, 1785 |
| Thomas Jefferson | Virginia | May 17, 1785 | Sept. 26, 1789 |
| William Short | Virginia | June 14, 1790 | May 15, 1792 |
| Gouverneur Morris | New York | June 3, 1792 | Apr. 8, 1794 |
| James Monroe | Virginia | Aug. 15, 1794 | Dec. 9, 1796 |
| Robert R. Livingston | New York | Dec. 6, 1801 | Nov. 18, 1804 |
| John Armstrong | New York | Nov. 18, 1804 | Sept. 14, 1810 |
| Jonathan Russell | Rhode Island | Feb. 13, 1811 | Nov. 17, 1811 |
| Joel Barlow | Wash., D.C. | Nov. 17, 1811 | Dec. 26, 1812 |
| William H. Crawford | Georgia | Dec. 14, 1813 | Apr. 26-30,1815 |
| Albert Gallatin | Pennsylvania | July 16, 1816 | May 16, 1823 |
| James Brown | Louisiana | Apr. 13, 1824 | June 28, 1829 |
| William C. Rives | Virginia | Oct. 25, 1829 | Sept. 27, 1832 |
| Levett Harris | New Jersey | Apr. 20, 1833 | Sept. 30, 1833 |
| Edward Livingston | Louisiana | Sept. 30, 1833 | Apr. 29, 1835 |
| Lewis Cass | Michigan | Dec. 1, 1836 | Nov. 12, 1842 |
| William R. King | Alabama | July 1, 1844 | Sept. 15, 1846 |
| Richard Rush | Pennsylvania | July 31, 1847 | Oct. 8, 1849 |
| William C. Rives | Virginia | July 20, 1849 | May 12, 1853 |
| John Y. Mason | Virginia | Jan. 22, 1854 | Oct. 3, 1859 |
| Charles J. Faulkner | Virginia | Mar. 4, 1860 | May 12, 1861 |
| William L. Dayton | New Jersey | May 19, 1861 | Dec. 1, 1864 |
| John Bigelow | New York | Apr. 23, 1865 | Dec. 23, 1866 |
| John A. Dix | New York | Dec. 23, 1866 | May 23, 1869 |
| Elihu B. Washburne | Illinois | May 23, 1869 | Sept. 5, 1877 |
| Edward F. Noyes | Ohio | Sept. 5, 1877 | Aug. 5, 1881 |
| Levi P. Morton | New York | Aug. 5, 1881 | May 14, 1885 |
| Robert M. McLane | Maryland | May 14, 1885 | May 20, 1889 |
| Whitelaw Reid | New York | May 21, 1889 | Mar. 25, 1892 |
| T. Jefferson Coolidge | Massachusetts | June 10, 1892 | May 4, 1893 |
| James B. Eustis | Louisiana | May 6, 1893 | May 24, 1897 |
| Horace Porter | New York | May 25, 1897 | May 2, 1905 |
| Robert S. McCormick | Illinois | May 2, 1905 | Mar. 2, 1907 |
| Henry White | Rhode Island | Mar. 23, 1907 | Nov. 3, 1909 |
| Robert Bacon | New York | Dec. 31, 1909 | Apr. 19, 1912 |
| Myron T. Herrick | Ohio | Apr. 29, 1912 | Nov. 28, 1914 |
| William G. Sharp | Ohio | Dec. 4, 1914 | Apr. 14, 1919 |
| Hugh Campbell Wallace | Washington | Apr. 22, 1919 | July 5, 1921 |
| Myron T. Herrick | Ohio | July 15, 1921 | Mar. 31, 1929 |
| Walter E. Edge | New Jersey | Dec. 18, 1929 | Apr. 13, 1933 |
| Jesse Isidor Straus | New York | June 8, 1933 | Aug. 5, 1936 |
| William Christian Bulitt | Pennsylvania | Oct. 13, 1936 | July 11, 1940 |
| William D. Leahy | Georgia | Jan. 8, 1941 | May 1, 1942 |

Table 4.2 (continued)

| Name | Home State | Dates of Service | |
|------|-----------|------|-----|
| | | From | To |

France

| Name | Home State | From | To |
|------|-----------|------|-----|
| Jefferson Caffery | Louisiana | Dec. 30, 1944 | May 13, 1949 |
| David K. E. Bruce | Virginia | May 17, 1949 | Mar. 10, 1952 |
| James Clement Dunn | New York | Mar. 27, 1952 | Mar. 2, 1953 |
| C. Douglas Dillon | New Jersey | Mar. 13, 1953 | Jan. 28, 1957 |
| Amory Houghton | New York | Apr. 17, 1957 | Jan. 19, 1961 |
| James M. Gavin | Massachusetts | Mar. 21, 1961 | Sept. 26, 1962 |
| Charles E. Bohlen | Wash., D.C. | Oct. 27, 1962 | Feb. 9, 1968 |
| Robert Sargent Shriver, Jr. | Illinois | May 25, 1968 | Mar. 25, 1970 |
| Arthur K. Watson | Connecticut | May 6, 1970 | Oct. 30, 1972 |
| John N. Irwin II | New York | Mar. 23, 1973 | Oct. 20, 1974 |
| Kenneth Rush | New York | Nov. 21, 1974 | Mar. 14, 1977 |
| Arthur A. Hartman | New Jersey | July 7, 1977 | Oct. 14, 1981 |
| Evan Griffith Galbraith | Connecticut | Dec. 2, 1981 | |

Germany

| Name | Home State | From | To |
|------|-----------|------|-----|
| John Quincy Adams | Massachusetts | Dec. 5, 1797 | May 5, 1801 |
| Henry Wheaton | New York | June 9, 1835 | July 18, 1846 |
| Andrew J. Donelson | Tennessee | July 18, 1846 | Nov. 2, 1849 |
| Edward A. Hannegan | Indiana | June 30, 1849 | Jan. 13, 1850 |
| Daniel D. Barnard | New York | Dec. 10, 1850 | Sept. 21, 1853 |
| Peter D. Vroom | New Jersey | Nov. 4, 1853 | Aug. 10, 1857 |
| Joseph A. Wright | Indiana | Sept. 3, 1857 | July 1, 1861 |
| Norman B. Judd | Illinois | July 1, 1861 | Sept. 3, 1865 |
| Joseph A. Wright | Indiana | Sept. 3, 1865 | May 11, 1867 |
| George Bancroft | New York | Aug. 28, 1867 | June 30, 1874 |
| J. C. Bancroft Davis | Massachusetts | Aug. 28, 1874 | Sept. 26, 1877 |
| Bayard Taylor | Pennsylvania | May 7, 1878 | Dec. 19, 1878 |
| Andrew D. White | New York | June 19, 1879 | Aug. 15, 1881 |
| A. A. Sargent | California | May 18, 1882 | June 6, 1884 |
| John A. Kasson | Iowa | Sept. 10, 1884 | June 21, 1885 |
| George H. Pendleton | Ohio | June 21, 1885 | Apr. 25, 1889 |
| William Walter Phelps | New Jersey | Sept. 26, 1889 | June 4, 1893 |
| Theodore Runyon | New Jersey | June 4, 1893 | Jan. 27, 1896 |
| Edwin F. Uhl | Michigan | May 3, 1896 | June 8, 1897 |
| Andrew D. White | New York | June 12, 1897 | Nov. 27, 1902 |
| Charlemagne Tower | Pennsylvania | Dec. 19, 1902 | June 8, 1908 |
| David Jayne Hill | New York | June 14, 1908 | Sept. 2, 1911 |
| John G. A. Leishman | Pennsylvania | Oct. 24, 1911 | Oct. 4, 1913 |
| James W. Gerard | New York | Oct. 29, 1913 | Feb. 5, 1917 |
| Ellis Loring Dressel | Massachusetts | Dec. 10, 1921 | Apr. 18, 1922 |
| Alanson B. Houghton | New York | Apr. 22, 1922 | Feb. 21, 1925 |
| Jacob Gould Schurman | New York | June 29, 1925 | Jan. 21, 1930 |
| Frederic M. Sackett | Kentucky | Feb. 12, 1930 | Mar. 24, 1933 |
| William E. Dodd | Illinois | Aug. 30, 1933 | Dec. 29, 1937 |
| Hugh R. Wilson | Illinois | Mar. 3, 1938 | Nov. 16, 1938 |
| James B. Conant | Massachusetts | May 14, 1955[c] | Feb. 19, 1957 |
| David K. E. Bruce | Maryland | Apr. 17, 1957 | Oct. 29, 1959 |
| Walter C. Dowling | Georgia | Dec. 3, 1959 | Apr. 21, 1963 |
| George C. McGhee | Texas | May 18, 1963 | May 21, 1968 |
| Henry Cabot Lodge | Massachusetts | May 27, 1968 | Jan. 14, 1969 |
| Kenneth Rush | New York | July 22, 1969 | Feb. 20, 1972 |
| Martin J. Hillenbrand | Illinois | June 27, 1972 | Oct. 18, 1976 |
| Walter J. Stoessel, Jr. | California | Oct. 27, 1976 | Jan. 5, 1981 |
| Arthur F. Burns | Wash., D.C. | June 30, 1981 | |

Table 4.2 (continued)

| Name | Home State | Dates of Service | |
|------|------------|------|-----|
| | | From | To |

### India

| Name | Home State | From | To |
|------|------------|------|-----|
| Henry F. Grady | California | July 1, 1947 | June 22, 1948 |
| Loy W. Henderson | Colorado | Nov. 19, 1948 | Sept. 21, 1951 |
| Chester Bowles | Connecticut | Nov. 1, 1951 | Mar. 23, 1953 |
| George V. Allen | North Carolina | May 4, 1953 | Nov. 30, 1954 |
| John Sherman Cooper | Kentucky | Apr. 9, 1955 | Apr. 23, 1956 |
| Ellsworth Bunker | Vermont | Mar. 4, 1957 | Mar. 23, 1961 |
| J. Kenneth Galbraith | Massachusetts | Apr. 18, 1961 | July 12, 1963 |
| Chester Bowles | Connecticut | July 19, 1963 | Apr. 21, 1969 |
| Kenneth B. Keating | New York | July 2, 1969 | July 26, 1972 |
| Daniel P. Moynihan | New York | Feb. 28, 1973 | Dec. 2, 1974 |
| William B. Saxbe | Ohio | Mar. 8, 1975 | Nov. 20, 1976 |
| Robert F. Goheen | New Jersey | May 26, 1977 | Dec. 10, 1980 |
| Harry G. Barnes, Jr. | Maryland | Nov. 17, 1981 | |

### Israel

| Name | Home State | From | To |
|------|------------|------|-----|
| James Grover McDonald | New York | Mar. 28, 1949 | Dec. 13, 1950 |
| Monnett B. Davis | Colorado | Feb. 26, 1951 | Dec. 26, 1953 |
| Edward B. Lawson | Wash., D.C. | Nov. 12, 1954 | Feb. 17, 1959 |
| Ogden Rogers Reid | New York | July 2, 1959 | Jan. 19, 1961 |
| Walworth Barbour | Massachusetts | June 12, 1961 | Jan. 19, 1973 |
| Kenneth B. Keating | New York | Aug. 28, 1973 | May 5, 1975 |
| Malcolm Toon | Maryland | July 10, 1975 | Dec. 27, 1976 |
| Samuel W. Lewis | Texas | May 25, 1977 | |

### Italy

| Name | Home State | From | To |
|------|------------|------|-----|
| Hezekiah Gold Rogers | n.a. | Sept. 15, 1840 | Nov. 22, 1841 |
| Ambrose Baber | Georgia | Dec. 1, 1841 | Jan. 10, 1844 |
| Robert Wickliffe, Jr. | Kentucky | Jan. 10, 1844 | n.a. 1847 |
| Nathaniel Niles | Vermont | Apr. 28, 1848 | Aug. 20, 1850 |
| William B. Kinney | New Jersey | Aug. 21, 1850 | Oct. 8, 1853 |
| John M. Daniel | Virginia | Oct. 10, 1853 | Jan. 10, 1861 |
| George P. Marsh | Vermont | June 23, 1861 | July 23, 1882 |
| William Waldorf Astor | New York | Nov. 21, 1882 | Mar. 1, 1885 |
| John B. Stallo | Ohio | Nov. 27, 1885 | June 6, 1889 |
| Albert G. Porter | Indiana | June 6, 1889 | July 9, 1892 |
| William Potter | Pennsylvania | Dec. 28, 1892 | Mar. 8, 1894 |
| Wayne MacVeagh | Pennsylvania | Mar. 11, 1894 | Mar. 4, 1897 |
| William F. Draper | Massachusetts | June 29, 1897 | June 5, 1900 |
| George v. L. Meyer | Massachusetts | Feb. 4, 1901 | Apr. 1, 1905 |
| Henry White | Rhode Island | Apr. 16, 1905 | Feb. 26, 1907 |
| Lloyd C. Griscom | Pennsylvania | Mar. 17, 1907 | June 14, 1909 |
| John G. A. Leishman | Pennsylvania | July 4, 1909 | Oct. 7, 1911 |
| Thomas J. O'Brien | Michigan | Nov. 13, 1911 | Sept. 17, 1913 |
| Thomas Nelson Page | Virginia | Oct. 12, 1913 | June 21, 1919 |
| Robert Underwood Johnson | New York | Apr. 22, 1920 | May 20, 1921 |
| Richard Washburn Child | Massachusetts | July 28, 1921 | Jan. 20, 1924 |
| Henry P. Fletcher | Pennsylvania | Apr. 3, 1924 | Aug. 3, 1929 |
| John W. Garrett | Maryland | Nov. 20, 1929 | May 22, 1933 |
| Breckinridge Long | Missouri | May 31, 1933 | Apr. 23, 1936 |
| William Phillips | Massachusetts | Nov. 4, 1936 | Oct. 6, 1941 |
| Alexander C. Kirk | Illinois | Jan. 8, 1945 | Mar. 5, 1946 |
| James Clement Dunn | New York | Feb. 6, 1947 | Mar. 17, 1952 |

Table 4.2 (continued)

| Name | Home State | Dates of Service | |
|------|------------|------|-----|
| | | From | To |

### Italy

| Name | Home State | From | To |
|------|-----------|------|-----|
| Ellsworth Bunker | New York | May 7, 1952 | Apr. 3, 1953 |
| Clare Boothe Luce | Connecticut | May 4, 1953 | Dec. 27, 1956 |
| James David Zellerbach | California | Feb. 6, 1957 | Dec. 10, 1960 |
| G. Frederick Reinhardt | California | May 17, 1961 | Mar. 3, 1968 |
| H. Gardner Ackley | Michigan | Apr. 3, 1968 | Aug. 27, 1969 |
| Graham A. Martin | North Carolina | Oct. 30, 1969 | Feb. 10, 1973 |
| John A. Volpe | Massachusetts | Mar. 6, 1973 | Jan. 24, 1977 |
| Richard N. Gardner | North Carolina | Mar. 21, 1977 | Feb. 27, 1981 |
| Maxwell M. Rabb | New York | July 1, 1981 | |

### Japan

| Name | Home State | From | To |
|------|-----------|------|-----|
| Townsend Harris | New York | Nov. 5, 1858 | Apr. 26, 1862 |
| Robert H. Pruyn | New York | May 17, 1862 | Apr. 28, 1865 |
| Robert B. Van Valkenburgh | New York | May 4, 1867 | Nov. 11, 1869 |
| Charles E. De Long | Nevada | Nov. 11, 1869 | Oct. 7, 1873 |
| John A. Bingham | Ohio | Oct. 7, 1873 | July 2, 1885 |
| Richard B. Hubbard | Texas | July 2, 1885 | May 15, 1889 |
| John F. Swift | California | May 15, 1889 | Mar. 10, 1891 |
| Frank L. Coombs | California | June 13, 1892 | July 14, 1893 |
| Edwin Dun | Ohio | July 14, 1893 | July 2, 1897 |
| Alfred E. Buck | Georgia | July 3, 1897 | Dec. 4, 1902 |
| Lloyd C. Griscom | Pennsylvania | June 22, 1903 | Nov. 19, 1905 |
| Luke E. Wright | Tennessee | May 26, 1906 | Aug. 13, 1907 |
| Thomas J. O'Brien | Michigan | Oct. 15, 1907 | Aug. 31, 1911 |
| Charles Page Bryan | Illinois | Nov. 22, 1911 | Oct. 1, 1912 |
| Larz Anderson | Wash., D.C. | Feb. 1, 1913 | Mar. 15, 1913 |
| George W. Guthrie | Pennsylvania | Aug. 7, 1913 | Mar. 8, 1917 |
| Roland S. Morris | Pennsylvania | Oct. 30, 1917 | May 15, 1920 |
| Charles Beecher Warren | Michigan | Sept. 24, 1921 | Jan. 28, 1922 |
| Cyprus E. Woods | Pennsylvania | July 21, 1923 | June 5, 1924 |
| Edgar A. Bancroft | Illinois | Nov. 19, 1924 | July 27, 1925 |
| Charles MacVeagh | New Hampshire | Dec. 9, 1925 | Dec. 6, 1928 |
| William R. Castle, Jr. | Wash., D.C. | Jan. 24, 1930 | May 27, 1930 |
| W. Cameron Forbes | Massachusetts | Sept. 25, 1930 | Mar. 22, 1932 |
| Joseph C. Grew | New Hampshire | June 14, 1932 | Dec. 8, 1941 |
| Robert D. Murphy | Wisconsin | May 9, 1952 | Apr. 28, 1953 |
| John M. Allison | Nebraska | May 29, 1953 | Feb. 2, 1957 |
| Douglas MacArthur 2d | Wash., D.C. | Feb. 25, 1957 | Mar. 12, 1961 |
| Edwin O. Reischauer | Massachusetts | Apr. 27, 1961 | Aug. 19, 1966 |
| U. Alexis Johnson | California | Nov. 8, 1966 | Jan. 15, 1969 |
| Armin H. Meyer | Illinois | July 3, 1969 | Mar. 27, 1972 |
| Robert Stephen Ingersoll | Illinois | Apr. 12, 1972 | Nov. 8, 1973 |
| James D. Hodgson | California | July 19, 1974 | Feb. 5, 1977 |
| Michael J. Mansfield | Montana | June 10, 1977 | |

### Mexico

| Name | Home State | From | To |
|------|-----------|------|-----|
| Joel R. Poinsett | South Carolina | June 1, 1825 | Oct. 17, 1829 |
| Anthony Butler | Mississippi | Jan. 29, 1830 | Oct. 21, 1835 |
| Powhatan Ellis | Mississippi | May 11, 1836 | Apr. 21, 1842 |
| Waddy Thompson | South Carolina | Apr. 21, 1842 | Mar. 9-10, 1844 |
| Wilson Shannon | Ohio | Sept. 1, 1844 | Mar. 28, 1845 |
| Nathan Clifford | Maine | Oct. 2, 1848 | Sept. 6, 1849 |
| Robert P. Letcher | Kentucky | Feb. 7, 1850 | Aug. 2, 1852 |

Table 4.2 (continued)

| Name | Home State | Dates of Service | |
| | | From | To |
|------|------------|------|-----|

### Mexico

| Name | Home State | From | To |
|------|------------|------|-----|
| Alfred Conkling | New York | Nov. 30, 1852 | Aug. 17, 1853 |
| James Gadsden | South Carolina | Aug. 17, 1853 | Oct. 23, 1856 |
| John Forsyth | Alabama | Oct. 23, 1856 | June 21, 1858 |
| Robert M. McLane | Maryland | Apr. 6, 1859 | Dec. 22, 1860 |
| John B. Weller | California | Jan. 30, 1861 | May 14, 1861 |
| Thomas Corwin | Ohio | May 21, 1861 | Apr. 27, 1864 |
| Marcus Otterbourg | Wisconsin | Aug. 19, 1867 | Aug. 28, 1867 |
| William S. Rosecrans | Ohio | Dec. 10, 1868 | June 26, 1869 |
| Thomas H. Nelson | Indiana | June 26, 1869 | June 16, 1873 |
| John W. Foster | Indiana | June 16, 1873 | Mar. 2, 1880 |
| Philip H. Morgan | Louisiana | Apr. 21, 1880 | June 6, 1885 |
| Henry R. Jackson | Georgia | June 11, 1885 | Oct. 7, 1886 |
| Thomas C. Manning | Louisiana | Oct. 26, 1886 | Sept. 21, 1887 |
| Edward S. Bragg | Wisconsin | Mar. 3, 1888 | May 27, 1889 |
| Thomas Ryan | Kansas | May 27, 1889 | May 9, 1893 |
| Isaac P. Gray | Indiana | May 9, 1893 | Dec. 7, 1894 |
| Matt W. Ransom | North Carolina | Apr. 18, 1895 | Feb. 13, 1897 |
| Powell Clayton | Arkansas | May 13, 1897 | May 26, 1905 |
| Edwin H. Conger | Iowa | June 15, 1905 | Aug. 3, 1905 |
| David E. Thompson | Nebraska | Mar. 8, 1906 | Dec. 1, 1909 |
| Henry Lane Wilson | Washington | Mar. 5, 1910 | July 17, 1913 |
| Henry P. Fletcher | Pennsylvania | Mar. 3, 1917 | Jan. 25, 1919 |
| Charles Beecher Warren | Michigan | Mar. 31, 1924 | July 22, 1924 |
| James Rockwell Sheffield | New York | Oct. 15, 1924 | June 5, 1927 |
| Dwight W. Morrow | New Jersey | Oct. 29, 1927 | Sept. 17, 1930 |
| J. Reuben Clark, Jr. | Utah | Nov. 28, 1930 | Feb. 14, 1933 |
| Josephus Daniels | North Carolina | Apr. 24, 1933 | Nov. 9, 1941 |
| George S. Messersmith | Delaware | Feb. 25, 1942 | May 15, 1946 |
| Walter Thurston | Arizona | June 17, 1946 | Nov. 4, 1950 |
| William O'Dwyer | New York | Nov. 23, 1950 | Dec. 6, 1952 |
| Francis White | Maryland | Apr. 28, 1953 | June 30, 1957 |
| Robert C. Hill | New Hampshire | July 25, 1957 | Dec. 1, 1960 |
| Thomas C. Mann | Texas | May 8, 1961 | Dec. 22, 1963 |
| Fulton Freeman | California | Apr. 6, 1964 | Jan. 6, 1969 |
| Robert H. McBride | Wash., D.C. | July 22, 1969 | Jan. 25, 1974 |
| Joseph J. Jova | Florida | Jan. 30, 1974 | Feb. 21, 1977 |
| Patrick J. Lucey | Wisconsin | July 19, 1977 | Oct. 31, 1979 |
| Julian Nava | California | May 7, 1980 | Apr. 3, 1981 |
| John A. Gavin | California | June 5, 1981 | |

### New Zealand

| Name | Home State | From | To |
|------|------------|------|-----|
| Patrick J. Hurley | Oklahoma | Apr. 24, 1942 | Aug. 12, 1942 |
| William C. Burdett | Tennessee | Dec. 4, 1943 | Jan. 14, 1944 |
| Kenneth S. Patton | Virginia | Aug. 15, 1944 | Oct. 22, 1945 |
| Avra M. Warren | Maryland | Feb. 27, 1946 | July 15, 1947 |
| Robert M. Scotten | Michigan | Apr. 7, 1948 | Feb. 1, 1955 |
| Robert C. Hendrickson | New Jersey | Feb. 16, 1955 | Nov. 20, 1956 |
| Francis H. Russell | Maine | June 5, 1857 | Nov. 28, 1960 |
| Anthony B. Akers | New York | July 1961 | Aug. 25, 1963 |
| Herbert B. Powell | Oregon | Oct. 23, 1963 | Feb. 28, 1967 |
| John F. Henning | California | Apr. 5, 1967 | Sept. 9, 1969 |
| Kenneth Franzheim II | Texas | Oct. 7, 1969 | Nov. 1, 1972 |
| Armistead I. Selden | Alabama | Apr. 22, 1974 | Apr. 23, 1979 |
| Anne Clark Martindell | New Jersey | Aug. 28, 1979 | May 7, 1981 |
| H. Monroe Browne | California | Aug. 11, 1981 | |

Table 4.2 (continued)

| Name | Home State | Dates of Service From | To |
|---|---|---|---|
| | | Pakistan | |
| Paul H. Alling | Connecticut | Feb. 26, 1948 | June 27, 1948 |
| Avra M. Warren | Maryland | Feb. 25, 1950 | Nov. 26, 1952 |
| Horace A. Hildreth | Maine | May 18, 1953 | May 1, 1957 |
| James M. Langley | New Hampshire | July 27, 1957 | July 29, 1959 |
| William M. Rountree | Maryland | Aug. 17, 1959 | Feb. 7, 1962 |
| Walter P. McConaughy | Alabama | Mar. 20, 1962 | May 17, 1966 |
| Eugene Murphy Locke | Texas | June 9, 1966 | Apr. 16, 1967 |
| Benjamin H. Oehlert, Jr. | Georgia | Aug. 16, 1967 | June 17, 1969 |
| Joseph S. Farland | Wash., D.C. | Nov. 15, 1969 | Apr. 30, 1972 |
| Henry A. Byroade | Indiana | Dec. 5, 1973 | Apr. 23, 1977 |
| Arthur W. Hummel, Jr. | Maryland | June 28, 1977 | July 19, 1981 |
| Ronald I. Spiers | Vermont | Oct. 29, 1981 | n.a. 1983 |
| Dean Hinton | Florida | Nov. 18, 1983 | |
| | | Russia (Soviet Union) | |
| John Quincy Adams | Massachusetts | Nov. 5, 1809 | Apr. 28, 1814 |
| William Pinkney | Maryland | Jan. 13, 1817 | Feb. 14, 1818 |
| Geo. Washington Campbell | Tennessee | Feb. 7, 1819 | July 8, 1820 |
| Henry Middleton | South Carolina | June 17, 1821 | Aug. 3, 1830 |
| James Buchanan | Pennsylvania | June 11, 1832 | Aug. 5, 1833 |
| William Wilkins | Pennsylvania | Dec. 14, 1834 | Dec. 24, 1835 |
| John Randolph Clay | Pennsylvania | Sept. 2, 1836 | Aug. 5, 1837 |
| George M. Dallas | Pennsylvania | Aug. 6, 1837 | July 29, 1839 |
| Churchill C. Cambreleng | New York | Sept. 21, 1840 | July 13, 1841 |
| Charles S. Todd | Kentucky | Nov. 28, 1841 | Jan. 27, 1846 |
| Ralph I. Ingersoll | Connecticut | May 30, 1847 | July 1, 1848 |
| Arhtur P. Bagby | Alabama | Jan. 14, 1849 | May 14, 1849 |
| Neill S. Brown | Tennessee | Aug. 13, 1850 | June 23, 1853 |
| Thomas H. Seymour | Connecticut | Apr. 2, 1854 | July 17, 1858 |
| Francis W. Pickens | South Carolina | July 18, 1858 | Sept. 9, 1860 |
| John Appleton | Maine | Sept. 9, 1860 | June 8, 1861 |
| Cassius M. Clay | Kentucky | July 14, 1861 | June 25, 1862 |
| Simon Cameron | Pennsylvania | June 25, 1862 | Sept. 18, 1862 |
| Cassius M. Clay | Kentucky | May 7, 1863 | Oct. 1, 1869 |
| Andrew G. Curtin | Pennsylvania | Oct. 28, 1869 | July 1, 1872 |
| James L. Orr | South Carolina | Mar. 18, 1873 | May 6, 1873 |
| Marshall Jewell | Connecticut | Dec. 9, 1873 | July 19, 1874 |
| George H. Boker | Pennsylvania | July 24, 1875 | Jan. 24, 1878 |
| Edwin W. Stoughton | New York | Jan. 15, 1878 | Mar. 2, 1879 |
| John W. Foster | Indiana | June 11, 1880 | Aug. 1, 1881 |
| William H. Hunt | Louisiana | Aug. 23, 1882 | Feb. 27, 1884 |
| Alphonso Taft | Ohio | Sept. 3, 1884 | July 31, 1885 |
| George V. N. Lothrop | Michigan | July 31, 1885 | Aug. 1, 1888 |
| Lambert Tree | Illinois | Jan. 4, 1889 | Feb. 2, 1889 |
| Charles Emory Smith | Pennsylvania | May 14, 1890 | Apr. 17, 1892 |
| Andrew D. White | New York | Nov. 7, 1892 | Oct. 1, 1894 |
| Clifton R. Breckinridge | Arkansas | Nov. 1, 1894 | Dec. 10, 1897 |
| Ethan A. Hitchcock | Missouri | Dec. 16, 1897 | Jan. 28, 1899 |
| Charlemagne Tower | Pennsylvania | Mar. 19, 1899 | Nov. 19, 1902 |
| Robert S. McCormick | Illinois | Jan. 12, 1903 | Mar. 27, 1905 |
| George v. L. Meyer | Massachusetts | Apr. 12, 1905 | Jan. 26, 1907 |
| John W. Riddle | Minnesota | Feb. 8, 1907 | Sept. 8, 1909 |
| William Woodville Rockhill | Wash., D.C. | Jan. 11, 1910 | June 17, 1911 |
| Curtis Guild | Massachusetts | Aug. 17, 1911 | Apr. 24, 1913 |
| George T. Marye | California | Oct. 30, 1914 | Mar. 28, 1916 |
| David R. Francis | Missouri | May 5, 1916 | Nov. 7, 1918 |

Table 4.2 (continued)

| Name | Home State | Dates of Service | |
|------|------------|------------------|---|
| | | From | To |

### Russia (Soviet Union)

| Name | Home State | From | To |
|------|------------|------|-----|
| William Christian Bullitt | Pennsylvania | Dec. 13, 1933 | May 16, 1936 |
| Joseph E. Davies | Wash., D.C. | Jan. 25, 1937 | June 11, 1938 |
| Lawrence A. Steinhardt | New York | Aug. 11, 1939 | Nov. 12, 1941 |
| William H. Standley | California | Apr. 14, 1942 | Sept. 19, 1943 |
| W. Averell Harriman | New York | Oct. 23, 1943 | Jan. 24, 1946 |
| Walter Bedell Smith | Indiana | Apr. 3, 1946 | Dec. 25, 1948 |
| Alan G. Kirk | Wash., D.C. | July 4, 1949 | Oct. 6, 1951 |
| George F. Kennan | Pennsylvania | May 14, 1952 | Sept. 19, 1952 |
| Charles E. Bohlen | Wash., D.C. | Apr. 20, 1953 | Apr. 18, 1957 |
| Llewellyn E. Thompson | Colorado | July 16, 1957 | July 27, 1962 |
| Foy D. Kohler | Ohio | Sept. 27, 1962 | Nov. 14, 1966 |
| Llewellyn E. Thompson | Colorado | Jan. 23, 1967 | Jan. 14, 1969 |
| Jacob D. Beam | New Jersey | Apr. 18, 1969 | Jan. 24, 1973 |
| Walter J. Stoessel, Jr. | California | Mar. 4, 1974 | Sept. 13, 1976 |
| Malcolm Toon | New York | Jan. 18, 1977 | Oct. 16, 1979 |
| Thomas J. Watson, Jr. | Connecticut | Oct. 29, 1979 | Jan. 15, 1981 |
| Arthur Adair Hartman | Maryland | Oct. 26, 1981 | |

### United Kingdom

| Name | Home State | From | To |
|------|------------|------|-----|
| John Adams | Massachusetts | June 1, 1785 | Feb. 20, 1788 |
| Thomas Pinckney | South Carolina | Aug. 9, 1792 | July 27, 1796 |
| Rufus King | New York | July 27, 1796 | May 16, 1803 |
| James Monroe | Virginia | Aug. 17, 1803 | Oct. 7, 1807 |
| William Pinkney | Maryland | Apr. 27, 1808 | May 7, 1811 |
| Jonathan Russell | Massachusetts | Nov. 15, 1811 | July 29, 1812 |
| John Q. Adams | Massachusetts | June 8, 1815 | May 14, 1817 |
| Richard Rush | Pennsylvania | Feb. 12, 1818 | Apr. 27, 1825 |
| Rufus King | New York | Nov. 11, 1825 | June 16-23, 1826 |
| Albert Gallatin | Pennsylvania | Sept. 1, 1826 | Oct. 4, 1827 |
| James Barbour | Virginia | Nov. 24, 1828 | Oct. 1, 1829 |
| Louis McLane | Delaware | Oct. 12, 1829 | June 13, 1831 |
| Martin Van Buren | New York | Sept. 21, 1831 | Mar. 19, 1832 |
| Aaron Vail | n.a. | Apr. 4, 1832 | July 13, 1836 |
| Andrew Stevenson | Virginia | July 13, 1836 | Oct. 21, 1841 |
| Edward Everett | Massachusetts | Dec. 16, 1841 | Aug. 8, 1845 |
| Louis McLane | Maryland | Aug. 8, 1845 | Aug. 18, 1846 |
| George Bancroft | New York | Nov. 12, 1846 | Aug. 31, 1849 |
| Abbott Lawrence | Massachusetts | Oct. 20, 1849 | Oct. 12, 1852 |
| Joseph R. Ingersoll | Pennsylvania | Oct. 16, 1852 | Aug. 23, 1853 |
| James Buchanan | Pennsylvania | Aug. 23, 1853 | Mar. 15, 1856 |
| George M. Dallas | Pennsylvania | Apr. 4, 1856 | May 16, 1861 |
| Charles Francis Adams | Massachusetts | May 16, 1861 | May 13, 1868 |
| Reverdy Johnson | Maryland | Sept. 14, 1868 | May 13, 1869 |
| J. Lothrop Motley | Massachusetts | June 18, 1869 | Dec. 6, 1870 |
| Robert C. Schenck | Ohio | June 23, 1871 | Mar. 3, 1876 |
| Edwards Pierrepont | New York | July 11, 1876 | Dec. 22, 1877 |
| John Welsh | Pennsylvania | Dec. 22, 1877 | Aug. 14, 1879 |
| James Russell Lowell | Massachusetts | May 11, 1880 | May 19, 1885 |
| Edward J. Phelps | Vermont | May 18, 1885 | Jan. 31, 1889 |
| ARobert T. Lincoln | Illinois | May 25, 1889 | May 4, 1893 |
| Thomas F. Bayard | Delaware | June 22, 1893 | Mar. 17, 1897 |
| John Hay | Wash., D.C. | May 3, 1897 | Sept. 12, 1898 |
| Joseph H. Choate | New York | Mar. 6, 1899 | May 23, 1905 |
| Whitelaw Reid | New York | June 5, 1905 | Dec. 15, 1912 |
| Walter Hines Page | New York | May 30, 1913 | Oct. 3, 1918 |
| John W. Davis | West Virginia | Dec. 18, 1918 | Mar. 9, 1921 |

Table 4.2 (continued)

| Name | Home State | Dates of Service From | To |
|---|---|---|---|
| | | United Kingdom | |
| George Harvey | New Jersey | May 12, 1921 | Nov. 3, 1923 |
| Frank B. Kellogg | Minnesota | Jan. 14, 1924 | Feb. 10, 1925 |
| Alanson B. Houghton | New York | Apr. 27, 1925 | Mar. 28, 1929 |
| Charles G. Dawes | Illinois | June 15, 1929 | Dec. 30, 1931 |
| Andrew W. Mellon | Pennsylvania | Apr. 9, 1932 | Mar. 17, 1933 |
| Robert Worth Bingham | Kentucky | May 23, 1933 | Nov. 19, 1937 |
| Joseph P. Kennedy | New York | Mar. 8, 1938 | Oct. 22, 1940 |
| John G. Winant | New Hampshire | Mar. 1, 1941 | Apr. 10, 1946 |
| W. Averell Harriman | New York | Apr. 30, 1946 | Oct. 1, 1946 |
| Lewis W. Douglas | Arizona | Mar. 25, 1947 | Nov. 16, 1950 |
| Walter S. Gifford | New York | Dec. 21, 1950 | Jan. 23, 1953 |
| Winthrop W. Aldrich | New York | Feb. 20, 1953 | Feb. 1, 1957 |
| John Hay Whitney | New York | Feb. 28, 1957 | Jan. 14, 1961 |
| David K. E. Bruce | Maryland | Mar. 17, 1961 | Mar. 20, 1969 |
| Walter H. Annenberg | Pennsylvania | Apr. 29, 1969 | Oct. 30, 1974 |
| Elliot Richardson | Massachusetts | Mar. 21, 1975 | Jan. 16, 1976 |
| Anne L. Armstrong | Texas | Mar. 17, 1976 | Mar. 3, 1977 |
| Kingman Brewster | Connecticut | June 3, 1977 | Feb. 23, 1981 |
| John J. Louis, Jr. | Illinois | May 27, 1981 | n.a. 1983 |
| Charles Price II | Missouri | Nov. 11, 1983 | |

n.a. Data not available.

[a]U.S. severed official relations with the National Republic of China (Taiwan) on January 1, 1979. The embassy closed February 28, 1979.

[b]U.S. began official relations with the People's Republic of China on January 1, 1979. Before this date, the official position was Chief Liaison Officer. On February 26, 1979, Leonard Woodcock, the Chief Liaison Officer since June 1977, was confirmed as the First American ambassador to mainland China since the 1949 Communist takeover. The U.S. Liaison Office became Embassy Beijing on March 1, 1979.

[c]West Germany since this date. Another ambassador is assigned in East Germany. See Table 4.3.

Table 4.3

Current United States Ambassadors *
(effective September, 1984)

| Country | Ambassador |
|---------|-----------|
| Afghanistan | Vacant |
| Albania[a] | |
| Algeria | Michael H. Newlin |
| Angola[b] | |
| Antigua & Barbuda | Thomas Anderson, Jr. |
| Australia | Robert D. Nesen |
| Austria | Helene von Damm |
| Bahamas | Lev E. Dobriansky |
| Bahrain | Donald Leidel |
| Bangladesh | Howard Schaffer |
| Barbados | Thomas Anderson, Jr. |
| Belgium | Geoffrey Swaebe |
| Belize | Malcolm R. Barnebey |
| Benin | George Moose |
| Bermuda | Max L. Friedersdorf |
| Bolivia | Edwin G. Corr |
| Botswana | Theodore C. Miano |
| Brunei | Barrington King |
| Bulgaria | Robert L. Barry |
| Burma | Daniel O'Donohue |
| Burundi | James Bullington |
| Cambodia[c] | |
| Cameroon | Myles Frechette |
| Cape Verde | John Yates |
| Central African Republic | Edmund DeJarnette |
| Chad | Jay Moffat |
| Chile | James D. Theberge |
| China (Taiwan)[d] | |
| China, People's Republic of | Arthur W. Hummel, Jr. |
| Colombia | Lewis Tambs |
| Comoros | Robert Keating |
| Congo | Alan Lukens |
| Costa Rica | Curtin Winsor, Jr. |
| Cuba[e] | |
| Cyprus | Richard Boehm |
| Czechoslovakia | William Luers |
| Denmark | Terence Todman |
| Djibouti | Alvin Adams |
| Dominica | Thomas Anderson, Jr. |

Table 4.3 (continued)

| Country | Ambassador |
| --- | --- |
| Dominican Republic | Robert Anderson |
| Ecuador | Samuel F. Hart |
| Egypt | Nicholas Veliotes |
| El Salvador | Thomas R. Pickering |
| Equatorial Guinea | Alan M. Hardy |
| Estonia[f] | |
| Ethiopia | Vacant |
| Fiji | Fred J. Eckert |
| Finland | Keith F. Nyborg |
| France | Evan G. Galbraith |
| Gabon | Larry Williamson |
| Gambia | Robert Hennemeyer |
| Germany, East | Rozanne L. Ridgway |
| Ghana | Robert Fritts |
| Greece | Monteagle Stearns |
| Grenada | Vacant |
| Guatemala | Alberto Piedra |
| Guinea | James Rosenthal |
| Guinea-Bissau | Wesley Egan, Jr. |
| Guyana | Clint Lauderdale |
| Haiti | Clayton McManaway, Jr. |
| Honduras | John D. Negroponte |
| Hungary | Nicolas Salgo |
| Iceland | Marshall Brement |
| India | Harry G. Barnes |
| Indonesia | John H. Holdridge |
| Iran[g] | |
| Iraq[h] | |
| Ireland | Robert Kane |
| Ivory Coast | Robert Miller |
| Jamaica | William A. Hewitt |
| Japan | Michael J. Mansfield |
| Jordan | Paul Boeker |
| Kampuchea[c] | |
| Kenya | Gerald Thomas |
| Kiribati | William Bodde, Jr. |
| Korea, South | Richard L. Walker |
| Kuwait | Anthony Quainton |
| Laos | Vacant |

Table 4.3 (continued)

| Country | Ambassador |
|---|---|
| Latvia[f] | |
| Lebanon | Reginald Bartholomew |
| Lesotho | S. L. Abbott |
| Liberia | William L. Swing |
| Libya[i] | |
| Lithuania[f] | |
| Luxembourg | John E. Dolibois |
| Madagascar | Robert Keating |
| Malawi | Weston Adams |
| Malaysia | Thomas Shoesmith |
| Maldives, Republic | John H. Reed |
| Mali | Robert Ryan, Jr. |
| Malta | James M. Rentschler |
| Mauritania | Edward L. Peck |
| Mauritius | George Andrews |
| Mexico | John A. Gavin |
| Morocco | Joseph V. Reed, Jr. |
| Mozambique | Peter Jon de Vos |
| Nauru | Robert D. Nesen |
| Nepal | Leon Weil |
| Netherlands | L. Paul Bremer III |
| New Zealand | H. Monroe Browne |
| Nicaragua | Harry Bergold, Jr. |
| Niger | William R. Casey, Jr. |
| Nigeria | Thomas Smith |
| Norway | Robert Stuart |
| Oman | John R. Countryman |
| Pakistan | Dean Hinton |
| Panama | Everett E. Briggs |
| Papua New Guinea & Solomon Islands | Paul Gardner |
| Paraguay | Arthur H. Davis, Jr. |
| Peru | David Imus |
| Philippines | Stephen Bosworth |
| Poland | Francis J. Meehan |
| Portugal | Henry Allen Holmes |
| Qatar | Charles Dunbar |
| Romania | David B. Funderburk |
| Rwanda | John Blane |
| Samoa | Anne C. Martindale |
| Sao Tome and Principe | Larry Williamson |

Table 4.3 (continued)

| Country | Ambassador |
|---|---|
| Saudi Arabia | Walter Cutler |
| Senegal | Charles W. Bray III |
| Seychelles | David J. Fischer |
| Sierra Leone | Arthur Winston Lewis |
| Singapore | Harry E. Thayer |
| Somalia | Robert B. Oakley |
| South Africa | Herman W. Nickel |
| Spain | Thomas Enders |
| Sri Lanka (Ceylon) | John H. Reed |
| St. Christopher & Nevis | Thomas Anderson, Jr. |
| St. Lucia | Thomas Anderson, Jr. |
| St. Vincent & Grenadines | Thomas Anderson, Jr. |
| Sudan | Hume Horan |
| Surinam | Robert W. Duemling |
| Swaziland | Robert H. Phinny |
| Sweden | Franklin S. Forsberg |
| Switzerland | John Lodge |
| Syrian Arab Republic | Robert P. Paganelli |
| Tanzania | John Shirley |
| Thailand | John G. Dean |
| Togo | Owen Roberts |
| Tonga | Fred J. Eckert |
| Trinidad and Tobago | Sheldon J. Krys |
| Tunisia | Peter Sebastina |
| Turkey | Robert Strausz-Hupe |
| Tuvalu | Fred J. Eckert |
| Uganda | Allen Clayton Davis |
| USSR | Arthur A. Hartman |
| United Arab Emirates | G. Quincy Lumsden, Jr. |
| United Kingdom | Charles Price II |
| Upper Volta | Leonard Neher |
| Uruguay | Thomas Aranda, Jr. |
| Venezuela | George W. Landua |
| Vietnam[c] | |
| Yemen, South[c] | |
| Yemen Arab Republic | David E. Zweifel |
| Yugoslavia | David Anderson |
| Zaire | Brandon Grove, Jr. |
| Zambia | Nicholas Platt |
| Zimbabwe | David Miller, Jr. |

Table 4.3 (continued)

---

\*For current ambassadors to Argentina, Australia, Austria, Brazil, National Republic of China, People's Republic of China, France, Germany (West), India, Israel, Italy, Japan, Mexico, New Zealand, Pakistan, USSR, and United Kingdom, see table 4.2.

[a]U.S. severed relations in 1969.

[b]U.S. embassy closed in 1975.

[c]U.S. embassy closed in 1975 during Communist takeover.

[d]U.S. severed relations in 1978. Unofficial commercial and other relations with the people of Taiwan are maintained through a private instrumentality, the American Institute in Taiwan.

[e]U.S. relations severed in 1961; limited ties restored in 1977.

[f]U.S. does not officially recognize 1940 annexations by USSR.

[g]U.S. severed relations on April 7, 1980, as a result of the Iranian Hostage Crisis.

[h]Relations severed in 1967; limited staff returned in 1972. Belgium protects U.S. interests.

[i]U.S. withdrew all embassy personnel on May 2, 1980.

Table 4.4

United States Economic Assistance, 1946-1982
(in millions of dollars)

| Periods | Dates | Country | | | | | |
|---------|-------|----------|-----------|---------|--------|---------------------|----------|
| | | Argentina | Australia | Austria | Brazil | Republic of China | France |
| Post war relief period | 1946-1948 | 0.2 | 6.7 | 341.0 | 73.9 | 535.5 | 1,909.1 |
| Marshall Plan period | 1949-1952 | 101.5 | 1.3 | 679.8 | 112.1 | 467.8 | 2,714.6 |
| Mutual Security Act period | 1953-1957 | 175.4 | 5.9 | 107.9 | 850.5 | 529.5 | 508.1 |
| | 1958 | 0.2 | -- | 30.7 | 26.9 | 99.8 | 12.4 |
| | 1959 | 140.6 | -- | 1.1 | 134.1 | 99.0 | 0.3 |
| | 1960 | 1.0 | 1.5 | 1.0 | 20.5 | 120.7 | -5.5 |
| | 1961 | 38.5 | -- | 0.8 | 280.0 | 110.8 | 0.3 |
| Foreign Assistance Act period | 1962 | 27.9 | -- | 4.0 | 208.0 | 72.6 | 0.1 |
| | 1963 | 132.9 | -- | 31.4 | 142.5 | 80.4 | 0.1 |
| | 1964 | 10.9 | -- | -- | 381.8 | 48.2 | 0.1 |
| | 1965 | 9.5 | -- | -- | 273.3 | 60.4 | * |
| | 1966 | 27.8 | 134.0 | -- | 383.6 | 68.9 | 11.0 |
| | 1967 | 1.6 | -- | -- | 240.0 | 4.6 | -- |
| | 1968 | 2.8 | -- | -- | 280.7 | 6.8 | -- |
| | 1969 | 1.9 | -- | -- | 29.2 | -- | -- |
| | 1970 | 1.0 | -- | -- | 154.0 | -- | -- |
| | 1971 | 0.5 | -- | -- | 117.6 | 19.2 | -- |
| | 1972 | -- | -- | -- | 21.0 | -- | -- |
| | 1973 | -- | -- | -- | 53.8 | -- | -- |
| | 1974 | * | -- | -- | 17.2 | -- | -- |
| | 1975 | 0.1 | -- | -- | 14.7 | -- | -- |
| | 1976 | -- | -- | -- | 1.0 | -- | -- |
| | 1977 | -- | -- | -- | 1.0 | -- | -- |
| | 1978 | -- | -- | -- | -- | -- | -- |
| | 1979 | -- | -- | -- | -- | -- | -- |
| | 1980 | -- | -- | -- | -- | -- | -- |
| | 1981 | -- | -- | -- | -- | -- | -- |
| | 1982 | -- | -- | -- | -- | 70.0 | -- |

Table 4.4 (continued)

| Period | Dates | Germany (Federal Republic) | India | Israel | Italy | Japan | Mexico |
|---|---|---|---|---|---|---|---|
| | | | | | Country | | |
| Post war relief period | 1946-1948 | 1,344.4 | 39.9 | -- | 1,271.2 | 979.7 | 95.3 |
| Marshall Plan period | 1949-1952 | 2,491.8 | 248.7 | 221.5 | 1,520.4 | 1,220.7 | 178.7 |
| Mutual Security Act period | 1953-1957 | 176.4 | 700.4 | 292.6 | 435.4 | 218.3 | 94.2 |
| | 1958 | 16.1 | 307.6 | 85.3 | 73.7 | 63.8 | 64.5 |
| | 1959 | 9.1 | 366.0 | 52.5 | 42.1 | 25.1 | 107.4 |
| | 1960 | 3.2 | 725.9 | 54.2 | 56.0 | 22.3 | 46.6 |
| | 1961 | 1.4 | 592.1 | 77.9 | 30.6 | 48.2 | 31.1 |
| Foreign Assistance Act period | 1962 | 0.7 | 763.1 | 80.3 | 21.6 | 65.3 | 49.8 |
| | 1963 | 0.2 | 705.8 | 78.0 | 127.2 | 117.2 | 46.6 |
| | 1964 | -- | 685.4 | 39.8 | 131.4 | 22.3 | 104.3 |
| | 1965 | -- | 721.2 | 57.8 | 6.1 | 64.7 | 110.2 |
| | 1966 | 2.5 | 913.1 | 36.9 | 64.7 | 52.4 | 128.2 |
| | 1967 | -- | 577.6 | 6.1 | 1.4 | -- | 0.3 |
| | 1968 | -- | 632.1 | 51.8 | -- | -- | 0.2 |
| | 1969 | -- | 477.5 | 36.7 | -- | -- | 0.2 |
| | 1970 | -- | 449.7 | 41.1 | -- | -- | 1.0 |
| | 1971 | -- | 444.5 | 55.8 | -- | -- | -- |
| | 1972 | -- | 113.5 | 104.2 | -- | 320.0 | 0.5 |
| | 1973 | -- | 81.7 | 109.8 | -- | -- | * |
| | 1974 | -- | 137.3 | 51.5 | -- | -- | 0.4 |
| | 1975 | -- | 249.4 | 353.1 | -- | -- | 0.2 |
| | 1976 | -- | -- | 700.0 | -- | -- | -- |
| | 1977 | -- | -- | 735.0 | 1.0 | -- | -- |
| | 1978 | -- | 60.0 | 785.0 | 3.0 | -- | -- |
| | 1979 | -- | 91.0 | 785.0 | 4.0 | -- | -- |
| | 1980 | -- | 103.0 | 785.0 | 3.0 | -- | -- |
| | 1981 | -- | 105.0 | 764.0 | 5.0 | -- | -- |
| | 1982 | -- | 99.0 | 806.0 | 52.0 | -- | -- |

414

Table 4.4 (continued)

| | | Country | | |
|---|---|---|---|---|
| Period | Dates | New Zealand | Pakistan | United Kingdom |
| Post war relief period | 1946-1948 | 4.3 | 0.1 | 3,836.9 |
| Marshall Plan period | 1949-1952 | -- | 11.1 | 3,190.0 |
| Mutual Security Act period | 1953-1957 | 12.1 | 566.3 | 645.0 |
| | 1958 | * | 158.2 | * |
| | 1959 | * | 229.5 | 2.1 |
| | 1960 | * | 291.8 | -- |
| | 1961 | * | 167.8 | -- |
| Foreign Assistance Act period | 1962 | * | 422.2 | -- |
| | 1963 | * | 355.2 | -- |
| | 1964 | -- | 380.1 | ᵀ⁻ |
| | 1965 | -- | 348.2 | 250.0 |
| | 1966 | 6.5 | 141.6 | 86.1 |
| | 1967 | -- | 230.4 | -- |
| | 1968 | -- | 295.2 | -- |
| | 1969 | -- | 111.4 | -- |
| | 1970 | -- | 209.8 | -- |
| | 1971 | -- | 107.9 | -- |
| | 1972 | -- | 165.1 | -- |
| | 1973 | -- | 177.9 | -- |
| | 1974 | -- | 101.8 | -- |
| | 1975 | -- | 180.9 | -- |
| | 1976 | -- | 106.0 | -- |
| | 1977 | -- | 71.0 | -- |
| | 1978 | -- | 20.0 | -- |
| | 1979 | -- | 9.0 | -- |
| | 1980 | -- | -- | -- |
| | 1981 | -- | -- | -- |
| | 1982 | -- | 100.0 | -- |

*Less than $50,000

# CHAPTER FIVE

☆         ☆

## *Armed Forces*

Military affairs across United States history are featured in this chapter. Table 5.1 presents the estimated number of military personnel in the armed forces, by year, from 1789 to 1982. The heads of various branches of the armed services are listed in table 5.2. Tables 5.3 and 5.4 document the estimated casualties and costs (respectively) of the major wars in which the United States has participated (including one domestic conflict, the Civil War).

Table 5.1

Military Personnel on Active Duty,
1789-1982[a]

| Year | Total | Year | Total |
|------|-------|------|-------|
| 1789 | 718 | 1843 | 20,741 |
| 1794 | 5,669 | 1844 | 20,919 |
| 1795 | 5,296 | 1845 | 20,726 |
| 1798 | n.a. | 1846 | 39,165 |
| 1799 | n.a. | 1847 | 57,761 |
| 1800 | n.a. | 1848 | 60,308 |
| 1801 | 7,108 | 1849 | 23,165 |
| 1802 | 5,432 | 1850 | 20,824 |
| 1803 | 4,528 | 1851 | 20,699 |
| 1804 | 5,323 | 1852 | 21,349 |
| 1805 | 6,498 | 1853 | 20,667 |
| 1806 | 4,076 | 1854 | 21,134 |
| 1807 | 5,323 | 1855 | 26,402 |
| 1808 | 8,200 | 1856 | 25,867 |
| 1809 | 12,375 | 1857 | 27,345 |
| 1810 | 11,554 | 1858 | 29,014 |
| 1811 | 11,528 | 1859 | 28,978 |
| 1812 | 12,631 | 1860 | 27,958 |
| 1813 | 25,152 | 1861 | 217,121 |
| 1814 | 46,858 | 1862 | 673,124 |
| 1815 | 40,885 | 1863 | 960,061 |
| 1816 | 16,743 | 1864 | 1,031,724 |
| 1817 | 14,606 | 1865 | 1,062,848 |
| 1818 | 14,260 | 1866 | 76,749 |
| 1819 | 13,259 | 1867 | 74,786 |
| 1820 | 15,113 | 1868 | 66,412 |
| 1821 | 10,587 | 1869 | 51,632 |
| 1822 | 9,863 | 1870 | 50,348 |
| 1823 | 10,871 | 1871 | 42,238 |
| 1824 | 11,008 | 1872 | 42,205 |
| 1825 | 11,089 | 1873 | 43,228 |
| 1826 | 11,586 | 1874 | 43,609 |
| 1827 | 11,627 | 1875 | 38,105 |
| 1828 | 11,431 | 1876 | 40,591 |
| 1829 | 12,096 | 1877 | 34,094 |
| 1830 | 11,942 | 1878 | 36,444 |
| 1831 | 11,173 | 1879 | 38,022 |
| 1832 | 12,478 | 1880 | 37,894 |
| 1833 | 12,895 | 1881 | 37,845 |
| 1834 | 13,396 | 1882 | 37,850 |
| 1835 | 14,311 | 1883 | 37,278 |
| 1836 | 16,874 | 1884 | 39,400 |
| 1837 | 22,464 | 1885 | 39,098 |
| 1838 | 17,948 | 1886 | 38,636 |
| 1839 | 19,317 | 1887 | 38,763 |
| 1840 | 21,616 | 1888 | 39,035 |
| 1841 | 20,79 | 1889 | 39,452 |
| 1842 | 22,851 | 1890 | 38,666 |

Table 5.1 (continued)

| Year | Total | Year | Total |
|------|-------|------|-------|
| 1891 | 37,868 | 1937 | 311,808 |
| 1892 | 38,677 | 1938 | 322,932 |
| 1893 | 39,492 | 1939 | 334,473 |
| 1894 | 42,101 | 1940 | 458,365 |
| 1895 | 42,226 | 1941 | 1,801,101 |
| 1896 | 41,680 | 1942 | 3,858,791 |
| 1897 | 43,656 | 1943 | 9,044,745 |
| 1898 | 235,785 | 1944 | 11,451,719 |
| 1899 | 100,166 | 1945 | 12,123,455 |
| 1900 | 125,923 | 1946 | 3,030,088 |
| 1901 | 112,322 | 1947 | 1,582,999 |
| 1902 | 111,145 | 1948 | 1,445,910 |
| 1903 | 106,043 | 1949 | 1,615,360 |
| 1904 | 110,129 | 1950 | 1,460,261 |
| 1905 | 108.301 | 1951 | 3,249,455 |
| 1906 | 112,216 | 1952 | 3,635,912 |
| 1907 | 108,375 | 1953 | 3,555,067 |
| 1908 | 128,500 | 1954 | 3,302,104 |
| 1909 | 142,200 | 1955 | 2,935,107 |
| 1910 | 139,344 | 1956 | 2,806,441 |
| 1911 | 144,846 | 1957 | 2,795,798 |
| 1912 | 153,174 | 1958 | 2,600,581 |
| 1913 | 154,914 | 1959 | 2,504,310 |
| 1914 | 165,919 | 1960 | 2,476,435 |
| 1915 | 174,112 | 1961 | 2,483,771 |
| 1916 | 179,376 | 1962 | 2,807,819 |
| 1917 | 643,833 | 1963 | 2,699,677 |
| 1918 | 2,897,167 | 1964 | 2,687,409 |
| 1919 | 1,172,602 | 1965 | 2,655,389 |
| 1920 | 343,302 | 1966 | 3,094,058 |
| 1921 | 386,542 | 1967 | 3,376,880 |
| 1922 | 270,207 | 1968 | 3,547,902 |
| 1923 | 247,011 | 1969 | 3,460,162 |
| 1924 | 261,189 | 1970 | 3,066,294 |
| 1925 | 251,756 | 1971 | 2,714,000 |
| 1926 | 247,396 | 1972 | 2,322,000 |
| 1927 | 248,943 | 1973 | 2,252,000 |
| 1928 | 250,907 | 1974 | 2,161,000 |
| 1929 | 255,031 | 1975 | 2,127,000 |
| 1930 | 255,648 | 1976 | 2,087,000 |
| 1931 | 252,605 | 1977 | 2,075,000 |
| 1932 | 244,902 | 1978 | 2,062,000 |
| 1933 | 243,845 | 1979 | 2,027,000 |
| 1934 | 247,137 | 1980 | 2,051,000 |
| 1935 | 251,799 | 1981 | 2,083,000 |
| 1936 | 291,356 | 1982 | 2,109,000 |

n.a. Information not available.

[a]As of June 30, beginning 1878 for Army, 1900 for Navy, and 1798 for Marine Corps. For prior years the month for which most complete records were available was used. Coast Guard Personnel are excluded.

Table 5.2

Heads of Branches of the United States
Armed Services, 1775-1984

| Name | Years Served | Rank |
|------|-------------|------|

### Army[a]

| Name | Years Served | Rank |
|------|-------------|------|
| George Washington | 1775-1783 | General |
| Henry Knox | 1783-1784 | Major General |
| Josiah Harmar | 1784-1791 | Lieutenant Colonel |
| Arthur St. Clair | 1791-1792 | Major General |
| Anthony Wayne | 1792-1796 | Major General |
| James Wilkinson | 1796-1798 | Brigadier General |
| George Washington | 1798-1799 | Lieutenant General |
| Alexander Hamilton | 1799-1800 | Major General |
| James Wilkinson | 1800-1812 | Brigadier General |
| Henry Dearborn | 1812-1815 | Major General |
| Jacob Brown | 1815-1828 | Major General |
| Alexander Macomb | 1828-1841 | Major General |
| Winfield Scott | 1841-1861 | Major General |
| G. B. McClellan | 1861-1862 | Major General |
| Henry W. Halleck | 1862-1864 | Major General |
| Ulysses S. Grant | 1864-1869 | General |
| William T. Sherman | 1869-1883 | General |
| Philip H. Sheridan | 1883-1888 | General |
| James McA. Schofield | 1888-1895 | Lieutenant General |
| Nathan A. Miles | 1895-1903 | Lieutenant General |
| Samuel B. M. Young | 1903-1904 | Lieutenant General |
| Adna R. Chaffee | 1904-1906 | Lieutenant General |
| John C. Bates | 1906-1906 | Lieutenant General |
| J. Franklin Bell | 1906-1910 | Major General |
| Leonard Wood | 1910-1914 | Major General |
| William W. Witherspoon | 1914-1914 | Major General |
| Hugh L. Scott | 1914-1917 | Major General |
| Tasker H. Bliss | 1917-1918 | General |
| Peyton C. March | 1918-1921 | General |
| John J. Pershing | 1921-1924 | Gen. of the Armies |
| John L. Hines | 1924-1926 | Major General |
| Charles P. Summerall | 1926-1930 | General |
| Douglas MacArthur | 1930-1935 | General |
| Malin Craig | 1935-1939 | General |
| George C. Marshall | 1939-1945 | Gen. of the Army |
| Dwight D. Eisenhower | 1945-1948 | Gen. of the Army |
| Omar N. Bradley | 1948-1949 | Gen. of the Army |
| J. Lawton Collins | 1949-1953 | General |
| Matthew B. Ridgway | 1953-1955 | General |
| Maxwell D. Taylor | 1955-1959 | General |
| Lyman L. Lemnitzer | 1959-1960 | General |
| George H. Decker | 1960-1962 | General |
| Earle G. Wheeler | 1962-1964 | General |
| Harold K. Johnson | 1964-1968 | General |
| William C. Westmoreland | 1968-1972 | General |
| Bruce Palmer, Jr. | 1972-1972 | General |
| Creighton W. Abrams | 1972-1974 | General |
| Fred C. Weyand | 1974-1977 | General |
| Bernard W. Rogers | 1977-1979 | General |
| Edward C. Meyer | 1979-1983 | General |
| John A. Wickham, Jr. | 1983-date | General |

Table 5.2 (continued)

| Name | Years Served | Rank |
|------|--------------|------|

### Air Force[b]

| Name | Years Served | Rank |
|------|--------------|------|
| Carl Spaatz | 1947-1948 | General |
| Hoyt S. Vandenberg | 1948-1953 | General |
| Nathan F. Twining | 1953-1957 | General |
| Thomas D. White | 1957-1961 | General |
| Curtis E. LeMay | 1961-1965 | General |
| John P. McConnell | 1965-1969 | General |
| John D. Ryan | 1969-1974 | General |
| David C. Jones | 1974-1977 | General |
| Lew Allen, Jr. | 1977-1982 | General |
| Charles A. Gabriel | 1982- | General |

### Navy[c]

| Name | Years Served | Rank |
|------|--------------|------|
| William S. Benson | 1915-1919 | Admiral |
| Robert E. Coontz | 1919-1923 | Admiral |
| Edward W. Eberle | 1923-1927 | Admiral |
| Charles F. Hughes | 1927-1930 | Admiral |
| William V. Pratt | 1930-1933 | Admiral |
| William H. Standley | 1933-1937 | Admiral |
| William D. Leahy | 1937-1939 | Fleet Admiral |
| Harold R. Stark | 1939-1942 | Admiral |
| Ernest J. King | 1942-1945 | Fleet Admiral |
| Chester W. Nimitz | 1945-1947 | Fleet Admiral |
| Louis E. Denfield | 1947-1949 | Admiral |
| Forrest P. Sherman | 1949-1951 | Admiral |
| William M. Fechteler | 1951-1953 | Admiral |
| Robert B. Carney | 1953-1955 | Admiral |
| Arleigh A. Burke | 1955-1961 | Admiral |
| George W. Anderson | 1961-1963 | Admiral |
| David L. McDonald | 1963-1967 | Admiral |
| Thomas H. Moorer | 1967-1970 | Admiral |
| Elmo R. Zumwalt | 1970-1974 | Admiral |
| James L. Holloway | 1974-1978 | Admiral |
| Thomas B. Hayward | 1978-1982 | Admiral |
| James D. Watkins | 1982- | Admiral |

Table 5.2 (continued)

| Name | Years Served | Initial Rank as Commandant | Final Rank as Commandant |
|---|---|---|---|
| Marine Corps[d] | | | |
| Samuel Nicholas | 1775-1781 | Captain | Major |
| William Ward Burrows | 1798-1804 | Major | Lt. Colonel |
| Franklin Wharton | 1804-1818 | Lt. Colonel | Lt. Colonel |
| Anthony Gale | 1819-1920 | Lt. Colonel | Lt. Colonel |
| Archibald Henderson | 1820-1859 | Lt. Colonel | Colonel |
| John Harris | 1859-1864 | Colonel | Colonel |
| Jacob Zeilin | 1864-1876 | Colonel | Brigadier Gen. |
| Charles G. McCawley | 1876-1891 | Colonel | Colonel |
| Charles Heywood | 1891-1903 | Colonel | Maj. Gen. |
| George Elliott | 1903-1910 | Brigadier Gen. | Maj. Gen. |
| William P. Biddle | 1911-1914 | Maj. Gen. | Maj. Gen. |
| George Barnett | 1914-1920 | Maj. Gen. | Maj. Gen. |
| John A. Lejeune | 1920-1929 | Maj. Gen. | Maj. Gen. |
| Wendell C. Neville | 1929-1930 | Maj. Gen. | Maj. Gen. |
| Ben H. Fuller | 1930-1934 | Maj. Gen. | Maj. Gen. |
| John H. Russell | 1934-1936 | Maj. Gen. | Maj. Gen. |
| Thomas Holcomb | 1936-1943 | Maj. Gen. | Lt. General |
| Alexander A. Vandegrift | 1944-1947 | Lt. General | General |
| Clifton B. Cates | 1948-1951 | General | General |
| Lemuel C. Shepherd, Jr. | 1952-1955 | General | General |
| Randolph McCall Pate | 1956-1959 | General | General |
| David M. Shoup | 1960-1963 | General | General |
| Wallace M. Green, Jr. | 1964-1967 | General | General |
| Leonard F. Chapman, Jr. | 1968-1971 | General | General |
| Robert E. Cushman, Jr. | 1972-1975 | General | General |
| Louis H. Wilson | 1975-1978 | General | General |
| Robert H. Barrow | 1978-1983 | General | General |
| Paul X. Kelley | 1983- | General | General |

[a]From 1775 to 1903 the head of the Army was titled "Commanding General of the Army." In 1903 a General Staff Corps was created and the commander of the Army was given the title of "Army Chief of Staff."

[b]Until 1947, the Air Force was a branch of the Army and was entitled the Army Air Corps. With the establishment of the Department of Defense, in 1947, came the creation of the Air Force as a separate branch of the Armed Services, entitled the United States Air Force. The commanding officer is called the Chief of Staff of the Air Force.

[c]Until 1900 the United States Navy was directed by various boards rather than one commander. In 1900 a General Navy Board was created, with Admiral George Dewey serving as its President from 1900-1917. The position of Chief of Naval Operations was created in 1915 and became the supreme command post of the Navy.

[d]The head of the Marine Corps is entitled Commandant of the United States Marine Corps.

Table 5.3

American Military Personnel and Casualties
During Selected Wars

| | Total Military Personnel (est.) | Casualties | | |
|---|---|---|---|---|
| War | | Total Deaths | Battle Deaths | Wounds Not Mortal |
| American Revolution | a | n.a. | n.a. | n.a. |
| War of 1812 | 286,730 | n.a. | n.a. | n.a. |
| Mexican War | 78,718 | n.a. | n.a. | n.a. |
| Civil War | 2,218,000[b] | 364,511 | 140,414 | 281,881 |
| Spanish-American War | 307,000 | 2,446 | 385 | 1,662 |
| World War I | 4,744,000 | 116,516 | 53,402 | 204,002 |
| World War II | 16,354,000 | 405,399 | 291,557 | 670,846 |
| Korean conflict | 5,764,000 | 54,246 | 33,629 | 103,284 |
| Vietnam conflict | 8,744,000 | 56,886 | 46,498 | 153,329 |

[a]The number of personnel serving in the American Revolution is not known, but estimates range from 184,000 to 250,000.

[b]This is for the Union forces only. Estimates for Confederate forces range from 600,000 to 1,500,000.

422

Table 5.4

Total Costs of United States Wars
(in millions of dollars, except percent)

| War | Estimated Total War Costs | Original War Costs | Veterans' Benefits | | | Estimated Interest Payments on War Loans | |
| --- | --- | --- | --- | --- | --- | --- | --- |
| | | | Total Costs Under Present Laws | Percent of Original War Costs | Total Costs to 1970 | Total | Percent of Original War Costs |
| American Revolution | 190 | 100 | 70 | 70 | 70 | 20 | 20 |
| War of 1812 | 158 | 93 | 49 | 53 | 49 | 16 | 17 |
| Mexican War | 147 | 73 | 64 | 88 | 64 | 10 | 14 |
| Civil War (Union only) | 12,952 | 3,200 | 8,580 | 260 | 8,570 | 1,172 | 37 |
| Spanish-American War | 6,460 | 400 | 6,000 | 1,505 | 5,436 | 60 | 15 |
| World War I | 112,000 | 26,000 | 75,000 | 290 | 45,585 | 11,000 | 42 |
| World War II | 664,000 | 288,000 | 290,000 | 100 | 87,445 | 86,000 | 30 |
| Korean conflict | 164,000 | 54,000 | 99,000 | 184 | 15,016 | 11,000 | 20 |
| Vietnam conflict | 352,000 | 107,800 | 220,000[a] | 200[a] | 2,461 | 22,000[a] | 20[a] |

[a]This is the average of the high and low estimates.

# CHAPTER SIX

☆　　　☆

## Wealth, Revenue, Taxation, and Public Expenditure

The tables contained in this chapter document economic and fiscal trends across the nation's history. Included are statistics relating to personal wealth and income (table 6.1); federal government receipts by source (table 6.2); federal, state, and local governmental expenditure by function (table 6.3); and federal government outlays by major function (tables 6.4a–6.4d). Most of the early figures in these tables are estimates, and many begin with figures dating only from the mid to late nineteenth century.

Table 6.1

Per Capita Personal Income by State, 1929-1982
(in current dollars)

| State | 1929 | 1940 | 1948 | 1949 | 1950 | 1951 | 1952 | 1953 |
|---|---|---|---|---|---|---|---|---|
| Alabama | 322 | 278 | 866 | 880 | 880 | 1,006 | 1,071 | 1,124 |
| Alaska | --- | --- | --- | 2,384 | 2,384 | 2,836 | 2,612 | 2,492 |
| Arizona | 593 | 502 | 1,274 | 1,330 | 1,330 | 1,566 | 1,662 | 1,654 |
| Arkansas | 306 | 254 | 875 | 825 | 825 | 927 | 992 | 1,035 |
| California | 995 | 835 | 1,752 | 1,730 | 1,852 | 2,044 | 2,167 | 2,204 |
| Colorado | 644 | 544 | 1,433 | 1,487 | 1,487 | 1,745 | 1,830 | 1,767 |
| Connecticut | 994 | 885 | 1,713 | 1,875 | 1,875 | 2,137 | 2,263 | 2,346 |
| Delaware | 1,037 | 1,023 | 1,720 | 2,132 | 2,132 | 2,209 | 2,293 | 2,379 |
| Dist. of Columbia | 1,292 | 1,198 | 1,958 | 2,221 | 2,221 | 2,378 | 2,457 | 2,363 |
| Florida | 525 | 507 | 1,180 | 1,281 | 1,281 | 1,359 | 1,442 | 1,526 |
| Georgia | 349 | 336 | 968 | 1,034 | 1,034 | 1,167 | 1,241 | 1,288 |
| Hawaii | --- | --- | 1,407 | 1,386 | 1,386 | 1,580 | 1,748 | 1,795 |
| Idaho | 502 | 450 | 1,315 | 1,295 | 1,295 | 1,443 | 1,588 | 1,509 |
| Illinois | 959 | 754 | 1,815 | 1,825 | 1,825 | 2,015 | 2,078 | 2,186 |
| Indiana | 615 | 550 | 1,451 | 1,512 | 1,512 | 1,694 | 1,766 | 1,930 |
| Iowa | 589 | 502 | 1,590 | 1,485 | 1,485 | 1,577 | 1,652 | 1,598 |
| Kansas | 543 | 423 | 1,333 | 1,443 | 1,443 | 1,578 | 1,783 | 1,722 |
| Kentucky | 394 | 317 | 990 | 933 | 981 | 1,143 | 1,229 | 1,293 |
| Louisiana | 414 | 360 | 1,032 | 1,084 | 1,120 | 1,205 | 1,279 | 1,346 |
| Maine | 597 | 515 | 1,235 | 1,174 | 1,186 | 1,297 | 1,411 | 1,421 |
| Maryland | 780 | 709 | 1,467 | 1,456 | 1,602 | 1,769 | 1,888 | 1,964 |
| Massachusetts | 912 | 780 | 1,500 | 1,470 | 1,633 | 1,793 | 1,866 | 1,910 |
| Michigan | 794 | 676 | 1,560 | 1,520 | 1,701 | 1,874 | 1,962 | 2,161 |
| Minnesota | 602 | 529 | 1,431 | 1,310 | 1,410 | 1,548 | 1,592 | 1,665 |
| Mississippi | 287 | 216 | 790 | 691 | 755 | 830 | 886 | 923 |
| Missouri | 631 | 521 | 1,389 | 1,339 | 1,431 | 1,556 | 1,656 | 1,728 |
| Montana | 601 | 566 | 1,616 | 1,385 | 1,622 | 1,761 | 1,786 | 1,779 |
| Nebraska | 602 | 436 | 1,509 | 1,304 | 1,490 | 1,571 | 1,668 | 1,612 |
| Nevada | 896 | 890 | 1,814 | 1,823 | 2,018 | 2,249 | 2,429 | 2,462 |
| New Hampshire | 682 | 571 | 1,284 | 1,259 | 1,323 | 1,497 | 1,557 | 1,616 |
| New Jersey | 929 | 816 | 1,689 | 1,663 | 1,834 | 2,028 | 2,134 | 2,247 |
| New Mexico | 381 | 373 | 1,084 | 1,117 | 1,117 | 1,306 | 1,367 | 1,386 |
| New York | 1,164 | 871 | 1,797 | 1,749 | 1,873 | 2,015 | 2,067 | 2,139 |
| North Carolina | 333 | 323 | 973 | 940 | 1,037 | 1,139 | 1,181 | 1,223 |
| North Dakota | 365 | 340 | 1,401 | 1,130 | 1,263 | 1,314 | 1,217 | 1,244 |
| Ohio | 782 | 660 | 1,558 | 1,474 | 1,620 | 1,848 | 1,926 | 2,028 |
| Oklahoma | 454 | 366 | 1,144 | 1,169 | 1,143 | 1,284 | 1,391 | 1,467 |
| Oregon | 689 | 618 | 1,621 | 1,573 | 1,620 | 1,789 | 1,875 | 1,867 |
| Pennsylvania | 776 | 648 | 1,431 | 1,401 | 1,541 | 1,697 | 1,773 | 1,870 |
| Rhode Island | 871 | 739 | 1,493 | 1,437 | 1,605 | 1,765 | 1,804 | 1,878 |
| South Carolina | 269 | 301 | 891 | 850 | 893 | 1,071 | 1,160 | 1,199 |
| South Dakota | 417 | 360 | 1,497 | 1,091 | 1,242 | 1,438 | 1,272 | 1,376 |
| Tennessee | 375 | 334 | 944 | 927 | 994 | 1,081 | 1,137 | 1,229 |
| Texas | 480 | 430 | 1,199 | 1,291 | 1,349 | 1,469 | 1,544 | 1,583 |
| Utah | 558 | 480 | 1,241 | 1,244 | 1,309 | 1,491 | 1,542 | 1,578 |
| Vermont | 625 | 505 | 1,133 | 1,074 | 1,121 | 1,275 | 1,324 | 1,374 |
| Virginia | 434 | 458 | 1,130 | 1,108 | 1,228 | 1,387 | 1,470 | 1,488 |
| Washington | 749 | 655 | 1,600 | 1,569 | 1,674 | 1,821 | 1,919 | 2,001 |
| West Virginia | 460 | 402 | 1,120 | 1,033 | 1,065 | 1,192 | 1,258 | 1,282 |
| Wisconsin | 684 | 552 | 1,418 | 1,366 | 1,477 | 1,697 | 1,757 | 1,787 |
| Wyoming | 683 | 606 | 1,595 | 1,605 | 1,668 | 1,911 | 1,866 | 1,892 |

Table 6.1 (continued)

| State | 1954 | 1955 | 1956 | 1957 | 1958 | 1959 | 1960 | 1961 |
|---|---|---|---|---|---|---|---|---|
| Alabama | 1,099 | 1,233 | 1,304 | 1,371 | 1,405 | 1,467 | 1,493 | 1,515 |
| Alaska | 2,300 | 2,273 | 2,446 | 2,323 | 2,357 | 2,507 | 2,824 | 2,659 |
| Arizona | 1,623 | 1,677 | 1,767 | 1,802 | 1,861 | 1,947 | 1,030 | 2,065 |
| Arkansas | 1,044 | 1,142 | 1,194 | 1,207 | 1,280 | 1,378 | 1,376 | 1,497 |
| California | 2,172 | 2,313 | 2,419 | 2,489 | 2,508 | 2,648 | 2,704 | 2,764 |
| Colorado | 1,718 | 1,814 | 1,887 | 2,023 | 2,114 | 2,194 | 2,271 | 2,329 |
| Connecticut | 2,294 | 2,414 | 2,603 | 2,712 | 2,635 | 2,689 | 2,800 | 2,880 |
| Delaware | 2,328 | 2,519 | 2,754 | 2,641 | 2,621 | 2,725 | 2,772 | 2,765 |
| Dist. of Columbia | 2,423 | 2,483 | 2,660 | 2,701 | 2,817 | 2,927 | 3,023 | 3,059 |
| Florida | 1,520 | 1,620 | 1,723 | 1,768 | 1,826 | 1,935 | 1,946 | 1,955 |
| Georgia | 1,259 | 1,375 | 1,445 | 1,469 | 1,516 | 1,606 | 1,637 | 1,680 |
| Hawaii | 1,802 | 1,838 | 1,900 | 1,944 | 1,981 | 2,156 | 2,366 | 2,481 |
| Idaho | 1,503 | 1,539 | 1,667 | 1,720 | 1,797 | 1,867 | 1,846 | 1,916 |
| Illinois | 2,154 | 2,243 | 2,416 | 2,488 | 2,463 | 2,579 | 2,646 | 2,713 |
| Indiana | 1,795 | 1,894 | 1,991 | 2,028 | 2,006 | 2,128 | 2,198 | 2,229 |
| Iowa | 1,723 | 1,608 | 1,694 | 1,869 | 1,920 | 1,948 | 1,986 | 2,083 |
| Kansas | 1,762 | 1,732 | 1,795 | 1,882 | 2,074 | 2,076 | 2,159 | 2,232 |
| Kentucky | 1,272 | 1,328 | 1,417 | 1,465 | 1,500 | 1,556 | 1,581 | 1,683 |
| Louisiana | 1,346 | 1,396 | 1,500 | 1,614 | 1,618 | 1,671 | 1,662 | 1,700 |
| Maine | 1,417 | 1,552 | 1,635 | 1,679 | 1,734 | 1,772 | 1,834 | 1,817 |
| Maryland | 1,888 | 1,994 | 2,126 | 2,198 | 2,202 | 2,268 | 2,340 | 2,456 |
| Massachusetts | 1,893 | 2,026 | 2,146 | 2,247 | 2,283 | 2,369 | 2,453 | 2,533 |
| Michigan | 2,031 | 2,183 | 2,214 | 2,229 | 2,165 | 2,264 | 2,338 | 2,311 |
| Minnesota | 1,671 | 1,729 | 1,783 | 1,874 | 1,988 | 2,016 | 2,110 | 2,182 |
| Mississippi | 908 | 1,020 | 1,026 | 1,040 | 1,126 | 1,202 | 1,205 | 1,278 |
| Missouri | 1,715 | 1,802 | 1,884 | 1,922 | 2,021 | 2,099 | 2,113 | 2,165 |
| Montana | 1,729 | 1,852 | 1,891 | 1,944 | 2,057 | 2,009 | 2,036 | 1,969 |
| Nebraska | 1,681 | 1,594 | 1,628 | 1,876 | 1,962 | 1,974 | 2,108 | 2,107 |
| Nevada | 2,437 | 2,549 | 2,502 | 2,588 | 2,645 | 2,760 | 2,848 | 2,893 |
| New Hampshire | 1,651 | 1,765 | 1,829 | 1,927 | 1,948 | 2,076 | 2,135 | 2,193 |
| New Jersey | 2,231 | 2,306 | 2,443 | 2,536 | 2,517 | 2,635 | 2,708 | 2,767 |
| New Mexico | 1,412 | 1,504 | 1,593 | 1,702 | 1,826 | 1,914 | 1,886 | 1,939 |
| New York | 2,167 | 2,283 | 2,396 | 2,493 | 2,513 | 2,655 | 2,742 | 2,803 |
| North Carolina | 1,239 | 1,313 | 1,377 | 1,369 | 1,431 | 1,506 | 1,558 | 1,629 |
| North Dakota | 1,254 | 1,378 | 1,437 | 1,479 | 1,699 | 1,536 | 1,714 | 1,504 |
| Ohio | 1,961 | 2,081 | 2,171 | 2,227 | 2,150 | 2,278 | 2,338 | 2,335 |
| Oklahoma | 1,445 | 1,507 | 1,580 | 1,641 | 1,764 | 1,807 | 1,865 | 1,917 |
| Oregon | 1,821 | 1,927 | 2,016 | 1,996 | 2,070 | 2,179 | 2,223 | 2,264 |
| Pennsylvania | 1,804 | 1,889 | 2,032 | 2,137 | 2,134 | 2,200 | 2,247 | 2,260 |
| Rhode Island | 1,866 | 1,962 | 1,993 | 1,998 | 2,038 | 2,152 | 2,216 | 2,289 |
| South Carolina | 1,119 | 1,181 | 1,210 | 1,236 | 1,252 | 1,329 | 1,372 | 1,432 |
| South Dakota | 1,398 | 1,293 | 1,365 | 1,603 | 1,668 | 1,471 | 1,783 | 1,770 |
| Tennessee | 1,222 | 1,281 | 1,368 | 1,419 | 1,448 | 1,532 | 1,544 | 1,624 |
| Texas | 1,611 | 1,667 | 1,752 | 1,823 | 1,856 | 1,919 | 1,931 | 1,997 |
| Utah | 1,554 | 1,625 | 1,707 | 1,794 | 1,833 | 1,929 | 1,971 | 2,041 |
| Vermont | 1,395 | 1,463 | 1,586 | 1,647 | 1,648 | 1,736 | 1,839 | 1,875 |
| Virginia | 1,501 | 1,571 | 1,634 | 1,652 | 1,684 | 1,770 | 1,842 | 1,899 |
| Washington | 2,001 | 2,038 | 2,092 | 2,170 | 2,205 | 2,309 | 2,340 | 2,447 |
| West Virginia | 1,232 | 1,326 | 1,491 | 1,610 | 1,565 | 1,600 | 1,612 | 1,658 |
| Wisconsin | 1,722 | 1,816 | 1,927 | 1,991 | 2,018 | 2,153 | 2,175 | 2,216 |
| Wyoming | 1,818 | 1,857 | 1,938 | 2,054 | 2,148 | 2,239 | 2,267 | 2,304 |

Table 6.1 (continued)

| State | 1962 | 1963 | 1964 | 1965 | 1966 | 1967 | 1968 | 1969 |
|---|---|---|---|---|---|---|---|---|
| Alabama | 1,587 | 1,687 | 1,799 | 1,950 | 2,092 | 2,215 | 2,429 | 2,664 |
| Alaska | 2,699 | 2,744 | 2,997 | 3,154 | 3,380 | 3,675 | 3,899 | 4,223 |
| Arizona | 2,160 | 2,210 | 2,268 | 2,382 | 2,547 | 2,743 | 3,010 | 3,319 |
| Arkansas | 1,564 | 1,655 | 1,785 | 1,188 | 2,106 | 2,228 | 2,417 | 2,616 |
| California | 2,867 | 2,973 | 3,111 | 3,234 | 3,447 | 3,640 | 3,956 | 4,214 |
| Colorado | 2,410 | 2,451 | 2,530 | 2,668 | 2,839 | 2,982 | 3,233 | 3,519 |
| Connecticut | 3,022 | 3,098 | 3,218 | 3,418 | 3,671 | 3,987 | 4,276 | 4,606 |
| Delaware | 2,879 | 3,009 | 3,141 | 3,362 | 3,469 | 3,585 | 3,876 | 4,205 |
| Dist. of Columbia | 3,223 | 3,353 | 3,542 | 3,725 | 3,934 | 4,198 | 4,551 | 4,908 |
| Florida | 2,025 | 2,107 | 2,245 | 2,382 | 2,569 | 2,796 | 3,077 | 3,394 |
| Georgia | 1,782 | 1,892 | 2,028 | 2,200 | 2,413 | 2,618 | 2,852 | 3,153 |
| Hawaii | 2,567 | 2,641 | 2,813 | 2,885 | 3,185 | 3,409 | 3,755 | 4,097 |
| Idaho | 2,038 | 2,062 | 2,145 | 2,431 | 2,440 | 2,602 | 2,712 | 3,038 |
| Illinois | 2,816 | 2,901 | 3,042 | 3,280 | 3,531 | 3,711 | 3,970 | 4,279 |
| Indiana | 2,368 | 2,473 | 2,603 | 2,858 | 3,056 | 3,167 | 3,419 | 3,716 |
| Iowa | 2,182 | 2,310 | 2,419 | 2,757 | 3,011 | 3,047 | 3,258 | 3,532 |
| Kansas | 2,323 | 2,403 | 2,527 | 2,733 | 3,000 | 3,141 | 3,397 | 3,639 |
| Kentucky | 1,768 | 1,857 | 1,916 | 2,087 | 2,288 | 2,450 | 2,666 | 2,881 |
| Louisiana | 1,766 | 1,865 | 1,973 | 2,120 | 2,323 | 2,528 | 2,744 | 2,864 |
| Maine | 1,887 | 1,937 | 2,105 | 2,269 | 2,433 | 2,534 | 2,779 | 3,010 |
| Maryland | 2,556 | 2,646 | 2,792 | 2,967 | 3,158 | 3,351 | 3,675 | 3,991 |
| Massachusetts | 2,637 | 2,716 | 2,825 | 2,985 | 3,200 | 3,448 | 3,747 | 4,058 |
| Michigan | 2,467 | 2,611 | 2,810 | 3,094 | 3,314 | 3,438 | 3,775 | 4,075 |
| Minnesota | 2,237 | 2,351 | 2,418 | 2,651 | 2,866 | 3,047 | 3,296 | 3,595 |
| Mississippi | 1,327 | 1,466 | 1,526 | 1,667 | 1,836 | 1,986 | 2,185 | 2,370 |
| Missouri | 2,271 | 2,370 | 2,483 | 2,681 | 2,846 | 3,047 | 3,300 | 3,478 |
| Montana | 2,264 | 2,258 | 2,255 | 2,439 | 2,652 | 2,731 | 2,899 | 3,170 |
| Nebraska | 2,236 | 2,263 | 2,349 | 2,618 | 2,914 | 3,029 | 3,172 | 3,594 |
| Nevada | 3,188 | 3,185 | 3,177 | 3,229 | 3,385 | 3,521 | 3,862 | 4,264 |
| New Hampshire | 2,282 | 2,326 | 2,414 | 2,556 | 2,797 | 2,982 | 3,224 | 3,418 |
| New Jersey | 2,890 | 2,966 | 3,089 | 3,267 | 3,483 | 3,701 | 3,995 | 4,288 |
| New Mexico | 2,011 | 2,053 | 2,102 | 2,242 | 2,364 | 2,463 | 2,672 | 2,877 |
| New York | 2,921 | 3,010 | 3,183 | 3,354 | 3,571 | 3,828 | 4,157 | 4,470 |
| North Carolina | 1,732 | 1,815 | 1,935 | 2,075 | 2,316 | 2,481 | 2,711 | 2,989 |
| North Dakota | 2,151 | 2,006 | 1,985 | 2,319 | 2,424 | 2,549 | 2,667 | 3,006 |
| Ohio | 2,438 | 2,522 | 2,666 | 2,880 | 3,117 | 3,245 | 3,528 | 3,827 |
| Oklahoma | 1,936 | 2,004 | 2,138 | 2,323 | 2,508 | 2,682 | 2,886 | 3,088 |
| Oregon | 2,358 | 2,457 | 2,591 | 2,753 | 2,925 | 3,081 | 3,309 | 3,528 |
| Pennsylvania | 2,371 | 2,440 | 2,599 | 2,749 | 2,982 | 3,173 | 3,402 | 3,688 |
| Rhode Island | 2,422 | 2,504 | 2,650 | 2,804 | 3,048 | 3,287 | 3,546 | 3,705 |
| South Carolina | 1,541 | 1,597 | 1,719 | 1,885 | 2,104 | 2,261 | 2,483 | 2,718 |
| South Dakota | 1,996 | 1,906 | 1,883 | 2,208 | 2,461 | 2,580 | 2,819 | 2,987 |
| Tennessee | 1,703 | 1,786 | 1,893 | 2,067 | 2,267 | 2,405 | 2,634 | 2,882 |
| Texas | 2,047 | 2,131 | 2,251 | 2,405 | 2,638 | 2,832 | 3,079 | 3,321 |
| Utah | 2,162 | 2,213 | 2,270 | 2,377 | 2,495 | 2,622 | 2,810 | 2,976 |
| Vermont | 1,976 | 2,010 | 2,146 | 2,365 | 2,638 | 2,785 | 3,035 | 3,262 |
| Virginia | 2,020 | 2,101 | 2,273 | 2,430 | 2,622 | 28,26 | 3,098 | 3,351 |
| Washington | 2,583 | 2,618 | 2,721 | 2,908 | 3,231 | 3,431 | 3,690 | 3,924 |
| West Virginia | 1,727 | 1,819 | 1,943 | 2,087 | 2,250 | 2,403 | 2,545 | 2,738 |
| Wisconsin | 2,321 | 2,350 | 2,509 | 2,681 | 2,911 | 3,043 | 3,270 | 3,495 |
| Wyoming | 2,386 | 2,419 | 2,435 | 2,571 | 2,765 | 2,895 | 3,077 | 3,380 |

428

Table 6.1 (continued)

| State | 1970 | 1971 | 1972 | 1973 | 1974 | 1975 | 1976 | 1977 |
|---|---|---|---|---|---|---|---|---|
| Alabama | 2,913 | 3,087 | 3,333 | 3,864 | 4,198 | 4,635 | 5,105 | 5,622 |
| Alaska | 4,603 | 4,875 | 5,162 | 5,926 | 7,023 | 9,636 | 10,178 | 10,586 |
| Arizona | 3,631 | 3,913 | 4,300 | 4,687 | 4,989 | 5,391 | 5,817 | 6,509 |
| Arkansas | 2,869 | 3,078 | 3,357 | 3,956 | 4,280 | 4,510 | 5,073 | 5,540 |
| California | 4,467 | 4,640 | 5,002 | 5,508 | 5,997 | 6,575 | 7,164 | 7,911 |
| Colorado | 3,839 | 4,153 | 4,449 | 4,966 | 5,343 | 5,987 | 6,503 | 7,160 |
| Connecticut | 4,871 | 4,995 | 5,342 | 5,931 | 6,471 | 6,799 | 7,373 | 8,061 |
| Delaware | 4,483 | 4,673 | 4,983 | 5,813 | 6,227 | 6,547 | 7,290 | 7,697 |
| Dist. of Columbia | 5,333 | 5,870 | 6,383 | 6,566 | 7,479 | 7,262 | 8,648 | 8,999 |
| Florida | 3,692 | 3,930 | 4,188 | 4,820 | 5,235 | 5,631 | 6,108 | 6,684 |
| Georgia | 3,318 | 3,599 | 3,846 | 4,343 | 4,662 | 5,029 | 5,571 | 6,014 |
| Hawaii | 4,562 | 4,738 | 4,995 | 5,525 | 5,882 | 6,708 | 6,969 | 7,677 |
| Idaho | 3,280 | 3,409 | 3,635 | 4,381 | 4,934 | 5,179 | 5,726 | 5,980 |
| Illinois | 4,492 | 4,775 | 5,126 | 5,801 | 6,337 | 6,735 | 7,432 | 7,768 |
| Indiana | 3,752 | 4,027 | 4,391 | 4,998 | 5,263 | 5,609 | 6,257 | 6,921 |
| Iowa | 3,749 | 3,877 | 4,318 | 5,347 | 5,302 | 5,894 | 6,439 | 6,878 |
| Kansas | 3,841 | 4,192 | 4,593 | 5,338 | 5,406 | 5,958 | 6,495 | 7,134 |
| Kentucky | 3,104 | 3,306 | 3,601 | 4,050 | 4,470 | 4,887 | 5,423 | 5,945 |
| Louisiana | 3,068 | 3,252 | 3,528 | 3,950 | 4,310 | 4,803 | 5,386 | 5,913 |
| Maine | 3,272 | 3,375 | 3,571 | 4,040 | 4,439 | 4,766 | 5,385 | 5,734 |
| Maryland | 4,281 | 4,522 | 4,897 | 5,446 | 5,881 | 6,403 | 7,036 | 7,572 |
| Massachusetts | 4,340 | 4,562 | 4,870 | 5,268 | 5,731 | 6,077 | 6,585 | 7,258 |
| Michigan | 4,156 | 4,430 | 4,817 | 5,540 | 5,928 | 5,991 | 6,994 | 7,619 |
| Minnesota | 3,848 | 4,032 | 4,332 | 5,144 | 5,450 | 5,779 | 6,153 | 7,129 |
| Mississippi | 2,596 | 2,788 | 3,063 | 3,546 | 3,764 | 4,047 | 4,575 | 5,030 |
| Missouri | 3,768 | 3,940 | 4,206 | 4,831 | 5,056 | 5,476 | 6,005 | 6,654 |
| Montana | 3,498 | 3,629 | 3,897 | 4,626 | 4,776 | 5,388 | 5,600 | 6,125 |
| Nebraska | 3,794 | 4,030 | 4,341 | 5,299 | 4,877 | 5,882 | 6,240 | 6,720 |
| Nevada | 4,452 | 4,822 | 5,215 | 5,712 | 6,073 | 6,625 | 7,337 | 7,988 |
| New Hampshire | 3,745 | 3,796 | 4,092 | 4,615 | 5,143 | 5,417 | 5,973 | 6,536 |
| New Jersey | 4,635 | 4,811 | 5,126 | 5,874 | 6,384 | 6,794 | 7,269 | 7,994 |
| New Mexico | 3,117 | 3,298 | 3,656 | 3,877 | 4,137 | 4,843 | 5,213 | 5,857 |
| New York | 4,714 | 5,000 | 5,319 | 5,720 | 6,244 | 6,519 | 7,100 | 7,537 |
| North Carolina | 3,218 | 3,424 | 3,721 | 4,258 | 4,612 | 4,940 | 5,409 | 5,935 |
| North Dakota | 3,120 | 3,538 | 3,718 | 5,730 | 5,547 | 5,888 | 5,400 | 6,190 |
| Ohio | 3,992 | 4,175 | 4,512 | 5,070 | 5,549 | 5,778 | 6,432 | 7,084 |
| Oklahoma | 3,350 | 3,515 | 3,802 | 4,331 | 4,566 | 5,280 | 5,657 | 6,346 |
| Oregon | 3,694 | 3,959 | 4,296 | 4,845 | 5,270 | 5,769 | 6,331 | 7,007 |
| Pennsylvania | 3,943 | 4,147 | 4,447 | 5,010 | 5,490 | 5,841 | 6,466 | 7,011 |
| Rhode Island | 3,941 | 4,126 | 4,399 | 4,869 | 5,376 | 5,709 | 6,498 | 6,775 |
| South Carolina | 2,963 | 3,142 | 3,448 | 3,885 | 4,258 | 4,665 | 5,126 | 5,628 |
| South Dakota | 3,124 | 3,441 | 3,716 | 4,771 | 4,218 | 5,009 | 4,796 | 5,957 |
| Tennessee | 3,082 | 3,300 | 3,640 | 4,124 | 4,484 | 4,804 | 5,432 | 5,785 |
| Texas | 3,576 | 3,726 | 4,045 | 4,558 | 4,790 | 5,584 | 6,243 | 6,803 |
| Utah | 3,228 | 3,442 | 3,745 | 4,096 | 4,452 | 4,900 | 5,482 | 5,923 |
| Vermont | 3,311 | 3,638 | 3,865 | 4,185 | 4,588 | 4,924 | 5,480 | 5,823 |
| Virginia | 3,653 | 3,899 | 4,258 | 4,868 | 5,265 | 5,772 | 6,276 | 6,865 |
| Washington | 4,022 | 4,132 | 4,476 | 5,151 | 5,651 | 6,298 | 6,772 | 7,528 |
| West Virginia | 3,047 | 3,275 | 3,574 | 3,974 | 4,390 | 4,962 | 5,394 | 5,986 |
| Wisconsin | 3,794 | 3,912 | 4,207 | 4,781 | 5,120 | 5,616 | 6,293 | 6,890 |
| Wyoming | 3,796 | 3,929 | 4,345 | 4,696 | 5,156 | 6,123 | 6,723 | 7,562 |

429

Table 6.1 (continued)

| State | 1978 | 1979 | 1980 | 1981 | 1982 |
|---|---|---|---|---|---|
| Alabama | 6,247 | 6,976 | 7,477 | 8,284 | 8,649 |
| Alaska | 10,851 | 11,252 | 12,916 | 14,904 | 16,257 |
| Arizona | 7,374 | 8,305 | 8,832 | 9,871 | 10,173 |
| Arkansas | 6,183 | 6,785 | 7,166 | 8,178 | 8,479 |
| California | 8,850 | 9,913 | 10,920 | 12,064 | 12,567 |
| Colorado | 8,001 | 8,945 | 10,042 | 11,389 | 12,302 |
| Connecticut | 8,914 | 9,959 | 11,536 | 12,844 | 13,748 |
| Delaware | 8,604 | 9,557 | 10,066 | 11,033 | 11,731 |
| Dist. of Columbia | 10,022 | 10,911 | 12,296 | 13,672 | 14,550 |
| Florida | 7,505 | 8,532 | 9,201 | 10,438 | 10,978 |
| Georgia | 6,700 | 7,515 | 8,061 | 9,012 | 9,583 |
| Hawaii | 8,380 | 9,353 | 10,222 | 11,068 | 11,652 |
| Idaho | 6,813 | 7,446 | 8,044 | 8,875 | 9,029 |
| Illinois | 8,745 | 9,823 | 10,471 | 11,616 | 12,100 |
| Indiana | 7,696 | 8,686 | 9,430 | 10,274 | 10,677 |
| Iowa | 7,873 | 8,589 | 9,336 | 10,749 | 10,791 |
| Kansas | 8,001 | 9,055 | 9,942 | 11,237 | 11,765 |
| Kentucky | 6,615 | 7,342 | 7,648 | 8,567 | 8,934 |
| Louisiana | 6,640 | 7,477 | 8,525 | 9,778 | 10,231 |
| Maine | 6,333 | 7,057 | 7,672 | 8,494 | 9,042 |
| Maryland | 8,306 | 9,150 | 10,385 | 11,522 | 12,238 |
| Massachusetts | 8,063 | 8,844 | 10,089 | 11,248 | 12,088 |
| Michigan | 8,442 | 9,269 | 9,872 | 10,620 | 10,956 |
| Minnesota | 7,847 | 8,760 | 9,688 | 10,684 | 11,175 |
| Mississippi | 5,736 | 6,167 | 6,680 | 7,414 | 7,778 |
| Missouri | 7,342 | 8,132 | 8,720 | 9,764 | 10,170 |
| Montana | 7,051 | 7,412 | 8,361 | 9,252 | 9,580 |
| Nebraska | 7,391 | 8,341 | 9,137 | 10,331 | 10,683 |
| Nevada | 9,032 | 10,204 | 10,761 | 11,816 | 11,981 |
| New Hampshire | 7,277 | 8,231 | 9,010 | 10,051 | 10,729 |
| New Jersey | 8,818 | 9,702 | 10,976 | 12,230 | 13,089 |
| New Mexico | 6,505 | 7,294 | 7,891 | 8,707 | 9,190 |
| New York | 8,267 | 9,098 | 10,283 | 11,473 | 12,314 |
| North Carolina | 6,607 | 7,359 | 7,753 | 8,648 | 9,044 |
| North Dakota | 7,478 | 7,774 | 8,759 | 10,911 | 10,872 |
| Ohio | 7,812 | 8,775 | 9,430 | 10,274 | 10,677 |
| Oklahoma | 6,951 | 8,226 | 9,187 | 10,606 | 11,370 |
| Oregon | 7,839 | 8,842 | 9,356 | 10,017 | 10,335 |
| Pennsylvania | 7,733 | 8,559 | 9,389 | 10,423 | 10,955 |
| Rhode Island | 7,526 | 8,266 | 9,174 | 10,129 | 10,723 |
| South Carolina | 6,242 | 7,027 | 7,298 | 8,128 | 8,502 |
| South Dakota | 6,841 | 7,334 | 8,028 | 9,245 | 9,666 |
| Tennessee | 6,489 | 7,299 | 7,662 | 8,516 | 8,906 |
| Texas | 7,697 | 8,649 | 9,538 | 10,954 | 11,419 |
| Utah | 6,622 | 7,185 | 7,656 | 8,478 | 8,875 |
| Vermont | 6,541 | 7,280 | 7,832 | 8,877 | 9,507 |
| Virginia | 7,624 | 8,605 | 9,357 | 10,450 | 11,905 |
| Washington | 8,450 | 9,435 | 10,198 | 11,163 | 11,560 |
| West Virginia | 6,456 | 7,470 | 7,665 | 8,336 | 8,769 |
| Wisconsin | 7,597 | 8,419 | 9,347 | 10,227 | 10,774 |
| Wyoming | 9,096 | 9,657 | 11,042 | 12,217 | 12,372 |

Table 6.2

Federal Government Receipts,

by Source, 1789-1982[a]

| | | | | Other Receipts | |
| | | | | | |
| Year or Period | Total[b] | Customs | Internal Revenue | Total, Excl. Sales of Public Lands | Sales of Public Lands |
| --- | --- | --- | --- | --- | --- |
| 1789-1791 | 4,419 | 4,399 | n.a. | 19 | n.a. |
| 1792 | 3,670 | 3,443 | 209 | 18 | n.a. |
| 1793 | 4,653 | 4,255 | 338 | 60 | n.a. |
| 1794 | 5,432 | 4,801 | 274 | 357 | n.a. |
| 1795 | 6.115 | 5,588 | 338 | 188 | n.a. |
| 1796 | 8,378 | 6,568 | 475 | 1,334 | 5 |
| 1797 | 8,689 | 7,550 | 575 | 564 | 84 |
| 1798 | 7,900 | 7,106 | 644 | 150 | 12 |
| 1799 | 7,547 | 6,610 | 779 | 157 | n.a. |
| 1800 | 10,849 | 9,081 | 809 | 958 | * |
| 1801 | 12,935 | 10,751 | 1,048 | 1,137 | 168 |
| 1802 | 14,996 | 12,438 | 622 | 1,936 | 189 |
| 1803 | 11,064 | 10,479 | 215 | 370 | 166 |
| 1804 | 11,826 | 11,099 | 51 | 677 | 488 |
| 1805 | 13,561 | 12,936 | 22 | 602 | 540 |
| 1806 | 15,560 | 14,668 | 20 | 8721 | 765 |
| 1807 | 16,398 | 15,846 | 13 | 539 | 466 |
| 1808 | 17,061 | 16,364 | 8 | 689 | 648 |
| 1809 | 7,773 | 7,296 | 4 | 473 | 442 |
| 1810 | 9,384 | 8,583 | 7 | 793 | 697 |
| 1811 | 14,424 | 13,313 | 2 | 1,108 | 1,040 |
| 1812 | 9,801 | 8,959 | 5 | 837 | 710 |
| 1813 | 14,340 | 13,225 | 5 | 1,111 | 836 |
| 1814 | 11,182 | 5,999 | 1,663 | 3,520 | 1,136 |
| 1815 | 15,729 | 7,283 | 4,678 | 3,768 | 1,288 |
| 1816 | 47,678 | 36,307 | 5,125 | 6,246 | 1,718 |
| 1817 | 33,099 | 26,283 | 2,678 | 4,138 | 1,991 |
| 1818 | 21,585 | 17,176 | 955 | 3,454 | 2,607 |
| 1819 | 24,603 | 20,284 | 230 | 4,090 | 3,274 |
| 1820 | 17,881 | 15,006 | 106 | 2,769 | 1,636 |
| 1821 | 14,573 | 13,004 | 69 | 1,500 | 1,213 |
| 1822 | 20,232 | 17590 | 68 | 2,575 | 1,804 |
| 1823 | 20,541 | 19,088 | 34 | 1,418 | 917 |
| 1824 | 19,381 | 17,878 | 35 | 1,468 | 984 |
| 1825 | 21,841 | 20,099 | 26 | 1,716 | 1,216 |
| 1826 | 25,260 | 23,341 | 22 | 1,898 | 1,394 |
| 1827 | 22,966 | 19,712 | 20 | 3,234 | 1,496 |
| 1828 | 24,764 | 23,206 | 17 | 1,541 | 1,018 |
| 1829 | 24,828 | 22,682 | 15 | 2,131 | 1,517 |
| 1830 | 24,844 | 21,922 | 12 | 2,910 | 2,329 |
| 1831 | 28,527 | 24,224 | 7 | 4,295 | 3,211 |
| 1832 | 31,866 | 28,465 | 12 | 3,389 | 2,623 |
| 1833 | 33,948 | 29,033 | 3 | 4,913 | 3,968 |
| 1834 | 21,792 | 16,215 | 4 | 5,573 | 4,858 |

Table 6.2 (continued)

| Year or Period | Total[b] | Customs | Internal Revenue | Other Receipts Total, Excl. Sales of Public Lands | Sales of Public Lands |
|---|---|---|---|---|---|
| 1835 | 35,430 | 19,3919 | 10 | 16,028 | 14,758 |
| 1836 | 50,827 | 23,410 | * | 27,416 | 24,877 |
| 1837 | 24,954 | 11,169 | 5 | 13,779 | 6,776 |
| 1838 | 26,303 | 16,159 | 2 | 10,141 | 3,082 |
| 1839 | 31,483 | 23,138 | 3 | 8,342 | 7,076 |
| 1840 | 19,480 | 13,500 | 2 | 5,979 | 3,293 |
| 1841 | 16,860 | 14,487 | 3 | 2,370 | 1,366 |
| 1842 | 19,976 | 18,188 | * | 1,788 | 1,336 |
| 1843 | 8,303 | 7,047 | * | 1,256 | 898 |
| 1844 | 29,321 | 26,184 | 2 | 3,136 | 2,060 |
| 1845 | 29,970 | 27,528 | 4 | 2,438 | 2,077 |
| 1846 | 29,700 | 26,713 | 3 | 2,984 | 2,694 |
| 1847 | 26,496 | 23,748 | * | 2,748 | 2,498 |
| 1848 | 35,736 | 31,757 | * | 3,978 | 3,329 |
| 1849 | 31,208 | 28,347 | n.a. | 2,861 | 1,689 |
| 1850 | 43,603 | 39,669 | n.a. | 3,935 | 1,860 |
| 1851 | 52,559 | 49,018 | n.a. | 3,542 | 2,352 |
| 1852 | 49,847 | 47,339 | n.a. | 2,507 | 2,043 |
| 1853 | 61,587 | 58,932 | n.a. | 2,655 | 1,667 |
| 1854 | 73,800 | 64,224 | n.a. | 9,576 | 8,471 |
| 1855 | 65,351 | 53,026 | n.a. | 12,325 | 11,497 |
| 1856 | 74,057 | 64,023 | n.a. | 10,034 | 8,918 |
| 1857 | 68,965 | 63,876 | n.a. | 5,089 | 3,829 |
| 1858 | 46,655 | 41,790 | n.a. | 4,866 | 3,154 |
| 1859 | 53,486 | 49,566 | n.a. | 3,921 | 1,757 |
| 1860 | 56,065 | 53,188 | n.a. | 2,877 | 1,779 |
| 1861 | 41,510 | 39,582 | n.a. | 1,928 | 871 |
| 1862 | 51,987 | 49,056 | n.a. | 2,931 | 152 |
| 1863 | 112,697 | 69,060 | 37,641 | 5,997 | 168 |
| 1864 | 264,627 | 102,316 | 109,741 | 52,569 | 588 |
| 1865 | 333,715 | 84,928 | 209,464 | 39,322 | 997 |
| 1866 | 558,033 | 179,047 | 309,227 | 69,759 | 665 |
| 1867 | 490,634 | 176,418 | 266,028 | 48,189 | 1,164 |
| 1868 | 408,638 | 164,465 | 191,088 | 50,086 | 1,349 |
| 1869 | 370,944 | 180,048 | 158,356 | 32,539 | 4,020 |
| 1870 | 411,255 | 194,538 | 184,900 | 31,817 | 3,350 |
| 1871 | 383,324 | 206,270 | 143,098 | 33,955 | 2,389 |
| 1872 | 374,107 | 216,370 | 130,642 | 27,094 | 2,576 |
| 1873 | 333,738 | 188,090 | 113,729 | 31,919 | 2,882 |
| 1874 | 304,979 | 163,104 | 102,410 | 29,465 | 1,852 |
| 1875 | 288,000 | 157,168 | 110,007 | 20,825 | 1,414 |
| 1876 | 294,096 | 148,072 | 116,701 | 29,323 | 1,129 |
| 1877 | 281,406 | 130,956 | 118,620 | 31,820 | 976 |
| 1878 | 257,764 | 130,171 | 110,82 | 17,012 | 1,080 |
| 1879 | 273,827 | 137,250 | 113,562 | 23,016 | 925 |
| 1880 | 333,522 | 186,522 | 124,009 | 22,995 | 1,017 |
| 1881 | 360,782 | 198,160 | 135,264 | 27,358 | 2,202 |
| 1882 | 403,525 | 220,411 | 146,498 | 36,617 | 4,753 |
| 1883 | 398,288 | 314,706 | 144,720 | 38,861 | 7,956 |
| 1884 | 348,520 | 195,067 | 121,586 | 31,866 | 9,811 |
| 1885 | 323,691 | 181,472 | 112,499 | 29,720 | 5,706 |
| 1886 | 336,440 | 192,905 | 16,806 | 26,729 | 5,631 |
| 1887 | 371,403 | 217,287 | 118,823 | 35,293 | 9,254 |

Table 6.2 (continued)

| Year or Period | Total[b] | Customs | Internal Revenue | Other Receipts | |
|---|---|---|---|---|---|
| | | | | Total, Excl. Sales of Public Lands | Sales of Public Lands |
| 1888 | 397,266 | 219,091 | 124,297 | 35,878 | 11,202 |
| 1889 | 387,050 | 223,833 | 130,882 | 32,336 | 8,039 |
| 1890 | 403,081 | 229,669 | 142,607 | 30,806 | 6,358 |
| 1891 | 392,612 | 219,522 | 145,686 | 27,404 | 4,030 |
| 1892 | 354,938 | 177,453 | 153,971 | 23,514 | 3,262 |
| 1893 | 385,820 | 203,355 | 161,028 | 21,437 | 3,182 |
| 1894 | 306,355 | 131,819 | 147,111 | 27,426 | 1,674 |
| 1895 | 324,729 | 152,159 | 143,422 | 29,149 | 1,103 |

Table 6.2 (continued)

| Year or Period | Total[b] | Customs | Internal Revenue | Other Receipts Total, Excl. Sales of Public Lands | Sales of Public Lands | Refunds, Transfers, Interfund Transactions |
|---|---|---|---|---|---|---|
| 1896 | 338,142 | 160,022 | 146,763 | 31,358 | 1,006 | n.a. |
| 1897 | 347,722 | 176,554 | 146,89 | 24,479 | 865 | n.a. |
| 1898 | 405,321 | 149,575 | 170,901 | 84,846 | 1,243 | n.a. |
| 1899 | 515,961 | 206,128 | 273,437 | 36,395 | 1,78 | n.a. |
| 1900 | 567,241 | 233,165 | 295,328 | 38,748 | 1,837 | n.a. |
| 1901 | 587,685 | 238,585 | 307,181 | 41,919 | 2,965 | n.a. |
| 1902 | 562,478 | 254,445 | 271,880 | 36,153 | 4,144 | n.a. |
| 1903 | 561,881 | 284,480 | 230,810 | 46,591 | 8,926 | n.a. |
| 1904 | 541,087 | 261,275 | 232,904 | 46,908 | 7,453 | n.a. |
| 1905 | 544,275 | 261,799 | 234,096 | 48,380 | 4,859 | n.a. |
| 1906 | 594,984 | 300,252 | 249,150 | 45,582 | 4,880 | n.a. |
| 1907 | 665,860 | 332,233 | 269,667 | 63,960 | 7,879 | n.a. |
| 1908 | 601,862 | 286,113 | 251,711 | 64,038 | 9,732 | n.a. |
| 1909 | 604,320 | 300,712 | 246,213 | 57,396 | 7,01 | n.a. |
| 1910 | 675,512 | 333,683 | 289,934 | 51,895 | 6,356 | n.a. |
| 1911 | 701,833 | 314,497 | 322,529 | 64,807 | 5,732 | n.a. |
| 1912 | 692,609 | 311,322 | 321,612 | 59,657 | 5,393 | n.a. |
| 1913 | 714,463 | 318,891 | 344,417 | 60,803 | 2,910 | -9,648 |
| 1914 | 725,117 | 292,320 | 380,041 | 62,312 | 2,572 | -9,556 |
| 1915 | 683,417 | 209,787 | 415,670 | 72,455 | 2,167 | -14,494 |
| 1916 | 761,445 | 213,186 | 512,702 | 56,647 | 1,888 | -21,089 |
| 1917 | 1,100,500 | 225,962 | 809,366 | 88,996 | 1,893 | -23,825 |
| 1918 | 3,645,240 | 179,998 | 3,186,034 | 298,550 | 1,969 | -19,343 |
| 1919 | 5,130,042 | 184,458 | 4,315,285 | 652,514 | 1,405 | -22,215 |
| 1920 | 6,648,898 | 322,903 | 5,405,032 | 966,631 | 1,910 | -45,667 |
| 1921 | 5,570,790 | 308,564 | 4,596,426 | 719,943 | 1,530 | -54,143 |
| 1922 | 4,025,901 | 356,443 | 3,213,253 | 539,408 | 895 | -83,203 |
| 1923 | 3,852,795 | 561,929 | 2,624,473 | 820,734 | 657 | -154,341 |
| 1924 | 3,871,214 | 545,638 | 2,795,157 | 671,250 | 522 | -140,381 |
| 1925 | 3,640,805 | 547,561 | 2,589,176 | 643,412 | 624 | -139,343 |
| 1926 | 3,795,108 | 579,430 | 2,837,639 | 545,686 | 754 | -167,648 |
| 1927 | 4,012,794 | 605,500 | 3,869,414 | 654,480 | 621 | -116,601 |
| 1928 | 3,900,329 | 568,986 | 2,794,971 | 678,391 | 385 | -142,019 |
| 1929 | 3,861,589 | 602,263 | 2,938,019 | 492,968 | 315 | -171,661 |
| 1930 | 4,057,884 | 587,001 | 3,039,295 | 551,646 | 396 | -120,058 |
| 1931 | 3,115,557 | 378,354 | 2,429,781 | 381,504 | 230 | -74,082 |
| 1932 | 1,923,892 | 327,755 | 1,561,006 | 116,964 | 170 | -81,834 |
| 1933 | 1,996,844 | 250,750 | 1,604,424 | 224,523 | 103 | -82,853 |
| 1934 | 3,014,970 | 313,434 | 2,640,604 | 161,516 | 99 | -100,584 |
| 1935 | 3,705,956 | 343,353 | 3,277,690 | 179,424 | 87 | -94,512 |
| 1936 | 3,997,059 | 386,812 | 3,512,852 | 216,293 | 74 | -118,898 |
| 1937 | 4,955,613 | 486,357 | 4,597,140 | 210,094 | 71 | -337,978 |
| 1938 | 5,588,012 | 359,187 | 5,674,318 | 208,156 | 96 | -653,649 |
| 1939 | 4,979,066 | 318,837 | 5,161,221 | 187,765 | 248 | -688,758 |

Table 6.2 (continued)

| Year | Total | Customs | Individual Income Taxes | Corporation Income Taxes | Social Insurance Taxes & Contributions | Excise Taxes | Estate & Gift Taxes | Deposit of Earnings of the Federal Reserve System | Other |
|---|---|---|---|---|---|---|---|---|---|
| 1940 | 6,879 | 331 | 1,110 | 978 | 1,715 | 1,844 | 353 | n.a. | 548 |
| 1941 | 9,202 | 365 | 1,589 | 1,849 | 2,004 | 2,386 | 403 | n.a. | 606 |
| 1942 | 15,104 | 369 | 3,238 | 4,740 | 2,429 | 3,121 | 420 | n.a. | 787 |
| 1943 | 25,097 | 308 | 6,473 | 9,587 | 3,013 | 3,769 | 441 | n.a. | 1,506 |
| 1944 | 47,818 | 417 | 20,179 | 15,255 | 3,428 | 4,379 | 507 | n.a. | 3,653 |
| 1945 | 50,162 | 341 | 18,396 | 16,360 | 3,438 | 5,893 | 637 | n.a. | 5,097 |
| 1946 | 43,537 | 424 | 16,132 | 12,235 | 3,078 | 6,646 | 668 | n.a. | 4,354 |
| 1947 | 43,531 | 477 | 17,930 | 8,614 | 3,333 | 7,182 | 771 | 15 | 5,209 |
| 1948 | 45,357 | 403 | 19,310 | 9,678 | 3,966 | 7,356 | 890 | 100 | 3,654 |
| 1949 | 41,576 | 367 | 15,544 | 11,192 | 3,809 | 7,502 | 780 | 187 | 2,195 |
| 1950 | 40,940 | 407 | 15,747 | 10,449 | 4,386 | 7,550 | 698 | 192 | 1,511 |
| 1951 | 53,390 | 609 | 21,604 | 14,101 | 5,714 | 8,648 | 708 | 189 | 1,817 |
| 1952 | 68,011 | 533 | 27,918 | 21,226 | 6,496 | 8,852 | 818 | 278 | 1,890 |
| 1953 | 71,495 | 596 | 29,780 | 21,238 | 6,821 | 9,878 | 881 | 298 | 2,003 |
| 1954 | 69,719 | 542 | 29,542 | 21,101 | 7,210 | 9,945 | 934 | 341 | 104 |
| 1955 | 65,469 | 585 | 28,747 | 17,861 | 7,866 | 9,131 | 924 | 251 | 104 |
| 1956 | 74,547 | 682 | 32,188 | 20,880 | 9,323 | 9,929 | 1,161 | 287 | 97 |
| 1957 | 79,990 | 735 | 35,620 | 21,167 | 9,997 | 10,534 | 1,365 | 434 | 138 |
| 1958 | 79,636 | 782 | 34,724 | 20,074 | 11,239 | 10,638 | 1,393 | 664 | 122 |
| 1959 | 79,249 | 925 | 36,776 | 17,309 | 11,722 | 10,578 | 1,333 | 491 | 114 |
| 1960 | 92,492 | 1,105 | 40,741 | 21,494 | 14,684 | 11,676 | 1,606 | 1,093 | 94 |
| 1961 | 94,389 | 982 | 41,338 | 20,954 | 16,438 | 11,860 | 1,896 | 788 | 131 |
| 1962 | 99,676 | 1,142 | 45,571 | 20,523 | 17,046 | 12,534 | 2,016 | 718 | 125 |
| 1963 | 106,560 | 1,205 | 47,588 | 21,579 | 19,804 | 13,194 | 2,167 | 828 | 194 |
| 1964 | 112,662 | 1,252 | 48,697 | 23,493 | 22,012 | 13,731 | 2,394 | 947 | 138 |
| 1965 | 116,883 | 1,442 | 48,792 | 25,461 | 22,258 | 14,570 | 2,716 | 1,372 | 222 |
| 1966 | 130,856 | 1,767 | 55,446 | 30,073 | 25,567 | 18,062 | 3,006 | 1,713 | 162 |
| 1967 | 149,552 | 1,901 | 61,526 | 33,971 | 33,349 | 13,719 | 2,978 | 1,805 | 303 |

Table 6.2 (continued)

| Year | Total | Customs | Individual Income Taxes | Corporation Income Taxes | Social Insurance Taxes & Contributions | Excise Taxes | Estate & Gift Taxes | Deposit of Earnings of the Federal Reserve System | Other |
|------|-------|---------|-------------------------|--------------------------|----------------------------------------|--------------|---------------------|---------------------------------------------------|-------|
| 1968 | 153,671 | 2,038 | 68,726 | 28,665 | 34,622 | 14,079 | 3,051 | 2,091 | 400 |
| 1969 | 187,784 | 2,319 | 87,249 | 36,678 | 39,918 | 15,222 | 3,491 | 2,662 | 247 |
| 1970 | 193,743 | 2,430 | 90,412 | 32,829 | 45,298 | 15,705 | 3,644 | 3,266 | 158 |
| 1971 | 188,392 | 2,591 | 86,230 | 26,785 | 48,578 | 16,614 | 3,735 | 3,532 | 335 |
| 1972 | 208,649 | 3,287 | 94,737 | 32,166 | 53,914 | 15,477 | 5,436 | 3,252 | 380 |
| 1973 | 232,192 | 3,175 | 103,261 | 36,096 | 64,545 | 16,272 | 4,899 | 3,495 | 449 |
| 1974 | 264,932 | 3,334 | 118,952 | 36,620 | 65,892 | 16,844 | 5,035 | 4,845 | 13,410 |
| 1975 | 280,921 | 3,666 | 122,322 | 40,627 | 75,204 | 16,542 | 4,589 | 5,777 | 12,194 |
| 1976 | 300.0 | 4.1 | 131.6 | 41.4 | 92.7 | 17.0 | 5.2 | 5.5 | 8.0 |
| 1977 | 357.8 | 5.2 | 157.6 | 54.9 | 108.7 | 17.5 | 7.3 | 5.9 | 6.5 |
| 1978 | 402.0 | 6.6 | 181.0 | 60.0 | 123.4 | 18.4 | 5.3 | 6.6 | 7.4 |
| 1979 | 463.3 | 7.4 | 217.8 | 65.7 | 138.9 | 18.7 | 5.4 | 8.3 | 9.3 |
| 1980 | 517.1 | 7.2 | 244.1 | 64.6 | 157.8 | 24.3 | 6.4 | 11.8 | 12.7 |
| 1981 | 599.3 | 8.1 | 285.9 | 61.1 | 182.7 | 40.8 | 6.8 | 12.8 | 13.8 |
| 1982 | 617.8 | 8.9 | 297.7 | 49.2 | 201.5 | 36.3 | 8.0 | 15.2 | 16.2 |

* Less than $500

n.a. Data not available

[a] Figures reported for the period 1789 to 1939 are in thousands of dollars; the figures from 1940 to 1975 are in millions of dollars; the figures from 1976 to 1982 are in billions of dollars.

[b] Refunds of receipts are excluded starting in 1913; comparable data are not available for prior years. Certain interfund transactions are also excluded starting in 1932; for prior years, the amounts of such transactions are insignificant.

Table 6.3

Federal, State, and Local Government Expenditure,
by Function, 1902-1981
(in millions of dollars)

| | | | | | General Expenditure | | |
| | | | | | | Education | |
| Year | Total Expend- iture[a] | Total General Expend- iture | National Defense and Inter- national Relations | Postal Service | State Institu- tions of Higher Education | Local Schools | Other Education |
|------|------|------|------|------|------|------|------|
| 1902 | 1,660 | 1,578 | 165 | 126 | 13 | 238 | 7 |
| 1913 | 3,215 | 3,022 | 250 | 270 | 49 | 522 | 11 |
| 1922 | 9,297 | 8,854 | 875 | 553 | 143 | 1,541 | 29 |
| 1927 | 11,220 | 10,590 | 616 | 711 | 196 | 2,017 | 30 |
| 1932 | 12,437 | 11,748 | 721 | 794 | 234 | 2,050 | 41 |
| 1934 | 12,807 | 12,086 | 553 | 651 | 177 | 1,623 | 205 |
| 1936 | 16,758 | 15,835 | 932 | 751 | 231 | 1,904 | 230 |
| 1938 | 17,675 | 16,273 | 1,041 | 776 | 268 | 2,172 | 213 |
| 1940 | 20,417 | 18,125 | 1,590 | 808 | 290 | 2,292 | 245 |
| 1942 | 45,576 | 43,483 | 26,555 | 878 | 296 | 2,225 | 175 |
| 1944 | 109,947 | 107,823 | 85,503 | 1,085 | 380 | 2,344 | 81 |
| 1946 | 79,707 | 75,582 | 50,461 | 1,381 | 397 | 2,886 | 428 |
| 1948 | 55,081 | 50,088 | 16,075 | 1,715 | 895 | 4,363 | 2,463 |
| 1950 | 70,334 | 60,701 | 18,355 | 2,270 | 1,107 | 5,906 | 2,634 |
| 1952 | 99,847 | 91,291 | 48,187 | 2,612 | 1,267 | 6,862 | 1,469 |
| 1953 | 110,054 | 100,733 | 53,583 | 2,686 | 1,361 | 7,822 | 934 |
| 1954 | 111,332 | 100,365 | 49,265 | 2,669 | 1,418 | 8,947 | 831 |
| 1955 | 110,717 | 97,828 | 43,472 | 2,726 | 1,570 | 10,129 | 1,012 |
| 1956 | 115,796 | 102,156 | 43,388 | 2,899 | 1,814 | 11,165 | 1,182 |
| 1957 | 125,463 | 109,765 | 47,500 | 3,034 | 2,206 | 11,657 | 1,235 |
| 1958 | 134,931 | 115,714 | 47,626 | 3,327 | 2,582 | 13,032 | 1,222 |
| 1959[b]* | 145,748 | 124,217 | 49,688 | 3,499 | 2,920 | 14,034 | 1,165 |
| 1960 | 151,288 | 128,600 | 48,922 | 3,730 | 3,202 | 15,166 | 1,036 |

Table 6.3 (continued)

| Year | General Expenditure | | | | | |
| | High- ways | Public Welfare | Hos- pitals | Health | Police | Local Fire Protection |
|------|------|------|------|------|------|------|
| 1902 | 175 | 41 | 45 | 18 | 50 | 40 |
| 1913 | 419 | 57 | 80 | 33 | 92 | 76 |
| 1922 | 1,296 | 128 | 287 | 65 | 204 | 158 |
| 1927 | 1,819 | 161 | 347 | 84 | 290 | 203 |
| 1932 | 1,766 | 445 | 462 | 121 | 349 | 210 |
| 1934 | 1,829 | 979 | 416 | 119 | 306 | 189 |
| 1936 | 1,945 | 997 | 461 | 131 | 331 | 205 |
| 1938 | 2,150 | 1,233 | 496 | 182 | 378 | 231 |
| 1940 | 2,177 | 1,314 | 537 | 195 | 386 | 235 |
| 1942 | 1,765 | 1,285 | 517 | 197 | 444 | 236 |
| 1944 | 1,215 | 1,150 | 568 | 289 | 497 | 251 |
| 1946 | 1,680 | 1,435 | 762 | 380 | 549 | 294 |
| 1948 | 3,071 | 2,144 | 1,398 | 536 | 724 | 406 |
| 1950 | 3,872 | 2,964 | 2,050 | 661 | 864 | 488 |
| 1952 | 4,714 | 2,830 | 2,460 | 739 | 1,080 | 586 |
| 1953 | 5,053 | 2,956 | 2,548 | 698 | 1,160 | 598 |
| 1954 | 5,586 | 3,103 | 2,676 | 692 | 1,254 | 653 |
| 1955 | 6,520 | 3,210 | 2,721 | 707 | 1,358 | 694 |
| 1956 | 7,035 | 3,184 | 3,068 | 671 | 1,486 | 737 |
| 1957 | 7,931 | 3,534 | 3,416 | 735 | 1,623 | 810 |
| 1958 | 8,702 | 3,866 | 3,805 | 761 | 1,769 | 873 |
| 1959[b] | 9,726 | 4,193 | 4,074 | 993 | 1,880 | 914 |
| 1960* | 9,565 | 4,462 | 4,213 | 1,031 | 2,030 | 995 |

Table 6.3 (continued)

| | General Expenditure | | | | |
|---|---|---|---|---|---|
| Year | Local Sanitation | Natural Resources | Local Parks and Recreation | Housing and Urban Renewal | Veterans' Services, Not Elsewhere Classified |
| 1902 | 51 | 17 | 29 | -- | 141 |
| 1913 | 97 | 44 | 57 | -- | 177 |
| 1922 | 189 | 140 | 85 | 1 | 505 |
| 1927 | 312 | 206 | 153 | 1 | 572 |
| 1932 | 223 | 326 | 147 | -- | 928 |
| 1934 | 177 | 1,241 | 126 | 3 | 508 |
| 1936 | 204 | 2,158 | 104 | 71 | 1,699 |
| 1938 | 226 | 2,089 | 130 | 109 | 590 |
| 1940 | 207 | 2,730 | 162 | 267 | 501 |
| 1942 | 229 | 2,468 | 128 | 622 | 481 |
| 1944 | 245 | 2,731 | 123 | 574 | 530 |
| 1946 | 370 | 3,111 | 179 | 221 | 2,588 |
| 1948 | 670 | 2,223 | 243 | 245 | 3,926 |
| 1950 | 834 | 5,005 | 304 | 573 | 3,258 |
| 1952 | 992 | 3,252 | 324 | 875 | 2,570 |
| 1953 | 908 | 4,816 | 374 | 768 | 2,823 |
| 1954 | 1,058 | 6,377 | 424 | 742 | 2,913 |
| 1955 | 1,142 | 6,338 | 509 | 611 | 3,058 |
| 1956 | 1,326 | 6,630 | 541 | 562 | 3,185 |
| 1957 | 1,443 | 6,137 | 608 | 624 | 3,224 |
| 1958 | 1,505 | 6,160 | 685 | 801 | 3,576 |
| 1959[b] | 1,609 | 7,966 | 729 | 838 | 3,706 |
| 1960[*] | 1,727 | 7,087 | 770 | 1,142 | 3,801 |

## 439

Table 6.3 (continued)

| Year | General Expenditure | | | | |
|------|------|------|------|------|------|
| | Financial Admin- istration and General Control | Interest on General Debt[c] | Air and Water Transport and Terminals[d] | Other and Unallocable[d] | Utility and Liquor Stores Expenditure |
| 1902 | 175 | 97 | 22 | 128 | 82 |
| 1913 | 256 | 170 | 90 | 272 | 186 |
| 1922 | 439 | 1,370 | 302 | 544 | 359 |
| 1927 | 526 | 1,348 | 254 | 737 | 491 |
| 1932 | 601 | 1,323 | 198 | 809 | 518 |
| 1934 | 533 | 1,473 | 213 | 765 | 528 |
| 1936 | 662 | 1,455 | 269 | 1,095 | 701 |
| 1938 | 725 | 1,513 | 266 | 1,485 | 848 |
| 1940 | 739 | 1,552 | 374 | 1,524 | 1,324 |
| 1942 | 828 | 1,591 | 890 | 1,672 | 1,106 |
| 1944 | 1,087 | 2,650 | 4,741 | 1,779 | 1,281 |
| 1946 | 1,163 | 4,286 | 1,190 | 1,821 | 1,733 |
| 1948 | 1,325 | 4,722 | 550 | 2,394 | 2,379 |
| 1950 | 1,555 | 4,862 | 624 | 2,515 | 2,739 |
| 1952 | 1,801 | 4,814 | 1,070 | 2,784 | 3,067 |
| 1953 | 1,866 | 5,477 | 1,305 | 2,998 | 3,316 |
| 1954 | 1,997 | 5,515 | 1,137 | 3,105 | 3,482 |
| 1955 | 2,060 | 5,684 | 1,066 | 3,242 | 3,886 |
| 1956 | 2,235 | 6,297 | 1,358 | 3,394 | 4,065 |
| 1957 | 2,405 | 6,603 | 1,370 | 3,669 | 4,429 |
| 1958[b] | 2,536 | 7,360 | 1,409 | 4,117 | 4,693 |
| 1959[*] | 2,750 | 6,959 | 1,755 | 4,821 | 4,901 |
| 1960 | 2,859 | 9,332 | 1,984 | 5,546 | 5,088 |

440

Table 6.3 (continued)

| | Insurance Trust Expenditure | | | |
|---|---|---|---|---|
| Year | Employee Retirement | Unemployment Compensation | Old-age and Survivors' Insurance | Other |
| 1902 | -- | -- | -- | -- |
| 1913 | 7 | -- | -- | -- |
| 1922 | 36 | -- | -- | 48 |
| 1927 | 64 | -- | -- | 75 |
| 1932 | 103 | -- | -- | 68 |
| 1934 | 135 | -- | -- | 58 |
| 1936 | 157 | -- | -- | 65 |
| 1938 | 193 | 202 | 5 | 154 |
| 1940 | 209 | 509 | 16 | 234 |
| 1942 | 247 | 386 | 110 | 243 |
| 1944 | 298 | 70 | 185 | 289 |
| 1946 | 503 | 985 | 321 | 584 |
| 1948 | 541 | 821 | 512 | 740 |
| 1950 | 629 | 1,980 | 726 | 3,559 |
| 1952 | 831 | 1,022 | 1,983 | 1,653 |
| 1953 | 948 | 1,008 | 2,728 | 1,321 |
| 1954 | 1,090 | 1,648 | 3,276 | 1,471 |
| 1955 | 1,152 | 1,990 | 4,333 | 1,527 |
| 1956 | 1,332 | 1,383 | 5,361 | 1,500 |
| 1957 | 1,534 | 1,633 | 6,515 | 1,589 |
| 1958[b] | 1,773 | 2,979 | 8,043 | 1,728 |
| 1959[b][*] | 1,936 | 3,523 | 9,388 | 1,784 |
| 1960 | 2,161 | 2,639 | 10,798 | 1,997 |

Table 6.3 (continued)

| Year | Total Expenditure | Total General Expenditure | National Defense and International Relations | Postal Service | Education | | |
|------|------|------|------|------|------|------|------|
| | | | | | State Institutions of Higher Education | Local Schools | Other Education |
| 1961 | 164,875 | 139,161 | 51,210 | 4,025 | 3,570 | 16,608 | 1,036 |
| 1962 | 176,240 | 149,159 | 55,172 | 4,101 | 4,042 | 17,739 | 1,032 |
| 1963 | 184,996 | 156,002 | 56,386 | 4,402 | 4,466 | 18,759 | 1,255 |
| 1964 | 196,431 | 166,088 | 57,326 | 4,775 | 5,278 | 20,399 | 1,665 |
| 1965 | 205,550 | 173,613 | 55,810 | 5,261 | 5,863 | 21,966 | 1,785 |
| 1966 | 224,813 | 189,406 | 60,832 | 5,706 | 7,207 | 25,091 | 2,539 |
| 1967 | 257,800 | 216,888 | 74,638 | 6,227 | 8,932 | 27,590 | 3,692 |
| 1968 | 282,645 | 236,348 | 83,874 | 6,485 | 10,214 | 29,305 | 4,095 |
| 1969 | 308,344 | 255,924 | 84,496 | 6,993 | 11,551 | 33,752 | 5,074 |
| 1970 | 332,985 | 275,017 | 84,253 | 7,722 | 12,924 | 37,461 | 5,386 |
| 1971 | 372,100 | 303,800 | 83,100 | 8,700 | 14,800 | 41,800 | 7,300 |
| 1972 | 400,400 | 324,400 | 81,700 | 9,400 | 15,900 | 45,700 | 7,800 |
| 1973 | 436,800 | 348,400 | 83,000 | 9,600 | 17,200 | 48,800 | 8,900 |
| 1974 | 480,100 | 378,900 | 87,000 | 11,200 | 18,900 | 53,100 | 9,700 |
| 1975 | 559,800 | 443,300 | 93,900 | 12,700 | 21,700 | 61,500 | 11,800 |
| 1976 | 625,000 | 476,100 | 98,000 | 13,700 | 24,300 | 67,700 | 14,300 |
| 1977 | 682,500 | 514,200 | 105,600 | 14,600 | 26,000 | 71,500 | 13,100 |
| 1978 | 745,400 | 564,300 | 114,800 | 15,300 | 28,400 | 76,700 | 13,700 |
| 1979 | 832,300 | 630,600 | 128,500 | 16,600 | 30,100 | 83,400 | 16,000 |
| 1980 | 958,400 | 722,800 | 149,500 | 18,200 | 33,900 | 92,900 | 17,000 |
| 1981 | 1,109,800 | 827,900 | 174,600 | 20,500 | 38,100 | 100,500 | 19,400 |

Table 6.3 (continued)

| | | | General Expenditure | | | |
|---|---|---|---|---|---|---|
| Year | Highways | Public Welfare | Hospitals | Health | Police | Local Fire Protection |
| 1961 | 9,995 | 4,779 | 4,549 | 1,132 | 2,210 | 1,087 |
| 1962 | 10,508 | 5,147 | 4,791 | 1,344 | 2,326 | 1,124 |
| 1963 | 11,315 | 5,538 | 5,106 | 1,540 | 2,446 | 1,161 |
| 1964 | 11,828 | 5,880 | 5,461 | 1,618 | 2,586 | 1,222 |
| 1965 | 12,348 | 6,420 | 5,865 | 1,805 | 2,792 | 1,306 |
| 1966 | 12,895 | 6,965 | 6,297 | 2,065 | 3,033 | 1,376 |
| 1967 | 14,033 | 9,592 | 6,951 | 2,506 | 3,331 | 1,499 |
| 1968 | 14,654 | 11,245 | 7,801 | 2,778 | 3,700 | 1,623 |
| 1969 | 15,738 | 14,730 | 8,593 | 3,337 | 4,242 | 1,793 |
| 1970 | 16,746 | 17,517 | 9,693 | 3,895 | 4,903 | 2,024 |
| 1971 | 18,300 | 20,400 | 11,100 | 3,700 | 6,100 | 2,300 |
| 1972 | 19,300 | 23,600 | 12,600 | 4,400 | 6,900 | 2,600 |
| 1973 | 18,900 | 27,000 | 13,700 | 5,000 | 7,700 | 2,800 |
| 1974 | 20,200 | 31,000 | 15,300 | 6,400 | 8,300 | 3,000 |
| 1975 | 22,800 | 39,400 | 17,400 | 7,500 | 9,600 | 3,500 |
| 1976 | 24,200 | 45,100 | 18,900 | 8,600 | 10,700 | 3,900 |
| 1977 | 23,300 | 49,400 | 21,300 | 9,300 | 11,800 | 4,400 |
| 1978 | 24,900 | 54,200 | 22,800 | 10,200 | 12,900 | 4,800 |
| 1979 | 29,000 | 59,100 | 25,700 | 11,400 | 13,900 | 5,100 |
| 1980 | 33,700 | 64,800 | 29,200 | 14,100 | 15,200 | 5,700 |
| 1981 | 34,900 | 74,600 | 32,100 | 15,200 | 16,900 | 6,300 |

Table 6.3 (continued)

| | | | | General Expenditure | | | |
|---|---|---|---|---|---|---|---|
| Year | Local Sanitation | National Resources | Local Parks and Recreation | Housing and Urban Renewal | Veterans' Services, Not Elsewhere Classified | Financial Administration and General Control | Interest on General Debt |
| 1961 | 1,774 | 9,756 | 857 | 1,320 | 4,049 | 3,025 | 9,309 |
| 1962 | 1,958 | 10,468 | 886 | 1,701 | 1,224 | 3,187 | 9,173 |
| 1963 | 1,996 | 9,511 | 902 | 1,688 | 3,961 | 3,362 | 9,846 |
| 1964 | 2,267 | 10,042 | 1,022 | 2,037 | 4,208 | 3,583 | 10,649 |
| 1965 | 2,360 | 10,990 | 1,104 | 2,198 | 4,210 | 3,842 | 11,430 |
| 1966 | 2,571 | 10,301 | 1,187 | 2,415 | 4,531 | 4,105 | 12,278 |
| 1967 | 2,523 | 10,145 | 1,291 | 2,413 | 4,448 | 4,537 | 13,406 |
| 1968 | 2,707 | 9,200 | 1,412 | 2,841 | 4,773 | 4,966 | 14,873 |
| 1969 | 2,969 | 10,024 | 1,645 | 2,505 | 5,097 | 5,563 | 16,992 |
| 1970 | 3,413 | 11,469 | 1,888 | 3,189 | 5,455 | 6,370 | 18,411 |
| 1971 | 4,100 | 14,000 | 2,100 | 4,400 | 6,400 | 7,200 | 21,700 |
| 1972 | 4,700 | 14,600 | 2,300 | 5,200 | 6,900 | 8,100 | 23,100 |
| 1973 | 5,300 | 16,700 | 2,600 | 6,900 | 7,400 | 9,200 | 25,100 |
| 1974 | 6,000 | 15,800 | 3,000 | 7,600 | 7,700 | 10,000 | 30,100 |
| 1975 | 7,500 | 18,100 | 3,500 | 5,900 | 8,600 | 11,900 | 33,800 |
| 1976 | 8,200 | 19,400 | 3,900 | 5,400 | 9,300 | 13,400 | 39,600 |
| 1977 | 9,400 | 22,400 | 5,700 | 5,600 | 10,800 | 14,800 | 44,500 |
| 1978 | 9,900 | 26,300 | 6,700 | 6,000 | 10,800 | 16,700 | 51,300 |
| 1979 | 11,800 | 30,300 | 7,400 | 8,000 | 11,600 | 18,700 | 61,800 |
| 1980 | 13,200 | 35,200 | 8,200 | 12,100 | 12,500 | 20,700 | 76,000 |
| 1981 | 14,900 | 43,600 | 8,500 | 13,900 | 13,800 | 22,500 | 97,600 |

Table 6.3 (continued)

| | General Expenditure | | | | Insurance Trust Expenditure | | |
|---|---|---|---|---|---|---|---|
| Year | Air and Water Transport and Terminals[d] | Other and Unallocable[d] | Utility and Liquor Stores Expenditure | Employee Retirement | Unemployment Compensation | Old-age and Survivors' Insurance | Other |
| 1961 | 2,338 | 6,530 | 5,523 | 2,339 | 3,715 | 11,889 | 2,248 |
| 1962 | 2,470 | 7,764 | 5,453 | 2,642 | 3,019 | 13,669 | 2,298 |
| 1963 | 2,481 | 9,879 | 5,736 | 2,848 | 2,927 | 15,015 | 2,470 |
| 1964 | 2,513 | 11,729 | 6,184 | 3,170 | 2,772 | 15,830 | 2,388 |
| 1965 | 2,727 | 13,533 | 7,058 | 3,455 | 2,413 | 16,618 | 2,393 |
| 1966 | 2,899 | 15,113 | 7,282 | 3,915 | 1,981 | 19,793 | 2,437 |
| 1967 | 3,212 | 15,924 | 7,350 | 4,584 | 2,012 | 23,919 | 3,045 |
| 1968 | 3,343 | 16,459 | 8,170 | 4,979 | 2,126 | 27,951 | 3,071 |
| 1969 | 3,623 | 17,207 | 8,820 | 5,641 | 2,089 | 32,474 | 3,396 |
| 1970 | 3,969 | 18,329 | 9,447 | 6,399 | 2,816 | 35,828 | 3,478 |
| 1971 | n.a. | 23,100 | 10,300 | 7,400 | 4,800 | 42,000 | 3,900 |
| 1972 | n.a. | 26,200 | 11,400 | 8,600 | 4,900 | 46,900 | 4,300 |
| 1973 | n.a. | 29,300 | 13,000 | 10,400 | 4,200 | 56,400 | 4,400 |
| 1974 | n.a. | 31,300 | 14,400 | 12,300 | 4,800 | 64,700 | 5,000 |
| 1975 | 5,200 | 37,000 | 17,300 | 14,600 | 12,400 | 76,600 | 5,600 |
| 1976 | 5,400 | 42,100 | 19,500 | 16,800 | 18,100 | 88,300 | 6,200 |
| 1977 | 5,700 | 45,600 | 24,200 | 19,200 | 14,900 | 103,200 | 6,800 |
| 1978 | 6,100 | 51,800 | 26,300 | 21,800 | 10,900 | 115,000 | 7,100 |
| 1979 | 7,000 | 55,200 | 30,000 | 24,800 | 9,000 | 129,200 | 7,900 |
| 1980 | 8,300 | 62,400 | 36,200 | 28,900 | 12,300 | 149,500 | 8,700 |
| 1981 | 11,700 | 68,300 | 43,000 | 33,600 | 18,200 | 177,500 | 9,600 |

Table 6.3 (continued)

---

*Denotes first year for which figures include Alaska and Hawaii.

n.a. Data not available.

--Represents zero.

$^a$To avoid duplication, transactions between governments are excluded.

$^b$Includes Alaska.

$^c$Excludes interest on Federal securities held by Federal agencies and funds.

$^d$Any state and local amounts for "Air and water transport and terminals" prior to 1951 are included under "Other and unallocable."

Table 6.4A

Outlays of the Federal Government by Major Function,
1789-1899
(in thousands of dollars)

| Year | Total | Department of the Army (formerly War Department) | Department of the Navy | Interest on the Public Debt | Other | |
|---|---|---|---|---|---|---|
| | | | | | Total | Veterans' Compensation and Pensions[a] |
| 1789-91 | 4,269 | 633 | 1 | 2,349 | 1,286 | 176 |
| 1792 | 5,080 | 1,101 | * | 3,202 | 777 | 109 |
| 1793 | 4,482 | 1,130 | n.a. | 2,772 | 580 | 80 |
| 1794 | 6,991 | 2,639 | 61 | 3,490 | 800 | 81 |
| 1795 | 7,540 | 2,481 | 411 | 3,189 | 1,459 | 69 |
| 1796 | 5,727 | 1,260 | 275 | 3,195 | 997 | 101 |
| 1797 | 6,134 | 1,039 | 383 | 3,300 | 1,412 | 92 |
| 1798 | 7,677 | 2,010 | 1,381 | 3,053 | 1,232 | 105 |
| 1799 | 9,666 | 2,467 | 2,858 | 3,186 | 1,155 | 95 |
| 1800 | 10,786 | 2,561 | 3,449 | 3,375 | 1,402 | 64 |
| 1801 | 9,395 | 1,673 | 2,111 | 4,413 | 1,197 | 74 |
| 1802 | 7,862 | 1,179 | 916 | 4,125 | 1,642 | 85 |
| 1803 | 7,852 | 822 | 1,215 | 3,849 | 1,966 | 63 |
| 1804 | 8,719 | 875 | 1,190 | 4,267 | 2,388 | 80 |
| 1805 | 10,506 | 713 | 1,598 | 4,149 | 4,047 | 82 |
| 1806 | 9,804 | 1,224 | 1,650 | 3,723 | 3,206 | 82 |
| 1807 | 8,354 | 1,289 | 1,722 | 3,370 | 1,974 | 71 |
| 1808 | 9,932 | 2,901 | 1,884 | 3,428 | 1,719 | 83 |
| 1809 | 10,281 | 3,346 | 2,428 | 2,866 | 1,641 | 88 |
| 1810 | 8,157 | 2,294 | 1,654 | 2,845 | 1,363 | 84 |
| 1811 | 8,058 | 2,033 | 1,966 | 2,466 | 1,594 | 75 |
| 1812 | 20,281 | 11,818 | 3,959 | 2,451 | 2,052 | 91 |
| 1813 | 31,682 | 19,652 | 6,447 | 3,599 | 1,984 | 87 |

| | | | | | | |
|---|---|---|---|---|---|---|
| 1814 | 34,721 | 20,351 | 7,311 | 4,593 | 2,466 | 90 |
| 1815 | 32,708 | 14,794 | 8,660 | 5,755 | 3,499 | 70 |
| 1816 | 30,587 | 16,012 | 3,908 | 7,213 | 3,453 | 189 |
| 1817 | 21,844 | 8,004 | 3,315 | 6,389 | 4,136 | 297 |
| 1818 | 19,825 | 5,623 | 2,954 | 6,016 | 5,232 | 891 |
| 1819 | 21,464 | 6,506 | 3,848 | 5,164 | 5,946 | 2,416 |
| 1820 | 18,261 | 2,630 | 4,388 | 5,126 | 6,116 | 3,208 |
| 1821 | 15,811 | 4,461 | 3,319 | 5,087 | 2,943 | 243 |
| 1822 | 15,000 | 3,112 | 2,224 | 5,173 | 4,491 | 1,948 |
| 1823 | 14,707 | 3,097 | 2,504 | 4,923 | 4,183 | 1,781 |
| 1824 | 20,327 | 3,341 | 2,905 | 4,997 | 9,085 | 1,499 |
| 1825 | 15,857 | 3,660 | 3,049 | 4,367 | 4,781 | 1,309 |
| 1826 | 17,036 | 3,943 | 4,219 | 3,973 | 4,900 | 1,557 |
| 1827 | 16,139 | 3,939 | 4,264 | 3,486 | 4,450 | 976 |
| 1828 | 16,395 | 4,146 | 3,919 | 3,099 | 5,232 | 851 |
| 1829 | 15,203 | 4,724 | 3,309 | 2,543 | 4,627 | 950 |
| 1830 | 15,143 | 4,767 | 3,239 | 1,914 | 5,223 | 1,363 |
| 1831 | 15,248 | 4,842 | 3,856 | 1,384 | 5,166 | 1,171 |
| 1832 | 17,289 | 5,446 | 3,956 | 773 | 7,114 | 1,184 |
| 1833 | 23,018 | 6,704 | 3,901 | 304 | 12,108 | 4,589 |
| 1834 | 18,628 | 5,696 | 3,956 | 202 | 8,773 | 3,364 |
| 1835 | 17,573 | 5,759 | 3,865 | 58 | 7,891 | 1,955 |
| 1836 | 30,868 | 12,169 | 5,808 | n.a. | 12,891 | 2,883 |
| 1837 | 37,243 | 13,683 | 6,647 | n.a. | 16,914 | 2,672 |
| 1838 | 33,865 | 12,897 | 6,132 | 15 | 14,821 | 2,156 |
| 1839 | 26,899 | 8,917 | 6,182 | 400 | 11,400 | 3,143 |
| 1840 | 24,318 | 7,097 | 6,114 | 175 | 10,932 | 2,604 |
| 1841 | 26,566 | 8,806 | 6,001 | 285 | 11,474 | 2,388 |
| 1842 | 25,206 | 6,612 | 8,397 | 774 | 9,423 | 1,379 |
| 1843 | 11,858 | 2,957 | 3,728 | 524 | 4,649 | 843 |
| 1844 | 22,338 | 5,179 | 6,498 | 1,834 | 8,826 | 2,031 |
| 1845 | 22,937 | 5,753 | 6,297 | 1,040 | 9,847 | 2,397 |
| 1846 | 27,767 | 10,793 | 6,455 | 843 | 9,676 | 1,810 |
| 1847 | 57,281 | 38,306 | 7,901 | 1,119 | 9,956 | 1,748 |
| 1848 | 45,377 | 25,502 | 9,408 | 2,391 | 8,076 | 1,211 |
| 1849 | 45,052 | 14,853 | 9,787 | 3,566 | 16,846 | 1,330 |
| 1850 | 39,543 | 9,400 | 7,905 | 3,782 | 18,456 | 1,870 |
| 1851 | 47,709 | 11,812 | 9,006 | 3,697 | 23,195 | 2,290 |

Table 6.4A (continued)

| Year | Total | Department of the Army (formerly War Department) | Department of the Navy | Interest on the Public Debt | Other | |
|---|---|---|---|---|---|---|
| | | | | | Total | Veterans' Compensation and Pensions [a] |
| 1852 | 44,195 | 8,225 | 8,953 | 4,000 | 23,017 | 2,404 |
| 1853 | 48,184 | 9,947 | 10,919 | 3,666 | 23,652 | 1,778 |
| 1854 | 58,045 | 11,734 | 10,799 | 3,071 | 32,442 | 1,238 |
| 1855 | 59,743 | 14,774 | 13,312 | 2,314 | 29,342 | 1,450 |
| 1856 | 69,571 | 16,948 | 14,092 | 1,954 | 36,577 | 1,298 |
| 1857 | 67,796 | 19,262 | 12,748 | 1,678 | 34,108 | 1,312 |
| 1858 | 74,185 | 25,485 | 13,985 | 1,567 | 33,148 | 1,217 |
| 1859 | 69,071 | 23,244 | 14,643 | 2,638 | 28,546 | 1,220 |
| 1860 | 63,131 | 16,410 | 11,515 | 3,177 | 32,029 | 1,103 |
| 1861 | 66,547 | 22,981 | 12,421 | 4,000 | 27,144 | 1,036 |
| 1862 | 474,762 | 394,368 | 42,668 | 13,190 | 24,535 | 853 |
| 1863 | 714,741 | 599,299 | 63,222 | 24,730 | 27,490 | 1,079 |
| 1864 | 865,323 | 690,792 | 85,726 | 53,685 | 35,119 | 4,984 |
| 1865 | 1,297,555 | 1,031,323 | 122,613 | 77,398 | 66,221 | 16,339 |
| 1866 | 520,809 | 284,450 | 43,324 | 133,068 | 59,968 | 15,605 |
| 1867 | 357,543 | 95,224 | 31,034 | 143,782 | 87,503 | 20,937 |
| 1868 | 377,340 | 123,247 | 25,776 | 140,424 | 87,894 | 23,782 |
| 1869 | 322,865 | 78,502 | 20,001 | 130,694 | 93,668 | 28,477 |
| 1870 | 309,654 | 57,656 | 21,780 | 129,235 | 100,982 | 28,340 |
| 1871 | 292,177 | 35,800 | 19,431 | 125,577 | 111,370 | 34,444 |
| 1872 | 277,518 | 35,372 | 21,250 | 117,358 | 103,538 | 28,533 |
| 1873 | 290,345 | 46,323 | 23,526 | 104,751 | 115,745 | 29,359 |
| 1874 | 302,634 | 42,314 | 30,933 | 107,120 | 122,268 | 29,038 |
| 1875 | 274,623 | 41,121 | 21,498 | 103,094 | 108,912 | 29,456 |
| 1876 | 265,101 | 38,071 | 18,963 | 100,243 | 107,824 | 28,257 |
| 1877 | 241,334 | 37,083 | 14,960 | 97,125 | 92,167 | 27,964 |

| | | | | | |
|---|---|---|---|---|---|
| 1878 | 236,964 | 32,154 | 17,365 | 102,501 | 84,944 | 27,137 |
| 1879 | 266,948 | 40,426 | 15,125 | 105,328 | 106,069 | 35,121 |
| 1880 | 267,643 | 38,117 | 13,537 | 95,758 | 120,231 | 56,777 |
| 1881 | 260,713 | 40,466 | 15,687 | 82,509 | 122,051 | 50,059 |
| 1882 | 257,981 | 43,570 | 15,032 | 71,077 | 128,302 | 61,345 |
| 1883 | 265,408 | 48,911 | 15,283 | 59,160 | 142,053 | 66,013 |
| 1884 | 244,126 | 39,430 | 17,293 | 54,578 | 132,826 | 55,429 |
| 1885 | 260,227 | 42,671 | 16,021 | 51,386 | 150,149 | 56,102 |
| 1886 | 242,483 | 34,324 | 13,908 | 50,580 | 143,671 | 63,405 |
| 1887 | 267,932 | 38,561 | 15,141 | 47,742 | 166,488 | 75,029 |
| 1888 | 267,925 | 38,522 | 16,926 | 44,715 | 167,761 | 80,289 |
| 1889 | 299,289 | 44,435 | 21,379 | 41,001 | 192,473 | 87,625 |
| 1890 | 318,041 | 44,583 | 22,006 | 36,099 | 215,352 | 106,937 |
| 1891 | 365,774 | 48,720 | 26,114 | 37,547 | 253,393 | 124,416 |
| 1892 | 345,023 | 46,895 | 29,174 | 23,378 | 245,576 | 134,583 |
| 1893 | 383,478 | 49,642 | 30,136 | 27,264 | 276,436 | 159,358 |
| 1894 | 367,525 | 54,568 | 31,701 | 27,841 | 253,415 | 141,177 |
| 1895 | 356,195 | 51,805 | 28,798 | 30,978 | 244,615 | 141,395 |
| 1896 | 352,179 | 50,831 | 27,148 | 35,385 | 238,816 | 139,434 |
| 1897 | 365,774 | 48,950 | 34,562 | 37,791 | 244,471 | 141,053 |
| 1898 | 443,369 | 91,992 | 58,824 | 37,585 | 254,968 | 147,452 |
| 1899 | 605,072 | 229,841 | 63,942 | 39,897 | 271,392 | 139,395 |

n.a. Data not available.

*Less than $500

aExcludes education and training.

Table 6.4B

Outlays of the Federal Government, by Major Function, 1900-1939
(in millions of dollars for years ending June 30)

| Year | Total | Major National Security | Inter-National Affairs and Finance[a] | Veterans' Services and Benefits | Interest | All Other |
|------|-------|-------------------------|---------------------------------------|----------------------------------|----------|-----------|
| 1900 | 521 | 191 | | 141 | 40 | 149[a] |
| 1901 | 525 | 206 | | 139 | 32 | 148[a] |
| 1902 | 485 | 180 | | 138 | 29 | 138[a] |
| 1903 | 517 | 202 | | 138 | 29 | 148[a] |
| 1904 | 584 | 268 | | 143 | 25 | 148[a] |
| 1905 | 567 | 244 | | 142 | 25 | 156[a] |
| 1906 | 570 | 247 | | 141 | 24 | 158[a] |
| 1907 | 579 | 247 | | 139 | 24 | 169[a] |
| 1908 | 659 | 294 | | 154 | 21 | 190[a] |
| 1909 | 694 | 308 | | 162 | 22 | 202[a] |
| 1910 | 694 | 284 | | 161 | 21 | 228[a] |
| 1911 | 691 | 283 | | 158 | 21 | 229[a] |
| 1912 | 690 | 284 | 5 | 154 | 23 | 224 |
| 1913 | 715 | 293 | 5 | 175 | 23 | 219 |
| 1914 | 725 | 298 | 5 | 173 | 23 | 226 |
| 1915 | 746 | 297 | 5 | 176 | 23 | 245 |
| 1916 | 713 | 305 | 6 | 171 | 23 | 208 |
| 1917 | 1,954 | 602 | 891 | 171 | 25 | 265 |
| 1918 | 12,662 | 7,110 | 4,748 | 235 | 198 | 371 |
| 1919 | 18,448 | 13,548 | 3,500 | 324 | 616 | 460 |
| 1920 | 6,357 | 3,997 | 435 | 332 | 1,024 | 569 |
| 1921 | 5,058 | 2,581 | 83 | 646 | 999 | 749 |
| 1922 | 3,285 | 929 | 10 | 686 | 991 | 669 |
| 1923 | 3,137 | 680 | 14 | 747 | 1,056 | 640 |
| 1924 | 2,890 | 647 | 15 | 676 | 941 | 611 |
| 1925 | 2,881 | 591 | 15 | 741 | 882 | 652 |
| 1926 | 2,888 | 586 | 17 | 772 | 832 | 681 |
| 1927 | 2,837 | 578 | 17 | 786 | 787 | 669 |
| 1928 | 2,933 | 656 | 12 | 806 | 731 | 728 |
| 1929 | 3,127 | 696 | 14 | 812 | 719 | 886 |
| 1930 | 3,320 | 734 | 14 | 821 | 697 | 1,054 |
| 1931 | 3,578 | 733 | 16 | 1,040 | 628 | 1,161 |
| 1932 | 4,659 | 703 | 19 | 985 | 619 | 2,333 |
| 1933 | 4,623 | 648 | 16 | 863 | 701 | 2,395 |
| 1934 | 6,694 | 540 | 12 | 557 | 770 | 4,815 |
| 1935 | 6,521 | 711 | 19 | 607 | 826 | 4,358 |
| 1936 | 8,494 | 914 | 18 | 2,350 | 756 | 4,456 |
| 1937 | 7,756 | 937 | 18 | 1,137 | 872 | 4,792 |
| 1938 | 6,792 | 1,030 | 19 | 581 | 933 | 4,229 |
| 1939 | 8,858 | 1,075 | 20 | 560 | 950 | 6,254 |

[a]Figures for "International Affairs and Finance" included with "All Other" for 1900-1911.

Table 6.4C

Outlays of the Federal Government, by Major Function, 1940–1967
(in millions of dollars for years ending June 30)

| Function | 1940 | 1941 | 1942 | 1943 | 1944 |
|---|---|---|---|---|---|
| Total outlays | 9,589 | 13,980 | 34,500 | 78,909 | 93,956 |
| National defense | 1,504 | 6,062 | 23,970 | 63,212 | 76,874 |
| International affairs and finance | 52 | 146 | 1,841 | 3,320 | 3,642 |
| Space research and technology | 3 | 8 | 12 | 23 | 30 |
| Veterans' benefits and services | 628 | 629 | 603 | 613 | 709 |
| Health | 48 | 53 | 61 | 73 | 152 |
| Income security | 1,460 | 1,628 | 1,454 | 1,136 | 1,080 |
| Education and manpower | 73 | 142 | 188 | 198 | 197 |
| Agriculture and rural development | 1,580 | 1,530 | 1,833 | 785 | 1,228 |
| Natural resources and environment | 481 | 459 | 541 | 510 | 412 |
| Commerce and transportation | 2,643 | 2,152 | 3,549 | 7,515 | 7,740 |
| Community development and housing | 28 | 122 | 207 | 297 | 307 |
| General government | 354 | 384 | 480 | 791 | 886 |
| Interest | 1,049 | 1,116 | 1,263 | 1,786 | 2,544 |
| Undistributed governmental transactions[a] | -224 | -258 | -308 | -366 | -503 |
| Unallocable[b] | -90 | -193 | -1,194 | -984 | -1,342 |

Table 6.4C (continued)

| Function | 1945 | 1946 | 1947 | 1948 | 1949 |
|---|---|---|---|---|---|
| Total outlays | 95,184 | 61,738 | 36,931 | 36,493 | 40,570 |
| National defense | 81,585 | 44,731 | 13,059 | 13,015 | 13,097 |
| International affairs and finance | 3,312 | 2,739 | 4,552 | 4,651 | 6,121 |
| Space science and technology | 38 | 32 | 35 | 38 | 49 |
| Veterans' benefits and services | 1,132 | 3,364 | 6,907 | 6,445 | 6,601 |
| Health | 186 | 173 | 146 | 150 | 183 |
| Income security | 1,173 | 2,509 | 2,762 | 2,782 | 3,580 |
| Education and manpower | 234 | 110 | 97 | 171 | 165 |
| Agriculture and rural development | 1,623 | 478 | 1,274 | 604 | 2,547 |
| Natural resources and environment | 329 | 322 | 554 | 770 | 1,089 |
| Commerce and transportation | 4,147 | 849 | 664 | 1,063 | 1,482 |
| Community development and housing | -191 | -597 | 260 | 100 | 295 |
| General government | 758 | 885 | 1,224 | 1,294 | 1,060 |
| Interest | 3,549 | 4,694 | 4,903 | 5,135 | 5,414 |
| Undistributed governmental transactions[a] | -624 | -813 | -904 | -998 | -1,074 |
| Unallocable[b] | -2,067 | 2,244 | 1,398 | 1,273 | -39 |

Table 6.4C (continued)

| Function | 1950 | 1951 | 1952 | 1953 | 1954 |
|---|---|---|---|---|---|
| Total outlays | 43,147 | 45,797 | 67,962 | 76,760 | 70,890 |
| National defense | 13,119 | 22,544 | 44,015 | 50,413 | 46,645 |
| International affairs and finance | 4,775 | 3,822 | 2,954 | 2,268 | 1,503 |
| Space research and technology | 54 | 62 | 67 | 79 | 90 |
| Veterans' benefits and services | 8,837 | 5,530 | 5,350 | 4,522 | 4,341 |
| Health | 252 | 307 | 330 | 318 | 288 |
| Income security | 4,707 | 4,442 | 5,206 | 6,128 | 7,760 |
| Education and manpower | 219 | 221 | 322 | 425 | 437 |
| Agriculture and rural development | 2,818 | 691 | 1,086 | 2,965 | 2,373 |
| Natural resources and environment | 1,246 | 1,311 | 1,409 | 1,409 | 941 |
| Commerce and transportation | 1,618 | 1,482 | 1,807 | 1,807 | 1,118 |
| Community development and housing | 250 | 501 | 589 | 397 | -639 |
| General government | 1,174 | 1,312 | 1,463 | 1,497 | 1,247 |
| Interest | 5,744 | 5,628 | 5,834 | 6,450 | 6,012 |
| Undistrubuted governmental transactions[a] | -1,189 | -1,204 | -1,302 | -1,422 | -1,226 |
| Unallocable[b] | -477 | -852 | -1,168 | -614 | --- |

Table 6.4C (continued)

| Function | 1955 | 1956 | 1957 | 1958 | 1959 |
|---|---|---|---|---|---|
| Total outlays | 68,509 | 70,460 | 76,741 | 82,575 | 92,104 |
| National defense | 40,245 | 40,305 | 42,760 | 44,371 | 46,617 |
| International affairs and finance | 2,038 | 2,181 | 3,074 | 3,063 | 3,267 |
| Space research and technology | 74 | 71 | 76 | 89 | 145 |
| Veterans' benefits and services | 4,522 | 4,810 | 4,870 | 5,184 | 5,428 |
| Health | 271 | 342 | 461 | 540 | 654 |
| Income security | 9,122 | 9,789 | 11,522 | 15,016 | 17,247 |
| Education and manpower | 573 | 674 | 672 | 820 | 870 |
| Agriculture and rural development | 4,023 | 3,991 | 3,082 | 3,224 | 5,365 |
| National resources and environment | 493 | 251 | 752 | 870 | 1,193 |
| Commerce and transportation | 1,218 | 1,791 | 2,171 | 3,033 | 4,467 |
| Community development and housing | 12 | 80 | 832 | 109 | 851 |
| General government | 1,187 | 1,331 | 1,643 | 1,243 | 1,168 |
| Interest | 6,030 | 6,292 | 6,679 | 6,944 | 7,070 |
| Undistributed governmental transactions[a] | -1,209 | -1,448 | -1,853 | -1,931 | -2,238 |
| Unallocable[b] | --- | --- | --- | --- | --- |

Table 6.4C (continued)

| Function | 1960 | 1961 | 1962 | 1963 | 1964 |
|---|---|---|---|---|---|
| Total outlays | 92,223 | 97,795 | 106,813 | 111,311 | 118,584 |
| National defense | 45,908 | 47,381 | 51,097 | 52,257 | 53,591 |
| International affairs and finance | 3,054 | 3,357 | 4,492 | 4,115 | 4,177 |
| Space research and technology | 401 | 744 | 1,257 | 2,552 | 4,170 |
| Veterans' benefits and services | 5,426 | 5,638 | 5,625 | 5,520 | 5,681 |
| Health | 756 | 873 | 1,130 | 1,379 | 1,716 |
| Income security | 18,203 | 21,227 | 22,530 | 24,084 | 25,110 |
| Education and manpower | 1,060 | 1,227 | 1,406 | 1,502 | 1,751 |
| Agriculture and rural development | 3,322 | 3,340 | 4,122 | 5,138 | 5,184 |
| Natural resources and environment | 1,002 | 1,554 | 1,675 | 1,498 | 1,966 |
| Commerce and transportation | 4,790 | 5,062 | 5,430 | 5,765 | 6,511 |
| Community development and housing | 971 | 191 | 589 | -880 | -185 |
| General government | 1,327 | 1,491 | 1,650 | 1,810 | 2,040 |
| Interest | 8,299 | 8,108 | 8,321 | 9,215 | 9,810 |
| Undistributed governmental transactions[a] | -2,296 | -2,449 | -2,513 | -2,644 | -2,877 |
| Unallocable[b] | --- | --- | --- | --- | --- |

Table 6.4C (continued)

| Function | 1965 | 1966 | 1967 |
|---|---|---|---|
| Total outlays | 118,430 | 134,652 | 158,254 |
| National defense | 49,578 | 56,785 | 70,081 |
| International affairs and finance | 4,340 | 4,490 | 4,547 |
| Space research and technology | 5,091 | 5,933 | 5,423 |
| Veterans' benefits and services | 5,722 | 5,920 | 6,897 |
| Health | 1,704 | 2,509 | 6,667 |
| Income security | 25,702 | 29,016 | 31,164 |
| Education and manpower | 2,284 | 4,258 | 5,853 |
| Agriculture and rural development | 4,805 | 3,676 | 4,373 |
| National resources and environment | 2,056 | 2,036 | 1,878 |
| Commerce and transportation | 7,399 | 7,171 | 7,594 |
| Community development and housing | 288 | 2,644 | 2,616 |
| General government | 2,210 | 2,292 | 2,510 |
| Interest | 10,357 | 11,285 | 12,588 |
| Undistributed governmental transactions[a] | -3,109 | -3,364 | -3,936 |
| Unallocable[b] | --- | --- | --- |

[a]Represents employer share of employee retirement received by trust funds.

[b]Allowance for differences between the unified budget and the consolidated ,statement.

Table 6.4D

Outlays of the Federal Government, by Major Function, 1968-1982
(in millions of dollars for years ending June 30)

| Function | 1968 | 1969 | 1970 | 1971 |
|---|---|---|---|---|
| Total outlays by function | 178,800 | 184,500 | 196,600 | 211,400 |
| Federal funds | 143,100 | 148,800 | 156,300 | 163,700 |
| Trust funds[a] | 41,500 | 43,300 | 49,100 | 59,400 |
| Interfund transactions | -5,800 | -7,500 | -8,800 | -11,600 |
| National defense | 79,400 | 80,200 | 79,300 | 76,800 |
| International affairs | 4,600 | 3,800 | 3,600 | 3,100 |
| General science, space, and technology | 5,600 | 5,100 | 4,600 | 4,300 |
| Agriculture | 4,500 | 5,800 | 5,200 | 4,300 |
| Natural resources, environ., and energy | 3,600 | 3,500 | 3,600 | 4,400 |
| Commerce and transportation | 10,600 | 7,100 | 9,100 | 10,400 |
| Community and regional development | 2,200 | 2,500 | 3,500 | 4,000 |
| Education, manpower, and social services | 7,000 | 6,900 | 7,900 | 9,000 |
| Health | 9,700 | 11,800 | 13,100 | 14,700 |
| Income security | 33,700 | 37,300 | 43,100 | 55,400 |
| Veterans' benefits and services | 6,900 | 7,600 | 8,700 | 9,800 |
| Law enforcement and justice | 700 | 800 | 1,000 | 1,300 |
| General government | 1,700 | 1,600 | 1,900 | 2,200 |
| Revenue sharing and general purpose fiscal assistance | 300 | 400 | 500 | 500 |
| Interest | 13,800 | 15,800 | 18,300 | 19,600 |
| Allowances | 0 | 0 | 0 | 0 |
| Undistributed offsetting receipts | -5,500 | -5,500 | -6,600 | -8,400 |

458

Table 6.4D (continued)

| Function | 1972 | 1973 | 1974 | 1975 |
|---|---|---|---|---|
| Total outlays by function | 231,900 | 246,500 | 268,400 | 313,400 |
| Federal funds | 178,000 | 186,400 | 198,700 | 229,000 |
| Trust funds[a] | 67,100 | 81,400 | 90,800 | 110,300 |
| Interfund transactions | -13,200 | -21,300 | -21,100 | -25,900 |
| National defense | 77,400 | 75,100 | 78,600 | 85,300 |
| International affairs | 3,700 | 3,000 | 3,600 | 4,900 |
| General science, space, and technology | 4,300 | 4,200 | 4,200 | 4,200 |
| Agriculture | 5,300 | 4,900 | 2,200 | 1,800 |
| Natural resource, environ., and energy | 5,000 | 5,500 | 6,400 | 9,400 |
| Commerce and transportation | 10,600 | 9,900 | 13,100 | 11,800 |
| Community and regional development | 4,700 | 5,900 | 4,900 | 4,900 |
| Education, manpower, and social services | 11,700 | 11,900 | 11,600 | 14,700 |
| Health | 17,500 | 18,800 | 22,100 | 26,500 |
| Income security | 63,900 | 73,000 | 84,400 | 106,700 |
| Veterans' benefits and services | 10,700 | 12,000 | 13,400 | 15,500 |
| Law enforcement and justice | 1,700 | 2,100 | 2,500 | 3,000 |
| General government | 2,500 | 2,700 | 3,300 | 2,600 |
| Revenue sharing and general purpose fiscal assistance | 500 | 7,200 | 6,700 | 7,000 |
| Interest | 20,600 | 22,800 | 28,100 | 31,300 |
| Allowances | 0 | 0 | 0 | 700 |
| Undistributed offsetting receipts | -8,200 | -12,300 | -16,700 | -16,800 |

Table 6.4D (continued)

| Function | 1976 | 1977 | 1978 | 1979 |
|---|---|---|---|---|
| Total outlays by function | 366,400 | 402,700 | 450,800 | 491,000 |
| Federal funds | 269,900 | 295,800 | 332,000 | 362,400 |
| Trust funds[a] | 131,300 | 143,300 | 155,300 | 168,700 |
| Interfund transactions | -34,800 | -36,300 | -36,500 | -40,100 |
| National defense | 89,400 | 97,500 | 105,200 | 117,700 |
| International affairs | 5,600 | 4,800 | 5,900 | 6,100 |
| General science, space and technology | 4,400 | 4,700 | 4,700 | 5,000 |
| Agriculture | 2,500 | 5,500 | 7,700 | 6,200 |
| Natural resources, environ., and energy | 11,200 | 14,200 | 16,800 | 19,000 |
| Commerce and transportation | 17,200 | 14,600 | 18,700 | 20,100 |
| Community and regional development | 4,700 | 6,300 | 11,000 | 9,500 |
| Education, manpower, and social services | 18,700 | 21,000 | 26,500 | 29,700 |
| Health | 33,400 | 38,800 | 43,700 | 47,000 |
| Income security | 127,400 | 137,900 | 146,200 | 160,200 |
| Veterans' benefits and services | 18,400 | 18,000 | 19,000 | 19,900 |
| Law enforcement and justice | 3,300 | 3,600 | 3,800 | 4,200 |
| General government | 3,000 | 3,300 | 3,700 | 4,100 |
| Revenue sharing and general purpose fiscal assistance | 7,200 | 9,500 | 9,600 | 8,400 |
| Interest | 34,500 | 38,000 | 44,000 | 52,600 |
| Allowances | 0 | 0 | 0 | 0 |
| Undistributed offsetting receipts | -14,700 | -15,100 | -15,800 | -18,500 |

Table 6.4D (continued)

| Function | 1980 | 1981 | 1982 |
|---|---|---|---|
| Total outlays by function | 576,700 | 657,200 | 728,400 |
| Federal funds | 419,200 | 475,200 | 526,100 |
| Trust funds[a] | 202,100 | 232,600 | 262,200 |
| Interfund transactions | -44,700 | -50,600 | -59,900 |
| National defense | 135,900 | 159,800 | 187,400 |
| International affairs | 10,700 | 11,100 | 10,000 |
| General science, space and technology | 5,700 | 6,400 | 7,100 |
| Agriculture | 4,800 | 5,600 | 14,900 |
| Natural resources, environ., and energy | 20,100 | 23,800 | 17,600 |
| Commerce and transportation | 28,900 | 27,300 | 24,500 |
| Community and regional development | 10,100 | 9,400 | 7,200 |
| Education, manpower, and social services | 30,800 | 31,400 | 26,300 |
| Health | 55,200 | 66,000 | 74,000 |
| Income security | 193,100 | 225,100 | 248,300 |
| Veterans' benefits and services | 21,200 | 23,000 | 24,000 |
| Law enforcement and justice | 4,600 | 4,700 | 4,700 |
| General government | 4,500 | 4,600 | 4,700 |
| Revenue sharing and general purpose fiscal assistance | 8,600 | 6,900 | 6,400 |
| Interest | 64,000 | 82,500 | 100,700 |
| Allowances | 0 | 0 | 0 |
| Undistributed offsetting receipts | -21,900 | -30,300 | -29,300 |

[a]Includes airports, airways, and highways.

☆          CHAPTER SEVEN          ☆

# Demographic Information

Demographic and social characteristics of the population of the United States are described in the seven tables of this chapter. Most of the data reported here were originally collected in connection with the decennial population censuses conducted in the nation beginning in 1790. While the United States censuses have usually been considered authoritative sources for the information collected by them, it should be noted that faulty and under-enumeration characteristic of all censuses render even these seemingly "factual" data less than precisely accurate. Therefore, the data presented in these tables must be seen as estimates of the numbers and characteristics of the population reported upon.

Table 7.1 covers annual population figures, table 7.2 breaks down U.S. population by sex and race, table 7.3 presents black population figures, table 7.4 presents annual national immigration statistics, table 7.5 shows the number of immigrants from selected countries by decade, table 7.6 has national-level labor force and unemployment statistics, and table 7.7 presents labor force and unemployment figures by state.

Table 7.1

Annual Estimated Population
of the United States, 1790-1983

| Year | Total | Year | Total |
|------|-------|------|-------|
| 1790 | 3,929,000 | 1846 | 20,794,000 |
| 1791 | 4,056,000 | 1847 | 21,406,000 |
| 1792 | 4,194,000 | 1848 | 22,018,000 |
| 1793 | 4,332,000 | 1849 | 22,631,000 |
| 1794 | 4,469,000 | 1850 | 23,261,000 |
| 1795 | 4,607,000 | 1851 | 24,086,000 |
| 1796 | 4,745,000 | 1852 | 24,911,000 |
| 1797 | 4,883,000 | 1853 | 25,736,000 |
| 1798 | 5,021,000 | 1854 | 26,561,000 |
| 1799 | 5,159,000 | 1855 | 27,386,000 |
| 1800 | 5,297,000 | 1856 | 28,212,000 |
| 1801 | 5,486,000 | 1857 | 29,037,000 |
| 1802 | 5,679,000 | 1858 | 29,862,000 |
| 1803 | 5,872,000 | 1859 | 30,687,000 |
| 1804 | 6,065,000 | 1860 | 31,513,000 |
| 1805 | 6,258,000 | 1861 | 32,351,000 |
| 1806 | 6,451,000 | 1862 | 33,188,000 |
| 1807 | 6,644,000 | 1863 | 34,863,000 |
| 1808 | 6,838,000 | 1865 | 35,701,000 |
| 1809 | 7,031,000 | 1866 | 36,538,000 |
| 1810 | 7,224,000 | 1867 | 37,376,000 |
| 1811 | 7,460,000 | 1868 | 38,213,000 |
| 1812 | 7,700,000 | 1869 | 39,051,000 |
| 1813 | 7,939,000 | 1870 | 39,905,000 |
| 1814 | 8,179,000 | 1871 | 40,938,000 |
| 1815 | 8,419,000 | 1872 | 41,972,000 |
| 1816 | 8,659,000 | 1873 | 43,006,000 |
| 1817 | 8,899,000 | 1874 | 44,040,000 |
| 1818 | 9,139,000 | 1875 | 45,073,000 |
| 1819 | 9,379,000 | 1876 | 46,107,000 |
| 1820 | 9,618,000 | 1877 | 47,141,000 |
| 1821 | 9,939,000 | 1878 | 48,174,000 |
| 1822 | 10,268,000 | 1879 | 49,208,000 |
| 1823 | 10,596,000 | 1880 | 50,262,090 |
| 1824 | 10,924,000 | 1881 | 51,542,000 |
| 1825 | 11,252,000 | 1882 | 52,821,000 |
| 1826 | 11,580,000 | 1883 | 54,100,000 |
| 1827 | 11,909,000 | 1884 | 55,379,000 |
| 1828 | 12,237,000 | 1885 | 56,658,000 |
| 1829 | 12,565,000 | 1886 | 57,938,000 |
| 1830 | 12,901,000 | 1887 | 59,217,000 |
| 1831 | 13,321,000 | 1888 | 60,496,000 |
| 1832 | 13,742,000 | 1889 | 61,775,000 |
| 1833 | 14,162,000 | 1890 | 63,056,000 |
| 1834 | 14,582,000 | 1891 | 64,361,000 |
| 1835 | 15,003,000 | 1892 | 65,666,000 |
| 1836 | 15,423,000 | 1893 | 66,970,000 |
| 1837 | 15,843,000 | 1894 | 68,275,000 |
| 1838 | 16,264,000 | 1895 | 69,580,000 |
| 1839 | 16,684,000 | 1896 | 70,885,000 |
| 1840 | 17,120,000 | 1897 | 72,189,000 |
| 1841 | 17,733,000 | 1898 | 73,494,000 |
| 1842 | 18,345,000 | 1899 | 74,799,000 |
| 1843 | 18,957,000 | 1900 | 76,094,000 |
| 1844 | 19,569,000 | 1901 | 77,584,000 |
| 1845 | 20,182,000 | 1902 | 79,163,000 |

Table 7.1 (continued)

| Year | Total | Year | Total |
|------|-------|------|-------|
| 1903 | 80,632,000 | 1945 | 132,481,000 |
| 1904 | 82,166,000 | 1946 | 140,054,000 |
| 1905 | 83,822,000 | 1947 | 143,446,000 |
| 1906 | 85,450,000 | 1948 | 146,093,000 |
| 1907 | 87,008,000 | 1949 | 148,665,000 |
| 1908 | 88,710,000 | 1950 | 151,235,000 |
| 1909 | 90,490,000 | 1951 | 153,310,000 |
| 1910 | 92,407,000 | 1952 | 155,687,000 |
| 1911 | 93,863,000 | 1953 | 158,242,000 |
| 1912 | 95,335,000 | 1954 | 161,164,000 |
| 1913 | 97,225,000 | 1955 | 164,308,000 |
| 1914 | 99,111,000 | 1956 | 167,306,000 |
| 1915 | 100,546,000 | 1957 | 170,371,000 |
| 1916 | 101,961,000 | 1958 | 173,320,000 |
| 1917 | 103,268,000 | 1959 | 176,289,000 |
| 1918 | 103,208,000 | 1959[a] | 177,135,000 |
| 1919 | 104,514,000 | 1960 | 179,979,000 |
| 1920 | 106,461,000 | 1961 | 182,992,000 |
| 1921 | 108,538,000 | 1962 | 188,771,000 |
| 1922 | 110,049,000 | 1963 | 188,483,000 |
| 1923 | 111,947,000 | 1964 | 191,141,000 |
| 1924 | 114,109,000 | 1965 | 193,526,000 |
| 1925 | 115,829,000 | 1966 | 195,576,000 |
| 1926 | 117,397,000 | 1967 | 197,457,000 |
| 1927 | 119,035,000 | 1968 | 199,399,000 |
| 1928 | 120,509,000 | 1969 | 210,385,000 |
| 1929 | 121,767,000 | 1970 | 203,810,000 |
| 1930 | 123,077,000 | 1971 | 206,219,000 |
| 1931 | 124,040,000 | 1972 | 208,234,000 |
| 1932 | 124,840,000 | 1973 | 209,859,000 |
| 1933 | 125,597,000 | 1974 | 211,389,000 |
| 1934 | 126,374,000 | 1975 | 215,465,000 |
| 1935 | 127,250,000 | 1976 | 217,563,000 |
| 1936 | 128,053,000 | 1977 | 219,760,000 |
| 1937 | 128,825,000 | 1978 | 222,095,000 |
| 1938 | 129,825,000 | 1979 | 224,567,000 |
| 1939 | 130,880,000 | 1980 | 227,202,000 |
| 1940 | 131,954,000 | 1981 | 229,348,000 |
| 1941 | 133,121,000 | 1982 | 231,059,000 |
| 1942 | 133,920,000 | 1983 | 233,267,000 |
| 1943 | 134,245,000 | 1984 | 236,681,000 |
| 1944 | 132,885,000 | | |

[a]Denotes first year for which figures include Alaska and Hawaii.

Table 7.2

Population of the United States by Sex and Race,
1790-1980

| | | | Male | | Other Races | | |
| Year | All Races | White | Black | Total[a] | Native American | Japanese | Chinese |
|---|---|---|---|---|---|---|---|
| 1790 | 3,929,214[b] | 1,615,434 | 757,208[b] | n.a. | n.a. | n.a. | n.a. |
| 1800 | 5,308,483[b] | 2,195,305 | 1,002,037[b] | n.a. | n.a. | n.a. | n.a. |
| 1810 | 7,239,881[b] | 2,988,130 | 1,377,808[b] | n.a. | n.a. | n.a. | n.a. |
| 1820 | 4,696,605 | 3,995,809 | 900,796 | n.a. | n.a. | n.a. | n.a. |
| 1830 | 6,532,489 | 5,366,213 | 1,166,276 | n.a. | n.a. | n.a. | n.a. |
| 1840 | 8,688,532 | 7,255,544 | 1,432,988 | n.a. | n.a. | n.a. | n.a. |
| 1850 | 11,837,660 | 10,026,402 | 1,811,258 | n.a. | n.a. | n.a. | n.a. |
| 1860[c] | 16,085,204 | 13,811,387 | 2,216,744 | 57,073 | 23,924 | n.a. | 33,149 |
| 1870[c] | 19,493,565 | 17,029,088 | 2,393,263 | 71,214 | 12,534 | 47 | 58,633 |
| 1880 | 25,518,820 | 22,130,900 | 3,253,115 | 134,805 | 33,985 | 134 | 100,686 |
| 1890 | 32,237,101 | 28,270,379 | 3,735,603 | 231,119 | 125,719 | 1,780 | 103,620 |
| 1900 | 38,816,448 | 34,210,735 | 4,386,547 | 228,166 | 119,484 | 23,341 | 85,341 |
| 1910 | 47,332,277 | 42,178,245 | 4,885,881 | 268,151 | 135,133 | 63,070 | 66,856 |
| 1920 | 53,900,431 | 48,430,655 | 5,209,436 | 260,340 | 125,068 | 72,707 | 53,891 |
| 1930 | 62,137,080 | 55,922,528 | 5,855,669 | 358,883 | 170,350 | 81,771 | 59,802 |
| 1940 | 66,061,592 | 59,448,548 | 6,269,038 | 344,006 | 171,427 | 71,967 | 57,389 |
| 1950 | 74,833,239 | 67,129,192 | 7,298,722 | 405,325 | 178,824 | 76,649 | 77,008 |
| 1960* | 87,864,510 | 78,153,040 | 9,105,702 | 605,768 | 255,677 | 124,323 | 115,849 |
| 1960[c] | 88,331,494 | 78,367,149 | 9,113,408 | 850,937 | 263,369 | 224,828 | 135,549 |
| 1970[d] | 98,912,192 | 86,720,987 | 10,748,316 | 1,442,889 | 388,691 | 271,300 | 228,565 |
| 1980 | 110,053,161 | 91,685,333 | 12,519,189 | 5,848,639 | 673,517 | 320,941 | 407,544 |

Table 7.2 (continued)

| | | Female | | Other Races | | | |
|---|---|---|---|---|---|---|---|
| Year | All Races | White | Black | Total[a] | Native American | Japanese | Chinese |
| 1790 | 3,929,214[b] | 1,556,572 | 757,208[b] | n.a. | n.a. | n.a. | n.a. |
| 1800 | 5,308,483[b] | 2,111,141 | 1,002,037[b] | n.a. | n.a. | n.a. | n.a. |
| 1810 | 7,239,881 | 2,873,943 | 1,377,808[b] | n.a. | n.a. | n.a. | n.a. |
| 1820 | 4,741,848 | 3,870,988 | 870,860 | n.a. | n.a. | n.a. | n.a. |
| 1830 | 6,333,531 | 5,171,165 | 1,162,366 | n.a. | n.a. | n.a. | n.a. |
| 1840 | 8,380,921 | 6,940,261 | 1,440,660 | n.a. | n.a. | n.a. | n.a. |
| 1850 | 11,354,216 | 9,526,666 | 1,827,550 | n.a. | n.a. | n.a. | n.a. |
| 1860[c] | 15,358,117 | 13,111,150 | 2,225,086 | 21,881 | 20,097 | n.a. | 1,784 |
| 1870[c] | 19,064,806 | 16,560,289 | 2,486,746 | 17,771 | 13,197 | 8 | 4,566 |
| 1880 | 24,636,963 | 21,272,070 | 3,327,678 | 37,215 | 32,422 | 14 | 4,779 |
| 1890 | 30,710,613 | 26,830,879 | 3,753,073 | 126,661 | 122,534 | 259 | 3,868 |
| 1900 | 37,178,127 | 32,607,461 | 4,447,447 | 123,219 | 117,712 | 985 | 4,522 |
| 1910 | 44,639,989 | 39,553,712 | 4,941,882 | 144,395 | 130,550 | 9,087 | 4,675 |
| 1920 | 51,810,189 | 46,390,260 | 5,253,695 | 166,234 | 119,369 | 38,303 | 7,748 |
| 1930 | 60,637,966 | 54,364,212 | 6,035,474 | 238,280 | 162,047 | 57,063 | 15,152 |
| 1940 | 65,607,683 | 58,766,322 | 6,596,480 | 244,881 | 162,542 | 54,980 | 20,115 |
| 1950 | 75,864,122 | 67,812,836 | 7,743,564 | 307,722 | 164,586 | 65,119 | 40,621 |
| 1960* | 90,599,726 | 80,301,916 | 9,754,415 | 543,395 | 252,998 | 135,736 | 83,109 |
| 1960[d] | 90,991,681 | 80,464,583 | 9,758,423 | 768,675 | 260,222 | 239,504 | 101,743 |
| 1970[d] | 104,299,734 | 91,027,988 | 11,831,973 | 1,439,773 | 404,039 | 319,990 | 206,497 |
| 1980 | 116,492,644 | 96,686,289 | 13,975,836 | 5,830,519 | 690,516 | 380,033 | 398,496 |

Table 7.2 (continued)

n.a. Data not available.

* Denotes first year for which figures include Alaska and Hawaii.

[a] Includes races not shown separately, of which Filipinos are most numerous. Filipino males: 1910-144; 1920-5,232; 1930-42,268; 1940-39,723; 1950-46,101; 1960 (conterminous U.S.)-67,351; 1960 (including Alaska and Hawaii)-112,286;1970-189,498; 1980-374,191. Filipino females: 1910-16; 1920-371; 1930-2,940; 1940-5,840; 1950-15,535; 1960 (conterminous U.S.)-369,075; 1960 (including Alaska and Hawaii)-64,024; 1970-153,562; 1980-400,461.

[b] Prior to 1820, sex was only reported for whites. Consequently, this represents the total for both male and female.

[c] Revisions to include adjustments for underenumeration in the Southern States show a total (both sexes) of 34,337,292 for white and 5,392,172 for Negro.

[d] The population of other races (i.e., neither white nor black) was overstated by about 327,000 in the 1970 census. Excludes 23,372 persons for whom sex and race are not available.

Table 7.3

Black Population, by State, 1790-1980
(in thousands)

| State | 1790 | 1800 | 1810 | 1820 | 1830 | 1840 | 1850 | 1860 | 1870 | 1880 |
|---|---|---|---|---|---|---|---|---|---|---|
| Alabama | — | — | — | 42 | 119 | 256 | 345 | 438 | 476 | 600 |
| Alaska | — | — | — | — | — | — | — | — | — | — |
| Arizona | — | — | — | — | — | — | — | — | — | 0 |
| Arkansas | — | — | — | 2 | 5 | 20 | 48 | 111 | 122 | 211 |
| California | — | — | — | — | — | — | 1 | 4 | 4 | 6 |
| Colorado | — | — | — | — | — | — | — | 0 | 0 | 2 |
| Connecticut | 6 | 6 | 7 | 8 | 8 | 8 | 8 | 9 | 10 | 12 |
| Delaware | 13 | 14 | 17 | 17 | 19 | 20 | 20 | 22 | 23 | 26 |
| Dist. of Columbia | — | 2 | 5 | 7 | 9 | 10 | 14 | 14 | 43 | 60 |
| Florida | — | — | — | — | 16 | 27 | 40 | 63 | 92 | 127 |
| Georgia | 30 | 60 | 107 | 151 | 220 | 284 | 385 | 466 | 545 | 725 |
| Hawaii | — | — | — | — | — | — | — | — | — | — |
| Idaho | — | — | — | — | — | — | — | — | 0 | 0 |
| Illinois | — | 0 | 1 | 1 | 2 | 4 | 5 | 8 | 29 | 46 |
| Indiana | — | — | 1 | 1 | 4 | 7 | 11 | 11 | 25 | 39 |
| Iowa | — | — | — | — | — | 0 | 0 | 1 | 6 | 10 |
| Kansas | — | — | — | — | — | — | — | 1 | 17 | 43 |
| Kentucky | 13 | 41 | 82 | 129 | 170 | 190 | 221 | 236 | 222 | 271 |
| Louisiana | — | — | 42 | 80 | 126 | 194 | 262 | 350 | 364 | 484 |
| Maine | 1 | 1 | 1 | 1 | 1 | 1 | 1 | 1 | 2 | 1 |
| Maryland | 111 | 125 | 145 | 147 | 156 | 152 | 165 | 171 | 175 | 210 |
| Massachusetts | 5 | 6 | 7 | 7 | 7 | 9 | 9 | 10 | 14 | 19 |
| Michigan | — | — | 0 | 0 | 0 | 1 | 3 | 7 | 12 | 15 |
| Minnesota | — | — | — | — | 0 | 1 | — | 0 | 2 | 2 |
| Mississippi | — | 4 | 17 | 33 | 66 | 197 | 311 | 437 | 444 | 650 |
| Missouri | — | — | 4 | 11 | 26 | 60 | 90 | 119 | 118 | 145 |
| Montana | — | — | — | — | — | — | — | — | — | 1 |
| Nebraska | — | — | — | — | — | — | — | 0 | 0 | 2 |
| Nevada | — | — | — | — | — | — | — | 0 | 1 | 0 |
| New Hampshire | 1 | 1 | 1 | 1 | 1 | 1 | 1 | 0 | 0 | 1 |
| New Jersey | 14 | 17 | 19 | 20 | 21 | 22 | 24 | 25 | 31 | 39 |

Table 7.3 (continued)

| State | 1790 | 1800 | 1810 | 1820 | 1830 | 1840 | 1850 | 1860 | 1870 | 1880 |
|---|---|---|---|---|---|---|---|---|---|---|
| New Mexico | -- | -- | -- | -- | -- | -- | 0 | 0 | 0 | 1 |
| New York | 26 | 31 | 40 | 39 | 45 | 50 | 49 | 49 | 52 | 65 |
| North Carolina | 106 | 140 | 179 | 220 | 265 | 269 | 316 | 362 | 392 | 531 |
| North Dakota | -- | -- | -- | -- | -- | -- | -- | -- | 0 | 0 |
| Ohio | -- | 0 | 2 | 5 | 10 | 17 | 25 | 37 | 63 | 80 |
| Oklahoma | -- | -- | -- | -- | -- | -- | -- | -- | -- | -- |
| Oregon | -- | -- | -- | -- | -- | -- | 0 | 0 | 0 | 0 |
| Pennsylvania | 10 | 16 | 23 | 30 | 38 | 48 | 54 | 57 | 65 | 86 |
| Rhode Island | 4 | 4 | 4 | 4 | 4 | 3 | 4 | 4 | 5 | 6 |
| South Carolina | 109 | 149 | 201 | 265 | 323 | 335 | 394 | 412 | 416 | 604 |
| South Dakota | -- | -- | -- | -- | -- | -- | 0 | -- | 0 | 0 |
| Tennessee | 4 | 14 | 46 | 83 | 146 | 189 | 246 | 283 | 322 | 403 |
| Texas | -- | -- | -- | -- | -- | -- | 59 | 183 | 253 | 393 |
| Utah | 0 | -- | -- | -- | -- | -- | 0 | 0 | 0 | 0 |
| Vermont | 306 | 1 | 1 | 1 | 1 | 1 | 1 | 1 | 1 | 1 |
| Virginia | 306 | 367 | 426 | 465 | 520 | 502 | 527 | 549 | 513 | 632 |
| Washington | -- | -- | -- | -- | -- | -- | -- | 0 | 0 | 0 |
| West Virginia | -- | -- | -- | -- | -- | 0 | 1 | 1 | 18 | 26 |
| Wisconsin | -- | -- | -- | -- | -- | -- | 1 | 1 | 2 | 3 |
| Wyoming | -- | -- | -- | -- | -- | -- | -- | -- | 0 | 0 |

Table 7.3 (continued)

| State | 1890 | 1900 | 1910 | 1920 | 1930 | 1940 | 1950 | 1960 | 1970 | 1980 |
|---|---|---|---|---|---|---|---|---|---|---|
| Alabama | 678 | 827 | 908 | 901 | 945 | 983 | 980 | 980 | 903 | 996 |
| Alaska | -- | 0 | 0 | 0 | 0 | 0 | -- | 7 | 9 | 14 |
| Arizona | 1 | 2 | 2 | 8 | 11 | 15 | 26 | 43 | 53 | 75 |
| Arkansas | 309 | 367 | 443 | 472 | 478 | 483 | 427 | 389 | 352 | 373 |
| California | 11 | 11 | 22 | 39 | 81 | 124 | 462 | 884 | 1,400 | 1,819 |
| Colorado | 6 | 9 | 11 | 11 | 12 | 12 | 20 | 40 | 66 | 102 |
| Connecticut | 12 | 15 | 15 | 21 | 29 | 33 | 53 | 107 | 181 | 217 |
| Delaware | 28 | 31 | 31 | 30 | 33 | 36 | 44 | 61 | 78 | 96 |
| Dist. of Columbia | 76 | 87 | 94 | 110 | 132 | 187 | 281 | 412 | 538 | 448 |
| Florida | 166 | 231 | 309 | 329 | 432 | 514 | 603 | 880 | 1,042 | 1,342 |
| Georgia | 859 | 1,035 | 1,177 | 1,206 | 1,071 | 1,085 | 1,063 | 1,123 | 1,187 | 1,465 |
| Hawaii | -- | 0 | 0 | 1 | 1 | 0 | 3 | 5 | 8 | 17 |
| Idaho | 0 | 0 | 1 | 1 | 1 | 1 | 1 | 2 | 2 | 3 |
| Illinois | 57 | 85 | 109 | 182 | 329 | 387 | 646 | 1,037 | 1,426 | 1,675 |
| Indiana | 45 | 58 | 60 | 81 | 112 | 122 | 174 | 269 | 357 | 415 |
| Iowa | 11 | 13 | 15 | 19 | 17 | 17 | 20 | 25 | 33 | 42 |
| Kansas | 50 | 52 | 54 | 58 | 66 | 65 | 73 | 91 | 107 | 126 |
| Kentucky | 268 | 285 | 262 | 236 | 226 | 214 | 202 | 216 | 231 | 259 |
| Louisiana | 559 | 651 | 714 | 700 | 776 | 849 | 882 | 1,039 | 1,087 | 1,237 |
| Maine | 1 | 1 | 1 | 1 | 1 | 1 | 1 | 3 | 3 | 3 |
| Maryland | 216 | 235 | 232 | 244 | 276 | 302 | 386 | 518 | 699 | 958 |
| Massachusetts | 22 | 32 | 38 | 45 | 45 | 55 | 73 | 112 | 176 | 221 |
| Michigan | 15 | 16 | 17 | 60 | 169 | 208 | 442 | 718 | 991 | 1,199 |
| Minnesota | 4 | 5 | 7 | 9 | 9 | 10 | 14 | 22 | 35 | 53 |
| Mississippi | 743 | 908 | 1,009 | 935 | 1,010 | 1,075 | 986 | 916 | 816 | 887 |
| Missouri | 150 | 161 | 157 | 178 | 224 | 244 | 297 | 391 | 480 | 514 |
| Montana | 1 | 2 | 2 | 2 | 1 | 1 | 1 | 1 | 2 | 2 |
| Nebraska | 9 | 6 | 8 | 13 | 14 | 14 | 19 | 29 | 40 | 48 |
| Nevada | 0 | 0 | 1 | 0 | 1 | 1 | 4 | 13 | 28 | 51 |
| New Hampshire | 1 | 1 | 1 | 1 | 1 | 0 | 1 | 2 | 3 | 4 |
| New Jersey | 48 | 70 | 90 | 117 | 209 | 227 | 319 | 515 | 770 | 925 |
| New Mexico | 2 | 2 | 2 | 6 | 3 | 5 | 8 | 17 | 20 | 24 |
| New York | 70 | 99 | 134 | 198 | -413 | 571 | 918 | 1,418 | 2,169 | 2,402 |

Table 7.3 (continued)

| State | 1890 | 1900 | 1910 | 1920 | 1930 | 1940 | 1950 | 1960 | 1970 | 1980 |
|---|---|---|---|---|---|---|---|---|---|---|
| North Carolina | 561 | 624 | 698 | 763 | 919 | 981 | 1,047 | 1,116 | 1,126 | 1,316 |
| North Dakota | 0 | 0 | 1 | 0 | 0 | 0 | 0 | 1 | 2 | 3 |
| Ohio | 87 | 97 | 111 | 186 | 309 | 339 | 513 | 786 | 970 | 1,077 |
| Oklahoma | 22 | 56 | 138 | 149 | 172 | 169 | 146 | 153 | 172 | 205 |
| Oregon | 1 | 1 | 1 | 2 | 2 | 3 | 12 | 18 | 26 | 37 |
| Pennsylvania | 108 | 157 | 194 | 285 | 431 | 470 | 638 | 853 | 1,017 | 1,048 |
| Rhode Island | 7 | 9 | 10 | 10 | 10 | 11 | 14 | 18 | 25 | 28 |
| South Carolina | 689 | 782 | 836 | 865 | 794 | 814 | 822 | 829 | 789 | 948 |
| South Dakota | 1 | 0 | 1 | 1 | 1 | 0 | 1 | 1 | 2 | 2 |
| Tennessee | 431 | 480 | 473 | 452 | 478 | 509 | 531 | 587 | 621 | 726 |
| Texas | 488 | 621 | 690 | 742 | 855 | 924 | 977 | 1,187 | 1,399 | 1,710 |
| Utah | 1 | 1 | 1 | 1 | 1 | 1 | 3 | 4 | 7 | 9 |
| Vermont | 1 | 1 | 2 | 1 | 1 | 0 | 0 | | 1 | 1 |
| Virginia | 635 | 661 | 671 | 690 | 650 | 661 | 734 | 816 | 861 | 1,008 |
| Washington | 2 | 3 | 6 | 7 | 7 | 7 | 31 | 49 | 71 | 106 |
| West Virginia | 33 | 43 | 64 | 86 | 115 | 118 | 115 | 89 | 67 | 65 |
| Wisconsin | 2 | 3 | 3 | 5 | 11 | 12 | 28 | 75 | 128 | 183 |
| Wyoming | 1 | 1 | 2 | 1 | 1 | 1 | 3 | 2 | 3 | 3 |

Table 7.4

Total Number of Immigrants Arriving Annually
in the United States, 1820-1980

| Year | Total | Year | Total |
|------|-------|------|-------|
| 1820 | 8,385 | 1875 | 227,498 |
| 1821 | 9,127 | 1876 | 169,986 |
| 1822 | 6,911 | 1877 | 141,857 |
| 1823 | 6,354 | 1878 | 138,469 |
| 1824 | 7,912 | 1879 | 177,826 |
| 1825 | 10,199 | 1880 | 457,257 |
| 1826 | 10,837 | 1881 | 669,431 |
| 1827 | 18,875 | 1882 | 788,992 |
| 1828 | 27,382 | 1883 | 603,322 |
| 1829 | 22,520 | 1884 | 518,592 |
| 1830 | 23,332 | 1885 | 392,346 |
| 1831 | 22,633 | 1886 | 334,203 |
| 1832 | 60,482 | 1887 | 490,109 |
| 1833 | 58,640 | 1888 | 546,889 |
| 1834 | 65,365 | 1889 | 444,427 |
| 1835 | 45,374 | 1890 | 455,302 |
| 1836 | 76,242 | 1891 | 560,319 |
| 1837 | 79,340 | 1892 | 579,663 |
| 1838 | 38,914 | 1893 | 439,730 |
| 1839 | 68,069 | 1894 | 285,631 |
| 1840 | 84,066 | 1895 | 258,536 |
| 1841 | 80,289 | 1896 | 343,267 |
| 1842 | 104,565 | 1897 | 230,832 |
| 1843 | 52,496 | 1898 | 229,299 |
| 1844 | 78,615 | 1899 | 311,715 |
| 1845 | 114,371 | 1900 | 448,572 |
| 1846 | 154,416 | 1901 | 487,918 |
| 1847 | 234,968 | 1902 | 648,743 |
| 1848 | 226,527 | 1903 | 857,046 |
| 1849 | 297,024 | 1904 | 812,870 |
| 1850 | 369,980 | 1905 | 1,026,499 |
| 1851 | 379,466 | 1906 | 1,100,735 |
| 1852 | 371,603 | 1907 | 1,285,349 |
| 1853 | 368,645 | 1908 | 782,870 |
| 1854 | 427,833 | 1909 | 751,786 |
| 1855 | 200,877 | 1910 | 1,041,570 |
| 1856 | 200,436 | 1911 | 878,587 |
| 1857 | 251,306 | 1912 | 838,172 |
| 1858 | 123,126 | 1913 | 1,197,892 |
| 1859 | 121,282 | 1914 | 1,218,480 |
| 1860 | 153,640 | 1915 | 326,700 |
| 1861 | 91,918 | 1916 | 298,826 |
| 1862 | 91,985 | 1917 | 295,403 |
| 1863 | 176,282 | 1918 | 110,618 |
| 1864 | 193,418 | 1919 | 141,132 |
| 1865 | 248,120 | 1920 | 430,001 |
| 1866 | 318,568 | 1921 | 805,228 |
| 1867 | 315,722 | 1922 | 309,556 |
| 1868 | 138,840 | 1923 | 522,919 |
| 1869 | 352,768 | 1924 | 706,896 |
| 1870 | 387,203 | 1925 | 294,314 |
| 1871 | 321,350 | 1926 | 304,488 |
| 1872 | 404,806 | 1927 | 335,175 |
| 1873 | 459,803 | 1928 | 307,255 |
| 1874 | 313,339 | 1929 | 279,678 |

Table 7.4 (continued)

| Year | Total | Year | Total |
|------|-------|------|-------|
| 1930 | 241,700 | 1956 | 321,625 |
| 1931 | 97,139 | 1957 | 326,867 |
| 1932 | 35,576 | 1958 | 253,265 |
| 1933 | 23,068 | 1959 | 260,686 |
| 1934 | 29,470 | 1960 | 265,398 |
| 1935 | 34,956 | 1961 | 271,344 |
| 1936 | 36,329 | 1962 | 283,763 |
| 1937 | 50,244 | 1963 | 306,260 |
| 1938 | 67,895 | 1964 | 292,248 |
| 1939 | 82,998 | 1965 | 296,697 |
| 1940 | 70,756 | 1966 | 323,040 |
| 1941 | 51,776 | 1967 | 361,972 |
| 1942 | 28,781 | 1968 | 454,448 |
| 1943 | 23,725 | 1969 | 358,579 |
| 1944 | 28,551 | 1970 | 373,326 |
| 1945 | 38,119 | 1971 | 370,478 |
| 1946 | 108,721 | 1972 | 384,685 |
| 1947 | 147,292 | 1973 | 400,063 |
| 1948 | 170,570 | 1974 | 394,861 |
| 1949 | 188,317 | 1975 | 386,194 |
| 1950 | 249,187 | 1976 | 502,289 |
| 1951 | 205,717 | 1977 | 462,315 |
| 1952 | 265,520 | 1978 | 601,442 |
| 1953 | 170,434 | 1979 | 460,348 |
| 1954 | 208,177 | 1980 | 530,639 |
| 1955 | 237,790 | | |

Table 7.5

Number of Immigrants from Selected Countries
Arriving in the United States by Decade, 1820-1980

| Year | Great Britain | Ireland | Scandinavia | Germany | Poland | U.S.S.R. and Baltic States |
|---|---|---|---|---|---|---|
| 1820-1830 | 27,489 | 54,338 | 283 | 7,729 | 21[a] | 89 |
| 1831-1840 | 75,810 | 207,381 | 2,264 | 152,454 | 369[b] | 277[c] |
| 1841-1850 | 267,044 | 780,719 | 14,442 | 434,626 | 105[d] | 551 |
| 1851-1860 | 423,974 | 914,119 | 24,680 | 951,667 | 1,164[f] | 457 |
| 1861-1870 | 606,896 | 435,778 | 126,392 | 787,468 | 2,027[f] | 2,512 |
| 1871-1880 | 548,043 | 436,871 | 243,016 | 691,813 | 12,970 | 39,284 |
| 1881-1890 | 807,357 | 655,482 | 656,494 | 1,452,970 | 51,876[i] | 213,282 |
| 1891-1900 | 271,538 | 388,416 | 371,512 | 505,152 | 96,720[j] | 505,290 |
| 1901-1910 | 525,950 | 399,065 | 505,324 | 341,498 | n.a. | 1,597,306 |
| 1911-1920 | 341,408 | 146,181 | 203,452 | 143,945 | n.a. | 921,957 |
| 1921-1930 | 330,213 | 220,591 | 198,210 | 412,202 | 227,734 | 89,423 |
| 1931-1940 | 29,378 | 13,167 | 11,286 | 114,058 | 17,026 | 7,401 |
| 1941-1950 | 131,592 | 27,503 | 26,901 | 226,578 | 7,571 | 4,307 |
| 1951-1960 | 191,614 | 57,332 | 57,101 | 477,765 | 9,985 | 6,288 |
| 1961-1970 | 206,353 | 40,435 | 43,458 | 190,796 | 53,539 | 7,763 |
| 1971-1980 | 121,700 | 10,100 | 15,100 | 63,900 | 34,900 | 36,800 |

Table 7.5 (continued)

| Year | Italy | China | Japan | Canada and Newfoundland | Mexico | Australia and New Zealand |
|---|---|---|---|---|---|---|
| 1820-1830 | 439 | n.a. | n.a. | 2,486 | 4,818 | n.a. |
| 1831-1840 | 2,253 | n.a. | n.a. | 13,624 | 6,599 | n.a. |
| 1841-1850 | 1,870 | 35[d] | n.a. | 41,723 | 3,271 | n.a. |
| 1851-1860 | 9,231 | 41,397[e] | 186[g] | 59,309 | 3,078 | n.a. |
| 1861-1870 | 11,725 | 64,301 | 149 | 153,878 | 2,191 | 9,886 |
| 1871-1880 | 55,759 | 123,201 | 2,270[j] | 383,640 | 5,162[h] | 7,017 |
| 1881-1890 | 307,309 | 61,711[j] | 25,942[j] | 393,304 | 1,913[h] | 2,740 |
| 1891-1900 | 651,893 | 14,799[j] | 129,797 | 3,311[k] | 971[i] | 11,975 |
| 1901-1910 | 2,045,877 | 20,605 | 83,337 | 179,226 | 49,642 | 12,348 |
| 1911-1920 | 1,109,524 | 21,278 | 33,462 | 742,185 | 219,004 | 8,299 |
| 1921-1930 | 455,315 | 29,907 | 1,948 | 924,515 | 459,287 | 2,231 |
| 1931-1940 | 68,028 | 4,928 | 1,555 | 108,527 | 22,319 | 13,805 |
| 1941-1950 | 57,661 | 16,709 | 46,250 | 171,718 | 60,589 | 11,506 |
| 1951-1960 | 185,491 | 9,657 | 39,988 | 377,952 | 299,811 | 19,562 |
| 1961-1970 | 214,111 | 34,764 | 43,800 | 413,310 | 453,937 | 20,900 |
| 1971-1980 | 104,600 | 113,800 |  | 143,600 | 54,700 |  |

Table 7.5 (continued)

| Year | Vietnam | Korea | Philippines | Other Asia | Africa | Cuba | Haiti and Dom. Rep. | Other W. Indies |
|---|---|---|---|---|---|---|---|---|
| 1820-1830 | n.a. | n.a. | n.a. | n.a. | n.a. | n.a. | n.a. | n.a. |
| 1831-1840 | n.a. | n.a. | n.a. | n.a. | n.a. | n.a. | n.a. | n.a. |
| 1841-1850 | n.a. | n.a. | n.a. | n.a. | n.a. | n.a. | n.a. | n.a. |
| 1851-1860 | n.a. | n.a. | n.a. | n.a. | n.a. | n.a. | n.a. | n.a. |
| 1860-1870 | n.a. | n.a. | n.a. | n.a. | n.a. | n.a. | n.a. | n.a. |
| 1871-1880 | n.a. | n.a. | n.a. | n.a. | n.a. | n.a. | n.a. | n.a. |
| 1881-1890 | n.a. | n.a. | n.a. | n.a. | n.a. | n.a. | n.a. | n.a. |
| 1891-1900 | n.a. | n.a. | n.a. | n.a. | n.a. | n.a. | n.a. | n.a. |
| 1900-1910 | n.a. | n.a. | n.a. | 15,800 | 7,400 | n.a. | n.a. | 107,500 |
| 1910-1920 | n.a. | n.a. | n.a. | 8,100 | 8,400 | n.a. | n.a. | 123,400 |
| 1920-1930 | n.a. | n.a. | n.a. | 14,900 | 6,300 | n.a. | n.a. | 74,900 |
| 1931-1940 | n.a. | n.a. | n.a. | 8,100 | 1,700 | n.a. | n.a. | 15,500 |
| 1941-1950 | n.a. | n.a. | n.a. | 13,300 | 8,200 | n.a. | n.a. | 47,700 |
| 1950-1960 | n.a. | 6,200 | 19,300 | 11,700 | 14,100 | 78,900 | 14,300 | 29,800 |
| 1961-1970 | 4,200 | 34,500 | 98,400 | 36,700 | 29,000 | 208,500 | 127,800 | 133,900 |
| 1971-1980 | 169,700 | 247,100 | 317,700 | 162,200 | 74,100 | 236,500 | 181,000 | 233,100 |

n.a.Data not available.

aData not available for the years 1826 and 1829.

bData not available for 1831.

cData not available for 1840.

dData not available for 1848.

eData not available for the years 1851 and 1852.

fData not available for 1868.

gData not available for the years 1862 to 1865 and 1868.

hData not available for the years 1886 to 1890.

iData not available for the years 1899 and 1900.

jData not available for 1892.

kData not available for the years 1892 and 1893.

lData not available for the years 1891 to 1893.

Table 7.6

Estimated Civilian Labor Force in the United States
and Percentage of Labor Force Unemployed,
1900-1982[a]

| Year | Number in Labor Force | % Un- employed | Year | Number in Labor Force | % Un- employed |
|------|-----------------------|----------------|------|-----------------------|----------------|
| 1900 | 28,376,000 | 5.0 | 1942 | 56,410,000 | 4.7 |
| 1901 | 29,153,000 | 4.0 | 1943 | 55,540,000 | 1.9 |
| 1902 | 29,904,000 | 3.7 | 1944 | 54,630,000 | 1.2 |
| 1903 | 30,698,000 | 3.9 | 1945 | 53,860,000 | 1.9 |
| 1904 | 31,441,000 | 5.4 | 1946 | 57,520,000 | 3.9 |
| 1905 | 32,299,000 | 4.3 | 1947 | 60,168,000 | 3.9 |
| 1906 | 33,212,000 | 1.7 | 1948 | 60,621,000 | 3.8 |
| 1907 | 34,183,000 | 2.8 | 1949 | 61,286,000 | 5.9 |
| 1908 | 34,916,000 | 8.0 | 1950 | 62,208,000 | 5.3 |
| 1909 | 35,721,000 | 5.1 | 1951 | 62,017,000 | 3.3 |
| 1910 | 36,709,000 | 5.9 | 1952 | 62,138,000 | 3.0 |
| 1911 | 37,478,000 | 6.7 | 1953 | 63,015,000 | 2.9 |
| 1912 | 37,932,000 | 4.6 | 1954 | 63,643,000 | 5.5 |
| 1913 | 38,675,000 | 4.3 | 1955 | 65,023,000 | 4.4 |
| 1914 | 39,401,000 | 7.9 | 1956 | 66,552,000 | 4.1 |
| 1915 | 39,600,000 | 8.5 | 1957 | 66,929,000 | 4.3 |
| 1916 | 40,057,000 | 5.1 | 1958 | 67,639,000 | 6.8 |
| 1917 | 40,023,000 | 4.6 | 1959 | 68,369,000 | 5.5 |
| 1918 | 39,076,000 | 1.4 | 1960 | 69,628,000 | 5.5 |
| 1919 | 39,696,000 | 1.4 | 1961 | 70,459,000 | 6.7 |
| 1920 | 41,340,000 | 5.2 | 1962 | 70,614,000 | 5.5 |
| 1921 | 41,979,000 | 11.7 | 1963 | 71,833,000 | 5.7 |
| 1922 | 42,496,000 | 6.7 | 1964 | 73,091,000 | 5.2 |
| 1923 | 43,444,000 | 2.4 | 1965 | 74,455,000 | 4.5 |
| 1924 | 44,235,000 | 5.0 | 1966 | 75,770,000 | 3.8 |
| 1925 | 45,169,000 | 3.2 | 1967 | 77,347,000 | 3.8 |
| 1926 | 45,629,000 | 1.8 | 1968 | 78,737,000 | 3.6 |
| 1927 | 46,375,000 | 3.3 | 1969 | 80,734,000 | 3.5 |
| 1928 | 47,105,000 | 4.2 | 1970 | 82,715,000 | 4.9 |
| 1929 | 47,757,000 | 3.2 | 1971 | 84,113,000 | 5.9 |
| 1930 | 48,523,000 | 8.7 | 1972 | 86,542,000 | 5.6 |
| 1931 | 49,325,000 | 15.9 | 1973 | 88,714,000 | 4.9 |
| 1932 | 50,098,000 | 23.6 | 1974 | 91,011,000 | 5.6 |
| 1933 | 50,882,000 | 24.9 | 1975 | 91,369,000 | 8.6 |
| 1934 | 51,650,000 | 21.7 | 1976 | 96,158,000 | 7.7 |
| 1935 | 52,283,000 | 20.1 | 1977 | 99,009,000 | 7.1 |
| 1936 | 53,019,000 | 16.9 | 1978 | 102,251,000 | 6.1 |
| 1937 | 53,768,000 | 14.3 | 1979 | 104,962,000 | 5.8 |
| 1938 | 54,532,000 | 19.0 | 1980 | 106,940,000 | 7.1 |
| 1939 | 55,218,000 | 17.2 | 1981 | 108,670,000 | 7.6 |
| 1940 | 55,640,000 | 14.6 | 1982 | 110,204,000 | 9.7 |
| 1941 | 55,910,000 | 9.9 | | | |

[a]For the period 1900 to 1947, the data include all persons 14 years old
and over, for 1948 to 1982, all persons 16 years old and over.

Table 7.7

Estimated Civilian Labor Force and Percentage
of Labor Force Unemployed, by State,
1930-1980

| State | 1930 | | 1940 | | 1950 | |
|-------|------------|----------|------------|----------|------------|----------|
| | Labor Force | % Unemp. | Labor Force | % Unemp. | Labor Force | % Unemp. |
| Alabama | 1,026,320 | 2.9 | 1,017,188 | 12.1 | 1,076,406 | 4.2 |
| Alaska | --- | --- | --- | --- | 46,969 | 9.8 |
| Arizona | 165,304 | 5.7 | 180,247 | 16.7 | 258,216 | 7.6 |
| Arkansas | 667,870 | 2.7 | 678,859 | 14.0 | 646,124 | 4.7 |
| California | 2,500,969 | 7.6 | 2,948,427 | 14.4 | 4,237,703 | 7.9 |
| Colorado | 402,894 | 7.5 | 421,493 | 17.0 | 497,648 | 4.2 |
| Connecticut | 677,292 | 7.5 | 770,003 | 11.6 | 874,661 | 5.4 |
| Delaware | 98,104 | 3.9 | 114,260 | 10.2 | 130,694 | 3.1 |
| Florida | 599,010 | 6.4 | 786,804 | 13.2 | 1,057,479 | 4.5 |
| Georgia | 1,162,174 | 3.4 | 1,225,705 | 9.7 | 1,299,254 | 3.4 |
| Hawaii | --- | --- | --- | --- | 185,115 | 9.5 |
| Idaho | 162,223 | 4.6 | 191,196 | 17.0 | 217,895 | 5.5 |
| Illinois | 3,184,875 | 8.9 | 3,360,823 | 14.5 | 3,693,948 | 4.0 |
| Indiana | 1,251,177 | 7.0 | 1,331,378 | 13.5 | 1,567,227 | 3.1 |
| Iowa | 912,832 | 3.4 | 957,869 | 9.9 | 1,020,881 | 1.8 |
| Kansas | 694,276 | 4.1 | 669,815 | 12.8 | 725,509 | 2.5 |
| Kentucky | 907,166 | 4.6 | 998,700 | 15.1 | 991,071 | 3.6 |
| Louisiana | 815,725 | 4.8 | 884,164 | 12.8 | 917,802 | 4.6 |
| Maine | 308,617 | 6.8 | 330,421 | 15.6 | 342,442 | 8.8 |
| Maryland | 672,906 | 4.7 | 767,091 | 9.9 | 938,305 | 4.6 |
| Massachusetts | 1,814,422 | 8.9 | 1,844,260 | 16.8 | 1,938,611 | 5.8 |
| Michigan | 1,927,498 | 10.2 | 2,125,877 | 14.2 | 2,530,060 | 5.4 |
| Minnesota | 992,847 | 5.6 | 1,101,464 | 15.4 | 1,185,767 | 3.5 |
| Mississippi | 844,887 | 1.9 | 808,462 | 10.0 | 742,827 | 3.5 |
| Missouri | 1,458,054 | 5.5 | 1,521,086 | 14.7 | 1,574,167 | 3.3 |
| Montana | 216,471 | 7.0 | 224,994 | 17.5 | 230,143 | 5.1 |
| Nebraska | 507,022 | 3.7 | 501,013 | 13.5 | 523,329 | 2.2 |
| Nevada | 42,885 | 7.3 | 47,979 | 13.6 | 68,206 | 6.7 |

Table 7.7 (continued)

| State | 1930 Labor Force | % Unemp. | 1940 Labor Force | % Unemp. | 1950 Labor Force | % Unemp. |
|---|---|---|---|---|---|---|
| New Hampshire | 192,671 | 7.0 | 206,919 | 14.9 | 216,960 | 6.6 |
| New Jersey | 1,712,125 | 8.2 | 1,857,340 | 15.5 | 2,067,912 | 5.1 |
| New Mexico | 142,866 | 4.6 | 177,908 | 21.2 | 218,276 | 5.4 |
| New York | 5,523,085 | 7.7 | 5,962,199 | 16.6 | 6,325,213 | 6.0 |
| North Carolina | 1,141,129 | 3.9 | 1,333,773 | 9.4 | 1,512,924 | 3.3 |
| North Dakota | 240,317 | 3.1 | 235,661 | 15.0 | 232,353 | 3.8 |
| Ohio | 2,615,938 | 8.2 | 2,765,687 | 15.2 | 3,201,109 | 4.4 |
| Oklahoma | 828,029 | 5.5 | 804,582 | 18.1 | 783,123 | 3.8 |
| Oregon | 409,680 | 7.7 | 453,382 | 14.0 | 616,733 | 6.5 |
| Pennsylvania | 3,722,426 | 8.8 | 3,986,000 | 19.0 | 4,157,543 | 5.4 |
| Rhode Island | 297,168 | 12.2 | 321,644 | 17.7 | 328,015 | 7.2 |
| South Carolina | 687,721 | 2.8 | 730,780 | 9.5 | 782,066 | 3.4 |
| South Dakota | 247,678 | 1.8 | 239,826 | 14.7 | 249,141 | 2.8 |
| Tennessee | 958,209 | 3.1 | 1,071,904 | 12.1 | 1,182,068 | 3.9 |
| Texas | 2,207,118 | 4.3 | 2,454,924 | 12.9 | 2,870,605 | 3.9 |
| Utah | 170,013 | 6.4 | 181,244 | 17.9 | 241,487 | 5.2 |
| Vermont | 141,190 | 5.8 | 141,407 | 11.5 | 145,190 | 5.5 |
| Virginia | 880,276 | 4.0 | 1,031,289 | 9.5 | 1,196,676 | 3.9 |
| Washington | 664,813 | 7.0 | 716,501 | 15.2 | 900,746 | 6.7 |
| West Virginia | 570,459 | 6.1 | 634,957 | 18.2 | 659,613 | 4.8 |
| Wisconsin | 1,129,546 | 5.7 | 1,227,552 | 13.6 | 1,396,383 | 2.9 |
| Wyoming | 92,451 | 5.3 | 100,409 | 13.8 | 112,666 | 4.3 |

Table 7.7 (continued)

| State | 1960 Labor Force | % Unemp. | 1970 Labor Force | % Unemp. | 1980 Labor Force | % Unemp. |
|---|---|---|---|---|---|---|
| Alabama | 1,065,897 | 5.7 | 1,249,195 | 4.5 | 1,634,743 | 7.5 |
| Alaska | 58,243 | 12.8 | 98,296 | 9.2 | 182,679 | 9.7 |
| Arizona | 429,862 | 5.3 | 641,000 | 4.2 | 1,186,832 | 6.2 |
| Arkansas | 565,491 | 6.0 | 688,630 | 5.7 | 940,880 | 6.9 |
| California | 5,761,433 | 6.1 | 7,992,168 | 6.3 | 11,386,075 | 6.5 |
| Colorado | 626,769 | 4.0 | 862,133 | 4.2 | 1.433,731 | 5.0 |
| Connecticut | 1,010,444 | 4.6 | 1,298,483 | 3.5 | 1,554,810 | 4.7 |
| Delaware | 162,950 | 4.6 | 219,155 | 3.8 | 280,437 | 6.3 |
| Florida | 1,719,591 | 5.0 | 2,521,245 | 3.8 | 4,217,665 | 5.1 |
| Georgia | 1,385,047 | 4.5 | 1,805,019 | 3.2 | 2,481,298 | 5.9 |
| Hawaii | 209,370 | 4.2 | 294,484 | 3.0 | 435,780 | 4.7 |
| Idaho | 232,858 | 5.7 | 271,593 | 5.2 | 416,891 | 8.0 |
| Illinois | 3,899,472 | 4.5 | 4,591,634 | 3.7 | 5,458,785 | 7.2 |
| Indiana | 1,717,241 | 4.2 | 2,103,434 | 4.1 | 2,566,755 | 7.8 |
| Iowa | 1,019,002 | 3.2 | 1,127,433 | 3.5 | 1,373,914 | 5.0 |
| Kansas | 783,877 | 3.7 | 886,624 | 3.9 | 1,123,496 | 4.0 |
| Kentucky | 935,944 | 6.0 | 1,141,594 | 4.6 | 1,517,653 | 8.5 |
| Louisiana | 1,007,812 | 6.1 | 1,224,186 | 5.4 | 1,744,102 | 6.0 |
| Maine | 330,584 | 6.5 | 381,714 | 4.2 | 497,401 | 7.6 |
| Maryland | 1,133,968 | 4.8 | 1,590,094 | 3.2 | 2,065,512 | 5.8 |
| Massachusetts | 2,000,312 | 4.2 | 2,389,419 | 3.8 | 2,816,374 | 5.0 |
| Michigan | 2,726,864 | 6.9 | 3,455,346 | 5.9 | 4,211,997 | 11.0 |
| Minnesota | 1,233,408 | 5.0 | 1,528,436 | 4.2 | 1,993,352 | 5.4 |
| Mississippi | 682,339 | 5.4 | 756,487 | 5.0 | 1,009,374 | 7.1 |
| Missouri | 1,571,900 | 4.1 | 1,845,402 | 4.2 | 2,259,764 | 6.9 |
| Montana | 231,270 | 6.8 | 260,649 | 6.2 | 357,846 | 8.3 |
| Nebraska | 525,938 | 3.1 | 592,142 | 2.7 | 744,195 | 3.7 |
| Nevada | 112,451 | 6.2 | 208,996 | 5.4 | 423,688 | 5.9 |
| New Hampshire | 234,444 | 4.3 | 304,713 | 3.5 | 454,430 | 4.8 |
| New Jersey | 2,345,496 | 4.6 | 2,972,561 | 3.8 | 3,523,255 | 6.7 |
| New Mexico | 287,904 | 5.9 | 342,482 | 5.7 | 547,074 | 7.1 |
| New York | 6,599,462 | 5.2 | 7,421,579 | 4.0 | 8,012,824 | 7.1 |

Table 7.7 (continued)

| State | 1960 | | 1970 | | 1980 | |
|-------|------|------|------|------|------|------|
| | Labor Force | % Unemp. | Labor Force | % Unemp. | Labor Force | % Unemp. |
| North Carolina | 1,605,478 | 4.5 | 2,054,838 | 3.4 | 2,759,197 | 5.5 |
| North Dakota | 213,661 | 5.6 | 214,344 | 4.6 | 288,011 | 5.3 |
| Ohio | 3,504,880 | 5.5 | 4,234,458 | 4.0 | 4,953,353 | 8.0 |
| Oklahoma | 785,948 | 4.4 | 968,430 | 4.2 | 1,343,066 | 4.1 |
| Oregon | 638,824 | 6.0 | 837,069 | 7.0 | 1,241,025 | 8.3 |
| Pennsylvania | 4,127,208 | 6.2 | 4,712,303 | 3.7 | 5,358,609 | 7.4 |
| Rhode Island | 317,272 | 5.3 | 388,002 | 4.0 | 459,146 | 7.0 |
| South Carolina | 803,733 | 4.1 | 991,844 | 3.8 | 1,405,262 | 6.1 |
| South Dakota | 238,173 | 4.1 | 249,360 | 3.7 | 312,022 | 4.9 |
| Tennessee | 1,222,257 | 5.2 | 1,526,055 | 4.4 | 2,067,882 | 7.4 |
| Texas | 3,318,503 | 4.5 | 4,297,786 | 3.6 | 6,574,676 | 4.0 |
| Utah | 302,147 | 4.1 | 399,162 | 5.2 | 619,738 | 5.5 |
| Vermont | 141,596 | 4.5 | 174,802 | 4.1 | 242,456 | 6.3 |
| Virginia | 1,340,800 | 4.2 | 1,766,740 | 3.0 | 2,471,158 | 5.0 |
| Washington | 1,001,909 | 6.6 | 1,338,513 | 7.9 | 1,937,615 | 7.4 |
| West Virginia | 538,214 | 8.3 | 579,316 | 5.1 | 753,076 | 8.4 |
| Wisconsin | 1,468,631 | 3.9 | 1,774,008 | 4.0 | 2,263,413 | 6.6 |
| Wyoming | 120,812 | 5.1 | 129,577 | 4.8 | 226,762 | 4.1 |

# *APPENDIX*

## Declaration of Independence
IN CONGRESS, JULY 4, 1776
A DECLARATION
By the REPRESENTATIVES of the
UNITED STATES OF AMERICA,
In GENERAL CONGRESS assembled

When in the Course of human Events, it becomes necessary for one People to dissolve the Political Bands which have connected them with another, and to assume among the Powers of the Earth, the separate and equal Station to which the Laws of Nature and of Nature's God entitle them, a decent Respect to the Opinions of Mankind requires that they should declare the causes which impel them to the Separation.

We hold these truths to be self-evident, that all Men are created equal, that they are endowed by their Creator with certain unalienable Rights, that among them are Life, Liberty, and the Pursuit of Happiness—That to secure these Rights, Governments are instituted among Men, deriving their just Powers from the Consent of the Governed, that whenever any form of Government becomes destructive of these Ends, it is the Right of the People to alter or to abolish it, and to institute new Government, laying its Foundation on such Principles, and organizing its Powers in such Form, as to them shall seem most likely to effect their Safety and Happiness. Prudence, indeed, will dictate that Governments long established should not be changed for light and transient Causes; and accordingly all Experience hath shewn, that Mankind are more disposed to suffer, while Evils are sufferable, than to right themselves by abolishing the Forms to which they are accustomed. But when a long Train of Abuses and Usurpations, pursuing invariably the same Object, evinces a Design to reduce them under absolute Despotism, it is their Right, it is their Duty, to throw off such Government, and to provide new Guards for their future Security. Such has been the patient Sufferance of these Colonies; and such is now the Necessity which constrains them to alter their former Systems of Government. The History of the present King of Great-

Britain is a History of repeated Injuries and Usurpations, all having in direct Object the Establishment of an absolute Tyranny over these States. To prove this, let Facts be submitted to a candid World.

He has refused his Assent to Laws, the most wholesome and necessary for the public Good.

He has forbidden his Governors to pass Laws of immediate and pressing Importance, unless suspended in their Operation, till his Assent should be obtained; and when so suspended, he has utterly neglected to attend to them.

He has refused to pass other Laws for the Accommodation of large Districts of People, unless those People would relinquish the Right of Representation in the Legislature, a Right inestimable to them, and formidable to Tyrants only.

He has called together Legislative Bodies at Places unusual, uncomfortable, and distant from the Depository of their Public Records, for the sole Purpose of fatiguing them into Compliance with his Measures.

He has dissolved Representative Houses repeatedly, for opposing with manly Firmness his Invasions on the Rights of the People.

He has refused for a long Time, after such Dissolutions, to cause others to be elected; whereby the Legislative Powers, incapable of Annihilation, have returned to the People at large for their exercise; the State remaining in the mean time exposed to all the Dangers of Invasion from without, and Convulsions within.

He has endeavoured to prevent the Population of these States; for that Purpose obstructing the Laws for Naturalization of Foreigners; refusing to pass others to encourage their Migrations hither, and raising the Conditions of new Appropriations of Lands.

He has obstructed the Administration of Justice, by refusing his Assent to Laws for establishing Judiciary Powers.

He has made judges dependent on his Will alone, for the Tenure of their Offices, and the Amount and payment of their Salaries.

He has erected a Multitude of new Offices, and sent hither Swarms of Officers to harrass our People, and eat out their Substance.

He has kept among us, in Times of Peace, Standing Armies, without the consent of our Legislatures.

He has affected to render the Military independent of, and superior to the Civil Power.

He has combined with others to subject us to a Jurisdiction foreign to our Constitution, and unacknowledged by our Laws; giving his Assent to their Acts of pretended Legislation:

For quartering large Bodies of Armed Troops among us:

For protecting them, by a mock Trial, from Punishment for any Murders which they should commit on the Inhabitants of these States:

For cutting off our Trade with all Parts of the World:

For imposing Taxes on us without our Consent:

For depriving us, in many Cases, of the Benefits of Trial by Jury:

For transporting us beyond Seas to be tried for pretended Offences:

For abolishing the free System of English Laws in a neighbouring Province, establishing therein an arbitrary Government, and enlarging its Boundaries, so as to render it at once an Example and fit Instrument for introducing the same absolute Rule into these Colonies:

For taking away our Charters, abolishing our most valuable Laws, and altering fundamentally the Forms of our Governments:

For suspending our own Legislatures, and declaring themselves invested with Power to legislate for us in all Cases whatsoever.

He has abdicated Government here, by declaring us out of his Protection and waging War against us.

He has plundered our Seas, ravaged our Coasts, burnt our towns, and destroyed the Lives of our People.

He is, at this Time, transporting large Armies of foreign Mercenaries to compleat the works of Death, Desolation, and Tyranny, already begun with circumstances of Cruelty and Perfidy, scarcely paralleled in the most barbarous Ages, and totally unworthy the Head of a civilized Nation.

He has constrained our fellow Citizens taken Captive on the high Seas to bear Arms against their Country, to become the Executioners of their Friends and Brethren, or to fall themselves by their Hands.

He has excited domestic Insurrections amongst us, and has endeavoured to bring on the Inhabitants of our Frontiers, the merciless Indian Savages, whose known Rule of Warfare, is an undistinguished Destruction, of all Ages, Sexes, and Conditions.

In every stage of these Oppressions we have Petitioned for Redress in the most humble Terms: Our repeated Petitions have been answered only by repeated Injury. A Prince, whose Character is thus marked by every act which may define a Tyrant, is unfit to be the Ruler of a free People.

Nor have we been wanting in Attentions to our British Brethren.

We have warned them from Time to Time of Attempts by their Legislature to extend an unwarrantable Jurisdiction over us. We have reminded them of the Circumstances of our Emigration and Settlement here. We have appealed to their native Justice and Magnanimity, and we have conjured them by the Ties of our common Kindred to disavow these Usurpations, which, would inevitably interrupt our Connections and Correspondence. They too have been deaf to the Voices of Justice and Consanguinity. We must, therefore, acquiesce in the Necessity, which denounces our Separation, and hold them as we hold the rest of Mankind, Enemies in War, in Peace, Friends.

We, therefore, the Representatives of the UNITED STATES OF AMERICA, in General Gongress, Assembled, appealing to the Supreme Judge of the World for the Rectitude of our Intentions, do, in the Name, and by Authority of the good People of these Colonies, solemnly Publish and Declare, That these United States are, and of Right ought to be, Free and Independent States; that they are absolved from all Allegiance to the British Crown, and that all political Connection between them and the State of Great Britain, is and ought to be totally dissolved; and that as Free and Independent States, they have full Power to levy War, conclude Peace, contract Alliances, establish Commerce, and to do all other Acts and Things which Independent States may of right do. And for the support of this declaration, with a firm Reliance on the Protection of divine Providence, we mutually pledge to each other our lives, our Fortunes, and our sacred Honor.

JOHN HANCOCK, President

Attest. CHARLES THOMSON, Secretary

# CONSTITUTION OF THE UNITED STATES

## The Original 7 Articles

### *Preamble*

We, the People of the United States, in Order to form a more perfect Union, establish Justice, and insure domestic Tranquility, provide for the common defence, promote the general Welfare, and secure the Blessings of Liberty to ourselves and our Posterity do ordain and establish this Constitution for the United States of America.

### *Article I*

Section 1. All legislative Powers herein granted shall be vested in a Congress of the United States, which shall consist of a Senate and House of Representatives.

Section 2. The House of Representatives shall be composed of members chosen every second Year by the People of the several States, and the Electors in each State shall have the Qualifications requisite for Electors of the most numerous Branch of the State Legislature.

No Person shall be a Representative who shall not have attained the Age of twenty-five Years, and been seven Years a Citizen of the United States, and who shall not, when elected, be an inhabitant of that State in which he shall be chosen.

Representatives and direct Taxes shall be apportioned among the several States which may be included within this Union, according to their respective Numbers, [which shall be determined by adding to the whole Number of free Persons including those bound to Service for a Term of Years, and excluding Indians not taxed, three-fifths of all other Persons.][1] The actual Enumeration shall be made within three Years after the first Meeting of the Congress of the United States, and within every subsequent Term of ten Years, in such Manner as they shall by law direct. The Number of Representatives shall not exceed one for every thirty Thousand, but each State shall have at least one Representative; and until such enumeration shall be made, the State of New Hampshire shall be entitled to choose three, Massachusetts eight, Rhode Island and Providence Plantations one, Connecticut five, New York six, New Jersey four, Pennsylvania eight, Delaware one, Maryland six, Virginia ten, North Carolina five, South Carolina five, and Georgia three.

When vacancies happen in the Representation from any State, the Executive Authority thereof shall issue Writs of Election to fill such Vacancies.

The House of Representatives shall choose their Speaker and other Officers; and shall have the sole Power of Impeachment.

Section 3. The Senate of the United States shall be composed of two Senators from each State, [chosen by the Legislature thereof][2] for six Years; and each Senator shall have one Vote.

Immediately after they shall be assembled in Consequence of the first Election, they shall be divided as equally as may be into three Classes. The Seats of the Senators of the first Class shall be vacated at the Expiration of the second year, of the second Class at the Expiration of the fourth Year, and of the third Class at the Expiration of the sixth Year, so that one third may be chosen every second Year; [and if Vacancies happen by Resignation, or otherwise, during the Recess of the Legislature of any State, the Executive thereof may make temporary Appointments until the next Meeting of the Legislature, which shall then fill such Vacancies.][3]

No Person shall be a Senator who shall not have attained to the Age of thirty Years, and been nine Years a Citizen of the United States, and who shall not, when elected, be an Inhabitant of that State for which he shall be chosen.

The Vice President of the United States shall be President of the Senate, but shall have no Vote, unless they be equally divided.

The Senate shall chuse their other Officers, and also a President pro tempore, in the Absence of the Vice President, or when he shall exercise the Office of President of the United States.

The Senate shall have the sole Power to try all Impeachments. When sitting for that Purpose, they shall be on Oath or Affirmation. When the President of the United States is tried, the Chief Justice shall preside: and no Person shall be convicted without the Concurrence of two thirds of the Members present.

Judgment in Cases of Impeachment shall not extend further than to removal from Office, and disqualification to hold and enjoy any Office of honor, Trust or Profit under the United States: but the Party convicted shall nevertheless be liable and subject to Indictment, Trial, Judgment and Punishment, according to Law.

Section 4. The Times, Places and Manner of holding Elections for Senators and Representatives, shall be prescribed in each State by the Legislature thereof; but the Congress may at any time by Law make or alter such Regulations, except as to the Places of Chusing Senators.

[The Congress shall assemble at least once in every Year, and such Meeting shall be on the first Monday in December, unless they shall by Law appoint a different Day.]⁴

Section 5. Each House shall be the Judge of the Elections, Returns, and Qualifications of its own Members, and a Majority of each shall constitute a Quorum to do Business; but a small Number may adjourn from day to day, and may be authorized to compel the Attendance of absent Members, in such Manner, and under such Penalties as each House may provide.

Each House may determine the Rules of its Proceedings, punish its Members for disorderly Behaviour, and, with the Concurrence of two thirds, expel a Member.

Each House shall keep a Journal of its Proceedings, and from time to time publish the same, excepting such Parts as may in their Judgment require Secrecy; and the Yeas and Nays of the Members of either House on any question shall, at the Desire of one fifth of those Present, be entered on the Journal.

Neither House, during the Session of Congress, shall, without the Consent of the other, adjourn for more than three days, nor to any other Place than that in which the two Houses shall be sitting.

Section 6. The Senators and Representatives shall receive a compensation for their Services, to be ascertained by Law, and paid out of the Treasury of the United States. They shall in all Cases, except Treason, Felony and Breach of the Peace, be privileged from Arrest during their Attendance at the Session of their respective Houses, and in going to and returning from the same; and for any Speech or Debate in either House, they shall not be questioned in any other Place.

No Senator or Representative shall, during the Time for which he was elected, be appointed to any civil Office under the Authority of the United States, which shall have been created, or the Emoluments whereof shall have been increased during such time; and no Person holding any Office under the United States, shall be a Member of either House during his Continuance in Office.

Section 7. All bills for raising Revenue shall originate in the House of Representatives; but the Senate may propose or concur with Amendments as on other Bills.

Every Bill which shall have passed the House of Representatives and the Senate, shall, before it becomes a Law, be presented to the President of the United States; If he approve he shall sign it, but if not he shall return it, with his Objections to that House in which it shall have originated, who shall enter the Objections at large on their Journal, and proceed to reconsider it. If after such Reconsideration two thirds of that House shall agree to pass the Bill, it shall be sent, together with the Objections, to the other House, by which it shall likewise be reconsidered, and if approved by two thirds of that House, it shall become a Law. But in all such Cases the Votes of both Houses shall be determined by yeas and Nays, and the Names of the Persons voting for and against the Bill shall be entered on the Journal of each House respectively. If any Bill shall not be returned by the President within ten Days (Sundays excepted) after it shall have been presented to him, the Same shall be a Law, in like Manner as if he had signed it, unless the Congress by their Adjournment prevent its Return, in which Case it shall not be a Law.

Every Order, Resolution, or Vote to which the Concurrence of the Senate and House of Representatives may be necessary (except on a question of Adjournment) shall be presented to the President of the United States; and before the Same shall take Effect, shall be approved by him, or being disapproved by him, shall be repassed by two thirds of the Senate and House of Representatives, according to the Rules and Limitations prescribed in the Case of a Bill.

Section 8. The Congress shall have Power To lay and collect Taxes, Duties, Imposts and Excises, to pay the Debts and provide for the common Defence and general Welfare of the United States; but all Duties, Imposts and Excises shall be uniform throughout the United States;

To borrow money on the credit of the United States;

To regulate Commerce with foreign Nations, and among the several States, and with the Indian Tribes;

To establish a uniform Rule of Naturalization, and uniform Laws on the subject of Bankruptcies throughout the United States;

To coin Money, regulate the Value thereof, and of foreign Coin, and fix the Standard of Weights and Measures;

To provide for the Punishment of counterfeiting the Securities and current Coin of the United States;

To establish Post Offices and post Roads;

To promote the Progress of Science and useful Arts, by securing for limited Times to Authors and Inventors the exclusive Right to their respective Writings and Discoveries;

To constitute Tribunals inferior to the supreme Court;

To define and punish Piracies and Felonies committed on the high Seas, and Offences against the Law of Nations;

To declare War, grant Letters of Marque and Reprisal, and make Rules concerning Captures on Land and Water;

To raise and support Armies, but no Appropriation of Money to that Use shall be for a longer Term than two Years;

To provide and maintain a Navy;

To make Rules for the Government and Regulation of the land and naval Forces;

To provide for calling forth the Militia to execute the Laws of the Union, suppress Insurrections and repel Invasions;

To provide for organizing, arming, and disciplining, the Militia, and for governing such Part of them as may be employed in the Service of the United States, reserving to the States respectively, the Appointment of the Officers, and the Authority of training the Militia according to the discipline prescribed by Congress;

To exercise exclusive Legislation in all Cases whatsoever, over such District (not exceeding ten Miles square) as may, by Cession of particular States, and the Acceptance of Congress, become the Seat of the Government of the United States, and to exercise like Authority over all Places purchased by the Consent of the Legislature of the State in which the Same shall be, for the Erection of Forts, Magazines, Arsenals, dock-Yards, and other needful Buildings;—And

To make all Laws which shall be necessary and proper for carrying into Execution the foregoing Powers, and all other Powers vested by this Constitution in the Government of the United States, or in any Department or Officer therof.

Section 9. The Migration or Importation of such Persons as any of the States now existing shall think proper to admit, shall not be prohibited by the Congress prior to the Year one thousand eight hundred and eight, but a Tax or duty may be imposed on such Importation, not exceeding ten dollars for each Person.

The Privilege of the Writ of Habeas Corpus shall not be suspended, unless when in Cases of Rebellion or Invasion the public safety may require it.

No Bill of Attainder or ex post facto Law shall be passed.

No Capitation, or other direct, Tax shall be laid, unless in Proportion to the Census or Enumeration herein before directed to be taken.[5]

No Tax or Duty shall be laid on Articles exported from any State.

No Preference shall be given by any Regulation of Commerce or Revenue to the Ports of one State over those of another; nor shall Vessels bound to, or from, one State be obliged to enter, clear, or pay Duties in another.

No money shall be drawn from the Treasury, but in Consequence of Appropriations made by Law; and a regular Statement and Account of the Receipts and Expenditures of all public Money shall be published from time to time.

No Title of Nobility shall be granted by the United States: And no Person holding any Office of Profit or Trust under them, shall without the Consent of the Congress, accept any present, Emolument, Office, or Title, of any kind whatever, from any King, Prince, or foreign State.

Section 10. No State shall enter into any Treaty, Alliance, or Confederation; grant Letters of Marque and Reprisal; coin Money; emit Bills of Credit; make any Thing but gold and silver Coin a Tender in Payment of Debts; pass any Bill of Attainder, ex post facto Law, or Law impairing the Obligation of Contracts, or grant any Title of Nobility.

No State shall, without the Consent of the Congress, lay any Imposts or Duties on Imports or Exports, except what may be absolutely necessary for executing its inspection laws; and the net Produce of all Duties and Imposts, laid by any State on Imports or Exports, shall be for the Use of the Treasury of the United States; and all such Laws shall be subject to the Revision, and Control of the Congress.

No State shall, without the Consent of Congress, lay any Duty of Tonnage, keep Troops, or Ships of War in time of Peace, enter into any Agreement or Compact with another State, or with a foreign

Power, or engage in War, unless actually invaded, or in such imminent Danger as will not admit of delay.

## *Article II*

Section 1. The executive Power shall be vested in a President of the United States of America. He shall hold his Office during the Term of four Years, and, together with the Vice President, chosen for the same Term, be elected as follows.

Each State shall appoint, in such Manner as the Legislature thereof may direct, a Number of Electors, equal to the whole Number of Senators and Representatives to which the State may be entitled in the Congress: but no Senator or Representative, or Person holding an Office of Trust or Profit under the United States, shall be appointed an Elector.

[The Electors shall meet in their respective States, and vote by Ballot for two Persons, of whom one at least shall not be an Inhabitant of the same State with themselves. And they shall make a List of all the Persons voted for, and the Number of Votes for each; which list they shall sign and certify, and transmit sealed to the Seat of the Government of the United States, directed to the President of the Senate. The President of the Senate shall, in the Presence of the Senate and House of Representatives, open all the Certificates, and the Votes shall then be counted. The person having the greatest Number of Votes shall be the President, if such Number be a Majority of the whole Number of Electors appointed; and if there be more than one who have such Majority, and have an equal Number of Votes, then the House of Representatives shall immediately chuse by Ballot one of them for President; and if no Person have a Majority, then from the five highest on the List the said House shall in like Manner chuse the President. But in chusing the President, the Votes shall be taken by States, the Representation from each State having one Vote; A quorum for this purpose shall consist of a Member or Members from two thirds of the States, and a Majority of all the States shall be necessary to a Choice. In every Case, after the Choice of the President, the Person having the greatest Number of Votes of the Electors shall be the Vice President. But if there should remain two or more who have equal Votes, the Senate chuse from them by Ballot the Vice President.][6]

The Congress may determine the Time of chusing the Electors, and the Day on which they shall give their Votes; which Day shall be the same throughout the United States.

No Person except a natural born Citizen, or a Citizen of the United States, at the time of the Adoption of this Constitution, shall be eligible to the Office of President; neither shall any Person be eligible to that Office who shall not have attained to the Age of thirty five Years, and been fourteen Years a Resident within the United States.

In Case of the Removal of the President from Office, or of his Death, Resignation, or Inability to discharge the Powers and Duties of the said Office, the Same shall devolve on the Vice President, and the Congress may by Law provide for the Case of Removal, Death, Resignation or Inability, both of the President and Vice President, declaring what Officer shall then act as President, and such Officer shall act accordingly, until the Disability be removed, or a President shall be elected.

The President shall, at stated Times receive for his Services, a Compensation, which shall neither be encreased nor diminished during the Period for which he shall have been elected, and he shall not receive within that Period any other Emolument from the United States, or any of them.

Before he enter on the Execution of his Office, he shall take the following Oath or Affirmation:—"I do solemnly swear (or affirm) that I will faithfully execute the Office of President of the United States, and will to the best of my Ability, preserve, protect, and defend the Constitution of the United States."

Section 2. The President shall be Commander in Chief of the Army and Navy of the United States, and of the Militia of the several States, when called into the actual Service of the United States; he may require the Opinion, in writing, of the principal Officer in each of the executive Departments, upon any Subject relating to the Duties of their respective Offices, and he shall have Power to grant Reprieves and Pardons for Offenses against the United States, except in Cases of Impeachment.

He shall have Power, by and with the Advice and Consent of the Senate, to make Treaties, provided two thirds of the Senators present concur; and he shall nominate, and by and with the Advice and Consent of the Senate, shall appoint Ambassadors, other public Ministers and Consuls, Judges of the supreme Court, and all other Officers of the United States, whose Appointments are not herein otherwise provided for, and which shall be established by Law: but the Congress may by Law vest the Appointment of such inferior Officers, as they think proper, in the President alone, in the Courts of Law, or in the Heads of Departments.

The President shall have Power to fill up all Vacancies that may happen during the Recess of the Senate, by granting Commissions which shall expire at the End of their next Session.

Section 3. He shall from time to time give to the Congress Information of the State of the Union, and recommend to their Consideration such Measures as he shall judge necessary and expedient; he may, on extraordinary Occasions, convene both Houses, or either of them, and in Case of Disagreement between them, with Respect to the Time of Adjournment, he may adjourn them to such Time as he shall think proper; he shall receive Ambassadors and other public Ministers; he shall take Care that the Laws be faithfully executed, and shall Commission all Officers of the United States.

Section 4. The President, Vice President and all civil Officers of the United States, shall be removed from Office on Impeachment for, and Conviction of, Treason, Bribery, or other high Crimes and Misdemeanors.

## Article III

Section 1. The judicial Power of the United States, shall be vested in one supreme Court, and in such inferior Courts as the Congress may from time to time ordain and establish. The Judges, both of the supreme and inferior Courts, shall hold their Offices during good Behaviour, and shall, at stated Times, receive for their Services, a Compensation, which shall not be diminished during their Continuance in Office.

Section 2. The judicial Power shall extend to all Cases, in Law and Equity, arising under this Constitution, the Laws of the United States, and Treaties made, or which shall be made, under their Authority;—to all Cases affecting Ambassadors, other public Ministers and Consuls;—to all Cases of admiralty and maritime Jurisdiction;—to Controversies to which the United States shall be a Party;—to Controversies between two or more States;—between a State and Citizens of another State;[7]—between Citizens of different States,—between Citizens of the same State claiming Lands under Grants of different States, and between a State, or the Citizens thereof, and foreign States, Citizens, or Subjects.

In all cases affecting Ambassadors, other public Ministers and Consuls, and those in which a State shall be Party, the supreme Court shall have original jurisdiction. In all the other Cases before mentioned, the supreme Court shall have appellate Jurisdiction, both as to Law and Fact, with such Exceptions, and under such Regulations as the Congress shall make.

The Trial of all Crimes, except in Cases of Impeachment, shall be by Jury; and such Trial shall be held in the State where the said Crimes shall have been committed; but when not committed within any State, the Trial shall be at such Place or Places as the Congress may by Law have directed.

Section 3. Treason against the United States, shall consist only in levying War against them, or in adhering to their Enemies, giving them Aid and Comfort. No Person shall be convicted of Treason unless on the Testimony of two Witnesses to the same overt Act, or on Confession in open Court.

The Congress shall have Power to declare the Punishment of Treason, but no Attainder of Treason shall work Corruption of Blood, or Forfeiture except during the Life of the Person attainted.

## Article IV

Section 1. Full Faith and Credit shall be given in each State to the public Acts, Records, and judicial Proceedings of every other State. And the Congress may by general Laws prescribe the Manner in which such Acts, Records and Proceedings shall be proved, and the Effect thereof.

Section 2. The Citizens of each State shall be entitled to all Privileges and Immunities of Citizens in the several States.

A Person charged in any State with Treason, Felony, or other Crime, who shall flee from Justice, and be found in another State, shall on Demand of the executive Authority of the State from which he fled, be delivered up, to be removed to the State having Jurisdiction of the Crime.

No Person held to Service or Labour in one State, under the Laws thereof, escaping into another, shall, in Consequence of any Law or Regulation therein, be discharged from such Service or Labour, but shall be delivered up on Claim of the Party to whom such Service or Labour may be due.

Section 3. New States may be admitted by the Congress into this Union; but no new State shall be formed or erected within the Jurisdiction of any other State; nor any State be formed by the Junction of two or more States, or Parts of States, without the Consent of the Legislatures of the States concerned as well as of the Congress.

The Congress shall have Power to dispose of and make all needful Rules and Regulations respecting the Territory or other Property belonging to the United States; and nothing in this Constitution shall be so construed as to Prejudice any Claims of the United States, or of any particular State.

Section 4. The United States shall guarantee to every State in this Union a Republican Form of Government, and shall protect each of them against Invasion; and on Application of the Legislature, or of the Executive (when the Legislature cannot be convened) against domestic Violence.

## Article V

The Congress, whenever two thirds of both Houses shall deem it necessary, shall propose Amendments to this Constitution, or, on the Application of the Legislatures of two thirds of the several States, shall call a Convention for proposing Amendments, which, in either Case, shall be valid to all Intents and Purposes, as Part of this Constitution, when ratified by the Legislatures of three fourths of the several States, or by Conventions in three fourths thereof, as the one or the other Mode of Ratification may be proposed by the Congress; Provided that no Amendment which may be made prior to the Year One thousand eight hundred and eight shall in any Manner affect the first and fourth Clauses in the Ninth Section of the first Article; and that no State, without its Consent, shall be deprived of its equal Suffrage in the Senate.

## Article VI

All Debts contracted and Engagements entered into, before the Adoption of this Constitution, shall be as valid against the United

States under this Constitution, as under the Confederation.

This Constitution, and the Laws of the United States which shall be made in Pursuance thereof; and all Treaties made, or which shall be made, under the Authority of the United States, shall be the supreme Law of the Land; and the Judges in every State shall be bound thereby, any Thing in the Constitution or Laws of any State to the Contrary notwithstanding.

The Senators and Representatives before mentioned, and the Members of the several State Legislatures, and all executive and judicial Officers, both of the United States and of the several States, shall be bound by Oath or Affirmation, to support this Constitution; but no religious Test shall ever be required as a Qualification to any Office or public Trust under the United States.

## Article VII

The Ratification of the Conventions of nine States, shall be sufficient for the Establishment of this Constitution between the States so ratifying the Same.
[Signatures omitted.]

## [Amendments]

ARTICLES in addition to, and Amendment of the Constitution of the United States of America, proposed by Congress and ratified by the Legislatures of the several States, pursuant to the fifth Article of the original Constitution.
[The first ten articles proposed 25 September, 1789; declared in force 15 December, 1791].

## Article I

Congress shall make no law respecting an establishment of religion, or prohibiting the free exercise thereof; or abridging the freedom of speech, or of the press; or the right of the people peaceably to assemble, and to petition the Government for a redress of grievances.

## *Article II*

A well regulated Militia, being necessary to the security of a free State, the right of the people to keep and bear Arms, shall not be infringed.

## *Article III*

No Soldier shall, in time of peace, be quartered in any house, without the consent of the Owner, nor in time of war, but in a manner to be prescribed by law.

## *Article IV*

The right of the people to be secure in their person, houses, papers, and effects, against unreasonable searches and seizures, shall not be violated, and no Warrants shall issue, but upon probable cause, supported by Oath or affirmation, and particularly describing the place to be searched, and the persons or things to be seized.

## *Article V*

No person shall be held to answer for a capital, or otherwise infamous crime, unless on a presentment or indictment of a Grand Jury, except in cases arising in the land or naval forces, or in the Militia, when in actual service in time of War or public danger; nor shall any person be subject for the same offense to be twice put in jeopardy of life or limb; nor shall be compelled in any criminal case to be a witness against himself, nor be deprived of life, liberty, or property, without due process of law; nor shall private property be taken for public use, without just compensation.

## *Article VI*

In all criminal prosecutions, the accused shall enjoy the right to a speedy and public trial, by an impartial jury of the State and district wherein the crime shall have been committed, which district shall have been previously ascertained by law, and to be informed of the nature and cause of the accusation; to be confronted with the witnesses against him; to have compulsory process for obtaining witnesses in his favor, and to have the Assistance of Counsel for his defense.

## Article VII

In Suits at common law, where the value in controversy shall exceed twenty dollars, the right of trial by jury shall be preserved, and no fact tried by a jury, shall be otherwise re-examined in any Court of the United States, than according to the rules of the common law.

## Article VIII

Excessive bail shall not be required, nor excessive fines imposed, nor cruel and unusual punishments inflicted.

## Article IX

The enumeration in the Constitution, of certain rights, shall not be construed to deny or disparage others retained by the people.

## Article X

The powers not delegated to the United States by the Constitution, nor prohibited by it to the States, are reserved to the States respectively, or to the people.

## Article XI
[proposed 5 March, 1794;
declared ratified 8 January, 1798]

The Judicial power of the United States shall not be construed to extend to any suit in law or equity, commenced or prosecuted against one of the United States by Citizens of another State, or by Citizens or Subjects of any Foreign State.

### *Article XII*
[proposed 12 December, 1803; declared ratified 25 September, 1804]

The Electors shall meet in their respective states, and vote by ballot for President and Vice-President, one of whom, at least shall not be an inhabitant of the same state with themselves; they shall name in their ballots the person voted for as President, and in distinct ballots the person voted for as Vice-President, and they shall make distinct lists of all persons voted for as President, and of all persons voted for as Vice-President, and of the number of votes for each, which lists they shall sign and certify, and transmit sealed to the seat of the government of the United States, directed to the President of the Senate;—The President of the Senate shall, in the presence of the Senate and House of Representatives, open all certificates and the votes shall then be counted;—The person having the greatest number of votes for President, shall be the President, if such number be a majority of the whole number of Electors appointed; and if no person have such majority, then from the persons having the highest numbers not exceeding three on the list of those voted for as President, the House of Representatives shall choose immediately, by ballot, the President. But in choosing the President, the votes shall be taken by states, the representation from each state having one vote; a quorum for this purpose shall consist of a member or members from two-thirds of the states, and a majority of all the states shall be necessary to a choice. And if the House of Representatives shall not choose a President whenever the right of choice shall devolve upon them, before the fourth day of March next following, then the Vice-President shall act as President, as in the case of the death or other constitutional disability of the President.—The person having the greatest number of votes as Vice-President, shall be the Vice-President, if such number be a majority of the whole number of Electors appointed, and if no person have a majority, then from the two highest numbers on the list, the Senate shall choose the Vice-President; a quorum for the purpose shall consist of two-thirds of the whole number of Senators, and a majority of the whole number shall be necessary to a choice. But no person constitutionally ineligible to the office of President shall be eligible to that of Vice-President of the United States.

## Article XIII
[proposed 1 February, 1865; declared ratified 18 December, 1865]

Section 1. Neither slavery nor involuntary servitude, except as a punishment for crime whereof the party shall have been duly convicted, shall exist within the United States, or any place subject to their jurisdiction.

Section 2. Congress shall have power to enforce this article by appropriate legislation.

## Article XIV
[proposed 16 June, 1866; declared ratified 28 July, 1868]

Section 1. All persons born or naturalized in the United States, and subject to the jurisdiction thereof, are citizens of the United States and of the State wherein they reside. No State shall make or enforce any law which shall abridge the privileges or immunities of citizens of the United States; nor shall any State deprive any person of life, liberty, or property, without due process of law; nor deny to any person within its jurisdiction the equal protection of the laws.

Section 2. Representatives shall be apportioned among the several States according to their respective numbers, counting the whole number of persons in each State, excluding Indians not taxed. But when the right to vote at any election for the choice of electors for President and Vice President of the United States, Representatives in Congress, the Executive and Judicial officers of a State, or the members of the Legislature thereof, is denied to any of the male inhabitants of such State, being twenty-one years of age, and citizens of the United States, or in any way abridged, except for participation in rebellion or other crime, the basis of representation therein shall be reduced in the proportion which the number of such male citizens shall bear to the whole number of male citizens twenty-one years of age in such State.

Section 3. No person shall be a Senator or Representative in Congress, or elector of President and Vice President, or hold any office, civil or military, under the United States, or under any State, who, having previously taken an oath, as a member of Congress, or as an officer of the United States, or as a member of any State legislature, or as an executive or judicial office of any State, to support the Constitution of the United States, shall have engaged in insurrection or rebellion against the same, or given aid and comfort to the enemies thereof. But Congress may by a vote of two-thirds of each House, remove such disability.

Section 4. The validity of the public debt of the United States, authorized by law, including debts incurred for payment of pensions and bounties for services in suppressing insurrection or rebellion, shall not be questioned. But neither the United States nor any state shall assume or pay any debt or obligation incurred in aid of insurrection or rebellion against the United States, or any claim for the loss or emancipation of any slave; but all such debts, obligations and claims shall be held illegal and void.

Section 5. The Congress shall have power to enforce, by appropriate legislation, the provisions of this article.

### Article XV
[proposed 27 February, 1869;
declared ratified 30 March, 1870]

Section 1. The right of citizens of the United States to vote shall not be denied or abridged by the United States or by any State on account of race, color, or previous condition of servitude.

Section 2. The Congress shall have power to enforce this article by appropriate legislation.

### Article XVI
[proposed 12 July 1909;
declared ratified 25 February, 1913]

The Congress shall have power to lay and collect taxes on incomes, from whatever source derived, without apportionment among the several States, and without regard to any census or enumeration.

## Article XVII
[proposed 16 May;
declared ratified 31 May, 1913]

The Senate of the United States shall be composed of two Senators from each State, elected by the people thereof, for six years; and each Senator shall have one vote. The electors in each State shall have the qualifications requisite for electors of the most numerous branch of the State legislatures.

When vacancies happen in the representation of any State in the Senate, the executive authority of such State shall issue writs of election to fill such vacancies: Provided, That the legislature of any State may empower the executive thereof to make temporary appointments until the people fill the vacancies by election as the legislature may direct.

This amendment shall not be so construed as to affect the election or term of any Senator chosen before it becomes valid as part of the Constitution.

## Article XVIII
[proposed 18 December, 1917;
declared ratified 29 January, 1919;
repealed by the 21st Amendment]

Section 1. After one year from the ratification of this article the manufacture, sale, or transportation of intoxicating liquors within, the importation thereof into, or the exportation thereof from the United States and all territory subject to the jurisdiction thereof for beverage purposes is hereby prohibited.

Section 2. The Congress and the several States shall have concurrent power to enforce this article by appropriate legislation.

Section 3. This article shall be inoperative unless it shall have been ratified as an amendment to the Constitution by the legislatures of the several States, as provided in the Constitution, within seven years from the date of the submission hereof to the States by the Congress.[8]

## Article XIX
[proposed 4 June, 1919;
declared ratified 26 August, 1920]

The right of citizens of the United States to vote shall not be denied or abridged by the United States or by any State on account of sex. Congress shall have power to enforce this article by appropriate legislation.

### *Article XX*
[proposed 2 March, 1932;
declared ratified 6 February, 1933]

Section 1. The terms of the President and Vice President shall end at noon on the 20th day of January, and the terms of Senators and Representatives at noon on the 3d day of January, of the years in which such terms would have ended if this article had not been ratified; and the terms of their successors shall then begin.

Section 2. The Congress shall assemble at least once in every year, and such meeting shall begin at noon on the 3d day of January, unless they shall by law appoint a different day.

Section 3. If, at the time fixed for the beginning of the term of the President, the President elect shall have died, the Vice President elect shall become President. If a President shall not have been chosen before the time fixed for the beginning of his term, or if the President elect shall have failed to qualify, then the Vice President elect shall act as President until a President shall have qualified; and the Congress may by law provide for the case wherein neither a President elect nor a Vice President elect shall have qualified, declaring who shall then act as President, or the manner in which one who is to act shall be selected, and such person shall act accordingly until a President or Vice President shall have qualified.

Section 4. The Congress may by law provide for the case of the death of any of the persons from whom the House of Representatives may choose a President whenever the right of choice shall have devolved upon them, and for the case of the death of any of the persons from whom the Senate may choose a Vice President whenever the right of choice shall have devolved upon them.

Section 5. Sections 1 and 2 shall take effect on the 15th day of October following the ratification of this article.

Section 6. This article shall be inoperative unless it shall have been ratified as an amendment to the Constitution by the legislatures of three-fourths of the several States within seven years from the date of its submission.

## Article XXI
[proposed 20 February, 1933;
declared ratified 5 December, 1933]

Section 1. The Eighteenth article of amendment to the Constitution of the United States is hereby repealed.

Section 2. The transportation or importation into any State, Territory, or possession of the United States for delivery or use therein of intoxicating liquors, in violation of the laws thereof, is hereby prohibited.

Section 3. This article shall be inoperative unless it shall have been ratified as an amendment to the Constitution by conventions in the several States, as provided in the Constitution, within seven years from the date of the submission hereof to the States by the Congress.


## Article XXII
[proposed 24 March, 1947;
declared ratified 26 February, 1951]

Section 1. No person shall be elected to the office of the President more than twice, and no person who has held the office of President, or acted as President for more than two years of a term to which some other person was elected President shall be elected to the office of the President more than once. But this Article shall not apply to any person holding the office of President or acting as President, during the term within which this Article becomes operative from holding the office of President or acting as President during the remainder of such term.

Section 2. This article shall be inoperative unless it shall have been ratified as an amendment to the Constitution by the legislatures of three-fourths of the several States within seven years from the date of its submission to the States by the Congress.


## Article XXIII
[proposed 16 June, 1960;
ratified 29 March, 1961]

Section 1. The district constituting the seat of government of the United States shall appoint in such manner as the Congress may direct:

A number of electors of President and Vice President equal to the whole number of Senators and Representatives in Congress to which the District would be entitled if it were a State, but in no event more than the least populous state; they shall be in addition to those appointed by the States, but they shall be considered, for the purpose of the election of President and Vice President, to be electors appointed by a State; and they shall meet in the District and perform such duties as provided by the twelfth article of amendment.

Section 2. The Congress shall have power to enforce this article by appropriate legislation.

### Article XXIV
[proposed 27 August, 1962;
ratified 23 January, 1964]

Section 1. The right of citizens of the United States to vote in any primary or other election for President or Vice President, for electors for President or Vice President, or for Senator or Representative in Congress, shall not be denied or abridged by the United States or any State by reason of failure to pay any poll tax or other tax.

Section 2. The Congress shall have power to enforce this article by appropriate legislation.

### Article XXV
[proposed 6 July, 1965;
ratified 10 February, 1967]

Section 1. In case of the removal of the President from office or of his death or resignation, the Vice President shall become President.

Section 2. Whenever there is a vacancy in the office of the Vice President, the President shall nominate a Vice President who shall take office upon confirmation by a majority vote of both houses of Congress.

Section 3. Whenever the President transmits to the President pro tempore of the Senate and the Speaker of the House of Representatives his written declaration that he is unable to discharge the powers and duties of his office, and until he transmits to them a written declaration to the contrary, such powers and duties shall be discharged by the Vice President as Acting President.

Section 4. Whenever the Vice President and a majority of either the principal officers of the executive departments or of such other body as Congress may by law provide, transmit to the President pro tempore of the Senate and the Speaker of the House of Representatives their written declaration that the President is unable to discharge the powers and duties of his office, the Vice President shall immediately assume the powers and duties of the office as Acting President.

Thereafter, when the President transmits to the President pro tempore of the Senate and the Speaker of the House of Representatives his written declaration that no inability exists, he shall resume the powers and duties of his office unless the Vice President and majority of either the principal officers of the executive department or of such other body as Congress may by law provide, transmit within four days to the President pro tempore of the Senate and the Speaker of the House of Representatives their written declaration that the President is unable to discharge the powers and duties of his office. Thereupon, Congress shall decide the issue, assembling within forty-eight hours for that purpose if not in session. If the Congress, within twenty-one days after receipt of the latter written declaration, or, if Congress is not in session, within twenty-one days after Congress is required to assemble, determines by two-thirds vote of both houses that the President is unable to discharge the powers and duties of his office, the Vice President shall continue to discharge the same as Acting President; otherwise, the President shall assume the powers and duties of his office.

## Article XXVI
[proposed 8 March, 1971;
ratified 1 July, 1971]

Section 1. The right of citizens of the United States, who are 18 years of age or older, to vote shall not be denied or abridged by the United States or any state on account of age.

Section 2. The Congress shall have the power to enforce this article by appropriate legislation.

## Proposed D.C. Representation Amendment
[proposed 11 August, 1978;
ratified by 13 states as of March 1984]

Section 1. For purposes of representation in the Congress, election of the President and Vice President, and article V of this Constitution, the District constituting the seat of government of the United States shall be treated as though it were a State.

Section 2. The exercise of the rights and powers conferred under this article shall be by the people of the District constituting the seat of government, and as shall be provided by the Congress.

Section 3. The twenty-third article of amendment to the Constitution of the United States is hereby repealed.

Section 4. This article shall be inoperative, unless it shall have been ratified as an amendment to the Constitution by the legislatures of three-fourths of the several States within seven years from the date of its submission.

# Notes

1. Superseded by the Fourteenth Amendment.
2. Superseded by the Seventeenth Amendment.
3. Modified by the Seventeenth Amendment.
4. Superseded by the Twentieth Amendment.
5. Modified by the Sixteenth Amendment.
6. Superseded by the Twelfth Amendment.
7. Modified by the Eleventh Amendment.
8. Superseded by the Twenty-first Amendment.

# Sources

## Chapter 1

*General:*

*Congressional Quarterly's Guide to U.S. Elections* (Washington, D.C.: Congressional Quarterly, Inc., 1975). Hereafter referred to as *"C.Q.'s Guide to U.S. Elections."*

Richard B. Morris, ed., *Encyclopedia of American History.* Revised Edition (New York: Harper and Row, 1965).

United States Senate, 92d Congress, 1st Session, *Biographical Directory of the American Congresses, 1774–1971.* Senate Document No. 92–8 (Washington, D.C.: U.S. Government Printing Office, 1971). Hereafter referred to as *"Biographical Directory."*

*The World Almanac and Book of Facts, 1984* (New York: Newspaper Enterprise Association, Inc., 1983), p. 301. Hereafter referred to as *"World Almanac, [year]."*

*Table 1.1:*

*C.Q.'s Guide to U.S. Elections,* p. 200.
*Biographical Directory,* pp. 13–36.
*World Almanac, 1976,* p. 320.
*World Almanac, 1984,* p. 260.

*Table 1.2:*

*C.Q.'s Guide to U.S. Elections,* p. 200.
*Biographical Directory,* pp. 13–36.
*World Almanac, 1976,* p. 320.
*C.Q. Weekly Report,* July 19, 1980, p. 1988.
Feerick, John D., *The Twenty-Fifth Amendment* (New York: Fordham University Press, 1976), p. 33.

*Table 1.3:*

*American Assassins: The Darker Side of Politics,* James W. Clarke, Princeton University Press, 1982.

*Table 1.4:*

*Biographical Directory,* pp. 13–16.
*World Almanac, 1978,* pp. 300–305.
*World Almanac, 1984,* pp. 296–300.
*C.Q.'s Weekly Reports,* December 1984.
*C.Q.'s Weekly Reports,* January 1985.

*Table 1.5:*

*Congressional Quarterly's Guide to the Congress of the United States* (Washington, D.C.: Congressional Quarterly Service, 1971), pp. 230–231. Hereafter referred to as *"C.Q.'s Guide to Congress."*
*World Almanac, 1978,* p. 253.
*C.Q.'s Guide to Congress, 3d ed., 1982,* p. 788.
*World Almanac, 1984,* p. 319.

*Tables 1.6–1.17:*

*C.Q.'s Guide to Congress,* pp. 230a–231a.
*Biographical Directory,* pp. 51–482.
United States Congress, *Congressional Directory* [separate volumes for each of the Congresses from the 44th to the 94th, 1875–1976] (Washington, D.C.: U.S. Government Printing Office). Hereafter *"Congressional Directory,* [Congress number]."
*World Almanac, 1984,* pp. 302, 305, 307, 314.
*C.Q.'s Guide to Congress, 3d ed., 1982,* pp. 894, 895, 898–901.
*C.Q.'s Weekly Reports,* December 1984.
*C.Q.'s Weekly Reports,* January 1985.

*Table 1.18:*

*Historical Statistics,* pp. 1081–1082.
*Statistical Abstract, 1977,* p. 502.
United States Congress, *Calendars of the U.S. House of Representatives and History of Legislation,* 95th Congress, 1st Session.
*Statistical Abstract, 1984,* p. 256.

United States *Congressional Record*, 97th Congress, 2d Session, December 23, 1982.

United States *Congressional Record*, 98th Congress, December 14, 1983 and October 12, 1984.

*Table 1.19:*

*Statistical Abstract, 1977*, p. 502.

United States Congress, *Calendars of the U.S. House of Representatives and History of Legislation*, 95th Congress, 1st Session.

*Statistical Abstract, 1984*, p. 256.

United States *Congressional Record*, 97th Congress, 2d Session, December 23, 1982.

United States *Congressional Record*, 98th Congress, December 14, 1983 and October 12, 1984.

*Tables 1.20–1.21:*

Inter-university Consortium for Political and Social Research (ICPSR), "Roster of Congressional Office Holders, 1789–1984" (ICPSR Study Number 7803). These and other ICPSR "studies" cited below are computer-readable data files which were obtained (and are available) from ICPSR by the authors. Tabular displays appearing in this volume were produced by the authors as a result of computer-aided manipulations of the basic data files.

Inter-university Consortium for Political and Social Research (ICPSR), "United States Congressional Roll Call Voting Records, 1789–1984" (ICPSR Study Number 4).

*Table 1.22:*

United States Senate, 53d Congress, 1st Session, 1893, *Document 49*, "Dockery Report" (Washington, D.C.: U.S. Government Printing Office, 1893).

*United States Statutes at Large* (various)

*United States Code*, Title 5: 5312, 2885, and Title 3: 102, 104.

United States Bureau of the Census, *Statistical Abstract of the United States, 1974* (Washington, D.C.: U.S. Government Printing Office, 1977), p. 240. Hereafter called "*Statistical Abstract*, [year]."

*Statistical Abstract, 1984*, p. 338.

*World Almanac, 1974–1983.*

*Table 1.23:*

*Statistical Abstract 1984,* p. 338.

*Organizational Charts A-D:*

*Congressional Directory, 1983–1984.*
Congressional Quarterly, Inc. *The Supreme Court Justice and the Law* (3d ed., 1983) p. 4.
*World Almanac, 1985,* pp. 324–325.

## Chapter 2

*Table 2.1:*

*World Almanac, 1976,* pp. 152–153, 202–203.

*Table 2.2:*

United States Bureau of the Census, *Historical Statistics of the United States, Colonial Times to 1970.* Part 1 (Washington, D.C.: U.S. Government Printing Office, 1975), pp. 24–36. Hereafter called *"Historical Statistics."*
*World Almanac, 1984,* pp. 197–199.

*Table 2.3:*

*Encyclopedia Brittanica,* various volumes.
*World Almanac, 1975,* pp. 702–704.
*World Almanac, 1984,* pp. 631–634.

## Chapter 3

*General:*

Morris, *Encyclopedia of American History.*

*C.Q.'s Guide to U.S. Elections,* pp. 1–119, 177–188.

*Table 3.1:*

*Historical Statistics,* pp. 1073–1075.

Petersen, Svend. *A Statistical History of the American Presidential Elections 1968*, pp. 11–115.
*Statistical Abstract, 1984*, p. 249.
Secretary of State's Office (final election returns from individual states).
*New York Times*, November 8, 1984.
*American National Election Studies Data Sourcebook*, 1952–1978 (Cambridge, Mass.: Harvard University Press, 1980); American National Election Study, Center for Political Studies, University of Michigan (various documents for 1980–1984 elections).

*Table 3.2:*

*Historical Statistics Colonial Times to 1973*, p. 1075.
Petersen, Svend. *A Statistical History of the American Presidential Elections 1968*, pp. 11–115.
*Statistical Abstract, 1984*, p. 249.

*Table 3.3:*

ICPSR, "State-level Presidential Election Data for the United States, 1824–1972" (ICPSR Study Number 19). Hereafter called "ICPSR Study 19."
ICPSR, "United States Historical Election Returns, 1788–1982" (ICPSR Study Number 1). Hereafter called "ICPSR Study 1."
Clerk of the United States House of Representatives, Statistics of the Presidential and Congressional Election of November 2, 1976 (Washington, D.C.: U.S. Government Printing Office, 1977). Hereafter called "Statistics of the (Presidential and) Congressional Elections of [date]."
Secretary of State's Office (final election returns from individual states).
*New York Times*, November 8, 1984.

*Tables 3.4–3.7:*

ICPSR, "State-level Congressional, Gubernatorial and Senatorial Elections Data for the United States, 1824–1972" (ICPSR Study Number 75). Hereafter called "ICPSR Study 75."
*Statistics of the Congressional Elections of November 4, 1974.*
*Statistics of the Presidential and Congressional Elections of November 2, 1976.*

Secretary of State's Office (final election returns from individual states).
*C.Q.'s Weekly Report,* November 10, 1984.

*Table 3.8:*

*Historical Statistics,* pp. 1084–1085.
*World Almanac, 1984,* pp. 307–313.

*Table 3.9:*

*Historical Statistics,* p. 1081.
*Congressional Quarterly Weekly Report,* December 13, 1973 (Washington, D.C.: Congressional Quarterly, Inc., 1973), p. 2382.
*The New York Times,* February 20, 1977, p. 2.
*C.Q.'s Guide to Congress, 3d ed., 1982,* p. 655.
*C.Q.'s Weekly Report,* August 4, 1984.

*Table 3.10:*

Congressional Quarterly Inc., *National Party Conventions, 1831–1980,* pp. 8–9.

*Table 3.11:*

Porter, Kirk, *A History of Suffrage in the United States* (Chicago, Ill.: University of Chicago Press, 1918), p. 148.
McCulloch, Albert J., *Suffrage and its Problems* (Baltimore, Md.: Warwick and York, Inc., 1929), pp. 34, 44–45, 54–59, 67–69.
Albright, Spencer Delaney, *The American Ballot* (Washington, D.C.: American Council of Political Affairs, 1942), p. 82.
Harris, Joseph, *Election Administration in the United States* (Washington, D.C.: Brookings Institution, 1934), p. 247.
League of Women Voters, miscellaneous unpublished reports relating to suffrage and registration requirements.
*The Book of the States,* 1982–1983 (Lexington, Kentucky: The Council of State Governments, 1982), p. 105.

*Tables 3.12–3.13:*

ICPSR Study 19 (see above).
ICPSR Study 75 (see above).

ICPSR Study 1 (see above).
*Statistical Abstract, 1982–1983,* p. 490.
*Statistical Abstract, 1984,* p. 263.
Secretary of State's Office (final election returns from individual states).
*New York Times,* November 8, 1984.
*C.Q.'s Weekly Reports,* October 27, 1984 and November 10, 1984.

*Table 3.14:*

George Gallup, *The Political Almanac, 1952* (New York: Forbes Co., 1952), p. 37.
Flanigan, William H., *Political Behavior of the American Electorate* (New York: Allyn and Bacon Co., 1971), p. 52.
Survey Research Center/Center for Political Studies, Codebooks for the American National Election Studies of 1952–1982 (Institute for Social Research, The University of Michigan).

*Table 3.15:*

*The Book of the States, 1975–1976* (Lexington, Kentucky: The Council of State Governments, 1975), p. 212.
*The Book of the States, 1982–1983,* p. 104.

## Chapter 4

*Tables 4.1–4.2:*

Dougall, Richard and Mary Patricia Chapman, *"United States Chiefs of Mission, 1778–1973"* (United States Department of State, 1973).
*Congressional Directory,* 94th and 95th Congresses.
Gale Research Co., *Countries of the World and their Leaders, 1983.* pp. 166–185: Supplement, 1983, pp. 154–173.
*World Almanac, 1981–1984.*
*Congressional Quarterly Almanac, 1975–1983.*
*Congressional Quarterly Weekly Reports,* January–September 1984.
*Who's Who in America* (42nd edition, Marquis Who's Who Inc., Chicago, Illinois, 1982–1983).
*The International Who's Who, 1984–1985* (48th ed., Europa Publications Limited, London, England).

United States Department of State, *United States Chiefs of Mission, 1778–1982.*

*Table 4.3:*

*World Almanac, 1984,* pp. 562–563.
Gale Research Co., *Countries of the World and their Leaders, 1983* pp. 166–185: Supplement, 1983, pp. 154–173.
*Congressional Quarterly Weekly Reports,* January-September 1984.

## Chapter 5

*Table 5.1:*

*Historical Statistics,* pp. 1141–1143.
*Statistical Abstract, 1984,* p. 352.

*Table 5.2:*

Mimeograph information supplied by the U.S. Army Historical Division, U.S. Marine Corps Historical Division, and the office of the Chiefs of Naval Operation.
Alfred Goldberg, ed., *A History of the United States Air Force* (Princeton, N.J.: Van Nostrand, Inc., 1957).
U.S. Air Force, *Air Force Register,* 1962, 1966, 1970, 1974.
*World Almanac, 1984,* p. 326.
*World Almanac, 1983,* p. 329.
*World Almanac, 1982,* p. 327.
*World Almanac, 1979,* p. 325.
*World Almanac, 1978,* p. 321.

*Tables 5.3–5.4:*

*Historical Statistics,* p. 1140.
*World Almanac, 1976,* p. 364.

## Chapter 6

*Table 6.1:*

*Statistical Abstract, 1975,* pp. 383–388.

*Statistical Abstract, 1977,* p. 437.
*Statistical Abstract, 1978,* p. 449.
*Statistical Abstract, 1979,* p. 445.
*Statistical Abstract, 1980,* p. 447.
*Statistical Abstract, 1984,* p. 457.

*Table 6.2:*

*Statistical Abstract, 1975,* pp. 1104–1106.
*Statistical Abstract, 1982–1983,* p. 249.
*Statistical Abstract, 1984,* p. 316.
*World Almanac, 1979,* p. 92.
*World Almanac, 1982,* p. 99.

*Table 6.3:*

*Historical Statistics,* pp. 1120–1129.
*Statistical Abstract, 1942,* p. 248.
*Statistical Abstract, 1951,* p. 363.
*Statistical Abstract, 1976,* pp. 266–268.
*Statistical Abstract, 1984,* p. 273.

*Table 6.4:*

*Historical Statistics,* pp. 1114–1116, 1120–1129.
*Statistical Abstract, 1941,* p. 243.
*Statistical Abstract, 1952,* p. 306.
*Statistical Abstract, 1975,* p. 226.
*Statistical Abstract, 1976,* pp. 266–268.
*Statistical Abstract, 1979,* pp. 254, 258.
*Statistical Abstract, 1980,* pp. 263, 266.
*Statistical Abstract, 1981,* pp. 246, 249.
*Statistical Abstract, 1982–1983,* pp. 246, 249.
*Statistical Abstract, 1984,* pp. 315–316.

## *Chapter 7*

*Table 7.1:*

*Historical Statistics,* p. 8.
*Statistical Abstract, 1976,* p. 5.

*Statistical Abstract, 1984,* pp. 11, 34.

U.S. Bureau of the Census, *Current Population Report, Population Profile, 1982,* p. 42.

U.S. Bureau of the Census, *Current Population Reports,* p. 25, No. 965.

*Table 7.2:*

*Historical Statistics,* p. 14.

U.S. Bureau of the Census, *1980 Census of Population,* vol. 1, chapter B, p. 20.

*Table 7.3:*

*Historical Statistics,* pp. 24–37.

*World Almanac, 1984,* p. 200.

*Table 7.4–7.5:*

*Historical Statistics,* pp. 105–109.

*World Almanac, 1984,* p. 568.

*World Almanac, 1984,* p. 204.

*Table 7.6:*

*Historical Statistics,* pp. 127, 135.

*Statistical Abstract, 1982–1983,* p. 376.

*Statistical Abstract, 1984,* pp. 406–407.

*Table 7.7:*

Fifteenth Census (1930), Volume 1, Unemployment, pp. 18–22.

Sixteenth Census (1940), Volume 3, Population, p. 27.

*County and City Data Book, 1952,* p. 4.

*County and City Data Book, 1962,* p. 4.

*County and City Data Book, 1972,* p. 4.

*County and City Data Book, 1983,* p. 8.

*Appendix:*

Constitution and Declaration of Independence

*Encyclopedia of American History,* Richard B. Morris, p. 476.

*The World Almanac, 1984,* p. 442.